8th Joint SIGHUM Workshop on Computational Linguistics for Cultural Heritage, Social Sciences, Humanities and Literature (LaTeCH-CLfL-2024)

St. Julian's, Malta
22 March 2024

ISBN: 978-1-7138-9441-4

Printed from e-media with permission by:

Curran Associates, Inc.
57 Morehouse Lane
Red Hook, NY 12571

Some format issues inherent in the e-media version may also appear in this print version.

Association for Computational Linguistics
209 N. Eighth Street
Stroudsburg, Pennsylvania 18360

Phone: 1-570-476-8006
Fax: 1-570-476-0860

acl@aclweb.org

Additional copies of this publication are available from:

Curran Associates, Inc.
57 Morehouse Lane
Red Hook, NY 12571 USA
Phone: 845-758-0400
Fax: 845-758-2633
Email: curran@proceedings.com
Web: www.proceedings.com

LaTeCH-CLfL 2024

The 8th Joint SIGHUM Workshop on Computational Linguistics for Cultural Heritage, Social Sciences, Humanities and Literature

Proceedings of the Workshop

March 22, 2024

The LaTeCH-CLfL organizers gratefully acknowledge the support from the following sponsors.

IDeaL
SFB 1102

Association for Computational Linguistics (ACL)
209 N. Eighth Street
Stroudsburg, PA 18360
USA
Tel: +1-570-476-8006
Fax: +1-570-476-0860
acl@aclweb.org

Introduction

Welcome to the 2024 edition of LaTeCH-CLfL! Whether you are coming back or joining us for the first time, we are delighted to have you here. This workshop, with a history of nearly two decades, continues to serve as home for a wide spectrum of discussions. This year is no exception, with a lineup of topics that span the intersection of language technology, computational linguistics and the broadly conceived humanities.

This year, we keep studying literature through the computational lens, exploring the complex interplay of literary devices, individual style and the markers of narrative structures. This group of works includes papers that focus on quantitative analyses and experiments to study literary texts or verify literary hypotheses, such as automatic recognition of knowledge transfer in German drama, authorship verification models for quotation attribution, and sentiment analysis in a low resource setting. These papers demonstrate the application of computational methods in the analysis of literary texts and authors' styles.

Computational methods are increasingly prominent in the study of history, reporting new dimensions of large-scale phenomena and their development across centuries. Papers in this category apply computational techniques to historical and cultural sources, including handwritten text recognition in marginalia, named entity recognition in historical texts, topic modelling to explore historical portrayals, the analysis of diachronic scientific writing and the study of parliamentary debates. This research showcases the intersection of digital humanities with computational linguistics to uncover insights from historical and cultural texts.

This year, we highlight the latest innovations in language processing tools and digital resources to cover both diachronic and synchronic differences. This group of papers focuses on the development and evaluation of computational tools and resources, such as coreference resolution in a corpus of long documents, entity linking in digital content, PoS tagging of Latin texts through GPT and the OCR correction of historical text transcripts. These contributions are essential for advancing methodologies in text analysis and improving the accuracy of computational models.

Last but not least, the workshop encompasses papers dealing with sociopolitical and cultural text analysis. Included here are papers that analyze contemporary themes and emergent phenomena through computational methods, such as the dehumanization of Ukrainians on social media, metaphorical framing in media, topic modelling of newspapers, and the effects of the Plain English Movement on legal and scientific articles. This research highlights the role of computational linguistics in understanding contemporary events and how they are discussed in the public forum.

As you can see, there is something for everyone (all things considered) but do keep an open mind and read all papers, if you have the time. You will be glad you did.

Do not forget to visit our Web site HERE – and check out past workshops too.

It goes without saying that whatever success our workshop enjoys is due to the authors (thank you for staying with us or for trusting us the first time), and without question to the reviewers. A special shout-out to our wonderful program committee!

Yuri, Stefania, Anna, Stan

Organizing Committee

Organizers

Yuri Bizzoni, Aarhus University
Stefania Degaetano-Ortlieb, Saarland University
Anna Kazantseva, National Research Council Canada
Stan Szpakowicz, EECS, University of Ottawa

Program Committee

Program Committee

Diego Alves, Saarland University
Melanie Andresen, Universität Stuttgart
Jinyeong Bak, Sungkyunkwan University
Paul Buitelaar, University of Galway
Miriam Butt, University of Konstanz
Florian Cafiero, Ecole nationale des chartes - PSL
Jacob Eisenstein, Google
Anna Feldman, Montclair State University
Mark Finlayson, FIU
Stefan Fischer, Universität des Saarlandes
Antske Fokkens, VU Amsterdam
Francesca Frontini, Istituto di Linguistica Computazionale A. Zampolli"- ILC Consiglio Nazionale delle Ricerche - CNR
Udo Hahn, Friedrich-Schiller-Universitaet Jena
Serge Heiden, ENS de Lyon
Rebecca Hicke, Cornell University
Labiba Jahan, Southern Methodist University
Fotis Jannidis, Universität Würzburg
Dimitrios Kokkinakis, University of Gothenburg
Stasinos Konstantopoulos, NCSR Demokritos
Marie-Pauline Krielke, Saarland University
Maria Kunilovskaya, Saarland University
John Ladd, Washington and Jefferson College
John Lee, City University of Hong Kong
Chaya Liebeskind, Jerusalem College of Technology , Lev Academic Center
Thomas Lippincott, Johns Hopkins University
Barbara Mcgillivray, King's College London
David Mimno, Cornell University
Vivi Nastase, University of Geneva
Borja Navarro-Colorado, University of Alicante
Pierre Nugues, Lund University
Petya Osenova, Sofia University St. Kl. Ohridskiand IICT-BAS
Janis Pagel, Department of Digital Humanities, University of Cologne
Andrew Piper, McGill University
Petr Plecháč, Institute of Czech Literature CAS
Thierry Poibeau, LATTICE (CNRS and ENS/PSL)
Jelena Prokic, Leiden University
Georg Rehm, DFKI
Nils Reiter, University of Cologne
Martin Reynaert, ILLC - Universiteit van Amsterdam / DCA - Tilburg University
Pablo Ruiz Fabo, LiLPa, Université de Strasbourg
Marijn Schraagen, Utrecht University
Artjoms Šeļa, Institute of Polish Language (PAN)
Daniil Skorinkin, Higher School of Economics (Moscow, Russia)
Pia Sommerauer, Vrije Universiteit Amsterdam
Elke Teich, Universität des Saarlandes

Laure Thompson, University of Massachusetts Amherst
Ulrich Tiedau, University College London
Rob Voigt, Northwestern University
Albin Zehe, University of Wuerzburg
Heike Zinsmeister, Universitaet Hamburg

Additional Reviewers

Sam Backer, John Hopkins University
Pascale Feldkamp, Center for Humanities Computing, Aarhus University
Jörg Knappen, Saarland University
Ida-Marie Lassen, Center for Humanities Computing, Aarhus University
Craig Messner, John Hopkins University
Hale Sirin, John Hopkins University

Keynote Talk: The Impresso Project's Approach to Historical Media Analysis

Marten Düring and Maud Ehrmann
Luxembourg Centre for Contemporary and Digital History (C2DH) // Digital Humanities Laboratory of the Ecole Polytechnique Fédérale de Lausanne

Abstract: In the impresso project, a team of computational linguists, historians and designers strive to enable data-driven analyses of historical media across time, institutional silos, media types and languages. To this end we compile a corpus of historical newspaper and radio collections with the help of Western European partners, enrich it using text mining techniques and develop user interfaces for their exploration and computational analysis.

Bio:

Marten has a robust background at the crossroads of cultural history, digital humanities, and computational methods. He has a rich academic trajectory, including a PhD in Contemporary History from the University of Mainz, with his dissertation focusing on the emergence of covert networks during World War II. Marten has contributed his expertise to various institutions, such as Radboud University and the University of North Carolina at Chapel Hill, and has been integral to digital history initiatives at C2DH since 2016.
At C2DH, Marten serves as a principal investigator for the impresso project, which seeks to revolutionize the way historical newspaper and radio collections are accessed and analyzed, transcending barriers of language and national borders. His role encompasses coordinating interface development and steering digital history research within the team. Additionally, Marten is a founding editor of the Journal of Historical Network Research and leads the coordination of the Historical Network Research Community. His commitment to the field is also evident through his involvement in the Hands-on History lecture series and his proactive engagement in support activities for Ukrainian scholars by the C2DH center following the 2021 crisis.
Marten's work not only reflects his dedication to enhancing the tools available for historical research but also underscores the potential of interdisciplinary approaches that meld historical inquiry with technological innovation. His presence as a speaker is a testament to his leadership in shaping the future of digital history.

Maud is a research scientist and lecturer at the Digital Humanities Laboratory of the Ecole Polytechnique Federale de Lausanne. She holds a PhD in Computational Linguistics from the Paris Diderot University (Paris 7) and has been engaged in a large number of scientific projects centred on information extraction and text analysis, both for present-time and historical documents. Before joining the DHLAB, she worked at the Linguistics Computing Laboratory at the Sapienza University of Rome where she worked on the BabelNet resource and contributed to the LIDER project (2013-2014). Prior to that, she worked at the European Commission's Joint Research Centre in Ispra, Italy, as member of the OPTIMA unit (now Text and Data mining unit) which develops innovative and application-oriented solutions (Europe Media Monitor) for retrieving and extracting information from the Internet with a focus on high multilinguality (2009-2013). Previously, she worked at the Xerox Europe Research Centre in Grenoble, France (now Naver Labs Europe) in the Parsing and Semantics unit, first as PhD candidate supported by a CIFRE grant (2005-2008), then as a post-doctoral researcher (2008-2009). There, her research focused mainly on the automatic processing and fine-grained analysis of entities of interest, specifically named entities and temporal expressions.

Table of Contents

Evaluating In-Context Learning for Computational Literary Studies: A Case Study Based on the Automatic Recognition of Knowledge Transfer in German Drama

Janis Pagel and **Axel Pichler** and **Nils Reiter**
Department for Digital Humanities
University of Cologne
{janis.pagel,axel.pichler,nils.reiter}@uni-koeln.de

Abstract

In this paper, we evaluate two different natural language processing (NLP) approaches to solve a paradigmatic task for computational literary studies (CLS): the recognition of knowledge transfer in literary texts. We focus on the question of how adequately large language models capture the transfer of knowledge about family relations in German drama texts when this transfer is treated as a classification or textual entailment task using in-context learning (ICL). We find that a 13 billion parameter LLAMA 2 model performs best on the former, while GPT-4 performs best on the latter task. However, all models achieve relatively low scores compared to standard NLP benchmark results, struggle from inconsistencies with small changes in prompts and are often not able to make simple inferences beyond the textual surface, which is why an unreflected generic use of ICL in the CLS seems still not advisable.

1 Introduction

Computational literary studies (CLS) is a subfield of Digital Humanities. CLS attempts to expand the traditional methods of literary studies to include quantitative approaches with the help of statistical methods and machine learning or natural language processing (NLP) (Piper et al., 2021; Jannidis, 2022). The latter has made enormous progress in recent years: at the latest since the development of the transformer architecture (Vaswani et al., 2017) large language models (LLMs) based on it have been breaking traditional NLP-benchmarks. Until 2020, the development and domain-adaption of these models was dominated by an approach that emerged as a result of the bidirectional encoder representations from transformer models (BERT, Devlin et al., 2018), which has been termed the *pre-training* and *fine-tuning* paradigm. This practice has now also arrived in CLS, as a recent survey on machine learning in CLS shows (Hatzel et al., 2023). However, another paradigm shift in NLP appeared when the developers of GPT-3 (Brown et al., 2020), an autoregressive LLM with around 175 billion parameters, showed in 2020 that with the help of a few examples ('few-shot learning') without fine-tuning and exclusively through natural language interaction, the model not only corresponded to the performance of predecessor models in numerous NLP tasks, but even outperformed them. This type of conditioning of a LLM to perform a specific task using only a natural language input and no gradient update is called 'in-context learning' (ICL, Dong et al., 2023). With the publication of ChatGPT, ICL has gained popularity among the general public, but its potential and limits for CLS has yet to be determined.

Use of Language Models in CLS

Especially for the often highly individualized research questions of CLS, it is tempting to provide a natural language description of the task in order to analyze literary texts. On the first sight, such an approach does not require in-depth knowledge of LLMs and NLP, and even the output – human-readable language – can be interpreted directly, without requiring quantitative and/or statistical analysis. Furthermore, this approach seemingly gets rid of the need to formulate unambigouous and precise definitions, which are tested via annotation and – due to the explication – open for critique by other researchers (cf. Reiter et al., 2019). Thus, in order to include ICL in the CLS method arsenal, it is necessary to disclose the potentials and limitations of this method properly. With this paper, we want to take a first step in this direction by testing a representative CLS-task – knowledge transfer between literary characters in German theatre plays – with the help of three different LLMs using ICL-methods.

We consider this task representative for many CLS tasks: i) It revolves around literary characters,

Proceedings of LaTeCH-CLfL 2024, pages 1–10
March 22, 2024

which are one of the most important 'anchors' for literary interpretation. Their knowledge about the world they live in is an important property if one understands literary characters as representations of human beings. ii) While some CLS tasks (e.g., authorship or genre attribution) assign properties to the entire text, many focus on smaller units such as scenes or events, which are represented by a small number of tokens. iii) Finally, corpus sizes in CLS are typically rather small, as much of the work is focused on historic data.

The paper directly links to the flourishing drama research in literary studies and CLS (Moretti, 2011; Fischer et al., 2017; Krautter, 2018; Andresen et al., 2022; Dennerlein et al., 2023). The goal of this study is two-fold: (i) evaluating if LLMs are able to sufficiently solve the task out-of-the-box, and (ii) investigating the problems and pitfalls that may arise when utilizing LLMs for such a CLS task.

2 Related Work

While prompt engineering, which is often equated with ICL, recently gained a lot of traction, studies based on it are still rare in DH in general and CLS in particular. Initial reflections and experiments can be found in Computational Science Studies (CSS). Ziems et al. (2023) investigate the potential of LLMs for CSS by investigating the viability of zero-shot-learning for sociological research. Overall, they posit that LLMs perform well in certain zero-shot classification tasks within the context of social studies research, but "do not match or exceed the performance of carefully fine-tuned classifiers" (Ziems et al., 2023, p. 2). Across their experiments, models demonstrate optimal performance in tasks related to misinformation classification, stance detection, and emotion classification. The authors attribute this success to the presence of either a ground truth (as in the case of misinformation) or an annotation schema that corresponds to (implicit) definitions of everyday concepts.[1] However, they also note that models perform worse in tasks requiring intricate expert taxonomies. This difficulty arises from the complex nature of expert-informed annotation guidelines, which may not align semantically with much of the LLM's training data.

In the realm of NLP, several papers have explored ICL for solving sets of diverse tasks (cf. Ye et al., 2021; Chen et al., 2022; Wei et al., 2022; Sanh et al., 2022; Min et al., 2022), investigated methods for constructing reliable prompts (cf. Schick and Schütze, 2021; Zhao et al., 2021; Perez et al., 2021; Lu et al., 2022) and choosing suitable evaluation metrics (Schaeffer et al., 2023). In terms of related tasks, the `implicit_relations` task from the BIG-bench benchmark (Srivastava et al., 2023) seems to be closest to our setup, with Hoffmann et al. (2022) achieving an accuracy score of 49.4% using a 70B parameter Chinchilla model and Rae et al. (2021) an accuracy score of 36.4% using a 280B parameter Gopher model.

3 Task

We work on a paradigmatic task for Computational Literary Studies: the transfer of knowledge about family relationships in German theatre plays. This type of task is paradigmatic for CLS insofar as research questions from literary studies often focus on particular realizations of concepts in specific literary contexts or specific particularities of genres and single texts which are difficult to generalize and thus data sparsity becomes an issue. We conduct two experiments within the framework of ICL in order to gain insights into how LLMs can be applied here:

- **Experiment 1: Classification**: For our first approach, we aim to investigate if LLMs are able to correctly predict family relations between characters. The task for the models is to decide which family relation holds between two characters given the context in a dialogue snippet taken from a German drama. In the last scene of the last act of Lessing's *Nathan the Wise*, for instance, Nathan reveals that Recha and the Templar are siblings (see appendix A for the relevant segment). In this case, the classification goal would be to assign the class `siblings`.

- **Experiment 2: Textual entailment**: Textual entailment recognition (TER), also known as natural language inference (NLI), is a task that has been established in NLP since 2005 (Dagan et al., 2006). It refers to the ability of a model to determine whether a hypothesis is entailed by another sentence or short text. As part of this task, we reformulated the classification task from Experiment 1 so that it

[1]These assumptions correlate with the initial research into why and how ICL works, summarized and brought together by Xie et al. (2021) and Xie and Min (2021) who interpret this ability as Bayesian inference of a latent concept conditioned on the prompt – a capability that arises from structure in the pretraining data.

becomes an entailment task. The text snippet from the play becomes the premise, and the family relationship it conveys is formulated as a proposition that serves as the hypothesis (e.g. "Iphigenia is the child of Agamemnon.").

4 Data

We make use of one pre-existing dataset, a corpus of knowledge transfer annotations on German theatre plays pertaining to family relations (Andresen et al., 2022). The authors understand knowledge in a broad way to be beliefs that are thought to be true by a certain character at a certain point in time but might later turn out to be wrong during the advance of the plot. The corpus contains 30 texts sampled from the German Drama Corpus (GerDraCor, Fischer et al., 2019). For each family relation that a character learns about, an annotation marks the source and target of the knowledge transfer, which family relation is being transferred and who is part of this relation, as well as additional, optional properties like lies or uncertainty. While the dataset in total contains 1277 annotated text passages, we removed the infrequent relation types as well as all annotations that do not represent knowledge transfer. This yields 89 annotations for our experiments, which are divided into four categories: *parent of* (29), *child of* (26), *siblings* (23) and *spouses* (11). While this is a rather small dataset, it is suitable for our premise of evaluating a typical CLS task, since data sparsity is a common — and perhaps inherent — feature of CLS tasks, as also mentioned earlier. The same dataset is used for Experiments 1 and 2, whereby in the case of Experiment 2, 39 instances are changed so that they are classified as propositions that are not entailed by the text snippet. For instance, if an annotation contains a *parent of* relationship, the proposition is changed to "[Character X] is not the parent of [Character Y]".

5 Experiments

5.1 Models

For deciding on which model to use, we looked at the rankings of the HuggingFace LLM leaderboard[2] and chose the top three performing models for their performance on the HellaSwag benchmark[3] (Zellers et al., 2019). Since HellaSwag contains common sense inferences, it appeared to be the benchmark most closely related to our task. Thus, we compare three different LLM architectures, namely the open source models LLAMA 2 (Touvron et al., 2023), in a version optimized for chatting, Platypus2 (Lee et al., 2023), which is a derivative of LLAMA 2, and the closed source model GPT-4 (OpenAI, 2023).[4]

5.2 Experimental Setup

We test different model sizes, namely LLAMA 2 7B and 13B, as well as Platypus2 7B and 13B and compare their best results to GPT-4 with roughly 1.8T parameters. In addition to the sentence containing an annotation, we provide the models with context sentences and experiment with one and two context sentences on each side of the target sentence. We experiment with different prompts and prompt formats by utilizing the structures used for initially instructing the LLMs (LLAMA 2 and Alpaca prompt formats) as well as re-formulating in order to entice the model to generate a certain output format. In particular, we test the effects of providing the models with the names of the characters involved in the relationship (w/ character name), or not (wo/ character name). The specific prompt setups we used are documented in the appendix (see C.2). Lastly, we experiment with zero shot and few shot learning and test the effects on model performance. For the few shot setups, we provide the models with four examples chosen randomly from the development set. The code to re-run all experiments can be found on `https://zenodo.org/doi/10.5281/zenodo.10581289`.

6 Results

Table 1 shows the best results by each model architecture for predicting family relations.[5] The best F1 and accuracy scores with values of 66% and 68% in a zero shot setting and of 68% and 66% in a few shot setting were obtained with LLAMA 2 (13b) based on prompts in which the names of the characters whose family relationship is transmitted are input to the model. They thus achieve higher performance scores than are reported for the BIG-bench benchmark (49% accuracy) and are also at the upper end of the scores achieved by

[2]`https://huggingface.co/spaces/HuggingFaceH4/open_llm_leaderboard`

[3]Effective September 13, 2023.

[4]We believe that proprietary models such as OpenAI's GPT-4 are not suitable as a valid basis for scientific experiments due to their opacity, but can serve as a good benchmark for comparison with open source models due to their performance.

[5]For a complete list of results see Table 3 in the appendix.

Model	Context	Learning method	Prompt	F1	Prec.	Rec.	Acc.
Majority Baseline	–	–	–	0.16	0.10	0.33	0.33
Llama-2-13b	1	zero shot	v2 w/ character	0.66	0.69	**0.68**	**0.68**
Llama-2-13b	2	few shot	w/ character	**0.68**	**0.74**	0.66	0.66
Platypus2-13b	2	zero shot	w/o character	0.53	0.60	0.54	0.54
GPT-4	2	zero shot	w/ character	0.52	0.55	0.51	0.55

Table 1: Results of Experiment 1: Classification.

Model	F1	Prec.	Rec.	Acc.
Maj. Baseline	0.72	0.56	1.00	0.56
Llama-2-13b	0.38	0.49	0.45	0.45
Platypus-2-13b	0.26	0.19	0.43	0.44
GPT-4	**0.50**	**0.74**	**0.56**	**0.56**

Table 2: Results of Experiment 2: Textual entailment. All models were used with a context window of one sentence. All scores are weighted-scores.

Ziems et al. (2023, p. 14) (58 % to 64 %). Note, however, that Ziems et al. did not aim at the classification of implicit meta-knowledge. Nevertheless, the results are still below the scores achieved for other text-classification tasks with smaller pre-trained language models (PLMs). Platypus2 and GPT-4 are generally outperformed by LLAMA 2, but achieve results similar to the baselines established by Hoffmann et al. (2022) and Ziems et al. (2023).

Table 2 shows the results for the textual entailment task. The data set for this task consists of 89 text-sentence pairs, of which 50 sentences are entailed from the snippets of the drama texts and 39 are not entailed. We compare the models to a baseline that classifies all instances as "entailed" (majority baseline). All three models perform poorly at the textual entailment task: While GPT-4 achieves an accuracy of 56% (baseline: 56%), LLAMA 2 classifies a larger number of sentences as not entailed, but only has a recall of 45% and therefore achieves F1 and accuracy scores far below the baseline. Platypus2 performs worst and classifies all instances as "not entailed".

LLAMA 2 even explicitly justifies why it classifies actually entailed sentences as non-implied, as the following example shows: "The text does not explicitly state that Iphigenie and Orest are siblings. While it mentions "Schwestern" (sisters) and "Bruder" (brother) in the same sentence, it does not explicitly state their relationship. Therefore, the proposition that Iphigenie and Orest are siblings is not entailed by the given text."[6]

7 Discussion

Our experiments show that the performance of an LLM is strongly affected by its potential lack of 'understanding' of the task, or particular words in the prompt as well as minor changes in the prompt templates. This is insofar not surprising, as the dramas date from the period 1750-1910 – with the majority dating from the turn of the 18th and 19th centuries – and therefore use a language that is also literary in style and in some cases versified, for which there were most likely no examples in the training data of the models. Recent studies investigating ICL argue that both semantic priors and input-label mapping in the prompts influence the ICL competence of LLMs, although the latter only applies to very large LLMs (Zhao et al., 2021; Xie et al., 2021; Wei et al., 2023). With regard to our experiments, one can assume that in the training data of LLAMA 2 the connection between the classification of an implicit knowledge transfer of a family relation and the fact that the same text snippet entails this family relation formulated in the form of a proposition, which is self-evident for a human speaker, was not represented.

8 Conclusion

It is worth noting that one of the dangers of ICL (and generative models in general) is the seemingly straightforward use of their output. We believe that using natural language output of such models is a regression compared to properly defined, symbolic output, as it requires interpretation and naturally

[6]As experiments have shown, in the case of LLAMA 2 this also applies sometimes to very simple material inferences. For example, when asked whether "Peter is taller than Fritz" implies that "Fritz is smaller than Peter", LLAMA 2 answers: "To entail the latter proposition, the text would need to explicitly state that Fritz is smaller than Peter [. . .]" GPT-4 does classify these sentences correctly.

contains ambiguities and terminological vagueness. "The worst dangers may lie in the humanist's ability to interpret nearly any result" (Sculley and Pasanek, 2008, 409), and this holds even more when the result comes in the form of natural language.

It also follows from our experiments that an unreflected and generic out-of-the-box use of ICL – even with open-source LLMs – for the automation of analytical sub-steps in the CLS is not yet recommended. The accuracy and F1-scores, although respectable per se, are still too low for this. Methodologically, it follows that for each task-specific use of ICL in the CLS, it must be clarified in each specific case whether and how the selected LLMs represent the subject-specific vocabulary for this task validly and with a high degree of accuracy. For certain tasks, it should also be considered whether the breakdown of a complex concept into simpler everyday concepts potentially mastered by the model – an LLM-specific operationalization of the complex concepts – does not achieve better scores.

In the background of this methodological recommendation lie the following open research questions: Is it really the case that LLMs perform better with ICL if the models already have semantic prior knowledge of the task-specific concepts/vocabulary? What does this mean for the domain-specific vocabulary of CLS? Can this be generically categorized in such a way that a distinction is made between everyday concepts, which are likely to be represented by LLMs or can be represented in principle, and complex concepts, which are likely to be difficult to represent by LLMs? How suitable are more recent low-resource 'fine-tuning-methods' such as PEFT (Lester et al., 2021) or LoRA (Hu et al., 2021) for CLS? The highly successful instruction-fine-tuning paradigm is rarely applicable in CLS due to a lack of available data, but alternatives such as PEFT have so far only been tested on standard NLP benchmarks like SuperGLUE. The extent to which these methods increase the accuracy of LLMs in CLS tasks will have to be examined in the future.

Acknowledgements

The research in this paper has been carried out within the Q:TRACK project funded by the German Research Foundation (DFG) in the context of SPP 2207 *Computational Literary Studies*. We thank the foundation for making this possible. We would also like to thank Melanie Andresen and Benjamin Krautter as well as the anonymous reviewers for their valuable and helpful feedback.

References

Melanie Andresen, Benjamin Krautter, Janis Pagel, and Nils Reiter. 2022. Who Knows What in German Drama? A Composite Annotation Scheme for Knowledge Transfer - Annotation, Evaluation, and Analysis. *Journal of Computational Literary Studies (JCLS)*, 1(1).

Tom B. Brown, Benjamin Mann, Nick Ryder, Melanie Subbiah, Jared Kaplan, Prafulla Dhariwal, Arvind Neelakantan, Pranav Shyam, Girish Sastry, Amanda Askell, Sandhini Agarwal, Ariel Herbert-Voss, Gretchen Krueger, Tom Henighan, Rewon Child, Aditya Ramesh, Daniel M. Ziegler, Jeffrey Wu, Clemens Winter, Christopher Hesse, Mark Chen, Eric Sigler, Mateusz Litwin, Scott Gray, Benjamin Chess, Jack Clark, Christopher Berner, Sam McCandlish, Alec Radford, Ilya Sutskever, and Dario Amodei. 2020. Language models are few-shot learners. In *Proceedings of the 34th International Conference on Neural Information Processing Systems*, NIPS'20, Red Hook, NY, USA. Curran Associates Inc.

Mingda Chen, Jingfei Du, Ramakanth Pasunuru, Todor Mihaylov, Srini Iyer, Veselin Stoyanov, and Zornitsa Kozareva. 2022. Improving in-context few-shot learning via self-supervised training. In *Proceedings of the 2022 Conference of the North American Chapter of the Association for Computational Linguistics: Human Language Technologies*, pages 3558–3573, Seattle, United States. Association for Computational Linguistics.

Ido Dagan, Oren Glickman, and Bernardo Magnini. 2006. The pascal recognising textual entailment challenge. In *Machine Learning Challenges. Evaluating Predictive Uncertainty, Visual Object Classification, and Recognising Tectual Entailment*, pages 177–190, Berlin, Heidelberg. Springer Berlin Heidelberg.

Katrin Dennerlein, Thomas Schmidt, and Christian Wolff. 2023. Computational emotion classification for genre corpora of German tragedies and comedies from 17th to early 19th century. *Digital Scholarship in the Humanities*, 38(4):1466–1481.

Jacob Devlin, Ming-Wei Chang, Kenton Lee, and Kristina Toutanova. 2018. BERT: Pre-training of Deep Bidirectional Transformers for Language Understanding. Publisher: arXiv Version Number: 2.

Qingxiu Dong, Lei Li, Damai Dai, Ce Zheng, Zhiyong Wu, Baobao Chang, Xu Sun, Jingjing Xu, Lei Li, and Zhifang Sui. 2023. A Survey on In-context Learning. Publisher: arXiv Version Number: 3.

Frank Fischer, Ingo Börner, Mathias Göbel, Angelika Hechtl, Christopher Kittel, Carsten Milling, and Peer Trilcke. 2019. Programmable corpora: Introducing

DraCor, an infrastructure for the research on European drama. In *Proceedings of DH2019: "Complexities"*.

Frank Fischer, Mathias Göbel, Dario Kampkaspar, Christopher Kittel, and Peer Trilcke. 2017. Network dynamics, plot analysis. approaching the progressive structuration of literary texts. In *Book of Abstracts of the DH2017 conference*.

Hans Ole Hatzel, Haimo Stiemer, Chris Biemann, and Evelyn Gius. 2023. Machine learning in computational literary studies. *it - Information Technology*.

Jordan Hoffmann, Sebastian Borgeaud, Arthur Mensch, Elena Buchatskaya, Trevor Cai, Eliza Rutherford, Diego de Las Casas, Lisa Anne Hendricks, Johannes Welbl, Aidan Clark, Tom Hennigan, Eric Noland, Katie Millican, George van den Driessche, Bogdan Damoc, Aurelia Guy, Simon Osindero, Karen Simonyan, Erich Elsen, Jack W. Rae, Oriol Vinyals, and Laurent Sifre. 2022. Training compute-optimal large language models.

Edward J. Hu, Yelong Shen, Phillip Wallis, Zeyuan Allen-Zhu, Yuanzhi Li, Shean Wang, Lu Wang, and Weizhu Chen. 2021. LoRA: Low-Rank Adaptation of Large Language Models. Publisher: arXiv Version Number: 2.

Fotis Jannidis, editor. 2022. *Digitale Literaturwissenschaft: DFG-Symposion 2017*. Germanistische Symposien. J.B. Metzler, Stuttgart.

Benjamin Krautter. 2018. Quantitative microanalysis? Different methods of digital drama analysis in comparison. In *Book of Abstracts of DH 2018*, pages 225–228.

Ariel N. Lee, Cole J. Hunter, and Nataniel Ruiz. 2023. Platypus: Quick, cheap, and powerful refinement of LLMs.

Brian Lester, Rami Al-Rfou, and Noah Constant. 2021. The Power of Scale for Parameter-Efficient Prompt Tuning. Publisher: arXiv Version Number: 2.

Yao Lu, Max Bartolo, Alastair Moore, Sebastian Riedel, and Pontus Stenetorp. 2022. Fantastically ordered prompts and where to find them: Overcoming few-shot prompt order sensitivity. In *Proceedings of the 60th Annual Meeting of the Association for Computational Linguistics (Volume 1: Long Papers)*, pages 8086–8098, Dublin, Ireland. Association for Computational Linguistics.

Sewon Min, Mike Lewis, Luke Zettlemoyer, and Hannaneh Hajishirzi. 2022. MetaICL: Learning to learn in context. In *Proceedings of the 2022 Conference of the North American Chapter of the Association for Computational Linguistics: Human Language Technologies*, pages 2791–2809, Seattle, United States. Association for Computational Linguistics.

Franco Moretti. 2011. Network theory, plot analysis. *Pamphlets of the Stanford Literary Lab*, 2:2–11.

OpenAI. 2023. GPT-4 technical report.

Ethan Perez, Douwe Kiela, and Kyunghyun Cho. 2021. True few-shot learning with language models. In *Advances in Neural Information Processing Systems*.

Andrew Piper, Richard Jean So, and David Bamman. 2021. Narrative theory for computational narrative understanding. In *Proceedings of the 2021 Conference on Empirical Methods in Natural Language Processing*, pages 298–311, Online and Punta Cana, Dominican Republic. Association for Computational Linguistics.

Jack W. Rae, Sebastian Borgeaud, Trevor Cai, Katie Millican, Jordan Hoffmann, H. Francis Song, John Aslanides, Sarah Henderson, Roman Ring, Susannah Young, Eliza Rutherford, Tom Hennigan, Jacob Menick, Albin Cassirer, Richard Powell, George van den Driessche, Lisa Anne Hendricks, Maribeth Rauh, Po-Sen Huang, Amelia Glaese, Johannes Welbl, Sumanth Dathathri, Saffron Huang, Jonathan Uesato, John Mellor, Irina Higgins, Antonia Creswell, Nat McAleese, Amy Wu, Erich Elsen, Siddhant M. Jayakumar, Elena Buchatskaya, David Budden, Esme Sutherland, Karen Simonyan, Michela Paganini, Laurent Sifre, Lena Martens, Xiang Lorraine Li, Adhiguna Kuncoro, Aida Nematzadeh, Elena Gribovskaya, Domenic Donato, Angeliki Lazaridou, Arthur Mensch, Jean-Baptiste Lespiau, Maria Tsimpoukelli, Nikolai Grigorev, Doug Fritz, Thibault Sottiaux, Mantas Pajarskas, Toby Pohlen, Zhitao Gong, Daniel Toyama, Cyprien de Masson d'Autume, Yujia Li, Tayfun Terzi, Vladimir Mikulik, Igor Babuschkin, Aidan Clark, Diego de Las Casas, Aurelia Guy, Chris Jones, James Bradbury, Matthew J. Johnson, Blake A. Hechtman, Laura Weidinger, Iason Gabriel, William Isaac, Edward Lockhart, Simon Osindero, Laura Rimell, Chris Dyer, Oriol Vinyals, Kareem Ayoub, Jeff Stanway, Lorrayne Bennett, Demis Hassabis, Koray Kavukcuoglu, and Geoffrey Irving. 2021. Scaling language models: Methods, analysis & insights from training gopher. *CoRR*, abs/2112.11446.

Nils Reiter, Marcus Willand, and Evelyn Gius. 2019. A shared task for the digital humanities chapter 1: Introduction to annotation, narrative levels and shared tasks. *Journal of Cultural Analytics*, 4(3).

Victor Sanh, Albert Webson, Colin Raffel, Stephen Bach, Lintang Sutawika, Zaid Alyafeai, Antoine Chaffin, Arnaud Stiegler, Arun Raja, Manan Dey, M Saiful Bari, Canwen Xu, Urmish Thakker, Shanya Sharma Sharma, Eliza Szczechla, Taewoon Kim, Gunjan Chhablani, Nihal Nayak, Debajyoti Datta, Jonathan Chang, Mike Tian-Jian Jiang, Han Wang, Matteo Manica, Sheng Shen, Zheng Xin Yong, Harshit Pandey, Rachel Bawden, Thomas Wang, Trishala Neeraj, Jos Rozen, Abheesht Sharma, Andrea Santilli, Thibault Fevry, Jason Alan Fries, Ryan Teehan, Teven Le Scao, Stella Biderman, Leo Gao, Thomas Wolf, and Alexander M Rush. 2022. Multitask prompted training enables zero-shot task generalization. In *International Conference on Learning Representations*.

Rylan Schaeffer, Brando Miranda, and Sanmi Koyejo. 2023. Are emergent abilities of large language models a mirage?

Timo Schick and Hinrich Schütze. 2021. Few-shot text generation with natural language instructions. In *Proceedings of the 2021 Conference on Empirical Methods in Natural Language Processing*, pages 390–402, Online and Punta Cana, Dominican Republic. Association for Computational Linguistics.

D. Sculley and Bradley M. Pasanek. 2008. Meaning and mining: the impact of implicit assumptions in data mining for the humanities. *Literary and Linguistic Computing*, 23(4):409–424.

Aarohi Srivastava et al. 2023. Beyond the imitation game: Quantifying and extrapolating the capabilities of language models. *Transactions on Machine Learning Research.*

Hugo Touvron, Louis Martin, Kevin Stone, Peter Albert, Amjad Almahairi, Yasmine Babaei, Nikolay Bashlykov, Soumya Batra, Prajjwal Bhargava, Shruti Bhosale, Dan Bikel, Lukas Blecher, Cristian Canton Ferrer, Moya Chen, Guillem Cucurull, David Esiobu, Jude Fernandes, Jeremy Fu, Wenyin Fu, Brian Fuller, Cynthia Gao, Vedanuj Goswami, Naman Goyal, Anthony Hartshorn, Saghar Hosseini, Rui Hou, Hakan Inan, Marcin Kardas, Viktor Kerkez, Madian Khabsa, Isabel Kloumann, Artem Korenev, Punit Singh Koura, Marie-Anne Lachaux, Thibaut Lavril, Jenya Lee, Diana Liskovich, Yinghai Lu, Yuning Mao, Xavier Martinet, Todor Mihaylov, Pushkar Mishra, Igor Molybog, Yixin Nie, Andrew Poulton, Jeremy Reizenstein, Rashi Rungta, Kalyan Saladi, Alan Schelten, Ruan Silva, Eric Michael Smith, Ranjan Subramanian, Xiaoqing Ellen Tan, Binh Tang, Ross Taylor, Adina Williams, Jian Xiang Kuan, Puxin Xu, Zheng Yan, Iliyan Zarov, Yuchen Zhang, Angela Fan, Melanie Kambadur, Sharan Narang, Aurelien Rodriguez, Robert Stojnic, Sergey Edunov, and Thomas Scialom. 2023. Llama 2: Open foundation and fine-tuned chat models.

Ashish Vaswani, Noam Shazeer, Niki Parmar, Jakob Uszkoreit, Llion Jones, Aidan N. Gomez, Lukasz Kaiser, and Illia Polosukhin. 2017. Attention Is All You Need. Publisher: arXiv Version Number: 5.

Jason Wei, Maarten Bosma, Vincent Zhao, Kelvin Guu, Adams Wei Yu, Brian Lester, Nan Du, Andrew M. Dai, and Quoc V Le. 2022. Finetuned language models are zero-shot learners. In *International Conference on Learning Representations*.

Jerry Wei, Jason Wei, Yi Tay, Dustin Tran, Albert Webson, Yifeng Lu, Xinyun Chen, Hanxiao Liu, Da Huang, Denny Zhou, and Tengyu Ma. 2023. Larger language models do in-context learning differently.

Sang Michael Xie and Sewon Min. 2021. How does in-context learning work? a framework for understanding the differences from traditional supervised learning. `http://ai.stanford.edu/blog/understanding-incontext/`.

Sang Michael Xie, Aditi Raghunathan, Percy Liang, and Tengyu Ma. 2021. An Explanation of In-context Learning as Implicit Bayesian Inference. Publisher: arXiv Version Number: 6.

Qinyuan Ye, Bill Yuchen Lin, and Xiang Ren. 2021. CrossFit: A few-shot learning challenge for cross-task generalization in NLP. In *Proceedings of the 2021 Conference on Empirical Methods in Natural Language Processing*, pages 7163–7189, Online and Punta Cana, Dominican Republic. Association for Computational Linguistics.

Rowan Zellers, Ari Holtzman, Yonatan Bisk, Ali Farhadi, and Yejin Choi. 2019. HellaSwag: Can a machine really finish your sentence? In *Proceedings of the 57th Annual Meeting of the Association for Computational Linguistics*, pages 4791–4800, Florence, Italy. Association for Computational Linguistics.

Tony Z. Zhao, Eric Wallace, Shi Feng, Dan Klein, and Sameer Singh. 2021. Calibrate before use: Improving few-shot performance of language models. In *Proceedings of International Conference on Machine Learning 2021 (ICML).*

Caleb Ziems, William Held, Omar Shaikh, Jiaao Chen, Zhehao Zhang, and Diyi Yang. 2023. Can large language models transform computational social science?

A Example Knowledge Transfer

Excerpt from Lessing's *Nathan the Wise*. English translation by W. Taylor.

> NATHAN. He called himself Leonard of Filnek, but he was no German.
>
> TEMPLAR. You know that too?
>
> NATHAN. He had espoused a German, And followed for a time your mother thither.
>
> TEMPLAR. No more I beg of you—But Recha's brother—
>
> NATHAN. Art thou
>
> TEMPLAR. I, I her brother—
>
> RECHA. He, my brother?

This segment has been annotated by Andresen et al. (2022) with the following predicate:

```
transfer(nathan, saladin,
siblings(tempelherr, recha))
```

B Complete Results

Table 3 shows the complete results for Experiment 1.

Model	Context window	Learning method	Prompt	F1	Precision	Recall	Accuracy
Majority Baseline	–	–	–	0.16	0.10	0.33	0.33
Llama-2-7b	1	zero shot	w/o character	0.46	0.49	0.45	0.45
Llama-2-7b	1	zero shot	v2 w/o character	0.37	0.57	0.36	0.36
Llama-2-7b	1	few shot	w/o character	0.28	0.35	0.32	0.32
Llama-2-7b	1	zero shot	v2 w/ character	0.58	**0.74**	0.49	0.49
Llama-2-7b	1	few shot	w/ character	0.29	0.41	0.32	0.32
Llama-2-13b	1	zero shot	w/o character	0.48	0.60	0.51	0.50
Llama-2-13b	1	zero shot	v2 w/o character	0.56	0.56	0.56	0.56
Llama-2-13b	1	few shot	w/o character	0.41	0.41	0.44	0.44
Llama-2-13b	1	zero shot	v2 w/ character	0.66	0.69	**0.68**	**0.68**
Llama-2-13b	1	few shot	w/ character	0.63	0.71	0.63	0.63
Llama-2-7b	2	zero shot	w/o character	0.47	0.48	0.47	0.47
Llama-2-7b	2	zero shot	v2 w/o character	0.35	0.65	0.33	0.33
Llama-2-7b	2	few shot	w/o character	0.19	0.27	0.24	0.24
Llama-2-7b	2	zero shot	v2 w/ character	0.51	0.52	0.49	0.49
Llama-2-7b	2	few shot	w/ character	0.20	0.28	0.25	0.25
Llama-2-13b	2	zero shot	w/o character	0.44	0.51	0.47	0.47
Llama-2-13b	2	zero shot	v2 w/o character	0.51	0.50	0.53	0.53
Llama-2-13b	2	few shot	w/o character	0.38	0.36	0.4	0.4
Llama-2-13b	2	zero shot	v2 w/ character	0.67	0.70	0.65	0.65
Llama-2-13b	2	few shot	w/ character	**0.68**	**0.74**	0.66	0.66
Platypus2-7b	1	zero shot	w/ character	0.26	0.51	0.19	0.19
Platypus2-7b	1	zero shot	w/o character	0.37	0.47	0.37	0.37
Platypus2-7b	2	zero shot	w/ character	0.29	0.31	0.33	0.33
Platypus2-7b	2	zero shot	w/o character	0.26	0.46	0.25	0.25
Platypus2-13b	1	zero shot	w/ character	0.41	0.50	0.46	0.46
Platypus2-13b	1	zero shot	w/o character	0.44	0.50	0.51	0.50
Platypus2-13b	2	zero shot	w/ character	0.42	0.49	0.46	0.46
Platypus2-13b	2	zero shot	w/o character	0.53	0.60	0.54	0.54
GPT-4	2	zero shot	w/ character	0.52	0.51	0.55	0.55
GPT-4	2	zero shot	w/o character	0.52	0.50	0.55	0.55

Table 3: Complete results for Experiment 1.

C Prompts

C.1 Used Prompts

C.1.1 Experiment 1: LLAMA 2

```
<s>[INST]
What kind of family relationship between
    {person_1} and {person_2} is
    conveyed in the following German {
    drama_snippet}?

Choose one of the following labels:
A: "child_of"
B: "parent_of"
C: "siblings"
D: "spouses".
JUST name the label and nothing else!
Family relation:
[/INST]
```

Listing 1: "Zero shot prompt template w/o person; v2"

```
<s>[INST]
What kind of family relationship is
    conveyed in the following German {
    drama_snippet}?

Choose one of "parent_of", "child_of", "
    siblings", "spouses".
JUST name the label and nothing else!
Family relation:
[/INST]
```

Listing 2: "Zero shot prompt template w/ person"

C.1.2 Experiment 1: Platypus2

```
Instruction: You are a literary scholar.
What is the family relation in the
    German text {drama_snippet}?
The possible family relations are parent
    , child, uncle, siblings, cousins.
Answer in a single sentence in the
    following format: The family
    relation is >>correct family
    relation<<.
Do NOT write code.
Do NOT write anything before or after
    the answer sentence.
```

Listing 3: "Zero shot prompt template w/ person"

```
Instruction: You are a literary scholar.
What is the family relation between {person1} and {person2} in the German text {drama_snippet}?
The possible family relations are parent, child, uncle, siblings, cousins.
Answer in a single sentence in the following format: The family relation between {person1} and {person2} is >>correct family relation<<.
Do NOT write code.
Do NOT write anything before or after the answer sentence.
Response:
```

Listing 4: "Zero shot prompt template w/o person"

C.1.3 Experiment 2: LLAMA 2

```
<s>[INST]

Consider the following two texts:

1. German text: {text}
2. {proposition}

Can you determine whether the second proposition {proposition} is entailed by the German text {text}?

Please provide your answer in the form of a logical statement:
a.) Yes, the proposition is entailed by the given text.
b.) No, the proposition is not entailed by the given text.
Your answer:
[/INST]
```

Listing 5: "Textual Entailment prompt "

C.1.4 Experiment 2: Platypus2

```
<s>[INST]

A text T textually entails a proposition P, iff typically, a human would be justified in reasoning from the propositions expressed by T to the proposition expressed by H.

Is the proposition {proposition} entailed by the following piece of German text: {text}?
Answer with:
a.) Yes, the proposition is entailed by the given text.
b.) No, the proposition is not entailed by the given text.
Your answer:
[/INST]
```

Listing 6: "Textual Entailment prompt "

C.1.5 Experiment 2: GPT-4

```
Common sense reasoning exam
###
Explain your reasoning in detail than answer with "Yes, the proposition is entailed by the given text" or "No, the proposition is not entailed by the given text".
Your answer should follow this 4-line format:

Premise: <some sentences from a German play>.
Question: <question requiring logical deduction>.
Reasoning: <an explanation of what you understand about the possible scenarios>.
Answer: <"Yes, the proposition is entailed by the given text" or "No, the proposition is not entailed by the given text">.

###
Premise: German {text}
Question: {proposition}
Reasoning: Let's think logically step by step.
Answer:
```

Listing 7: "Textual Entailment prompt

C.2 Different Prompting Setups

C.2.1 LLAMA 2

- Use of the Llama-specific prompt templates:
  - A prompt opens with the tags <s> [INST] and ends with [/INST]. A complete user/-model interaction is contained between the <s> and </s> tags.
- Enumeration of possible labels in a sentence vs. declared list
  - Prompt Template Version 1 (v1): “Choose one of "parent_of", "child_of", "siblings", "spouses".” vs. Prompt Template Version 2 (v2): Choose one of the following labels cf. Ziems et al. (2023, p. 12):

    A : "child_of"

    B : "parent_of"

    C : "siblings"

    D : "spouses".
- Instructions for generating desired output
  - *JUST name the label, do NOT generate any more text!*

C.2.2 Platypus

- Use Alpaca-specific prompt template:
  - A prompt with *Instruction* and *Response* directives
- Instructions for generating desired output
  - *Do NOT output anything after the family relation*
  - *Do NOT output programming code*
- Inserting information about the characters in a family relation
  - *identify the type of family relation and the characters involved* vs. *identify the type of family relation between person {person1} and person {person2}*

C.2.3 GPT-4

- Here we follow the OpenAI prompting principles as taught in the prompting course with Deeplearning.ai.
  - Give the model a role: “You are a literary scholar. ”.
  - Use of delimiters: ###.
  - Asking for structured output: “JUST name the label without quotation marks and nothing else!”

Coreference in Long Documents using Hierarchical Entity Merging

Talika Gupta[†*] and **Hans Ole Hatzel** [‡] and **Chris Biemann** [‡]
[†] IIIT Guwahati, Assam, India
[‡] Language Technology Group, Universität Hamburg, Germany
talika.gupta@iiitg.ac.in,
{hans.ole.hatzel, chris.biemann}@uni-hamburg.de

Abstract

Current top-performing coreference resolution approaches are limited with regard to the maximum length of texts they can accept. We explore a recursive merging technique of entities that allows us to apply coreference models to texts of arbitrary length, as found in many narrative genres. In experiments on established datasets, we quantify the drop in resolution quality caused by this approach. Finally, we use an under-explored resource in the form of a fully coreference-annotated novel to illustrate our model's performance for long documents in practice. Here, we achieve state-of-the-art performance, outperforming previous systems capable of handling long documents.

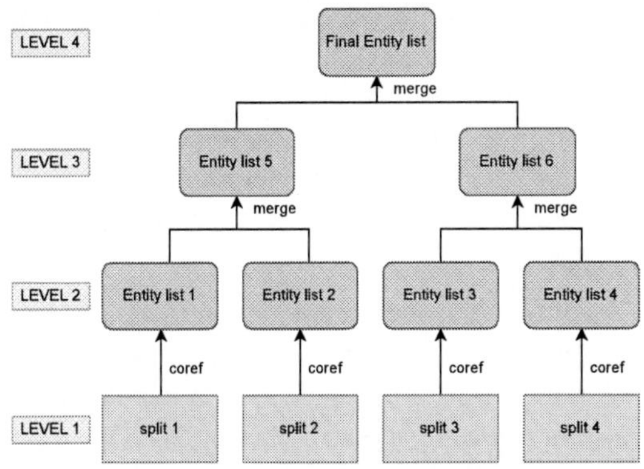

Figure 1: Our hierarchical merging approach iteratively merges pairs of entity lists until we arrive at a single set of entities that spans the full document. The first sets of weight denoted by "coref" is used while generating entity lists in each split. The second sets of weight denoted by "merge" is used while merging the entity lists across splits.

1 Introduction

Coreference resolution has significant time and memory requirements which, in currently released models, typically increase at least quadratically with the length of the document, resulting in inefficient systems. These substantial computational requirements make coreference resolution impractical for long documents such as novels. The task of establishing coreference links in such texts is important to enable a wide range of downstream tasks such as extracting character interaction networks (e.g. Konle and Jannidis, 2022). We propose a novel hierarchical algorithm for coreference resolution, to conserve computational resources while still achieving good performance. Our approach allows the models to – in principle – scale to documents of arbitrary length, outperforming existing long-document approaches.

Our proposed approach works by splitting a long document into multiple splits and then running an existing coreference resolution model on each split, thereby extracting the entities in each of them. We then propose a merging approach, where we pairwise merge the entities across splits by leveraging existing mention linking models, applying them to the merging of clusters instead. We experiment by splitting a document into a varying number of constituent parts and document the effectiveness of the merging approach as the length of the split decreases.

2 Background & Related Work

Coreference resolution is the task of identifying corefering spans in a text, that is to say, those groups of spans that refer to the same entity. Traditional coreference resolution comprises of two phases: span extraction from the text and the subsequent identification of coreference links among the extracted spans. The Word-Level Coreference (subsequently wl-coref) Resolution model (Dobrovolskii, 2021) separates the task of coreference resolution from span extraction and solves it on the word level, hence lowering the time complexity of the

[*]Work conducted as part of an internship at Universität Hamburg

Proceedings of LaTeCH-CLfL 2024, pages 11–17
March 22, 2024 ©2024 Association for Computational Linguistics

model to $O(n^2)$, where n is the length of the document. The span extraction is performed separately only for those words that are found to be coreferent to some other words. We will base our experiments on this model, but note that our hierarchical approach can in principle also be used with the other major coreference resolution model architectures, with the only requirement being that mentions can be represented by fixed-length embeddings. The models by Bohnet et al. (2023); Zhang et al. (2023) are recent sequence-to-sequence coreference models, but are impractical for long documents due to their memory requirements, with even short document processing being very resource-intensive. Our proposed hierarchical merging strategy could potentially help to apply these models to long documents.

We train our English model on the OntoNotes dataset (Pradhan et al., 2012) and the LitBank (Bamman et al., 2020) dataset, the latter containing coreference annotations for literary texts. We evaluate our approach on LitBank, and observe competitive performance to the state-of-the-art coreference models while being memory efficient. For training our German models, we employ the TüBa-DZ news dataset (Telljohann et al., 2004) and the DROC literature dataset (Krug et al., 2018).

Efficient coreference resolution in long documents is a task that current models struggle with, due to their memory-intensive nature. Traditional incremental coreference resolution models use global entity representations, but their performance lags behind compared to other models (Toshniwal et al., 2020). Thirukovalluru et al. (2021) propose a scalable coreference resolution approach that works on the token level instead of the span level, and drops non-essential candidate antecedents to improve memory and time requirements. They test their system on a long book for which no annotations are available. Their code is not available as open source, which prevented us from testing it on the full book data that we use.

3 Methodology

In this section, we describe our coreference approach in detail. We build upon the wl-coref model (Dobrovolskii, 2021), picking it over alternatives due to its quick inference and relative simplicity in conjunction with competitive performance. Our code is publicly available.[*] We split each document evenly into n splits, ensuring an equal number of sentences in each, where $n \in \{2, 4, 8\}$. Treating each split as an independent document, the model performs inference as normal on each of them, ideally yielding one cluster for each entity in each split. That is to say, the model predicts pairwise scores for whether two words co-refer and builds a transitive closure over those connections that exceed a certain threshold.

Now, since some entities in one split may refer to the same entity as entities in another split, we develop a merging approach to merge such coreferring entities across splits. This process is similar to linking two mentions, except that instead of passing mention embeddings, we pass entity embeddings to the model. Hence, we need a way to represent individual entities as vectors. In this work, we only evaluate the approach of creating entity embeddings by means of averaging over all embeddings in a cluster.

Next, we merge the entities from two splits at a time, by passing the entity embeddings in the same way that the model takes in the word embeddings to create links among them. This results in an entity list that spans both the splits. The merging process is repeated for all such disjoint pairs of splits in each level, resulting in $n/2$ splits in the subsequent level if the previous level had n splits. Consequently, the last level of our hierarchical approach results in entities that encompass the entire document. This is illustrated in Figure 1.

4 Experiments

We conduct a set of experiments to evaluate the efficacy of the proposed hierarchical merging approach. First, we train the standard wl-coref model, which is pre-trained on the OntoNotes dataset, for an additional 10 epochs on the LitBank dataset. The resulting model is evaluated on the test split of LitBank, from which we exclude the singleton mentions since the original wl-coref architecture removes singletons during the span extraction step. That is to say we evaluate on a version of the texts without singleton mentions.

In terms of merging approaches, we follow the process laid out in Section 3. We document the results under three scenarios: **(a)** without merging entities across splits, **(b)** merging entities without

[*] https://github.com/uhh-lt/hierarchical-coref

training the model for merging (i.e. using the same model twice), and **(c)** merging entities after training the model for merging.

We expect the merging approach to have a negative impact on prediction quality, at least for short documents. To quantify said impact of merging on the prediction quality, we split the documents into n equal-sized splits and experiment with different values of n, specifically 2, 4, and 8.

We set a baseline result by refraining from merging the entities across splits. For the merging module, we experimented with and without training the model specifically for merging. For training data, we use 2-way splits and use gold entities in the individual splits, rather than predicted ones. We subsequently average the span embeddings in each entity to obtain the entity embeddings in each split. As these embeddings are handled analogously to word embeddings in the original setup, the model creates links between the entities in the same way that it does so for the words. We evaluate the entities now spanning the entire documents on the gold data. Our merging model is trained for 10 epochs using 2-way split documents, on top of the existing word-level weights.

As we found the model to lose its span prediction capabilities after training the merging module, we use two distinct sets of weights for the two tasks. For the first level of our approach, where the model generates an entity list, we employ the first sets of weights, which was trained on LitBank but not trained specifically for merging entities (this is denoted as "coref" in Figure 1). For subsequent levels of our approach, where entity lists from two splits are merged to produce an entity list that spans both the splits, we use the second set of weights, which was specifically trained for merging entities (indicated by "merge" in Figure 1). We refer to the recursive application of the merging step as hierarchical entity merging.

Our approach is primarily evaluated on the standard CoNLL-F1 score. Additionally, we provide LEA, an evaluation metric that focuses on coreference links and resolves several issues that CoNLL-F1 constituent scores suffer from (Moosavi and Strube, 2016).

4.1 German Data

The main advantage of our model lies in its modest memory consumption, enabling the processing of documents of arbitrary length. Accordingly,

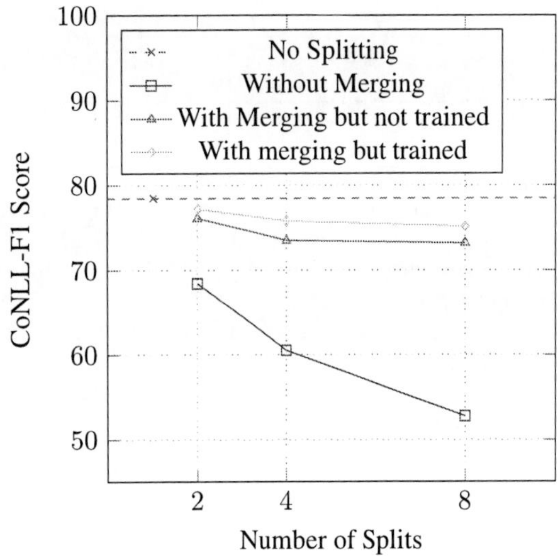

Figure 2: Comparison of CoNLL-F1 scores across varying numbers of splits, with and without merging the entity lists across splits

it is important to understand the performance on book-length literary texts. We are not aware of any such dataset in English, so instead we evaluate our model on two German texts: **(a)** the fairy tale "Der blonde Eckbert" by Ludwig Tieck (subsequently *Eckbert*) and **(b)** the full novel "Effi Briest" by Theodor Fontane (subsequently *Briest*). The two texts have around 7,000 and more than 100,000 tokens, respectively, and provide a good, if small-scale, benchmark for long-document coreference systems. For both novels, despite the coreference data being publicly available* we only know of results from a single system (Krug, 2020) on the data. For comparison, we provide the performance numbers of the system by Schröder et al. (2021) in Table 1, which was trained on German data, including the DROC corpus. Other models are generally not applicable to the full novel due to memory requirements. We train our hierarchical model on 2 and 4 splits of DROC, after training it on TüBa-D/Z using the German model gelectra-large as a foundation model (Chan et al., 2020). We chose 32 as a split size as it was the smallest number of splits to not cause memory errors at inference time for both texts. For comparison, we also provide numbers for 64 splits. Operating on split numbers that are not powers of two would also be possible

*https://gitlab2.informatik.uni-wuerzburg.de/kallimachos/AnnotierteDaten/-/tree/master/komplett

Text	System	CoNLL-F1	LEA
Eckbert	wl-coref	66.91	63.06
Eckbert	Schröder et al. (2021)	66.74	59.27
Briest	Schröder et al. (2021)	44.71	15.92
Briest	Krug (2020)	51.76	-

Table 1: Performance comparison of existing systems on the full stories. The system by Schröder et al. (2021) is the incremental system capable of handling arbitrary-length texts in constant memory. The rule-based system by Krug (2020) includes singletons in its evaluation and is therefore not directly comparable. Wl-coref is the word-level coreference model trained on DROC and TüBa-D/Z.

Text	Num-Splits	CoNLL-F1	LEA
Eckbert	32	51.56	59.06
Eckbert	64	57.27	50.78
Briest	32	52.89	36.75
Briest	64	54.17	39.12

Table 2: Performance of our system on the full German stories using either 32 or 64 splits of the original text. For detailed results see Appendix A, Table 5.

and would result in leaf nodes at varying depths of the merging tree. Our implementation omits this option for simplicity.

5 Results

All the scores have been obtained using the official CoNLL-2012 scorer (Pradhan et al., 2014). We perform experiments with varying numbers of splits, specifically splitting the document into 1 (i.e. not splitting it), 2, 4, and 8 segments, as can be seen in Figure 2.

For the unsplit document, we achieve a CoNLL-F1 score of 78.45. For two splits, we achieve a score of 76.06 if we employ merging without specifically training the merging module (using only first sets of weights). We achieve an improved F1 score of 77.30 if we additionally train the merging module (using two sets of weights). As a control experiment where we do not merge entity lists at all, we unsurprisingly obtain a much worse F1 score of 70.27. Similarly, for four and eight splits, the scores increase by two points on average as we go from one set of weights approach to the two sets of weights approach. The best F1 score we achieve is 74.52 and 73.96 respectively, by using two sets of weights. The scores when not conducting a merging step are unsurprisingly far below those with a

Num Splits	Merger trained	CoNLL-F1	LEA
1	Not needed	78.45	**78.37**
	appended	70.27	64.78
2	✗	76.06	74.68
	✓	77.30	**76.17**
	appended	60.54	50.20
4	✗	73.49	71.53
	✓	75.80	**74.52**
	appended	52.75	40.35
8	✗	73.18	72.52
	✓	75.13	**73.96**

Table 3: LEA and CoNLL-F1 scores for a varying number of document splits on the LitBank data. For detailed results see Appendix A, Table 4.

merging step and also drastically decrease as we split the text into more sections.

Our results for "Der Blonde Eckbert" using the word-level system also illustrate that the incremental system yields competitive results for short texts. With regard to the full-book data "Effi Briest", our approach was able to set a new state-of-the-art result, outperforming the incremental model as well as the rule-based model by Krug (2020), in terms of both CoNLL-F1 and LEA scores. While the CoNLL-F1 score is already considerably better than with the incremental system, moving from 44.71 to 54.17 (see Table 2), we see a much more substantial improvement in the LEA score, from 15.92 to 39.12, which we attribute to LEA's approach of marking down split entities. Our model outperforms the rule-based model, moving from a 51.76 CoNLL-F1 score to 54.17, although results are not directly comparable because Krug (2020) includes singleton mentions in his evaluation. These results were attained by further training the merging module of our model, first using the four splits of "Effi Briest" and then the two splits. In this experiment, shorter splits, generally, have a positive impact on performance. We attribute this to our average-pooling approach, which presumably results in worse embeddings in longer texts.

In practice, our model is very run-time efficient and inference for the whole book "Effi Briest" takes just under two minutes on a single A6000 GPU.

6 Conclusion

Our results demonstrate a potential path for applying state-of-the-art models to longer text without vast increases in memory requirements. We use existing systems to provide a baseline result for coreference resolution on a fully-annotated novel and set new state-of-the-art results. There is further headroom, as we are – for reasons of simplicity – not using the best available model for within-split resolution. Our training process could also be improved, for example by randomly splitting documents (rather than into roughly equal portions) to create more training data. While our approach exhibits reasonable coreference resolution quality for novels, it still does not suffice for use as a pre-processing step in most literary computing applications. We suspect that a substantial improvement of our approach would be possible by creating specialized embeddings for merging rather than averaging mention embeddings; additional error analysis will be needed to verify this intuition. Our general idea of hierarchical merging could also potentially be adapted to the very recent seq2seq coreference architectures (Zhang et al., 2023; Bohnet et al., 2023) where they could help overcome the model's maximum input lengths.

Acknowledgements

This work was, in part, funded through the project "Evaluating Events in Narrative Theory (EvENT)" (grant `BI 1544/11-1`) funded by the DFG.

References

David Bamman, Olivia Lewke, and Anya Mansoor. 2020. An annotated dataset of coreference in English literature. In *Proceedings of the Twelfth Language Resources and Evaluation Conference*, pages 44–54, Marseille, France. European Language Resources Association.

Bernd Bohnet, Chris Alberti, and Michael Collins. 2023. Coreference resolution through a seq2seq transition-based system. *Transactions of the Association for Computational Linguistics*, 11:212–226.

Branden Chan, Stefan Schweter, and Timo Möller. 2020. German's next language model. In *Proceedings of the 28th International Conference on Computational Linguistics*, pages 6788–6796, Barcelona, Spain (Online). International Committee on Computational Linguistics.

Vladimir Dobrovolskii. 2021. Word-level coreference resolution. In *Proceedings of the 2021 Conference on Empirical Methods in Natural Language Processing*, pages 7670–7675, Online and Punta Cana, Dominican Republic. Association for Computational Linguistics.

Leonard Konle and Fotis Jannidis. 2022. Modeling Plots of Narrative Texts as Temporal Graphs. In *Proceedings of the Computational Humanities Research Conference 2022*, volume 3290 of *CEUR Workshop Proceedings*, pages 318–336, Antwerp, Belgium. CEUR.

Markus Krug. 2020. *Techniques for the Automatic Extraction of Character Networks in German Historic Novels*. Ph.D. thesis, Julius Maximilians University Würzburg, Germany.

Markus Krug, Lukas Weimer, Isabella Reger, Luisa Macharowsky, Stephan Feldhaus, Frank Puppe, and Fotis Jannidis. 2018. Description of a corpus of character references in German novels-DROC [Deutsches ROman Corpus]. *DARIAH-DE Working Papers*, 27.

Nafise Sadat Moosavi and Michael Strube. 2016. Which Coreference Evaluation Metric Do You Trust? A Proposal for a Link-based Entity Aware Metric. In *Proceedings of the 54th Annual Meeting of the Association for Computational Linguistics (Volume 1: Long Papers)*, pages 632–642, Berlin, Germany. Association for Computational Linguistics.

Sameer Pradhan, Xiaoqiang Luo, Marta Recasens, Eduard Hovy, Vincent Ng, and Michael Strube. 2014. Scoring coreference partitions of predicted mentions: A reference implementation. In *Proceedings of the 52nd Annual Meeting of the Association for Computational Linguistics (Volume 2: Short Papers)*, pages 30–35, Baltimore, Maryland, USA. Association for Computational Linguistics.

Sameer Pradhan, Alessandro Moschitti, Nianwen Xue, Olga Uryupina, and Yuchen Zhang. 2012. CoNLL-2012 shared task: Modeling multilingual unrestricted coreference in OntoNotes. In *Joint Conference on EMNLP and CoNLL - Shared Task*, pages 1–40, Jeju Island, Korea. Association for Computational Linguistics.

Fynn Schröder, Hans Ole Hatzel, and Chris Biemann. 2021. Neural end-to-end coreference resolution for German in different domains. In *Proceedings of the 17th Conference on Natural Language Processing (KONVENS 2021)*, pages 170–181, Düsseldorf, Germany. KONVENS 2021 Organizers.

Heike Telljohann, Erhard Hinrichs, and Sandra Kübler. 2004. The Tüba-D/Z Treebank: Annotating German with a Context-Free Backbone. In *Proceedings of the Fourth International Conference on Language Resources and Evaluation (LREC'04)*, pages 2229–2232, Lisbon, Portugal. European Language Resources Association.

Raghuveer Thirukovalluru, Nicholas Monath, Kumar Shridhar, Manzil Zaheer, Mrinmaya Sachan, and Andrew McCallum. 2021. Scaling within document coreference to long texts. In *Findings of the Association for Computational Linguistics: ACL-IJCNLP 2021*, pages 3921–3931, Online. Association for Computational Linguistics.

Shubham Toshniwal, Sam Wiseman, Allyson Ettinger, Karen Livescu, and Kevin Gimpel. 2020. Learning to Ignore: Long Document Coreference with Bounded Memory Neural Networks. In *Proceedings of the 2020 Conference on Empirical Methods in Natural Language Processing (EMNLP)*, pages 8519–8526, Online. Association for Computational Linguistics.

Wenzheng Zhang, Sam Wiseman, and Karl Stratos. 2023. Seq2seq is all you need for coreference resolution. In *Proceedings of the 2023 Conference on Empirical Methods in Natural Language Processing*, pages 11493–11504, Singapore. Association for Computational Linguistics.

A Full Results

Num Splits	Merger trained	CoNLL MUC	CoNLL CEAFE	CoNLL B^3	CoNLL F1	LEA
1	Not needed	90.06	65.80	79.55	78.45	78.37
2	appended	89.03	60.77	66.48	70.27	64.78
	✗	89.45	63.95	76.14	76.06	74.68
	✓	89.56	65.91	77.57	77.30	76.17
4	appended	87.12	52.26	52.56	60.54	50.20
	✗	88.63	60.65	73.14	73.49	71.53
	✓	88.94	63.74	75.98	75.80	74.52
8	appended	84.08	43.05	43.51	52.75	40.35
	✗	87.64	58.32	74.25	73.18	72.52
	✓	88.02	62.94	75.59	75.13	73.96

Table 4: Detailed results for our LitBank experiment.

Text	System	CoNLL MUC	CoNLL CEAFE	CoNLL B^3	CoNLL F1	LEA
Eckbert	wl-coref	93.17	28.23	67.79	66.91	63.06
Eckbert	Schröder et al. (2021)	93.80	46.44	59.97	66.74	59.27
Briest	Schröder et al. (2021)	86.79	29.19	18.16	44.71	15.92
Briest	Krug (2020)	85.8	29.9	39.6	51.76	-

Table 5: Detailed performance comparison of existing systems on the full German stories.

Text	Num-Splits	CoNLL MUC	CoNLL CEAFE	CoNLL B^3	CoNLL F1	LEA
Eckbert	32	91.67	32.80	52.71	51.56	59.06
Eckbert	64	91.74	28.38	51.69	57.27	50.78
Briest	32	89.96	31.22	37.50	52.89	36.75
Briest	64	90.24	32.40	39.87	54.17	39.12

Table 6: Performance of our system on the full document using varying number of initial splits.

Metaphorical Framing of Refugees, Asylum Seekers and Immigrants in UK's Left and Right-Wing Media

Yunxiao Wang
Shanghai International Studies University
yxwang@shisu.edu.cn

Abstract

The metaphorical framing of refugees, asylum seekers, and immigrants (RASIM) has been widely explored in academia, but mainly through close analysis. The present research outlines a large-scale computational investigation of RASIM metaphors in UK's media discourse. We experiment with a method that facilitates automatic identification of RASIM metaphors in 21 years of RASIM-related news reports from eight popular UK newspapers. From the metaphors extracted, four overarching frames are identified. Further analysis reveals correlations between political bias and metaphor usage: overall, right-biased newspapers use RASIM metaphors more frequently than their left-biased counterparts. Within the metaphorical frames, water, disaster, and non-human metaphors are more prevalent in right-biased media. Additionally, diachronic analysis illustrates that the distinctions between left and right media have evolved over time. Water metaphors, for example, have become increasingly more representative of the political right in the past two decades.

1 Introduction

Issues regarding refugees, asylum seekers, and immigrants (henceforth RASIM) have been widely debated for their social, cultural, and economic implications. Metaphors, in particular, have received much scrutiny for their ability to link conceptualizations of immigration to personal and cultural experiences. As repositories of cultural understandings, they allow dominant ideologies and prejudices to be represented and reinforced in a transparent fashion, shaping public opinion without drawing attention to themselves (Ana, 1999; Cisneros, 2008).

Discussions concerning the metaphorical framing of immigrants, especially in political and media discourse, have primarily been carried out under the Critical Discourse Analysis (CDA) framework (Chilton, 2005; Hart, 2010, 2011; Hawkins, 2001; Cisneros, 2008; KhosraviNik, 2010; Musolff, 2015). Most of the metaphors identified and discussed so far represent dehumanizing or stigmatizing frames for immigrants and refugees, such as animals (Ana, 1999), diseases (Santa Ana et al., 1998), enemies and invaders (Parker, 2015), pollution (Cisneros, 2008), or other destructive forces like flood (Santa Ana et al., 1998; Charteris-Black, 2006). Another point of interest lies in how metaphors may be connected to the ideological compositions of texts (Charteris-Black, 2004, pp. 27-28). Charteris-Black (2006), for example, observes differences between UK's centre-right and far-right discourses in terms of their use of immigration metaphors, arguing that they contribute to the formation of legitimacy in right-wing political communication. However, this analysis does not cover data from left-wing media.

Partly due to the complexity of metaphorical language, most research in this field so far has relied on close analysis of small datasets. In this research, we conduct a large-scale computational investigation into the metaphorical framing of RASIM in British media. Our data comprises RASIM-related articles published in eight prominent UK newspapers over a span of 21 years from 2000 to 2020. From the text material, metaphorical expressions related to RASIM are automatically identified using both construction pattern matching and a fine-tuned RoBERTa model. The main research questions can be outlined as: (1) How have RASIM been metaphorically framed in the UK media? (2) Are distinctions among the newspapers' political stances reflected in their use of RASIM metaphors?

In summary, by incorporating computational methods in the analysis of RASIM metaphors, we aim to move beyond the limitations of small-scale studies, exploring how metaphors contribute to shaping public perceptions and investigating potential connections between metaphorical language and political stance.

Proceedings of LaTeCH-CLfL 2024, pages 18–27
March 22, 2024 ©2024 Association for Computational Linguistics

2 Related Work

Traditionally, analysis of metaphors in naturally occurring language has relied primarily on close examination of small datasets. With the development of corpus tools and the increasing accessibility of large corpora, corpus methods have been employed to extend such analysis to a greater scale (Charteris-Black, 2004; Deignan, 2005; Koller et al., 2008; Krennmayr, 2015; Musolff, 2015; Salahshour, 2016). Most research in this direction has taken a lexical approach by analyzing concordances of several specific search terms, defined either by drawing upon the researcher's knowledge of the source and target domains, or through close analysis of a sample of the corpus (Jaworska, 2017). However, this method has an inherent limitation – it confines the analysis to predetermined search strings, making it challenging to identify new metaphorical patterns (Koller et al., 2008).

A more sophisticated approach involves the use of WMatrix (Rayson, 2008), a corpus tool capable of assigning tokens to semantic domains based on the UCREL semantic annotation scheme (USAS). Initially put forward by Koller et al. (2008), this method builds upon the assumption that semantic tags allocated by WMatrix correspond to the source domains of metaphoric expressions. Instead of searching for specific word terms, this approach seeks domain tags, enabling the discovery of a broader spectrum of metaphors beyond predefined word lists. Demmen et al. (2015) start by identifying a list of metaphorical expressions from a small sample of the entire corpus, from which source domains and corresponding USAS tags are derived for query and analysis. Similarly, Jaworska (2017) follows a similar procedure to identify metaphors in promotional tourism discourse. However, since the USAS tagger itself cannot make predictions about metaphoricity, extensive human efforts are still required for disambiguating the candidate metaphors, which is not ideal for larger datasets.

Within computational linguistics, automatic identification and interpretation of metaphors have been a challenging and widely discussed topic (e.g., Choi et al., 2021; Dodge et al., 2015; Hong, 2016; Su et al., 2020). In recent years, efforts have been made to incorporate such advancements in the analysis of metaphorical framing in public discourse. Mendelsohn et al. (2020), for example, put forward a computational framework for investigating the dehumanization of LGBTQ people in the New York Times articles. Recognizing vermin metaphors as an important component of dehumanization, the authors use word embeddings to measure the metaphorical relationship between LGBTQ people and vermin. Specifically, a vermin concept vector is calculated by averaging the vectors of a predefined list of vermin terms. The intuition is that, the more closely a group is related to vermin through metaphors, the larger the cosine similarity will be between the group label vector and the vermin vector.

In a similar vein, Card et al. (2022) investigate how Republicans and Democrats frame immigrants differently using dehumanizing metaphors such as "animal" and "cargo". In order to detect implicit metaphorical language, mentions of immigrants and immigrant groups are masked from the sentences. A neural language model, BERT (Devlin et al., 2018), is then used to predict the mask words based on the surrounding contexts. From BERT's predictions, metaphoricity is calculated from the probabilities assigned to terms related to the predefined source domains. In this way, they essentially measure how much mentions of immigrants "sound like" particular types of dehumanizing metaphors.

In order to provide a comprehensive account of the metaphorical language related to RASIM, we hope that our identification system should be capable of unveiling novel metaphorical expressions, rather than relying on a fixed set of keywords or key domains. For this purpose, we experiment with a system based on finetuning RoBERTa, a Transformer-based language model capable of encoding nuanced contextual information. The setup is further introduced in Section 3.2.

3 Data and Method

3.1 Data Collection

In this study, the texts are collected from eight popular UK newspapers: *The Guardian*, *The Mirror*, *The Independent*, *The Times*, *The Telegraph*, *The Sun*, *The Daily Express*, and *The Daily Mail*. In general, within the relevant time frame, *The Guardian* and *The Mirror* are overall perceived as aligning with the Labour or the political left; on the other side, *The Times*, *The Telegraph*, *The Sun*, and *The Daily Express* are more often recognized as favourable to the Conservative or the political right; finally, *The Independent* is generally described as centre to centre-left (Forman and Baldwin, 2007).

While some level of consensus can be reached

regarding the overall political bias of a newspaper, there is no easy way to quantify such bias. As a rough point of reference, we refer to a survey conducted by YouGov in 2017 [1], which asked Britons about their perceptions of the eight newspapers' political biases. According to the survey results, *The Guardian* and *The Mirror* are perceived as predominantly left-wing, with a slightly higher percentage of people rating *The Guardian* as "very left-wing" than *The Mirror*. For *The Independent*, the majority of responses classify it as "centre", followed by "slightly left-of-centre". All the other five news media are predominantly conceived as right-wing. Ranked by the percentage of people who rate the newspaper as "very right-wing", *The Daily Mail* is considered to be the most right-biased, followed by *The Daily Express*, *The Sun*, *The Telegraph* and finally *The Times*.

To collect the data, we employ a procedure similar to the one adopted by Gabrielatos and Baker (2008). Using the news query interface provided by LexisNexis, we scrape all news articles that contain at least one of the RASIM terms, which are "immigrant", "migrant", "refugee", "asylum seeker" and all their inflections. The range of publication date is set between Jan. 1st, 2000 and Dec. 31st, 2020, spanning a total of 21 years. The sources of the articles are limited to the aforementioned eight newspapers. Altogether, over 570,000 articles are collected, amounting to over 380 million words after removing duplicate paragraphs. From these articles, approximately 638,000 mentions of RASIM terms are identified.

3.2 Identifying RASIM Metaphors

Lakoff and Johnson (1980) introduced the idea of conceptual metaphor mapping. In this framework, concepts originating from the source domain are employed figuratively to express aspects of the target domain. For example, consider the phrase "flow of immigrants", where the mapping IMMIGRANT IS WATER is instantiated. In this context, the term "flow" invokes associations with the source domain of WATER, which are then extended to the target domain of IMMIGRANT. This mapping allows immigrants to be discussed in relation to concepts and impressions drawn from the source domain, such as being mass in quantity and difficult to control.

Based on the conceptual metaphor theory, our goal can be summarized as follows: Given a sentence that contains a RASIM term (target word), the task is to identify all the words in the sentence (source words) capable of evoking a conceptual mapping to the RASIM domain. For a candidate source word to satisfy this requirement, both of the following conditions have to be satisfied:

First, it must be syntactically possible for the candidate word pair to form a linguistic metaphor. Previous research has illustrated that metaphors tend to be expressed in certain construction patterns (Sullivan, 2007, 2013), and certain syntactic relations can distinguish metaphorical uses from literal ones (Hovy et al., 2013). Drawing from these insights, we follow the procedure in Dodge et al. (2015), where a set of grammatical patterns are used to filter the word pairs before feeding them to a metaphoricity evaluation component. For each candidate word pair, we use the NLP package spaCy to extract the shortest dependency path (SDP) between the source and target words, and check whether the path is present in a predefined list (see Appendix A). Since the target words are limited to one of the RASIM terms, we only consider patterns where the target is a noun.

Second, the source word should be metaphorically used. That is, instead of conveying the literal sense, its meaning is context-specific and has to be interpreted in relation to the target domain. To capture the nuanced contextual information, we build upon a pretrained neural language model, RoBERTa (Liu et al., 2019), by finetuning it to classify the metaphoricity of a given token in a sentence. Concretely, taking a sentence as the input, RoBERTa encodes each (sub)token into a dense vector representation; a linear classification layer is then applied to the vector representation of the candidate source token to predict its metaphoricity. Despite its simplicity, this model architecture has served as a strong baseline in multiple metaphor identification tasks (Choi et al., 2021; Leong et al., 2020; Su et al., 2020).

For training, we use a free portion of the LCC metaphor dataset (Mohler et al., 2016), as it is close to the collected texts in terms of topic and style. The dataset contains around 7,500 sentences, each marked with a candidate source/target pair. For each candidate pair, its metaphoricity is annotated on a four-point scale from 0 to 3, where 0 stands for no metaphoricity, 1 for possible/weak metaphors, 2 for likely/conventional metaphors, and 3 for clear

[1] https://yougov.co.uk/politics/articles/17715-how-left-or-right-wing-are-uks-newspapers

Label	P	R	F1
0	0.80	0.93	0.86
1	0.49	0.33	0.39
2	0.48	0.23	0.31
3	0.63	0.76	0.69
>=1	0.91	0.76	0.83

Table 1: Classification results for all labels.

metaphors. Our model is trained to predict the level of metaphoricity of the candidate source token in a given sentence. The dataset is randomly split into 80% for training, 10% for validation, and 10% for testing. On the test split, the finetuned RoBERTa model achieves around 71% accuracy when predicting the fine-grained levels of metaphoricity, and around 87% accuracy when results are aggregated to a binary classification between non-metaphor (0) and metaphor (1-3). Detailed results for different metaphoricity labels are shown in Table 1. Overall, while the model struggles to assert the exact metaphor strength, resulting in lower accuracy, the coarse classification between metaphorical and literal usage is more reliable.

In summary, to identify RASIM metaphors from our corpus, we first use construction patterns to select the word pairs syntactically capable of forming metaphors. The finetuned RoBERTa model then predicts the metaphoricity of each candidate source word. For each identified metaphor pair, the lemmas corresponding to the source and target words, the sentential context, along with other necessary meta-information are stored in a data frame to be queried and analyzed later. Based on this procedure, a total of 55,344 RASIM metaphors are identified.

3.3 Identifying Frames

To curate frames from the metaphors identified by the model, we employ a qualitative procedure where the lemmas are clustered into different groups based on the source domains they evoke. To rule out coincidental occurrences, only those which have appeared at least 30 times are considered. Originally, we weighted the raw frequencies with predicted metaphoricity to help elevate stronger metaphors. However, given the high level of confusion the model exhibits with different levels of metaphor strengths, it is decided that the weighting scheme may not be robust enough.

For each candidate lemma, 15 sentences are randomly sampled where the corresponding word is predicted as a metaphor. A lemma is only considered a valid metaphor if it evokes a conceptual mapping to RASIM in at least half of the sentences. It is then allocated to the existing clusters based on resemblance to their members in terms of the source domain evoked; if no appropriate cluster exists, the lemma is assigned a new cluster. The general principle is that each cluster, representing a frame, should have a distinct focus shared by all members within.

3.4 Methodological Limitations

In this part, we review the potential inaccuracies and biases that may be involved in the research design, and discuss how these limitations may affect the validity of the results.

During data collection, eight newspapers are selected to represent the discourse of UK's left- and right-wing media. However, this may not be enough to sufficiently address some potential confounding factors such as the distinctions between broadsheet and tablet (Gabrielatos and Baker, 2008). Indeed, later analysis shows that the stylistic difference could be linked to the use of certain metaphors.

For metaphor identification, the model's ability to generalize knowledge from the training set to real-world data can be essential for the identification of novel metaphors. As a rough reference, among the 100 metaphors presented in Table 2, 56 of them have not appeared in the training split, including strong metaphors such as "magnet" and "dump". This suggests at least a certain level of ability to adapt to unseen data. However, a more rigorous evaluation, specifically regarding how many and what kind of metaphors may be missed, would require a manually annotated test set from the RASIM news reports.

Another issue relates to the judgement of whether a metaphor is directed to RASIM, which is done by matching construction patterns. However, even when the syntactic requirements are satisfied, it does not necessarily guarantee the existence of a conceptual mapping. Initially, other than the frames outlined in Table 2, we also identified three frames which are victim (e.g., "abuse", "exploit"), protection (e.g., "shield", "harbour"), and traveller (e.g., "journey"). After more careful consideration, however, we recognized that while such expressions are metaphorical, they represent more gen-

Frame	Source domain lemmas	%
Water	flow, wave, flood, influx, surge, pour, tide, stream, inflow, fill, trickle, swell, pool, outflow, tsunami	44.1
Non-human	magnet, drive, cap, caravan, trap, push, control, draw, attract, flee, smuggle, backlog, swarm, curb, catch, spread, lure, lock, flock, hunt, cram, strip, throw, dump, traffic, horde, mass, track, trafficking, boat, wash, ground, flight, weed, smuggling, brake, column, boatload, herd, cling, bottleneck	22.7
Disaster	flood, swamp, burden, impact, swarm, pressure, spread, overrun, storm, threat, overwhelm, drain, boom, chaos, sweep, tsunami, crush	15.0
Enemy	crackdown, block, ban, attack, deter, touch, invasion, sneak, fight, curb, catch, backlash, lock, bar, storm, battle, army, gang, disperse, slip, drain, defence, clampdown, play, tackle, break, round, harbour, war, barrier, sweep, camp, mob, chase, assault, besiege, bash	18.2

Table 2: Metaphorical frames and the corresponding source domain lemmas, arranged by raw frequency in descending order.

eral conceptual relations rather than being directed to RASIM. For example, although "shield" as in "shield the immigrants" is a metaphor, the mapping is between the idea of a physical barrier and the abstract concept of protection; and while this expression frames immigrants as being protected, the effect is literal rather than metaphorical. More intricate methods are therefore needed to better address the complexity of conceptual mapping.

Finally, we have not been able to systematically evaluate whether the inaccuracies may be distributed unevenly in different publications. For example, it could be possible that some metaphors used predominantly by either side have not been detected, or that certain expressions carry mainly literal senses in one side but metaphorical ones in the other. In both cases, it may lead to bias in the estimation of metaphor distributions among left- and right-wing media. It should be noted therefore that the following quantitative analyses are based on the assumption of even distributions of errors in different publications.

4 Results and Discussions

4.1 Metaphorical Frames

Following the procedure outlined in the previous section, four main frames are identified, as presented in Table 2. Note that the categories are not mutually exclusive, as a few words, depending on the context, can be representative of more than one type of metaphors.

Among the seven categories, water or liquid metaphors are the most prominent in terms of overall frequency. Words in this category illustrate a diverse range of conceptualizations for varying aspects of RASIM. For example, words like "flood", "swamp", and "tsunami" describe RASIM as destructive natural forces, expressing strongly negative sentiments. On the other hand, words like "flow", "stream", and "trickle" serve as more affectively neutral ways to describe their movements at different scales. Additionally, words like "surge", "swell" and "tide" focus on the temporal changes in the numbers of RASIM, typically sudden increases over a short period. Despite such variations, the water metaphors are dehumanizing in general, expressing neutral to strongly negative sentiments.

The non-human frame is characterized by the portrayal of RASIM as animals or inanimate entities that are denied agency and subject to manipulation from others. It can be viewed as an abstraction over several dehumanizing metaphors, such as animals ("flock"), cargo ("boatload"), plants ("weed"), or other inanimate objects. Although less frequent than the water metaphors, the non-human metaphors are characterized by the most diverse vocabulary. Some of them represent images of RASIM, for example, the size of their groups and communities (e.g., dehumanizing quantifiers including "swarm", "flock" and "horde"), as well as their reactions towards outside disturbances (e.g., "magnet", "flee", "lure"). Others, on the other hand, represent images of actions imposed upon immigrants and refugees, which are commonly used in relation to non-human entities such as animals (e.g., "trap", "hunt", "catch", "herd") and cargo (e.g., "smuggle", "dump", "traffic").

The disaster metaphors generally depict RASIM

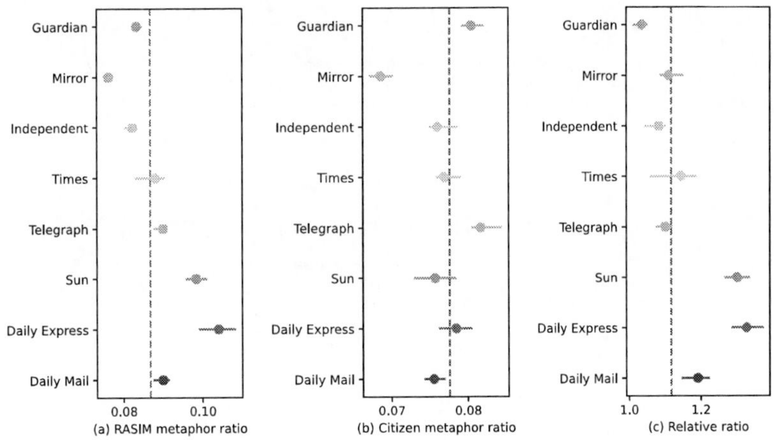

Figure 1: (a) Frequency of RASIM metaphors; (b) Frequency of "citizen" metaphors; (c) Relative frequency ratio between RASIM and "citizen" metaphors. In plots (a) and (b), farther to the left represents less frequent metaphor use. In plot (c), the closer to 1.0, the greater "similarity" there is between RASIM and citizens in terms of metaphor frequency. The grey dashed vertical lines represent the global averages calculated from the entire corpus. To ensure that the findings do not over-represent data from a short period of time, we leave out every two consecutive years in turn, and the full range of possible values obtained are shown using the horizontal lines.

as destructive forces such as flood (e.g., "swamp", "flood", "tsunami"), disease (e.g., "spread") or parasites (e.g., "swarm"). In addition to these words that directly frame RASIM to natural or man-made disasters, some words focus on representing the negative effects they bring to their destinations, for instance, imposing "burden(s)" upon citizens, "drain(ing)" the resources, and "overwhelm(ing)" the social and economic systems. In general, these metaphors emphasize how RASIM may disrupt life in the countries that they migrate to.

The enemy metaphors, likewise, can be further categorized into smaller groups concerned with different aspects of RASIM: First, their large quantities (e.g., "army", "gang" and "mob"); second, their hostile or illegal actions and the undesirable consequences (e.g., "invasion", "sneak", "storm", "drain"); finally, the government's actions in response to their "invasions" and "attacks", for instance fighting back ("crackdown", "battle", "war", "defend"), keeping them out ("block", "bar", "barrier") or containing them ("catch", "lock", "camp"). Overall, metaphors in this frame represent stigmatizing conceptualizations of RASIM, characterized by a strong sense of hostility.

Other than these four main frames, we also identify a small group of metaphors that do not fit into these categories. "Scapegoat" and "exodus", for example, frame RASIM under certain religious contexts (Ana, 1999). Given the relatively small number of occurrences, these metaphors are not included in the following quantitative analysis.

4.2 Political Bias and RASIM Metaphors

4.2.1 Overall Metaphor Frequency

To quantitatively assess the use of metaphors, a simple yet informative metric is their frequency. Figure 1(a) illustrates how often RASIM terms are accompanied by metaphors in each of the eight newspapers. A strong correlation is observed between political bias and metaphor frequency. Calculating the Pearson correlation coefficient yields r=.77, p=.02. Specifically, all three left-leaning newspapers—*The Guardian*, *The Mirror*, and *The Independent*—exhibit frequencies below the global average (indicated by the grey dashed line), while the five right-leaning newspapers consistently surpass this average. Among all eight publications, *The Daily Express* is the most frequent user of RASIM metaphors, with over one metaphor for every ten RASIM mentions. Conversely, *The Mirror* employs RASIM metaphors with the lowest frequency.

It could be argued though that this correlation might be influenced by other confounding factors, such as how inclined a newspaper is to use rhetorical devices. To explore this alternative hypothesis, we employ "citizen(s)" as a contrasting term and calculate the frequency with which it is accompanied by metaphors. This choice is informed by Ana

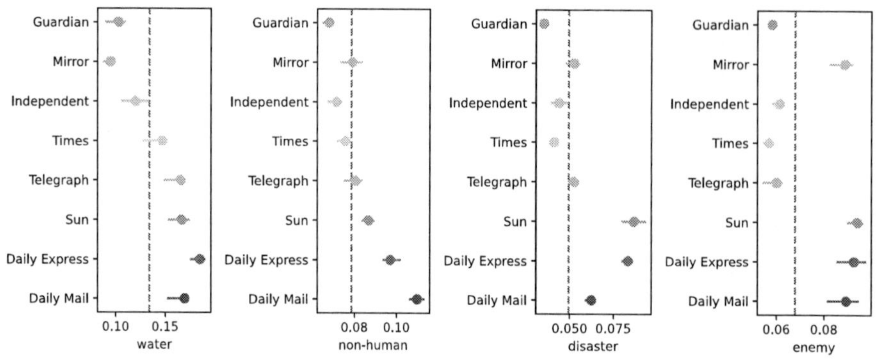

Figure 2: Frequency of each frame among all identified metaphors in each newspaper. The grey dashed vertical lines represent the global averages calculated from the entire corpus. Horizontal lines represent all possible values obtained by leaving out every two consecutive years. Farther to the right indicates higher frequency.

(1999) who observed different narratives between immigrants and citizens marked by the use of animal metaphors. The result is shown in Figure 1(b), and the correlation is no longer present.

Figure 1(c) offers insight into the relative ratio between the frequencies of RASIM metaphors and citizen metaphors, which can be interpreted as the "distance" between citizens and RASIM in terms of metaphor usage. For all newspapers, the relative ratios exceed 1.0, suggesting that RASIM terms are generally more likely to be depicted using metaphors in comparison to citizens. Notably, the correlation with political bias remains discernible, with a particularly pronounced effect observed among far-right newspapers, specifically, *The Sun*, *The Daily Express*, and *The Daily Mail*. Conversely, in *The Guardian*, RASIM and citizens are approximately equally likely to be accompanied by metaphors, with the relative ratio only slightly exceeding 1.0.

In summary, Figure 1 underscores two key findings: first, in comparison to citizens, RASIM are more likely to be subjects of metaphorical discourse; second, this distinction is notably more conspicuous within right-biased newspapers. A plausible explanation can be drawn from Dann's (1996) proposition that metaphor usage tends to increase when dealing with greater cultural distance as an attempt to mitigate the effect of strangeness. This claim has been supported by empirical evidence from Jaworska (2017), which shows that descriptions of faraway tourist locations are significantly more loaded with metaphors than those of "home" destinations. Although originating from the rhetorical language of tourism, this argument presents a reasonable rationale for our findings regarding the language of immigration. The higher frequency of RASIM metaphors may be interpreted as a reflection of the strangeness surrounding the images of immigrants and refugees, who are often portrayed as the social and cultural "other", subject to an alienating discourse. Consequently, the higher occurrence of RASIM metaphors in right-biased newspapers could be indicative of a heightened sense of cultural distance or unfamiliarity, contributing to a discourse that accentuates the perceived "otherness" of immigrants and refugees.

4.2.2 Frame Frequency

After investigating the overall metaphor frequencies, we turn our focus to whether newspapers with different political stances may show different "preferences" towards specific metaphorical frames. For each frame, we calculate its relative frequency against all metaphors identified in each newspaper. The results are shown in Figure 2. Clear correlations between political bias and metaphor frequency can be observed for water, disaster, and non-human metaphors: generally, right-biased newspapers are more likely to employ these types of metaphors. Such divergence in the use of dehumanizing metaphors may find its root in the broader ideological stance on immigration: right-leaning outlets may be inclined to present them as potential threats or crises, which resonates with narratives emphasizing security and stricter immigration measures.

Interestingly, for the enemy metaphors, their relative frequencies seem to be more closely connected to style (broadsheet vs. tabloid) rather than polit-

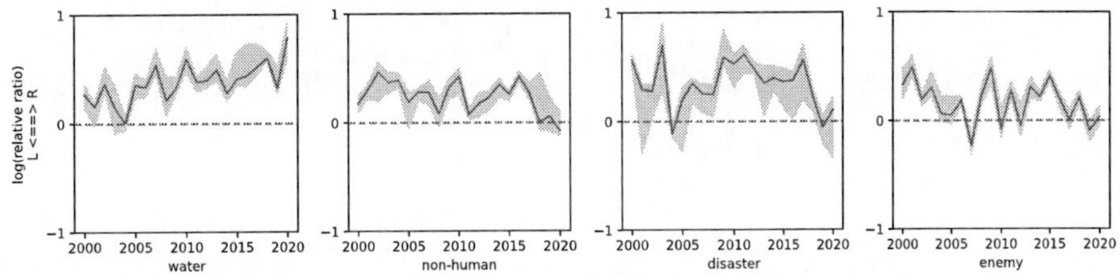

Figure 3: Logarithm of the relative usage frequency for each type of metaphors by left- and right-biased newspapers. For each subplot, greater values represent more frequent usage by right-biased newspapers and vice-versa. 0 represents equal frequency from both sides. Shaded areas represent all possible values obtained by leaving out each word in turn to ensure that the patterns are not overly influenced by single terms.

ical bias, with all four tabloids (*The Mirror*, *The Sun*, *The Daily Express* and *The Daily Mail*) well above the average, and all four broadsheets (*The Guardian*, *The Independent*, *The Times* and *The Telegraph*) below the average. However, more data are required to determine whether this correlation is statistically significant or merely due to chance.

Figure 3 illustrates how the partisan preference for each frame has evolved over time. Throughout the 21-year period, water metaphors have become increasingly more prominent in right-biased newspapers compared to their left-biased counterparts. On the other hand, disaster, non-human, and enemy metaphors have also shown higher frequencies in right-leaning publications, but their temporal trends show a tendency to move towards a more "neutral" position. These findings further demonstrate that the links between political bias and the use of RASIM metaphors are not static, but instead dynamic and subject to change over time.

5 Conclusions

In this research, we utilized a computational approach to analyze 21 years of UK news reports on refugees, asylum seekers, and immigrants (RASIM), revealing four key metaphorical frames: water, disaster, non-human, and enemy. Overall, the metaphorical representation of RASIM in British media has been predominantly stigmatizing and dehumanizing. Further analysis shows a correlation between political bias and RASIM metaphors: while both left- and right-wing newspapers exhibit increased metaphorical language when discussing RASIM compared to "citizen", this difference is more pronounced in right-wing discourse. Investigations of individual frames reveal that the dehumanizing frames are generally more common in right-biased media. Additionally, such connections have changed over time. Water metaphors, for example, have become increasingly more representative of the political right in the past two decades. Such divergences can be illustrative of the broad ideological stances on immigration.

With the help of computational modelling, we were able to extend the analysis of metaphorical framing to a large dataset, enabling a broader account of the interplay between language and ideology. This scaling-up, however, comes with trade-offs. First, we had to restrict ourselves to a closed set of syntactic structures, which is far from enough to fully address the richness and flexibility of metaphorical expressions in real life. How to strike a balance between the need for formalization and the high variability of real-world language can be a challenge for similar research. Second, to better understand how the use of metaphors relates and contributes to the sociopolitical environment, it can be important to examine the specific contexts, such as the event being described or the attitude of the authors. However, as we have only focused on individual metaphorical words, such contextual information has not been taken into consideration. Future research can therefore seek to establish links between text and context for a more nuanced analysis of language as a social practice.

References

Otto Santa Ana. 1999. 'like an animal i was treated': Anti-immigrant metaphor in us public discourse. *Discourse & Society*, 10(2):191–224.

Dallas Card, Serina Chang, Chris Becker, Julia Mendelsohn, Rob Voigt, Leah Boustan, Ran Abramitzky, and Dan Jurafsky. 2022. Computational analysis of 140 years of us political speeches reveals more positive but increasingly polarized framing of immigration. *Proceedings of the National Academy of Sciences*, 119(31):e2120510119.

Jonathan Charteris-Black. 2004. *Corpus Approaches to Critical Metaphor Analysis*. Palgrave Macmillan UK, London. DOI: 10.1057/9780230000612.

Jonathan Charteris-Black. 2006. Britain as a container: immigration metaphors in the 2005 election campaign. *Discourse & Society*, 17(5):563–581.

Paul A Chilton. 2005. Manipulation, memes and metaphors. *Manipulation and ideologies in the twentieth century*, page 15–43. Publisher: John Benjamins Amsterdam.

Minjin Choi, Sunkyung Lee, Eunseong Choi, Heesoo Park, Junhyuk Lee, Dongwon Lee, and Jongwuk Lee. 2021. MelBERT: Metaphor detection via contextualized late interaction using metaphorical identification theories. In *Proceedings of the 2021 Conference of the North American Chapter of the Association for Computational Linguistics: Human Language Technologies*, pages 1763–1773, Online. Association for Computational Linguistics.

J. David Cisneros. 2008. Contaminated communities: The metaphor of "immigrant as pollutant" in media representations of immigration. *Rhetoric & Public Affairs*, 11(4):569–601.

G. Dann. 1996. *The Language of Tourism: A Sociolinguistic Perspective*. A CAB International Publication. CAB International. LCCN: lc96206040.

Alice Deignan. 2005. *Metaphor and Corpus Linguistics*. John Benjamins Publishing. Google-Books-ID: bp3dHiJEUNQC.

Jane Demmen, Elena Semino, Zsófia Demjén, Veronika Koller, Andrew Hardie, Paul Rayson, and Sheila Payne. 2015. A computer-assisted study of the use of violence metaphors for cancer and end of life by patients, family carers and health professionals. *International Journal of Corpus Linguistics*, pages 205–231.

Jacob Devlin, Ming-Wei Chang, Kenton Lee, and Kristina Toutanova. 2018. Bert: Pre-training of deep bidirectional transformers for language understanding. *arXiv preprint arXiv:1810.04805*.

Ellen Dodge, Jisup Hong, and Elise Stickles. 2015. MetaNet: Deep semantic automatic metaphor analysis. In *Proceedings of the Third Workshop on Metaphor in NLP*, pages 40–49, Denver, Colorado. Association for Computational Linguistics.

Francis Nigel Forman and Nicholas Baldwin. 2007. *Mastering British Politics*. Bloomsbury Publishing.

Costas Gabrielatos and Paul Baker. 2008. Fleeing, sneaking, flooding: A corpus analysis of discursive constructions of refugees and asylum seekers in the uk press, 1996-2005. *Journal of English Linguistics*, 36(1):5–38.

C. Hart. 2010. *Critical Discourse Analysis and Cognitive Science: New Perspectives on Immigration Discourse*. Springer.

Christopher Hart. 2011. Force-interactive patterns in immigration discourse: A cognitive linguistic approach to cda. *Discourse & Society*, 22(3):269–286. Publisher: SAGE Publications Sage UK: London, England.

Bruce Hawkins. 2001. Ideology, metaphor and iconographic reference. *AMSTERDAM STUDIES IN THE THEORY AND HISTORY OF LINGUISTIC SCIENCE SERIES 4*, page 27–50. Publisher: Amsterdam; Philadelphia; J. Benjamins Pub. Co; 1999.

Jisup Hong. 2016. Automatic metaphor detection using constructions and frames. *Constructions and Frames*, 8(2):295–322.

Dirk Hovy, Shashank Srivastava, Sujay Kumar Jauhar, Mrinmaya Sachan, Kartik Goyal, Huying Li, Whitney Sanders, and Eduard Hovy. 2013. Identifying metaphorical word use with tree kernels. In *Proceedings of the First Workshop on Metaphor in NLP*, pages 52–57.

Sylvia Jaworska. 2017. Metaphors we travel by: A corpus-assisted study of metaphors in promotional tourism discourse. *Metaphor and Symbol*, 32(3):161–177.

Majid KhosraviNik. 2010. The representation of refugees, asylum seekers and immigrants in british newspapers: A critical discourse analysis. *Journal of Language and Politics*, 9(1):1–28.

Veronika Koller, Andrew Hardie, Paul Rayson, and Elena Semino. 2008. Using a semantic annotation tool for the analysis of metaphor in discourse. *Metaphorik. de*, 15(1):141–160.

Tina Krennmayr. 2015. What corpus linguistics can tell us about metaphor use in newspaper texts. *Journalism Studies*, 16(4):530–546.

George Lakoff and Mark Johnson. 1980. *Metaphors We Live By*. University of Chicago Press. Google-Books-ID: iyZgQgAACAAJ.

Chee Wee (Ben) Leong, Beata Beigman Klebanov, Chris Hamill, Egon Stemle, Rutuja Ubale, and Xianyang Chen. 2020. A report on the 2020 VUA and TOEFL metaphor detection shared task. In *Proceedings of the Second Workshop on Figurative Language Processing*, pages 18–29, Online. Association for Computational Linguistics.

Yinhan Liu, Myle Ott, Naman Goyal, Jingfei Du, Mandar Joshi, Danqi Chen, Omer Levy, Mike Lewis, Luke Zettlemoyer, and Veselin Stoyanov. 2019. Roberta: A robustly optimized bert pretraining approach. *arXiv preprint arXiv:1907.11692*.

Julia Mendelsohn, Yulia Tsvetkov, and Dan Jurafsky. 2020. A framework for the computational linguistic analysis of dehumanization. *Frontiers in Artificial Intelligence*, 3:55.

Michael Mohler, Mary Brunson, Bryan Rink, and Marc Tomlinson. 2016. Introducing the lcc metaphor datasets. In *Proceedings of the Tenth International Conference on Language Resources and Evaluation (LREC'16)*, pages 4221–4227.

Andreas Musolff. 2015. Dehumanizing metaphors in uk immigrant debates in press and online media. *Journal of Language Aggression and Conflict*, 3(1):41–56.

Samuel Parker. 2015. 'unwanted invaders': The representation of refugees and asylum seekers in the uk and australian print media. *ESharp*, 23(1):1–21.

Paul Rayson. 2008. From key words to key semantic domains. *International Journal of Corpus Linguistics*, 13(4):519–549.

Neda Salahshour. 2016. Liquid metaphors as positive evaluations: A corpus-assisted discourse analysis of the representation of migrants in a daily new zealand newspaper. *Discourse, Context & Media*, 13:73–81.

Otto Santa Ana, Juan Moran, and Cynthia Sanchez. 1998. Awash under a brown tide: Immigration metaphors in california public and print media discourse. *Aztlán: A Journal of Chicano Studies*, 23(2):137–176.

Chuandong Su, Fumiyo Fukumoto, Xiaoxi Huang, Jiyi Li, Rongbo Wang, and Zhiqun Chen. 2020. DeepMet: A reading comprehension paradigm for token-level metaphor detection. In *Proceedings of the Second Workshop on Figurative Language Processing*, pages 30–39, Online. Association for Computational Linguistics.

Karen Sullivan. 2007. *Grammar in metaphor: A construction grammar account of metaphoric language*. dissertation, University of California, Berkeley.

Karen Sullivan. 2013. Frames and constructions in metaphoric language. *Frames and Constructions in Metaphoric Language*, page 1–192. Publisher: John Benjamins Publishing Company.

A Construction Patterns

The LCC dataset is utilized for the compilation of this construction pattern list. Concretely, the LCC dataset provides samples where the candidate source/target word pairs are syntactically impossible to form metaphors. Such samples are labeled with score -1. We start from a list complete with all construction patterns extracted from the positive samples, i.e. those with score greater than -1. Then, we iteratively remove patterns which, after removal, improve F1 on the entire dataset. Finally, we remove infrequent patterns as well as those which are results of parse errors. The final list of patterns recovers 90% of the positive sentences from the dataset.

Construction patterns
S_NOUN-prep-ADP-pobj-T_NOUN
S_VERB-dobj-T_NOUN
T_NOUN-nsubj-S_VERB
T_NOUN-compound-S_NOUN
S_ADJ-amod-T_NOUN
T_NOUN-nsubj-AUX-attr-S_NOUN
S_VERB-agent-ADP-pobj-T_NOUN
S_VERB-amod-T_NOUN
S_NOUN-compound-T_NOUN
T_NOUN-nsubjpass-S_VERB
T_NOUN-nsubj-AUX-acomp-S_ADJ
T_NOUN-poss-S_NOUN

Table 3: Construction patterns for the initial selection of metaphor candidates.

Computational Analysis of Dehumanization of Ukrainians on Russian Social Media

Kateryna Burovova
LetsData / Lviv, Ukraine
kate.burovova@gmail.com

Mariana Romanyshyn
Grammarly / Kyiv, Ukraine
mariana.scorp@gmail.com

Abstract

Dehumanization is a pernicious process of denying some or all attributes of humanness to the target group. It is frequently cited as a common hallmark of incitement to commit genocide. The international security landscape has seen a dramatic shift following the 2022 Russian invasion of Ukraine. This, coupled with recent developments in the conceptualization of dehumanization, necessitates the creation of new techniques for analyzing and detecting this extreme violence-related phenomenon on a large scale. Our project pioneers the development of a detection system for instances of dehumanization. To achieve this, we collected the entire posting history of the most popular bloggers on Russian Telegram and tested classical machine learning, deep learning, and zero-shot learning approaches to explore and detect the dehumanizing rhetoric. We found that the transformer-based method for entity extraction SpERT shows a promising result of $F_1 = 0.85$ for binary classification. The proposed methods can be built into the systems of anticipatory governance, contribute to the collection of evidence of genocidal intent in the Russian invasion of Ukraine, and pave the way for large-scale studies of dehumanizing language. This paper contains references to language that some readers may find offensive.

1 Introduction

Dehumanization has been frequently proposed as a mechanism that mitigates or eliminates moral concern about cruel behavior, thus playing a crucial role in war, genocide, and other forms of extreme violence (Bandura, 1999). Recent research (Mendelsohn et al., 2020; Markowitz and Slovic, 2020; Magnusson et al., 2021) focuses on more subtle forms of dehumanization; those are considered both a precursor and a consequence of discrimination, violence, and other forms of day-to-day abuse outside of the context of armed conflicts. This shift in focus resulted in a simultaneously more nuanced and broad definition of dehumanization, inviting new approaches to operationalization. Multiple investigations (Diamond et al., 2022; Hook et al., 2023) have been conducted regarding the 2022 Russian invasion of Ukraine to determine if the Russian Federation is responsible for violating the Genocide Convention[1]. Central to these inquiries is the role of dehumanizing rhetoric in the direct and public encouragement of genocide. According to these reports, Russian officials and State media repeatedly described Ukrainians as subhuman ("bestial," "zombified"), contaminated or sick ("filth," "disorder"), or existential threats and the epitome of evil ("Hitler youth," "Third Reich," "Nazi"), rendering them legitimate or necessary targets for destruction. Hence, detecting the dehumanizing rhetoric at scale within this particular context can provide comprehensive evidence for further inquiries, as well as empirically support or challenge the assumptions of existing dehumanization frameworks.

2 Background

The concept of dehumanization has developed through cross-disciplinary conversations, integrating perspectives from various fields such as philosophy, psychology, sociology, and more. In the field of social psychology, Bandura (1999) investigated how people can psychologically detach themselves from others, viewing them as less than human, which can result in violence, bias, and discrimination. In sociology and critical theory, dehumanization was first scrutinized in relation to power dynamics, social disparities, and oppressive structures. Academics and thinkers such as Fanon (1967), Arendt (1963), and Bauman (1989) examined how dehumanization contributes to the marginalization, subjugation, and violence in sce-

[1] https://www.un.org/en/genocideprevention/genocide-convention.shtml

Proceedings of LaTeCH-CLfL 2024, pages 28–39
March 22, 2024

narios of colonialism, totalitarianism, and genocide.

Dehumanization is often seen as a key stage leading to genocide[2]. However, Haslam (2019) argues that dehumanization is not just a precursor but is intertwined throughout the entire genocidal process. Our research shows that the temporal change of dehumanizing rhetoric on Russian Telegram conforms with this view.

3 Definition and Operationalization

Dehumanization is commonly defined as the denial of humanness to others (Haslam, 2006). Currently accepted frameworks mainly differ in understanding of "humanness" and of the ways in which this denial is taking place.

Kelman (1973) defines dehumanization as denying an individual both "identity" and "community"; Opotow (1990) introduces "moral exclusion" as an extension. Bandura (1999, 2002) argues that dehumanization relaxes moral self-sanctions and prevents self-condemnation. Harris and Fiske (2006, 2011) relate dehumanization to mental-state attribution, suggesting that dehumanized groups are perceived as having fewer mental states. This aligns with the mind perception theory by Gray et al. (2007), which categorizes perceptions into two dimensions: agency and experience.

The integrative review on dehumanization by Haslam (2006) proposes two distinct senses of humanness that can be denied in order to dehumanize persons or groups: human uniqueness **(UH)** and human nature **(NH)**. According to Haslam, the line dividing people from the related category of animals is defined by traits that are "uniquely human" (UH). Refined emotions, higher-order cognition, and language can all be considered uniquely human. Human-nature attributes (NH) are those that characterize humans in general and include emotional responsiveness, interpersonal warmth, openness, and emotional depth. Building on that, Haslam (2006) proposed two corresponding types of dehumanization: animalistic dehumanization, in which people or groups are thought to have fewer characteristics that make them uniquely human (and are perceived as vermin, animals, or disease), and mechanistic dehumanization, in which people or groups are thought to have fewer characteristics that describe people in general (and are perceived as automata or objects).

Li (2014) proposed the mixed model of dehumanization to address existing variability in the literature on dehumanization. This model is informed by framework by Haslam (2006); it contains four quadrants, formed by the level of Human Nature and Human Uniqueness attribution. We found this framework consistent with the most recent empirical evidence found in historical documents (Landry et al., 2022).

Genocide researchers highlight the limitations of using dehumanization as an early warning sign for atrocities. Neilsen (2015) introduced *toxification* as a more precise indicator. This concept goes beyond viewing victims as merely non-human and suggests that perpetrators see eradicating victims as essential for their survival, for two main reasons: victims are "toxic to the ideal" (threatening beliefs) or "toxic to the self" (posing harm).

Drawing from from Li (2014), Haslam (2006), and Neilsen (2015), we define *dehumanization* as the representation of the target group as existentially threatening and/or morally deficient by blatantly or subtly manipulating the features of its human uniqueness (including relevant elements in agency and competence) and/or human nature (including relevant elements in experience and warmth). Figure 1 summarizes all types with corresponding metaphors.

We chose the representation of Ukrainians in Russian Telegram as the target of our research. Below are some common blatantly dehumanizing metaphors used towards Ukrainians broken into types of dehumanization. Of type $\downarrow$ UH $\uparrow$ NH: укропитеки[3], свинорез[4], бандерлоги[5]; of type $\downarrow$ UH $\downarrow$ NH: расходный материал[6], майданутые[7], горящее сало[8], and of type $\uparrow$ UH

[2] http://genocidewatch.net/genocide-2/8-stages-of-genocide/

[3] [ukropiteki] — a derogatory term, combining "ukro" for "Ukrainian" and "piteki," which refers to early hominids

[4] [svinorez] — "pig slaughter," implying that Ukrainians are similar to pigs

[5] [banderlogi] — a play on Kipling's monkeys "Bandar-log" and "Bandera" (Ukrainian nationalist and the leader of the Ukrainian Insurgent Army)

[6] [raskhodnyy material] — "expendable material"

[7] [maidanutye] — the term is derived from "Maidan," the center of the Euromaidan protests in 2013-2014. The ending "-nutye" is common in Russian slang words meaning "crazy" or "nuts". Thus, the word can be translated as mentally ill with Maidan.

[8] [goryashcheye salo] — "burning lard," used to refer to Ukrainian people dying at the battlefield

↓ NH: укронацики[9], сатанисты[10], шайтаны[11]. ↑ UH ↑ NH means the absence of dehumanization.

In the case of укропитеки[3] , by being likened to pre-humans, Ukrainians are shown as lacking competence (dehumanized along the UH axis). Desires or experience are not denied, so NH axis position is unaffected; thus, we assign the label ↓ UH ↑ NH. The укронацики[9] metaphor demonizes Ukrainians and shapes an image of the epitome of evil, exaggerating competence and agency but reducing perceived warmth, affect, and shared human experience; thus we assign the label ↑ UH ↓ NH.

We treat dehumanization signals as additive. Therefore, compound words like Свинорейх[12], which consist of dehumanizing metaphors of ↓ UH ↑ NH and ↑ UH ↓ NH, are considered ↓ UH ↓ NH.

Table A.2 outlines a detailed description.

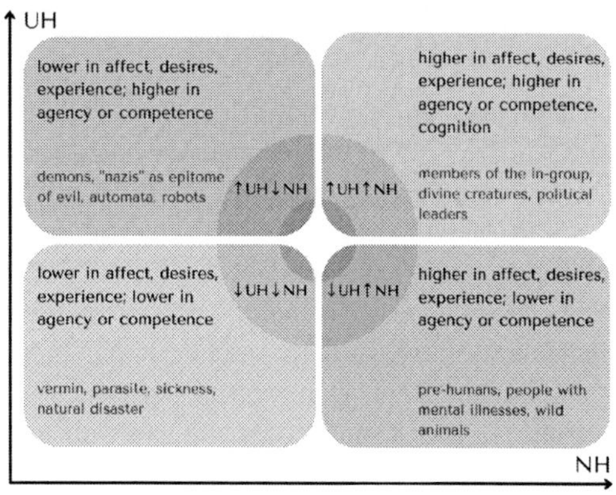

Figure 1: Four quadrants of dehumanization. ↑ UH ↑ NH represents the absence of dehumanization. The other three quadrants represent three types of dehumanization.

4 Related Computational Work

To the best of our knowledge, the first and only computational analysis framework focusing on dehumanization was proposed by Mendelsohn et al. (2020). It was applied to the analysis of discussions of LGBTQ people in the New York Times from 1986 to 2015. The authors identified linguistic correlates of salient components of dehumanization (negative evaluation, denial of agency, and metaphors of moral disgust and vermin) and then analyzed linguistic variation and change in discourses surrounding the chosen marginalized group.

In the study on dehumanization toward immigrants, Markowitz and Slovic (2020) attempted to evaluate the psychology of dehumanizers through language patterns, hypothesizing that three language dimensions reflect those who tend to dehumanize immigrants: (i) prevalence of impersonal pronouns, (ii) use of power words (e.g., "pitiful," "victim," "weak"), and (iii) emotion terms, evaluated through the affect category in LIWC (Pennebaker et al., 2015).

The study of Card et al. (2022) identifies dehumanizing metaphors by measuring the likelihood of a word denoting foreigners being related to a number of well-known dehumanizing metaphors (like "animals" and "cargo") in immigration-related sentences. The approach is best suited for the research setting where exhaustive lists of the considered metaphors are available.

Work by Magnusson et al. (2021) is informed by Bandura (1999); it presents a knowledge graph schema, dataset, and transformer-based NLP model SpERT to identify and represent indicators of moral disengagement and dehumanization in text. They define the multi-attribute knowledge graph extraction task as predicting the set of entities, the set of relations over entities, and the set of attributes over entities in a given text span. Among other indicators, they detect dehumanization based on the cumulative semantics of these attributes, entities, and relationships.

In the study of Nazi propaganda documents, Landry et al. (2022) analyzed the prevalence of agency and experience mental state terms used when referring to Jews in Nazi Germany, building on the moral disengagement theory by Bandura (1999) and mind perception theory introduced by Gray et al. (2007).

5 Research Setting

Existing solutions by Mendelsohn et al. (2020); Magnusson et al. (2021) have not yet been tested on cross-domain tasks. Computational analysis of dehumanization in the context of extreme violence (Landry et al., 2022) so far relied only on dictionary and lexicon-based approaches, and few dehumanization frameworks have been tested. Moreover, state-of-the-art large language models (LLMs) showing promising results across diverse

[9] [ukronatsiki] — a derogatory term which is a portmanteau of Ukrainian and Nazi

[10] [satanisty] — "satanists"

[11] [shaytany] — derived from the word "Shaytan" of Arabic origin, which means "devil" or "demon"

[12] [svinoreikh] — "Pig Reich" referencing the Nazi regime

domains were not yet tested for this task.

5.1 Methodology

Our approach is grounded in the definition of dehumanization proposed in Section 3. We narrow down the scope of the dehumanization to the context of extreme violence (hence, we consider only negative valence) but include both the subtle form expressed via metaphors and stylistic devices and the blatant form (e.g., directly likening the target group to inanimate objects).

We frame our primary task as the binary classification at the sentence level — detecting sentences containing at least one instance of dehumanization of Ukrainians. Building on the developed binary classification system, we work on a supplementary multi-class classification system that receives a sentence in Russian and classifies it by type according to the chosen dehumanization framework. We then investigate the explanatory potential of the chosen dehumanization framework.

Approach to Solution We start with collecting the data from selected social media sources. We proceed with the annotation project to obtain training data of the required granularity and format. We begin experimentation with the classical machine learning models to establish baseline performance and leverage their interpretability.

We experiment with enhancements like augmentation and feature engineering to improve performance. We then proceed with the deep learning approach by testing the SpERT model, applied for computational analysis of dehumanization for similar tasks by Magnusson et al. (2021). Next, we test the zero-shot learning approach using OpenAI (2022) GPT-3.5 Turbo[13]. We conclude experiments for the binary classification of dehumanization at the sentence level by comparing the results in the same setting. Next, we use the best model to explore the evolution of dehumanizing rhetoric within the timeframe of our dataset to test the explanatory potential of existing dehumanization frameworks.

For **quantitative evaluation** we rely on F_1, precision, and recall as our evaluation metrics. We adhere to an 80/20 train/test split with five folds for cross-validation.

Magnusson et al. (2021) reported micro-averaged F_1 = 50.12, precision 51.30, and recall of 51.29 for dehumanization relation for the SpERT model trained to extract signs of moral disengagement. We cannot treat these results as state-of-the-art and report these values purely as a reference, given that our results can not be directly compared due to the different contexts, underlying entity and relation schemes, and annotation approaches. Comparison with the commonly used methods is also impossible since we are pioneering binary dehumanization classification.

To further investigate the performance of the best-performing models, we perform a **qualitative error analysis** to identify the patterns in dehumanization not adequately captured by our models.

6 Dataset

For our analysis, we chose a group of 299 most popular political and news Telegram channels[14] (based on the ratings in the largest Telegram channels and groups catalog TGStat[15]) and collected their entire posting history spanning from 22 September 2015 to 25 November 2022, yielding 6.8M posts (23.91M sentence-level samples).

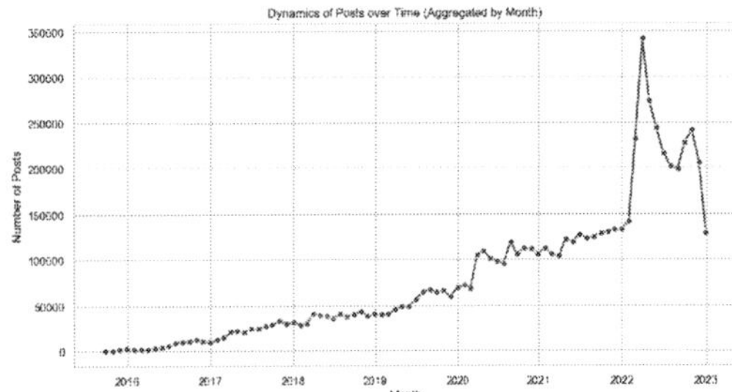

Figure 2: Dynamics of posts in the initial unlabeled dataset over time. Y-axis shows the absolute number of posts, and X-axis represents the time scale.

Several advantages arise from using social media as a data source for our task. Social media platforms provide (i) a dataset encompassing many different perspectives; (ii) an authentic snapshot of people's attitudes and behaviors; (iii) better accessibility with the APIs for ethical data collection.

While choosing a particular platform, we considered algorithmic contamination and the sanctions against Russia, due to which big social media companies have been limiting their functionalities[16].

Telegram is beneficial for our task due to (i) broad geographical scope and growth; (ii) being

[13]https://platform.openai.com/docs/models

[14]Unidirectional messaging platform where administrators can post exclusively.

[15]https://tgstat.com/

[16]https://www.npr.org/2022/02/26/1083291122/russia-ukraine-facebook-google-youtube-twitter

a primary messenger for most Russians (Newman et al., 2022); (iii) state role in decentralized content discovery: the Russian state uses the centralized endorsement by influencers, further amplifying their messages (Vavryk, 2022).

6.1 Data Annotation

To obtain training datasets we undertook the Annotation Project consisting of two sub-projects. First, we compiled a dataset of sentences and crowdsourced annotation with binary labels for the presence of dehumanization using Labelbox (2023). Then for the positive class sentences, we annotated dehumanizing spans by type of dehumanization.

We crowdsourced labels for this project from Ukrainian volunteers from the Ukrainian NLP community. We made this decision after carefully considering the alternatives: inviting Russian citizens (which would also introduce bias but would be much more difficult to set up) or inviting Russian-speaking annotators from other countries (who do not possess the needed level of context immersion). Since dehumanization is often expressed through the literary devices rooted in a particular culture, we clearly articulated how to handle the popular ambiguities in the annotation guidelines.

We evaluate the labels with Cohen's Kappa (Cohen, 1960), developed to account for the possibility that annotators guess on at least some variables due to uncertainty. The original annotation guidelines in Ukrainian for all sub-projects can be accessed via our GitHub repository[17]. All questions included the option to refuse answering if unsure, and all workers were clearly warned about the highly offensive content.

6.1.1 Part I of Annotation Project

The annotation schema for Part I of the annotation project (AP1) included three questions (listed here in translation from Ukrainian):

Q1 Does this sentence contain any mentions of Ukraine or Ukrainians?

Q2 Are there any comparisons that reduce Ukrainians to inanimate objects or individuals devoid of their distinctive human characteristics?

Q3 Is there an emotional evaluation of Ukrainians present in the text, and of what kind?

The full dataset encompasses various writing styles and spans years of posting history; thus, we expected the signals of dehumanization to be sparse. AP1 included two preselection phases. We started with a semi-manual random sentence sampling across the entire timeline and author set. To reduce the potential bias that this approach may impose on our training data, we finetuned transformer models for Russian on tasks of sentiment classification[18] and detection of mention of Ukrainians[19] using the Q1 and Q3 answers from the previous step. We then randomly sampled from the sentences from the full dataset classified by these models as containing a negative sentiment and a mention of Ukrainians.

Nine volunteers worked on AP1, annotating 4,111 samples in total. 39.28% of samples are positive dehumanization class, 20% of all samples were annotated by two workers. The overall inter-annotator agreement (IAA) is calculated as the pairwise mean. The labels for AP1 sentence-level classification are of high quality with Cohen's Kappa coefficients equal to 0.85 and 0.97 for dehumanization labels for the two preselection phases and the average of 0.90 and 0.92 for Q1 and Q3 respectively. Figure A.4 shows the distribution of classes for AP1.

6.1.2 Part II of Annotation Project

Our goal for Part II of the Annotation Project (AP2) was twofold: (i) to facilitate experimentation with entity classifiers, we need to obtain a dataset with spans labeled in the CoNLL04 format (Carreras and Màrquez, 2004); (ii) to track the evolution of dehumanizing rhetoric over time, we need to separate dehumanizing spans of different types. We used positive dehumanization class sentences from AP1 as the dataset for AP2 span annotation. The task was to identify spans of text that are dehumanizing towards Ukrainians and assign the correct dehumanization type to each span according to the three dehumanization quadrants of Figure 1. The guidelines contain detailed explanations for each type of dehumanization, provide examples, and cover instructions for edge cases, such as spans that combine multiple dehumanization types. These guidelines can be accessed through our GitHub

[17] https://github.com/kateburovova/dehumanization/tree/mainbranch/docs/annotation_guidelines

[18] https://huggingface.co/blanchefort/rubert-base-cased-sentiment

[19] https://huggingface.co/DeepPavlov/rubert-base-cased

repository[20]. A total of 478 sentences were annotated by one annotator. The majority class is ↑ UH ↓ NH. Figure A.5 shows the distribution of classes for AP2.

7 Experiments

7.1 Enhancements

In the initial phase of our research, we explored strategies to enhance the training by (1) extracting features with potentially stronger dehumanization signals and (2) generating synthetic training samples to reduce overfitting.

For the former, we drew from Mendelsohn et al. (2020) collocation extraction approach to extract four collocation types using spaCy[21]. We experimented with adding as features (i) verb-object or verb-adjunct collocations (ii) subject-verb collocations (iii) noun phrases where a noun is modified by another nominal element (iv) adjective-noun collocations.

For data augmentation, we employed an oversampling technique where we collected common non-dehumanizing mentions of Ukrainians or Ukraine and randomly replaced them in the data, thus generating new examples and reducing the reliance of the models on the context.

7.2 Classical Machine Learning

7.2.1 Logistic Regression

We started with Logistic Regression (LR) as the baseline classifier; the text was vectorized using the TF-IDF method. For this task, we used the dataset annotated during the AP1.

We experimented with clean lowercase (but not lemmatized) text, and then added lemmas and collocations as features. For each feature set, we performed grid search with cross-validation over the set of values for the parameters C (regularization strength) and penalty type (L1, L2). GridSearch for LR with lemmas and collocations as features produced the best result of F_1 = 0.78.

7.2.2 SVM

For experiments with SVM, we extended the same feature engineering approach. We performed a grid search over the regularization parameter C, which determines the balance between the misclassification of training examples and the simplicity of the decision surface. In all cases, the grid search relies on the best F_1 on the full test set as a selection criterion for each feature column. The best F_1 = 0.80 was attained with C=100 and linear kernel with enhancements; see the results in Table 1.

7.3 Deep Learning Approach

For experimentation with transformer models, we chose SpERT by Eberts and Ulges (2020), the attention model for span-based joint entity and relation extraction which performs the reasoning on BERT embeddings. For SpERT training, we use AP2 dataset. SpERT draws negative samples from the same sentence in a single BERT pass (Eberts and Ulges, 2020), so no additional negative samples were needed for training. In terms of classification, SpERT's entity recognition is a multiclass problem, where each identified span is associated with one of a predefined set of entity labels (but the spans can overlap partially or fully). To use SpERT in our setting of binary classification, we use a mapping function. Let $f(s)$ be the binary classification function, and $E(s)$ be the set of entities identified in a sentence s by the SpERT model. The function $f(s)$ maps to 1 if any entities are found in a sentence (i.e., if $E(s)$ is not empty), and 0 otherwise. This can be expressed as:

$$f(s) = \{ 1 , if E(s) \neq \emptyset, 0, if E(s) = \emptyset.$$

We followed the authors' recommendations on hyperparameter tuning, provided in their GitHub repository[22]. We report the SpERT model's performance in two contexts: multiclass classification over text spans produced best F_{1micro} = 0.80 and F_{1macro} = 0.81 and in binary setting F_1 = 0.85 as shown in Table 1.

7.4 Zero-Shot Learning

For experiments with zero-shot learning, we used ChatGPT gpt-3.5-turbo developed by OpenAI (2022) through the chat completions API endpoint. For this task, we used the dataset annotated during the AP1. Our approach was defined by the recommendations supplied by the OpenAI team[23] as well as by the empirical evidence shared within the developers community.

We evaluated 80 different prompt combinations for the GPT-3.5 Turbo agent, varying across three

[20] https://github.com/kateburovova/dehumanization/blob/mainbranch/docs/annotation_guidelines/An_part_II.pdf

[21] https://spacy.io/models/ru#ru_core_news_md

[22] https://github.com/markus-eberts/spert

[23] https://www.deeplearning.ai/short-courses/chatgpt-prompt-engineering-for-developers/

main components: definition of dehumanization (ranging from no definition to detailed guidelines in English or Ukrainian), the agent's role (from no specified role to acting as a social scientist, psychologist, or NLP researcher), and the approach to thinking process decomposition (from no specific instructions to step-by-step analysis strategies). The output formatting instructions for the agent remained consistent across all variations.

We found that the perspective of the social scientist induced the desired behavior, as well as the additional step of extracting the dehumanizing metaphors, if there are any, producing the best $F_1 = 0.82$.

7.5 Results and Discussion

Model	F_1	Precision	Recall
Logistic Regression	0.75	0.79	0.72
Logistic Regression with enhancements	0.78	0.82	0.75
SVM	0.75	0.79	0.72
SVM with enhancements	0.80	0.87	0.74
SpERT via a mapping function $f(s)$	**0.85**	**0.86**	**0.85**
GPT-3.5 Turbo	0.82	0.86	0.82

Table 1: Results for all models in the binary setting on the test set.

Through the employment of LR as the baseline classifier, we confirmed lemmatization as a critical pre-processing step and subject-verb structures as key features. During experimentation with LR, we observed that the models detect blatant dehumanization (with dehumanization contained directly in group labels) better than subtle dehumanization (usually expressed via metaphors and stylistic devices). This encouraged us to split the test set into blatant and subtle dehumanization subsets based on the presence of dehumanization in group labels' spans and additionally test the models' performance on them.

The implementation of the SVM model revealed an improved performance over the LR baseline. The SVM model demonstrated a propensity towards precision, aiming to minimize false positives. Augmenting the dataset enhanced performance on the samples with subtle dehumanization. Using SpERT in the binary setting, we reached SOTA performance for the binary dehumanization classification task at the sentence level. We concluded our experimentation with GPT-3.5 Turbo. By testing various combinations of context prompts we observed that the perspective of a social scientist and additional steps for extracting dehumanizing metaphors produced the most desirable results.

We can report that SpERT and GPT-3.5 Turbo showed significantly better results for the detection of subtle dehumanization than Logistic Regression or SVM. While results for the blatant dehumanization subset were comparable, best SVM model attained only $F_1 = 0.51$ on the subtle dehumanization subset, GPT-3.5 Turbo showed significant improvement with $F_1 = 0.65$ and best SpERT model produced the result of $F_1 = 0.82$. Precision and recall are much better balanced for SpERT and GPT-3.5 Turbo than for LR or SVM as well.

We observed higher average performance of the GPT-3.5 Turbo model, when prompted with the original Ukrainian annotation instructions on the test subset featuring dehumanization in group labels. This implies that GPT-3.5 Turbo utilized the examples in the original text to effectively match phrases closely related to those examples.

8 Temporal Dynamics of Dehumanization

To investigate how types of dehumanization evolved over time, we used SpERT in the multiclass setting to detect instances of dehumanization throughout the initially collected Telegram dataset.

We calculated the representative sample size for each period to assess the dynamics of dehumanization by type for 95% confidence interval with 1% margin of error, accounting for the Bessel's correction. All required samples sizes were below 300 posts, we chose 1,000 posts per time period as a reasonable sample size.

Figure 3 shows the dynamics for dehumanization by type. We added two notable events to the plot: the vertical blue line signifies the date of publication of the essay "On the Historical Unity of Russians and Ukrainians"[24], in which Putin publicly questions the legitimacy of Ukraine as a state, and the vertical red line shows the start of the 2022 Russian invasion of Ukraine. We observe that the dehumanization rhetoric, manipulating both dimensions of humanity (LOW_UN_LOW_NH) is the only type following a stable growth pattern over time. This is the type of dehumanization that is con-

[24] http://en.kremlin.ru/events/president/news/66181

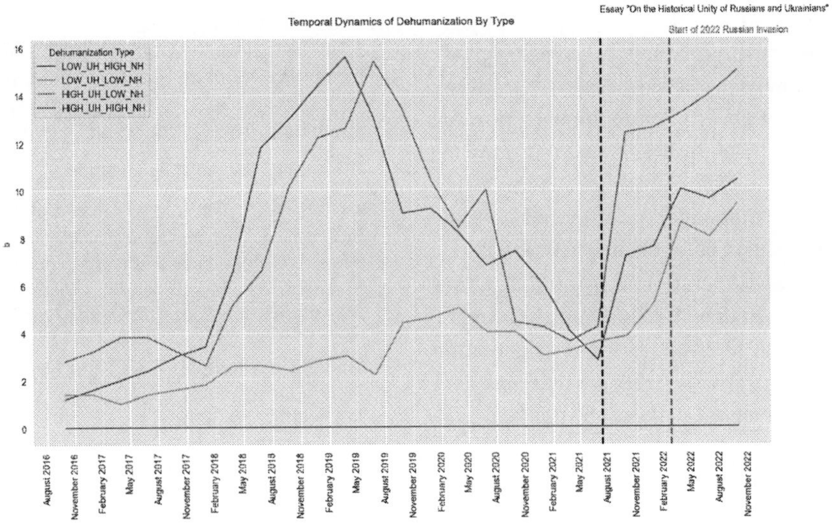

Figure 3: Dynamics of dehumanization. The X-axis represents a time scale, with data points aggregated over 3-month intervals with granularity of 1 month for random samples. The Y-axis depicts the mean number of positives.

sidered indicative of extreme violence risks and includes disgust-driven dehumanization and objectification. This dynamic does not appear to be defined by swift changes in political background or key policy-maker's decisions. The hyper-humanization (HIGH_UN_HIGH_NH) is not present due to its absence in the training data.

The two types of dehumanization that manipulate one of the two dimensions of dehumanization (HIGH_UN_LOW_NH and LOW_UN_HIGH_NH) demonstrate complex patterns. Their frequency starts to increase around 2017, and peaks in 2019 around the time of Ukrainian presidential elections[25], reaching the lowest point in 2021 by the time of the first wave of Russia's amassing troops at Ukraine's borders[26]. The rapid changes in these dehumanization types suggest that the dissemination of the imagery they supply may be orchestrated, or they are highly sensitive to the shifts in political reality. Figure 3 shows that these types start to increase not long before the 2022 invasion and drop at its start, confirming the idea of the preparatory role of dehumanizing rhetoric in sanctioning genocide. Notably, the dehumanization signals do not return to the pre-invasion levels with time, suggesting that this phenomenon cannot be localized as only the precursory stage in extreme violence. We observe that different types of dehumanization are evolving at different pace, suggesting that each fulfills a specific role.

9 Conclusion

In this research, we have delved into advanced techniques for dehumanization detection in the backdrop of extreme violence, culminating in the development of the first-ever dataset in the Russian language annotated at both sentence and span levels and a SpERT-based dehumanization detection model showing $F_1 = 0.85$. Leveraging our state-of-the-art model, our work offers a clear window into the temporal dynamics of dehumanizing rhetoric both before and during the 2022 Russian invasion of Ukraine, setting a precedent in the field. This system holds potential for integration into systems aimed at predicting and preventing extreme violence and creates a foundation for further research of computational analysis of dehumanization. Both best SpERT model and dataset are available for non-commercial use upon reasonable request and following the intended use; they have not been made publicly accessible to prevent potential malicious use.

10 Ethics and Limitations

We lack the instruments to compile a dataset representative of the general structure of the Russian population; instead, we focus on the most influen-

[25] https://www.bbc.com/news/world-europe-48007487

[26] https://www.iiss.org/online-analysis/online-analysis/2021/12/why-is-russia-amassing-troops-at-its-border-with-ukraine

tial media figures to infer the state of public thought from the speech patterns they are spreading. We do not intend to draw causal inferences between the magnitude of the type of dehumanization signal and the severity of violence toward Ukrainians. Instead, we seek to examine which dehumanizing perceptions are implicated in harm and how the change in degree and components can evolve.

Our toolkit and operationalization techniques can be extended to detect dehumanization in languages other than Russian. However, adaptation to other languages and contexts would require accounting for their unique cultural and political landscapes.

The annotated dataset was ensured to contain no publicly identifiable information (PII) other than widely available media coverage.

References

Hannah Arendt. 1963. *Eichmann in Jerusalem: A Report on the Banality of Evil.* Viking Press.

Albert Bandura. 1999. Moral Disengagement in the Perpetration of Inhumanities. *Pers Soc Psychol Rev*, 3(3):193–209.

Albert Bandura. 2002. Selective Moral Disengagement in the Exercise of Moral Agency. *Journal of Moral Education*, 31(2):101–119.

Zygmunt Bauman. 1989. *Modernity and the Holocaust.* Cornell University Press.

Dallas Card, Serina Chang, Chris Becker, Julia Mendelsohn, Rob Voigt, Leah Boustan, Ran Abramitzky, and Dan Jurafsky. 2022. Computational analysis of 140 years of us political speeches reveals more positive but increasingly polarized framing of immigration. *Proceedings of the National Academy of Sciences*, 119.

Xavier Carreras and Lluís Màrquez. 2004. Introduction to the CoNLL-2004 shared task: Semantic role labeling. In *Proceedings of the Eighth Conference on Computational Natural Language Learning (CoNLL-2004) at HLT-NAACL 2004*, pages 89–97, Boston, Massachusetts, USA. Association for Computational Linguistics.

Jacob Cohen. 1960. A coefficient of agreement for nominal scales. *Educational and Psychological Measurement*, 20:37–46. Place: US Publisher: Sage Publications.

Yonah Diamond, John Packer, Farrell Rosenberg, and Susan Benesch. 2022. An independent legal analysis of the russian federation's breaches of the genocide convention in ukraine and the duty to prevent.

Markus Eberts and Adrian Ulges. 2020. Span-based Joint Entity and Relation Extraction with Transformer Pre-training. *Santiago de Compostela.*

Frantz Fanon. 1967. *Black Skin, White Masks.* Grove Press.

Susan T. Fiske, Amy J. C. Cuddy, Peter Glick, and Jun Xu. 2002. A model of (often mixed) stereotype content: Competence and warmth respectively follow from perceived status and competition. *Journal of Personality and Social Psychology*, 82(6):878–902.

Heather M. Gray, Kurt Gray, and Daniel M. Wegner. 2007. Dimensions of Mind Perception. *Science*, 315(5812):619–619.

Lasana T. Harris and Susan T. Fiske. 2006. Dehumanizing the Lowest of the Low: Neuroimaging Responses to Extreme Out-Groups. *Psychol Sci*, 17(10):847–853.

Lasana T. Harris and Susan T. Fiske. 2011. Dehumanized Perception: A Psychological Means to Facilitate Atrocities, Torture, and Genocide? *Zeitschrift für Psychologie*, 219(3):175–181.

Nick Haslam. 2006. Dehumanization: An Integrative Review. *Pers Soc Psychol Rev*, 10(3):252–264.

Nick Haslam. 2019. The Many Roles of Dehumanization in Genocide. pages 119–138. Oxford University Press. Book Title: Confronting Humanity at its Worst.

Kristina Hook, John Packer, Farrell Rosenberg, and Susan Benesch. 2023. The russian federation's escalating commission of genocide in ukraine: A legal analysis.

Herbert G. Kelman. 1973. Violence without Moral Restraint: Reflections on the Dehumanization of Victims and Victimizers. *Journal of Social Issues*, 29(4):25–61.

Labelbox. 2023. Labelbox. [Online]. Available: https://labelbox.com/.

Alexander P. Landry, Ram I. Orr, and Kayla Mere. 2022. Dehumanization and mass violence: A study of mental state language in Nazi propaganda (1927–1945). *PLoS ONE*, 17(11):e0274957.

Mengyao Li. 2014. Towards a comprehensive taxonomy of dehumanization: Integrating two senses of humanness, mind perception theory, and stereotype content model.

Ian H. Magnusson, S. Schmer-Galunder, Ruta Wheelock, Jeremy Gottlieb, Pooja Patel, and Christopher Miller. 2021. Toward Transformer-Based NLP for Extracting Psychosocial Indicators of Moral Disengagement. In *Proceedings of the Annual Meeting of the Cognitive Science Society, 43.*

David M. Markowitz and Paul Slovic. 2020. Social, psychological, and demographic characteristics of dehumanization toward immigrants. *Proc. Natl. Acad. Sci. U.S.A.*, 117(17):9260–9269.

Julia Mendelsohn, Yulia Tsvetkov, and Dan Jurafsky. 2020. A Framework for the Computational Linguistic Analysis of Dehumanization. *Front. Artif. Intell.*, 3:55.

Rhiannon Neilsen. 2015. 'Toxification' as a More Precise Early Warning Sign for Genocide Than Dehumanization? An Emerging Research Agenda. In *Genocide Studies and Prevention*, volume 9, pages 83–95. ISSN: 1911-0359, 1911-9933 Issue: 1 Journal Abbreviation: GSP.

Nic Newman, Richard Fletcher, Antonis Kalogeropoulos, and Rasmus Kleis Nielsen. 2022. Digital news report 2022. Technical report, Reuters Institute for the Study of Journalism.

OpenAI. 2022. GPT-4 Technical Report. ArXiv:2303.08774 [cs].

Susan Opotow. 1990. Moral Exclusion and Injustice: An Introduction. *Journal of Social Issues*, 46(1):1–20.

James Pennebaker, Roger Booth, Ryan Boyd, and Martha Francis. 2015. *Linguistic Inquiry and Word Count: LIWC2015.*

Petro Vavryk. 2022. Mapping Growth of the Russian Domestic Propaganda Apparatus on Telegram. *Challenges to national defence in contemporary geopolitical situation*, 2022(1):227–231.

A Appendix

Label	Type
↓ UH ↓ NH	Low in Human Nature and Low in Human Uniqueness quadrant corresponds to disgust-driven dehumanization and objectification. Welfare recipients, drug users, and the homeless are among the social groups most at risk from this severe dehumanization (Fiske et al., 2002). These groups, which are perceived as detached and incapable, arouse intensely unpleasant emotions like disgust and hatred, which in turn predict both active harm (harassment) and passive harm (neglecting) behavioral patterns.
↑ UH ↓ NH	Low in Human Nature and High in Human Uniqueness quadrant corresponds to the mechanistic dehumanization, and members of groups dehumanized in this manner are often perceived as cold, rigid, passive, and yet highly competent (e.g., technicians, businesspeople). Mechanistic dehumanization denotes a horizontal social comparison to unfamiliar individuals and elicits responses like indifference and alienation instead of contempt and denigration (Haslam, 2006), in contrast to animalistic dehumanization, which reflects a downward social comparison. Superhumanization and demonization fall into this category. Demonization, in particular, is a common technique in acts of extreme violence, in which the target is branded as evil and incapable of change [(Li, 2014)]. The roles of perpetrators and victims are flipped completely when violence victims are demonized. For instance, during the Holocaust, the persecutors saw themselves as heroes for ensuring the survival of a superior race while portraying Jews as evil criminals (Landry et al., 2022). By doing this, demonization not only excludes victims from moral consideration (Opotow, 1990), but it also establishes a moral mandate that labels victims as evil and calls for action to be taken against them.
↓ UH ↑ NH	High in Human Nature, Low in Human Uniqueness quadrant corresponds to animalistic dehumanization. When UH is thought to be absent, people are frequently negatively viewed as unintelligent, impolite, or lacking in self-control resembling non-human animals. However, the perceived high levels of NH are linked to a concurrently neutral or even favorable assessment of others as warm, emotional, and creative. This form of dehumanization treats dehumanized targets as unrefined animals without necessarily subjecting them to malicious prejudice and inhumane treatment. This perception is consistent with the paternalistic stereotype in the Stereotype Content Model (SCM), which appears predominantly in traditional portrayals of women, elderly, or the disabled (Fiske et al., 2002).
↑ UH ↑ NH	High in Human Nature and high in Human Uniqueness quadrant corresponds to humanization and superhumanization. Some people and groups are seen as fully human on both dimensions, which is the opposite of the extreme dehumanization with both Human Nature and Human Uniqueness denied. According to the SCM, ingroup members are typically viewed as both warm and competent, which is consistent with the idea of ingroup favoritism, or the tendency to favor the ingroup over the outgroup.

Table A.2: Detailed Description of Dehumanization Types

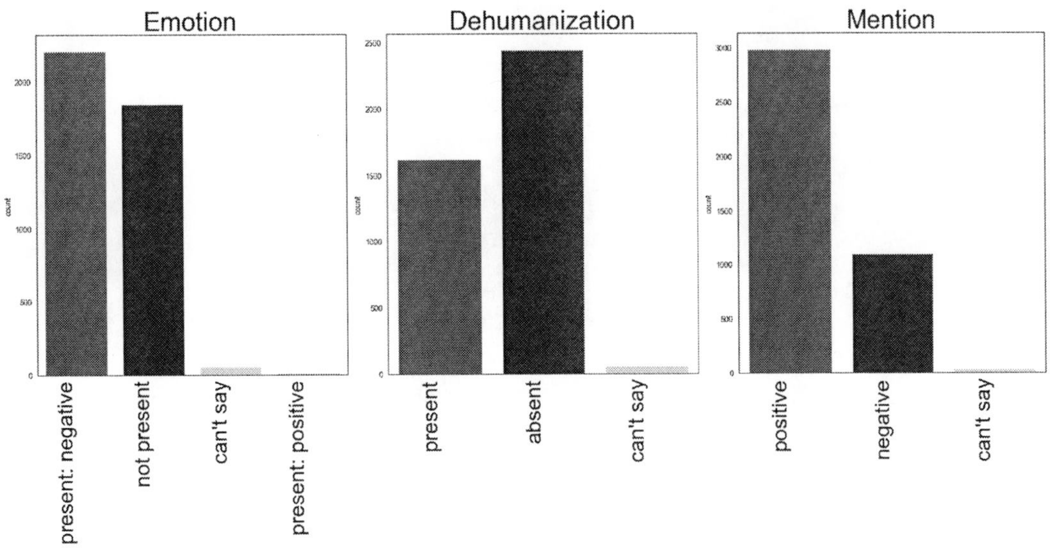

Figure A.4: The distribution of classes in the AP1.

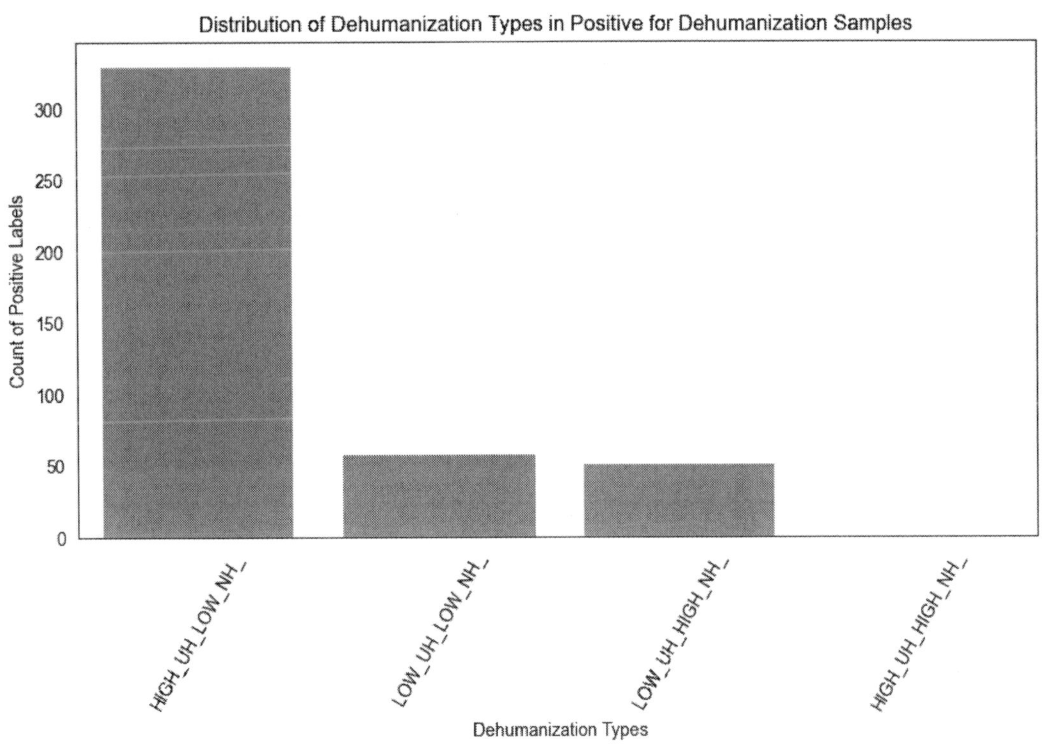

Figure A.5: The distribution of classes in the AP2.

Compilation of a Synthetic Judeo-French Corpus

Iglika Nikolova-Stoupak **Gaël Lejeune** **Eva Schaeffer-Lacroix**
Sens Texte Informatique Histoire, Sorbonne Université, Paris, France
iglika.nikolova-stoupak@etu.sorbonne-universite.fr,
{gael.lejeune, eva.lacroix}@sorbonne-universite.fr

Abstract

Judeo-French is one of a number of rare languages used in speaking and writing by Jewish communities as confined to a particular temporal and geographical frame (in this case, 11th- to 14th-century France). The number of resources in the language is very limited and its involvement in the contemporary domain of Natural Language Processing (NLP) is practically non-existent. This work outlines the compilation of a synthetic Judeo-French corpus. For the purpose, a pipeline of transformations is applied to Old French text belonging to the same general time period, leading to the derivation of text that is reliable in terms of phonological, morphological and lexical characteristics as witnessed in Judeo-French. A tradeoff is sought between authenticity and efficiency as the ultimate goal is for this synthetic corpus to be used in standard NLP tasks, such as Neural Machine Translation (NMT), as an instance of data augmentation.

1 Introduction

When prompted to translate a text from Old French to Judeo-French, ChatGPT offers a slightly altered and, strangely, modernised version of the source text, also written in Latin script. Asked to identify the rare language based on a short sample, it convincingly defines it as "Hebrew".

1.1 The Judeo-French Language

Judeo-French was in use between the 11th and 14th centuries by Jewish communities in the northern regions of France. In fact, its similarity to the Old French language is at times so striking as for Banitt (1963) to famously define it as "a ghost language". Despite the difference of opinions on the topic, for purposes of clarity, Judeo-French will be referred to as a "language" rather than a "variety" within this work. The key distinguishing feature of Judeo-French is its rendition into Hebrew rather than Latin script. The three main types of Judeo-French sources existent today are: isolated glosses (including those by the renowned rabbi Rashi), Biblical glossaries, and several texts compiled entirely in Judeo-French (such as "Elegy of Troyes", a lament about thirteen Jews burned in Troyes in 1288). Similarly to Old French, Judeo-French involved a number of dialects and was not uniform throughout the centuries that marked its use. Also, although both languages are written in a highly phonetic manner, not all texts reflect perfectly ongoing processes of linguistic change; in other words, the languages are "phonetic in intention, if not always in performance" (Pope 1934).

1.2 Data Augmentation

One of the main challenges in NMT and other state-of-the-art language models is their application to low-resource languages i.e. languages that lack sufficient corpora to guarantee the optimal function of models. Different solutions have been proposed to overcome this limitation, including "transfer learning" from a "parent" language model to a "child" model in a related lower-resource language. In this case, the two languages share the same vector space and, by extension, benefit from the same data used in the training process (Dabre et al 2020). Another approach to dealing with scarcely-resourced languages is the practice of data augmentation or

Proceedings of LaTeCH-CLfL 2024, pages 40–45
March 22, 2024

the enlargement of the existing corpus via a variety of methods, such as backtranslation (loop translation from the target language back to the source language) or the addition of alternative subcorpora of lower quality and relevance to the task at hand. For example, in their abstract text summarization model, Parida and Motlicek (2019) use synthetic data derived from the noisy Common Crawl corpus. Dai et al (2023) benefit from ChatGPT's state-of-the-art text generation abilities as they rephrase sentences for consequent use in text classification.

Rule-based approaches to data augmentation were especially common before the advancement of neural models; for instance, in their work on a Machine Translation system that involves minority languages, Probst et al (2002) choose to rely on "a set of human-readable rules rather than a set of statistics" in the syntactic transfer between a low-resource and high-resource language. In the current age of neural networks and large language models (LLMs), the elaboration of rules mostly comes in the face of attempts to decipher the inner workings of "black box" language models; the emphasis being on economy of labelled training data and domain expert contribution (Mishra, 2022). Yet, the preservation of historical and culturally significant languages is an example of a goal that mandates explainability, expertise, and ready application in linguistic research and education. In his work *Anaphora Resolution*, Mitkov (2014) expresses optimism about the ongoing presence of rule-based approaches in universities and academia.

2 Pipeline

2.1 Selection of Source Text

The portal "Base de français medieval" is selected as the most suitable available source in Old French to be used for the extraction of text to be converted into synthetic Judeo-French. It contains 219 texts (about 6.5 million words), composed between the 9th and 15th centuries, along with metadata (see Table 1).

Table 1: An overview of the source corpus.

1	id	auteur	titre	siècle	dialecte	domaine
2	adgar	Adgar (dit Guillaume)	Collection de miracles	12	anglo-normand	religieux
3	AlexisProlRaM	anonyme	Prologue de la Vie de saint Alexis	09-11	normand	religieux
4	AlexisRaM	anonyme	Vie de saint Alexis	09-11	normand	religieux
5	aliscans1	anonyme	Aliscans	12	picard	littéraire
6	aliscans2	anonyme	Aliscans	12	picard	littéraire

2.2 Preprocessing

Standard preprocessing is applied to a concatenated version of the texts, including the removal of capitalisaton and special symbols. The text is tokenised into sentences and the sentences are shuffled. A sample size is defined and extracted based on user input in function of the amount of augmented data that may be required by the NLP task at hand.

2.3 Transliteration

2.3.1 Into IPA Notation

As mentioned, the main difference setting apart Judeo-French text from Old French text is the script in which it is written. Therefore, the pipeline follows elaborate steps to guarantee the systematic transliteration of Latin to Hebrew letters. As an intermediary stage, the Old French text is converted into international IPA notation via the Python tool *epitran*. Specifically, the *fra-Latn-np* model for transliteration from French is applied, as it is highly based on the values of written letters as opposed to pronunciation as observable in the modern French language. To illustrate, the sentence "entre ses femmes appella cellui que elle avoit plus chiere" is rendered as "entrɛ sɛs fɛmɛs apɛla sɛlyi kɛ ɛlɛ avwat plys ʃirɛ".

2.3.2 Into Hebrew Script

The issuing text in IPA notation is then transliterated into Hebrew script on the basis of hand-crafted rules, derived from historical information about Judeo-French (see Figure 1). When applicable, decisions are taken to reduce ambiguity (e.g. פ is taken to correspond to the sound *p*, although a value of *f* is also possible, in order to differentiate it from its *rafe* version, פֿ). Where a symbol can be transliterated into multiple 'entrɛ sɛs fɛmɛs apɛla sɛlyi kɛ ɛlɛ avwat plys ʃirɛ. ɛt pɔse kɛ il et plesansɛ ɛn sa biote, il nɛ sɛnsyit pas pur sɛ kɛ il lemɛ. dɛdant la ditɛ mesɔn nabitɛ nyli dɛ prɛsɛnt; si i a ynɛ grant mɔnte dɛ dɛgrɛz d ɛvant la ditɛ mesɔn. si lɛs fist tus rɛturnɛr, vulsisissɛnt u nɔm.'

'אנטר שש פמש אפל שלי ק אל אבוונט פליש קר. אט פוש ק אל אט פלשנש אן ש בוט אל נ
שנשיט פש פור ש ק אל למ. דדנט ל דט משון נבט ניל ד פרשנט ש א א ין גרנט מונט ד דגרץ
דבנט ל דט משון. ש לש פשט טוש רטורנר בולששנט ו נום.'

Figure 1: Transliteration from IPA notation into Hebrew letters.

Hebrew letters (e.g. *v* into וו ,ב ,בֿ or ו), the most frequent mapping is used (in this case, בֿ). Given a larger sample, it is expected that it would be a better decision to also include the alternative renditions in a pre-defined proportion.

The automatised conversion pipeline includes the following steps: 1) vowels with IPA values that have the same Hebrew letter equivalents are made identical; 2) vowels are replaced with wildcards and consonants are replaced with their Hebrew equivalents while more wildcards are introduced for consonants that are interpreted as multiple symbols (e.g. those containing the *dagesh* diacritic); 3) where applicable, consonants are replaced with their *sofit* (end-of-word) versions; 4) initial vowels are replaced with א and the respective diacritic; 5) the *sheva* (vowel-less) diacritic is added to remaining consonants; 6) finally, remaining vowels are also replaced with א and the respective diacritic.

2.4 Simulation of Lexical Features

2.4.1 Lexical Borrowing

'entre ses femmes appella cellui que il ait plaisance en sa biauté aime. dedant la dite maison nabit

⇩

'אנטר שש **נשים** אפל שלי ק אל אבוונט פליש
שנשיט פש פור ש ק אל למ. דדנט ל דט משון
דבנט ל דט'

Figure 2: The French word "femmes" is replaced by the Hebrew word "נשים"

Another distinctive feature of the Judeo-French language is its occasional borrowing of Hebrew vocabulary. This phenomenon concerns particularly nouns and lexical fields associated with Jewish lifestyle and worship. Six out of the 80 nouns (i.e. 7.5 %) in "Elegy of Troyes" are such lexical borrowings: *torah* (Law), *tosafot* (additions, commentary), *hatan* (son-in-law), *sofer* (scribe), *cohen* (priest), and *qedushah* (holiness).

In order to mimic the phenomenon, Python's *spacy* library is used to derive words' part-of-speech tags. Then, a list of all nouns is produced and translated into Hebrew with the *googletrans* library. A set percentage of the produced Hebrew nouns are incorporated in the text in place of the original Old French nouns (see Figure 2).

Due to the scenario of data scarcity, it is recommended for informative features to be emphasised in the sample. For instance, in their recent article, Bansal and Sharma (2023) demonstrate the efficiency in selecting the most representative domain-specific data to annotate and consequently use in a language model, thus encouraging generalisation. For this reason, the percentage of instances of the feature is initially doubly increased in the synthetic sample (to 15%), with the ready possibility for modification based on performance of the sample in specific NLP tasks.

2.4.2 Words with Specific Spelling

Some commonly used words in Judeo-French tend to be spelled in a uniform way across dialects and time frames. A distinctive example is the word "God", which is counter-intuitively spelled as גֿי (in contrast with the common Latin-based spellings "Dé" or "Dieu"), thus demonstrating sensitivity to current linguistic processes.

2.5 Simulation of Morpho-Syntactic Features

2.5.1 Interrogative Particle

Occasionally, Judeo-French texts use the word "si" as a question particle, calquing the Hebrew equivalent, הֲ. A ratio of the questions in the synthetic sample are set to follow this pattern.

2.5.2 Graphical Separation

Another discernible feature of Judeo-French is that definite articles, the conjunction "and" and several prepositions are typically connected to the word that follows, mimicking the behaviour of their Hebrew counterparts. The feature is reflected in the entire synthetic text.

2.5.3 Nominal Expressions

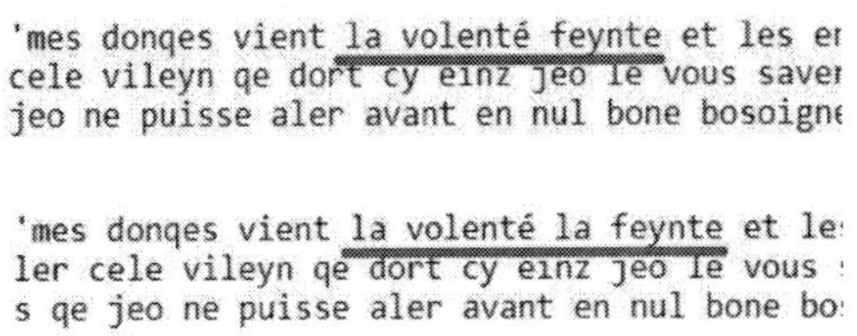

Figure 4: An example of a modified nominal expression.

Occasionally, Judeo-French nominal expressions follow the Hebrew structure of the definite article being repeated before both the noun and its attributive adjective (a necessity in the Hebrew language, as it does not feature the verb "to be" in the present tense, as a result of which it would otherwise be impossible to tell apart attributive from predicative adjectives).

In the compiled sample, combinations of consecutive *determinant* + *noun* + *adjective* and *determinant* + *adjective* + *noun* are sought and for a ratio of them, a second definite article is added accordingly (see Figure 3).

2.5.4 Plural Nouns

Commonly used nouns which are plural in Hebrew, such as "sky" and "water", are usually pluralised in Judeo-French. These nouns, along with possible articles that precede them, are specifically sought in the source text in all of their common spellings as found in Old French during the examined time period (e.g. "water" could be spelled as "eue", "eve" or "ewe") and then pluralised.

2.5.5 Feminine Nouns

The unpronounced consonant ה- is often used in Judeo-French to mark feminine nouns, similarly to its role in the Hebrew language. In "Elegy of Troyes", 3 out of 12 feminine nouns (25%) display the feature. A defined ratio (e.g. 50%) is made to comply to this rule in the assembled synthetic corpus. Firstly, a general assumption is made (and then verified manually) that nouns ending in the *e* or *ɛ* sound in the source text are feminine. A portion of these nouns are marked with a wildcard prior to transliteration into Hebrew letters, and it is eventually replaced by the letter ה.

2.6 Simulation of Scribal Errors

Scribal errors were a rather common occurrence in texts issuing from the discussed time period. Although their number varies significantly from text to text, they are all the more prominent when Hebrew script is involved due to the close resemblance of some letters. Consonants that were commonly confused include: ד and ז; ר and ץ; ב and ם; ן and ס. Coincidentally, mistakes (a.k.a. noise) are often regarded as a positive addition in machine learning models, as they ensure that the system does not overgeneralise the text it encounters during training. 10% of occurrences of each of the involved letters are set to be erroneous in order to for the tendency to be emphasised (see Figure 4). This step takes place before the consonants and the vowels' wildcards are replaced with Hebrew consonants carrying diacritics.

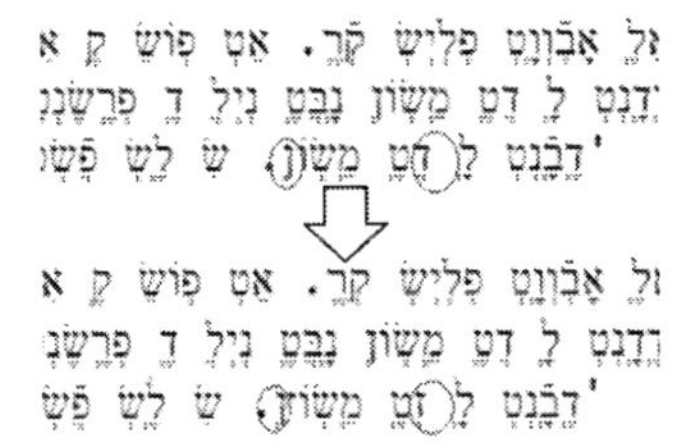

Figure 3: Simulation of scribal errors

3 Conclusion and Future Directions

The current study provides a basis for major extension in terms of both breadth and depth. On one hand, a number of rare Jewish languages share in their specificities as seen in relation to more common languages and language varieties spoken in the same time and geographical area. That is to say, Judeo-French relates to Old French in a similar manner that, for instance, Judeo-Italian relates to Italian or Judeo-Greek relates to Greek. Minor modifications in the presented pipeline can therefore allow for the derivation of synthetic corpora in these languages. From an even broader perspective, the authors hope that through its detailed documentation and shared code, the study can encourage similar work with rare languages that are not related to the discussed one.

On the other hand, this work's artefact in the face of a sample for data augmentation is only the beginning of what can become a larger and more sophisticated NLP system, such as a Machine Translation or summarisation model, whose usability would in turn be exponentially larger as authentic documents in Judeo-French and related languages become translatable or otherwise more easily accessible in today's digital context.

Limitations

To underline the Judeo-French language's uniqueness and linguistic unpredictability, Kiwitt (2015) notes that "[c]ette transposition en graphie courante ne peut pas être mise en œuvre en appliquant des règles de substitution de manière mécanique" ("This common graph transposition cannot be implemented by applying substitution rules mechanically"). However, whilst synthetic Judeo-French text cannot reach the point of having authentic value, a simulation of the language's distinguishing characteristics can enable its active participation in contemporary NLP tasks.

The proposed pipeline can clearly benefit from the involvement of more elaborate NLP tools. For instance, topic modelling may be applied in order for nouns to be associated to relevant lexical fields before being replaced by Hebrew translations.

Although the described system's output corresponds to the authors' expectations and is subjectively judged as resembling Judeo-French text, its quality can be estimated best in the framework of its involvement in NLP tasks.

Ethics Statement

The synthetic Judeo-French corpus presented in this work has no claims of authenticity or full plausibility. Instead, it is meant to be used as a tool that would allow for the integration of authentic Judeo-French text into the framework of contemporary NLP tools, such as Machine Translation systems.

Acknowledgments

This work has benefitted immensely from the lectures provided by the Oxford School of Rare Jewish Languages (OSRJL) and, in particular, the Judeo-French lectures of Dr. Sandra Hajek.

References

Menahem Banitt. 1963. Une langue fantôme: le judéo-français. *Revue de linguistique romane*, 27:245–294.

Parikshit Bansal and Amit Sharma. 2023. Large Language Models as Annotators: Enhancing Generalization of NLP Models at Minimal Cost.

David Simon Blondheim. 1926. Poésies judéo-françaises. *Romania LII*, 17-36.

Raj Dabre, Chenghui Chu and Anoop Kunchukuttan. 2020. A survey of multilingual neural machine translation. *ACM Computing Surveys*, 53(5).

Haixing Dai, Zhengliang Liu, Wenxiong Liao, Xiaoke Huang, Yihan Cao, Zihao Wu Lin Zhao, Shaochen Xu, Wei Liu, Ninghao Liu, Sheng Li, Dajiang Zhu, Hongmin Cai, Lichao Sun, Quanzheng Li, Dinggang Shen, Tianming Liu and Xiang Li. 2023. AugGPT: Leveraging ChatGPT for Text Data Augmentation, arXiv:2302.13007.

Stephen Dörr and Marc Kiwitt. 2016. Judeo-French. In Lily Kahn and Aaron D. Rubin (eds.): *Handbook of Jewish Languages*. Brill, Leiden: 138–177.

Kirsten A. Fudeman. 2008. Restoring a vernacular Jewish voice: The Old French Elegy of Troyes. *Jewish Studies Quarterly*, 15(3): 190-221.

Marc Kiwitt. 2015. L'ancien français en caractères hébreux. In David Trotter (ed.): *Manuel de la philologie de l'édition*. De Gruyter, Berlin: 219–236.

Ruslan Mitkov. 2014. *Anaphora Resolution*. Routledge.

Pradeepta Mishra. 2022, Model Explainability for Rule-Based Expert Systems. In *Practical Explainable AI Using Python*. Apress, Berkeley, CA: 315-326.

Shantipriya Parida and Petr Motlicek. 2019. Abstract Text Summarization: A low resource challenge. In *Proceedings of the 2019 Conference on Empirical Methods in Natural Language Processing and the 9th International Joint Conference on Natural Language Processing (EMNLP-IJCNLP)*, pages 5994-5998.

Heinz Pfaum. 1933. Deux hymnes judéo-français du moyen âge. *Romania*, 59: 389-422.

Mildred K. Pope. 1935. From Latin to Modern French with a special consideration of Anglo-Norman:

Phonology and morphology. *Modern Language Review*, 30: 385.

Katharina Probst, Lori Levin, Erik Peterson, Alon Lavie and Jaime Carbonell. 2002. MT for minority languages using elicitation-based learning of syntactic transfer rules. *Machine Translation*, 17: 245-270.

Detecting Structured Language Alternations in Historical Documents by Combining Language Identification with Fourier Analysis

Hale Sirin
Center for Digital Humanities
Johns Hopkins University
hsirin1@jhu.edu

Sabrina Li
Center for Digital Humanities
Johns Hopkins University
sli159@jhu.edu

Tom Lippincott
Center for Digital Humanities
Johns Hopkins University
tom@cs.jhu.edu

Abstract

In this study, we present a generalizable workflow to identify documents in a historic language with a nonstandard language and script combination, Armeno-Turkish. We introduce the task of detecting distinct patterns of multilinguality based on the frequency of structured language alternations within a document.

1 Introduction

This work emerges from the goal to create a corpus in Armeno-Turkish—vernacular Turkish written in Armenian script. This historic language was actively used from the early 18th century to the early 20th century in a variety of locations in the Middle East, Europe and the US, including Istanbul, Venice, Vienna and Boston (Der Matossian, 2020). There are lists of works in Armeno-Turkish available (Stepanyan, 2005), but searching HathiTrust manually points to the existence of works that are not recorded in these lists due to challenges in the bibliographical recording of these works in library catalogues (missing titles in the original script, wrong or missing language labels). Unable to collate works in Armeno-Turkish by using the metadata, we used language identification. This process did not produce a clean dataset in Armeno-Turkish, but showed that a significant portion of these works are multilingual. Based on this observation, this study is a first attempt at modeling some of the interesting multilingual phenomena with structured language alternations that emerge in this process: bilingual translations, dictionaries, original-language text followed by commentary in a different language, language study books.

As opposed to unstructured code switching (oral interviews), structured multilingual patterns involve an organized alternation of two or more languages. These language alternations may occur at different frequencies (every sentence, paragraph, every page, every chapter). A structured language alternation may serve various purposes, including making the content available in multiple languages in a legal document to reach its target audiences, as shown in the two-column Ottoman legal code in Armenian and Armeno-Turkish in Figure 1.

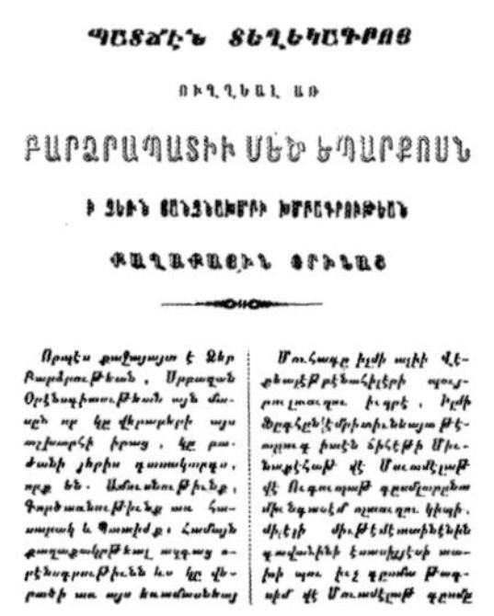

Figure 1: The first page of the Ottoman legal code, *Mejelle*, published in 1889 in a bi-column bilingual format, Armenian on the left and Armeno-Turkish on the right (mej, 1889).

Especially for historic languages, detecting structured language alternations is valuable for identifying clean monolingual segments which can then be used to create new resources for NLP tasks. This analysis also provides insight into material history of physical books and translation studies, by showcasing different formats of page segmentation in structured multilingual books (bi-column, top-bottom) (McConnaughey et al., 2017; Werner, 2012). This project introduces the task of detecting structured language alternations and makes the following contributions:

- We introduce an experiment that maps the language alternations in the time domain to the frequency domain to detect different patterns of structured language alternations in a corpus, and show that unsupervised clustering applied to the frequency spectra can be a simple and efficient first step in grouping documents with

Proceedings of LaTeCH-CLfL 2024, pages 46–50
March 22, 2024

different patterns of structured language alternations.

- We present a more comprehensive and nuanced Armeno-Turkish corpus from the HathiTrust Digital Repository, and compare the performance of a character n-gram model and a trained neural model for language identification of a historic language with a non-standard language and script combination.

2 Background

2.1 Language ID

Language identification is the task of determining the language(s) of a document and a crucial step in document classification in historical research. Character-based n-gram models are a performant statistical approach (Cavnar and Trenkle, 1994), and recent neural models offer a fast and efficient solution (Joulin et al., 2016).

While language identification of a document is mostly regarded as a solved task (McNamee, 2005), a near-perfect performance is only achieved when certain assumptions are made regarding the quantity and the quality of the data, and the monolinguality of the documents. However, historic and multilingual documents in low-resource languages motivate different approaches to language identification (Jauhiainen et al., 2018). Multilinguality of these documents is frequently overlooked, even though historic languages in non-standard scripts, such as Armeno-Turkish, represent territories that were predominantly multilingual. Despite the perceived monolingualism of 18th-and-19th-century books that are published in "national print-languages" (Anderson, 2006), multilingual activity persisted and even flourished during this period in commercial, legal, cultural and literary domains (Mende, 2023).

Research in multilingual language identification and code switching generally focuses on identifying the language, but not the relative location of these languages in each document (Lui et al., 2014). Kevers (2022) locates code switches, but primarily in multilingual documents when language diversity is unstructured. In this study, we focus on distinct patterns of structured language alternations that emerge in historical datasets (religious commentary, language study books, bilingual legal documents) in Armeno-Turkish, a low-resource language that falls outside the "national-print language" category.

2.2 Frequency Analysis

Discrete Fourier Transform (DFT) converts a time-domain sequence to a frequency domain sequence. It's defined by equation 1, mapping a sequence of N numbers $x_0, x_1 \dots, x_{N-1}$ to a new sequence of N numbers, for $0 \leq k \leq N-1$.

$$X_k = \sum_{n=0}^{N-1} x_n e^{-2\pi i k n / N} \tag{1}$$

Fast Fourier Transform (FFT) is an efficient algorithm used to calculate the DFT, reducing the time complexity from $O(N^2)$ to $O(N \log N)$ (Cooley and Tukey, 1965). Fourier transform has a wide range of applications in NLP. In this study, we approached the probability of a language label as a discrete signal at 50-word time steps in a document. Figure 2 shows a simulation of this approach, representing an idealized alternation of one language and another language as an array of alternating 0s and 1s and plotting its frequency domain representation using the Fourier Transform.

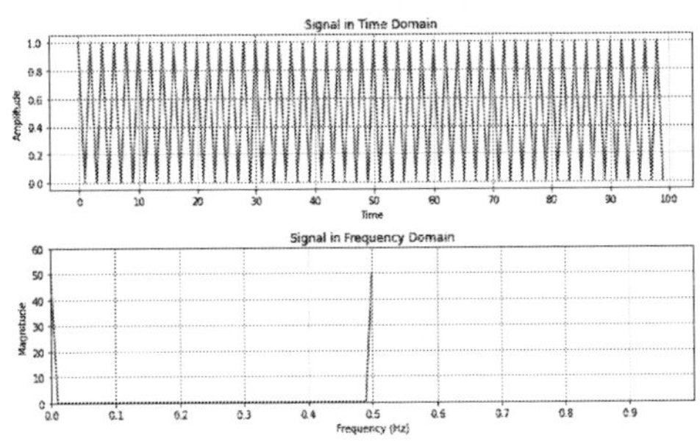

Figure 2: Time domain and frequency domain representations of an alternating discrete signal.

3 Materials and Methods [1]

3.1 Data

HathiTrust Digital Library (HT) (HathiTrust Foundation) offers unprecedented access to scholars who work with text as data in a variety of disciplines. However, corpus construction is a significant challenge when working with historic languages and multilingual documents (due to missing language and script information, OCR errors) and the overarching language label, even when it is correct, does not provide information regarding the multilingual composition of a given document.

[1] Code for the full experiment is available at `https://github.com/comp-int-hum/Armeno-Turkish-Collection`

The MARC 21 Bibliographic Record offers a limited structure to include script-related information, but it is not put to use systematically by cataloging librarians. The script information for the Armeno-Turkish works, if there is any, is occasionally found in the Notes section of the MARC record. This means that researchers' only recourse is to browse works in Armenian and in Turkish manually with the hopes of encountering Armeno-Turkish works.

3.2 Language ID Experimental Setup

We start by creating a training dataset of works labeled according to both language and script from the HT. For Armeno-Turkish, we use 97 expert-labeled documents. For negative examples, we first use the HT's MARC index to create a reverse mapping of languages (as assigned by librarians at the contributing institution) to documents, skipping anything dated before 1500 CE. We remove languages with less than 100 documents or whose code is not valid ISO-639. To ensure diverse temporal representation of each language, we split the range from the earliest to latest document in that language into 5 buckets covering equal time periods, and randomly select one document from each bucket. We then select an additional 5 documents at random from the overall remaining set, for a total of 10 documents per language. We split each document into sub-documents of contiguous script according to the Unicode script specification. This process results in 118 unique script and language combinations, serving as our training data. For the positive examples we only keep the Armenian script, since these are hand-annotated and does not rely on MARC metadata. At test time, we segment the document into smaller sections. By recording the segmentation offsets, the original documents can be reconstructed with the inferred language information.

We compare a trigram character language model with FastText neural language ID model (Joulin et al., 2016), trained on our labeled dataset in Table 1. We create a dataset of all documents in the HTC tagged as Turkish (tur), Ottoman Turkish (ota), or Armenian (arm), a total of 18367 records.

We apply the trained FastText model with a 0.91 fscore on the test set, to all documents in the HTC tagged as Turkish (tur), Ottoman Turkish (ota), or Armenian (arm) in 50-word windows. This process yields 95 works with Armeno-Turkish as the majority language label.

Model	Fscore (macro)
Multinomial NB	0.67
Char N-gram	0.83
Trained FastText	0.91

Table 1: Lang ID Model Performance Comparison

3.3 Frequency Analysis

The output of the FastText model is a grid of probability distributions over all possible language_script labels for each 50-word window in a document. In order to reach our goal of bringing out the periodic phenomena in these 95 works, we simplify this fairly noisy information. Since it is unclear how well-calibrated the model is, we calculate the majority language label of the whole document, and use the probability value of that language for each chunk. This language-agnostic approach radically simplifies the initial big grid of the full probability distribution, into a sequence of probabilities of that majority language for each 50-word chunk.

We transform each probability distribution array into a frequency domain, using FFT, and cluster each frequency spectrum using k-means clustering. Frequency domain transformation allows us to compare signals of different lengths.

4 Results and Discussion

The clustering of the frequency spectra yielded three coherent groups:

1. Works that are predominantly in Armeno-Turkish (59 documents)

2. Works that are bilingual, alternating between Armeno-Turkish and another language (10 documents: Language textbooks: alternating every few sentences, Bilingual editions: alternating every column or every page)

3. Works that are multilingual in languages other than Armeno-Turkish (13 documents: Language textbooks in Armenian-Greek, Armenian-Russian, Armenian-French)

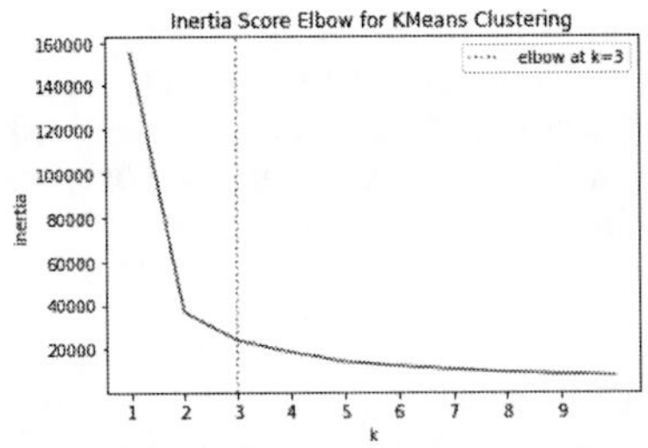

Figure 3: Visualization of k-elbow inertia metric for optimal k in k-means clustering.

As visualized in Figure 3, we selected the number of clusters based on the inertia metric for optimal k. While the clusters are relatively coarse-grained, this is a fast and efficient approach to historical datasets with unreliable metadata and high variation in genre and language composition. The frequency analysis combined with segmented language identification is a promising venue to explore documents in historic languages, since it lets us divide the corpora automatically into more distinct categories, revealing a variety of genres. Preserving the diversity of genres is valuable for low resource situations in which there is a risk of certain genres dominating the fine-tuning material.

This experiment identified 30 new records in Armeno-Turkish that were not in the training set, including translations of the Bible, dictionaries, textbooks for learning foreign languages, and legal documents.

4.1 Error Analysis

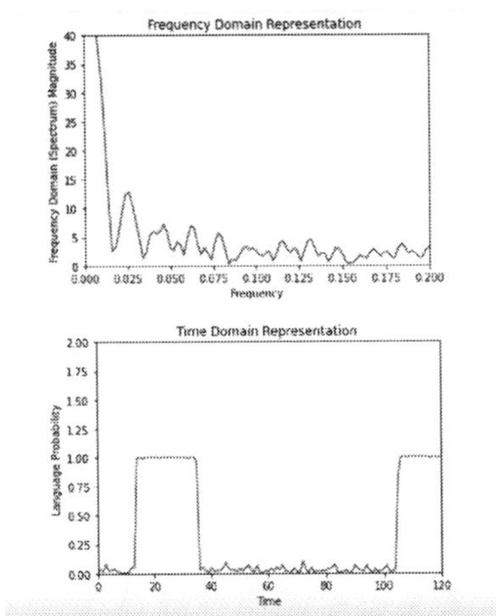

Figure 4: Time domain and frequency domain representations of the alternating language probability signal in a section of the monolingual book with page segmentation shown in Figure 4.

For example, Figure 4 shows a book that is entirely in Armeno-Turkish, but is segmented into four parts, with the lower two segments in a smaller font and occasionally in a different typeface, resulting in a significantly worse OCR output periodically. This creates a falsely identified language alternation pattern. Figure 5 shows the frequency and time domain representations of the Armeno-Turkish probability in the same book. In comparison, figure 6 shows the time-domain and frequency-domain signal representations of an actual bilingual book with an alternation pattern every sentence.

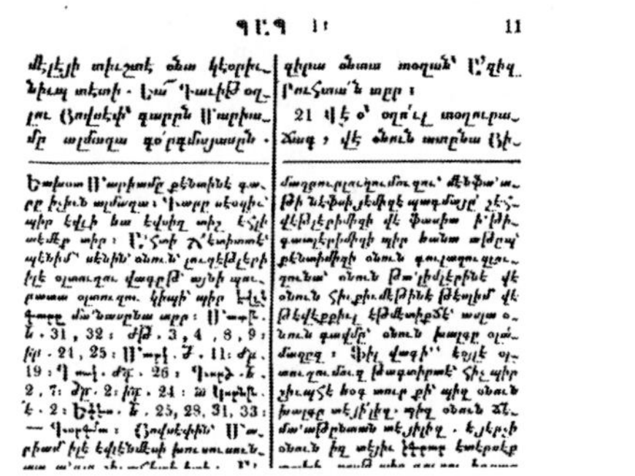

Figure 5: Page segmentation in the book, *Commentary On the Gospel of Matthew*, in Armeno-Turkish. (Goodell, 1851)

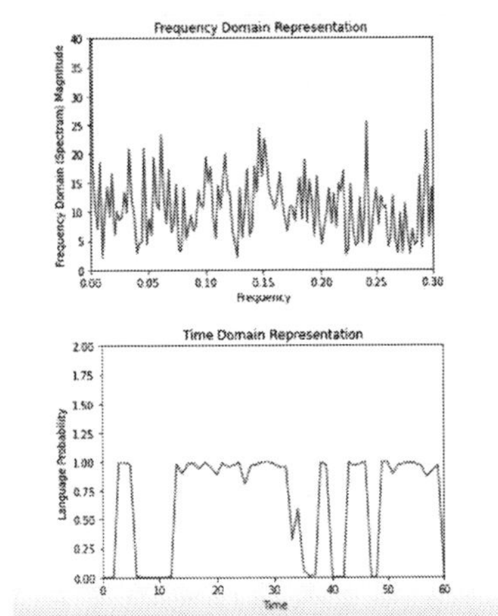

Figure 6: Time domain and frequency domain representations of the alternating language probability signal in a section of a bilingual book that alternates between Armenian and Armeno-Turkish every sentence. (Erg, 1881)

The patterns of language alternation that emerge are not very fine-grained, due to the high degree of noise in the HathiTrust corpus. In some cases, this leads to alternations in the lang ID probability results, not due to a change in the language, but due to a periodic noise in the post-OCR text (footnotes in smaller font, highly segmented pages).

5 Future Work

We plan to expand the frequency analysis approach by using a cleaner dataset and including different languages with the goal of reaching a more nuanced classification at the word or sentence level (such as dictionaries). This process has a potential to be applied as a feature extractor for a downstream classification task. Training a classifier on clean data, where the patterns of structured language alternations are known, could lead to a specific classifier (dictionary, bilingual, annotated edition). This process would require clean data, but we hypothesize that a model trained on carefully annotated high-resource data could then be used on a low-resource language, since the periodic signal would be the same across languages.

References

1881. *Erger Tghayots' Hamar*. Konstandnupolis: Tpagrut'iwn Aramean.

1889. *Mejelle [Ottoman Civil Law.]*.

B. Anderson. 2006. *Imagined Communities: Reflections on the Origin and Spread of Nationalism*. ACLS Humanities E-Book. Verso.

William B. Cavnar and John M. Trenkle. 1994. N-gram-based text categorization.

James W. Cooley and John W. Tukey. 1965. An algorithm for the machine calculation of complex Fourier series. *Mathematics of Computation*, 19(90):297–301.

Bedross Der Matossian. 2020. The development of armeno-turkish (hayatar t'rk'erēn) in the 19th century ottoman empire: Marking and crossing ethnoreligious boundaries. *Intellectual History of the Islamicate World*, 8(1):67–100.

William Goodell. 1851. *Madtéos Injilinin Tefsiri: [Commentary on the Gospel of Matthew]*. Smyrna: William Griffith.

HathiTrust Foundation. 2023. HathiTrust Digital Library.

Tommi Jauhiainen, Marco Lui, Marcos Zampieri, Timothy Baldwin, and Krister Lindén. 2018. Automatic language identification in texts: A survey.

Armand Joulin, Edouard Grave, Piotr Bojanowski, Matthijs Douze, Hérve Jégou, and Tomas Mikolov. 2016. Fasttext.zip: Compressing text classification models. *arXiv preprint arXiv:1612.03651*.

Laurent Kevers. 2022. CoSwID, a code switching identification method suitable for under-resourced languages. In *Proceedings of the 1st Annual Meeting of the ELRA/ISCA Special Interest Group on Under-Resourced Languages*, pages 112–121, Marseille, France. European Language Resources Association.

Marco Lui, Jey Han Lau, and Timothy Baldwin. 2014. Automatic detection and language identification of multilingual documents. *Transactions of the Association for Computational Linguistics*, 2:27–40.

Lara McConnaughey, Jennifer Dai, and David Bamman. 2017. The labeled segmentation of printed books. In *Proceedings of the 2017 Conference on Empirical Methods in Natural Language Processing*, pages 737–747, Copenhagen, Denmark. Association for Computational Linguistics.

Paul McNamee. 2005. Language identification: A solved problem suitable for undergraduate instruction. *J. Comput. Sci. Coll.*, 20(3):94–101.

Jana-Katharina Mende, editor. 2023. *Hidden Multilingualism in 19th-Century European Literature*. De Gruyter, Berlin, Boston.

Hasmik Stepanyan. 2005. *(Armenian-Turkish-French) Bibliographie des livres et de la presse armeno-turque, 1727–1968*. Istanbul: Turkuaz Yayınları.

Sarah Werner. 2012. Where material book culture meets digital humanities. *Journal of Digital Humanities*, 1.

EmotionArcs: Emotion Arcs for 9,000 Literary Texts

Emily Öhman[†]
School of International Liberal Studies
Waseda University, Japan
ohman@waseda.jp

Yuri Bizzoni[†]
Center for Humanities Computing
Aarhus University, Denmark
yuri.bizzoni@cc.au.dk

Pascale Feldkamp Moreira[†]
School of Communication and Culture
Aarhus University, Denmark
pascale.moreira@cc.au.dk

Kristoffer L. Nielbo
Center for Humanities Computing
Aarhus University, Denmark
kln@cas.au.dk

Abstract

We introduce 'EmotionArcs', a dataset comprising emotional arcs from over 9,000 English novels, assembled to understand the dynamics of emotions represented in text and how these emotions may influence a novel's reception and perceived quality. We evaluate emotion arcs manually by comparing them to human annotation and against other similar emotion modeling systems to show that our system produces coherent emotion arcs that correspond to human interpretation. We present and make this resource available for further studies of a large collection of emotion arcs and present one application, exploring these arcs for modeling reader appreciation. Using information-theoretic measures to analyze the impact of emotions on literary quality, we find that emotional entropy, as well as the skewness and steepness of emotion arcs, correlate with two proxies of literary reception. Our findings may offer insights into how quality assessments relate to emotional complexity and could help with the study of affect in literary novels.

1 Introduction

Sentiment analysis and emotion detection are subjective in nature, as not even humans can typically agree on which emotions any specific text contains (Campbell, 2004; Bayerl and Paul, 2011). There are also crucial distinctions between whether we are measuring the evocation or association of emotions and whether we are doing this from the reader's or the writer's perspective (Mohammad, 2016). Approaches to sentiment analysis garner critique both for inherent problems in, for example, word-based annotation (Swafford, 2015), but also for being overly focused on evaluation metrics over applicability to downstream tasks (Öhman, 2021b) and how the task of emotion detection to some degree constructs the phenomena it is trying to measure (Laaksonen et al., 2023). The importance of a literary text's emotional profile for its overall quality ("performance", reception) is hard to overestimate (Bal and Van Boheemen, 2009). While literary narratives are far from being only matters of emotions, the emotions touched upon in texts – in both explicit *and* evocative ways – determine essential aspects of the reader's experience at the structural and stylistic level (Mar et al., 2011). However, while this relation between emotions in literary texts and reader experience can seem relatively intuitive, it needs to be more obvious to test or quantify. This presents us with a few difficulties. The first difficulty is the modeling of "emotions in the text" – defining what we mean by that, deciding which emotions to define, and how to measure the emotional content of any given textual unit - word, phrase, sentence, or paragraph. Due to the complexity of human readers' interpretations and experiences of texts, this is a difficult task to model. The second difficulty is quantifying the relation between emotions in text and their reception or perceived quality of a literary narrative. In this paper, we introduce a new resource, 'EmotionArcs', to explore the relationship between these emotion arcs and literary quality complete with some early analyses. 'EmotionArcs', is a dataset that comprises emotional arcs constructed from over 9,000 English novels through a novel approach that utilizes emotion intensity lexicons enhanced by word embeddings fine-tuned for the domain of literature to construct emotion arcs. We use the dataset to analyze and measure how affective language impacts a novel's literary quality, measured both through library holding numbers and GoodReads ratings.

2 Related Work

Computational literary studies (CLS) is an active field of research affiliated with Digital Humanities

[†]These authors contributed equally to this work

Proceedings of LaTeCH-CLfL 2024, pages 51–66
March 22, 2024 ©2024 Association for Computational Linguistics

and applied Natural Language Processing. Sentiments, emotions, and affect are all common research topics within CLS and include work in emotion classification, genre classification, story-type clustering, sentiment tracking, and character analysis (Kim and Klinger, 2018).

2.1 Emotion Analysis

Previous work has tested the potential of sentiment analysis (Alm, 2008; Jain et al., 2017) at the word (Mohammad, 2018a), sentence (Mäntylä et al., 2018), or paragraph level (Li et al., 2019), for capturing meaningful aspects of the reading experience (Drobot, 2013; Cambria et al., 2017; Kim and Klinger, 2018; Brooke et al., 2015; Jockers, 2017; Reagan et al., 2016). Sentiment arcs have been used in multiple studies to model and evaluate narratives in terms of literary genre (Kim et al., 2017), plot archetypes (Reagan et al., 2016), dynamic properties (Hu et al., 2021), narrative mood (Öhman and Rossi, 2023), and reader preferences and perceived quality (Bizzoni et al., 2022a). Previous work has tested the potential of sentiment analysis (Alm, 2008; Jain et al., 2017) at the word (Mohammad, 2018a), sentence (Mäntylä et al., 2018), or paragraph level (Li et al., 2019), for capturing meaningful aspects of literary texts and the reading experience (Drobot, 2013; Cambria et al., 2017; Kim and Klinger, 2018; Brooke et al., 2015; Jockers, 2017; Reagan et al., 2016).

Because literary texts have additional layers of affective meaning (cf. the distinction between tone and mood) at more narrative levels, (narrator, character, style, etc.) than other texts, additional challenges accompany annotating emotions in them. However, some recent papers have shown that lexicon-based methods can produce accuracies comparable to machine learning and transformer-based methods using chunks or bin sizes (a set number of tokens) of only a few hundred tokens with the additional benefit of transparency and human interpretability (Teodorescu and Mohammad, 2023; Elkins, 2022; Öhman, 2021b).

2.2 Literary Quality

Studies that aim to forecast the perception of literary quality by relying on textual features[1] have mostly depended on stylistic features. This includes factors like sentence length and readability (Maharjan et al., 2017; Bizzoni et al., 2023a), the proportion of different classes of words (Koolen et al., 2020; Bizzoni et al., 2023c), and the frequency of word pairs (n-grams) (van Cranenburgh and Koolen, 2020). Other recent studies have explored the use of alternative textual or narrative elements such as sentiment analysis (Alm, 2008; Jain et al., 2017), to model as a significant aspect of the reading experience (Drobot, 2013; Cambria et al., 2017; Kim and Klinger, 2018; Brooke et al., 2015; Jockers, 2017; Reagan et al., 2016). This strand of research predominantly focuses on sentiment valence with the aim of roughly modeling the sentiment arcs – the ups and downs – of novels (Jockers, 2017), but without taking into account essential aspects like plot variability or the progression of the narrative. Once the arcs are computed, it is possible to cluster them based on similarities (Reagan et al., 2016). For example, a simple sentiment arc clustering approach by identified six fundamental narrative arcs that they speculated might form the basis of narrative construction. More recently, Hu et al. (2021) and Bizzoni et al. (2022a) applied fractal analysis, a technique to study complex systems' dynamics (Hu et al., 2009), to model the persistence, coherence, and predictability of sentiment arcsrelated to reader appreciation (Bizzoni et al., 2021, 2022b, 2023b). Systems to distinguish between different emotions have also been applied to study narratives (Somasundaran et al., 2020) and the aesthetics of literary works (Haider et al., 2020). Maharjan et al. (2018) modeled the "flow of emotions" in literary texts using the NRC lexicon, showing that the shape of emotion-specific arcs had an effect on predicting whether books were successful (based on GoodReads ratings). The distribution of emotions seemed particularly telling for the "success" of a work, as Maharjan et al. (2018) found emotion intensity and variation (std. deviation) higher for successful than for unsuccessful works. As it has been shown that emotion distribution and levels may vary across genres (Mohammad, 2011), it is particularly interesting for us to continue this line of assessing the importance of the shapes of emotion-specific arcs on quality perception, in our case examining novels only.

3 Dataset Construction

3.1 Selecting and Curating Novels

Our data comes from the "Chicago Corpus". This corpus consists of 9,089 novels published in the

[1] In contrast to the study of *extra-textual* features (Verdaasdonk, 1983; Lassen et al., 2022)

US between 1880 and 2000, making it an unusual collection for both size and modernity, as it contains both more and more recent novels than the works available on most other platforms. [2]. The corpus was compiled based on the number of libraries holding numbers worldwide, with a preference for more circulated works. It features works by Nobel laureates (i.e., Ernest Hemingway, Tony Morrison), widely popular works, and "genre literature", from Mystery to Science Fiction (e.g., from Agatha Christie to Philip K. Dick) (Long and Roland, 2016).[3] The use of more commonly available or "popular" books also means that the novels are more likely reviewed on tertiary platforms such as GoodReads, which facilitates the examination of correlations between public reception and novels' affective content. The dataset consists of 1,108,108,457 tokens, ranging from 246 tokens to 723,804 tokens per book with an average of 121,918 tokens per book. For parts of our analysis, we split the books into bins each containing 500 tokens, which means there are on average 244 bins per book. We chose a 500-bin size for both practical and theoretical reasons. Multiple studies have shown that using bin sizes of just 200-300 tokens can beat state-of-the-art machine learning models in accuracy (Teodorescu and Mohammad, 2023; ?; Öhman and Rossi, 2023) Using too large bin sizes, on the other hand, could misrepresent and muddle the emotion arcs. We determined 500 tokens, roughly corresponding to text subsets that are 1-2 paragraphs in length, to be suitable in order to strike a balance between theory, interpretability, and practice. Note that the token count will be much higher than the word count of the same text. This is especially true for literary texts which tend to have dialogue with quotation marks, dashes, and more punctuation marks all of which count as individual tokens.

3.2 Affective Word Embeddings

We utilize the NRC Affect Intensity Lexicon (Mohammad, 2018b) for emotion labels as it is the most extensive emotion intensity lexicon we are aware of. Moreover, both it and its sister lexicon EmoLex (Mohammad and Turney, 2013) have been used in countless emotion detection tasks and have proven their accuracy and usability in a variety of tasks. This lexicon was created with the help of human annotators using best-worst scaling. It contains 9,829 lexemes with at least one emotion association and a value between 0 and 1 for each emotion to represent the intensity of the labeled emotion. The emotions included are *anger*, *anticipation*, *disgust*, *fear*, *joy*, *sadness*, *surprise*, and *trust*. As this lexicon is not specific to the domain of literary texts, we used the novels in our dataset to create a semantic vector space model with Word2Vec (Mikolov et al., 2018) and then with the aid of cosine similarity measures expanded the lexicon to make it more domain-specific. Cosine similarity is a commonly used measurement to determine the similarity between two objects, in this case, lexemes, represented as vectors. For vectors a and b we can represent cosine similarity as follows: $\cos(\mathbf{a}, \mathbf{b}) = \frac{\mathbf{ab}}{\|\mathbf{a}\|\|\mathbf{b}\|}$ As there has been some criticism of using cosine similarity for similarity measures of high-frequency words (Zhou et al., 2022), we also conducted manual evaluations of the newly added terms to ensure the appropriateness of the modifications. The lexicon was checked for unsubstantiated emotion associations and the lemmas in the novels for words that have an emotion association but were not in the lexicon. Following this procedure, we created *emotion intensities* for the whole novels (e.g., see Fig. 1) as well as for each 500-token bin. For the former, the results were normalized by word count; for the latter, the results were simply sums of the word-emotion association intensities. These intensity calculations are available publicly[4].

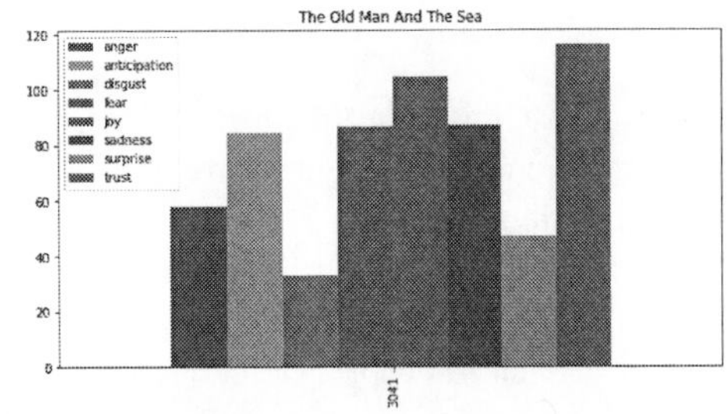

Figure 1: Emotion intensities for Hemingway's *The Old Man and The Sea*. For instance, the prevalence of trust might mirror the Santiago-Manolin relation and be a proxy for the protagonist's endurance.

[2]On average, studies on literary quality and success tend to rely on collections of tens to hundreds of novels, i.a., (Ashok et al., 2013).

[3]Other quantitative studies are based on this corpus (Underwood et al., 2018; Cheng, 2020), which can be viewed at `https://textual-optics-lab.uchicago.edu/us_novel_corpus`.

[4]https://github.com/yuri-bizzoni/EmoArc

4 Agreement and Validation

As the approach used in this project does not allow for traditional accuracy measures often used in machine learning (Öhman, 2021b), we focus our validation efforts on comparing human interpretations with those generated by our lexicon-based model, which has shown to be accurate in multiple prior studies (Teodorescu and Mohammad, 2023; Öhman and Rossi, 2023; Koljonen et al., 2022). We validated the EmotionArcs resource in three different ways:

(i) Two literary scholars inspected the emotion arcs of select novels, relating style and narrative events to the shapes of emotion arcs. One example of a manual annotation of the correspondence of our emotion arcs with narrative events is shown in Figure 4 (see another in the Appendix). Note that while at first sight, the co-occurrence of peaks in fear and joy (especially from chunk 80 on) may appear puzzling, it illustrates an important aspect of Hemingway's style in describing complex emotions and reflects the themes of the story overall: in moments of crisis and violence, Hemingway's protagonist still reflects on the natural beauty and his love for the sea. This creates a mix of complex feelings in key scenes (love and hatred, fear and admiration) so that intensities in these feelings co-occur (see, e.g., box 7 in Fig. 4), which is also a token of the protagonist's endurance and optimistic outlook on life. The slope and generally high levels of trust in the story also follow the progression of narrative events (see, e.g., box 5 in Fig. 4).

(ii) We randomly selected 11 passages from one novel: *The Old Man and the Sea*, asking 20 non-expert volunteer annotators to indicate, for each passage, which emotions were present from a pre-defined set and at what intensity on a 0-1 scale (for the agreement between model and annotator scores, see the Appendix). All passages received 3 to 6 annotations. After a first independent round, annotators were provided with the EmotionArcs scores for the same passage and asked whether they thought the model scores were present in the text, and whether they should be lower or higher (Moreira et al., 2023; Bizzoni and Feldkamp, 2023) Our annotators vastly agreed with the model's categorical choice (see Table 1), while agreement on their intensity varied. In 225 over 232 cases, annotators assessed that the model chose the correct emotions for the text. In 122 of these cases, the annotators also agreed with the intensity score assigned. Of the remaining 110 cases, 43 were given the assessment "could be higher" and 60 the assessment "could be lower".

	Agree			**Disagree**
	Higher	Lower	Correct	
Count	43	60	122	7
Total	225			7

Table 1: Annotators' agreement with EmotionArc's scores

Joy was the emotion that elicited most "could be lower" responses. We believe this is because in Plutchik's eight core emotions (Plutchik, 1980), *joy* is the only genuinely positive one.

(iii) Lastly, two novels were selected for close-reading evaluation. We evaluated the EmotionArcs by comparing their scores to valence scores produced by an independent (RoBERTa, fine-tuned for sentiment analysis on tweets (Barbieri et al., 2022)[5]) and average human annotations for valence of the same books.[6] As emotion annotation has been shown to correlate with valence scores – most notably joy and fear with positive and negative valence (Moreira et al., 2023) – we combined the emotion scores of joy and fear of our method to model arcs of novels, comparing them against the SA and human annotation of the same novel. An example can be seen in Figure 2, where human evaluation closely follows that of our model's *joy* values minus *fear* value as well as that of additional validation produced with the help of RoBERTa scores. In other words, by combining the most prevalent positive emotion and the most prevalent negative emotion, with a positive and negative sign respectively, it's possible to reproduce a novel's sentiment trendline [7]

[5]Note that to convert RoBERTa's categorical output we used the confidence score of labels as a proxy for sentiment intensity. If the model classifies a sentence as *positive* with a confidence of, for example, 0.89, we interpret it as a valence score of +0.89, and so on. Scores of the *neutral* category were converted to a score of 0.0. For further details SA with Transformers, see Bizzoni and Feldkamp (2023).

[6]Human annotators (n=2) read from beginning to end and scored sentences on a 1 to 10 valence scale.

[7]We focus our comparison on *joy* and *fear* as they are among the most frequent in text and we see them as the purest representatives of unambiguous valence in the available categories and highly representative of overall valence due to the overall overlap of emotions with *fear* and *joy* (Bizzoni and Feldkamp, 2023; Öhman, 2020a,b).

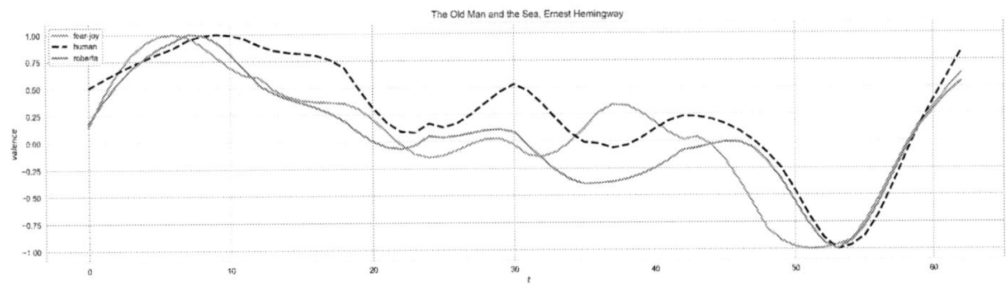

Figure 2: *The Old Man and the Sea*, manual evaluations, EmotionArcs (fear minus joy), and RoBERTa. Arcs were smoothed using adaptive filtering (Jianbo Gao et al., 2010).

4.1 Agreement in Emotions

Certain emotions are more likely to co-occur than others. This can lead to lower accuracy scores in multilabel machine learning models when the features of correlated emotions are muddled, but increased detail in lexicon-based models when we can differentiate better between closely related associations. Figure 3 shows the correlation of emotions in the entire 'EmotionArcs' corpus. The negative emotions *anger*, *disgust*, *fear*, and *sadness* show a high rate of co-occurrence as expected, while *joy* is negatively correlated with both *anger* and *fear* and positively so with *anticipation* and *trust*. *Anticipation* strongly correlates not only with *joy*, but also with *trust* [8], an emotion of more ambiguous valence. *Anger* correlates significantly also with *surprise*. It stands to reason that a passage expressing *anger* can be framed as sudden, surprising and, even cathartic.[9].

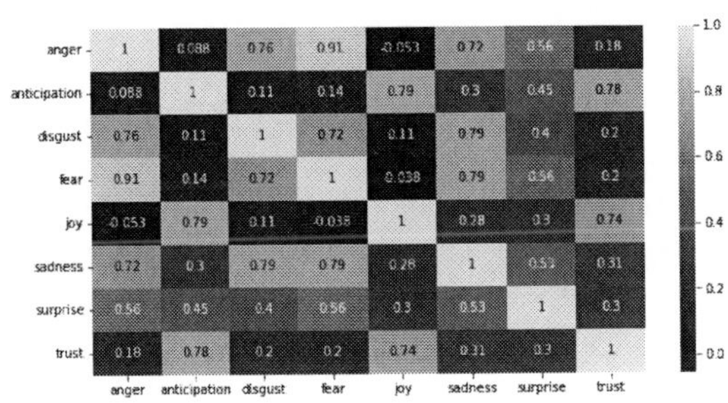

Figure 3: Correlation between emotions in all emotion arcs

[8] *trust* is commonly associated with its negative counterpart *distrust*, which is not a label in Plutchik

[9] Plutchik considers *anger* a positive emotion, counter to how it is used in most NLP models, and it is not immediately clear whether the valence in a literary setting should be reversed from its psychological roots as is standard practice (Plutchik, 1980; Öhman, 2021a).

5 Quality Proxies

5.1 Rationale

The idea that the distribution and dynamics of the emotions expressed in a text are related to the reception of that text is widespread, and several studies have used both sentiment analysis and emotion detection to capture meaningful aspects of the reading experience (Drobot, 2013; Cambria et al., 2017; Kim and Klinger, 2018; Brooke et al., 2015; Jockers, 2017; Öhman and Rossi, 2023). In this work, we tried several different resources that approximate the reception of a novel – specifically, its perceived overall quality – by either a large number of lay readers (crowd-based proxies) or a small number of expert readers (expert-based proxies).

5.2 Expert-based and crowd-based proxies

Expert-based judgments of literary works originate from a limited group of expert readers, such as editors, publishers (Karlyn and Keymer; Vulture, 2018), individual literary scholars (Bloom, 1995), and award committees like the Nobel prize. Crowd-based judgments, on the other hand, are formed by a large number of readers without a given literary expertise, and offer more inclusivity and statistical robustness. GoodReads, a social readership platform with over 90 million users, provides insight into such crowd-based judgments (Maharjan et al., 2017; Bizzoni et al., 2021; Jannatus Saba et al., 2021; Porter, 2018) and especially into reading culture "in the wild" (Nakamura, 2013), as it catalogs books from different genres and derives ratings from a heterogeneous pool of readers (Kousha et al., 2017). There are various issues with using GoodReads' ratings as a metric, among others, how this heterogeneity is conflated into one single score (0-5) that takes no account of differential rating behavior, for example across genres. Beyond the rating or "stars" on GoodReads, another option is to

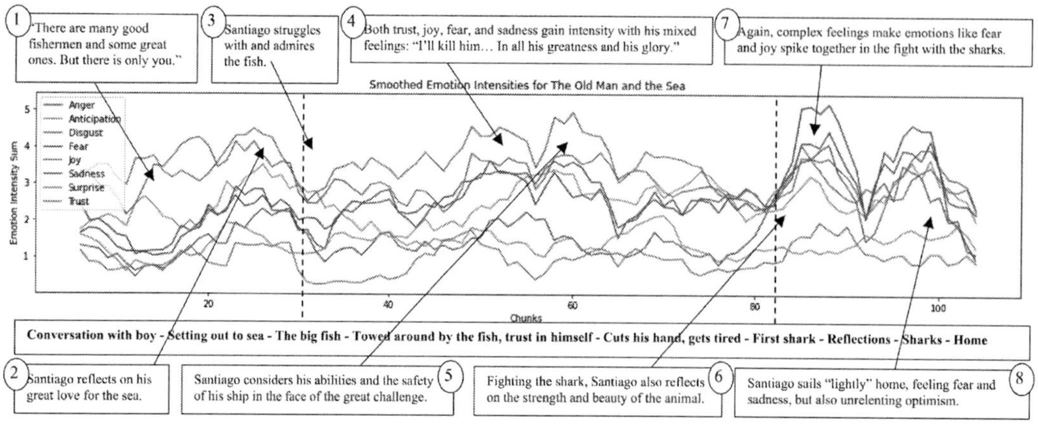

Figure 4: Arcs of *The Old Man and the Sea* annotated for narrative events.

use the rating count itself as a proxy of quality perception, supposing that more frequently rated titles are also more popular and liked. There are also less clear-cut, more nuanced measures of literary reception. For example, a conceptually hybrid measure between crowd- and expert-based is the number of libraries holding a given title worldwide, as indicated on WorldCat (Bennett et al., 2003). Expert choice and user demand may influence what titles are acquired by libraries, and since the libraries are many, the compound nature of all title selections approximates crowd-based judgment.

In this work, we selected the latter two proxies: for each book, we collected the number of ratings of GoodReads (as of December 2022) and libraries holdings of the title.[10]

6 Data Analysis

6.1 Emotion Distribution

Building on previous work (Maharjan et al., 2018), we examine the association between the emotional content of novels and their perceived quality, we examined the **overall intensity** of the eight emotions in each novel. As noted, intensity values were length-normalized to ensure comparability across texts of different sizes. To understand the variation in emotions in each novel, we computed the **entropy** of their emotion intensity distribution. In our context, the concept of entropy serves as a measure of the uncertainty of emotional intensities in novels: a low entropy value indicates that one emotion may dominate the text, being reliably more intense than other emotions. Conversely, high entropy indicates a more diverse emotional profile, where each emotion is represented with comparable intensity. In Fig. 1 the emotional profile of *The Old Man and the Sea* appears to have medium-high entropy.

6.2 Emotion Trends

Building on work examining the shape and dynamics of narrative arcs (Bizzoni et al., 2021; Öhman and Rossi, 2023; Moreira et al., 2023), we relate the linear shapes of the eight emotion arcs to quality perceptions, computing the **skewness** and **slope** steepness of each emotion arc; as a score for each emotion separately and as the average score of all eight emotions per novel. The slope value for each emotion is retrieved by linear regression and represents the development in intensity of that particular emotion across the narrative: if the joy arc increases or decreases linearly across a novel, the slope of its joy arc will be relatively steep (Su et al., 2012). Skewness captures the symmetry of an emotion arc: an arc with few large values or intensities but many small values is positively skewed, while an arc with an even distribution of large and small values has a skewness approximating 0 (Kokoska and Zwillinger, 2000).

6.3 Overall novel emotion

The intensity of most emotions appears to hold a correlation with the number of library holdings, but a weak one. There is also a weak negative correlation between library holdings and the overall entropy of the emotional values of a text (Table 2).

Yet it seems that the distribution of the data is unfit for standard correlation, as the relation be-

[10]Note that in our corpus, library holdings and rating count are correlated with a coefficient of 0.50 ($p<0.01$) using a simple Spearman correlation.

Emotion	Coefficient
Fear (sum)	0.14
Sadness (sum)	0.14
Anger (sum)	0.14
Disgust (sum)	0.13
Anticipation (sum)	0.13
Surprise (sum)	0.13
Joy (sum)	0.12
Entropy (all emotions)	-0.12

Table 2: Emotion intensities correlation with library holdings (Spearmann). For all correlations, $p < 0.01$.

Variable	rating count	libraries
mean skewness > 500	0.60*	0.50*
mean skewness < 100	-0.55*	-0.41*
mean slope inclination > 500	-0.81**	-0.71*
mean slope inclination < 100	0.83**	0.69*
mean entropy > 500	0.76*	0.29
mean entropy < 100	-0.69*	-0.63*

Table 3: Correlations of emotion arc features with reception proxies (Spearman correlation). $*p < 0.05$, $**p < 0.01$

tween emotion entropy and library holdings and GoodReads rating count is not linear. Different populations have different distributions: one group of titles with relatively low rating count and low library holdings is present at almost every level of entropy, while a group of titles with increasingly high rating count and library holdings cluster in a subset of the space.

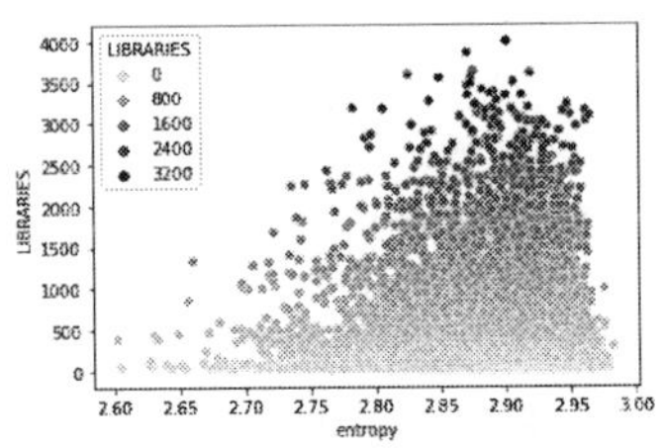

Figure 5: Distribution of library holdings with respect to emotion entropy.

To account for this hill-like distribution, we divided our data into two groups: one with low and the other with high rating counts (RC) and library holdings (LH), setting a threshold of ratings and library holdings at below 100 or above 500.[11] While these thresholds of 100 and 500 are somewhat arbitrary, they represent relatively robust trends in the data that can be reproduced with different cutoff points (see Fig 6 for the effect of different upper thresholds).

With this separation of marginally more "successful" and "unsuccessful" groups of titles, the relation between emotion entropy and quality perception is more evident: negative correlations of emotion entropy and the quality proxies continue only up to a certain entropy value, before which there is even a positive correlation between entropy and library holdings; and when looking at rating count, the correlation is almost completely positive. In general, it seems that titles with higher entropy of emotions receive a higher number of ratings and – up to a point – are held in more libraries (see Fig.7).

6.4 Emotion arcs

Using the same groupings of high and low rating and library holdings titles, we examined the correlation between our quality proxies and the average slope intensity, as well as the average skewness of arcs, averaging the values across slopes and skewness of each of the eight emotion for each title. Again, by grouping before correlating, we find a correlation between quality proxies and arc shape. It seems that more novels with more sloping arcs are rated less often and are held in fewer libraries; and where novels with more skewed emotions seem to have more ratings and library holdings (Table 3). We similarly correlated slopes of each emotion in a novel, as we might suppose that titles (or even genres) exhibit a steep slope for one emotion (not for others), making the mean unrepresentative. Here, we find that the average patterns represented in Table 3 hold for almost any single emotion: titles above 500 ratings and library holdings correlate negatively with slopes, and the reverse is true for titles below 100 ratings and library holdings, while the opposite appears true for skewness (Table 4).

7 Concluding Discussion

With 'EmotionArcs' we have presented a new resource for the study of emotions in literary novels that we hope will enable many other researchers to investigate how affect in literary works is intertwined with other aspects of literature. We have shown that our method produces reliable, useful, and easily interpretable emotion arcs that can help more traditional literary scholars compare larger corpora of literary works that are possible using only qualitative methods. It seems that overall emotional entropy, the slopes of emotion arcs, and their level of skewness hold some relation with the re-

[11]Number of books in each goup: RC<100 = 2978, RC>500 = 4340; LH<100 = 2206, LH>500 = 3464

	Joy	Anger	Sadness	Fear	Disgust	Surprise	Trust	Ant.
Rating count >500	-0.656**	-0.861**	-0.560*	-0.694**	-0.686**	-0.809**	-0.764**	-0.667**
Rating count <100	0.652**	0.886**	0.776**	0.721**	0.772**	0.765**	0.737**	0.589 **
Holdings >500	-0.938**	-0.953**	-0.913**	-0.885**	-0.875**	-0.835**	-0.839**	-0.794**
Holdings <100	0.935**	0.930**	0.749**	0.885**	0.782**	0.617*	0.757**	0.725**
Rating count >500	0.272*	0.068	0.288**	0.019	0.309**	0.453**	0.548**	-0.774*
Rating count <100	-0.272*	0.020	-0.199*	-0.020	-0.151	-0.516**	-0.550**	0.662*
Holdings >500	0.035	0.136	0.347**	0.247*	0.308**	0.427**	0.332**	0.92*
Holdings <100	0.047	-0.188*	-0.324**	-0.138	-0.233**	-0.527**	-0.477**	0.93*

Table 4: Correlation of the emotion arcs' slopes (rows 1-4) and skewness (rows 5-8) with Rating Count and libraries' holdings for both >500 and <100 values. Asterisks reflect p-value: * p<0.05, ** p<0.01.

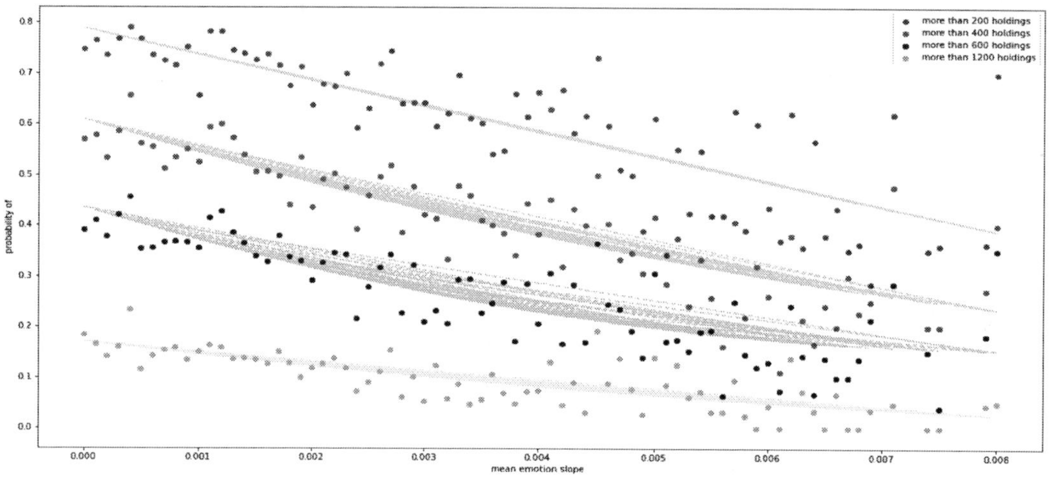

Figure 6: Trends in the probability of being in the high- or low-rating group at different cutting points of emotion slope value. While 100 and 500 rating counts and library holdings are somewhat arbitrary thresholds, trends in our data are reproduced at different cutoff points.

ception of the novels as measured via rating count and library holdings.

(i) **Entropy**. A novel with higher emotional entropy will have an overall higher probability of being rated more than five hundred times on GoodReads. The same holds for its likelihood of being held in a large number of libraries – up to a point: "too much entropy" is related to lower circulation in libraries.

(ii) **Slope**. A novel with steeper overall emotion arcs will have an overall lower probability of being rated more than five hundred times on GoodReads or being held by more than five hundred libraries; conversely, it will have an increased probability of being rated less than 100 times and held by less than 100 libraries.

(iii) **Skewness**. A novel with a low level of overall emotion skewness will have an overall lower probability of being rated more than five hundred times on GoodReads or being held in more than five hundred libraries; conversely, it will have an increased probability of being rated less than 100 times and being held by less than 100 libraries. Our results on entropy might bear a relation to Jautze et al. (2016) regarding topics: novels with relatively few, dominating topics are perceived as being less good than novels that use a larger topical palette. There may be a similar effect at the level of the emotions represented in a text. It is important to remember that we are talking about fine-grained emotions: a novel with a high level of fear does not necessarily correspond to a narrative where characters are constantly scared. Rather, because of its selection of certain events, a text may be more likely to sample from an emotional vocabulary of fear than from that of another emotion. Something similar might be inferred from the slopes' steepness and skewness: excessively predictable and smooth emotion arcs might not create as effective a reader experience. This interpretation is corrobo-

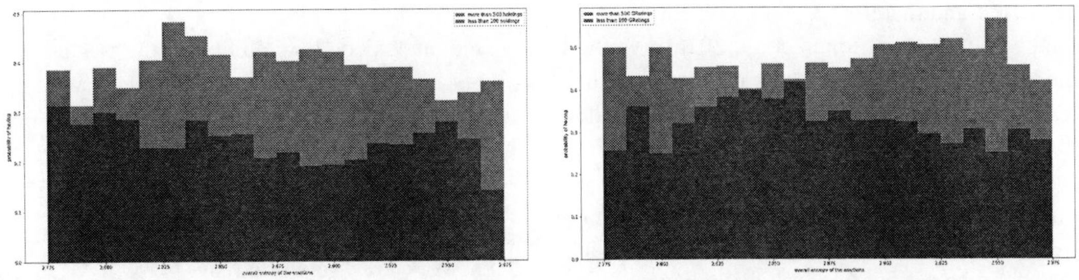

(a) Titles below 100 or above 500 holdings. (b) Titles below 100 or above 500 ratings.

Figure 7: Probability of having high/low number of library holdings or Goodreads ratings (below 100/above 500) at different values of emotional entropy. All probabilities were computed on populations of at least 10 different titles. The relation with the number of libraries' holdings might point to a "sweet spot".

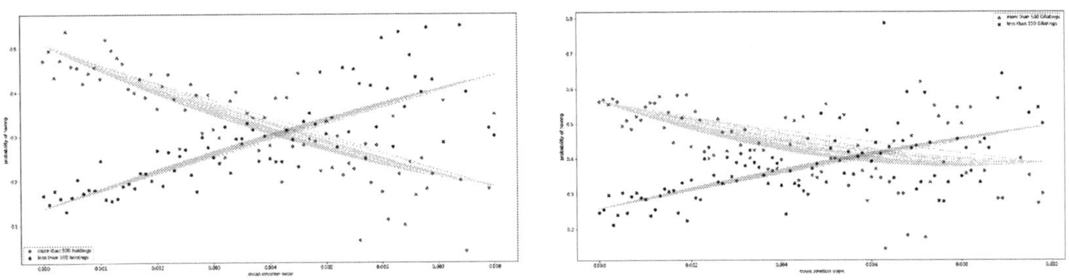

(a) Titles below 100 or above 500 holdings. (b) Titles below 100 or above 500 ratings.

Figure 8: Probability of having high/low library holdings or high/low number of GoodReads' ratings (below 100/above 500) at different levels of average slope steepness. All probabilities were computed on populations of at least 10 different titles.

rated by studies that have found that readers tend to prefer fractal story arcs but only with a moderate level of coherence (Hu et al., 2021; Bizzoni et al., 2021). Story arcs that monotonically focus on one emotion or have a very steep slope will either be overly predictable, and by extension overly coherent, or, at some point, too unpredictable and locally incoherent. Finally, in addition to a novel resource, the methods used in this study offer simple and robust tools that should be a part of any lexicon-based emotion projects. We strongly believe our methodology of fine-tuning existing lexicons to be more domain- and period-specific with the help of affective word embeddings should be the first step in any sentiment analysis or emotion detection task that utilizes lexicons as it not only makes the lexicons more attuned to the specific domain at hand but also increases precision and recall in general and can even negate some of the effects of semantic shifts in language. In the future, we aim to continue with similar projects further improving and enhancing the lexicon and extending the use cases of emotion arcs to, e.g., the exploration of narrative structure and differences in affective language used by individual authors and across genres. Emotional expectations are likely to vary greatly across genres and might yield further insight into the relation between affect, mood, and reception. We also aim to experiment with different proxies for perceived literary quality, including more expert-based resources such as canon lists and prestigious awards. Finally, we intend to combine our emotional arcs with more sophisticated modeling techniques for fractal analysis and time series forecasting in order to have a more complex view of the relation between the textual representation of emotions and reader experience.

Limitations

As emotion annotation is a notoriously difficult task, this study has attempted to make the process as robust as possible, regardless, emotions are always subjective and difficult to measure. Emotions are also partly constructed by the measuring process itself and therefore always a reflection of the methods used (Laaksonen et al., 2023). Methodologically, the choice of lemmatization, and to a lesser extent other preprocessing steps, affects how the semantic vector space is constructed and how words match the affective space. Although English is a comparatively easy language to lemmatize, there were instances of lexemes in the data that could have been further broken down.

Word embeddings are inherently contextual, however, they are not immune to polysemy, particularly when used with a hybrid lexicon-based approach. We reduced the effect of polysemous words and other similar artifacts with our iterative approach, however, it is unlikely we were completely able to remove the effects of semantic shifts or cultural biases that occur in language and stem from the original annotations of the NRC lexicon as well as the diverse nature of the data. Ultimately, unlimited iterations are possible, and we made a balanced choice between feasibility, time, cost, and practicality.

One important limitation of our corpus of novels is its strong Anglophone and American tilt: there are few non-American and non-Anglophone authors, which inevitably situates the entire analysis within the context of an "Anglocentric" literary field.

Regarding the proxies of reader appreciation used in this study, it is hard to control the demographics of each proxy for literary quality and reception. Generally, sources like GoodReads are more diverse and represent a more comprehensive demographic selection than awards committees or anthologies' editorial boards. Yet it should be noted that the majority of GoodReads users from the beginning of GoodReads in 2007 were anglophone. The number of library holdings as a proxy reflects a complex interaction of user demand and expert choice, where demographics are difficult to gauge.

It is also likely that there is a correlation between reviews on GoodReads and quality, but as with any proxy measurement, it is difficult to concretely distinguish popularity, success, and quality.

Ethics Statement

We strongly believe in reproducible and replicable science and are therefore making all data and code freely available where possible. We adhere to best practice guidelines in both the creation and publication of the datasets as suggested by Gebru et al. (2021) and Mohammad (2022). We have assessed the lexicon's suitability for the task at hand and tried to mitigate any inherent biases with our lexicon-enhancement process, however, we may have missed some details and welcome feedback.

Acknowledgements

This work was supported by JSPS KAKENHI Grant Number 22K18154.

References

Ebba Cecilia Ovesdotter Alm. 2008. *Affect in* text and speech*. Ph.D. thesis, University of Illinois at Urbana-Champaign.

Vikas Ganjigunte Ashok, Song Feng, and Yejin Choi. 2013. Success with style: Using writing style to predict the success of novels. In *Proceedings of the 2013 conference on empirical methods in natural language processing*, pages 1753–1764.

Mieke Bal and Christine Van Boheemen. 2009. *Narratology: Introduction to the theory of narrative*. University of Toronto Press.

Francesco Barbieri, Luis Espinosa Anke, and Jose Camacho-Collados. 2022. XLM-T: Multilingual language models in Twitter for sentiment analysis and beyond. In *Proceedings of the Thirteenth Language Resources and Evaluation Conference*, pages 258–266, Marseille, France. European Language Resources Association.

Petra Saskia Bayerl and Karsten Ingmar Paul. 2011. What determines inter-coder agreement in manual annotations? A meta-analytic investigation. *Computational Linguistics*, 37(4):699–725.

Rick Bennett, Brian F Lavoie, and Edward T O'Neill. 2003. The concept of a work in WorldCat: an application of FRBR. *Library collections, acquisitions, and technical services*, 27(1):45–59.

Yuri Bizzoni and Pascale Feldkamp. 2023. Comparing transformer and dictionary-based sentiment models for literary texts: Hemingway as a case-study. In *Proceedings of the 3rd International Workshop on Natural Language Processing for Digital Humanities*, pages 219–226, Tokyo, Japan. Association for Computational Linguistics.

Yuri Bizzoni, Pascale Moreira, Nicole Dwenger, Ida Lassen, Mads Thomsen, and Kristoffer Nielbo. 2023a. Good Reads and Easy Novels: Readability and Literary Quality in a Corpus of US-published Fiction. In *Proceedings of the 24th Nordic Conference on Computational Linguistics (NoDaLiDa)*, pages 42–51, Tórshavn, Faroe Islands. University of Tartu Library.

Yuri Bizzoni, Pascale Moreira, Mads Rosendahl Thomsen, and Kristoffer Nielbo. 2023b. Sentimental Matters - Predicting Literary Quality by Sentiment Analysis and Stylometric Features. In *Proceedings of the 13th Workshop on Computational Approaches to Subjectivity, Sentiment, & Social Media Analysis*, pages 11–18, Toronto, Canada. Association for Computational Linguistics.

Yuri Bizzoni, Pascale Feldkamp Moreira, Kristoffer Nielbo, Ida Marie Lassen, and Mads Thomsen. 2023c. Modeling Readers' Appreciation of Literary Narratives Through Sentiment Arcs and Semantic Profiles. In *Proceedings of the The 5th Workshop on Narrative Understanding*, pages 25–35, Toronto, Canada. Association for Computational Linguistics.

Yuri Bizzoni, Telma Peura, Kristoffer Nielbo, and Mads Thomsen. 2022a. Fractal sentiments and fairy tales-fractal scaling of narrative arcs as predictor of the perceived quality of andersen's fairy tales. *Journal of Data Mining & Digital Humanities*.

Yuri Bizzoni, Telma Peura, Kristoffer Nielbo, and Mads Thomsen. 2022b. Fractality of sentiment arcs for literary quality assessment: The case of nobel laureates. In *Proceedings of the 2nd International Workshop on Natural Language Processing for Digital Humanities*, pages 31–41, Taipei, Taiwan. Association for Computational Linguistics.

Yuri Bizzoni, Telma Peura, Mads Rosendahl Thomsen, and Kristoffer Nielbo. 2021. Sentiment dynamics of success: Fractal scaling of story arcs predicts reader preferences. In *Proceedings of the Workshop on Natural Language Processing for Digital Humanities*, pages 1–6, NIT Silchar, India. NLP Association of India (NLPAI).

Harold Bloom. 1995. *The Western Canon: The Books and School of the Ages*, first riverhead edition edition. Riverhead Books, New York, NY.

Julian Brooke, Adam Hammond, and Graeme Hirst. 2015. Gutentag: an nlp-driven tool for digital humanities research in the project gutenberg corpus. In *Proceedings of the Fourth Workshop on Computational Linguistics for Literature*, pages 42–47.

Erik Cambria, Dipankar Das, Sivaji Bandyopadhyay, and Antonio Feraco. 2017. Affective computing and sentiment analysis. In *A practical guide to sentiment analysis*, pages 1–10. Springer.

Nick Campbell. 2004. Perception of affect in speech-towards an automatic processing of paralinguistic information in spoken conversation. In *Eighth International Conference on Spoken Language Processing*.

Jonathan Cheng. 2020. Fleshing out models of gender in English-language novels (1850–2000). *Journal of Cultural Analytics*, 5(1):11652.

Irina-Ana Drobot. 2013. Affective narratology. the emotional structure of stories. *Philologica Jassyensia*, 9(2):338.

Katherine Elkins. 2022. *The Shapes of Stories: Sentiment Analysis for Narrative*. Cambridge University Press.

Timnit Gebru, Jamie Morgenstern, Briana Vecchione, Jennifer Wortman Vaughan, Hanna Wallach, Hal Daumé Iii, and Kate Crawford. 2021. Datasheets for datasets. *Communications of the ACM*, 64(12):86–92.

Thomas Haider, Steffen Eger, Evgeny Kim, Roman Klinger, and Winfried Menninghaus. 2020. Po-emo: Conceptualization, annotation, and modeling of aesthetic emotions in german and english poetry. *arXiv preprint arXiv:2003.07723*.

Jing Hu, Jianbo Gao, and Xingsong Wang. 2009. Multifractal analysis of sunspot time series: the effects of the 11-year cycle and Fourier truncation. *Journal of Statistical Mechanics: Theory and Experiment*, 2009(02):P02066.

Qiyue Hu, Bin Liu, Mads Rosendahl Thomsen, Jianbo Gao, and Kristoffer L Nielbo. 2021. Dynamic evolution of sentiments in never let me go: Insights from multifractal theory and its implications for literary analysis. *Digital Scholarship in the Humanities*, 36(2):322–332.

Swapnil Jain, Shrikant Malviya, Rohit Mishra, and Uma Shanker Tiwary. 2017. Sentiment analysis: An empirical comparative study of various machine learning approaches. In *Proceedings of the 14th International Conference on Natural Language Processing (ICON-2017)*, pages 112–121, Kolkata, India. NLP Association of India.

Syeda Jannatus Saba, Biddut Sarker Bijoy, Henry Gorelick, Sabir Ismail, Md Saiful Islam, and Mohammad Ruhul Amin. 2021. A Study on Using Semantic Word Associations to Predict the Success of a Novel. In *Proceedings of *SEM 2021: The Tenth Joint Conference on Lexical and Computational Semantics*, pages 38–51, Online. Association for Computational Linguistics.

Kim Jautze, Andreas van Cranenburgh, and Corina Koolen. 2016. Topic Modeling Literary Quality. In *Digital Humanities 2016: Conference Abstracts.*, pages 233–237, Kraków.

Jianbo Gao, H. Sultan, Jing Hu, and Wen-Wen Tung. 2010. Denoising Nonlinear Time Series by Adaptive Filtering and Wavelet Shrinkage: A Comparison. *IEEE Signal Processing Letters*, 17(3):237–240.

Matthew Jockers. 2017. Syuzhet: Extracts sentiment and sentiment-derived plot arcs from text (version 1.0. 1).

Matthew L Jockers. 2015. Some thoughts on Annie's thoughts . . . about Syuzhet. *M. Jockers' blog*.

Danny Karlyn and Tom Keymer. Chadwyck-Healey Literature Collection.

Evgeny Kim and Roman Klinger. 2018. A survey on sentiment and emotion analysis for computational literary studies. *arXiv preprint arXiv:1808.03137*.

Evgeny Kim, Sebastian Padó, and Roman Klinger. 2017. Investigating the Relationship between Literary Genres and Emotional Plot Development. In *Proceedings of the Joint SIGHUM Workshop on Computational Linguistics for Cultural Heritage, Social Sciences, Humanities and Literature*, pages 17–26, Vancouver, Canada. Association for Computational Linguistics.

Stephen Kokoska and Daniel Zwillinger. 2000. *CRC standard probability and statistics tables and formulae*. Crc Press.

Juha Koljonen, Emily Öhman, Pertti Ahonen, and Mikko Mattila. 2022. Strategic sentiments and emotions in post-Second World War party manifestos in Finland. *Journal of computational social science*, pages 1–26.

Corina Koolen, Karina van Dalen-Oskam, Andreas van Cranenburgh, and Erica Nagelhout. 2020. Literary quality in the eye of the Dutch reader: The National Reader Survey. *Poetics*, 79:101439.

Kayvan Kousha, Mike Thelwall, and Mahshid Abdoli. 2017. Goodreads reviews to assess the wider impacts of books. *Journal of the Association for Information Science and Technology*, 68(8):2004–2016.

Salla-Maaria Laaksonen, Juho Pääkkönen, and Emily Öhman. 2023. From hate speech recognition to happiness indexing: Critical issues in datafication of emotion in text mining. In *Handbook of Critical Studies of Artificial Intelligence*. Edward Elgar.

Ida Marie Schytt Lassen, Yuri Bizzoni, Telma Peura, Mads Rosendahl Thomsen, and Kristoffer Laigaard Nielbo. 2022. Reviewer Preferences and Gender Disparities in Aesthetic Judgments. In *CEUR Workshop Proceedings*, pages 280–290, Antwerp, Belgium.

Xin Li, Lidong Bing, Wenxuan Zhang, and Wai Lam. 2019. Exploiting BERT for end-to-end aspect-based sentiment analysis. *W-NUT 2019*, page 34.

Hoyt Long and Teddy Roland. 2016. US Novel Corpus. Technical report, Textual Optic Labs, University of Chicago.

Suraj Maharjan, John Arevalo, Manuel Montes, Fabio A. González, and Thamar Solorio. 2017. A multi-task approach to predict likability of books. In *Proceedings of the 15th Conference of the European Chapter of the Association for Computational Linguistics: Volume 1, Long Papers*, pages 1217–1227, Valencia, Spain. Association for Computational Linguistics.

Suraj Maharjan, Sudipta Kar, Manuel Montes, Fabio A. González, and Thamar Solorio. 2018. Letting emotions flow: Success prediction by modeling the flow of emotions in books. In *Proceedings of the 2018 Conference of the North American Chapter of the Association for Computational Linguistics: Human Language Technologies: Volume 2, Short Papers*, pages 259–265, New Orleans, Louisiana. Association for Computational Linguistics.

Raymond A Mar, Keith Oatley, Maja Djikic, and Justin Mullin. 2011. Emotion and narrative fiction: Interactive influences before, during, and after reading. *Cognition & emotion*, 25(5):818–833.

Tomáš Mikolov, Édouard Grave, Piotr Bojanowski, Christian Puhrsch, and Armand Joulin. 2018. Advances in pre-training distributed word representations. In *Proceedings of the Eleventh International Conference on Language Resources and Evaluation (LREC 2018)*.

Saif Mohammad. 2011. From Once Upon a Time to Happily Ever After: Tracking Emotions in Novels and Fairy Tales. In *Proceedings of the 5th ACL-HLT Workshop on Language Technology for Cultural Heritage, Social Sciences, and Humanities*, pages 105–114, Portland, OR, USA. Association for Computational Linguistics.

Saif Mohammad. 2016. A practical guide to sentiment annotation: Challenges and solutions. In *WASSA@ NAACL-HLT*, pages 174–179.

Saif M. Mohammad. 2018a. Obtaining reliable human ratings of valence, arousal, and dominance for 20,000 English words. In *Proceedings of The Annual Conference of the Association for Computational Linguistics (ACL)*, Melbourne, Australia.

Saif M. Mohammad. 2018b. Word affect intensities. In *Proceedings of the 11th Edition of the Language Resources and Evaluation Conference (LREC-2018)*, Miyazaki, Japan.

Saif M Mohammad. 2022. Ethics sheet for automatic emotion recognition and sentiment analysis. *Computational Linguistics*, 48(2):239–278.

Saif M Mohammad and Peter D Turney. 2013. NRC emotion lexicon. *National Research Council, Canada*, 2.

Pascale Feldkamp Moreira, Yuri Bizzoni, Emily Öhman, and Kristoffer L. Nielbo. 2023. Not just Plot(ting): A Comparison of Two Approaches for Understanding Narrative Text Dynamics. In *Computational Humanities Research 2023*, pages 191–205, Paris, France. CEUR Workshop Proceedings.

Mika V. Mäntylä, Daniel Graziotin, and Miikka Kuutila. 2018. The evolution of sentiment analysis—a review of research topics, venues, and top cited papers. *Computer Science Review*, 27:16–32.

Lisa Nakamura. 2013. "Words with friends": Socially networked reading on Goodreads. *PMLA*, 128(1):238–243.

Emily Öhman. 2020a. Challenges in Annotation: Annotator Experiences from a Crowdsourced Emotion Annotation Task. In *Digital Humanities in the Nordic Countries 2020*. CEUR Workshop Proceedings.

Emily Öhman. 2020b. Emotion Annotation: Rethinking Emotion Categorization. In *Digital Humanities in the Nordic Countries Post-Proceedings*, pages 134–144. CEUR WS.

Emily Öhman. 2021a. *The Language of Emotions: Building and Applying Computational Methods for Emotion Detection for English and Beyond*. Ph.D. thesis, University of Helsinki.

Emily Öhman. 2021b. The Validity of Lexicon-based Sentiment Analysis in Interdisciplinary Research. In *Proceedings of the Workshop on Natural Language Processing for Digital Humanities*, pages 7–12, NIT Silchar, India. NLP Association of India (NLPAI).

Emily Öhman and Riikka Rossi. 2023. Affect as Proxy for Mood. *Journal of Data Mining and Digital Humanities*, Special Issue: Natural Language Processing for Digital Humanities.

Robert Plutchik. 1980. A general psychoevolutionary theory of emotion. *Theories of emotion*, 1:3–31.

J.D. Porter. 2018. *Stanford Literary Lab Pamphlet 17: Popularity/Prestige*. Stanford Literary Lab.

Andrew J Reagan, Lewis Mitchell, Dilan Kiley, Christopher M Danforth, and Peter Sheridan Dodds. 2016. The Emotional Arcs of Stories Are Dominated by Six Basic Shapes. *EPJ Data Science*, 5(1):1–12.

Swapna Somasundaran, Xianyang Chen, and Michael Flor. 2020. Emotion arcs of student narratives. In *Proceedings of the First Joint Workshop on Narrative Understanding, Storylines, and Events*, pages 97–107, Online. Association for Computational Linguistics.

Xiaogang Su, Xin Yan, and Chih-Ling Tsai. 2012. Linear regression. *Wiley Interdisciplinary Reviews: Computational Statistics*, 4(3):275–294.

Annie Swafford. 2015. Problems with the syuzhet package. *Anglophile in Academia: Annie Swafford's Blog*.

Daniela Teodorescu and Saif M Mohammad. 2023. Generating high-quality emotion arcs for low-resource languages using emotion lexicons. *arXiv preprint arXiv:2306.02213*.

Ted Underwood, David Bamman, and Sabrina Lee. 2018. The transformation of gender in English-language fiction. *Journal of Cultural Analytics*, 3(2):11035.

Andreas van Cranenburgh and Corina Koolen. 2020. Results of a single blind literary taste test with short anonymized novel fragments. In *Proceedings of the The 4th Joint SIGHUM Workshop on Computational Linguistics for Cultural Heritage, Social Sciences, Humanities and Literature*, pages 121–126.

Hugo Verdaasdonk. 1983. Social and economic factors in the attribution of literary quality. *Poetics*, 12(4-5):383–395.

editors Vulture. 2018. A Premature Attempt at the 21st Century Literary Canon.

Kaitlyn Zhou, Kawin Ethayarajh, Dallas Card, and Dan Jurafsky. 2022. Problems with cosine as a measure of embedding similarity for high frequency words. In *Proceedings of the 60th Annual Meeting of the Association for Computational Linguistics (Volume 2: Short Papers)*, pages 401–423, Dublin, Ireland. Association for Computational Linguistics.

A Appendix

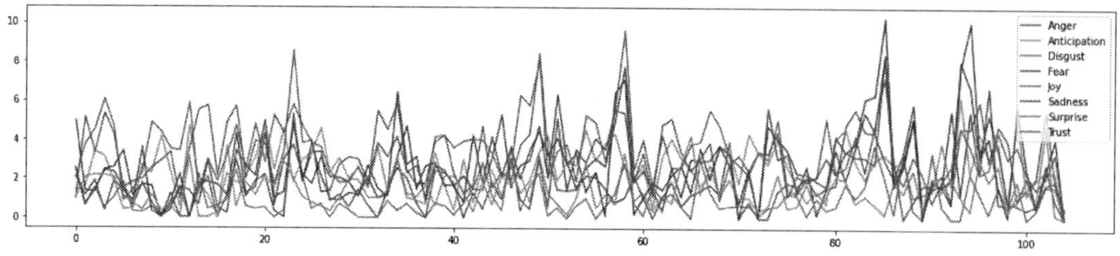

Figure 9: Unsmoothed emotion arcs for *The Old Man and the Sea*

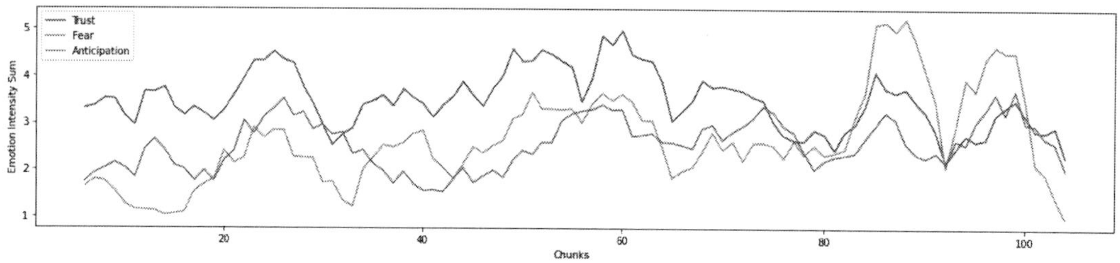

Figure 10: Smoothed arcs for trust, fear, and anticipation for *The Old Man and the Sea*

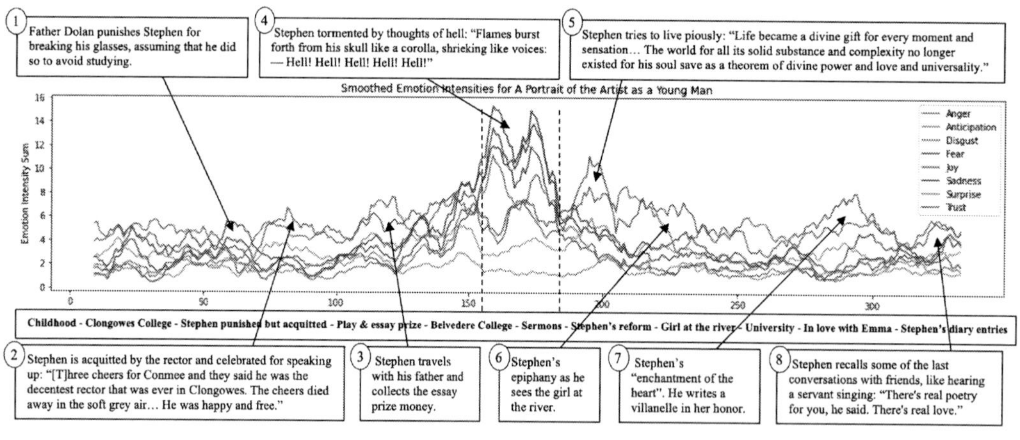

Figure 11: Another annotation of the novel *The Portrait of the Artist as a Young Man* by James Joyce. Note the peak of negative emotions in the center for this book, which Jockers (2015) has called a "man in a hole" narrative.

Pair	Coefficient	Type of Correlation
Anger, Fear	0.90	Strong Positive
Anticipation, Joy	0.77	Strong Positive
Disgust, Anger	0.77	Strong Positive
Disgust, Sadness	0.78	Strong Positive
Fear, Sadness	0.78	Strong Positive
Anticipation, Trust	0.76	Strong Positive
Joy, Trust	0.71	Strong Positive
Anger, Entropy	0.63	Moderate Positive
Entropy, Joy	-0.53	Moderate Negative
Entropy, Trust	-0.51	Moderate Negative

Table 5: Pairwise correlation of emotions

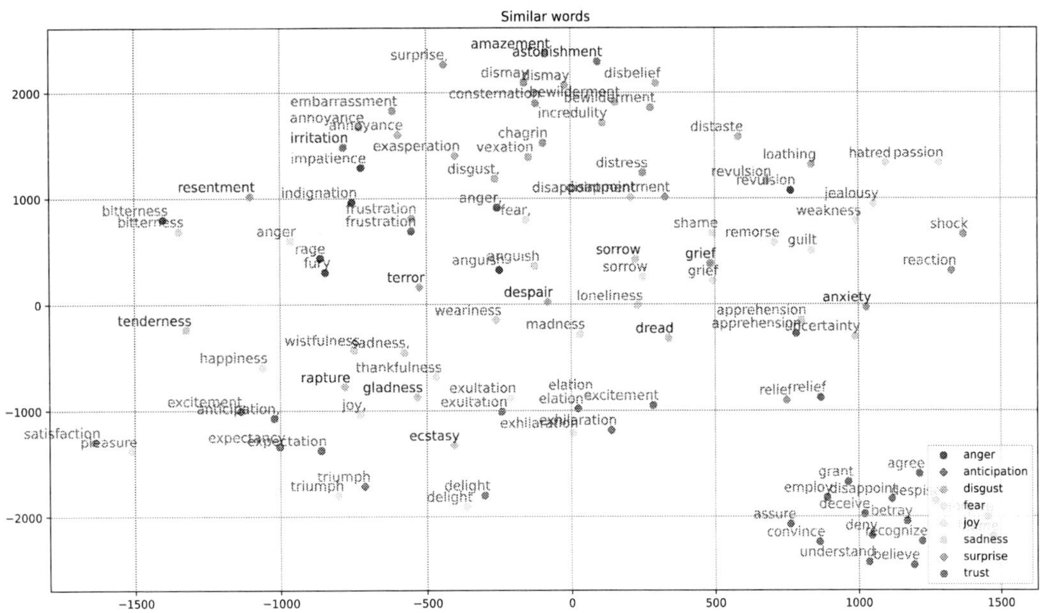

Figure 12: Word similarities for Plutchik's core emotions in the corpus in the affective semantic vector space as measured by cosine similarity. We can see that *trust*, although commonly co-occurring with both *joy* and *anticipation* does not overlap with these emotions. On the other hand, the negative emotions both overlap and co-occur.

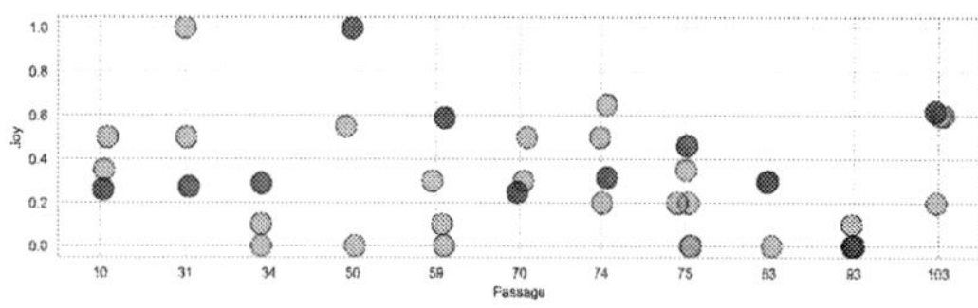

Figure 13: **Joy**, human and model scores.

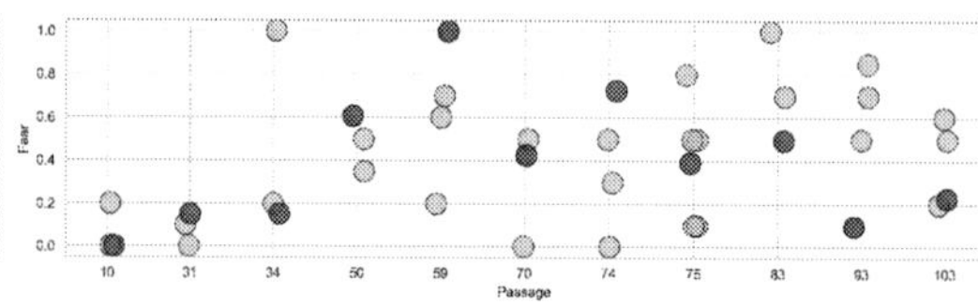

Figure 14: **Fear**, human and model scores.

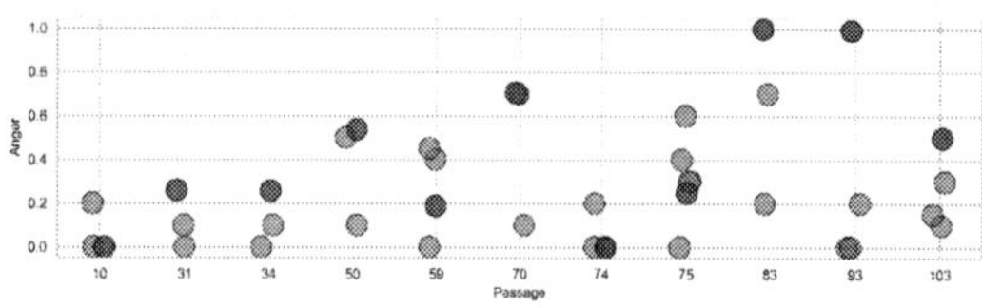

Figure 15: **Anger**, human and model scores.

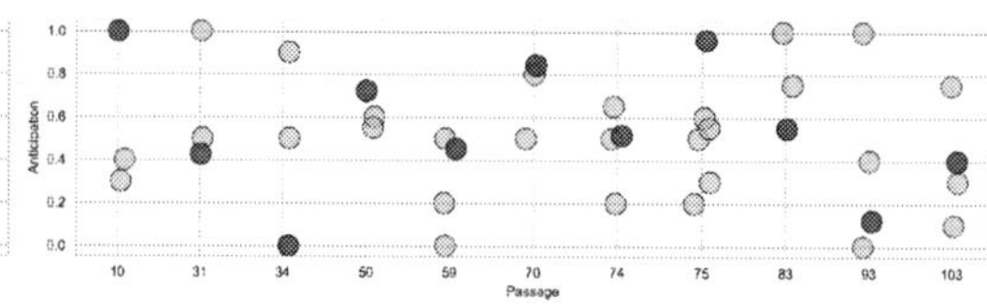

Figure 16: **Anticipation**, human and model scores.

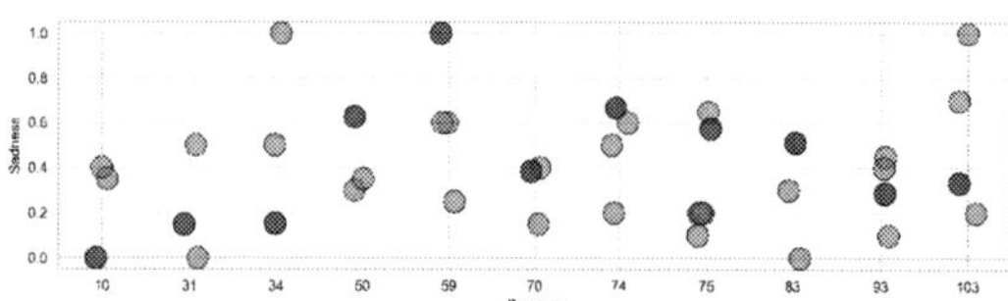

Figure 17: **Sadness**, human and model scores.

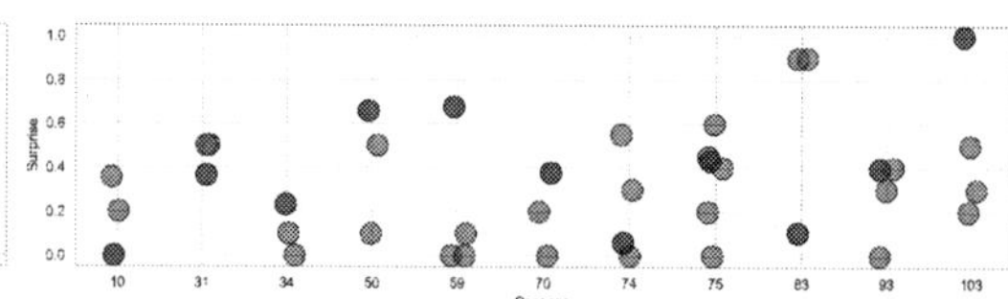

Figure 18: **Surprise**, human and model scores.

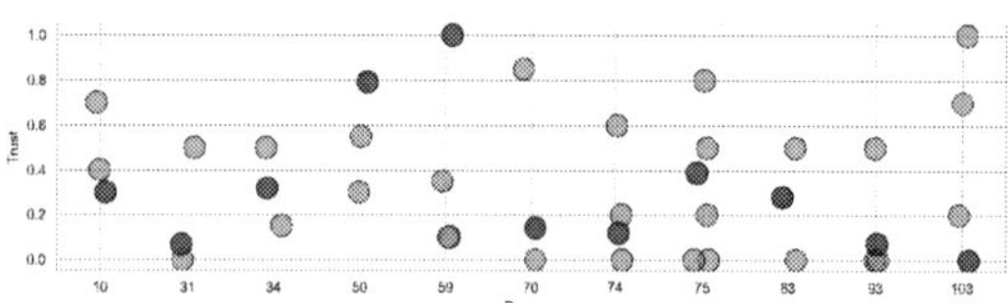

Figure 19: **Trust**, human and model scores.

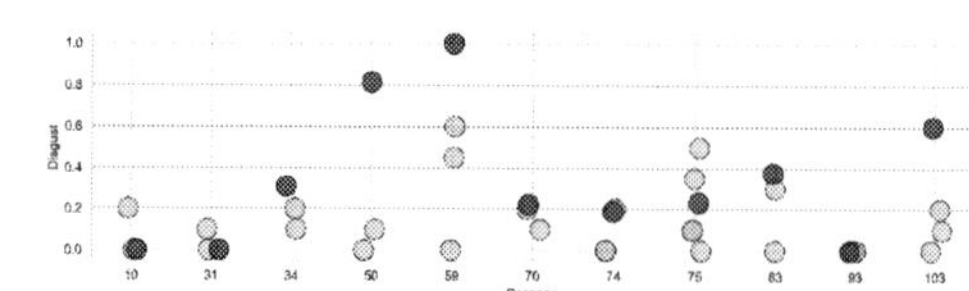

Figure 20: **Disgust**, human and model scores.

Annotator and model scores for 11 randomly selected passages per emotion. On the x-axis, each passage with scores arranged as increasing on the y-axis. For each passage, darker dots represent the EmotionArcs score for the emotion of the passage. Note that the number of annotators varies with respect to emotion and passage.

Multi-word Expressions in English Scientific Writing

Diego Alves
Saarland University, Germany
diego.alves@uni-saarland.de

Stefan Fischer
Saarland University, Germany
stefan.fischer@uni-saarland.de

Stefania Degaetano-Ortlieb
Saarland University, Germany
s.degaetano@mx.uni-saarland.de

Elke Teich
Saarland University, Germany
e.teich@mx.uni-saarland.de

Abstract

Multi-Word Expressions (MWEs) play a pivotal role in language use overall and in register formation more specifically, e.g. encoding domain-specific terminology. Our study focuses on the identification and categorization of MWEs used in English scientific writing, considering their formal characteristics as well as their developmental trajectory over time from the mid-17th century to the present. For this, we develop an approach combining three different types of methods to identify MWEs (Universal Dependency annotation, Partitioner and the Academic Formulas List) and selected measures to characterize MWE properties (e.g., dispersion by Kullback-Leibler Divergence and several association measures). This allows us to inspect MWE types in a novel data-driven way regarding their functions and change over time in specialized discourse.

1 Introduction

Regularity in language does not only concern structural aspects (syntax, morphology), but also the way we combine words. Some word combinations are perceived as patterns that are associated with specific meanings or connotations, collectively referred to as multi-word expressions (MWEs). MWEs range from idioms that are formally fixed and have a figurative meaning (e.g., *kick the bucket*) to compounds (*bus ticket*) or phrasal verbs (*take a ride*) that are typically compositional and often lexically fairly productive (cf. Avgustinova and Iomdin (2019)).

MWEs are ubiquitous since they contribute to language efficiency by having highly predictable transitions from one word to the next or, if highly conventionalized, they can be retrieved from the lexicon rather than processed incrementally, thus giving them a processing advantage over other word sequences. Furthermore, MWEs play a crucial role in register formation as they provide conventional encodings of context-specific meanings. For example, MWEs such as *in no event* or *said therein* are typical of legal language and rarely encountered elsewhere, while noun-noun and adjective-noun combinations such as *iron oxide* or *sulphuric acid* are a typical type of MWEs used in scientific language forming domain-specific terminology.

In particular, we are interested in MWEs in scientific English from a diachronic perspective (mid 17th century to today). Scientific English develops into a recognizable register during the late modern period and becomes highly conventionalized in modern times. Overall, we want to better understand the process of register formation and whether processing advantages might have an impact. Specifically, we ask (i) what are the MWEs used in scientific English, (ii) which specific *types* of MWEs are used in the scientific domain, and (iii) how to characterize the diachronic development of MWEs in this domain, e.g., do specific MWEs trend in particular periods, do MWEs become more/less fixed and/or productive over time, thus contributing to conventionalization. For instance, we expect that MWEs serving domain-specific terminology (such as noun-noun compounds) will be quite agile and productive, while others, e.g., expressions of stance (e.g. *it is interesting*) will change at a lower rate and be less varied. We develop an approach to identify MWEs in scientific texts in order to be able to address these questions and better understand the role MWEs play in register formation. The scientific domain is well-suited as it encompasses different types of MWEs ranging from scientific terms up to stylistic expressions. In this paper, we take a first step towards answering the above questions, focusing on the identification of MWEs and possibilities of categorization into types by applying dispersion and association measures to our diachronic data set.

The remainder of the paper is organized as

Proceedings of LaTeCH-CLfL 2024, pages 67–76
March 22, 2024 ©2024 Association for Computational Linguistics

follows. In Section 2 we discuss related work on MWEs in computational linguistics/NLP. Sections 3 and 4 presents our methods and results, including a preliminary diachronic analysis. We conclude with a summary and outlook (Section 5).

2 Related Work

From a linguistic perspective, there are numerous corpus-based accounts of MWEs in different registers, including the scientific one (e.g. Biber and Barbieri (2007); Hyland (2008); Liu (2012)). Some of these descriptions include lists of MWEs used in academic texts that are freely available. We make use of one specific list (Simpson-Vlach and Ellis, 2010) in our own approach (Section 3), but obviously such lists are always biased (time, corpus). Therefore, a sound, reusable computational method for identifying MWEs is needed, including analysis of their inherent properties (such as transparency, compositionality, fixedness; cf. also Schulte im Walde and Smolka (2019)).

From a computational point of view, MWEs have been considered "a pain in the neck" (Sag et al., 2002) because they are not trivial to identify, let alone classify, by standard language models or NLP tools. Two formal criteria of MWEs are *predictability* in a given context (e.g., register) and relative *fixedness* of the elements within the expression. In combination with relative frequency, well-established measures to assess MWE candidates are pointwise mutual information (PMI) and log-likelihood, commonly also applied to identify collocations (e.g., Evert (2008); Ramisch et al. (2010); Wahl and Gries (2018); Fabre et al. (2019)).

Regarding the identification of MWEs using machine-learning methods, Ramisch et al. (2023) conducted a survey on existing MWE corpora and evaluation methods. They showed that most of the existing tools for this specific NLP task are based either on DiMSUM (Schneider et al., 2016) or PARSEME (Savary et al., 2015) corpora and that, due to the complexity of the task and differences between approaches, results are not always comparable. PARSEME acknowledges discontinuity, variability, nesting, and overlaps and has a fine-grained MWE classification, however, it considers only verbal MWEs. On the other hand, DiMSUM corpus is annotated for most major MWE categories (i.e., nominal, verbal, adverbial, and functional), but does not include any category labels. Considering the scope of our study, the broader coverage of DiMSUM seems more relevant and aligned with our aims. The complexity of the automatic extraction of MWEs is noticeable in works such as Tanner and Hoffman (2023) where state-of-the-art tools have F1-scores below 65.

Given the complexity of the task, different approaches focus on different aspects of MWEs, so we decided to combine the state-of-the-art approaches for a more comprehensive treatment.

3 Methods

3.1 Dataset

As the main objective of this study is to investigate the role of MWEs in the development of English scientific writing, we decided to use the Royal Society Corpus (RSC) 6.0, a diachronic corpus of scientific English covering the period from 1665 until 1996. The RSC comprises 47 837 texts (295 895 749 tokens), mainly scientific articles covering a wide range of areas from both the mathematical and physical sciences and the biological sciences, and is based on the Philosophical Transactions and Proceedings of the Royal Society of London (Fischer et al., 2020).

Given its fair size and time coverage, the RSC is not only particularly relevant for diachronic linguistic analysis (e.g., Feltgen et al. (2017); Degaetano-Ortlieb and Teich (2018); Degaetano-Ortlieb and Teich (2022)), but also for historical and cultural analysis (e.g., Fyfe et al. (2015); Moxham and Fyfe (2018)).

3.2 Extraction of Multi-word Expressions

To identify and extract MWEs from the RSC corpus, we combined three different approaches which are schematised in Figure 1. The idea was to increase the number of identified MWEs, reducing biases related to the recall of each approach. From each method, we extract a list of MWEs which are, then, merged into the final RSC MWE list. For each method, MWEs are extracted in lowercase. Each method is described in detail in the subsections below.

3.2.1 Universal Dependencies Method

The Universal Dependencies[1] (UD) guidelines for the annotation of dependency relations (De Marneffe et al., 2021) include 5 dependency labels which concern MWEs: i) compound - combinations of tokens that morphosyntactically behave as single

[1]https://universaldependencies.org/

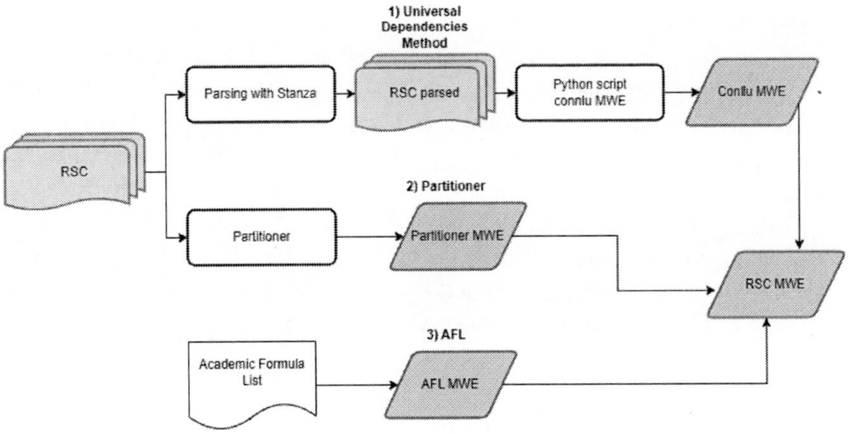

Figure 1: Methodology for extracting MWEs from the RSC corpus.

words. In English, we find most commonly nominal compounds written as separate words, for example, *orange juice*; b) compound:prt - phrasal verbs (e.g., *shut down* and *find out*); c) flat - this relation combines elements of an expression where none of the immediate components can be identified as the sole head using standard substitution tests. For example: *Hillary Clinton* and *San Francisco*; d) flat:foreign - sequences of foreign words; and e) fixed - used for certain fixed grammaticalized expressions which tend to behave like function words (e.g., *because of, in spite of, as well as*).

CoNNL-U is the standard format for texts containing morphosyntactic annotations following the UD guidelines. It is supported by state-of-the-art dependency parsers (e.g., Stanza) and can be easily queried for specific syntactic information. Thus, from a parsed corpus, it is possible to identify the word units composing the different types of MWE according to the UD framework.

The RSC 6.0 was parsed using Stanza tool (Qi et al., 2020) and the combined model for the English language provided by the developers which was trained with different UD corpora. Then, we developed a Python script using pyconll library[2] to identify and count the MWEs in the RSC texts per year and merged the results in a unified list of UD MWEs concerning all RSC.

The UD method for extracting MWEs depends on the accuracy of the parser, thus, although Stanza is a state-of-the-art tool for dependency annotation, some errors are inevitable. A manual evaluation of 70 sentences (10 per 50-year period of the RSC) showed that the accuracy of the parser is equal or higher than 85% for compound:prt, compound, and fixed MWEs, and equal to 75% for flat ones. The scores are quite consistent throughout the different time periods[3].

Another bias related to the UD method concerns the fact that many MWEs are not captured as they are described syntactically with dependency relations different from the 5 ones described above (e.g., *in terms of, so far, as so*). Therefore, this method alone is not enough for a global diachronic analysis of MWEs.

3.2.2 Partitioner

Partitioner 0.1.2[4] is a Python module that performs tokenization with generalisations into MWE segmentation using a supervised machine learning algorithm (Williams, 2016). It was presented by Tanner and Hoffman (2023) as one of the state-of-the-art tools for MWE extraction (evaluated using the DiMSUM corpus).

We applied the partitioner method to the RSC texts and, as was the case of the UD method, extracted the ensemble of MWEs in the RSC and also identified the MWEs occurring each year.

The partitioner memory overhead comes from the English Wikipedia data set, thus, it may also fail in identifying certain MWEs from the earlier periods of the RSC. Moreover, although it is a state-of-the-art tool (with better recall than the others listed by Tanner and Hoffman (2023)), it is clear that it is not possible to identify all MWEs in our corpus.

[2]https://github.com/pyconll/pyconll

[3]flat:foreign was not evaluated as this class is rare in the RSC and it did not appear in the evaluation set

[4]https://pypi.org/project/partitioner/

3.2.3 Academic Formulas List

The third approach that we selected regarding MWE identification in the RSC concerns the Academic Formulas List (AFL), which is a list of the most common formulaic sequences in academic English. It is composed of a core list of 207 formulaic expressions found in written and spoken academic language, a specific list of 200 expressions from written corpora, and another one (also with 200 expressions) based on spoken academic English texts (Simpson-Vlach and Ellis, 2010). The AFL multi-word expressions were identified by the authors with a special measure of usefulness called the formula teaching worth (FTW), which combines frequency and mutual information measures.

Using a Python script, we identified and counted all AFL MWEs in the RSC. In total, 506 out of the 607 MWEs in the AFL occur in our corpus. As expected, most of the AFL expressions that do not appear in the RSC concern the ones from the AFL spoken list (e.g., *I'll talk about*, *gonna talk about*, *let's look at*).

3.2.4 Merged MWEs

Once we identified and counted the MWEs in the RSC with the three methods, we merged the lists to create our final set of MWEs.

Since UD MWEs are grammatically motivated and AFL MWEs were selected using specific measures, we kept all the elements from these lists. However, regarding the partitioner method, we consider only the MWEs with frequency (in the whole corpus) >3, following the threshold defined by Gries (2022). The aim is to avoid, in our final list, syntagmas such as a determiner followed by a noun as well as other sequence of tokens which are not MWEs as they are not grammatically motivated like flat and compound structures and are not frequent in the text to be considered a collostructure. Moreover, we decided to exclude MWEs composed only of numbers.

Regarding the frequency values, if the MWE appeared in more than one list, we considered its frequency to be the highest number when comparing values from the different approaches.

3.3 Dimensions of Information

Several measures are described in the literature to characterize MWE properties. Gries (2022) defined eight different ones which he used to identify MWEs in the Brown corpus (Francis and Kucera, 1979) using a multi-dimensional strategy based on an information-theoretic approach.

In our case, MWEs were extracted using automatic methods, thus, our aim regarding dimensions of information is to use these metrics to describe the multi-word units identified in the RSC. Besides the MWE frequency provided by the scripts of the three approaches, we also calculated, for each MWE, its dispersion and association values across years.

3.3.1 Dispersion

The dispersion measure assesses the spread of an MWE within a corpus. It is defined by Gries (2022) as a normalized version of the Kullback–Leibler divergence (KLD), which is a unidirectional measure quantifying how much in percent of a word's total occurrences in each corpus part diverges from the corpus part sizes in percent. Dispersion values vary from 0 to 1, the higher that number, the more heterogeneously distributed the MWE is. In this study, dispersion for each MWE was calculated across time by subdividing the RSC per year.

Thus, with the frequency of each MWE and the size of each corpus part (number of tokens) per year, it was possible to calculate the normalized dispersion values of all MWEs of our merged list.

3.3.2 Association

The Association measures of bi-grams are defined as (i) the degree to which the first token attracts the second one, and (ii) the degree to which the second token of the MWE attracts the first. For n-grams with $n > 2$, we calculate as many association measures as necessary to describe the whole MWE, considering the whole left context. For example, for the MWE *in spite of*, we calculate: a) association of *in* and *spite*; b) Association of *spite* and *in*; c) association of *in spite* and *of*; and c) association of *of* and *in spite*.

Associations measures are also obtained using normalized KLD as described by Gries (2022). Thus, for each MWE from the merged list, we calculated the different association values considering the whole corpus and also for each 50-year period of the RSC.

4 Results

4.1 Extraction of MWEs

We present in Table 1 the details of the RSC MWE list in terms of the number of MWE types per class of MWE: (i) UD MWEs correspond to MWEs identified only with the UD method as well as the ones identified by both UD and partitioner approaches; (ii) Other MWEs are the partitioner MWEs which do not appear in the UD list; and (iii) AFL MWEs are the MWEs provided by the AFL approach.

Method	MWE
UD	3 147 597
Other	181 659
AFL	506
Total	3 329 762

Table 1: Number of MWE types of each extraction approach and for the RSC MWE merged list.

It is possible to notice that the majority of the RSC MWEs (94%) come from the UD method. This is due to our decision to keep even the MWEs extracted via this method with a frequency < 3. Moreover, most MWEs in our list (69%) appear only once in the whole corpus.

Table 2 presents the distribution of the number of MWE types regarding UD MWEs in terms of dependency relation.

Compound and flat are the UD MWE classes with the highest number of MWE types in the RSC, however, they have a high number of types that occur only once in the corpus (hapax percentage higher than 70%). Most of these MWEs correspond to specific entities that are only mentioned in the precise context of specific articles (e.g., *oligocene regime*; *wavelength translators*; *Prince Joseph Oscar*) and did not become part of scientific terminology. The flat:foreign class is essentially composed of hapaxes, thus, of lesser interest for our study. The flat:foreign MWEs with a frequency > 1 (8 in total) concern mostly parsing errors (e.g., *J. McLean*, *complete collection*, *rb 27*).

Figure 2 presents the relative frequency of each MWE class per year in the RSC. It is possible to notice a clear tendency of increasing the usage of compounds in scientific English (as observed previously by Degaetano-Ortlieb and Teich (2018)), with a more pronounced slope from the second half of the nineteenth century. Moreover, flat MWEs seem to become increasingly more common specially in the second half of the twentieth century.

UD MWE	MWE	%
compound	2 523 696	80.2
flat	604 057	19.2
compound:prt	16 337	0.5
fixed	3 107	0.1
flat:foreign	400	0.0

Table 2: Distribution of UD MWEs in terms of dependency relation.

Furthermore, applying the Mann-Kendall trend test to each class (Hussain and Mahmud, 2019), with the exception of phrasal verbs (i.e., compound:prt), all the other classes present an overall increasing tendency (p-value below 0.05) even though, in some cases, decreasing periods are observed.

4.2 Dimensions of Information

4.2.1 Dispersion and Association overview

As previously mentioned, we focus our analysis on two specific dimensions of information: dispersion and association. Thus, to have a graphic overview of the distribution of the different classes of MWEs identified in the RSC according to these metrics, we plotted the graphs presented in Figure 3.

Each graph represents the MWEs of the specific class in red, and in black, the other ones. To improve the visualisation, we plot only the types with a frequency > 10. For dispersion, each type has one value, while for association, the number depends on the number of words composing the MWE. Therefore, what is plotted corresponds to the mean of the different association values[5].

As expected, the different classes of MWEs behave differently in terms of distribution regarding dispersion and association metrics.

Most AFL MWEs are positioned in the lower left quadrant, thus indicating that these units are fairly well distributed within the RSC but with low mean association values. This is due to the fact that most of the AFL MWEs are composed of words that appear in many other contexts (e.g., *that is the*, *it is important*, *on the other*). The AFL elements with a mean association value around 0.5 are the ones where at least one word is more usually present in that specific construction (e.g., *in accordance with*). Few AFL MWEs are positioned in the upper left quadrant (i.e.; not homogeneously dispersed in the RSC) and usually concern MWEs with personal pronouns (mostly *I* and *you*).

Compound and flat classes are the ones with the highest number of MWE types. In both cases, most of the MWEs are positioned in the upper quadrants of the graphs. However, compound MWEs have a

[5]These graphs are available in the html format at: http://tinyurl.com/2pd8n7s8

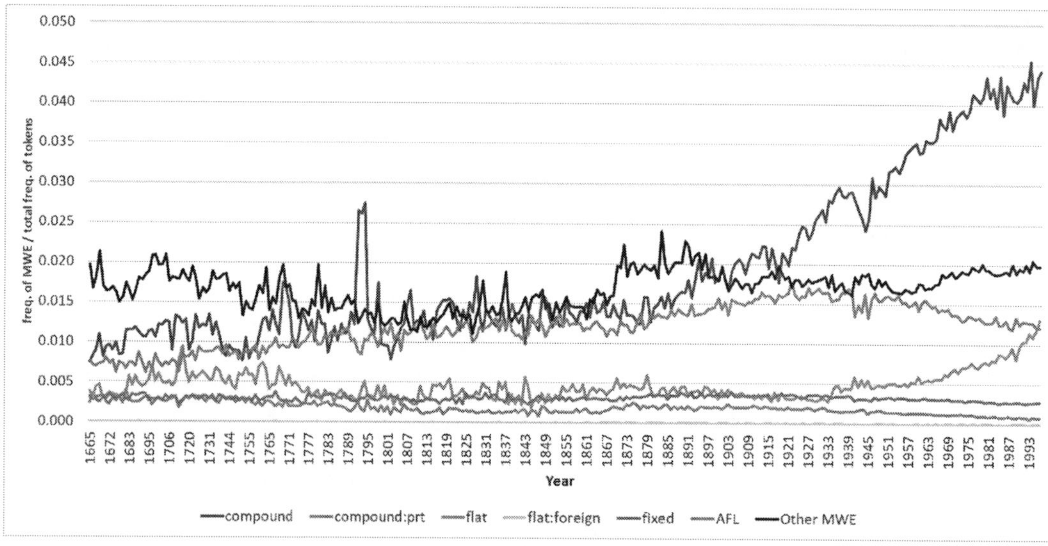

Figure 2: Relative frequency of the different classes of MWE per year in the RSC.

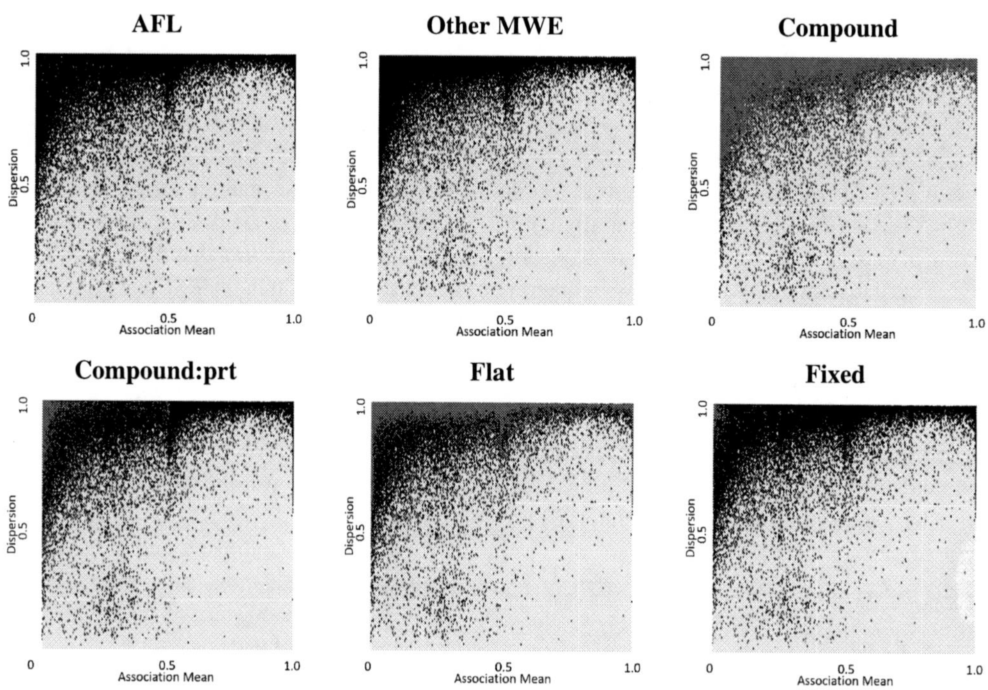

Figure 3: Distribution of the RSC MWEs in terms of Dispersion and Association. Each graph presents in red the class of MWE specified in its title.

better distribution in terms of dispersion in these quadrants. For these two classes, the elements in the upper right quadrant usually correspond to very specific scientific terms such as name of species (e.g., *Ambystoma mexicanum*), while the MWEs in the upper left side are composed of words that are more generic (e.g., *Mr Baker*, *Dr Davies*, *phase modulation*). The compound and flat MWEs in the lower right quadrant are very frequent terms that are quite homogeneously dispersed in the RSC, for example: *Royal Society*, *New York*, *refractive index*, *differential equations*, *standard deviation*. The scientific terms in the lower quadrants correspond to broad concepts usually applied in different fields.

Phrasal verbs (compound:prt) present a particular behaviour. Usually, the association value of its preposition in regard to the verb is very low as this element can appear in a large variety of other contexts. Thus, it explains the fact that most compound:prt MWEs are positioned in the left quadrants. More specifically, the vast majority of these MWEs are not well dispersed in the RSC, thus, the upper left quadrant is the most populated one with this class. Some specific phrasal verbs which are common in the scientific language are better distributed in our corpus, such as: *carried out*, *pointed out*, *depend on*. Phrasal verbs with mean association values close to 0.5 are the ones for which the verb is not encountered in other contexts in the RSC (e.g., *churned up*, *smoothes out*, *budded off*).

Regarding fixed MWEs, we observe a cluster of elements on the left upper side and many others spread over the left lower quadrant. The MWEs in the upper side correspond to unusual terms (frequency below 50) such as *according with*, *one other*, *without than*, while the ones in the lower part of the graph occur more frequently (more than 100 occurrences). Moreover, some fixed MWEs that are homogeneously distributed in the RSC have a mean association value closer to 0.5, indicating that at least one of its units is strongly attracted to the other words forming the MWE. This is the case for *due to*, *less than*, *rather than*, etc.

Finally, the MWEs from the "Other MWE" class (extracted using the partitioner tool) are mostly present on the left upper and lower parts of the graph. A qualitative analysis of these terms shows that some of them correspond to nominal phrases composed of an adjective and a noun (e.g., *electrical stimulation*, *practical applications*). Also, many of-genitive examples can be identified as "Other MWE" such as *University of Bristol* and *Department of Chemistry*. We also notice many cases of discourse markers such as *at first sight*, *for example*, etc.

4.2.2 Diachronic Analysis of Association Values

To analyse the diachronic evolution of MWEs in scientific English, we focus on the examination of the mean association values throughout the 50-year periods. As described in Section 3.3.2, for each period, we calculated the association metrics for each MWE present in the sub-corpus as well as its mean value.

Our aim is to check whether the identified MWEs became more or less fixed in time, a phenomenon that can indicate possible conventionalization processes in this specific register of the English language. Therefore, we used the Mann-Kendall trend test[6] which is suited to the analysis of time series data regarding increasing or decreasing trends (Hussain and Mahmud, 2019).

As we are interested in diachronic trends, only MWEs that appear in at least 2 periods were examined (316 390 out of 3 329 762). Thus, we applied the original Mann-Kendall test proposed by the pymannkendall module to these MWEs and extracted the following results: i) trend: increasing or decreasing (if p-value < 0.05) and no trend (if p-value > 0.05) and ii) slope: value representing the rate of change (positive for increasing values of mean association and negative when decreasing).

Table 3 presents the results for each class of MWE in the RSC with detailed information regarding the number of MWEs with increasing and decreasing trends as well as the number of elements where no trend was observed. Overall, it is possible to observe that, for all classes of MWEs, the number of elements presenting no statistically valid trend is higher than in the cases where an increase or decrease is attested. Moreover, considering the percentage of MWEs with an increasing or decreasing tendency, AFL is the class with the highest number of MWEs where changes have occurred (34%), Fixed and Compound:prt classes present changes for 5 to 8%, and for the other classes, the percentage is below 1%.

Besides having the highest percentage of statistically valid trends, AFL is the only class for which the amount of MWEs with an increasing trend is

[6] pymannkendall 1.4.3 Python module available at: https://pypi.org/project/pymannkendall/

Trend	Compound	Compound:prt	Flat	Fixed	AFL	Other MWE
Increasing	60	15	20	7	**149**	61
Decreasing	**437**	**181**	**84**	**40**	13	**365**
No trend	128 007	3 895	18 781	630	309	48 146
Total	128 504	4 091	18 885	677	471	48 572

Table 3: Mean Association values trends for each class of MWEs in the RSC. In bold are highlighted the highest values comparing increasing and decreasing trends.

MWE Class	Increasing Trend	Decreasing Trend
compound	*North Carolina, University College, Great Britain*	*os ilium, radius vector, os sacrum*
compound:prt	*depend upon, carry out, break down*	*set down, taken out, let loose*
flat	*St. Petersburgh, red deer, J. D.*	*Dr. Johnson, Thomas Barker, James Stirling*
fixed	*of course, no doubt, whether or not*	*as if, some other, it is*
AFL	*should be noted, the other hand, on the other hand*	*of the same, and if you, a kind of*
Other MWE	*prime minister, at first sight, give rise*	*at variance, inmost recesses, in all likelihood*

Table 4: Top-3 MWEs per class with increasing and decreasing trends in terms of mean association value.

higher than the decreasing one. As previously explained, AFL MWEs were identified in corpora of academic English using specific metrics, therefore, they correspond to formulaic expressions specific to this register, similar to RSC.

Table 4 presents, for each class, the three MWEs with the highest rate of increase and decrease of the mean value of association measures. These results show that, in the evolution of scientific writing, specific lexical groups regarding this domain became more fixed, thus, indicating a conventionalization process. For the other classes, changes are less significant and the predominance of decreasing trends can be due to the MWEs' semantic characteristics. Compound, flat, and some Other MWEs usually refer to entities, thus related to the evolution of research topics and their terminology. On the other hand, the decrease observed in phrasal verbs and fixed MWEs could be related to a tendency of standardisation in terms of lexical choices, with some specific elements from these classes being preferred over the others.

5 Conclusions and Future Work

We presented a multifaceted approach to identify MWEs in scientific English for analysing their evolution from the mid-17th century. Our approach uniquely combines three distinct methods: (1) Universal Dependency annotation, which was key in uncovering syntactic structures of MWEs, (2) Partitioner, segmenting texts to detect MWEs effectively, and (3) the Academic Formulas List, which further enriched our analysis by providing a benchmark for MWEs used in the scientific context. Our methodology went beyond identification; we used tools like Kullback-Leibler Divergence for dispersion analysis and various association measures to characterise MWEs (cf. Gries (2022)). This revealed their dynamic nature and evolving roles in scientific discourse. Some MWEs adapted over time, reflecting changes in scientific language, while others remained consistent, signifying their entrenched role in scientific communication.

Our findings not only enhance understanding of MWEs in scientific English but also pave the way for future linguistic research, particularly in language evolution and specialized registers. We currently work on integrating MWEs in word embeddings to classify them semantically and model their temporal dynamics in terms of productivity. Also, we intend to compute surprisal of MWEs to link up with processing explanations (e.g. Siyanova-Chanturia et al. (2017); Bhattasali et al. (2020)).

Acknowledgements

This research is funded by *Deutsche Forschungsgemeinschaft* (DFG, German Research Foundation) – Project-ID 232722074 – SFB 1102.

References

Tanya Avgustinova and Leonid Iomdin. 2019. Towards a typology of microsyntactic constructions. In *Proceedings of the International Conference on Computational and Corpus-Based Phraseology*, pages 15–30.

Shohini Bhattasali, Murielle Fabre, Christophe Pallier, and John Hale. 2020. Modeling conventionalization and predictability within MWEs at the brain level. In *Proceedings of the Society for Computation in Linguistics 2020*, pages 313–322, New York, New York. Association for Computational Linguistics.

Douglas Biber and Federica Barbieri. 2007. Lexical bundles in university spoken and written registers. *English for Specific Purposes*, 26:263–286.

Marie-Catherine De Marneffe, Christopher D. Manning, Joakim Nivre, and Daniel Zeman. 2021. Universal dependencies. *Computational Linguistics*, 47(2):255–308.

Stefania Degaetano-Ortlieb and Elke Teich. 2018. Using relative entropy for detection and analysis of periods of diachronic linguistic change. In *Proceedings of the 2nd SIGHUM LaTeCH-CLfL workshop*, pages 22–33.

Stefania Degaetano-Ortlieb and Elke Teich. 2022. Toward an optimal code for communication: The case of scientific English. *Corpus Linguistics and Linguistic Theory*, 18(1):175–207.

Stefan Evert. 2008. Corpora and collocations. In *Corpus linguistics. An international handbook*, volume 2, pages 1212–1248. Mouton de Gruyter.

Murielle Fabre, Shohini Bhattasali, Christophe Pallier, and John Hale. 2019. Modeling Conventionalization and Predictability in Multi-Word Expressions at Brain-level. Proceedings of the Society for Computation in Linguistics.

Quentin Feltgen, Benjamin Fagard, and Jean-Pierre Nadal. 2017. Frequency patterns of semantic change: corpus-based evidence of a near-critical dynamics in language change. *Royal Society Open Science*, 4(11):170830.

Stefan Fischer, Jörg Knappen, Katrin Menzel, and Elke Teich. 2020. The Royal Society Corpus 6.0: providing 300+ years of scientific writing for humanistic study. In *Proceedings of the Twelfth Language Resources and Evaluation Conference*, pages 794–802.

W. Nelson Francis and Henry Kucera. 1979. Brown corpus manual. *Letters to the Editor*, 5(2):7.

Aileen Fyfe, Julie McDougall-Waters, and Noah Moxham. 2015. 350 years of scientific periodicals. *Notes and Records: the Royal Society journal of the history of science*, 69(3):227–239.

Stefan Th. Gries. 2022. Multi-word units (and tokenization more generally): a multi-dimensional and largely information-theoretic approach. *Lexis. Journal in English Lexicology*, (19).

Md. Manjurul Hussain and Ishtiak Mahmud. 2019. pyMannKendall: a python package for non parametric Mann Kendall family of trend tests. *Journal of Open Source Software*, 4(39):1556.

Ken Hyland. 2008. As can be seen: Lexical bundles and disciplinary variation. *English for Specific Purposes*, 27:4–21.

Dilin Liu. 2012. The most frequently-used multi-word constructions in academic written English: A multi-corpus study. *English for Specific Purposes*, 31:25–35.

Noah Moxham and Aileen Fyfe. 2018. The Royal Society and the prehistory of peer review, 1665–1965. *The Historical Journal*, 61(4):863–889.

Peng Qi, Yuhao Zhang, Yuhui Zhang, Jason Bolton, and Christopher D. Manning. 2020. Stanza: A Python natural language processing toolkit for many human languages. In *Proceedings of the 58th Annual Meeting of the Association for Computational Linguistics: System Demonstrations*.

Carlos Ramisch, Aline Villavicencio, and Christian Boitet. 2010. MWEtoolkit: A framework for multiword expression identification. In *Proceedings of the Seventh International Conference on Language Resources and Evaluation (LREC'10)*, Valletta, Malta. ELRA.

Carlos Ramisch, Abigail Walsh, Thomas Blanchard, and Shiva Taslimipoor. 2023. A survey of MWE identification experiments: The devil is in the details. In *Proceedings of the 19th Workshop on Multiword Expressions (MWE 2023)*, pages 106–120, Dubrovnik, Croatia. Association for Computational Linguistics.

Ivan A. Sag, Tim Baldwin, Francis Bond, Ann Copestake, and Dan Flickinger. 2002. Multiword expressions: A pain in the neck for NLP. In *International conference on intelligent text processing and computational linguistics*, pages 1–15, Berlin. Springer.

Agata Savary, Manfred Sailer, Yannick Parmentier, Michael Rosner, Victoria Rosén, Adam Przepiórkowski, Cvetana Krstev, Veronika Vincze, Beata Wójtowicz, Gyri Smørdal Losnegaard, Carla Parra Escartín, Jakub Waszczuk, Matthieu Constant, Petya Osenova, and Federico Sangati. 2015. PARSEME – PARSing and Multiword Expressions within a European multilingual network. In *7th Language & Technology Conference: Human Language Technologies as a Challenge for Computer Science and Linguistics (LTC 2015)*, Poznań, Poland.

Nathan Schneider, Dirk Hovy, Anders Johannsen, and Marine Carpuat. 2016. Semeval-2016 task 10: Detecting minimal semantic units and their meanings (dimsum). In *Proceedings of the 10th International*

Workshop on Semantic Evaluation (SemEval-2016), pages 546–559.

Sabine Schulte im Walde and Eva Smolka, editors. 2019. *The role of constituents in multiword expressions*. Number 4 in Phraseology and Multiword Expressions. Language Science Press, Berlin.

Rita Simpson-Vlach and Nick C. Ellis. 2010. An academic formulas list: New methods in phraseology research. *Applied linguistics*, 31(4):487–512.

Anna Siyanova-Chanturia, Kathy Conklin, Sendy Caffarra, Edith Kaan, and Walter J.B. van Heuven. 2017. Representation and processing of multi-word expressions in the brain. *Brain and Language*, 175:111–122.

Joshua Tanner and Jacob Hoffman. 2023. MWE as WSD: Solving multiword expression identification with word sense disambiguation. *arXiv preprint arXiv:2303.06623*.

Alexander Wahl and Stefan Th. Gries. 2018. Multiword expressions: A novel computational approach to their bottom-up statistical extraction. In Pascual Cantos-Gómez and Moisés Almela-Sánchez, editors, *Lexical Collocation Analysis: Advances and Applications*, pages 85–109. Springer International Publishing, Cham.

Jake Ryland Williams. 2016. Boundary-based MWE segmentation with text partitioning. *arXiv preprint arXiv:1608.02025*.

EventNet-ITA: Italian Frame Parsing for Events

Marco Rovera
Fondazione Bruno Kessler, Trento, Italy
m.rovera@fbk.eu

Abstract

This paper introduces EventNet-ITA, a large, multi-domain corpus annotated *full-text* with event frames for Italian. Moreover, we present and thoroughly evaluate an efficient multi-label sequence labeling approach for Frame Parsing. Covering a wide range of individual, social and historical phenomena, with more than 53,000 annotated sentences and over 200 modeled frames, EventNet-ITA constitutes the first systematic attempt to provide the Italian language with a publicly available resource for Frame Parsing of events, useful for a broad spectrum of research and application tasks. Our approach achieves a promising 0.9 strict F1-score for frame classification and 0.72 for frame element classification, on top of minimizing computational requirements. The annotated corpus and the frame parsing model are released under open license.

1 Introduction

Frame Parsing is a powerful tool for real-world applications in that it enables deep grasp of the meaning of a textual statement and automatic extraction of complex semantic descriptions of situations, including events, and their relations with the entities involved. To this effect, Frame Parsing can effectively be used for Event Extraction, as the two tasks share the common goal of recognizing and classifying argument structures of a target predicate. However, training supervised models for Frame Parsing is a data-intensive task, which is why comprehensive linguistic resources are available in few languages, thereby limiting further research and application in downstream tasks. Furthermore, most existing corpora are created by targeting the annotation of one single frame (or event) class per sentence. While lexicographically motivated, this procedure makes the training of automatic models and their application to real-world scenarios more complicated and burdensome.

The contribution described in this paper is twofold: first, we present EventNet-ITA (EvN-ITA) a large-scale, multi-domain corpus annotated *full-text* (see Section 4) with over 200 semantic frames of events (Fillmore and Baker, 2001) and 3,600 specific frame elements in Italian, also discussing the motivation behind its creation, the annotation guidelines and the covered domains; secondly, we introduce an efficient multi-label sequential approach for eventive Frame Parsing and evaluate it on the dataset. This work aims at providing the community with a solid, manually-curated corpus and a ready-to-use model for frame-based event extraction for Italian, thus filling an existing data gap. In fact, recent works in application fields like computational social science (Minnema et al., 2021, 2022) or historical NLP (Sprugnoli and Tonelli, 2017; Menini et al., 2023) showed how semantic frames can be used as a powerful textual analysis tool to investigate a wide range of societal and historical phenomena. The annotated dataset, along with its full documentation, is released to the community under open license (see Section 7). The envisioned application purpose of EvN-ITA is that of enabling accurate mining of events from large collections of documents, with focus on individual, social and, in a broad sense, historical phenomena. The paper is structured as follows: Section 2 discusses existing work in Frame Parsing and Event Extraction, with a subsection focused on Italian; Section 3 introduces our annotated corpus and describes the motivations and design decisions that guided its creation, while Section 4 focuses on the annotation procedure. In Section 5 we discuss the methodology for Frame Parsing, a transformer-based multi-label sequence labeling approach. In Section 6 we evaluate our methodology and discuss the results. Section 7 provides the reader with pointers for the dataset and model release, while Section 8 concludes the paper and highlights future directions of our work.

Proceedings of LaTeCH-CLfL 2024, pages 77–90
March 22, 2024 ©2024 Association for Computational Linguistics

2 Related Work

The development of systems able to recognize and classify event mentions and their argument structure in text has been a long-term effort in computational linguistics and a variety of methods has been employed for the task of Event Extraction (Ahn, 2006; Liao and Grishman, 2010; Chen et al., 2015; Nguyen et al., 2016; Orr et al., 2018; Nguyen and Nguyen, 2019; Lu et al., 2021; Paolini et al., 2021). Event Extraction is the task of recognizing and classifying event mentions and entities involved in the event from a textual statement and it has seen applications in a wide range of fields, like social media analysis (de Bruijn et al., 2019), biomedical NLP (Li et al., 2019; Huang et al., 2020; Ramponi et al., 2020), history and humanities (Segers et al., 2011; Cybulska and Vossen, 2011; Sprugnoli and Tonelli, 2019; Lai et al., 2021; Rovera et al., 2021), as well as literary text mining (Sims et al., 2019). Although benchmark datasets exist, like Automatic Content Extraction (ACE) (Walker et al., 2006) for Event Extraction or TAC-KBP (Ellis et al., 2015) for multiple event-related tasks, they exhibit limitations in terms of size and domain coverage. Also, while they are well suited for evaluation campaigns, they have not been designed for use in real-world application tasks. Moreover, most of these corpora only exist for English, with few extensions for other languages (Ji et al., 2016).

2.1 Frame Parsing

Frame Parsing (Das et al., 2014; Swayamdipta et al., 2017, 2018) consists in recognizing, in a textual expression, a word or set of words (the *lexical unit*) as the predicate evoking a given frame and isolating the text spans that evoke the semantic arguments (*frame elements*) related to that frame. Frames are conceptual structures describing prototypical situations and their realizations in text. The reference linguistic resource for Frame Parsing in English is FrameNet (FN) (Baker et al., 1998; Fillmore and Baker, 2001; Ruppenhofer et al., 2006). In this work, we use Frame Parsing for extracting event frames. While event extraction initiatives have been based on a variety of models, approaches and schemes, which are not always interoperable or comparable, the advantage of using Frame Parsing for Event Extraction is the availability of an established resource, based on a unified, grounded theoretical framework (Fillmore et al., 1976). EvN-ITA differs from FN in that the latter is based on lexicographic annotation (one target lexical unit per sentence), providing only a small subset of full-text annotated data (Ruppenhofer et al., 2016), whereas EvN-ITA has been annotated by design in a *full-text* fashion (see Section 4). Also, it is important to point out that EvN-ITA is not meant to be a comprehensive Italian version of the popular English FN. Instead, in this work we adopt part of the FN schema but focus exclusively on event-denoting frames, aiming at providing a large, self-contained and robust tool for frame-based Event Extraction in Italian.

2.2 Italian Event Extraction and Frame Semantics

As for Italian, the Frame Labeling over Italian Texts Task (FLAIT) was organized at EVALITA in 2011 (Basili et al., 2012). Moreover, Event Extraction in Italian was the object of the EVENTI evaluation campaign at EVALITA 2014 (Caselli et al., 2014), which focused on temporal processing and was based on the Ita-TimeBank schema (Caselli et al., 2011). Later on, Caselli (2018) experimented with the same dataset using a neural architecture and evaluated the impact of different word embeddings for event extraction. While Italian Event Extraction approaches have traditionally been based on the TimeML (Saurí et al., 2006) classification scheme, which provides 7 broad, temporal-oriented classes, more recently the necessity has emerged of a more fine-grained annotation schema for event classification, as discussed by Sprugnoli and Tonelli (2017). Supported by a survey involving historians, the authors investigated the application of event extraction on historical texts. Sprugnoli and Tonelli (2019) describe a specific schema, adapting semantic categories provided by the Historical Thesaurus of the Oxford English Dictionary (HTOED) (Kay et al., 2009), resulting in 22 topic-driven event classes, thereby moving towards developing a richer and at the same time finer-grained inventory of classes for representing events in text. As for frame semantics, on the other hand, Basili et al. (2017) and Brambilla et al. (2020) described a work in progress for the creation of IFrameNet, a large scale Italian version of FN, by using semi-automatic methods and manual validation for frame induction, with 5,208 sentences annotated with at least one lexical unit. However, the dataset has not been released so far. In fact, despite the considerable amount of work in lexical (Lenci et al., 2012a;

Jezek et al., 2014) and frame semantics (Tonelli and Pianta, 2008; Tonelli et al., 2009; Lenci et al., 2010, 2012b), Italian still lacks an extensive, publicly available linguistic resource for Frame Parsing.

3 Dataset

3.1 EventNet-ITA

In order to ensure multilingual compatibility, we employ a selection of event frames from FN (Baker et al., 1998; Ruppenhofer et al., 2006), where available. This way, 85% of EvN-ITA classes are mapped to FN schema, either by direct match (59%) or by subclassing (26%). In a minor number of cases (15% of the schema), where target phenomena are not covered in FN, an *ad hoc* frame class has been created. Frame-to-frame mappings between EvN-ITA and FN are provided in the documentation of the resource. Table 1 offers a quantitative description of the corpus. EvN-ITA counts

Annotated sentences	53,854
Tokens	1,583,612
Vocabulary (words)	97,512
Avg. sentence length (tokens)	29
Modeled event frames	205
Modeled frame elements	3,571
Lexical units	837
Frame instances	102,294
Frame element instances	180,279
Frame instances per sentence (avg.)	1.9
Examples per class (avg.)	491

Table 1: Statistics of the EvN-ITA dataset.

53,854 annotated sentences, including negative examples (see Section 4.2), 102,294 event instances and over 1.5 million tokens, annotated by an experienced annotator (native speaker) with background in Frame Semantics. Each frame class has on average 491 annotated examples.

The corpus - as well as the annotation schema - has been created with the purpose of covering historical narratives in a broad sense, but without committing to a specific textual genre. For this reason, as well as for creating a releasable corpus, sentences for the annotation set of EvN-ITA have been sampled from a subset of the Italian Wikipedia edition. In order to filter out irrelevant documents, i.e. documents not likely to contain events, we collected Wikipedia pages falling under the categories *Events by country*[1] and *History by country*.[2] This choice ensures a wide variety of featured events, both temporally (from ancient history to the present days) and geographically.

Through standard pre-processing (tokenization, lemmatization and dependency parsing have been performed using TINT[3] (Palmero Aprosio and Moretti, 2018)), a pool of sentences, arranged by lemma, was generated, from which to pick for the annotation set. Annotated sentences are drawn from 16,309 different Wikipedia articles.

3.2 Domain coverage

In the design phase of the resource, a manual analysis was made of existing corpora in multiple languages, in order to circumscribe the domains and classes to be modelled. Resources as Automatic Content Extraction (Doddington et al., 2004; Consortium et al., 2005), Event Nugget (Mitamura et al., 2015), the Historical Thesaurus of the Oxford English Dictionary (HTOED) (Kay et al., 2009) and FN (Baker et al., 1998) were reviewed and compared. FN is currently the most complete, rich and established existing resource and has been taken as reference for the development of EvN-ITA. This choice is motivated by the opportunities it offers in terms of reuse, coverage and possible multilingual extensions. EvN-ITA's annotation schema covers 205 different event frames, each provided with a set of specific frame elements (unique modeled frame elements amount to 3,571), and has been extensively documented by providing, for each frame, its definition, the corresponding set of lexical units and frame elements associated to it. The distribution of classes, arranged by topic, is depicted in Figure 1. Beside conflict-related events, that hold a prominent place in historical accounts and journalistic narratives, we have taken care to extend the collection of event types to other aspects of the life of societies and individuals, such as legislative and legal processes, work, establishment of and membership in social organizations, life events, as well as events related to the arts, economic processes and cognitive processes such as decisions, skills, judgements, amongst others. In the design of the resource, attention has been paid also to maintain the balance between internal coherence and usabil-

[1] https://it.wikipedia.org/wiki/Categoria:Eventi_per_stato

[2] https://it.wikipedia.org/wiki/Categoria:Storia_per_stato

[3] https://dh.fbk.eu/research/tint/

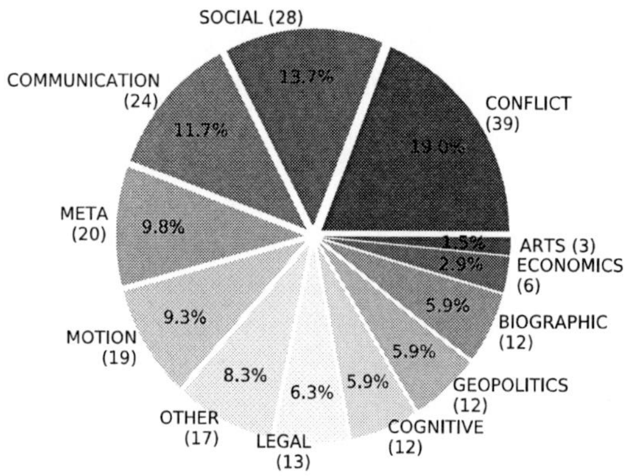

Figure 1: Macro-topics covered in EvN-ITA (in brackets, the number of frames belonging to each domain).

ity of the class schema. This has been achieved in multiple ways:

(a) by including for each class, where existing, also its opposite (HIRING / FIRING, CREATE SOCIAL ENTITY / END SOCIAL ENTITY, VEHICLE TAKE OFF / VEHICLE LANDING);

(b) by making possible narrative chains (e.g. COMMITTING CRIME, ARREST, TRIAL, SENTENCING, IMPRISONMENT, CAPTIVITY, RELEASING);

(c) by providing couples of classes representing an event and the subsequent logical state (e.g. BECOMING A MEMBER / MEMBERSHIP, BECOMING AWARE / AWARENESS, MAKE ACQUAINTANCE / ACQUAINTANCE).

(d) by ensuring a certain degree of redundancy and perspective (BEING IN PLACE / TEMPORARY STAY, BEING BORN / GIVING BIRTH).

4 Annotation

The textual corpus, generated as discussed in Section 3.1, has been manually annotated by labeling event triggers with their frame class and predicate arguments with the corresponding frame element. Annotation was performed at the sentence level and was conducted frame-driven, by first selecting significant event frames for the domain and subsequently identifying the most relevant lexical units for each frame. Given a sentence, *any* lexical units in our schema and all related frame elements are annotated, producing as many layers as there are event mentions (*full-text* annotation). Figure 2 shows an example of full-text annotation from EvN-ITA.

4.1 Format

The IOB2 annotation format is being used, in which the B-tag identifies the first token of a span, the I-tag identifies all tokens inside the span and the O-tag all out-of-mention tokens. Discontinuous mentions are allowed, both for frames and for frame elements. The only constraint for event mentions is that they cannot overlap: each token in a sentence can denote at most one event type. This does not hold for frame elements: in fact, given a sentence with multiple frame occurrences, frame elements from different annotation sequences (i.e. belonging to different frames) can always overlap, hence a token may be labeled with more than one frame element tag[4] (See Figure 2).

4.2 Guidelines

EvN-ITA is thoroughly documented, both in the form of general annotation guidelines (what to annotate) and at the annotation schema level (frame description, lexical units, frame elements).
As for lexical units, we exclusively focus on nouns, verbs and multi-word expressions. Although also other parts-of-speech (adverbs, for example) can be loosely event-evoking, this focus is motivated by practical reasons: nouns and verbs, along with multi-word expressions, are the most frequent triggers of event mentions in text and are characterized by a richer syntactic structure, which in turn is crucial for harvesting information related to frame elements. Nouns are annotated as event triggers only if they reference *directly* the occurrence of an event, but not when the reference is indirect, for example:

> [...] *culminarono a Blois nel 1171 con la [morte* **DEATH***] sul rogo di 31 ebrei.* (culminated in Blois in 1711 with the death at the stake of 31 Jews.)
>
> *Nell'aprile del 1700, Giovanni si ammalò terribilmente e si trovò quasi sul letto di [morte* **Ø***].* (In April 1700, John fell terribly ill and was nearly on his deathbed.)

[4] In addition, a frame element may overlap with a frame mention if they belong to different annotation sequences, which is quite often the case. Only an frame-frame overlap is excluded.

Figure 2: An example of full-text annotation in EvN-ITA (English translation: *The construction of the Alvitian fortification dates back to the time of the Norman invasion.).*

As for verbs, we annotate the main verb but not the auxiliary.

> *Appena ricostruita dalla devastazione del sisma la città fu [distrutta* **DESTROYING***] nuovamente* [...] (As soon as it was rebuilt from the devastation of the earthquake, the city was destroyed again [...])

Multi-word expressions are annotated when they break compositionality, for example in *radere al suolo* (raze to the ground) or *aprire il fuoco* (opening fire), or in verbal periphrastic use *essere al corrente* (being aware) or *fare visita* (paying a visit).
Frame mentions are annotated regardless of their factuality value, which means that also negated or hypotetical frame mentions must be annotated, as well as those introduced by modals. Conversely, in EvN-ITA we do not annotate as frame mention lexical units that are used with metaphorical meaning or in the form of rhetoric expression.[5]
EvN-ITA's annotation schema consists of 205 frames and 837 lexical units, out of which 358 have at least 100 annotations each, 191 have a number of annotations comprised between 50 and 99, and 288 have a number of annotations comprised between 20 an 40. The annotation process has been oriented to keep the balance between frame completion and polysemy preservation. For this reason, we also annotated less frequent lexical units encountered in the corpus, resulting in a long queue of lexical units with less than 20 occurrences each. This strategy was adopted in order both to increase the flexibility of the resource and to set the stage for its future extension. Also, with the aim of improving robustness, for each lexical unit we annotated a number of *negative examples*, i.e. sentences in which the given lexical unit occurs without triggering any of the corresponding frames.[6]
Within the scope of this work, we consider as events any accomplishment, achievement or process, without distinction. The schema additionally models a number of states (e.g. BEING IN PLACE, CAPTIVITY) and relations (LEADERSHIP, DURATION RELATION, POSSESSION). As for semantic roles, we referred to FN's frame elements, with minor adaptations or additions, which in most cases tend towards increased specificity.

4.3 Inter-Annotator Agreement

EvN-ITA was annotated by one single native speaker annotator with a solid background in Frame Semantics. For this reason, particular attention has been devoted to assessing the robustness, consistency and intelligibility of the resource by means of inter-annotator agreement analysis. We therefore validated our schema and guidelines by re-annotating 2,251 sentences, spanning over 61 classes, with a second (native speaker) annotator. When selecting classes to be included in this validation set, we paid attention to include pairs or triplets of frames with high semantic similarity,[7] in order to stress the test. We used two different metrics for assessing agreement: Jaccard Index (computed as the ratio between the number of items annotated with the same label and the sum of all annotated items) and Cohen's Kappa (Cohen, 1960). The scores have been computed both at token level (relaxed) and at span level (strict). Results are reported in Table 2. Considering the high number of

	Jaccard		**Cohen's K**	
	Token	Span	Token	Span
Lexical units	0.952	0.945	0.951	0.944
Frame elements	0.878	0.832	0.877	0.830

Table 2: Inter-annotator agreement scores.

different frames and frame elements in EvN-ITA, we observe that agreement values are high and indicate that the guidelines are sufficiently detailed in their description of the linguistic phenomena to be annotated. As expected, the annotation of frame elements has proven more challenging. A further manual analysis conducted on a sample of

[5]More annotation examples for such cases are provided in Appendix A.

[6]See Appendix A for negative examples.

[7]For example: BLAMING / ACCUSE, REPORTING / DENOUNCE, MARRIAGE / BEING_MARRIED.

245 sentence pairs with low agreement showed that disagreement had three main sources:

Ontological (67,5%) a textual span is recognized as frame or frame element by one annotator but not by the other;

Span Length (20,4%) annotators agree on the label but not on the exact span to annotate;

Classification (12%) annotators agree on the span to annotate but assign two different labels.

5 Methodology

A traditional approach for Frame Parsing, as well as for Event Extraction, is to break down the problem into sub-tasks (Das et al., 2014; Ahn, 2006), usually separating the steps of trigger identification, frame classification and argument extraction. However, a major downside of this approach, besides being more complex, is that it implies error propagation from higher-level sub-tasks downwards. Instead, we propose to learn all the tasks in one single step, allowing the model to simultaneously exploit tag relations on the time (sequence) axis and on the token axis. Thus, in this work Frame Parsing is approached end-to-end and is treated as a multi-label sequence tagging problem. The strength of this design option lies in its simplicity as it requires minimal pre-processing and does not imply the use of additional knowledge, as well as in its efficiency, as it minimizes computational requirements (see Section 5.2).

5.1 Preprocessing

The adoption of full-text annotation implies, at preprocessing time, the definition of each frame element as frame-specific, in order to avoid overlaps between frame elements with the same name but referring to different frames. In fact, many frames belonging to the same semantic area share a set of frame elements with the same name. For example, both motion frames FLEEING and MOTION_DOWNWARDS have a frame element called MOVER. In EvN-ITA, frame elements referring to the same *semantic role* (thus carrying the same name) but belonging to different frames are assigned different, frame-aware labels. Therefore, frame elements MOVER-FLEEING and MOVER-MOTION_DOWNWARDS will be assigned two different labels. This data encoding strategy, in return, allows us to minimize the need for post-processing (as each predicted frame element is implicitly linked to its frame) and enables the model to learn relationships between multiple frame elements occurring on the same token/span.

5.2 Experimental Setup

Our frame parser aims at jointly extracting all frame mentions and all related frame elements in a target sentence. In other words, given an input sentence, each token must be labeled according to the event frame and/or frame element(s) it denotes. The underlying idea is to leverage mutual co-occurrence between frame (and frame element) classes, as certain frames typically tend to appear more often with, or have a semantic preference for, other frames.[8] This way, the model is led to not only learn correspondences between a word and a given frame or frame element, but also local patterns of co-occurrence between different frame elements.

In order to provide a reliable performance assessment, we opted for an 80/10/10 *stratified* train/dev/test split, thus ensuring the same proportion of (frame) labels in each split. Moreover, we generate 4 folds from the dataset, the first used for hyperparmeter search and the remaining three for evaluation. To this purpose we fine-tune a BERT model[9] (Devlin et al., 2019) for Italian and show that the approach allows us to scale with thousands of (unique) labels without a remarkable computational and memory overhead. In this experimental setup we use MaChAmp, v 0.4 beta 2 (van der Goot et al., 2021), a toolkit supporting a variety of NLP tasks, including multi-label sequence labeling. We performed hyperparameter search by exploring the space with batch sizes between 8 and 256 and learning rates between 7.5e-4 and 7.5e-3. All other hyperparameters are left unchanged with respect to MaChAmp's default configuration for the multi-sequential task.[10] Overall, 64 configurations have been explored. The best hyperparameter values we found, according to the performance on the development set, are batch size of 64 and learning rate of 1.5e-3 and the resulting model has been used for the evaluation (Section 6). The training requires approximately 3.5 hours on an NVIDIA RTX A5000 GPU with 24 GB memory and 8192 CUDA cores.

[8]This assumption is mentioned in previous work (Liao and Grishman, 2010) and we verified it in our dataset by analysing frame relationships with several co-occurrence measures, such as Pointwise Mutual Information (see Appendix B).

[9]`https://huggingface.co/dbmdz/bert-base-italian-xxl-cased`

[10]`https://github.com/machamp-nlp/machamp/blob/master/docs/multiseq.md`

		Frames $n = 40$			Frame Elements $n = 200$		
		P	R	F1	P	R	F1
TEST	All classes	0.904	0.914	**0.907**	0.841	0.724	**0.761**
	All classes weighted	0.909	0.919	**0.913**	0.85	0.779	**0.804**
	Best *n* classes	0.974	0.982	0.978	0.938	0.912	0.923
	Worst *n* classes	0.811	0.808	0.806	0.72	0.441	0.516
	n most frequent classes	0.912	0.933	0.922	0.861	0.831	0.843
	n least frequent classes	0.865	0.871	0.865	0.781	0.493	0.575

Table 3: *Token-based* (*relaxed*) performance for multi-label sequential Frame Parsing (macro average, aggregate). Figures in bold represent the reference performance values for EventNet-ITA.

		Frames $n = 40$			Frame Elements $n = 200$		
		P	R	F1	P	R	F1
TEST	All classes	0.906	0.899	**0.901**	0.829	0.666	**0.724**
	All classes (weighted)	0.909	0.903	**0.905**	0.853	0.711	**0.768**
	Best *n* classes	0.975	0.976	0.975	0.937	0.867	0.898
	Worst *n* classes	0.81	0.789	0.796	0.673	0.398	0.476
	n most frequent classes	0.915	0.917	0.915	0.878	0.762	0.813
	n least frequent classes	0.879	0.866	0.87	0.743	0.441	0.529

Table 4: *Span-based* (*strict*) performance for multi-label sequential Frame Parsing (macro average, aggregate). Figures in bold represent the reference performance values for EventNet-ITA.

In terms of memory, the maximum requirement is 5 GB RAM.

6 Evaluation

In this section, we discuss the quantitative (Section 6.1) and qualitative (Section 6.2) performance of the multi-label sequence labeling approach on the EvN-ITA dataset.

6.1 Quantitative results

Evaluation results are reported in Table 3 and Table 4 in an aggregated fashion in order to provide the reader with different views on performance. Reported values have been obtained by separately computing the metrics class-wise on each fold, and then averaging the obtained scores. For each of the two groups of labels (frames and frame elements), beside the overall average performance, we provide the average of the *n*-best and *n*-worst performing classes and the average of the *n* most and least frequent classes in the dataset, on the three test sets, with $n = 40$ for frames and $n = 200$ for frame elements.[11] We also compute the macro average and the weighted macro average of all classes, the latter providing a more realistic view in a context of highly unbalanced label distribution. With a strict F1-score of 0.9 for frames and 0.724 for frame elements, our system shows very promising results for the task. Overall, the results show that, despite being fundamentally token-based, our multi-label sequence tagging approach proves effective also in the identification of (multiple) textual spans in a sentence, scaling well on a dataset involving a very high number of classes. This is further confirmed by the small delta between relaxed and strict performance values.

6.2 Error Analysis

To assess the potential of the proposed approach and the possible inconsistencies, we perform an error analysis on the test sets of the three folds,

[11] In the case of frame elements, given their extremely skewed distribution, resulting in a long tail of rare labels, we also apply a threshold, taking into account only labels occurring at least 5 times in the span-based setting and at least 20 times in the token-based setting.

Gold	Predicted
BLAMING	ACCUSE
HOSTILE_ENCOUNTER	WAR
CONQUERING	OCCUPANCY
ACCUSE	BLAMING
REPLACING	TAKE_PLACE_OF
OCCUPANCY	CONQUERING
BUILDING	MANUFACTURING
CREATE_ARTWORK	TEXT_CREATION
KILLING	DEATH
REQUEST	QUESTIONING

Table 5: Top 10 prediction errors between event frames.

at token level. Since in a multi-label setting it is not always possible to establish a univocal correspondence between labels in the gold and predicted sets (given the possibility of multiple assignments on both sides), we proceed as follows: for each token, we filter out from both sets of labels (gold and predicted) the correctly matched labels. Based on this output, we focus on a subset of tokens, those labeled, in both sets, with exactly one label and we use it as an approximation for identifying most common errors. This allows us to focus on specific one-to-one label mismatchings, both for event frames (Table 5) and for frame elements (Table 6). Considering only event frames, analysis reveals that only 4.8% of the identified mismatches involves two event labels, while 95.2% involves a mismatch between an event label and the O-tag (out-of-mention). This ratio becomes more balanced with regard to frame elements (39% and 61%, respectively). Also, the impact of errors referred to the IOB schema remains very low, amounting to 1.16% for event frames and 4.8% for frame elements.

Qualitatively, the analysis shows a clear pattern, namely that errors occur in most cases between frames with a high semantic similarity, like BLAMING/ACCUSE or HOSTILE_ENCOUNTER/WAR, which in some cases may be difficult to classify even for the human annotator. As for frame elements, errors occur mostly *a)* between the same frame element of two different event frames (for example MESSAGE-REQUEST vs. MESSAGE-QUESTIONING) or *b)* between frame elements that have a latent semantic correspondence in different frames (INTERLOCUTOR2-CONVERSATION vs. PARTY2-NEGOTIATION or REASON-BLAMING vs. OFFENSE-ACCUSE) or, still, *c)* between semantically close frame elements within the same frame (EXPLANATION-DEATH vs. CAUSE-DEATH). These quite subtle error types further reveal how the multi-label sequence labeling approach is capable of learning cross-frame correspondences of frame elements, an aspect that we plan to further investigate in future work.

Frame element - Event frame
(G) REASON-BLAMING (P) OFFENSE-ACCUSE
(G) INTERLOCUTOR2-CONVERSATION (P) PARTY2-NEGOTIATION
(G) LOCATION-BEINGLOCATED (P) RELATIVELOCATION-BEINGLOCATED
(G) MESSAGE-REQUEST (P) MESSAGE-QUESTIONING
(G) RELATIVELOCATION-BEINGLOCATED (P) LOCATION-BEINGLOCATED
(G) MESSAGE-ANSWER (P) MESSAGE-REPLY
(G) ISSUE-TAKINGSIDES (P) SIDE-TAKINGSIDES
(G) ARTWORK-CREATEARTWORK (P) TEXT-TEXTCREATION
(G) EVALUEE-BLAMING (P) ACCUSED-ACCUSE
(G) EXPLANATION-DEATH (P) CAUSE-DEATH

Table 6: Top 10 prediction errors between frame elements (G = Gold, P = Predicted).

7 Dataset and Model Release

The EvN-ITA annotated dataset, along with its documentation, is being released upon request[12], under CC-BY-SA 4.0 license[13]. The model of the frame parser, described in Section 5.2, is available on Huggingface[14].

8 Conclusion and Future Works

In this paper we presented EvN-ITA, a large corpus annotated with event frames in Italian, accompanied by an efficient multi-label sequential model for Frame Parsing, trained and evaluated on the

[12]The dataset can be requested by filling out the form at `https://forms.gle/qAgZsf4La9qdzETn6` or by emailing the author at eventnetita@gmail.com.

[13]`https://creativecommons.org/licenses/by-sa/4.0/deed.en`

[14]`https://huggingface.co/mrovera/eventnet-ita`

corpus. Future work includes extrinsic tests of the resource on new data from different textual genres and the reinforcement of the schema, in view of providing a wider domain coverage and increased adaptability of the model. Moreover, is our plan to employ EvN-ITA as a benchmark to investigate the performance of different methodologies and learning models for Frame Parsing, as well as to explore strategies for multilingual applications.

Limitations

The first limitation of this work lies in the unique source of the data, Wikipedia, that, if on the one end guarantees an ample variety of topics and types of events, on the other hand, from the linguistic point of view it sets a constraint on a homogeneous linguistic style. As mentioned above, this will be the focus of our future effort. Secondly, in case of multiple mentions of the *same* event frame in a given sentence (this case concerns 6% of the sentences in EvN-ITA), the currently adopted methodology does not support automatic linking of frame elements to the exact frame mention they refer to in the sentence. Future approaches will be geared to take this issue into account.

Acknowledgements

I owe my gratitude to Serena Cristoforetti, for her dedicated contribution to the inter-annotator assessment process, carried out as part of her curricular internship at the Digital Humanities (DH) group. I am equally thankful to Alan Ramponi and Sara Tonelli (DH) and to Enrica Troiano (Vrije Universiteit Amsterdam) for proofreading the manuscript and for their precious and constructive feedback. This work and the effort it represents are dedicated to the memory of Anna Goy.

References

David Ahn. 2006. The stages of event extraction. In *Proceedings of the Workshop on Annotating and Reasoning about Time and Events*, pages 1–8.

Collin F Baker, Charles J Fillmore, and John B Lowe. 1998. The berkeley framenet project. In *Proceedings of the 17th international conference on Computational linguistics-Volume 1*, pages 86–90. Association for Computational Linguistics.

Roberto Basili, Silvia Brambilla, Danilo Croce, and Fabio Tamburini. 2017. Developing a large scale framenet for italian: the iframenet experience. *CLiC-it 2017 11-12 December 2017, Rome*, page 59.

Roberto Basili, Diego De Cao, Alessandro Lenci, Alessandro Moschitti, and Giulia Venturi. 2012. Evalita 2011: The frame labelingover italian texts task. In *International Workshop on Evaluation of Natural Language and Speech Tool for Italian*, pages 195–204. Springer.

Silvia Brambilla, Danilo Croce, Fabio Tamburini, Roberto Basili, et al. 2020. Automatic induction of framenet lexical units in italian. In *CEUR WORKSHOP PROCEEDINGS*, volume 2769. CEUR-WS.

Tommaso Caselli. 2018. Italian event detection goes deep learning. *arXiv preprint arXiv:1810.02229*.

Tommaso Caselli, Valentina Bartalesi Lenzi, Rachele Sprugnoli, Emanuele Pianta, and Irina Prodanof. 2011. Annotating events, temporal expressions and relations in italian: the it-timeml experience for the ita-timebank. In *Proceedings of the 5th Linguistic Annotation Workshop*, pages 143–151. Association for Computational Linguistics.

Tommaso Caselli, Rachele Sprugnoli, Manuela Speranza, and Monica Monachini. 2014. Eventi: Evaluation of events and temporal information at evalita 2014. *EVENTI: EValuation of Events and Temporal INformation at Evalita 2014*, pages 27–34.

Yubo Chen, Liheng Xu, Kang Liu, Daojian Zeng, and Jun Zhao. 2015. Event extraction via dynamic multi-pooling convolutional neural networks. In *Proceedings of the 53rd Annual Meeting of the Association for Computational Linguistics and the 7th International Joint Conference on Natural Language Processing (Volume 1: Long Papers)*, pages 167–176.

Jacob Cohen. 1960. A coefficient of agreement for nominal scales. *Educational and psychological measurement*, 20(1):37–46.

Linguistic Data Consortium et al. 2005. Ace (automatic content extraction) english annotation guidelines for events. version 5.4. 3. *ACE*.

Agata Cybulska and Piek Vossen. 2011. Historical event extraction from text. In *Proceedings of the 5th ACL-HLT Workshop on Language Technology for Cultural Heritage, Social Sciences, and Humanities*, pages 39–43.

Dipanjan Das, Desai Chen, André FT Martins, Nathan Schneider, and Noah A Smith. 2014. Frame-semantic parsing. *Computational linguistics*, 40(1):9–56.

Jens A de Bruijn, Hans de Moel, Brenden Jongman, Marleen C de Ruiter, Jurjen Wagemaker, and Jeroen CJH Aerts. 2019. A global database of historic and real-time flood events based on social media. *Scientific data*, 6(1):311.

Jacob Devlin, Ming-Wei Chang, Kenton Lee, and Kristina Toutanova. 2019. BERT: Pre-training of deep bidirectional transformers for language understanding. In *Proceedings of the 2019 Conference of the North American Chapter of the Association for*

Computational Linguistics: Human Language Technologies, Volume 1 (Long and Short Papers), pages 4171–4186, Minneapolis, Minnesota. Association for Computational Linguistics.

George R Doddington, Alexis Mitchell, Mark A Przybocki, Lance A Ramshaw, Stephanie M Strassel, and Ralph M Weischedel. 2004. The automatic content extraction (ace) program-tasks, data, and evaluation. In *Lrec*, volume 2, page 1. Lisbon.

Joe Ellis, Jeremy Getman, Dana Fore, Neil Kuster, Zhiyi Song, Ann Bies, and Stephanie M Strassel. 2015. Overview of linguistic resources for the tac kbp 2015 evaluations: Methodologies and results. In *Tac*.

Charles J Fillmore and Collin F Baker. 2001. Frame semantics for text understanding. In *Proceedings of WordNet and Other Lexical Resources Workshop, NAACL*, volume 6.

Charles J Fillmore et al. 1976. Frame semantics and the nature of language. In *Annals of the New York Academy of Sciences: Conference on the origin and development of language and speech*, volume 280, pages 20–32. New York.

Kung-Hsiang Huang, Mu Yang, and Nanyun Peng. 2020. Biomedical event extraction with hierarchical knowledge graphs. In *Findings of the Association for Computational Linguistics: EMNLP 2020*, pages 1277–1285.

Elisabetta Jezek, Bernardo Magnini, Anna Feltracco, Alessia Bianchini, and Octavian Popescu. 2014. T-pas: A resource of corpus-derived types predicate-argument structures for linguistic analysis and semantic processing. In *Proceedings of LREC*, pages 890–895.

Heng Ji, Joel Nothman, H Trang Dang, and Sydney Informatics Hub. 2016. Overview of tac-kbp2016 trilingual edl and its impact on end-to-end cold-start kbp. *Proceedings of TAC*.

Christian Kay, Jane Roberts, Michael Samuels, and Irené Wotherspoon. 2009. *Historical thesaurus of the Oxford English dictionary*. Oxford University Press.

Viet Dac Lai, Minh Van Nguyen, Heidi Kaufman, and Thien Huu Nguyen. 2021. Event extraction from historical texts: A new dataset for black rebellions. In *Findings of the Association for Computational Linguistics: ACL-IJCNLP 2021*, pages 2390–2400, Online. Association for Computational Linguistics.

Alessandro Lenci, Martina Johnson, and Gabriella Lapesa. 2010. Building an italian framenet through semi-automatic corpus analysis. In *LREC*.

Alessandro Lenci, Gabriella Lapesa, and Giulia Bonansinga. 2012a. Lexit: A computational resource on italian argument structure. In *LREC*, pages 3712–3718.

Alessandro Lenci, Simonetta Montemagni, Giulia Venturi, and Maria Grazia Cutrulla. 2012b. Enriching the isst-tanl corpus with semantic frames. In *LREC*, pages 3719–3726.

Diya Li, Lifu Huang, Heng Ji, and Jiawei Han. 2019. Biomedical event extraction based on knowledge-driven tree-lstm. In *Proceedings of the 2019 Conference of the North American Chapter of the Association for Computational Linguistics: Human Language Technologies, Volume 1 (Long and Short Papers)*, pages 1421–1430.

Shasha Liao and Ralph Grishman. 2010. Using document level cross-event inference to improve event extraction. In *Proceedings of the 48th Annual Meeting of the Association for Computational Linguistics*, pages 789–797. Association for Computational Linguistics.

Yaojie Lu, Hongyu Lin, Jin Xu, Xianpei Han, Jialong Tang, Annan Li, Le Sun, Meng Liao, and Shaoyi Chen. 2021. Text2event: Controllable sequence-to-structure generation for end-to-end event extraction. In *Proceedings of the 59th Annual Meeting of the Association for Computational Linguistics and the 11th International Joint Conference on Natural Language Processing (Volume 1: Long Papers)*, pages 2795–2806.

Stefano Menini, Teresa Paccosi, Serra Sinem Tekiroğlu, and Sara Tonelli. 2023. Scent mining: Extracting olfactory events, smell sources and qualities. In *Proceedings of the 7th Joint SIGHUM Workshop on Computational Linguistics for Cultural Heritage, Social Sciences, Humanities and Literature*, pages 135–140.

Gosse Minnema, Sara Gemelli, Chiara Zanchi, Tommaso Caselli, Malvina Nissim, et al. 2022. Sociofillmore: A tool for discovering perspectives. In *The 60th Annual Meeting of the Association for Computational Linguistics Proceedings of System Demonstrations*, pages 240–250. Association for Computational Linguistics.

Gosse Minnema, Sara Gemelli, Chiara Zanchi, Viviana Patti, Tommaso Caselli, and Malvina Nissim. 2021. Frame semantics for social nlp in italian: Analyzing responsibility framing in femicide news reports. In *Italian Conference on Computational Linguistics 2021: CLiC-it 2021*. CEUR Workshop Proceedings (CEUR-WS. org).

Teruko Mitamura, Yukari Yamakawa, Susan Holm, Zhiyi Song, Ann Bies, Seth Kulick, and Stephanie Strassel. 2015. Event nugget annotation: Processes and issues. In *Proceedings of the The 3rd Workshop on EVENTS: Definition, Detection, Coreference, and Representation*, pages 66–76.

Thien Huu Nguyen, Kyunghyun Cho, and Ralph Grishman. 2016. Joint event extraction via recurrent neural networks. In *Proceedings of the 2016 Conference of the North American Chapter of the Association for Computational Linguistics: Human Language Technologies*, pages 300–309.

Trung Minh Nguyen and Thien Huu Nguyen. 2019. One for all: Neural joint modeling of entities and events. In *Proceedings of the AAAI Conference on Artificial Intelligence*, volume 33, pages 6851–6858.

Walker Orr, Prasad Tadepalli, and Xiaoli Fern. 2018. Event detection with neural networks: A rigorous empirical evaluation. In *Proceedings of the 2018 Conference on Empirical Methods in Natural Language Processing*, pages 999–1004, Brussels, Belgium. Association for Computational Linguistics.

Alessio Palmero Aprosio and Giovanni Moretti. 2018. Tint 2.0: an all-inclusive suite for nlp in italian. In *Proceedings of the Fifth Italian Conference on Computational Linguistics (CLiC-it 2018)*.

Giovanni Paolini, Ben Athiwaratkun, Jason Krone, Jie Ma, Alessandro Achille, Rishita Anubhai, Cicero Nogueira dos Santos, Bing Xiang, and Stefano Soatto. 2021. Structured prediction as translation between augmented natural languages. *arXiv preprint arXiv:2101.05779*.

Alan Ramponi, Rob van der Goot, Rosario Lombardo, and Barbara Plank. 2020. Biomedical event extraction as sequence labeling. In *Proceedings of the 2020 conference on empirical methods in natural language processing (emnlp)*, pages 5357–5367.

Marco Rovera, Federico Nanni, and Simone Paolo Ponzetto. 2021. Event-based access to historical italian war memoirs. *Journal on Computing and Cultural Heritage (JOCCH)*, 14(1):1–23.

Josef Ruppenhofer, Michael Ellsworth, Myriam Schwarzer-Petruck, Christopher R Johnson, and Jan Scheffczyk. 2006. Framenet ii: Extended theory and practice.

Josef Ruppenhofer, Michael Ellsworth, Myriam Schwarzer-Petruck, Christopher R Johnson, and Jan Scheffczyk. 2016. Framenet ii: Extended theory and practice. Technical report, International Computer Science Institute.

Roser Saurí, Jessica Littman, Bob Knippen, Robert Gaizauskas, Andrea Setzer, and James Pustejovsky. 2006. Timeml annotation guidelines. *Version*, 1(1):31.

Roxane Segers, Marieke Van Erp, Lourens Van Der Meij, Lora Aroyo, Jacco van Ossenbruggen, Guus Schreiber, Bob Wielinga, Johan Oomen, and Geertje Jacobs. 2011. Hacking history via event extraction. In *Proceedings of the sixth international conference on Knowledge capture*, pages 161–162.

Matthew Sims, Jong Ho Park, and David Bamman. 2019. Literary event detection. In *Proceedings of the 57th Annual Meeting of the Association for Computational Linguistics*, pages 3623–3634, Florence, Italy. Association for Computational Linguistics.

Rachele Sprugnoli and Sara Tonelli. 2017. One, no one and one hundred thousand events: Defining and processing events in an inter-disciplinary perspective. *Natural Language Engineering*, 23(4):485–506.

Rachele Sprugnoli and Sara Tonelli. 2019. Novel event detection and classification for historical texts. *Computational Linguistics*, 45(2):229–265.

Swabha Swayamdipta, Sam Thomson, Chris Dyer, and Noah A Smith. 2017. Frame-semantic parsing with softmax-margin segmental rnns and a syntactic scaffold. *arXiv preprint arXiv:1706.09528*.

Swabha Swayamdipta, Sam Thomson, Kenton Lee, Luke Zettlemoyer, Chris Dyer, and Noah A Smith. 2018. Syntactic scaffolds for semantic structures. In *Proceedings of the 2018 Conference on Empirical Methods in Natural Language Processing*, pages 3772–3782.

Sara Tonelli and Emanuele Pianta. 2008. Frame information transfer from english to italian. In *6th International Conference on Language Resources and Evaluation (LREC 2008)*.

Sara Tonelli, Daniele Pighin, Claudio Giuliano, and Emanuele Pianta. 2009. Semi-automatic development of framenet for italian. In *Proceedings of the FrameNet Workshop and Masterclass, Milano, Italy*.

Rob van der Goot, Ahmet Üstün, Alan Ramponi, Ibrahim Sharaf, and Barbara Plank. 2021. Massive choice, ample tasks (MaChAmp): A toolkit for multitask learning in NLP. In *Proceedings of the 16th Conference of the European Chapter of the Association for Computational Linguistics: System Demonstrations*, pages 176–197, Online. Association for Computational Linguistics.

Christopher Walker, Stephanie Strassel, Julie Medero, and Kazuaki Maeda. 2006. Ace 2005 multilingual training corpus. *Linguistic Data Consortium, Philadelphia*, 57:45.

A Examples of annotation

While the full documentation of EvN-ITA, including annotation guidelines, frame-based descriptions and examples is being released along with the resource, in this section we provide more details about the annotation process.
As mentioned in Section 4, in EvN-ITA target parts-of-speech are nouns, verbs and multiword expressions. In real-world data, however, beside events expressed in positive, factual form, there are often cases that raise exceptions. In EvN-ITA, event mentions are annotated regardless of their factuality value, which means that also *negated*, *abstract*, *hypotetical* event mentions must be annotated, as well as those introduced by modals verbs. Conversely, we do not annotate as event mention those lexical units that are used with *metaphorical meaning* or in the form of *rethoric expression*. In the following, we provide some examples[15]:

1. *negated events*

    [La Federazione russa, l'unico legale stato successore dell'Unione Sovietica PAYER], non ha mai riconosciuto le deportazioni degli estoni come un crimine e non ha [**pagato** PAY] [nessuna riparazione MONEY] [agli stati coinvolti BENEFICIARY].

    La persistente segregazione razziale negli Stati Uniti d'America in tutto il profondo sud significò che [la maggior parte degli afroamericani MEMBER] non poteva [**fare parte** MEMBERSHIP] [dei Grand Jury GROUP] i quali – totalmente composti da bianchi – continuarono ad emanare verdetti discriminatori e palesemente ingiusti.

    [Clary SPEAKER] però non può [**ribattere** REPLY] perché il suo cellulare squilla:

2. *hypothetical/possible events*

    Sull'orlo di una [**guerra** WAR], la Russia comunicò riluttante a Berlino e Vienna il suo consenso e, abbandonata a sé stessa, il 31 marzo, anche la Serbia si arrese.

    Nel gennaio 2008 hanno iniziato a rincorrersi notizie, via via sempre più insistenti e accreditate, che [ad Albano Laziale PLACE], [in prossimità della discarica sita in località "Roncigliano" della frazione di Cecchina RELATIVE_LOCATION], sarebbe stato [**realizzato** BUILDING] [un inceneritore CREATED_ENTITY] per smaltire i rifiuti, in vista dell'imminente chiusura della discarica di "Roncigliano" e di quella di Malagrotta a Roma.

    Il 22 novembre 1961 la polizia perquisì, senza risultato, il suo appartamento in cerca di [una pistola con cui MEANS] [Pasolini] avrebbe [**rapinato** ROBBERY], [il 18 sera TIME], [un distributore di benzina SOURCE] [di San Felice Circeo PLACE].

    La bomba non esplose, altrimenti [la detonazione CAUSE] avrebbe potuto effettivamente [**distruggere** DESTROYING] [la nave PATIENT].

    Il riluttante generale Raffaele Cadorna, per evitare che [Mussolini CAPTIVE] [**cadesse nelle mani** TAKING_CAPTIVE] [degli Alleati CAPTOR], rilasciò il salvacondotto necessario;

3. *events introduced by modals*

    Verosimilmente, si può presumere che [egli MOVER] dovette [**allontanarsi** QUITTING_A_PLACE [da Augsburg SOURCE] [in quanto cattolico EXPLANATION], dal momento c he, con quanto sancito dalla pace di Augusta, era in vigore il principio del "cuius regio, eius religio".

    Se l'indagine dimostrerà che sono stati commessi crimini di

[15]For the sake of readability, examples presented in this appendix are annotated with a single layer. Please see the documentation for more data samples.

guerra, [i responsabili DEFENDANT] dovranno essere trovati e [**processati** TRIAL] [conformemente alle norme in vigore BINDING_PRINCIPLE].

Conversely, we do *not* annotate as event mention occurrences used with *metaphorical meaning* or in the form of *rethoric expression*:

> Questa è [**la domanda** Ø] che Malone, Russo e Montague hanno cominciato a [**porsi** Ø] una volta esaurita la spinta idealistica dei primi anni di lavoro e la loro risposta è stata:
>
> Signor Presidente, il risultato delle elezioni in Israele ha [**fornito la risposta** Ø] della popolazione israeliana.
>
> Il visitatore / studioso poteva [**intraprendere** Ø] così [**un viaggio** Ø] dal microcosmo (la chimica), attraverso gli elementi primi della natura, al macrocosmo (l'astronomia) nel torrino che concludeva il percorso.
>
> Sostiene inoltre che, nonostante i problemi della filosofia della scienza e della ragione in generale, le "questioni morali" avranno [**risposte** Ø] oggettivamente giuste e sbagliate suffragate da fatti empirici su ciò che induce la gente a star bene e prosperare.

Finally, as mentioned in Section 4, in order to increase robustness, EvN-ITA contains many negative examples. Given a lexical unit, a negative example is an occurrence of the lexical unit which denotes a meaning not covered by the current schema. Negative examples are meant to improve the classifier's ability to work in an open-world setting and to generalize to extrinsic/unseen data.

Lexical unit: *istituire*

Positive example:

> La richiesta venne accolta e il papa diede l'autorizzazione a [**istituire** CREATE_SOCIAL_ENTITY] [in Inghilterra PLACE] [un tribunale ecclesiastico CREATED_ENTITY [per esaminare attentamente il caso PURPOSE], ...

Negative example:

> venne così [**istituito** Ø], nel 46 a.C., il calendario giuliano.

B Association between event frames

In this section we present numerical evidence of association between events, mentioned in Section 5.2. As stated above, patterns of association between frames can be identified by computing their co-occurrence. We choose 5 event frames and list the first 5 most related event frames and the 5 most unrelated frames, using Pointwise Mutual Information (PMI).

Target: INVEST

Related frames	PMI
BUY	2.87
GROWTH ON A SCALE	2.37
BUILDING	2.22
SELL	2.20
MANUFACTURING	1.79
...	
COMMUNICATION	-0.87
DEATH	-0.89
CONQUERING	-0.93
STATEMENT	-1.04
ATTACK	-1.38

Table 7: Correlation with the INVEST frame.

Target: ARRIVING

Related frames	PMI
DEPARTING	1.94
ENCOUNTER	1.86
MOVE AWAY	1.82
REMAIN IN PLACE	1.78
MOTION DOWNWARDS	1.75
...	
BEING MARRIED	-1.55
DECREASE ON A SCALE	-1.58
ACQUITTAL	-1.59
EARTHQUAKE	-1.62
TAKING SIDES	-1.79

Table 8: Correlation with the ARRIVING frame.

Target: CREATE ARTWORK

Related frames	PMI
PERFORMING ARTS	2.18
ASSIGN TASK	1.89
TEMPORAL ORIGIN	1.73
PUBLISHING	1.72
BEING LOCATED	1.67
...	
PURPOSE	-1.49
ROBBERY	-1.50
APPOINTING	-1.51
PROCESS END	-1.59
WAR	-1.70

Table 9: Correlation with the CREATE ARTWORK frame.

Target: TRIAL

Related frames	PMI
ACQUITTAL	3.81
SENTENCING	3.59
VERDICT	3.12
ACCUSE	2.99
EXECUTION	2.80
...	
FLEEING	-1.29
BEING LOCATED	-1.36
CREATE ARTWORK	-1.37
BEAT OPPONENT	-1.39
AGREEMENT	-1.41

Table 10: Correlation with the TRIAL frame.

Target: COMMUNICATION

Related frames	PMI
CONTACTING	2.64
QUESTIONING	2.09
ENCOUNTER	2.04
AWARENESS	2.02
GIVING	1.88
...	
EVENT ORDERING	-1.22
COUNTERATTACK	-1.24
APPOINTING ELECTION	-1.25
SUPPRESSING	-1.25
TAKE PLACE OF	-1.53

Table 11: Correlation with the COMMUNICATION frame.

Modeling Moravian Memoirs:
Ternary Sentiment Analysis in a Low Resource Setting

Patrick D. Brookshire
Digital Academy
Academy of Sciences and Literature | Mainz
patrick.brookshire@adwmainz.de

Nils Reiter
Department of Digital Humanities
University of Cologne
nils.reiter@uni-koeln.de

Abstract

The Moravians are a Christian group that has emerged from a 15th century movement. In this paper, we investigate how memoirs written by the devotees of this group can be analyzed with methods from computational linguistics, in particular sentiment analysis. To this end, we experiment with two different fine-tuning strategies and find that the best performance for ternary sentiment analysis (81 % accuracy) is achieved by fine-tuning a German BERT model, outperforming in particular models trained on much larger German sentiment datasets. We further investigate the model(s) using SHAP scores and find that the best performing model struggles with multiple negations and mixed statements. Finally, we show two application scenarios motivated by research questions from religious studies.

1 Introduction

While not entirely uncontroversial (cf. Mortimer, 2002, 189ff.), ego-documents (i.e. documents in which humans write about themselves and their experiences) are an important source of historical research (Burke, 2013; Farbstein, 1998; Kuromiya, 1985; Redlich, 1975). In this paper, we focus on one specific kind of ego-document, often called memoir: semi-autobiographical records written by members of the Moravian Church in the 18th century. In line with general migration movements at that time, many Moravians migrated from Europe to America. The semi-autobiographical records we investigate are the result of a custom among Moravians to document their lives in written form. As they were completed, compiled and collected by other members of the respective local church (Van Gent, 2017), we consider them semi-autobiographical. Religiously, the Moravians are connected to the so-called "Blood and Wounds" theology (Atwood, 2006), dating back to their founder, Nikolaus Ludwig von Zinzendorf (1700–1760). Next to blood, the "wounds Jesus suffered on the cross became the main focus of this religious attention" (Atwood, 2006, 38).

The memoirs are also believed to express a high degree of emotionality (Van Gent, 2017; Faull and McGuire, 2022), which is why we focus on sentiment analysis in this paper, while also taking into account that emotionality found in the text is not necessarily only rooted in emotions of the person the memoir is about. From a linguistic standpoint, these sources exhibit regional variation and domain-specific terms, some of them connected to the "Blood and Wounds" theology. We therefore experiment with multiple ways of assigning sentiment scores, and explore the gain by adapting these systems to the specific domain and text genre. We also investigate how to visualize what these models actually have learned, and provide two application scenarios motivated by research interests from religious and historical studies.

In the following sections, we outline connected fields of research first. Then, we go into details about how we compiled our dataset and what kind of analyses we conducted before discussing our findings.

2 Related Work

This paper has links to multiple research areas from Computational Linguistics (CL) and Digital Humanities (DH).

2.1 Digital Biographical Research

Biographical documents have been investigated in both disciplines for quite some time, often working with Wikipedia data (Biadsy et al., 2008; Palmero Aprosio and Tonelli, 2015; Chisholm et al., 2017) or focusing on digitization and editorial work which is often combined with Linked Open Data (Fokkens et al., 2014; Hyvonen et al., 2019). Targetwise, most works see biographies as factual texts from which facts can be extracted. Thus, there is a prevalence of spatio-temporal and social network

Proceedings of LaTeCH-CLfL 2024, pages 91–100
March 22, 2024 ©2024 Association for Computational Linguistics

analysis approaches (Faull, 2021; Windhager et al., 2017). To the best of our knowledge, there are only a few other studies that focus on emotions or sentiment in this area. One concerned Australian World War I diaries (Dennis-Henderson et al., 2020) and another one English Moravian memoirs from the 18th century (Faull and McGuire, 2022; McGuire, 2021). The latter is our main reference project.

2.2 Historical Sentiment Analysis

Sentiment analysis is a common CL task that has mainly been applied to news, product reviews and Social Media data (cf. Liu, 2012). Nevertheless, the number of studies devoted to historical domains increased over the past decade. An earlier application was a dictionary-based analysis of relationships between characters in Shakespeare's plays (Nalisnick and Baird, 2013). The former prevalence of sentiment dictionaries gave also rise to corpus-based domain adaptation methods that use seed lists (Hamilton et al., 2016). Regarding historical German data, one of the earliest approaches was a happy ending prediction based on a support vector machine (Zehe et al., 2016). More recent studies found that transformers outperform other approaches (Schmidt et al., 2021; Allaith et al., 2023). However, custom dictionaries are still used in particular for highly specific research questions or small heterogeneous datasets which are typical features of ego-document collections (Faull and McGuire, 2022; Dennis-Henderson et al., 2020).

2.3 Explainable AI

While dictionary-based approaches to sentiment analysis are inherently explainable, transformer-based ones are not, which raises questions about their trustworthyness. This is why various ways to explain a given model globally or locally (i.e. in relation to an individual prediction) have been proposed (Danilevsky et al., 2020; Linardatos et al., 2020). One such method relies on an architecture that not only predicts class labels but also summarizes its input (Bacco et al., 2021). A different one is `SHAP` (SHapley Additive exPlanations) which is an external explainability model that unifies several similar methods (Lundberg and Lee, 2017). Zielinski et al. (2023) evaluated it on a (non-historical) sentiment analysis application where it performed best with regard to BERT models in terms of plausibility and faithfulness.

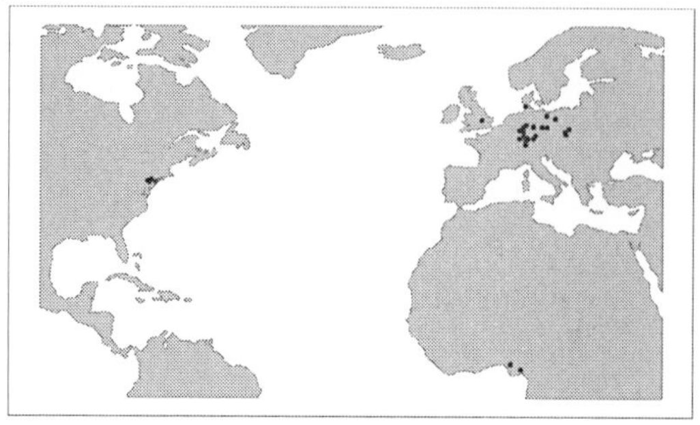

Figure 1: Birthplaces documented in the entire dataset

3 Data and Methodology

In this section, we first describe how we selected the data we wanted to analyze. Afterwards, we list the sentiment and explainability models we used and outline how we conducted our experiments.

3.1 Corpus Construction and Annotation

Due to the lack of German Moravian corpora with sentiment annotations, we needed to compile a new one ourselves. We started with 41 Moravian memoirs transcribed by Faull[1] and added 23 from the crowdsourcing project Moravian Lives[2]. This project lists 328 more documents as available but unpublished since their respective transcriptions are incomplete. Even more Moravian texts from various genres are in the process of digitization but not considered here (Lasch, 2023). To the best of our knowledge, there are at the moment only 64 German memoirs available in digital form, all of which include metadata about the person's gender as well as birth and death dates. This metadata was manually enriched by the place of birth and used to semi-randomly select a gender balanced subcorpus of 36 texts from people that lived in the 18th century. Figure 1 shows that people from various German speaking communities in Europe and New York/Pennsylvania are included but also a few Native Americans and two former African slaves.

Having selected our subcorpus, we first conduct sentence splitting using stanza (Qi et al., 2020). Since punctuation is often not normalized (or not used at all) in the data, we corrected the sentences semi-automatically, which yields 2210 sentences in total. Afterwards, we anonymized each sentence by masking names with `{NAME}` and annotated it with one of the three labels `negative`, `neutral` and

[1]https://katiefaull.com/moravian-materials

[2]http://moravianlives.org/

Dataset	Instances			
	neg	neut	pos	Total
Train	485	523	760	1768
Test	115	150	177	442
Total	600	673	937	2210

Table 1: Train/test dataset statistics

positive, making it a ternary classification task. It should be noted that the neutral class was used for sentences without sentiment bearing words, and not for mixed-sentiment sentences. In cases of mixed sentiment, we based our annotations on the final state or result of the action described in a given instance. For example, we annotated (1) as negative.

(1) Ich versuchte oft und viel mir selbst aus diesem Zustand zu helfen, aber vergebens, ('I tried often and hard to help myself out of this state, but in vain,')

Finally, we randomly split our data in 80 % training samples and 20 % used for testing. Both datasets show a positive bias (see Table 1) unlike the prevalence of negative samples in some literary corpora (Allaith et al., 2023; Schmidt et al., 2021).

3.2 Ternary Sentiment Analysis

In our experiment, we compare i) trained off-the-shelf models for sentiment analysis, ii) dictionary-based methods and iii) models fine-tuned to this specific dataset. We use the following systems:

ger-senti-bert. This BERT model was trained on 1.8M German samples from Social Media as well as app, hotel and movie reviews (Guhr et al., 2020).

senti-distilbert. This Hugging Face model[3] was distilled from the zero-shot classification pipeline on the Multilingual Sentiment dataset[4].

SentiWS. This dictionary lists polarity values within the interval [-1, 1] for 34.6k German word forms. It has a focus on financial data and product reviews (Remus et al., 2010).

GerVADER. VADER (Valence Aware Dictionary for sEntiment Reasoning) adds a few context-aware rules to a dictionary lookup (Hutto and Gilbert, 2014). The German adaptation builds on word forms from SentiWS as well as a few slang words all of which are re-rated in a crowdsourcing project and enriched with items commonly found in Social Media (Tymann et al., 2019).

We fine-tuned `bert-base-cased` (Devlin et al., 2019) and `gbert-base` (Chan et al., 2020) with the transformers library from Hugging Face using default parameter settings (i.e. 3 epochs). This took approximately 10 minutes on a T4 GPU. We also fine-tuned `ger-senti-bert` in the same way to evaluate whether this kind of transfer learning is a viable option.

3.3 Experimental Setup

The experiment we conduct is a **sentence-wise classification** experiment, to determine which of the systems/models mentioned above performs best. To this end, we transformed manual annotations as well as predicted sentiment labels into numbers (`-1` for the negative, `0` for the neutral and `1` for the positive class). In case of lexicon-based approaches we used a compound score per sentence instead, which already leads to values in the interval [-1, 1]. Afterwards, we calculated mean sentiment values per text and compared the values from our manual annotations to model predictions.

3.4 Explainability Analysis

In order to reach a deeper understanding of the main differences between the systems under investigation, we conducted various SHAP experiments. SHAP values are gained by masking an input as a whole before subsequently unmasking tokens. Thus, they measure the impact of a given token on the probability that the model under investigation predicts a given label on a range from -1 (negative impact) to 1 (positive impact) (Lundberg and Lee, 2017). It should also be noted that the sum of all SHAP values per class (three in our case) is always zero. Annotating all of our 442 test sentences this way took approximately one hour on a T4 GPU. We analyzed the enriched dataset by first looking at distributions per class. Afterwards, we calculated means per token, bigram and trigram and looked at the most impactful ones per class.

4 Results

We performed two types of model evaluations, namely looking at raw performance scores on the one hand and explainability attempts on the other. The following subsections present our findings.

[3] https://huggingface.co/lxyuan/distilbert-base-multilingual-cased-sentiments-student

[4] https://github.com/tyqiangz/multilingual-sentiment-datasets

Model	Acc	F1 Scores		
		neg	neut	pos
Random Baseline	.33	.33	.33	.33
Majority Baseline	.40	.00	.00	.57
SentiWS	.34	.03	.51	.00
GerVADER	.59	.46	.59	.65
ger-senti-bert	.37	.18	.51	.09
senti-distilbert	.45	.56	.00	.53
bert*	.63	.54	.72	.63
gbert*	**.81**	**.76**	**.84**	**.82**
ger-senti-bert*	.74	.69	.77	.75

Table 2: Sentiment classification results. Models marked with * are fine-tuned on Moravian data, best results are highlighted in bold.

4.1 Sentiment Classification

Table 2 lists accuracy and F1 scores per class for each model based on predictions on the test dataset as well as random and majority baselines. In order to compare the different approaches, the compound scores of lexicon-based approaches (`SentiWS` and `GerVADER`) were categorized with thresholds of ±.05 that are said to yield best results (Hutto and Gilbert, 2014).

It is worth noting that the addition of context-aware rules, which is the main difference between the two lexicon-based approaches led to an .25 increase in accuracy to .59. The individual F1 scores imply that this may be due to a better recognition of non-neutral instances. Similar issues can be seen in the scores of `ger-senti-bert` explaining why this transformer-based approach is also outperformed by `GerVADER`. The multilingual `senti-distilbert` by contrast hardly identifies any neutral samples at all which is another notable finding since this is the only model doing so. The scores can be improved by fine-tuning as we showed with `ger-senti-bert`. This model ranks between base cased BERT models which is in line with previous research (Schmidt et al., 2021). In our case `gbert` performed best with an accuracy of .81 and similar F1 scores. Looking at individual F1 scores, all fine-tuned models share the common trait of performing worst in recognizing negative samples. This may be due to the fact that this class is underrepresented in our dataset (see Table 1).

Figure 2 shows confusion matrices of our fine-tuned models which illustrate that neither one of them had problems distinguishing neutral from non-neutral samples. However, the English BERT model confused about one third of the negative samples with positive ones and vice versa. A similar but weaker trend is also observable for the other fine-tuned models.

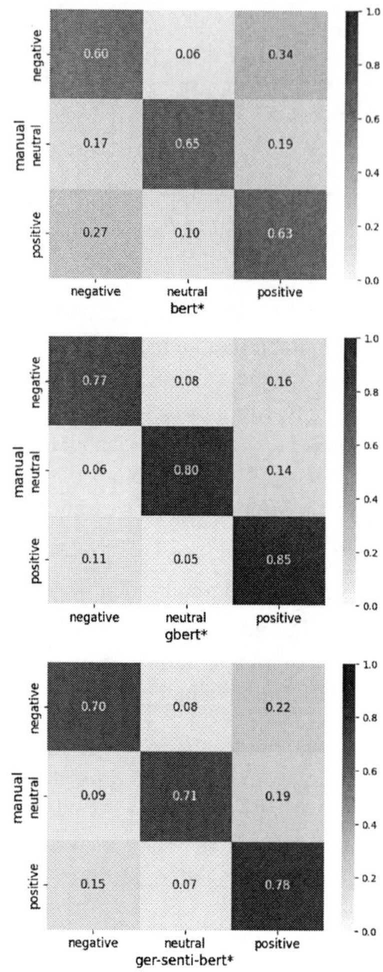

Figure 2: Confusion matrices of fine-tuned models

4.2 Error Analysis

Since the fine-tuned `gbert` model performed best, we focus our error analysis on this model. Even though many misclassifications cannot be categorized (see Table 3), we note that in a few cases, the model fails to consider the outcome in sentences with mixed sentiment. Example (1) from above is classified as `positive` but annotated as `negative`.

The most error-prone group were long sentences since they tend to contain mixed sentiment. Short sentences, by contrast, were classified wrongly in

Error	Confusion			
	neg/pos	neg/neut	neut/pos	**Total**
mixed	.08	.01	.01	.11
long	**.20**	.13	.02	.36
short	.01	.01	.07	.10
negated	.05	.04	–	.08
other	.10	**.14**	**.24**	**.48**
Total	**.44**	.33	.35	1.00

Table 3: Distribution of error types of the fine-tuned gbert model. Highest values are highlighted in bold.

a few cases where they were ambiguous without context. Finally, some errors can be explained by multiple negations as in (2).

(2) er würde nicht flüchten den er hätte den Indianern nichts böses sondern vielmehr gutes gethan,
('he would not flee because he had done the Native Americans no harm but rather good,')

4.3 Explaining Sentiment Predictions

Here, we present results from our explainability experiments. We start by using standard plotting functionality of the shap library[5] on a single prediction before analyzing SHAP value distributions and n-grams from our whole test dataset.

4.3.1 Explaining Individual Predictions

As SHAP is at its core a local explainability method, it offers ways to visualize which input features contributed to what degree to a model output. One such visualization can be seen in Figure 3 where (3) is analyzed.

(3) Die lezte Zeit kränckelte er.
('In recent times, he has been ailing.')

In this case, our fine-tuned English BERT model falsely predicts the positive class with 57.8 % confidence while the true label `negative` only reaches 34.7 %. The German model, by contrast, labels the sentence correctly with 99.8 % confidence. This difference between the two models is a typical one when considering their confusion matrices (see Figure 2) and can be explained in this specific instance. The former model focused on the wrong word forms namely *Die lezte* 'In recent' while the latter identified the correct sentiment anchor *kränckelte* 'ailing'. This can be seen by higher supporting SHAP values (colored in deeper red in Figure 3) attributed to the respective BERT tokens.

[5]https://shap.readthedocs.io/en/latest/

4.3.2 SHAP Value Distributions

To get insights into the general classification behavior of our fine-tuned models, we looked at the whole distribution of SHAP values (see Figure 4). As expected, the vast majority of individual tokens in our test dataset are non-discriminatory in nature. The means per class fall into the interval (-.01, .00) for the English BERT model and (-.01, .01) for the German one. Interestingly, the slightly negative mean SHAP value belongs to the neutral class in both cases. This trend is even more apparent when looking at outliers as the neutral class is the only one with considerably more negative outliers than positive ones. Thus, both models seem to recognize neutral samples stronger ex negativo which can be seen as a learning success since we used this class only in cases that lack sentiment bearing words.

Another interesting finding lies in the fact that fine-tuning `gbert` leads to considerably larger SHAP value intervals in all three classes. For example, the smallest range of this model was .94 with values between -.32 and .62 in case of attributions to the negative class. However, this is almost twice the maximum range of the fine-tuned `bert` (.56) that it reached with attributions to the neutral class with values between -.32 and .24. To sum it up, this implies that the German model was better at learning discriminatory tokens which matches our observations from looking at confusion matrices (see Figure 2) and will be investigated further in the following section.

4.3.3 N-gram Analysis

The additive nature of SHAP values enabled us to also look at token combinations (n-grams) that had the highest impact on predictions of our fine-tuned models. In Figure 5, we present SHAP values for single tokens and bigrams. Bigrams were added in order to get more interpretable results in our setting. This is due to the fact that especially tokens from `bert` were too ambiguous without context while an inclusion of trigrams led to a mere increase in variations of top ranking bigrams.

The English BERT has seemingly recognized the German negator *nicht* 'not' split into *ni* and *cht* as one of the most typical features of negative samples. This result was rather unexpected but gave

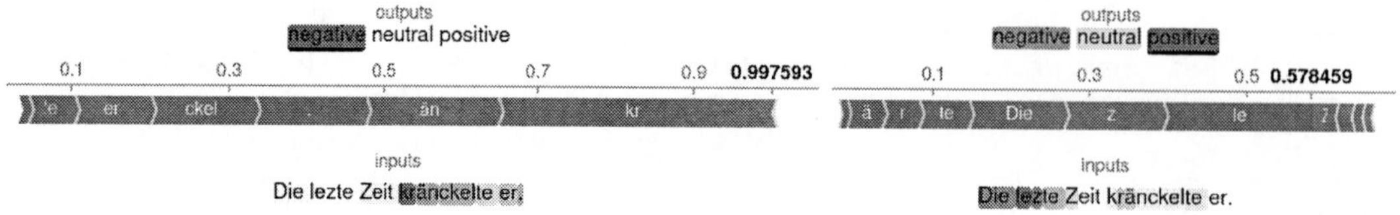

Figure 3: Default SHAP explanation plots per fine-tuned model (gbert* (left), bert* (right)). The predicted class is underlined and the confidence highlighted in bold. Negative SHAP values for the predicted class are colored blue and positive ones red. Lighter colors correspond to SHAP values closer to 0. The input sentence is shown in (3).

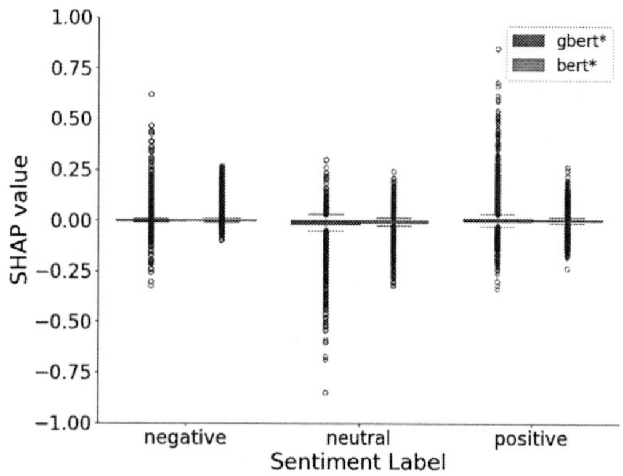

Figure 4: SHAP value distributions per model

insights into an imbalance in our train dataset as 29.5 % of the negative samples contain this type of negation but only 9.1 % percent of non-negative ones. Not only did gbert learn this feature but also some collocations of German words that bear negative sentiment like *Schmerz* 'pain', *verloren* 'lost', *Versuch[ung]* 'temptation', *Furcht* 'fear', *schwach* 'weak', *kon[fus]* 'confused', *schlecht* 'bad', *krank* 'sick' and *fehlen* 'to lack'.

With regard to neutral samples, it is worth mentioning that the English model considered dates and places as typical instances of this class. This is a learning success as such entities are commonly used in travel descriptions or introductory passages that tend to lack sentiment in Moravian memoirs. Interestingly, it also found the verb *heiraten* 'to marry' which accounts for the fact that marriages were indeed presented factually and not especially emotionalized in most memoirs. Top n-grams that contributed to neutral labeling of gbert on the other hand are harder to interpret. There is a prevalence of forms of the verb *wollen* 'to want' although they were similarly frequent in neutral annotations as in other ones.

The results for the positive class mirror those for the negative one. The English BERT seemed to have found another slight imbalance in our training corpus namely that exclamation marks occurred a little more frequently in positive samples (5.4 %) than in others (1.8 %). It might have also recognized the positively connoted noun *Herz* 'heart' as the trigram *zu +Her+zen* (.29) (c.f. *zu +Her* (.17) in Figure 5) implies. Still, gbert has once again learned more sentiment bearing lemmata like *lieben* 'to love', *gut* 'good', *willig* 'willing', *Vergnügen* 'pleasure', *helfen* 'to help', *Dank* 'gratitude', *Freude* 'joy' and *genießen* 'enjoy'.

Finally, we want to stress the fact that the mean SHAP values of n-grams from the German BERT model were consistently higher than ones from the English model even though is is less apparent for the neutral class. This is in line with our findings in section 4.3.1.

5 Applications

To illustrate some of the analyses made possible through sentiment assignments of the Moravian memoirs, we showcase two content-wise analyses of interest to the Moravian community.

5.1 Gender-based Sentiment Differences

We compared the German corpus with an English equivalent that was already analyzed (Faull and McGuire, 2022) by grouping sentiment annotations per gender. However, we did not limit our analysis to means but looked at whole distributions instead. Figure 6 shows the results with regard to manual annotations as well as ones generated from some of the models listed above. Note that we ignored the random and majority baselines since they are not expected to provide meaningful results. We also did not include SentiWS and our fine-tuned ger-senti-bert as they did not lead to insights that cannot be drawn from other models. This is due to the fact that the former classified almost anything as neutral and the latter was consistently in between the other two fine-tuned models.

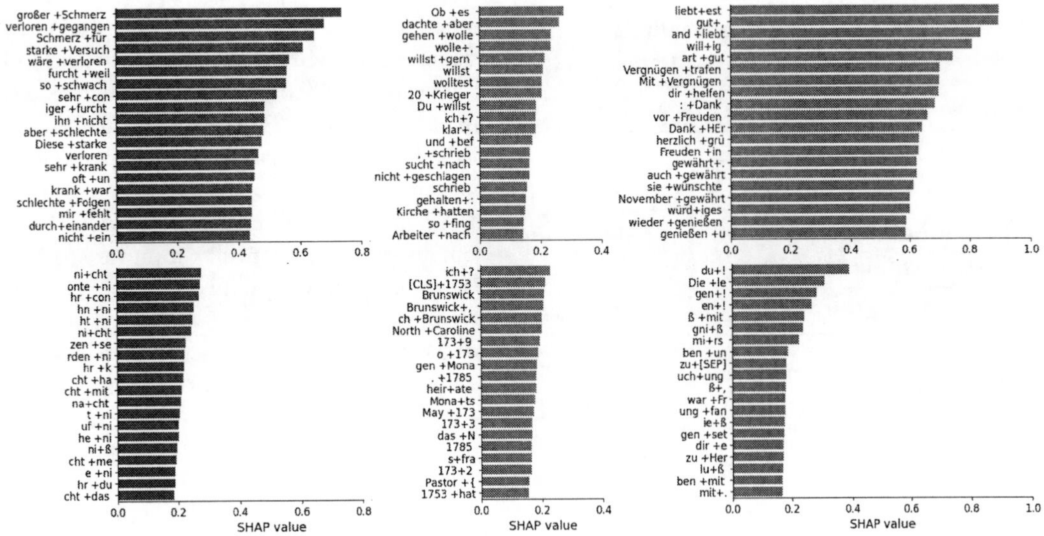

Figure 5: Single tokens and bigrams with highest SHAP values per class (negative (left), neutral (middle), positive (right)) and fine-tuned model (gbert* (top), bert* (bottom))

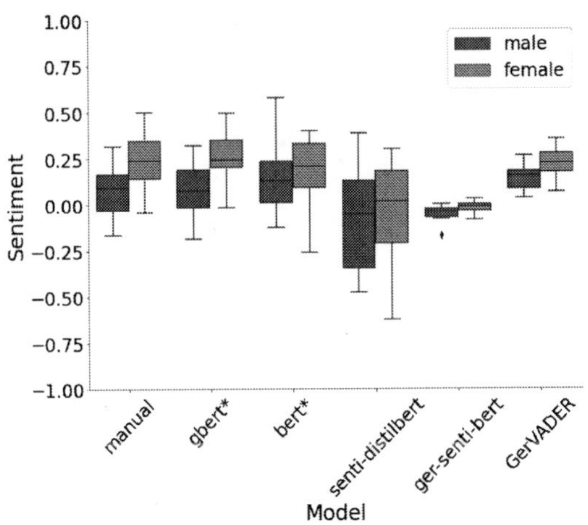

Figure 6: Sentiment distributions per gender and model

Our manual annotations are in line with the tendency found in the English corpus that lives of Moravian women are presented more positively than the ones of men (Faull and McGuire, 2022), especially when considering mean sentiment scores only. The fine-tuned gbert closely mirrored this distribution which was expected as it performed best (see Table 2). The same trend can however also be induced from most of the worse performing models although less overt. This is particularly true for the multilingual senti-distilbert which not only yields the highest range of sentiment values in general but also the biggest overlap between both distributions. On top of that, it leads to whiskers that are contrary to the general trend. Most of these findings are also true for classifications from the fine-tuned bert, albeit to a lesser extent. On the other hand, it is noteworthy that the sentiment values gained from senti-distilbert are more neutral (and negative). The former can also be seen by looking at the results of the other non-fine-tuned transformer model ger-senti-bert even though that model fails to identify most non-neutral samples (see Table 2). Interestingly, the lexicon-and-rule-based approach GerVADER performed almost as well on this task as our best fine-tuned model although its accuracy and F1 scores are worse.

5.2 Sentiment of "Blood and Wounds" Theology Related Words

Another research driven application is a quantitative analysis of the effects of "Blood and Wounds" theology on this corpus. The hypothesis is that tokens associated with this theology and accompanying themes are used in a positive context in memoirs of this specific time frame (Atwood, 2006; McGuire, 2021). Note that this was to the best of our knowledge not yet researched empirically, though. Nevertheless, most of the models we tested show this tendency as Table 4 illustrates.

Here, all fine-tuned models are able to confirm the hypothesis with mean sentiment values above .50. This suggests a strong positive sentiment towards the (sub)strings *[Bb]lut* 'blood'/'bleed' and *Wunden* 'wounds' which is in line with our man-

Model	Mean Sentiment	
	B&W	Dataset
manual	.52	.15
gbert*	**.52**	**.16**
bert*	.57	**.14**
senti-distilbert	.08	-.06
ger-senti-bert	-.01	-.04
GerVADER	.20	.18

Table 4: Mean sentiment per model of sentences with "Blood and Wounds" words (B&W) compared with the entire dataset. Models marked with * are fine-tuned on Moravian data, best results are highlighted in bold.

ual annotations. Our fine-tuned basic cased `bert` seemed to have indeed learned this very specific framing in Moravian memoirs of that time. It even slightly overrates the sentiment in relevant samples. It has to be noted, though, that both fine-tuned models have seen most of the samples as part of the train dataset. The other models we tested, on the other hand, hardly capture the fact that these tokens are as positively framed. This can be seen for example in the case of the weak positive sentiment attributed by `senti-distilbert`. This result is in line with its general performance on our data and the one on the previous task as the aggregation of mainly non-neutral annotations may lead to a mean value close to zero. `ger-senti-bert`, on the other hand, yields a very weak negative sentiment which can not only be explained in regard to its general classification tendency but also by the expected framing in non-Moravian data. Finally, `GerVADER` mirrors once again the general tendency but with a mean sentiment of .20 to a lesser extent.

6 Conclusion

In this paper, we introduced a manually annotated dataset for ternary sentiment analysis of German memoirs of Moravians that lived in the 18th century. The prevalence of non-neutral samples in it attest that sentiment in particular and emotions in general are important features of this domain which is in line with theological research (Van Gent, 2017; Faull and McGuire, 2022).

We also introduced BERT models fine-tuned on this dataset that not only outperform existing transformer models and lexicon-based approaches but also reach or even surpass state-of-the-art results (Allaith et al., 2023; Schmidt et al., 2021). This was not only true for performance statistics like accuracy and F1 scores but also for two research driven applications. Here, we found that German memoirs of women tend to be more positive than those of men and that a positively framed "Blood and Wounds" theology can be observed empirically. Both findings confirm results from various Moravian research projects (Atwood, 2006; Faull and McGuire, 2022; McGuire, 2021). They also show that the minimum performance level required may depend on the downstream task at hand.

Concerning model explainability, we showed that a deeper look at F1 score distributions and confusion matrices can already give some hints on the classification behavior and possible problems related to this. These results can be enriched by applying local explanation approaches like SHAP to a whole dataset. This revealed in our case that `gbert` actually learned sentiment bearing lemmata during fine-tuning and that a neutral class has to be inferred ex negativo. The base English BERT model, by contrast, focused more on rather random imbalances in our test dataset like negations and punctuation marks. The latter was also observed in a related NLP task (Inácio et al., 2023). We suspect that these differences might be due to the different tokenizers involved as the German one tends to split fewer word forms that may carry sentiment information.

From these observations we draw the conclusion that state-of-the-art performances for ternary sentiment analysis can already be reached with less than 2k fine-tuning samples. This makes transformer-based approaches feasible in low resource settings even more so since individual model predictions can be explained to a certain degree.

Limitations

This work should be seen as a case study that complements others like in the case of our performance comparisons (see Table 2) which confirmed trends from similar research projects. However, they are still only valid for our specific setting and thus we expect our fine-tuned models to perform worse when applied to strongly deviating domains. With regard to our explainability analysis, we want to stress the fact that the calculation of SHAP values is a resource-intensive task as also noted in another Sentiment Analysis application (Zielinski et al., 2023). In our case it was even more intensive than the main fine-tuning step. This could be accounted for in a future ablation study.

Ethics Statement

It should be noted that our fine-tuned models might have learned derogatory language in relation to Native Americans or immigrants with non-European origins which should be seen in the given historical context. We refrained from masking corresponding terms in order to enable future research especially since other projects already deal with framing and devaluation phenomena in Moravian missionary narratives (Lasch, 2023).

References

Ali Allaith, Kirstine Degn, Alexander Conroy, Bolette S. Pedersen, Jens Bjerring-Hansen, and Daniel Hershcovich. 2023. Sentiment Classification of Historical Danish and Norwegian Literary Texts. In *Nordic Conference of Computational Linguistics*, pages 324–334. University of Tartu Library.

Craig D. Atwood. 2006. Understanding Zinzendorf's Blood and Wounds Theology. *Journal of Moravian History*, 1:31–47.

Luca Bacco, Andrea Cimino, Felice Dell'Orletta, and Mario Merone. 2021. Explainable Sentiment Analysis: A Hierarchical Transformer-Based Extractive Summarization Approach. *Electronics*, 10(18).

Fadi Biadsy, Julia Hirschberg, and Elena Filatova. 2008. An unsupervised approach to biography production using Wikipedia. In *Proceedings of ACL-08: HLT*, pages 807–815, Columbus, Ohio. Association for Computational Linguistics.

Peter Burke. 2013. The rhetoric of autobiography in the seventeenth century. In Marijke J. van der Wal and Gijsbert Rutten, editors, *Touching the Past. Studies in the historical sociolinguistics of ego-documents*. John Benjamins Publishing Company, Amsterdam / Philadelphia.

Branden Chan, Stefan Schweter, and Timo Möller. 2020. German's Next Language Model. In *Proceedings of the 28th International Conference on Computational Linguistics*, pages 6788–6796, Barcelona, Spain (Online). International Committee on Computational Linguistics.

Andrew Chisholm, Will Radford, and Ben Hachey. 2017. Learning to generate one-sentence biographies from Wikidata. In *Proceedings of the 15th Conference of the European Chapter of the Association for Computational Linguistics: Volume 1, Long Papers*, pages 633–642, Valencia, Spain. Association for Computational Linguistics.

Marina Danilevsky, Kun Qian, Ranit Aharonov, Yannis Katsis, Ban Kawas, and Prithviraj Sen. 2020. A Survey of the State of Explainable AI for Natural Language Processing. In *Proceedings of the 1st Conference of the Asia-Pacific Chapter of the Association for Computational Linguistics and the 10th International Joint Conference on Natural Language Processing*, pages 447–459, Suzhou, China. Association for Computational Linguistics.

Ashley Dennis-Henderson, Matthew Roughan, Lewis Mitchell, and Jonathan Tuke. 2020. Life still goes on: Analysing Australian WW1 diaries through distant reading. In *Proceedings of the The 4th Joint SIGHUM Workshop on Computational Linguistics for Cultural Heritage, Social Sciences, Humanities and Literature*, pages 90–104, Online. International Committee on Computational Linguistics.

Jacob Devlin, Ming-Wei Chang, Kenton Lee, and Kristina Toutanova. 2019. Bert: Pre-training of Deep Bidirectional Transformers for Language Understanding. In *Proceedings of the 2019 Conference of the North American Chapter of the Association for Computational Linguistics: Human Language Technologies*, volume 1, pages 4171–4186, Minneapolis, Minnesota. Association for Computational Linguistics.

Esther Farbstein. 1998. Diaries and Memoirs as a Historical Source - The Diary and Memoir of a Rabbi at the "Konin House of Bondage". *Yad Vashem Studies*, XXVI:87–128.

Katherine Faull. 2021. *Visualizing religious networks, movements, and communities: building Moravian Lives*, pages 213–236. De Gruyter, Berlin, Boston.

Katherine Mary Faull and Michael A. McGuire. 2022. Analyzing Moravian Feelings Using Computational Methods to Ask Questions about Norms and Sentiments in Eighteenth-Century Moravian Lebensläufe. *Journal of Moravian History*, 22:125–149.

Antske Fokkens, Serge ter Braake, Niels Ockeloen, Piek Vossen, Susan Legêne, and Guus Schreiber. 2014. BiographyNet: Methodological Issues when NLP supports historical research. In *Proceedings of the Ninth International Conference on Language Resources and Evaluation (LREC'14)*, pages 3728–3735, Reykjavik, Iceland. European Language Resources Association (ELRA).

Oliver Guhr, Anne-Kathrin Schumann, Frank Bahrmann, and Hans Joachim Böhme. 2020. Training a Broad-Coverage German Sentiment Classification Model for Dialog Systems. In *Proceedings of The 12th Language Resources and Evaluation Conference*, pages 1620–1625, Marseille, France. European Language Resources Association.

William L. Hamilton, Kevin Clark, Jure Leskovec, and Dan Jurafsky. 2016. Inducing Domain-Specific Sentiment Lexicons from Unlabeled Corpora. In *Proceedings of the 2016 Conference on Empirical Methods in Natural Language Processing*, pages 595–605,

Austin, Texas. Association for Computational Linguistics.

Clayton J. Hutto and Eric Gilbert. 2014. VADER: A Parsimonious Rule-Based Model for Sentiment Analysis of Social Media Text. *Proceedings of the International AAAI Conference on Web and Social Media.*

Eero Hyvonen, Petri Leskinen, Minna Tamper, Heikki Rantala, Esko Ikkala, Jouni Tuominen, and Kirsi Keravuori. 2019. Linked Data – A Paradigm Shift for Publishing and Using Biography Collections on the Semantic Web. In *Proceedings of the Third Conference on Biographical Data in a Digital World*, pages 16–23, Varna, Bulgaria.

Marcio Inácio, Gabriela Wick-Pedro, and Hugo Goncalo Oliveira. 2023. What do Humor Classifiers Learn? An Attempt to Explain Humor Recognition Models. In *Proceedings of the 7th Joint SIGHUM Workshop on Computational Linguistics for Cultural Heritage, Social Sciences, Humanities and Literature*, pages 88–98, Dubrovnik, Croatia. Association for Computational Linguistics.

Hiroaki Kuromiya. 1985. Soviet Memoirs As A Historical Source. *Russian History*, 12:293–326.

Alexander Lasch. 2023. Unterschiede „zwischen uns & den weißen Leuten“. In *Die Herrnhuter Brüdergemeine im 18. und 19. Jahrhundert*, volume 69 of *Arbeiten zur Geschichte des Pietismus*, pages 531–550. Vandenhoeck & Ruprecht.

Pantelis Linardatos, Vasilis Papastefanopoulos, and Sotiris B. Kotsiantis. 2020. Explainable AI: A Review of Machine Learning Interpretability Methods. *Entropy*, 23.

Bing Liu. 2012. *Sentiment Analysis and Opinion Mining*, volume 5 of *Synthesis Lectures on Human Language Technologies*.

Scott M Lundberg and Su-In Lee. 2017. A Unified Approach to Interpreting Model Predictions. In *Advances in Neural Information Processing Systems*, volume 30. Curran Associates, Inc.

Michael McGuire. 2021. *Computational Sentiment Analysis of an 18th Century Corpus of Moravian English Memoirs.* Ph.D. thesis, Indiana University.

Geoff Mortimer. 2002. *Eyewitness Accounts of the Thirty Years War 1618–48.* Palgrave Macmillan.

Eric T. Nalisnick and Henry S. Baird. 2013. Character-to-Character Sentiment Analysis in Shakespeare's Plays. In *Proceedings of the 51st Annual Meeting of the Association for Computational Linguistics (Volume 2: Short Papers)*, pages 479–483, Sofia, Bulgaria. Association for Computational Linguistics.

Alessio Palmero Aprosio and Sara Tonelli. 2015. Recognizing biographical sections in Wikipedia. In *Proceedings of the 2015 Conference on Empirical Methods in Natural Language Processing*, pages 811–816, Lisbon, Portugal. Association for Computational Linguistics.

Peng Qi, Yuhao Zhang, Yuhui Zhang, Jason Bolton, and Christopher D. Manning. 2020. Stanza: A Python Natural Language Processing Toolkit for Many Human Languages. In *Proceedings of the 58th Annual Meeting of the Association for Computational Linguistics: System Demonstrations.*

Fritz Redlich. 1975. Autobiographies as sources for social history: A research program. *VSWG: Vierteljahrschrift für Sozial- und Wirtschaftsgeschichte*, 62(3):380–390.

Robert Remus, Uwe Quasthoff, and Gerhard Heyer. 2010. SentiWS: A Publicly Available German-language Resource for Sentiment Analysis. In *International Conference on Language Resources and Evaluation*, pages 1168–1171.

Thomas Schmidt, Katrin Dennerlein, and Christian Wolff. 2021. Using Deep Learning for Emotion Analysis of 18th and 19th Century German Plays. In *Fabrikation von Erkenntnis: Experimente in den Digital Humanities.* Melusina Press.

Karsten Tymann, Matthias Lutz, Patrick Palsbröker, and Carsten Gips. 2019. GerVADER: A German Adaptation of the VADER Sentiment Analysis Tool for Social Media Texts. In *Lernen, Wissen, Daten, Analysen.*

Jacqueline Van Gent. 2017. Moravian Memoirs and the Emotional Salience of Conversion Rituals. In *Emotion, Ritual and Power in Europe, 1200–1920: Family, State and Church*, pages 241–260.

Florian Windhager, Matthias Schlögl, Maximilian Kaiser, Ágoston Zénó Bernád, Saminu Salisu, and Eva Mayr. 2017. Beyond One-Dimensional Portraits: A Synoptic Approach to the Visual Analysis of Biography Data. In *Proceedings of the Second Conference on Biographical Data in a Digital World*, pages 67–75, Linz, Austria.

Albin Zehe, Martin Becker, Lena Hettinger, Andreas Hotho, Isabella Reger, and Fotis Jannidis. 2016. Prediction of Happy Endings in German Novels based on Sentiment Information. In *Proceedings of DMNLP, Workshop at ECML/PKDD*, pages 9–16, Riva del Garda, Italy.

Andrea Zielinski, Calvin Spolwind, Henning Kroll, and Anna Grimm. 2023. A Dataset for Explainable Sentiment Analysis in the German Automotive Industry. In *Proceedings of the 13th Workshop on Computational Approaches to Subjectivity, Sentiment, & Social Media Analysis*, pages 138–148, Toronto, Canada. Association for Computational Linguistics.

Applying Information-theoretic Notions to Measure Effects of the Plain English Movement on English Law Reports and Scientific Articles

Sergei Bagdasarov
Language Science and Technology
Saarland University
sergeiba@lst.uni-saarland.de

Stefania Degaetano-Ortlieb
Language Science and Technology
Saarland University
s.degaetano@mx.uni-saarland.de

Abstract

We investigate the impact of the Plain English Movement (PEM) on the complexity of legal language in UK law reports from the 1950s-2010s, contrasting it with the evolution of scientific language. The PEM, emerging in the late 20th century, advocated for clear and understandable legal language. We define complexity through the concept of surprisal – an information-theoretic measure correlating with cognitive processing difficulty. Our research contrasts surprisal with traditional readability measures, which often overlook content. We hypothesize that, if the PEM has influenced legal language, there would be a reduction in complexity over time and a shift from a nominal to a more verbal style. We analyze text complexity and lexico-grammatical changes in line with PEM recommendations. Results indicate minimal impact of the PEM on both legal and scientific domains. This finding suggests future research should consider processing effort when advocating for linguistic norms to enhance accessibility.

1 Introduction

Legal language has been notorious for its intricate syntax and specialized jargon, making it challenging for non-experts to comprehend. This complexity has not only been a barrier to understanding for the general public but has also posed significant challenges for computational analysis. In response to this, the Plain English Movement (PEM) emerged as a pivotal initiative in the latter half of the 20th century, advocating for clear, concise, and understandable legal language (cf. Mazur (2000)).

Our study is corpus-based and explores whether this movement has led to a measurable change in the complexity of legal language, specifically UK law reports, from the 1950s to the 2010s. We contrast this with scientific language, which we hypothesize has not been similarly influenced by the PEM. By comparing the evolution of language in these two domains, we work towards uncovering the unique trajectories of language complexity in response to professional and societal pressures.

We define complexity based on the concept of surprisal – an information-theoretic measure of unpredictability in language, which has shown to be proportional to cognitive effort and thus processing difficulty (Hale, 2001; Levy, 2008). Thus, high surprisal in a text, indicative of less predictable content, is associated with increased cognitive processing effort and serves as a reliable indicator of increased language complexity (Smith and Levy, 2013). We contrast surprisal with readability measures usually used to measure language complexity but often criticized for not taking into account the content of the text being evaluated (cf. Schriver (1997); Mazur (2000)). In fact, while recently, in the computational linguistic community text simplification systems have been applied to simplify legal language (Garimella et al., 2022), many open questions remain, for example, which information should be retained. Here, a measure of informativity could enhance approaches on the matter.

We introduce the PEM and work on the diachronic tendency of phrasal compression as a densification strategy in specialized discourse, which is an opposite trend to what the PEM advocates. We present our rationale putting forward two main hypotheses regarding law reports: If the PEM has an impact, then we assume (H1) reduced complexity over time and (H2) change from a heavy nominal towards a verbal involved style. For scientific articles, we hypothesize no PEM impact. We then present the corpora used and the methodology applied to measure text complexity and to analyze lexico-grammatical changes related to the suggestions of the PEM. Finally, our result section dives into a macro-analytical diachronic perspective and a micro-analysis of the linguistic features typical of contemporary law reports and scientific texts. Results show that the PEM had little to no impact on

Proceedings of LaTeCH-CLfL 2024, pages 101–110
March 22, 2024

language use in these two domains. From this, we derive implications for future research that should account for processing effort when implementing linguistic norms towards increased accessibility.

2 Background and Rationale

2.1 Plain English Movement

The Plain English Movement (PEM) originated in the second half of the 20th century in response to the writing style of legal documents, incomprehensible for a general audience. While there had been some critical voices already in the 1960s, it was not until the 1970s when the PEM began to gain momentum and resulted in the adoption of the first governmental regulations, mainly in the U.S., imposing the use of a more reader-friendly language (Mazur, 2000; Williams, 2005). In subsequent decades, many other laws, regulations and initiatives followed, which testifies to a broad acceptance of the PEM in the legal community.

Although the PEM is mainly concerned with legal documents, there have also been important efforts to influence the writing of scientific articles, another domain that can be hardly understood by a lay audience. Plain language can be highly advantageous to the scientific community, with its benefits ranging from the general popularization of scientific research to the better ability to obtain funding. Despite the lack of compelling legislation on this matter, many important journals encourage researchers to use plain language in their papers (Locke, 2003; Sedgwick et al., 2021).

In the last decades, many style guides and guidelines have appeared that present the main principles of plain writing (Garner, 2001; European Commission, 2016; Federal Government of the United States, 2011). These principles are mainly driven by reducing processing cost and can be summarized into the following suggestions:

S1: Use short sentences. As processing cost is proportional to sentence length, the PEM recommends a max. of 15-20 words per sentence on average.

S2: Use 1st and 2nd person pronouns for a more personal connection with the reader.

S3: Avoid nominalizations and use verbal style instead (e.g. *apply* instead of *submit an application*) to promote a verbal style of writing that should enhance clarity and reduce sentence length.

S4: Avoid compounds as they leave implicit the semantic relations between nouns.

S5: Avoid unnecessary jargon and terminology where these can be replaced with general language without semantic loss.

S6: Avoid unnecessary abbreviations for the sake of clarity.

S7: Use active voice. Active voice allows shorter and generally easier-to-process sentences.

S8: Avoid *shall* because of its semantic ambiguity resulting from a generalized overuse in legal texts.[1]

We will investigate, whether these recommendations are somehow reflected as possible tendencies over time for legal and scientific texts.

2.2 Phrasal compression in specialized discourse

Both law reports and scientific articles are considered to be rather complex registers that can be hardly understood by non-experts. The most distinctive feature of both is a style of writing that favors nominal phrases – a preference illustrated in a number of synchronic studies (Breeze, 2019; Gotti, 2012).

Diachronically, the shift towards increasing phrasal complexity has been especially notorious in the case of scientific articles. While they used to rely on a more verbal style of writing with long subordinate clauses in the 17th and 18th centuries, the 19th century saw a sharp increase of prepositional phrases functioning as postmodifiers at the cost of clausal elements (Biber and Gray, 2016; Degaetano-Ortlieb and Teich, 2019). The shift towards a major phrasal complexity consolidated in the 20th century, with compound nouns adopting an increasingly important role in scientific articles (Biber and Gray, 2016; Degaetano-Ortlieb, 2021).

Although there was no such a dramatic transformation in the history of law reports, this register did evolve to include more nominal elements in the last 300 years, with its most prominent features being prepositional postmodifiers, compounds (albeit to a lesser extent than in scientific articles), and nominalizations (Biber and Gray, 2019).

2.3 Rationale

Considering the PEM suggestions, we put forward the following hypotheses: (H1) *Reduced complexity:* If the PEM suggestions influenced language use in these two domains, results should show shorter sentences and a lower degree of complexity

[1] Consider the following example: *The applicant shall be notified by registered mail in all cases where ...* (Federal Government of the United States, 2011). Here, ***shall*** can denote an obligation or be just describing a future action.

Decade	CoCELD		RSC	
	Number of Tokens	Number of Texts	Number of Tokens	Number of Texts
1950s	101,770	40	23,760,143	3,656
1960s	102,093	40	28.695,408	4,168
1970s	101,621	40	40,611,994	5,231
1980s	101,707	40	44,035,328	5,488
1990s	102,083	40	34,915,666	4,925
2000s	101,629	40	-	-
2010s	122,324	48	-	-

Table 1: Number of tokens and texts in CoCELD and RSC

over time, which we aim to capture by readability formulas and surprisal. (H2) *Nominal vs. involved verbal style:* If suggestions S2-S8 have an impact, distinctive features of more contemporary periods would be 1st and 2nd person pronouns and verbal style, while distinctive of earlier periods would be nominalizations and a heavy nominal style with abbreviations as well as the use of *shall*. In general, we assume the impact of the PEM to be more pronounced for law reports than for scientific articles.

3 Data and Methods

3.1 Corpora

For law reports, the Corpus of Contemporary English Legal Decisions (CoCELD) is used (Rodríguez-Puente and Hernández-Coalla, 2023). It contains legal decisions produced by the Privy Council, the House of Lords and the UK Supreme Court between 1950 and 2021. For research articles, we used the 6.0 version of the Royal Society Corpus (RSC), comprising the Proceedings and Transactions of the Royal Society of London (Kermes et al., 2016; Fischer et al., 2020). We selected a subcorpus from the RSC including texts from 1950 to 1996, which partly corresponds with the time span of CoCELD. The distribution of texts and tokens across decades in both corpora is summarized in Table 1.

Both corpora were annotated with TreeTagger using the Penn Treebank Tagset (Schmid, 1995)[2]. The corpora feature metadata (publication date; for RSC also authors, titles, journal series, etc), linguistic annotation (word, lemma and part of speech), and surprisal annotation (see Section 3.2.1).

3.2 Methods

We analyze the possible impact of the PEM by considering (a) text complexity using readability measures and surprisal to address H1 (reduced complexity), and (b) changes in the use of lexicogrammatical features to address H2 (nominal vs. involved verbal style).

3.2.1 Measuring text complexity

For text complexity, three metrics are employed: sentence length, Dale-Chall readability formula[3], and sentence-based surprisal.

Sentence length is a parameter directly addressed by the PEM. It should go down if any significant PEM influence exists. In case of CoCELD, we calculated median sentence length values for each text (40 texts per decade in total) and then calculated a single median value for each decade. Since RSC is substantially larger than CoCELD, we randomly selected 40 texts[4] for each decade to ensure better comparability between the corpora. The values were subsequently computed following the same procedure. All calculations were performed using a Python script.

Dale-Chall readability formula (Dale and Chall, 1948) is a commonly used readability metric that attempts to capture both syntactic and lexical complexity.[5] The score ranges from 4.9 or lower (level of <=4th-graders) to 9.9 (level of an average college student), and is calculated as follows:

$$0.1579 \times \left(\frac{\text{difficult words}}{\text{total words}} \times 100\right) + 0.0496 \times \frac{\text{total words}}{\text{total sentences}}$$

Surprisal (Shannon, 1948) is an information-theoretic measure proportional to processing effort

[2]The RSC has been parsed using Universal Dependencies (UD) syntax; however, it is important to note that, at the time this paper was published, we are still in the process of evaluating this parsed version.

[3]Flesh Reading Ease and Gunning Fog Index were much less accurate, indicating law reports to being on par with high-school knowledge. Thus, we excluded them from the analysis.

[4]Dale-Chall readability scores and sentence-based surprisal for RSC are based on the same sample.

[5]For calculation we used the *Textatistic* Python package (Hengel, 2022), which contains an extended version of the original word list used in the formula (e.g., verb tense forms and plural noun forms).

(Hale, 2001; Levy, 2008). It measures the amount of information (in bits) transmitted by a word in context: $S(word) = -\log_2 p(\text{word}|\text{context})$. As context, we use a trigram of the preceding three words of the given word. Similarly to sentence length, we calculate one median sentence-based surprisal score for each decade, estimating the overall processing cost at the text level. High surprisal indicates higher processing effort, indicating a more complex text. To calculate surprisal values for texts within each decade, we first establish a reference corpus for that decade. This reference corpus is composed of all the texts (of the RSC or CoCELD respectively) from the decade, excluding the specific text for which we are calculating surprisal. We then use this reference corpus to generate probabilities for each word in our target text. These probabilities form the basis for calculating surprisal. This method of using a decade-specific reference corpus is advantageous because it provides a contextually relevant baseline for understanding linguistic patterns and changes over time. By comparing the language in a specific text against the broader linguistic trends of its time period, we can more accurately assess the relative novelty or commonality of its usage, thereby gaining deeper insights into the evolving dynamics of language use within that historical context.

3.2.2 Analyzing lexico-grammatical changes

At the lexico-grammatical level, we are interested in linguistic features distinctive of law reports and scientific texts over time. For this, we use Kullback-Leibler Divergence, which is commonly applied to compare two probability distributions of linguistic features (see Klingenstein et al. (2014); Fankhauser et al. (2014); Degaetano-Ortlieb and Teich (2018); Barron et al. (2018) for application across the digital humanities). KLD indicates the number of additional bits of information needed to encode one distribution (here of a decade) using another (a previous decade), and is formalized as:

$$D(A||B) = \sum_i p(\text{feature}_i|A) \log_2 \frac{p(\text{feature}_i|A)}{p(\text{feature}_i|B)} \quad (1)$$

where A stands for a decade and B for a previous decade. Advantageous for interpretability is that KLD calculates the contributions of individual features to a divergence, allowing us to generate feature rankings with the most distinctive features of a decade.

For the lexical level, we apply a unigram model (all words), and for the grammatical level a trigram model (sequences of three parts of speech) to analyze diachronic changes. Given the KLD scores, we subsequently identify those decade pairs that showed the most noticeable differences (high overall divergence) and analyze high-ranking features distinctive of the comparison.

To measure changes related to processing effort, we again use surprisal, but here calculated as the average amount of information that a word or part-of-speech trigram transmits across the whole time period (rather than in a single text). The average surprisal of individual words is calculated by summing the surprisal values of all occurrences of a word and dividing them by the total number of occurrences in a decade:

$$\text{AvSrp}(\text{word}) = \frac{1}{|\text{word}|} \sum_i -\log_2 p(\text{word}_i|\text{context}_i) \quad (2)$$

For part-of-speech trigrams, we first calculate the average surprisal of each of their individual words, sum all resulting values, and divide them by the number of occurrences N of the part-of-speech trigrams in a decade:

$$\text{AvSrp}(\text{postrigram}) = \frac{1}{|\text{N}|} \sum_i \left(\frac{\text{AvS}(\text{word}) + \text{AvS}(\text{word}) + \text{AvS}(\text{word})}{3} \right)_i \quad (3)$$

4 Results and Analysis

Considering the suggestions put forward by the PEM, first, we test whether the overall text complexity is reduced especially for law reports (H1). Second, an in-depth analysis of lexico-grammatical features will show whether the heavy nominal style changes towards a more involved verbal style (H2).

4.1 Overall text complexity

Considering sentence length (see Table 2), suggested to be kept short by the PEM, for law reports it stays relatively stable. For scientific articles, sentence length goes slightly down. However, both remain above the limit of 20 words recommended by the PEM. Based on the Dale-Chall formula, law reports show a continuous increase reaching 9.55 in the 2010s, matching almost the highest possible score and corresponding to language use at the level of a college student. The values for scientific articles are even higher (e.g., 10.08 in 1950s and 10.52

Decade	Sentence Length	
	Law	Science
1950s	31.0	27.0
1960s	30.0	27.0
1970s	29.0	26.5
1980s	30.0	27.8
1990s	29.5	25.0
2000s	27.0	-
2010s	32.0	-

Table 2: Median sentence length in law reports and scientific articles (as measured by the number of tokens)

in 1990s), indicating a major degree of complexity. These results are confirmed by sentence-based surprisal, showing a slight continuous increase for both domains (law: from 6.61 in the 1950s to 6.97 bits in the 2010s; science: from 6.41 to 6.85 bits).

This indicates no shift towards reduced complexity, on the contrary, both registers have become even more challenging to process over time.

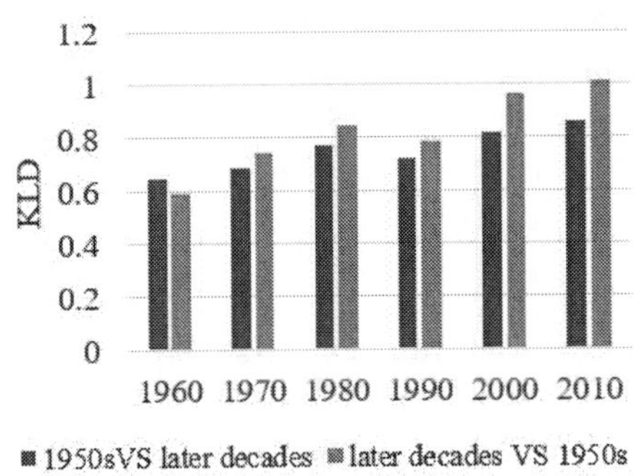

Figure 1: KLD comparison for the 1950s given the other periods and vice versa for law reports.

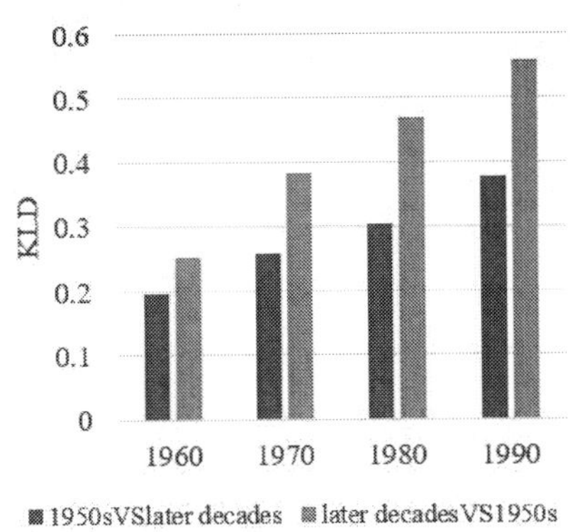

Figure 2: KLD comparison for the 1950s given the other periods and vice versa for scientific articles.

4.2 Changes at the lexico-grammatical level

4.2.1 General diachronic trends

We analyze changes at the lexical level by first asking (a) how much language use of the 1950s can be modeled by a more contemporary model, and (b) how well a language model of the 1950s can capture contemporary language use. Here, we make advantage of KLD's asymmetry (see Section 3), which allows us to model this directionality.

Figure 1 shows a comparison for law reports. For both directions, divergence increases, but in particular for the more contemporary models, which increasingly diverge from the 1950s model over time (orange bars). Thus, more contemporary language use is not well modeled by past language use.

Figure 2 shows a comparison for scientific articles. Again, KLD rises over time, with an even more pronounced tendency, showing how contemporary models are increasingly less well modeled by the 1950s model.

To better understand what drives an increase in divergence, we consider lexical features which are distinctive (i.e. have a major contribution to the increase in divergence). As depicted in Figure 3, law reports from the 1950s are characterized by the presence of words forming part of formulaic expressions (*lordship, noble*), auxiliary *be*, and pronouns (e.g., *I, my, me, their*, etc.). To a lesser extent also modal verbs (*must, can, shall*), mental verbs such as *think* and *agree*, and the relative pronoun *which* are distinctive.

On the contrary, the 2010s (see Figure 4) are characterized by the use of honorifics (*mr, ms*), abbreviations (*ltd, wlr, ukpc*, etc.) and a more pronounced use of nominalizations, especially those ending with *-tion* (*conviction, application, constitution*, etc.).

For scientific articles, the most distinctive feature in the later decades (see Figure 6) is *et* proba-

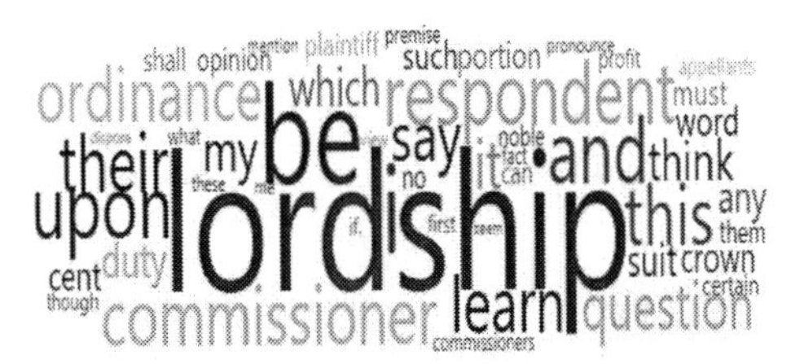

Figure 3: Lexical features distinctive of the 1950s when modeled by the 2010s for law reports

bly indicating an increase in multi-authored papers. Other relevant features include the conjunction *and*, prepositions *in* and *for* as well as the 1st person pronouns *I* and *we*. Both earlier and later decades include many terms of art, some of which are nominalizations (*absorption, bifurcation, selection*, etc). These tendencies seem to reflect the trend towards phrasal compression indicated by Biber and Gray (2016, 207), which is also depicted by the obvious amount of nominal lexis in the 1990s indicating an increased compound use (cf. Degaetano-Ortlieb (2021)). In contrast, we can observe a more varied use of word classes in the 1950s (see Figures 5) with the determiner *the*, the verb *be*, various prepositions (*of, about, at*), post-modification patterns (*by, which, to*), general verbs (*give, make, obtain, show*), and conjunctions (*but, so*).

4.2.2 Inspecting PEM influence

Let us now have a closer look at those features that are of particular interest to us in the context of the PEM. Here, we specifically address hypothesis H2, i.e. most of the PEM suggestions S2-S8 above for the use of a more involved less nominal style.

Use 1st and 2nd personal pronouns As illustrated in Figure 7, for law reports the overall frequency of personal pronouns[6] decreased, mainly due to the decline in 1st person pronouns, while 3rd person pronouns remained relatively stable over time. This is an indicator of a distant and objective style of writing as opposed to a more involved and subjective one recommended by the PEM (Rodríguez-Puente, 2019).

In scientific articles, 1st person pronouns, in contrast, became more common (see Figure 8). This trend has been observed in various studies on scientific writing (most prominently Hyland (2005)'s work) highlighting that by using personal pronouns, authors can create a sense of dialogue and interaction, making their writing more accessible and reader-friendly, which is in line with the PEM.

Avoid nominalizations Nominalizations[7] rise in frequency in both law reports (6,000 to 7,200 per million) and scientific articles (32,000 to 32,600 per million). This goes clearly against the PEM. We also consider the surprisal of nominalizations to observe tendencies in terms of processing effort. A rise in the use of conventionalized nominalizations would lead to a decrease in surprisal (enhanced predictability and lower processing effort). However, surprisal stays quite stable in both registers (see Figures 9 and 10), which seems to indicate a constant varied use of nominalizations.

Avoid compounds To inspect diachronic trends in compound use, we run KLD at the level of part-of-speech trigrams which allows us to determine distinctive grammatical features of variation for the more contemporary periods against the 1950s.

By inspecting the top ranking phrase and clause types[8], both law reports and scientific articles evolved quite similarly shifting even more towards a denser style of writing with a high proportion of nominal elements (see Figure 11). Importantly, most nominal trigrams characteristic of the later decades are either compounds (gray, NP (comp)) or complex noun phrases (orange, NP+)[9], which contradicts the suggestions of the PEM.

Compare also the top 5 most distinctive trigrams for law reports showing a varied set of trigrams distinctive of the 1960s, while the 2010s are marked by nominal trigrams (see Tables 3 and 4).

We also observe an increase in the frequency of two-noun and three-noun compounds in both registers (from 1,241 to 2,271 per million in law

Figure 4: Lexical features distinctive of the 2010s when modeled by the 1950s for law reports

[6]Following Rodríguez-Puente (2019), we focused on the nominative forms of personal pronouns (*I, you, he, she, we, they*), their accusative and genitive forms and the corresponding reflexive forms.

[7]We consider nouns with the following suffixes: $-ion$, $-ment$, $-al$, $-ibility$, $-ty$, $-ness$.

[8]We grouped part-of-speech trigrams into phrase and clause types as follows: NP: nominal phrase including premodification by adjective and use of determiner, NP+: nominal phrase with a postmodifier or conjunction, NP (comp): compound phrase, VP: clause, VP (modal/ing/ed): clause with modal verb, -ing or -ed forms, to-inf: to-infinitive clause, wh-clause, AdvP: adverbial phrase, CC: conjunction, PrepP: prepositional phrase, that-clause, AdjP: adjectival phrase

[9]Complex noun phrases are grouped under the NP+ label, which includes noun phrases with prepositional or non-finite postmodifiers or noun clauses with more than one head joined by a conjunction.

Figure 5: Lexical features distinctive of the 1950s when modeled by the 1990s for scientific articles

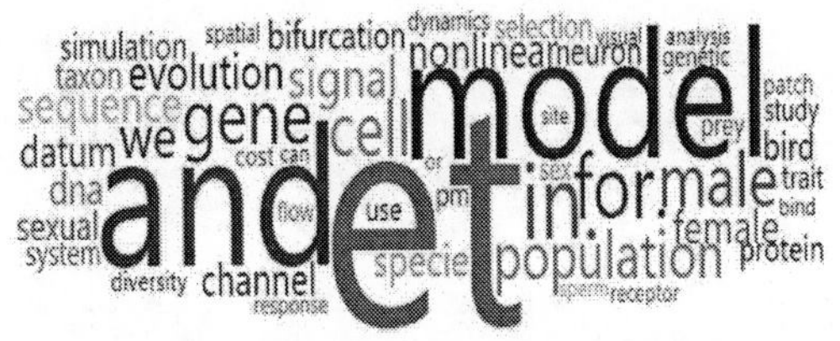

Figure 6: Lexical features distinctive of the 1990s when modeled by the 1950s for scientific articles

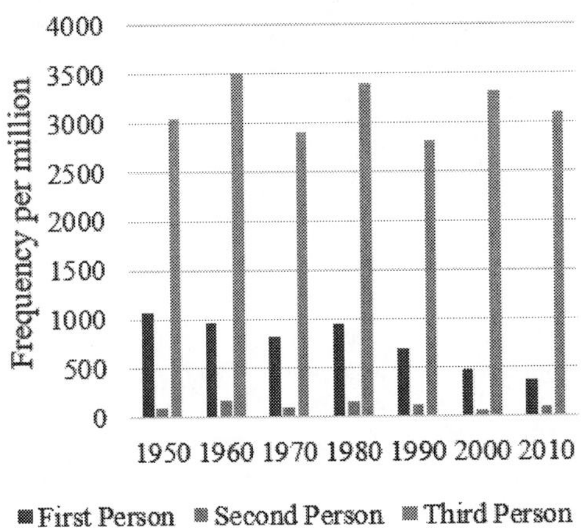

Figure 7: Evolution of personal pronouns in law reports

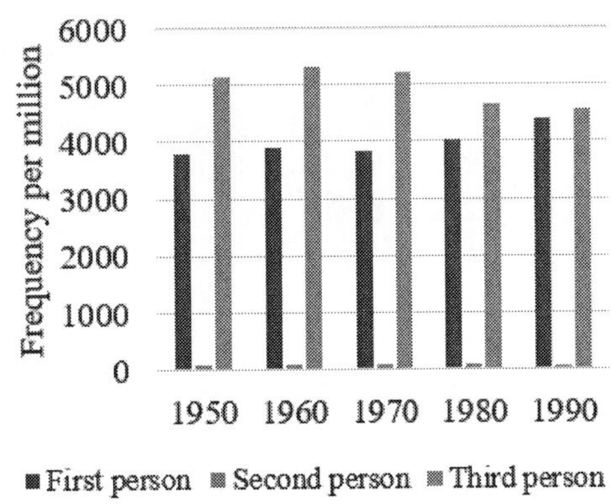

Figure 8: Evolution of personal pronouns in scientific articles

PoS	Example	KLD
VV.IN.DT	agree with the	0.0026
PP.MD.VV	I must regard	0.0023
DT.NN.WDT	this incident which	0.0022
CC.IN.DT	or by the	0.0019
PP.NNS.MD	their Lordships may	0.0019

Table 3: Top 5 trigrams characteristic of law reports drafted in 1960s

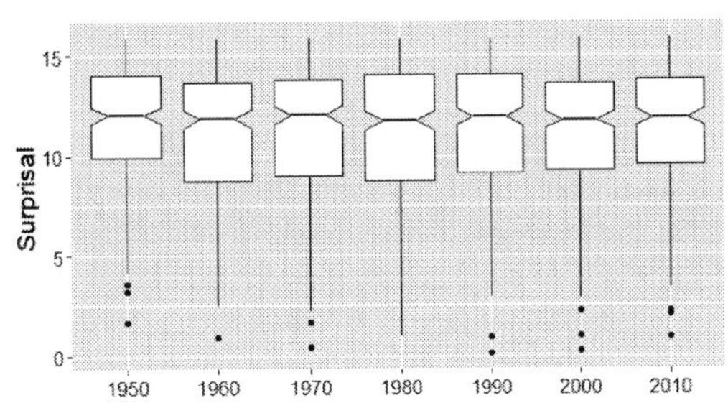

Figure 9: Average surprisal of nominalizations in law reports

reports and from 28,188 to 35,034 per million in scientific articles, X^2 p-value < 0.01), indicating a higher reliance on compact syntactic structures. To link this back to processing effort, we again consider surprisal. For illustration, we compare compound patterns distinctive of the recent decades with simple nominal phrases characteristic of the earlier decades (see Figure 12). There is a considerable difference in surprisal between compounds with three lexical words (e.g JJ.NN.NN: adjective+noun+noun) and simple nominal phrases. Even compound patterns with one function word (e.g., preposition (IN) or conjunction (CC)), which are lower in surprisal, have slightly higher surprisal values than simple nominal phrases.

Interestingly, this trend holds also for the NP+ category (i.e. complex nominal phrases such as NNS.IN.JJ): Patterns distinctive of the later periods tend to be more informationally loaded (higher surprisal) than those distinctive of the earlier periods. This is illustrated in the following examples, where example (1) shows one possible lexical realization of the DT.NNS.VVN trigram (characteristic of the earlier periods) and example (2) shows one possible realization of the NNS.IN.JJ trigram (characteristic of the later periods). The numbers indicate the average surprisal calculated on the decade basis for each element of the trigrams (average values over the trigram are provided in square brackets).

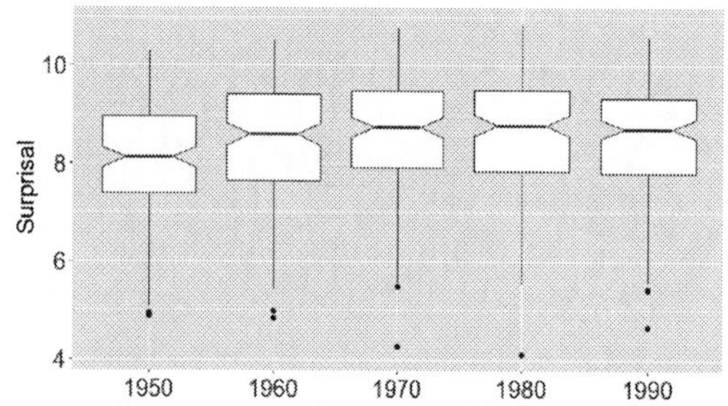

Figure 10: Average surprisal of nominalizations in scientific articles

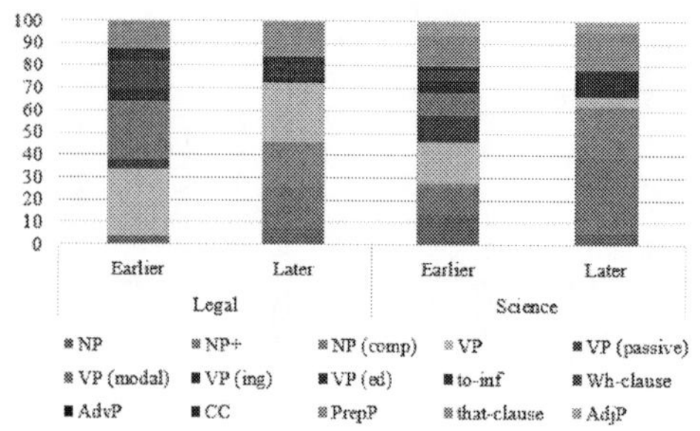

Figure 11: Proportion of the PoS trigrams in law reports and scientific articles

PoS	Example	KLD
NP.CC.NP	Regulations and Guidance	0.0072
NP.NP.NP	Land Registration Act	0.0062
IN.NP.NP.	by Theresa Henry	0.0058
NN.IN.NN	disclosure of information	0.0054
DT.NN.NN	the anonymity order	0.0046

Table 4: Top 5 trigrams characteristic of law reports drafted in 2010s

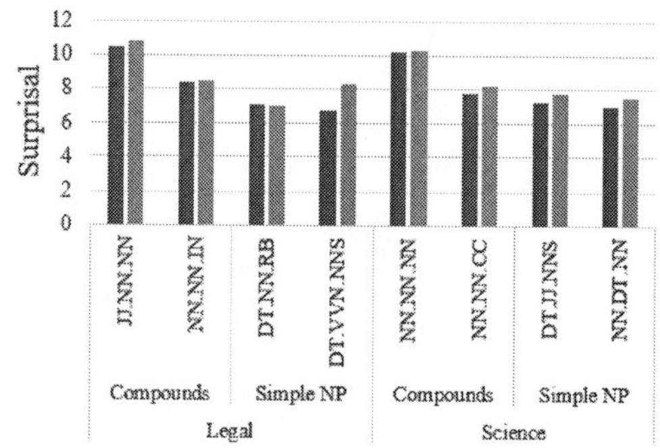

Figure 12: Surprisal of compound patterns and simple nominal phrases in law reports and scientific articles. The blue bars show the average surprisal for the first decade (1950s), the blue ones the average surprisal for the last decade (2010s for law reports and 1990s for scientific articles).

(1) *In the wheat grain a supplementary effect was demonstrated between **the/1.841 proteins/8.530 situated/11.447** [7.27] in the outer layers of the grain (bran) and those contained in the endosperm.* (RSC)

(2) *The importance of CMT was that it provided the first really practical means of detecting **bodies/8.902 at/6.034 normal/9.555** [8.16] room temperature.* (RSC)

In summary, compounds are not only more frequently used, which goes against the PEM suggestion but are also heavy in their informational content for both law reports and scientific articles.

Use active voice As already shown, verbal patterns become less distinctive of both domains over time at the expense of a pronounced nominal style. This applies also to passive constructions which dropped significantly in frequency (from 2,923 to 2,611 per million in law reports and from 17,574 to 12,720 per million in scientific articles, X^2 p-value < 0.01 for both registers). Although this is in line with the PEM, an inspection of general English as depicted by the LOB and FLOB corpora shows that this is more likely a general trend in the evolution of the English language, with a significant decrease in the use of passives (from 11,324 to 10,541 per million, X^2 p-value < 0.01).

Avoid *shall* As already suggested by the word clouds at the lexical level (see again Figure 3), *shall* has decreased in frequency over time and is distinctive (t-test with p-value < 0.01) for the 1950s. It primarily occurs in direct quotations from other legal documents (see Example (3)).[10]

(3) *Section 5 provided that "no owner **shall** ... convey [or] agree to convey ... any land in a new subdivision ... "* (CoCELD)

Thus, even though the decrease of *shall* might have been triggered by the PEM, the influence on law reports seems to be rather indirect.

5 Conclusion

We investigated the impact of the Plain English Movement (PEM) on the complexity of legal language in UK law reports from the 1950s to the 2010s, contrasting this with the evolution of scientific language. The study was grounded in the hy-

[10]Evaluated on a random sample of 50 occurrences of *shall* from the 1950s and 2010s each. The analysis yielded 82% and 88% of direct quotations in 1950s and 2010s, respectively.

pothesis that if the PEM had a significant influence, we should see a reduction in language complexity (H1) and a shift from a nominal to a more verbal style (H2) in legal texts. Conversely, we anticipated that scientific language, not being a direct target of the PEM, would not demonstrate similar changes.

Our findings, however, reveal that the impact of the PEM on the complexity of legal language has been minimal. Despite the efforts of the PEM, legal language has largely maintained its traditional complexity and style. This suggests that professional norms and the inherent nature of legal discourse may resist simplification efforts, even in the face of concerted campaigns like the PEM.

Surprisal and more elaborated notions of it (cf. Futrell (2023)) can serve as a robust indicator of the cognitive load imposed on readers, thereby guiding the development of more accessible yet accurate renditions of complex information, often not captured by readability measures. We have employed it to quantify complexity to account for the unpredictability and processing effort associated with language comprehension. However, its application would not only enhance readability but also ensure that critical nuances and technical accuracies are not lost in the process of simplification. For example, endeavors to produce simpler legal texts (cf. Garimella et al. (2022)) would profit from using approaches which reflect processing effort and measure its reduction. The approach is general in nature and can be applied across various fields.

References

Alexander T. J. Barron, Jenny Huang, Rebecca L. Spang, and Simon DeDeo. 2018. Individuals, institutions, and innovation in the debates of the French Revolution. *Proceedings of the National Academy of Sciences*, 115(18):4607–4612.

Douglas Biber and Bethany Gray. 2016. *Grammatical complexity in academic English: Linguistic change in writing*. Studies in English Language. Cambridge University Press, Cambridge.

Douglas Biber and Bethany Gray. 2019. Are law reports an 'agile' or an 'uptight' register? tracking patterns of historical change in the use of colloquial and complexity features. In Teresa Fanego and Paula Rodríguez-Puente, editors, *Corpus-based Research on Variation in English Legal Discourse*, number 91 in Studies in Corpus Linguistics, pages 147–170. John Benjamins Publishing Company.

Ruth Breeze. 2019. Part-of-speech patterns in legal genres: Text-internal dynamics from a corpus-based perspective. In Teresa Fanego and Paula Rodríguez-Puente, editors, *Corpus-based Research on Variation in English Legal Discourse*, number 91 in Studies in Corpus Linguistics, pages 79–104. John Benjamins Publishing Company.

Edgar Dale and Jeanne S. Chall. 1948. A formula for predicting readability: Instructions. *Educational Research Bulletin*, 27(2):37–54.

Stefania Degaetano-Ortlieb. 2021. Measuring informativity: The rise of compounds as informationally dense structures in 20th century scientific english. In Elena Soave and Douglas Biber, editors, *Corpus Approaches to Register Variation*, chapter 11, pages 291–312. John Benjamins Publishing Company.

Stefania Degaetano-Ortlieb and Elke Teich. 2018. Using relative entropy for detection and analysis of periods of diachronic linguistic change. In *Proceedings of the 2nd Joint SIGHUM Workshop on Computational Linguistics for Cultural Heritage, Social Sciences, Humanities and Literature at COLING*, pages 22–33, Santa Fe, NM. Association for Computational Linguistics.

Stefania Degaetano-Ortlieb and Elke Teich. 2019. Toward an optimal code for communication: The case of scientific English. *Corpus Linguistics and Linguistic Theory*, 0(0):1–33. Ahead of print.

European Commission. 2016. *English Style Guide: A Handbook for Authors and Translators in the European Commission*. European Union.

Peter Fankhauser, Jörg Knappen, and Elke Teich. 2014. Exploring and visualizing variation in language resources. In *Proceedings of the 9th Language Resources and Evaluation Conference (LREC)*, pages 4125–4128, Reykjavik, Iceland. European Language Resources Association.

Federal Government of the United States. 2011. *Federal Plain Language Guidelines*.

Stefan Fischer, Jörg Knappen, Katrin Menzel, and Elke Teich. 2020. The Royal Society Corpus 6.0: Providing 300+ years of scientific writing for humanistic study. In *Proceedings of the Language Resources and Evaluation Conference (LREC)*, pages 794–802, Marseille, France. European Language Resources Association.

Richard Futrell. 2023. Information-theoretic principles in incremental language production. *Proceedings of the National Academy of Sciences*, 120(39):e2220593120.

Aparna Garimella, Abhilasha Sancheti, Vinay Aggarwal, Ananya Ganesh, Niyati Chhaya, and Nandakishore Kambhatla. 2022. Text simplification for legal domain: Insights and challenges. In *Proceedings of the Natural Legal Language Processing Workshop 2022*, pages 296–304, Abu Dhabi, United Arab Emirates (Hybrid). Association for Computational Linguistics.

Bryan A. Garner. 2001. *Legal Writing in Plain English: A Text with Exercises*. University of Chicago Press.

Maurizio Gotti. 2012. Text And Genre. In *The Oxford Handbook of Language and Law*. Oxford University Press.

John Hale. 2001. A probabilistic Earley parser as a psycholinguistic model. In *Proceedings of the 2nd meeting of the North American Chapter of the Association for Computational Linguistics on Language technologies*, pages 1–8, Pittsburgh, PA.

Erin Hengel. 2022. Publishing While Female: are Women Held to Higher Standards? Evidence from Peer Review. *The Economic Journal*, 132(648):2951–2991.

Ken Hyland. 2005. *Metadiscourse: Exploring Interaction in Writing*. Continuum.

Hannah Kermes, Stefania Degaetano-Ortlieb, Ashraf Khamis, Jörg Knappen, and Elke Teich. 2016. The Royal Society Corpus: From uncharted data to corpus. In *Proceedings of the 10th International Conference on Language Resources and Evaluation (LREC)*, pages 1928–1931, Portorož, Slovenia. European Language Resources Association.

Sara Klingenstein, Tim Hitchcock, and Simon DeDeo. 2014. The civilizing process in London's Old Bailey. *Proceedings of the National Academy of Sciences*, 111(26):9419–9424.

Roger P. Levy. 2008. Expectation-based syntactic comprehension. *Cognition*, 106(3):1126–1177.

Joanne Locke. 2003. The plain language movement. *AMWA Journal*, 18(1):5–8.

Beth Mazur. 2000. Revisiting plain language. *Technical Communication*, 47:205–211.

Paula Rodríguez-Puente. 2019. Interpersonality in legal written discourse: A diachronic analysis of personal pronouns in law reports, 1535 to present. In Teresa Fanego and Paula Rodríguez-Puente, editors, *Corpus-based Research on Variation in English Legal Discourse*, number 91 in Studies in Corpus Linguistics, pages 171–200. John Benjamins Publishing Company.

Paula Rodríguez-Puente and David Hernández-Coalla. 2023. The : A new tool for analysing recent changes in english legal discourse. *ICAME Journal*, 47(1):109–117.

Helmut Schmid. 1995. Improvements in Part-of-Speech Tagging with an application to German. In *Proceedings of the ACL SIGDAT-Workshop*, Cambridge, MA.

Karen A. Schriver. 1997. *Dynamics in Document Design: Creating Text for Readers*. John Wiley Sons, New York, NY.

Cassie Sedgwick, Laura Belmonte, Amanda Margolis, Patricia Osborn Shafer, Jennifer Pitterle, and Barry E. Gidal. 2021. Extending the reach of science – talk in plain language. *Epilepsy Behavior Reports*, 16:100493.

Claude E. Shannon. 1948. A mathematical theory of communication. *Bell System Technical Journal*, 27:379–423, 623–656.

Nathaniel J. Smith and Roger Levy. 2013. The effect of word predictability on reading time is logarithmic. *Cognition*, 128(3):302–319.

Christopher Williams. 2005. *Tradition and Change in Legal English*. Peter Lang Verlag, Lausanne, Schweiz.

Uncovering the Handwritten Text in the Margins: End-to-end Handwritten Text Detection and Recognition

Liang Cheng[1,*], Jonas Frankemölle[2,*], Adam Axelsson[1,*] and Ekta Vats[1,†]
[1]Department of Information Technology, Uppsala University, Sweden
[2]Department of Archives, Libraries and Museums, Uppsala University, Sweden
[†]ekta.vats@it.uu.se

Abstract

The pressing need for digitization of historical documents has led to a strong interest in designing computerised image processing methods for automatic handwritten text recognition. However, not much attention has been paid on studying the handwritten text written in the margins, i.e. marginalia, that also forms an important source of information. Nevertheless, training an accurate and robust recognition system for marginalia calls for data-efficient approaches due to the unavailability of sufficient amounts of annotated multi-writer texts. Therefore, this work presents an end-to-end framework for automatic detection and recognition of handwritten marginalia, and leverages data augmentation and transfer learning to overcome training data scarcity. The detection phase involves investigation of R-CNN and Faster R-CNN networks. The recognition phase includes an attention-based sequence-to-sequence model, with ResNet feature extraction, bidirectional LSTM-based sequence modeling, and attention-based prediction of marginalia. The effectiveness of the proposed framework has been empirically evaluated on the data from early book collections found in the Uppsala University Library in Sweden. Source code and pre-trained models are available at Github[1].

1 Introduction

Libraries and archives across the globe are in possession of rich cultural heritage collections to be digitized for preservation and preventing degradation over time. For example, the Uppsala University Library in Sweden maintains several early book collections, dating back to the 1400s. An example of such a collection is the Walleriana book collection, encompassing medicine and science (uub). These collections are an important source of evidence for the European history and are valuable for researchers. Much of the content from these collections is well documented and is available online.

However, many books and documents, in addition to printed text, contain handwritten marginalia i.e. text written in the margins. This marginalia are also an important source of information for researchers, but is not as voluminous as the printed text. The presence of marginalia is sometimes mentioned, but its content is not. This is also due to poor readability of handwritten marginalia texts and challenges such as high variability in different writing styles, languages and scripts. Therefore, it is of great value to develop computational methods for digitization of the handwritten marginalia to make it as available as the printed text of these collections.

To do so, this work presents an end-to-end deep learning based approach for handwritten marginalia detection and recognition. Two different deep learning architectures: Region-based Convolutional Neural Network (R-CNN) and (Faster R-CNN) are studied for marginalia detection. The aim is for the networks to predict the coordinates of handwritten marginalia based on an input document image. To digitize the contents of the marginalia, there needs to be a way to automatically read it. To achieve this, an algorithm for segmenting handwritten text to individual words is also presented. Finally, when the marginalia have been identified and segmented, each word is fed in to an attention-based encoder-decoder network for handwritten text recognition (HTR), i.e. Attention-HTR introduced in our previous work in (Kass and Vats, 2022). The encoder block constitutes ResNet feature extraction and bidirectional LSTM-based sequence modeling stages, and the prediction stage consists of a decoder and a content-based attention mechanism.

To train the marginalia detector network, a sam-

*Equal contribution
[1]https://github.com/adamaxelsson/Project-Marginalia

Proceedings of LaTeCH-CLfL 2024, pages 111–120
March 22, 2024 ©2024 Association for Computational Linguistics

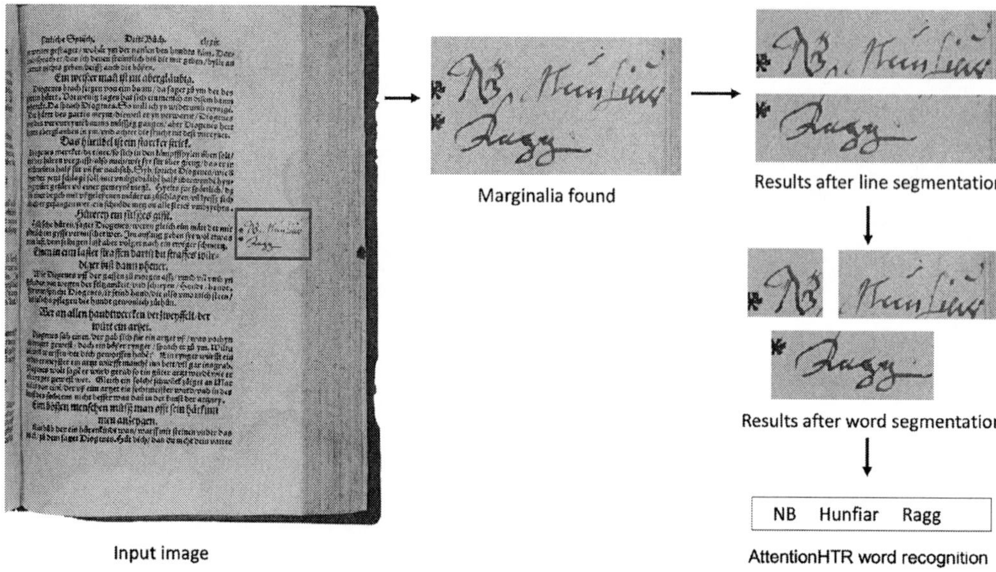

Figure 1: Overall pipeline of the end-to-end marginalia detection and recognition framework. The recognition result can be further improved using a suitable language model.

ple dataset of 513 scanned pages from Uppsala University Library's book collections is used. The dataset was labelled by an expert as part of this work using an open-source tool LabelMe (Russell et al., 2008), and the data thus obtained contains labeled coordinates for the marginalia, which are used as the targets for the network training. The overall pipeline of the end-to-end- marginalia detection and recognition framework is presented in Figure 1.

To the best of authors' knowledge, this is the first attempt at extracting the old historical handwritten text in the margins using an end-to-end detection and recognition pipeline. The research is reproducible, with user-friendly and modular designed code, and provide scope for future research and exploration of marginalias.

2 Related Work

Since the advent of deep neural networks, the HTR research has witnessed significant advancement in method design and development, with popular approaches such as Transformers based architectures TrOCR (Li et al., 2023) and attention-based sequence to sequence models (Kass and Vats, 2022; Bluche et al., 2017; Kang et al., 2019). Our previous work (Kass and Vats, 2022) introduced an end-to-end HTR system based on attention encoder-decoder networks, where the attention-based architecture is simple, modular, and reproducible, allowing more data to be added in the pipeline.

There have been other attempts at automatically reading historical handwritten documents (Nockels et al., 2022). For example, (Aradillas et al., 2020) discusses the challenge of dealing with different styles of handwriting. Since two documents can be from completely different centuries and countries, there is bound to be a lot of variability in the handwriting. The solution that is presented by the authors is to use transfer learning. First, a network is trained on a large set containing handwritten text of modern English. This base network can then be tweaked, depending on what kind of text will be processed. For example, if the network is to be used for a certain collection, a subset of this collection can be used to further train the network. Doing this can make the network significantly better at making predictions on that collection. The benefit of this technique is that since some collections can be very small, it can be difficult to train a network solely on that collection without running the risk of over-fitting. Transfer learning handles this problem by first creating a good general model, that is then tweaked and specialized to a certain dataset.

Another related work (Bluche, 2016) presents a joint line segmentation and transcription approach for end-to-end handwritten paragraph recognition. To do so, handwritten text is automatically segmented into individual lines by using Multi-Dimensional Long Short-Term Memory Recurrent

Neural Networks, or MDLSTM-RNN for short.

However, the problem of reading the text in the margins is relatively under-explored (Goodwin, 2021). The work (Bold and Wagstaff, 2017) highlighted the importance of marginal annotations for the community and how it benefits the readers and historians. For example, for historians working with texts, marginalia can provide insights into earlier readers and their perspectives. There have been some attempts at studying the marginalia notes and drafts by Moby-Dick author Herman Melville in (Ohge et al., 2018; Lambie et al., 2022; Hitchcock et al., 2023). These works focus on the visualization of marginalia, gender research and knowledge exploration for instance. On the other hand, our proposed work focuses on developing advanced computational methods for automatic detection and recognition of marginalia, leveraging modern deep learning models and our reproducible research.

3 Methodology

The methodology is divided into three parts: localizing the marginalia (using R-CNN and Faster R-CNN); segmenting the found text; and attention-based text recognition pipeline. In the following section, the methods that have been used to accomplish these functionalities will be presented.

3.1 Data Preprocessing

As part of the project, data was collected from the early book collections at Uppsala University Library that contain marginalia. The data was prepared and labelled by an expert using an open-source labelling tool *LabelMe* (Russell et al., 2008), where for an input image, the marginalia bounding box coordinates were obtained. A total of 513 labeled images were given, and they were randomly divided into training and test sets in the ratio of 9:1. Data augmentation was performed to supplement the training set, which involves flipping each training image horizontally, adding Gaussian noise, and randomly changing brightness or contrast. With data augmentation, the training set size was increased to 1848. In addition, the size of each image was re-scaled to 350*500 to reduce the computational cost.

3.2 Marginalia Detection: R-CNN

R-CNN uses cropped images, also known as regions of interest (ROI), as input. In localizing marginalia, R-CNN is a classification model in which the input images are classified into two categories: marginalia and non-marginalia, and AlexNet (Krizhevsky et al., 2012) is used as the network structure.

The first step in R-CNN experiments is to generate training samples, including ROI of marginalia and non-marginalia. To create ROI of marginalia, the pre-marked bounding box of marginalia is used. We first cut the marginalia parts from the image based on the bounding box coordinates, cropped it into different pieces according the the ratio of length and width, and resized them into 227*227. As for generating ROI of non-marginalia, all the images are processed by Maximally Stable Extremal Regions (MSER) algorithm (Matas et al., 2004). This algorithm is based on the concept of watershed: binarizing the image between the threshold $[0, 255]$, then the image would go through a process from completely black to completely white. In this process, the area of some connected regions change subtly with the increase of the threshold, and this kind of region is called MSER.

$$v_i = \frac{|Q_{i+\Delta} - Q_{i-\Delta}|}{|Q_i|} \quad (1)$$

where Q_i represents the area of the i-th connected region; Δ indicates a small threshold change (water injection); when v_i is less than a given threshold, the region is considered to be MSER. The segmentation of one image is shown in Figure 2.

After the bounding boxes are obtained, the tiny boxes are removed at first. Then *Intersection over Union*, or *IoU* is calculated for the rest of the bounding boxes, and 4 different boxes with $IoU = 0$ are selected as non-marginalia training samples for every image. Applying the same crop and resize procedure as marginalia part to acquire ROI of non-marginalia as the input for model training.

After the preparation of training samples is finished, the next step is to construct the neural network. This R-CNN model uses AlexNet as the network structure, which includes 1 input layer, 5 convolutional layers, 2 fully connected layers and 1 output layer. The basic structure of this network is similar to the original AlexNet (Krizhevsky et al., 2012), only the number of neurons on the fully connected layers and output layer are changed to 500, 20 and 2 according to the number of categories in the actual dataset.

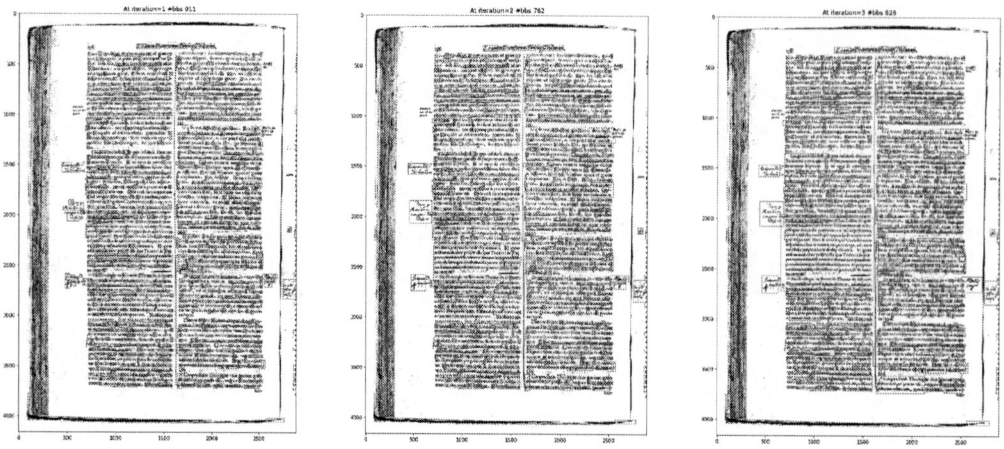

Figure 2: Result of MSER with iteration=3, Δ=1.1, i=0.1

3.3 Marginalia Detection: Faster R-CNN

R-CNN has drawbacks, most of all an expensive region proposal computation due to the selective search algorithm. To overcome this run-time issue, we investigated Faster R-CNN (Ren et al., 2015) that combines a region proposal network (RPN) with a Fast R-CNN. The Fast R-CNN runs a fully convolutional network to map an image into a lower resolution spatial feature map. Then, a region of interest (ROI) pooling operator converts each proposed region into a fixed dimensional representation which is the input to a neural network that predicts the object category and the box regression.

Instead of using the selective search algorithm, Faster R-CNN applies RPN, which is a fully convolutional network that generates region proposals with different scales and aspect ratios. The RPN can be trained and therefore produces better region proposals than the selective search algorithm in the R-CNN. It runs a sliding window over a feature map and determines for different anchor boxes whether there is an object. Further, it predicts deltas to the anchor box to improve its fit. It is a single, unified network that is computationally less expensive than a R-CNN, as the RPN and Fast R-CNN networks share the convolutional computations.

In our implementation, we use the pre-trained ResNet-50 as a network structure for the Faster R-CNN. As we are only interested in one object category, the network predicts 2 classes, marginalia or non-marginalia, as well as the 4 box coordinates. We trained the Faster R-CNN for 13 epochs and a learning rate of 0.001.

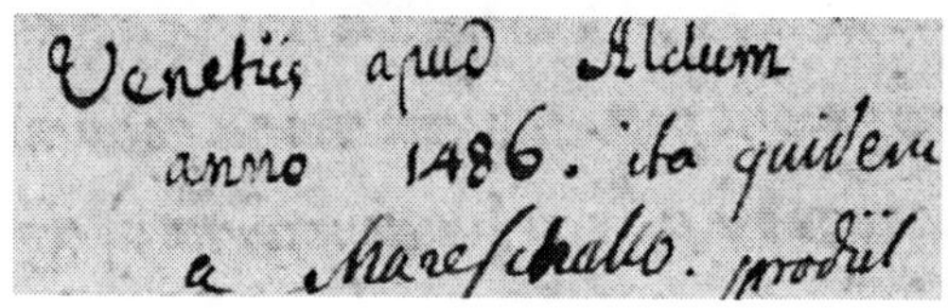

Figure 3: A sample image of marginalia found by the model.

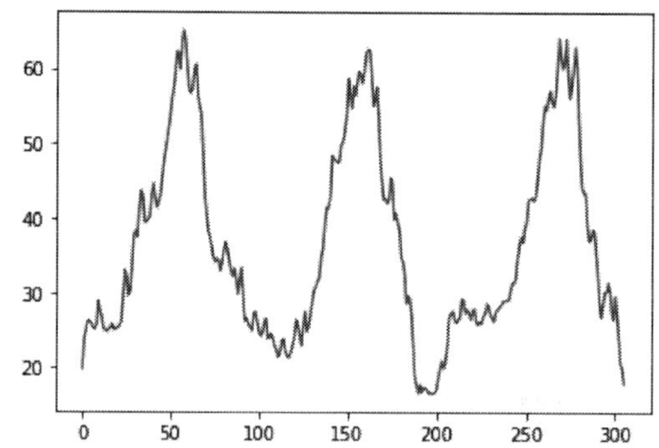

Figure 4: The result of horizontal projection on the image from Figure 3

3.4 Marginalia Segmentation

To segment the handwritten marginalia into individual words for further processing, each line of the text must first be identified. To do so, a *sobel* filter is used to emphasize the edges on an image. This is followed by a horizontal projection to the image, which is the sum of pixels on each pixel row. An example image and the result of this projection can be seen in figures 3 and 4 respectively.

The peaks that can be seen in the horizontal projection in Figure 4 shows us where the lines of text are located. This information is used to crop

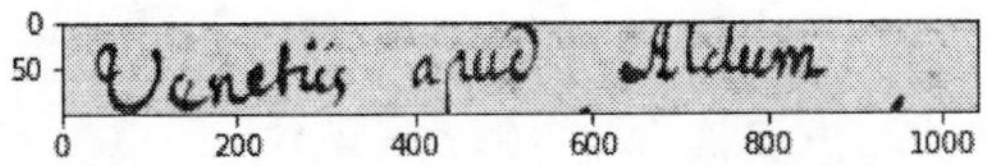

Figure 5: Row 1 obtained by line segmentation

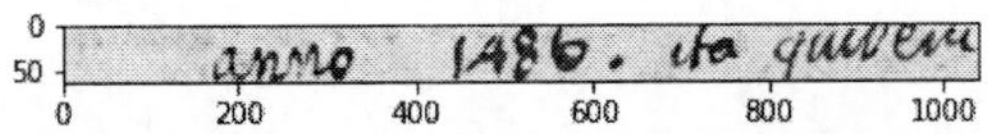

Figure 6: Row 2 obtained by line segmentation

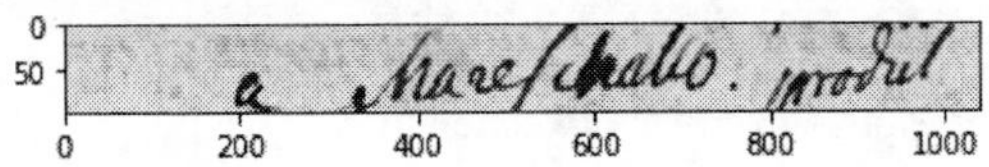

Figure 7: Row 3 obtained by line segmentation

the image to individual lines. A threshold must be set to decide how the rows should be divided. For this implementation the threshold is set to the value in the middle between the highest peak and the lowest value. In figures 5, 6 and 7, the resulting rows from the sample image can be seen.

Identification of the individual lines is followed by the identification of words. To begin with, the image containing the line is binarized and a vertical projection is applied. This allows observation of spaces in the lines, as can be observed in Figure 8. In the result from the projection one can see where the spaces between each word are located. However, since a word often has spaces between the letters, it is not suitable to divide on every empty space that is found. To solve this problem, the average length of all spaces is calculated and the line is only split on spaces that are larger than this average. An example of applying this to the line from Figure 5 can be seen in Figure 9.

3.5 Attention-based Recognition

After detecting the marginalia and segmenting the words, the goal is to correctly recognise these words. To do so, an end-to-end attention-based sequence-to-sequence model *AttentionHTR* introduced in (Kass and Vats, 2022) is used. The model architecture is presented in Figure 10, that consists of four stages: thin-plate spline (TPS) transformation, 32 layer ResNet based feature extraction, 2 layer bidirectional LSTM-based sequence modeling, and content-based attention mechanism for prediction. An attention-based decoder is used to improve character sequence predictions. The decoder is a unidirectional LSTM and attention is content-based. The segmented images of words are given as input into the AttentionHTR network, which produces the predicted word along with the confidence scores.

The main advantage of using AttentionHTR model for marginalia recognition is that the general purpose pre-trained model is able to cope with challenging examples due to insufficient annotated data. This is because to handle training data scarcity, AttentionHTR leverages transfer learning from scene images to handwriting images, and uses a multi-writer dataset (Imgur5K) that contains word examples from 5000 different writers. The architecture is modular and the integration with our pipeline was feasible and computationally inexpensive.

Epoch	Accuracy(%)	Loss
1	85.34	0.2120
2	89.35	0.1828
3	89.04	0.1257
4	89.19	0.138
5	90.74	0.2123

Table 1: R-CNN: Prediction accuracy and training loss

4 Results

4.1 Marginalia Detection

Table 1 shows the prediction accuracy and training loss of R-CNN on validation set after each epoch. The accuracy is calculated based on whether the predicted label (marginalia and non-marginalia) matches the pre-marked label.

As can be observed in Table 1, the model has been well trained after the third epoch. Although the accuracy on validation looks good, the result of the test samples needs improvement. The general situation is summarized into three categories, as shown in the Figure 11. In the figure, the green boxes are the originally marked marginalia and the red boxes are the predicted marginalia. The first category: the model is capable to make proper prediction though the predicted boxes don't 100% match the pre-marked boxes. The second category: the model is only able to mark down part of every marginalia bounding box. This is probably due to the input of this model is the small cropped image instead of the full image, the segmentation in the beginning may not cut down the whole marginalia. And the last category (the extreme case), for example, the majority of the image is marginalia. Under such kind of situation, the parameters in segmentation algorithm needs to be changed greatly, otherwise the image can't be segmented well.

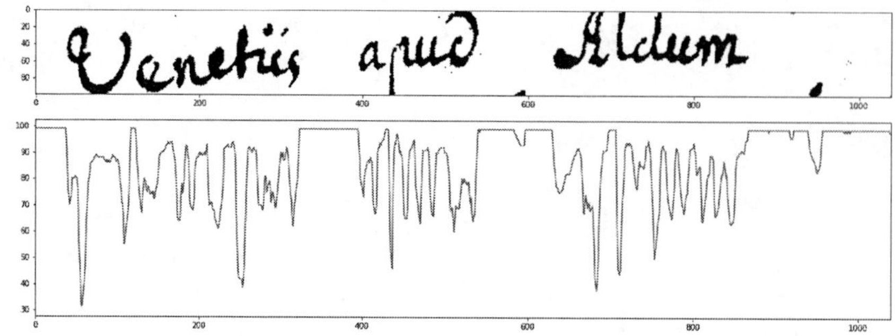

Figure 8: A binarized line and the result of applying vertical projection to it.

Figure 9: Word segmentation applied to Figure 5

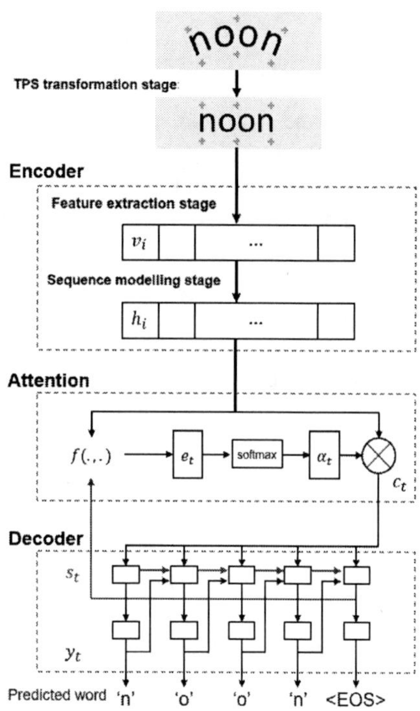

Figure 10: AttentionHTR (Kass and Vats, 2022).

The second set of experiments involve training a Faster R-CNN and applying on the test dataset. The training loss is plotted in Figure 12. Compared to the R-CNN, the Faster R-CNN performs better and shows a more accurate marginalia detection. An example of predicted marginalia is shown in Figure 13, where the labeled marginalia are marked in blue and the predicted marginalia in red. It can be observed that the Faster R-CNN is able to correctly fit the bounding boxes on the marginalia and to label them correctly in most cases. This is the case for different test images, such as images with large marginalia or images containing figures.

The good performance of the Faster R-CNN is also reflected by a high IoU score of **0.82**, which indicates that the predicted bounding boxes overlap with the labeled bounding boxes by a large amount.

4.2 Marginalia Segmentation

Due to the way that the segmentation algorithm is constructed, the results are highly dependant on that the rows do not cross over each other, such as in the example in Figure 3. However, this is not always the case since each author has a unique handwriting. One example of marginalia that has this problem can be seen in Figure 14. Since letters from two different lines are located at the same pixel rows the algorithm interprets the entire marginalia to be a single line.

Similarly, it is also important that separate words on the same line do not intersect. This problem does not seem to be as frequently occurring but it is still something that could be mentioned. An example is presented in Figure 15, where there is a line that is drawn above the middle word and the number at the right-hand side. Due to this line, the algorithm as it is constructed at the moment, is not able to separate the two words. A different method would be required to solve such problem.

4.3 Text Recognition using AttentionHTR

The segmented words were given as input into the AttentionHTR network. A selection of these results

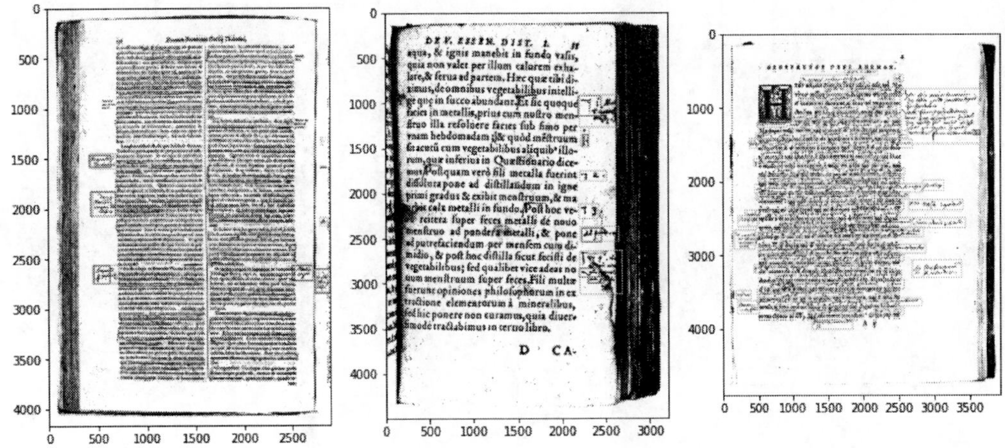

Figure 11: Visualization result: Prediction of marginalia on 3 test samples using a R-CNN.

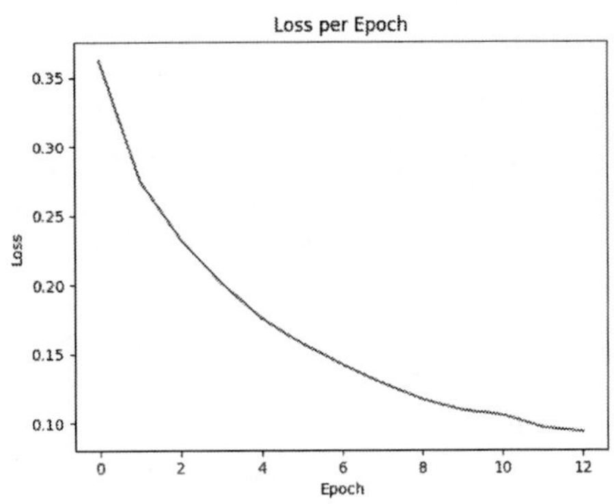

Figure 12: Faster R-CNN training loss.

can be seen in Figure 16, where the first column contains the input image, the second column contains the true word, and the third column presents the predicted word by AttentionHTR. As one can see, AttentionHTR labels the words and even numbers very reasonably. However, some of the words provided as input are not even readable for the human eye. As expected, AttentionHTR is not able to correctly label those input images. Further, it struggles if the input image is not perfectly segmented. For example, if the input image contains multiple words in different lines, the predicted text is inaccurate. Overall, AttentionHTR performs very well if the input image is clear, well segmented, and also readable for the human eye.

5 Discussion

In general, the R-CNN model works well if the input images have been well-cut. But the segmentation is not always perfect because the layout of each image is different. For instance, some have multiple marginalia outside of the printed text, some have a few marginalia inside the printed part, some have graphics besides handwritten and printed text, etc. The difference between each image requires adjustment of segmentation algorithm parameters for each image to make a good segmentation. Therefore, only with a better way to do the segmentation for an input image, can this model perform better.

In contrast to this, Faster R-CNN does not require the pre-segmentation operation, so it has a good chance to address the problem of not marking all potential marginalia before the images are input to the model. Instead, the regional proposal network of the Faster R-CNN does not only speed up computation, but also seems to propose more relevant sections of the image. Combined with the Fast R-CNN, the coordinate predictions for the marginalia are much more accurate than the ones of the R-CNN. The accuracy, together with the more efficient computation, lets the Faster R-CNN outperform the R-CNN. This is also reflected by a high IoU score (**0.82**) of the Faster R-CNN.

With regard to the marginalia segmentation, it was observed that the word segmentation algorithm struggles with lines and words that intersect with each other. These problems are very hard to solve with the current implementation, and requires more sophisticated algorithms. It would be interesting to try a R-CNN approach similar to the method for localizing the marginalia. However, this would require a good amount of time dedicated to creating training data for the algorithm by manually labeling

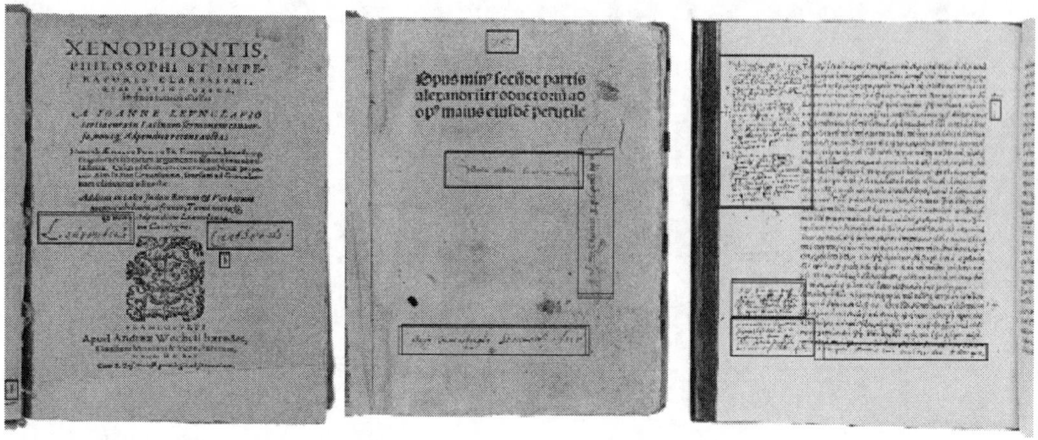

Figure 13: Visualization result: Prediction of marginalia on 3 test samples using the Faster R-CNN.

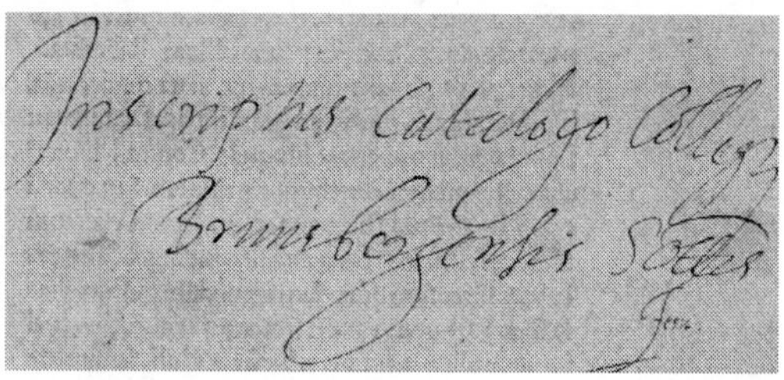

Figure 14: Handwriting with intersecting rows

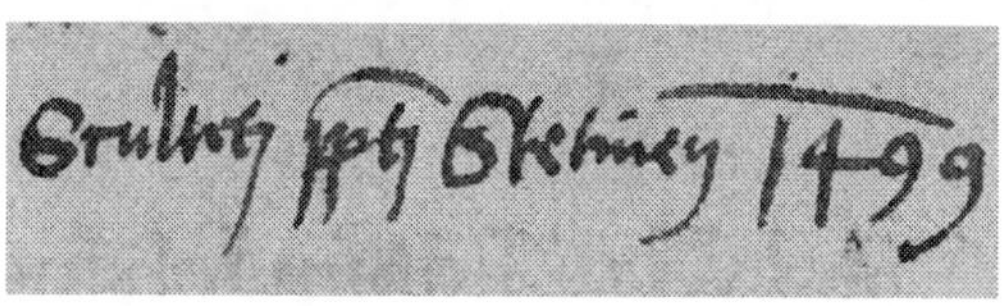

Figure 15: Handwriting with intersecting words

IMAGE	TRUE	PREDICTED
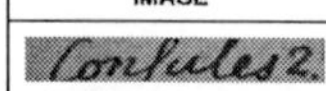	Confules2.	Confules2
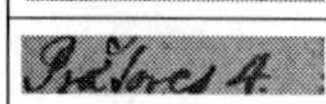	Pralores4.	Pritorest
	540.	540.
	hacde	back
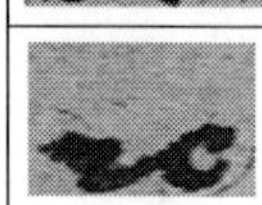	vc	is
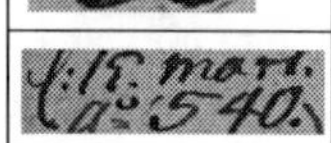	?	inimato

Figure 16: AttentionHTR word recognition results.

coordinates of the words.

While the Faster R-CNN was found to be well performing for our use-case, there also exists other object detection methods that were not explored in this study, such as Mask R-CNN (He et al., 2017) and YOLO (Redmon et al., 2016). However, the dataset is prepared in a format easily adaptable for different architectures, and other architectures such as Mask R-CNN and YOLO can be investigated as a potential future work. For text recognition, Transformer based methods such as TrOCR (Li et al., 2023) also exists, but this study focused on AttentionHTR due to a powerful in-house general purpose HTR multi-writer model, developed as part of our previous work (Kass and Vats, 2022). The experimental evaluation can be further extended with a comparison with other text recognition methods as future work.

The results show that the text recognition accuracy with AttentionHTR heavily depends on the quality of the segmented input image. If the image is clear and well segmented, i.e., only one word is visible, AttentionHTR provides accurate results, without the need for training from scratch. However, some output images of the marginalia segmentation algorithm were multiple lines long, or the quality of the given image was just not precise enough. In that latter case, even a human cannot correctly classify the text. Overall, AttentionHTR is highly accurate when the input was clear and well segmented. In future work, words in the dataset can be labeled, which would allow for training of the

AttentionHTR network on the given data. Also, the present study will be extended further to include annotated marginalia such as Melville (Norberg and Olsen-Smith, 2023) and Mill (Pionke, 2020).

5.1 Conclusion

This work presented an end-to-end framework for automatic detection and recognition of handwritten marginalia. The experimental results on the data from Uppsala University Library's early book collections demonstrate the effectiveness of the proposed method, where Faster R-CNN was found to perform better than R-CNN for marginalia localization, and AttentionHTR contributed towards the recognition performance. Under the experimental settings, the proposed HTR pipeline produced encouraging results for both marginalia detection and recognition. However, since the training data is limited and expert knowledge is needed for annotating the marginalia texts, the future work involves collaboration with the librarians and professionals to prepare training data for recognition of historical marginalia texts, written in both Swedish and English. Furthermore, language modeling, a different regularization method, and generative AI models for handwriting synthesis will be explored. The source code and pre-trained models are made available for advancing the research further at GitHub.

Limitations

Some of the limitations of this work include:

- The training data used in this work contains labeled bounding box coordinates for marginalia, but not the annotations representing what the marginalia reads. Unavailability of annotated marginalia is one of the main limitations of this work, making it challenging for the model to generalise on unseen data.

- It is not straightforward to annotate the marginalia text and is a time-consuming process. It requires expert knowledge, where an expert should be able to read a variety of handwriting, and is multi-lingual as one cannot know beforehand about the language used for marginalia (it can vary with different readers).

- To enhance the recognition performance, the authors have been investigating the integration of a language model (such as Skip-gram) in the pipeline. However, it was found to be more suitable as a post-processing step due to the architectural limitations with CNN-based feature extraction and sequential modeling. Also using a language model such as BERT at post-processing can enhance the accuracy, but it might also increase the computational cost, and the authors will investigate this further as future work.

- A limitation of an end-to-end detection and recognition pipeline is that it is challenging to tailor or tweak the models to handle cases with special scripts (e.g. Gothic, curlicue), blurry text, strike-through words, poor handwriting, etc. Therefore, we aim to have a general-purpose model that is good enough for a variety of data.

Ethics Statement

The research conducted in this work respects the rights and welfare of the society, general public and other stakeholders such as librarians, historians and research scholars. The languages studied herein includes Swedish and English, and the methods thus developed can be applied to other languages. The source code and pre-trained models are made public to the research community to benefit the research, future re-use, and for the dissemination of knowledge to the public. The research does not pose any risk or harm to anyone, and is conducted with honesty and integrity.

Acknowledgment

This research was partially supported by *Kjell och Märta Beijer Foundation* and *Uppsala-Durham Strategic Development Fund*: "Marginalia and Machine Learning: a Study of Durham University and Uppsala University Marginalia Collections". The computations were enabled by resources provided by the National Academic Infrastructure for Supercomputing in Sweden (NAISS) partially funded by the Swedish Research Council through grant agreement no. 2022-06725. The authors would like to thank Raphaela Heil and Peter Heslin for valuable suggestions and feedback.

References

Uppsala university library waller collections.

José Carlos Aradillas, Juan José Murillo-Fuentes, and Pablo M Olmos. 2020. Improving offline htr in small datasets by purging unreliable labels. In *2020 17th International Conference on Frontiers in Handwriting Recognition (ICFHR)*, pages 25–30. IEEE.

Théodore Bluche. 2016. Joint line segmentation and transcription for end-to-end handwritten paragraph recognition. *Advances in neural information processing systems*, 29.

Théodore Bluche, Jérôome Louradour, and Ronaldo Messina. 2017. Scan, attend and read: End-to-end handwritten paragraph recognition with mdlstm attention. In *2017 14th IAPR international conference on document analysis and recognition (ICDAR)*, volume 1, pages 1050–1055. IEEE.

Melanie Ramdarshan Bold and Kiri L Wagstaff. 2017. Marginalia in the digital age: Are digital reading devices meeting the needs of today's readers? *Library & Information Science Research*, 39(1):16–22.

Mia Goodwin. 2021. Locating digitised marginalia. *Marginal Notes: Social Reading and the Literal Margins*, pages 261–277.

Kaiming He, Georgia Gkioxari, Piotr Dollár, and Ross Girshick. 2017. Mask r-cnn. In *Proceedings of the IEEE international conference on computer vision*, pages 2961–2969.

Netanya Hitchcock, Steven Olsen-Smith, and Elisa Barney Smith. 2023. Gender and writing in melville's erased marginalia to shakespeare.

Lei Kang, J Ignacio Toledo, Pau Riba, Mauricio Villegas, Alicia Fornés, and Marçal Rusinol. 2019. Convolve, attend and spell: An attention-based sequence-to-sequence model for handwritten word recognition. In *Pattern Recognition: 40th German Conference, GCPR 2018, Stuttgart, Germany, October 9-12, 2018, Proceedings 40*, pages 459–472. Springer.

Dmitrijs Kass and Ekta Vats. 2022. Attentionhtr: handwritten text recognition based on attention encoder-decoder networks. In *International Workshop on Document Analysis Systems*, pages 507–522. Springer.

Alex Krizhevsky, Ilya Sutskever, and Geoffrey E Hinton. 2012. Imagenet classification with deep convolutional neural networks. *Advances in neural information processing systems*, 25.

Remington Lambie, Steven Olsen-Smith, and Elisa Barney Smith. 2022. Visualizing melville's marginalia: Visualizations.

Minghao Li, Tengchao Lv, Jingye Chen, Lei Cui, Yijuan Lu, Dinei Florencio, Cha Zhang, Zhoujun Li, and Furu Wei. 2023. Trocr: Transformer-based optical character recognition with pre-trained models. In *Proceedings of the AAAI Conference on Artificial Intelligence*, volume 37, pages 13094–13102.

Jiri Matas, Ondrej Chum, Martin Urban, and Tomás Pajdla. 2004. Robust wide-baseline stereo from maximally stable extremal regions. *Image and vision computing*, 22(10):761–767.

Joe Nockels, Paul Gooding, Sarah Ames, and Melissa Terras. 2022. Understanding the application of handwritten text recognition technology in heritage contexts: a systematic review of transkribus in published research. *Archival Science*, 22(3):367–392.

Peter Norberg and Steven Olsen-Smith. 2023. The technical development and expanding scope of melville's marginalia online. *Leviathan*, 25(2):61–85.

Christopher Ohge, Steven Olsen-Smith, Elisa Barney Smith, Adam Brimhall, Bridget Howley, Lisa Shanks, and Lexy Smith. 2018. At the axis of reality: Melville's marginalia in the dramatic works of william shakespeare. *Leviathan*, 20(2):37–67.

Albert D Pionke. 2020. Handwritten marginalia and digital search: The development and early research results of mill marginalia online. *ILCEA. Revue de l'Institut des langues et cultures d'Europe, Amérique, Afrique, Asie et Australie*, (39).

Joseph Redmon, Santosh Divvala, Ross Girshick, and Ali Farhadi. 2016. You only look once: Unified, real-time object detection. In *Proceedings of the IEEE conference on computer vision and pattern recognition*, pages 779–788.

Shaoqing Ren, Kaiming He, Ross Girshick, and Jian Sun. 2015. Faster r-cnn: Towards real-time object detection with region proposal networks. *Advances in neural information processing systems*, 28.

Bryan C Russell, Antonio Torralba, Kevin P Murphy, and William T Freeman. 2008. Labelme: a database and web-based tool for image annotation. *International journal of computer vision*, 77:157–173.

Historical Portrayal of Greek Tourism through Topic Modeling on International Newspapers

Eirini Karamouzi[1,2], **Maria Pontiki**[3,4], and **Yannis Krasonikolakis**[5]

[1]University of Sheffield, [2]American College of Greece,
[3]Panteion University of Social and Political Sciences, [4]Athena Research Center, [5]Grant Thornton

e.karamouzi@sheffield.ac.uk, m.pontiki@panteion.gr, yannis.krasonikolakis@gr.gt.com

Abstract

In this paper, we bridge computational linguistics with historical methods to explore the potential of topic modeling in historical newspapers. Our case study focuses on British and American newspapers published in the second half of the 20th century that debate issues of Greek tourism, but our method can be transposed to any diachronic data. We demonstrate that Non-negative Matrix Factorization (NMF) can generate interpretable topics within the historical period under examination providing a tangible example of how computational text analysis can assist historical research. Furthermore, we highlight the role of historical interpretation with regard to analyzing discourse dynamics through topic models. The results of our analysis provide interesting insights for academics and researchers in the field of (Digital) Humanities and Social Sciences, as well as for stakeholders in the tourism industry.

1 Introduction

Mass tourism has become a global phenomenon and a $9 trillion industry which, in 2022, accounted for 7.6% of the world's GDP according to the World Travel and Tourism Council.[1] It is vital to the well-being of individuals and nations, and of cultures, economies and societies, proven by the absence of travel during the pandemic and its revival since. Tourism is now in question as climate change forces the world to reconsider air miles and ecological footprints. It is more important than ever to understand tourism's history to inform decisions about its future. In this paper, we take Greece as a case study and we explore the country's transition to mass tourism from 1945 to 1989 for two reasons. First, it is widely accepted in tourism studies that modern international tourism began in earnest in the 1950s and grew exponentially thereafter, especially with the introduction of affordable package holidays (Zuelow, 2011). In Greece in 1950, visitor numbers were c. 33,000. Over the next four decades, that figure grew to c. 9 million. We also selected 1989 as an end date for practical research purposes since liberalization of air travel, end of Cold War divisions and the usage of the web changed the landscape of tourism and its promotion. There is also a methodological issue. In the second half of the 20th century, the newspapers played a central role in the political, economic and cultural life of Britain and the USA. For instance, the British read more newspapers per capita than any other people in the world (Bingham, 2010). Therefore analyzing the debates in these newspapers is an invaluable source of evidence for a wide range of historical investigations and in our case of Greek tourism.

Our focus is American and British newspapers, since the USA and UK were the main markets of tourists throughout this period, along with France and Germany. We experimented with LDA and NMF to uncover the main topics and narratives framing Greek tourism in international newspapers and explore the main textual representations of a tourist nation, their evolution over time, their cultural underpinnings, and how they were communicated to different audiences.

[1] https://wttc.org/research/economic-impact

Proceedings of LaTeCH-CLfL 2024, pages 121–132
March 22, 2024

The contribution of our work is two-fold; first, the extracted topics are evaluated both by a computational linguist and by a historian highlighting the crucial role of domain experts when interpreting topic modeling outputs. Second, the extracted topics are contextualized within the historical and political environment in which they appear, providing interesting insights about the historical representations of Greek tourism over the years, and about the development and the hallmarks of American and British tourism in Greece across different historical periods (from 1945 to 1989). The comparative analysis between the American and the British press reveals interesting insights including similar responses to specific events as well as notable differences between British and American tourism to Greece during the historical periods under examination. Overall, the results of our analysis can provide valuable information for academics and researchers in the field of (Digital) Humanities and Social Sciences, as well as for stakeholders in the tourism industry.

2 Background

Tourism has held a quasi-monopolistic status in Greece's development. While the promotion of tourism in Greece at times mirrored the agenda of the Greek state in the construction of its nation's image during its turbulent history of civil war, dictatorship, and democratization, it has also included the power of the market. After its emergence in the 1960s, almost 80% of Greek tourism has been inbound, which exemplifies the industry's exposure to international developments and events. How a nation depicts itself is not a value-free expression of identity, but a culmination of historical processes that 'reveal much about the social construction of space, cultural change, identity and discourse' (Pritchard & Morgan, 2001). The topic has been researched by visual artists, architects, ethnographers and economic historians of tourism who have looked at governmental archives, hotel/airline and tour operators repositories, posters, official and unsanctioned travel guides and personal travelogues and tourist documentaries and films (Tsartas, 2010; Vlachos, 2016; Alifragkis & Athanassiou, 2013). However, historical methods alone are insufficient for this study. By using computational approaches, it can advance the field of study beyond anthropology, ethnography and sociology to understand the major themes of how Greece promoted itself to different audiences, at different times.

Furthermore, newspapers constitute valuable sources in historical research, providing windows into the past, but also posing challenges for historians to go through their sheer volume of information page-by-page (Yang, Torgtet, & Mihalcea, 2011). Recent advancements in the field of historical research have witnessed a growing interest in leveraging topic modeling techniques to capture historical trends (e.g. Newman & Block, 2006; Oiva, 2021) and study discourse dynamics diachronically in newspapers collections (e.g. Marjanen et al., 2021; Viola & Verheul, 2019). In the tourism field, topic modeling is usually applied to travelogues and user comments on travel websites (e.g. Pang et al., 2011) as an important tourist attraction profiling technique facilitating personalized attraction recommendation services (Huang et al., 2018). Other approaches focus on online review platforms and social media data to analyze consumer perceptions and (dis)satisfaction of visitors of hospitality and tourism-related products, organizations and services (e.g., Guo, Barnes, & Jia, 2017; Kim, Kim & Park, 2021). To the best of our knowledge, topic modeling on historical newspapers has not been employed before in tourism studies. In the field of Digital Humanities, digital methods have been used to study travel and networks [2], but not the construction, transfer or consumption of a country's tourist destination within its ideological, political and cultural context.

3 Datasets

3.1 Data Collection and preparation

Based on a set of specific keywords related to Greece and Greek tourism (Appendix C) we collected a total of 1099 news articles from 11 sources for the period 1945-1989, as presented in Table 1. The digitized newspapers were from ProQuest Historical Newspapers and GALE Primary Sources, while New York Times has its own archival repository with paid subscription that we utilised. In order to ensure a balance of

[2] See https://grandtour.stanford.edu/

viewpoints, our selection of newspaper sources includes a range of broadsheets, economic newspapers, left and right on the political spectrum and magazines.

	American	British
Newspaper (number of articles)	Chicago Tribune (81), Los Angeles Times (60), New York Times (461), Wall Street Journal (26), Washington Post (44), Vogue (23)	Financial Times (82), Guardian Observer (86), Telegraph (49), The Economist (41), The Times (146)
Total	695	404

Table 1: Number of articles per newspaper.

Then, we applied OCR to transform the articles into machine readable format. For the American press, we used the *Tesseract* tool. For the British press, the same tool could not be applied for most of the newspapers (i.e. The Times, The Financial Times, Telegraph, and The Economist), so we used *ocrmypdf*, a Python library that adds an OCR text layer to scanned PDF files, allowing them to be searched. To estimate the quality of the extracted texts, we used the *enchant.Dict("en_US")* dictionary available at the *enchant* library, to determine the percentage of words that belong to the English vocabulary. The algorithm calculated the ratio of the recognized English words to the total number of words in each article providing a quantitative measure of the OCR text quality, with the percentage for the American articles being 93.47%, and for the British, 92.22%. In the list of the non-vocabulary words, there were some misspelled words (e.g.'Speciglists', instead of "Specialists"). To fix this issue we used the *pyspellchecker* Python library. After fixing misspellings, we observed that some of the remaining non-English words were names or places, so they should not be extracted from the text. We applied the Spacy Named Entity Recognizer to detect named entities using the "PERSON" and "LOC" (location) labels. The extracted terms were curated and cataloged within a non-English vocabulary list to ensure their retention within our corpus. Finally, we removed the list of non-vocabulary words left since it contained poorly extracted non-recognizable terms.

3.2 Data Organization

The data are organized in two main corpora per nationality (American and British), and further splitted according to specific periods. Breaking down news data into time windows that align with historically significant periods has previously been employed to uncover noteworthy historical trends (e.g. Yang, Torgtet, & Mihalcea, 2011; Hengchen, 2017). In our case, the following five periods have been set:

A. 1945-1949: Reconstruction of the country and first signs of tourism.
B. 1950-1966: Tourism takes off.
C. 1967-1974: Dictatorship.
D. 1975-1980: Democratisation & economic crisis.
E. 1981-1989: PASOK government.

Period	American		British	
	articles	tokens	articles	tokens
1945-49	16	10683	22	80375
1950-59	267	156684	164	527021
1960-69	133	96507	103	261726
1970-79	110	116601	42	88751
1980-89	169	180825	73	129181

Table 2: Number of articles and tokens per period.

4 Topic Modeling

Topic models provide an effective way to draw insights from large-scale collections and are widely used in digital humanities and social sciences (Brauer & Fridlund, 2013; Marjanen et al., 2020) to uncover the most prevalent themes on different types of data ranging from books, newspapers, and academic journals to parliament proceedings and social media. Since the inception of the term "topic model" along with the introduction of Latent Dirichlet Allocation (LDA) by Blei, Ng, and Jordan (2002), topic modeling research has evolved to address the challenges arising from different types of applications, since it became clear that not all algorithms are effective in all types of text (Churchill & Singh, 2022). In this paper, we experiment with LDA and Non-negative Matrix Factorization (NMF), two models that are very popular across various domains (e.g.

Pitichotchokphokhin et al., 2020; Egger & Yu, 2022).

The input for the topic models was preprocessed data. All the articles were lowercased, tokenized, part-of-speech tagged and lemmatized. Stop words were removed and bigrams were extracted to obtain topics with phrase-like keywords and not only single terms. After several iterations, the stop words list was enriched with more non content terms, and we decided to remove verbs and adverbs and to keep only nouns and adjectives. To find the best hyperparameters for LDA, we utilized Gensim's[3] LDA Model, focusing on optimizing the number of topics and the alpha parameter. Alpha, representing the document-topic density, influences how many topics a document potentially has. We experimented with values like 0.1 (indicating low topic density per document), 'symmetric' (assuming an equal distribution of topics across documents), and 'asymmetric' (allowing for a varied distribution of topics). The number of topics was also varied to identify the optimal structure for our datasets. This approach led us to identify a total of 18 topics in the American articles ranging from 2 to 5 per period, and a total of 24 topics in the British articles ranging from 2 to 7 per period. The results were visualized using pyLDAvis[4] to provide an intuitive understanding of the topics and their distribution.

For NMF, we employed the TfidfVectorizer from scikit-learn [5] to construct the terms-documents matrix. This matrix represents the importance of terms in each document, with higher weights assigned to terms that are frequent in a specific document but rare across the entire corpus. To estimate the optimal number of topics, we computed the highest coherence scores for each dataset and sub-corpus using Gensim's CoherenceModel. This model evaluates the coherence of topics by measuring the degree of semantic similarity between high scoring words in the topic. We identified a total of 39 topics in the American articles ranging from 6 to 9 per period, and a total of 34 topics in the British articles ranging from 3 to 9 per period.

The human evaluators concluded that NMF generates more interpretable topics than LDA on the specific datasets. A possible reason could be the fact that LDA is a static approach, whilst NMF can capture topic evolution in temporal data. Another possible explanation could be that, as reported in previous research (e.g. Young & Johnson, 2018), NMF performs better than LDA on a smaller number of documents. We plan to further explore the differences between the LDA and NMF outputs, considering also the unbalanced nature of our datasets (i.e. different number of articles from various newspapers for different periods). In the next section, we discuss findings based on the NMF results.

5 Results and Discussion

The topic modeling results for the American articles are presented in Appendix A and for the British articles in Appendix B. The extracted topics were qualitatively evaluated by a historian and a computational linguist. In this section we discuss the most important findings with the aim to highlight the potential of topic modeling in historical research, and the crucial role of domain experts when interpreting topic modeling outputs.

5.1 American Press

The results on the American press for the period **1945-1949** reveal 4 topics discussing the catastrophic damage wrought to the Greek economy during the Second World War, with tourism framed as potential means of partially mitigating Greece's balance of payments crisis, along with the restoration and cultivation of agricultural and industrial productivity (mainly of tobacco) (#A8). US aid provided to Greece and other European nations under the auspices of the Marshall Plan (Economic Recovery Programme) (#A1, #A6), following its inception in 1948 could in fact be used as a means of redeveloping a recipient's tourist industry despite the ongoing Civil War (1946-1949) (#A3). In topic #A7 which encompasses terms related to hospitality industry in Greece and other Mediterranean countries (e.g. hotel, restaurant, prices, currency), and in topic #A4 through terms reflecting aspects of transportation/travelings, one can detect the first signs of contemporaneous uptick in US travel to the Mediterranean with the majority of these journeys undertaken via cruise ships and other seagoing passenger vessels. Finally, topic #5 on Rhodes, recently returned to Greek sovereignty after Italian occupation, was given high priority as

[3] https://radimrehurek.com/gensim/

[4] https://pypi.org/project/pyLDAvis/

[5] https://scikit-learn.org/stable/

an already established popular tourist destination with the necessary infrastructure provided by the Italian administration.

In the **1950-1966** period, we can identify the onset of the jet age and the shifts in US tourist market (#B2). By 1953, air travel had made the tourism business a 12-month affair, and facilitated long trips while fostering off-season travel through reduced fares. That was further fortified by cruise-related travel services (#B9). Americans were encouraged to vacation in Greece for reasons of affordability where they would the 'most for their money' (#B3). This new reality pushed the Greek government in 1957 to put into operation a five year tourist investment plan, including the building of the Hilton hotel in Athens in addition to coastal areas near Athens (#B1, #B7). The focus on both the Delphi ancient site as well as the islands of Mykonos and Rhodes as tourist destinations (#B4), reflect how Greece was attempting to capture a larger portion of the growing international travel market by trumpeting the emergence of a 'modern' Greece that offered sea, sun and sand alongside its much-lauded antiquities and cultural politics. An interesting topic is #B6. Based on the top terms, the computational linguist recognised a topic discussing the legal status of Green-born citizens in the US, while the historian identified the issue of the Greek diaspora. Equally important are topics #B5, #B7, and #B8 that showcase the novel feature of the Greek tourism industry to target the diaspora in the USA and utilize its members for publicity events.

In the Dictatorship period (**1967-1974**), topics #C2, #C6 and #C4 indicate how the establishment of the regime of the Colonels in April 1967 did not hinder recently established relationships between US private investors and representatives of the Greek tourism and aviation sector. For example, a contract between the Greek government and Litton Industries Inc., pertaining to an ambitious 12-year 'nation building' project that focused *inter alia* on the development of tourism infrastructure within the western Peloponnese, was reaffirmed by the junta in short order. And while tourism to Greece to a 'nose dive right after the coup', it did not take long for normal service to be resumed with usual concerns of sightseeing, shopping and taverna comparings as we we can notice to the topics discussing again the islands of Mykonos, Rhodes and this time also Kos as tourist destinations in the Aegean Sea (#C1), on travel services (#C3), and heritage/gastronomy (#C7).

During the period of democratization and economic crisis (**1975-1980**) we identified 6 interpretable tourism related topics discussing this time Crete island as a tourist destination (#D1), hospitality services (#D2), cultural events (#D3), travel services (#D4), Athens and ancient Olympia (#D5) and touristic development of Pylos whilst for the first time we see environmental concerns over the touristification of places in Greece (#D6).

Finally, during the first socialist government of PASOK (**1981-1989**) along with the expected topics (#E1, #E5, #E4) discussing different aspects of Greek islands (i.e. sea, beach, town, village) and related travel (e.g. boat) and hospitality services (hotel, room, restaurant), we have two noteworthy developments. The depressive influence of a protracted economic recession in Europe, as indicated in topic #E6 on dollar and other countries continued to limit the growth of the Greek tourism industry until 1984. But the development of US tourism to Greece would, for the remainder of the decade, be defined primarily by debates concerning international terrorism, which achieved a degree of prominence hitherto unseen following the hijacking of TWA flight 847 shortly after its departure from Athens on 14 June 1985. The topics of cancellations (#E6) and hostage (#E8), refer to President Ronald Reagan's issuance of an injunction to US tourists to boycott Greece until security measures against terrorist attacks at Athens airport were improved (#E2). The effects of this intervention were felt immediately. With travel agents in Athens reporting mass cancellations of American bookings (#E8), and tensions escalating between the socialist government of Andreas Papandreou and the Reagan White House. The Greeks called upon George Lois to launch a campaign and attract much needed international visitors and their tourist dollars (#E7, #E9).

5.2 British Press

For the period **1945-1949**, we identified 2 topics focusing on governance and politics (#A2), and the economy and banking sector (#A3). The coverage underlines how an understanding of the economic realities imparted a sense of pragmatism among war-weary Greeks, for whom the exigencies of getting their country's economy back on its feet – which necessitated a rejuvenation of the tourist trade – superseded partisan politics, even during a period of deep internal unrest. The British are more interested than the Americans in the Greek political realities and challenges of governing. However, the Marshall plan, as with the American press, takes center stage in relation to its potential to tourist development.

The period of the tourist boom of **1950-1966**, is linked to economic policies (#B5). The 1955 annual review of the Bank of Greece revealed that earnings from tourism had increased by 164% between 1952 and 1954 on account of the devaluation of the drachma by fifty percent in April 1953 (#B4). It was not just domestic economic policy, private enterprise from Germany for instance also began to feature prominently in the development of tourist infrastructure (#B4). Equally important was the role of cruises (#B7). The Greek government hoped to maximize the impact of a recently discovered medium through which the natural beauty of Greece could be transmitted to international audiences – Hollywood motion pictures, as discussed in #B6 topic. The topic of destinations (Athens and Mykonos Island), archaeological sites (Parthenon and Delos), as well as the mention of sea and feeling good, reflects the element of duality: the allusion to two different concepts of Greece; one characterized by the ancient ruins that attracted 'ardent Hellenists', another comprised of picturesque scenery and the promise of relaxation on the cheap and in the sun (#B3, #B1). While the exponential growth of the Greek tourist industry would depend to a significant degree on marketing the latter to swelling ranks of sun worshippers, it would appear that, for British audiences, the former remained the predominant conception of Greece, its appeal as a tourist destination predicated on the cultural and historical significance of its antiquities. The rest of the topics revolve around impact of regional political tensions and political upheaval caused by the outbreak of political violence in Cyprus in November 1955 and 1964 (#B4).

During the Dictatorship period (**1967-1974**), we can identify the impactful role of political events on tourism with the Turkish invasion of Cyprus in 1974 that brought about the fall of the junta featuring in #C4. However, during the junta and in 1969, some 1,609,000 visited Greece, spending in excess of £80.6 million, making Greece (alongside Portugal) the fastest growing tourist center in Europe (The Economist, 1971). This influx, moreover, provided fresh impetus for renewed efforts to develop Greece's tourist infrastructure (#C2), with particular emphasis placed on the building of new hotels, beaches, and camping ground, as well as communications (#C6).

During the democratization and economic crisis period (**1975-1980**) similar tactics were employed in prioritizing particular regions for the development of tourism (#D1) like Crete and Corfu (#D4) and the investment of vast sums of money to provide the necessary infrastructure. Tourist figures duly returned to expected levels in 1975 and continued to rise sharply thereafter, leading to overcrowding and overbooking in several tourist resorts (#D5). As with the American press, the British discuss how by 1979 Greece was approaching an alarming milestone – six million visitors, or 'nearly two foreigners for every three Greeks'. The opening of the Porto Carras (#D6) tourist complex in Halkidiki in 1976, a conglomeration of hotels, villas, restaurants, swimming pools, golf courses and bathing beaches (#D4) represented a move towards a more sustainable approach to the development of the Greek tourism industry and a governmental effort to attract more 'affluent' holidaymakers and 'yuppify' (#D2). In addition, we can see an energy and oil industry related topic (#D3).

Finally, in the PASOK government period (**1981-1989**) we can see the British go back to the deeply rooted ideational associations with antiquity and cultural heritage (#E6, #E7). The economic downturn of the period is reflected on the topic of strikes in #E8 and the governmental response (#E1), as well as the impact on other European countries (#E3). We have again a general topic about islands and accommodation (#E2), but most importantly the issue of security and terrorism is discussed as with the American press (#E4).

5.3 Further Insights

In order to get additional insights from our datasets, we also calculated the term frequencies on the American and British articles for the whole period under examination (1945-1989). Overall, it is interesting that debates on Greek tourism don't prioritize the issue of cultural heritage, despite appearing in different topics in our analysis and giving us fresh insights on its meaning. As indicated by the following figures (font size indicates frequency), the American articles feature discourses on Greece as an opportunity for tourists to enjoy the country's 300 days of sunshine and the 1,416 islands available. Moreover, it confirms the analysis of the different topics that describe the American gaze on Greek tourism as a complex mosaic, ranging from fascination with antiquities to the natural beauty of landscapes and the warmth and hospitality of the people, depending on the needs of the audience across time.

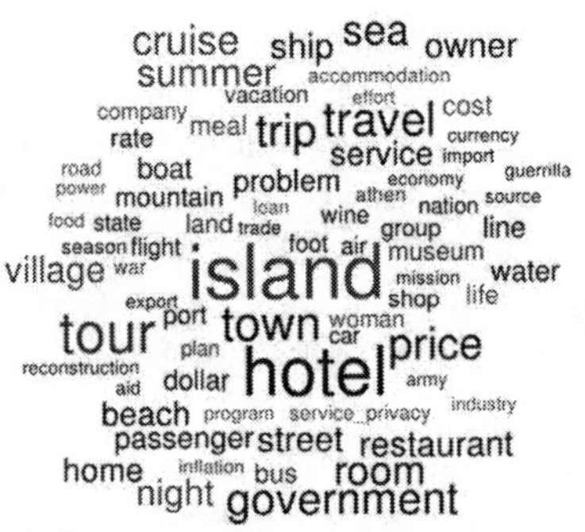

Figure 1. Summary of the most frequent terms in the American dataset.

The British articles diachronically focus on the Greek economic scene and the debates are quite consistent around governmental policy. There is preoccupation with Greece's investment in infrastructure, both public and private, with particular emphasis placed on the building of new hotels, roads and beaches. Also great attention is paid to the economic impact of the tourist industry and its dependency on international developments.

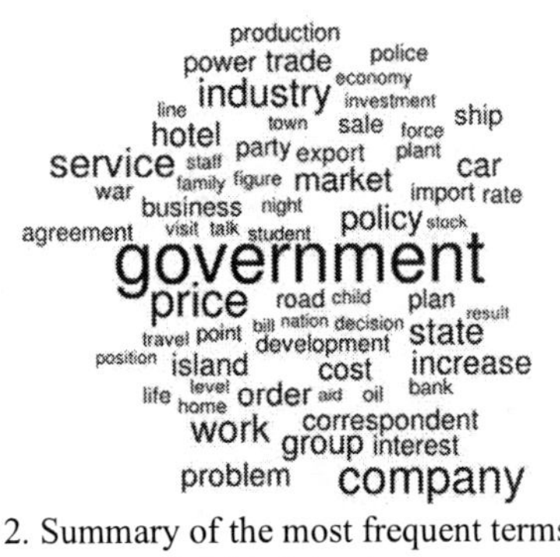

Figure 2. Summary of the most frequent terms in the British dataset.

Both American and British newspapers clearly show how the cultivation of Greece's tourist industry was seen as an economic imperative and an effective weapon in the battle against the country's perennial trade deficit and balancing the books. This was an orchestrated state endeavor as reflected in several topics in both USA and UK that focus on state-induced developments of a nation-wide network of modern leisure facilities, including hotels, motels, tourist pavilions, organized beaches and other infrastructural projects (roads, port facilities). The British are more interested in the Greek political and economic scene than the Americans in discussing tourism. Although technological advancements such as the onset of the jet age are seen as turning points on the increase of the tourists flows to Greece, it's interesting to see the complete omission of the role of other non-governmental stakeholders such as Olympic Airways, the country's flag-carrier from 1957 to 2009, that have been highlighted in most studies of the history of Greek tourism.

Beyond the economic function of tourism, the computational investigation in the foreign press confirms tourism's cultural, ideational and societal features. The results showed that most topics were on cultural politics of tourism promotion that should further encourage scholarship on tourist policy beyond the premises of the industry's significant multiplier effect on economic activity, which has been the focus of most of tourism literature.

The quantitative analysis of the newspapers showed how the debate on Greece as a tourist destination contributed to different notions of Greekness going back to the inception of the Greek state that sought to establish continuity between antiquity and modern Greek culture (Beaton, 2021). Early on, the Greek state utilized antiquity and the classical past as the cornerstone of the country's tourism policy, evident in several topics. However, our mixed methods research problematizes this cultural dualism following recent trends in Greek historiography that encourage more attention to diversity and plurality in the cultural politics of the country (Tziovas, 2021). Moreover, our research shows that the Greek tourism product was far from monolithic and was heavily dependent on international developments and changing attitudes of the tourist audiences.

The development of British tourism to Greece during 1945-1989 was characterized by a major shift from cultural tourism towards low-budget, mass tourism of the 'sun, sea and sand' variety. This transition was, for the most part, in keeping with the imperatives of the Greek tourism industry, which recognised that such a reorientation was required in order to sustain growth. However, the transformation (or transmogrification) of British tourism to Greece was so rapid and far reaching that, by the mid-1980s, there was a revival of the cultural tourism that had predominated during the post-war years. The growth of American tourism vis-à-vis Greece during the same period was a somewhat messier, amorphous process. Themes such a fascination with antiquities, the natural beauty of landscapes, and the warmth and hospitality of the Greek people were (inter)changeable depending on the perceived preferences of US audiences at the time. Common flashpoints, such as the military coup that installed the Regime of the Colonels and the spate of terrorist incidents during the 1980s, also yielded similar responses among British and American audiences, although as regards the fallout from terrorist violence, Greek stakeholders were undoubtedly more proactive in their attempts to assuage the concerns of US tourists through a series of publicity-related measures.

In fact, it could be argued that a major difference between the development of US tourism to Greece and the contemporaneous growth of the British variant was the more proactive efforts of representatives of the Greek tourism industry within the US to proselytise on behalf of their country. Another notable difference between British and American tourism to Greece during the period in question was the 'ethnic' tourism of the Greek diaspora in the US, for which no equivalent could be readily identified within Britain.

6 Conclusions

In this paper, we bridge computational linguistics with history with the aim to explore the potential of topic modeling in discovering significant topics and historical trends in newspapers on the representations of Greek tourism during the period 1945-1989. Overall, the qualitative evaluation of the extracted topics revealed that most of the NMF topics are interpretable. The computational linguist was able to provide descriptive labels (e.g. economy, transportation) to the majority of the topics, while the historian was able to identify more topics that required domain knowledge and also to contextualize them with the historical period under examination. Therefore, and in accord with Yang, Torgtet, & Mihalcea (2011), we agree with Block (2006) that "topic simulation is only a tool" and it is essential that an expert in the field contextualizes these topics and evaluates them for relevancy.

Furthermore, by contextualizing the extracted topics within the historical and political environment in which they appear, we highlighted the role of historical interpretation with regard to analyzing discourse dynamics through topic models. The analysis of our findings provides interesting insights about the main textual representations of Greece as a tourist nation, their evolution across different historical periods, their cultural underpinnings, and how they were communicated to different audiences, and offer a tangible example of how computational text analysis can assist historical research.

7. Limitations

The findings discussed in this paper are based on the NMF results on our datasets. We will further explore the capacity and the differences of both methods (LDA and NMF) also considering the size and the unbalanced nature of our datasets (i.e. different number of articles from various newspapers for different periods). A further limitation of our datasets arises from the OCR process; in addition to the quantitative evaluation of the OCR extracted texts, a qualitative one is also needed to check for irrelevant texts that might be included in our datasets due to unclear separation between different articles on the same page, thus affecting the quality of the topic modeling results (i.e. generating irrelevant or non-interpretable topics). In addition, the data collection method introduces limitations to our datasets, since the selected keywords may not capture the complexity of tourism as a multifaceted concept, other relevant articles might have been written using different terminology, and, given that we are dealing with historical data, some keywords may become outdated as language evolves and/or new terms may emerge. Taking into account the above limitations, the results presented in this paper are based on the specific articles that have been retrieved and analyzed from each newspaper; our findings cannot be considered representative of the coverage and the editorial stances of each newspaper included in our analysis for the period under examination and cannot be generalized to the whole spectrum of the American and the British press.

Acknowledgments

The authors are grateful to G.Kakavas, A. Vavadakis, C.Fragkiadiakis and A.Tsakiri for their valuable contribution in the data processing tasks. The work presented in this paper is supported by UKRI, Research England.

References

Stavros Alifragkis, and Emilia Athanassiou. 2011. Educating Greece in Modernity: Post-War Tourism and Western Politics. *The Journal of Architecture*. 18. 10.1080/13602365.2013.838285.

Roderick Beaton. 2021. *The Greeks: A Global History.* Basic Books, London, ISBN10: 1541618297.

Adrian Bingham. (2010). The Digitization of Newspaper Archives: Opportunities and Challenges for Historians. *Twentieth Century British History*, 21(2), pages 225–231.

David M. Blei, Andrew W. Ng, and Andrew M. Jordan. 2002. Latent Dirichlet Allocation. In *Advances in Neural Information Processing Systems (NIPS*), T. G. Dietterich, S. Becker, and Z. Ghahramani (Eds.). 601–608.

Sharon Block. 2006. Doing More with Digitization: An Introduction to Topic Modeling of Early American Sources. *Common-Place*, 6(2), January.

Rene Brauer and Mats Fridlund. 2013. Historicizing topic models, a distant reading of topic modeling texts within historical studies. In *International Conference on Cultural Research in the context of Digital Humanities*, St. Petersburg: Russian State Herzen University.

Rob Churchill and Lisa Singh. 2022. The Evolution of Topic Modeling. *ACM Computing Surveys*. 54. 10.1145/3507900.

Roman Egger and Joanne Yu. 2022. A Topic Modeling Comparison Between LDA, NMF, Top2Vec, and BERTopic to Demystify Twitter Posts. *Frontiers in Sociology*. 7. 10.3389/fsoc.2022.886498.

Yue Guo, Stuart S. Barnes, and Qiong Jia. 2017. Mining meaning from online ratings and reviews: Tourist satisfaction analysis using latent dirichlet allocation.*Tour. Manag*. 2017, 59, 467–483.

Simon Hengchen. 2017. When Does it Mean? Detecting Semantic Change in Historical Texts. Ph.D. thesis, Universite libre de Bruxelles.

Chao Huang, Qing Wang, Dongui Yanga, and Feifei Xu. 2018. Topic mining of tourist attractions based on a seasonal context aware LDA model. *Intelligent Data Analysis*. 22. 383-405. 10.3233/IDA-173364.

Woohyuk Kim, Sung-Bum Kim, and Eunhye Park. 2021. Mapping Tourists' Destination (Dis)Satisfaction Attributes with User-Generated Content. *Sustainability.* 3(22):12650.

Jani Marjanen, Elaine Zosa, Simon Hengchen, Lidia Pivovarova, and Mikko Tolonen. 2020. Topic Modelling Discourse Dynamics in Historical Newspapers. *ArXiv, abs/2011.10428*.

David J. Newman and Sharon Block (2006). Probabilistic topic decomposition of an eighteenth-century american newspaper. *Journal of the American Society for Information Science and Technology*, 57(6), 753–767.

Mila Oiva. 2021. Topic Modeling Russian History. In: Gritsenko, D., Wijermars, M., Kopotev, M. (eds) *The Palgrave Handbook of Digital Russia Studies*. Palgrave Macmillan, Cham.

Yanwei Pang, Qiang Hao, Yuan Yuan, Tanji Hu, Rui Cai, and Lei Zhang. 2011. Summarizing tourist destinations by mining user generated travelogues and photos. *Computer Vision and Image Understanding* 115 (3), pages 352 – 363, special issue on Feature-Oriented Image and Video Computing for Extracting Contexts and Semantics.

Pimpitcha Pitichotchokphokhin, Piyawat Chuangkrud, Kongkan Kalakan, Boontawee Suntisrivaraporn, Teerapong Leelanupab, and Nont Kanungsukkasem. 2020. Discover Underlying Topics in Thai News Articles: A Comparative Study of Probabilistic and Matrix Factorization Approaches. 759-762. 10.1109/ECTI-CON49241.2020.9158065.

Annette Pritchard, and Nigel Morgan. 2001. Culture, identity and tourism representation: Marketing Cymru or Wales?. *Tourism Management*. 22, pages 167-179. 10.1016/S0261-5177(00)00047-9.

Dimitris Tziovas. 2021. *Greece from Junta to Crisis: Modernization, Transition and Diversity*. Bloomsbury Publishing, London.

Paris Tsartas. 2010. *Greek Tourism Development* [in Greek] (Athens, 2010).

Lorella Viola and Jaap Verheul. 2019. Mining ethnicity: Discourse-driven topic modelling of immigrant discourses in the USA, 1898–1920. *Digital Scholarship in the Humanities*, Volume 35 (4), pages 921–943.

Angelos Vlachos. 2016. *Tourism, and the public policies in Contemporary Greece, 1914-1950* [in Greek] (Athens, 2016).

Tze-I Yang, Andrew Torget, and Rada Mihalcea. 2011. Topic Modeling on Historical Newspapers. In *Proceedings of the 5th ACL-HLT Workshop on Language Technology for Cultural Heritage, Social Sciences, and Humanities*, pages 96–104, Portland, OR, USA. Association for Computational Linguistics.

May Young, and David Johnson. 2018. A Comparison of LDA and NMF for Topic Modeling on Literary Themes. UBC Wiki: https://wiki.ubc.ca/Course:CPSC522/A_Comparison_of_LDA_and_NMF_for_Topic_Modeling_on_Literary_Themes

Eric E. G. Zuelow. 2011. *Touring Beyond the Nation: A Transnational Approach to European Tourism History*. Routledge, London.

Appendix A. Topic modeling results on the American articles.

topic ID	Top terms
A. Reconstruction of the country and first signs of tourism (1945-1949)	
#A1	war marshall_plan economic balance aid import state export price united foreign
#A2	like text document street letter old state despite mountain dress night little right
#A3	guerrilla five marshall aid program ration year army plan need current vehicle
#A4	service passenger air athens day new_york france army office cargo piraeus national
#A5	island italian currency problem beauty bank italy state occupation cause considerable point recovery
#A6	nation food loan united national economy industrial international special president resource truman
#A7	europe food business hotel france little situation restaurant italy price currency men problem
#A8	tobacco olive worth product germany export dollar government oil price united central living
B. Tourism takes off (1950-1966)	
#B1	hotel athens site festival ancient accommodation room price government road cost rate delphi
#B2	line passenger air ship atlantic flight charter vessel airline state united service
#B3	million foreign export income import common market economy economic trade industry government
#B4	island town rhodes ancient sea water cruise church mykonos aegean ruin small old
#B5	owner reproduction historical newspaper request chicago mayor tribune million dollar
#B6	draft united state regulation citizen greek born embassy citizenship law
#B7	publication condo document request white hilton database new_york publisher text woman
#B8	timesmachine home subject company reprint store date service privacy
#B9	travel new_york tour trip cruise agent round fare hotel jet
C. Dictatorship (1967-1974)	
#C1	island boat mykonos sea harbor rhodes village beach aegean ko water small town
#C2	junta military political government colonel regime communist athens coup new politics press state
#C3	cruise tour travel new_york ship agent line timesmachine service air travel agent
#C4	litton_contract development government investment nation project international development litton_industry proposal president industry
#C5	event reproduction owner reproduction historical newspaper historical owner million national newspaper period increase request historical request
#C6	million onassis refinery government nacho export loan oil foreign economic investment economy growth
#C7	acropolis athens museum street food ancient foot square like restaurant marble parthenon ate
D. Democratisation and economic crisis (1975-1980)	
#D1	island town village villa beach crete boat small street harbor water old hotel
#D2	departure transfer trip jet baggage round daily escort tax hotel continental breakfast
#D3	festival opera theater ballet ticket music orchestra athens concert program subject performance soloist
#D4	travel tour new_york fare price office cost vacation million charter europe
#D5	ancient bus temple ruin acropolis game athens museum site olympia mountain modern roman
#D6	environment development cultural touristic social economy pylos physical pollution economic natural environmental dilemma
E. PASOK government (1981-1989)	
#E1	island town beach village hotel small like church room sea restaurant boat old
#E2	security airport travel terrorist terrorism flight cancellation passenger airline athens twa incident president

#E3	timesmachine cruise home reprint store service privacy company tour brochure search archive caribbean
#E4	museum acropolis art street collection plaza athens admission open hall square folk restaurant
#E5	version section print archive parthenon turtle edition headline national
#E6	dollar europe travel european hotel france britain million price terrorism tour italy paris
#E7	document request condo film database text publisher publication image movie caption
#E8	philharmonic orchestra government hostage official sour state basis minister concert united cancel
#E9	lois advertising agency campaign commercial celebrity account unusual broadcast thing print born

Appendix B. Topic modeling results on the British articles.

topic ID	Top terms
A. Reconstruction of the country and first signs of tourism (1945-1949)	
#A1	government new service national policy night nation state lord office communist minister london
#A2	price profit tax million stock div gold steel market ordinary net dividend bank
#A3	guardian observer rhodes owner reproduction request historical newspaper village italian manchester
B. Tourism takes off (1950-1966)	
#B1	temp rain wind moderate shower cloudy editor government university deg sunny work midday
#B2	oil canadian stock steel company correspondent price industry canada market bank montreal sale
#B3	hotel island athens guardian mykonos classical class sea parthenon delos room cheap good
#B4	government minister correspondent state united party prime president soviet german police general
#B5	profit bank company dividend market increase account rate investment ordinary balance tax stock
#B6	news london daughter church engagement film work music service son daily salary car
#B7	cruise guinea travel agent hellenic southampton ship palma passenger madeira voyage london
#B8	allowance guardian observer owner reproduction newspaper travel historical sterling
#B9	hide cassock son spoof bros ord brit store stamp duty motor metal bargain
C. Dictatorship (1967-1974)	
#C1	government party minister new police vietnam state president student united court soviet press
#C2	million increase credit rate economy growth investment economic bank development deposit earnings
#C3	hotel cruise brochure travel beach island sun car agent street london villa sea
#C4	turkish cyprus cypriot base force united nation island deceit troop minister military
#C5	guardian newspaper observer historical reproduction owner hotel request
#C6	hotel development bed automatic astir athens ote island telecommunication beach national private five year
#C7	company industry market price new business profit investment plant group chemical government gold
D. Democratisation and economic crisis (1975-1980)	
#D1	hotel beach observer guardian like town island historical newspaper reproduction shop request night
#D2	party union government minister state french soviet eec leader foreign gas general france
#D3	bank ship hotel fleet foreign energy investment shipping oil million industry banking owner
#D4	corfu flower village club tour yacht mount golf near hotel available bird crete
#D5	london tel book street car brochure mon mile blue air travel great
#D6	arras porto village development island project service settlement hotel mainland cohen adrienne
E. PASOK government (1981-1989)	
#E1	minister government soviet president prime new state force party foreign prime minister talk nudist
#E2	island beach hotel town ferry road guide bay guardian village room observer like
#E3	rate germany jan australia france canada japan bank belgium billion holland sweden index
#E4	terrorist bomb security guardian hijack attack terrorism ship twa athens agency sentence group
#E5	hotel brochure tel travel london night flight tour company sale car football free
#E6	site cruise athens island crete ancient archaeological museum aegean eec professor problem foreign
#E7	rhodes stone fist mercury archaeologist limestone smith antiquity nationality statue bronze god kill

#E8	union government party worker strike company communist socialist solidarity social pay new employer
#E9	turtle austrian bay banana strauss egg chess bavaria breed steer west austria gentleman

Appendix C. Keywords used for Data Collection.

Greece Tourism
Greek Tourism
EOT/ GNTO
Greece-Olympic Airways
Greece-Cruises
Greece- Tourism exhibition
Greece- sun sea sand food
Greece-Mediterranean
Greece diaspora-tourism

Post-correction of Historical Text Transcripts with Large Language Models: An Exploratory Study

Emanuela Boros[1], **Maud Ehrmann**[1],
Matteo Romanello[2], **Sven Najem-Meyer**[1], **Frédéric Kaplan**[1]

[1]Digital Humanities Laboratory, EPFL, Lausanne, Switzerland
[2]Institute of Archeology and Classical Studies, University of Lausanne, Switzerland
{emanuela.boros,maud.ehrmann,sven.najem-meyer,frederic.kaplan}@epfl.ch
matteo.romanello@unil.ch

Abstract

The quality of automatic transcription of heritage documents, whether from printed, manuscripts or audio sources, has a decisive impact on the ability to search and process historical texts. Although significant progress has been made in text recognition (OCR, HTR, ASR), textual materials derived from library and archive collections remain largely erroneous and noisy. Effective post-transcription correction methods are therefore necessary and have been intensively researched for many years. As large language models (LLMs) have recently shown exceptional performances in a variety of text-related tasks, we investigate their ability to amend poor historical transcriptions. We evaluate fourteen foundation language models against various post-correction benchmarks comprising different languages, time periods and document types, as well as different transcription quality and origins. We compare the performance of different model sizes and different prompts of increasing complexity in zero and few-shot settings. Our evaluation shows that LLMs are anything but efficient at this task. Quantitative and qualitative analyses of results allow us to share valuable insights for future work on post-correcting historical texts with LLMs.

1 Introduction

Over the last two decades, heritage institutions have digitised their collections on a massive scale, yielding millions of historical documents in digital format along with their machine-readable text (Terras, 2011; Padilla, 2019). Whether obtained through optical character recognition (OCR, for printed documents), handwritten text recognition (HTR, for manuscripts) or automatic speech recognition techniques (ASR, for audio documents), the availability of textual transcriptions has not only improved the accessibility of historical documents, but has also opened up the possibility of applying machine-reading techniques to their content. Increasingly, research and initiatives are being undertaken to process and mine the rich information contained in unstructured heritage text data (Clausner et al., 2019; Ehrmann et al., 2022), or to develop computational approaches to its analysis (McGillivray et al., 2020; Bunout et al., 2022). While highly promising, these efforts face a persistent challenge that considerably impacts their effectiveness: the suboptimal quality of transcriptions.

Most text data derived from digitised historical documents contains transcription errors, for two reasons. Firstly, despite recent advances in the accuracy of text recognition –thanks to the adoption of neural approaches and robust transcription frameworks (Reul et al., 2019; Kahle et al., 2017; Engl, 2020) – the quality of digital documents and the diversity of document types, languages, scripts, fonts and handwriting still poses significant challenges to OCR, HTR and ASR approaches. Secondly, even though the latest transcription engines are much better than their predecessors, collections digitised long ago are rarely reprocessed, often for budgetary reasons. The impact of noisy transcriptions on downstream processes is well-documented, with a detrimental effect on search capacities (Chiron et al., 2017b), named entity processing (Linhares Pontes et al., 2019; Hamdi et al., 2020), language modeling (Todorov and Colavizza, 2022), and most natural language processing (NLP) tasks (van Strien et al., 2020).

Possible answers to this situation lie in the development of post-correction methods aimed at producing a better, corrected version of a transcription with respect to the corresponding original text and, more recently, in the targeted re-transcription of identified faulty text sections—a complex process that requires robust pipelines (Schneider and Maurer, 2022). Latest approaches to post-correction use sequence-to-sequence neural networks, with character-based translation models (Amrhein and Clematide, 2018) as well as LSTMs or transformer-

Proceedings of LaTeCH-CLfL 2024, pages 133–159
March 22, 2024 ©2024 Association for Computational Linguistics

based models (Nguyen et al., 2020; Rigaud et al., 2019). Despite significant progress, performances vary greatly across the variety of historical texts (Chiron et al., 2017a; Rigaud et al., 2019), and systems still have difficulties dealing with extreme noise (Amrhein and Clematide, 2018), generalising (Todorov and Colavizza, 2020) and avoiding undesired changes to error-free text, a particularly important requirement with historical sources (Schaefer and Neudecker, 2020).

At the core of many approaches to NLP, language representations have evolved from auxiliaries to machine learning systems, such as n-gram models and word vectors, to specialised experts fine-tuned for specific tasks, such as transformer-based pre-trained language models. Current efforts are aimed at more versatile systems, training autoregressive generative models on ever larger amounts of data and model sizes. This results in the emergence of large language models (LLMs) with exceptional robustness and generalisability capabilities, even in zero and few-shot settings (Brown et al., 2020; Chowdhery et al., 2022; Scao et al., 2022; Zhang et al., 2022, to cite but a few). Since the launch of the GPT (Generative Pre-Trained) model series by OpenAI in 2018, and in particular the ChatGPT conversational robot released in November 2022 based on the GPT-3.5 or GPT-4 models, the LLM race is on. More and more models are being released, with impressive performance on various text-related tasks and results close to the state of the art, e.g. in question answering (Bang et al., 2023), machine translation (Jiao et al., 2023) and stance detection (Zhang et al., 2023).

Of all the ways in which ChatGPT can be used, its ability to revise and improve the quality of texts was quickly noticed. Having been trained on hundreds of billions of tokens to predict the next word in a sequence, such text editing ability is hardly surprising. While evaluations have been carried out on tasks involving language editing capacities such as text summarisation and grammatical error correction—with fairly good results for some metrics (Gao et al., 2023; Wu et al., 2023; Laskar et al., 2023)—the ability of LLMs to amend historical transcriptions has not yet been systematically studied. Can large language models that have powerful capabilities for generating and understanding language in different contexts also help to correctly rewrite texts that have been poorly transcribed by automated processes? Capitalising on the recent rise of generative LLMs, this study aims to investigate, beyond anecdotal observations, the effectiveness of large language models to post-correct historical transcripts. In particular, we want to gain a better understanding of whether, to what extent, and under what conditions LLMs can produce good corrections of historical transcriptions, and seek to answer the following questions:

- **Ability to correct.** When prompted to correct the transcription of a given historical document, do LLMs improve, degrade, or leave the input text intact?
- **Sensitivity to variations in input text and instructions.** Does the correction performance depend on the time period, language, type and noise of the original document? How sensitive is LLM-based post-correction to prompt instructions?
- **Real-world applicability.** How do open-access models compare to OpenAI GPT models? Could LLM-based post-correction be a valid and cost-effective option for efficiently correcting backlogs of millions of noisy historical documents?

To this end, we evaluate fourteen foundation language models from four model series against various post-correction benchmarks comprising different languages, time periods, document types, and different transcription quality and origins. We compare the performance of different prompts of increasing complexity in zero and few-shot settings and provide quantitative and qualitative analyses of the results.

2 Background

We briefly highlight some key facets of LLMs and refer to Zhao et al. (2023) for a detailed survey. LLMs are text generators that are trained on massive plain text data. Based on well-established technology – deep neural networks and self-supervised learning – their success is mainly due to two key factors: scaling up model size and the amount of training data (Zhao et al., 2023). The former was made possible by the Transformer architecture (Vaswani et al., 2017) and the latter by 20 years' worth of internet text data. Coupled with optimisation frameworks (Rasley et al., 2020; Shoeybi et al., 2020), this has led to the rapid emergence of large language models with hundreds of billions of parameters, with increasing capacity to learn, generalise and act as general-purpose task solvers as more (clean) data is input. Quickly identified as a paradigm shift in artificial intelligence systems, LLMs, and more generally foundation models, possess the crucial ability to learn in context, i.e. to perform a task with only a few instructions and task demonstrations, generating the expected output without updating model parameters (Dong et al., 2023). Their behaviour is implicitly deduced and not explicitly constructed. Following OpenAI's initial releases, numerous models are being published by various commercial and academic players, sparking a global debate on the opportunities and risks from a scientific and societal point of view (Bommasani et al., 2022).

LLMs's text editing capabilities have particularly been assessed in the context of grammatical error correction (GEC). Several studies have compared state-of-the-art GEC systems with GPT models against various benchmarks and found that they can perform GEC tasks effectively (especially on sentence input) and that they are slightly better at error detection than at correction due to overcorrection (Ostling and Kurfalı, 2022; Wu et al., 2023), a tendency that can be controlled by optimising prompt and example selection (Fang et al., 2023; Loem et al., 2023; Coyne et al., 2023). Few attempts have been made to post-correct transcriptions with LLMs, including LLM-based selection of the best post-corrections for contemporary documents (Gupta et al., 2021), and fine-tuning the BART autoregressive Transformer to post-correct historical newspapers (Soper et al., 2021). To our knowledge, no previous study has explored LLM-based post-correction of historical transcripts.

3 Approach

We aim to assess the ability of generative LLMs to correct machine transcriptions of historical documents and to provide insights into what works best. Using post-correction transcription benchmarks, our approach is, essentially, to compare the similarities between original automated transcriptions and their ground truth (GT), and between LLM-corrected versions of the original transcriptions and the same GT, and to observe their variation, i.e. whether the LLM-corrected version is a degradation or an improvement of the original transcriptions.

To better reflect the diversity of archival collections and obtain results that are, to some extent, generalisable, we consider various post-correction benchmarks covering different document types, languages and periods, as well as different transcription qualities and origins. Their different formats are standardised to ensure consistent handling of the data, especially as far as different levels of text segmentation (line, sentence region) are concerned. The selection of LLMs is based on model size, training data, resource requirements and accessibility. We consider fourteen models from four series and craft five prompts to guide their text generation. Various post-processing heuristics are applied to clean up the output.

Despite their astonishing performance, we can hypothesise that post-correcting historical transcripts may pose several challenges for LLMs. First, unlike typical text generation tasks where multiple answers can be valid (summarisation, translation, dialogue systems), transcription correction requires a single correct answer that exactly matches the GT. This, of course, runs counter to LLM's tendency to hallucinate. Second, LLMs are not specifically trained for post-correction but learn in context through natural language instructions that they must understand – an ability that is unequal between models. Third, the level and nature of noise in historical transcripts vary considerably from document to document, i.e. texts can range from minimally to extremely noisy, with different forms of noise. While this challenge affects all approaches, LLMs may not have encountered many noisy historical transcripts during their training.

3.1 Datasets

We use eight post-correction benchmarks, each consisting of two historical transcriptions: one from an automated system (to be corrected) and its ground truth counterpart. The two versions are aligned at different levels, and there are no images of the original documents. Besides diversity, the choice of benchmarks was guided by the requirement that transcripts should not be too short to provide sufficient context for the LLMs. Table 1 outlines the datasets (six from OCR, one from ASR, and one from HTR), which are also presented below.

`icdar-2017` & `icdar-2019` Two ICDAR evaluation campaigns on post-OCR text correction published two benchmarks in 2017 and 2019 (Chiron et al., 2017a; Rigaud et al., 2019). `icdar-2017` (12M characters) comprises monographs and newspapers in English and French originating from a

Dataset Alias	Document Type	Origin	Time Period	Language	# Lines*	# Sentences*	# Regions*
icdar-2017	newspapers,monographies	OCR	17C-20C	en, fr	0	461	28
icdar-2019		OCR	not specified	bg,cz,en,fr,de,pl,sl	0	404	41
overproof	newspaper	OCR	19-20C	en	2,278	399	41
impresso-nzz	newspaper	OCR	18-20C	de	1,256	577	203
ajmc-mixed	class. commentaries	OCR	19C	grc, de, en, fr	535	379	33
ajmc-primary	class. commentaries	OCR	19C	grc, de, en, fr	40	27	9
htrec	papyri and manuscripts	HTR	10C-16C	grc	180	8	8
ina	radio programs	ASR	20C	fr	201	290	6

Table 1: Overview of the datasets. (*): Figures correspond to the data used in this study, except for `htrec`, `ina`, `ajmc-mixed`, and `ajmc-primary`, where they correspond to the full dataset.

range of heritage institutions and initiatives (Papadopoulos et al., 2013; Neudecker and Antonacopoulos, 2016), and `icdar-2019` (22M characters) expands to further types of printed documents, newspapers and shopping receipts in 10 European languages. No document dates are specified, but we estimate a 17C-20C time frame for `icdar-2017` based on the original datasets, assuming a similar range for the second. The documents in the dataset correspond to different segments of historical records, with OCR transcriptions and GT aligned at character level. Detailed information about data quality is unavailable, yet documents may contain up to 50% of misrecognised characters. In this study, we use samples of 12% and 20% of the 2017 and 2019 data, respectively.

`overproof` Published as part of an OCR evaluation, the Overproof benchmarks were extracted from the National Library of Australia's Trove digitised newspaper collection (Evershed and Fitch, 2014)[1]. In this study, we use a 20% random sample from the first dataset, which consists of medium-size articles from the *Sydney Morning Herald* from 1842 to 1945. The documents in the dataset correspond to articles, with OCR transcriptions and GT aligned at line level. The ground truth was crowd-sourced from users of the Trove website and may therefore be incomplete. We used the code of van Strien et al. (2020) to pre-process the data.

`impresso-nzz` Created as part of the first *impresso* project (Ehrmann et al., 2020), the `impresso-nzz` dataset consists of 167 front pages from the *Neue Zürcher Zeitung* newspaper, randomly selected from each year between 1780 and 1947 (Ströbel and Clematide, 2019)[2]. Documents correspond to pages, with OCR and GT aligned at region, line, and word levels. In this study, we use a 50% random sample of the data in its OCRed version from ABBYY FineReader Server11, that showed a low recognition rate on this black letter font (Ströbel et al., 2020).

`ajmc` This dataset was created as part of the Ajax Multi-Commentary project and consists of five 19C scholarly commentaries on Sophocles' *Ajax*. Commentaries are written in German, English, and Latin and contain a mix of Latin and polytonic Greek scripts (Romanello et al., 2021). Documents correspond to commentary pages, transcribed using Tesseract's `de`, `en`, `la` and `grc` models. OCR and GT are aligned at region and line level. In this study, we use two subsets: `ajmc-primary` with texts written only in Greek, and `ajmc-mixed` with mixed languages and scripts.

`htrec` Compiled for the Handwritten Text Recognition Error Correction (HTREC) shared task (Pavlopoulos et al., 2023), the `htrec` dataset comprises Byzantine papyri and manuscripts from 10C-16C in Byzantine Greek (between ancient and modern Greek) (Platanou et al., 2022). Documents correspond to pages, with HTR and GT transcriptions aligned at line level. In this study, we use the test set consisting of 180 lines.

`ina` Finally, the `ina` dataset consists of six French radio programmes of different types (political speech, news, fiction, entertainment), each from one decade between 1930 and 1980. Audio and ASR transcriptions were provided by the French National Audiovisual Institute to the authors, who transcribed them manually. Documents correspond to a programme, with ASR and GT aligned at the level of text 'sections'. These sections do not correspond to a speaker turn or anything else, and may contain less or more than one sentence. Background events (e.g. music) are not indicated.

[1] `https://overproof.projectcomputing.com/evaluation`

[2] Refer to the Zenodo and GitHub repositories.

Model	Release date	Used sizes	Access	Max length
GPT-2	11.2019	1.5B	open	1,024
GPT-3	06.2020	175B	limited	2,049
GPT-3.5	03.2023	unknown	limited	4,096
GPT-4	03.2023	unknown	limited	8,192
BLOOM	07.2022	560M, 3B, 7.1B	open	2,048
BLOOMZ	11.2022	560M, 3B, 7.1B	open	2,048
OPT	05.2022	350M, 6.7B	open	2,048
LLaMA	02.2023	7B	open	2,048
LLaMA-2	07.2023	7B	open	4,096

Table 2: Overview of LLMs used in this study.

Overall, these datasets provide challenging material for LLMs. In addition to the variety of error types and languages, models have to deal with a wide range of document lengths, some of which are exceptionally long, as well as with truncated text regions due to incorrect segmentation. We have not evaluated the ground truths of these benchmarks and assume that they are acceptable since they were created for evaluation purposes. It should be noted, however, that their quality is certainly not perfect.

3.2 Models

We consider fourteen LLMs from four model series, which differ in size, training settings, data, and accessibility. All models, summarised in Table 2, are decoder-only autoregressive LLMs.

GPT OpenAI's GPT model series consists of powerful models that grow in capability as training data and model size increase. In this study, we use GPT-2, GPT-3, GPT-3.5, and GPT-4. Only GPT-2 (Radford et al., 2019) is freely available to everyone, the others are accessible via OpenAI's commercial API and their training conditions and features have not been fully disclosed. While GPT-3 proved the impact of scaling and demonstrates in-context learning ability (Brown et al., 2020), the next capacity improvements came from training on code and reinforcement learning through human feedback (GPT-3.5), as well as increased maximum context length (Ouyang et al., 2022). GPT-4 has an even larger context window, and multimodal input (OpenAI, 2023).

BLOOM(Z) The BigScience Large Open-science Open-access Multilingual language model, developed by the BigScience project, handles 46 languages, is open source and, at the time of release, was larger than GPT-3 (176B). The initiative produced models of different sizes trained on the same dataset. Aimed at improving generalisation, the BLOOMZ series was subsequently released, with BLOOM and mT5 models fine-tuned on cross-lingual variants of the P3 dataset (a collection of prompts covering various NLP tasks) (Scao et al., 2022; Muennighoff et al., 2023). In this study, we use BLOOM(Z) 560M, 3B and 7.1B.

OPT The Open Pre-trained Transformers is a series of open-source LLMs developed by Meta AI. Trained on English data and ranging from 125M to 175B parameters, the OPT models are large causal language models designed to be comparable in size and performance to GPT-3, but transparent and with a lower training carbon footprint (Zhang et al., 2022). We use two model sizes.

LLaMA Also released openly and aimed at the research community, the Large Language Model Meta AI (LLaMA) model has been trained on twenty languages and, according to its developers, outperforms GPT-3 on many tasks while using fewer resources (Touvron et al., 2023a). LLaMA-2 is trained on 40% more data and with twice the context length (Touvron et al., 2023b).

4 Experimental Setting

4.1 Data Preparation

Data preparation consists of two processes: the homogenisation of text structures and their formats, and the definition of OCR quality bands.

Historical documents have different layouts (single or multiple columns, text subdivisions, presence of images), as do the selected datasets, with documents corresponding to different elements (page, article) and transcriptions corresponding to different levels of text segmentation (line, article, region). To ensure consistent data handling, facilitate fair performance comparison across datasets, and study the importance of context in post-correction with generative LLMs, we define three levels of text units. First, a line level – commonly found in historical documents – is already present in all datasets except `icdar`. Second, a sentence level, a linguistically meaningful unit of text that is not present in any of the datasets. For sentence splitting, we first align transcription and GT tokens using a fast recursive text alignment scheme (Yalniz and Manmatha, 2011), before applying a sentence splitter (Sadvilkar and Neumann, 2020). This process is applied to all datasets. Finally, we

Basic-1	`Correct the text:\n {{TEXT}}`
Basic-2	`Correct the spelling and grammar of the following text:\n {{TEXT}}`
Complex-1	`Correct the spelling and grammar of the following incorrect text from on optical character recognition (OCR) applied to a historical document:\n Incorrect text: {{TEXT}}\n The corrected text is:`
Complex-2	`Please assist with reviewing and correcting errors in texts produced by automatic transcription (OCR) of historical documents. Your task is to carefully examine the following text and correct any mistakes introduced by the OCR software. The text to correct appears after the segment "TEXT TO CORRECT:". Please place the corrected version of the text after the "CORRECTED TEXT:" segment. Do not write anything else than the corrected text.\n\n TEXT TO CORRECT:\n {{TEXT}} \n CORRECTED TEXT:`
Complex-3	Complex-2 translated to fr, de, etc.

Table 3: Prompt templates.

consider a region level, which corresponds to the whole text of a document in a dataset.

We further qualify each text unit according to its (original) transcription quality, expressed by the Levenshtein similarity measure between the transcription and the ground truth (the measure is presented in Section 4.3). Transcriptions are classified into one of five percentage quality bands: $0-40$, $40-60$, $60-80$, $80-99$ and $99-100$; the higher, the better.

4.2 Prompt Templates and Setup

Guiding models toward the intended output relies on prompts (Liu et al., 2023). Given a fixed LLM, prompting involves converting each test input into a prompt based on a template and inputting it into the model to generate the response.

We manually design five prompt templates that provide small to strong guidance, presented in Table 3. `Basic-1` simply instructs the model to correct any errors present in the input text. `Basic-2` is a bit more explicit and tells the model to focus on spelling and grammar errors. This prompt may be useful for text editing in general, but may still be too imprecise for OCR, ASR, and HTR material. `Complex-1` informs the model that the input is from an automatic transcription of a historical document (OCR, ASR or HTR), and `Complex-2` additionally asks it to shape its response according to an explicit format. Such context awareness and format guidance may improve the quality of corrections and the cleanliness of the output. Finally, `Complex-3` translates `Complex-2` in all languages of the datasets.

Models are prompted in zero-shot (ZS) and few-shot (FS) settings. In ZS, the model has access to the test input only, whereas in FS, three demonstration examples are provided. The examples are randomly selected from three of the lowest transcription quality bands for each dataset. For all experiments, we perform a single-pass generation, i.e. without aggregation of multiple runs.

LLM output often do not match the expected response shape and require post-processing. Where necessary, we trim the output from unnecessary spaces or response presentation formulas, remove repeated (parts of) the prompt, and discard any text that is longer than 1.5 times the input. Post-processing is further described in Appendix B.

4.3 Evaluation Metric

We determine the difference in quality between an LLM-generated post-correction of a transcription and the original automatic transcription using a Post-Correction Improvement Score (PCIS)[3]. This relative score measures the positive or negative improvement, in terms of Levenshtein similarity, between the two transcriptions and the same ground truth. The Levenshtein similarity (*lev_sim*) is based on the Levenshtein distance between a machine transcription (`transcr`) and a ground truth (`GT`), and is computed as follows:

$$lev\_sim = \frac{length - lev\_dist(\texttt{transc}, GT)}{length} \quad (1)$$

where *lev_dist* is a string metric that measures the difference between two textual sequences based on the number of single-character edits (Levenshtein, 1966) and *length* is the length of the longer string (*max(len(*`transc`*), len(*`GT`*))*). The Levenshtein similarity provides a measure between 0 and 1, with higher values indicating higher similarity.

The PCIS is calculated based on the Levenshtein similarity between an original transcription and the GT (*orig_sim*), and between the LLM-generated post-correction and the GT (*llm_sim*), as follows:

$$\text{PCIS} = \begin{cases} \min(\max(llm\_sim, -1), 1), \\ \quad if\, orig\_sim = 0 \\ \min(\max(\frac{llm\_sim - orig\_sim}{orig\_sim}, -1), 1), \\ \quad if\, orig\_sim \neq llm\_sim \\ 0, \quad if\, orig\_sim = llm\_sim. \end{cases} \quad (2)$$

The improvement score ranges from -1 to 1: negative values indicate deterioration, positive values indicate improvement, and 0 indicates no change.

[3]Please note that this measure is not our invention but a classical way to calculate the relative change or difference from an initial value to a new value.

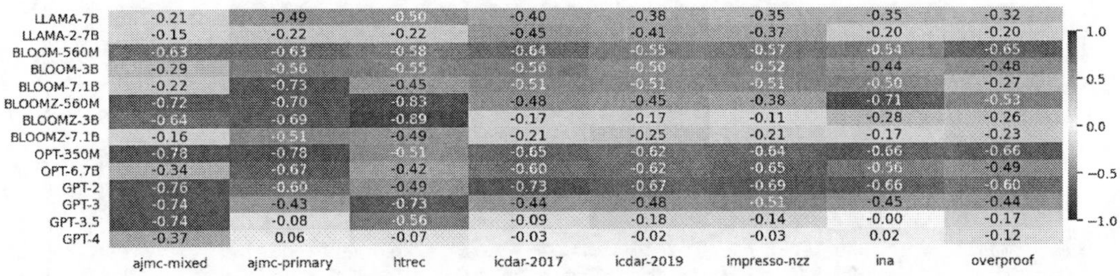

Figure 1: Average of post-correction improvement score per model and dataset, based on post-processed responses to sentence-level input with the best prompt template `Complex-2` in the zero-shot setting.

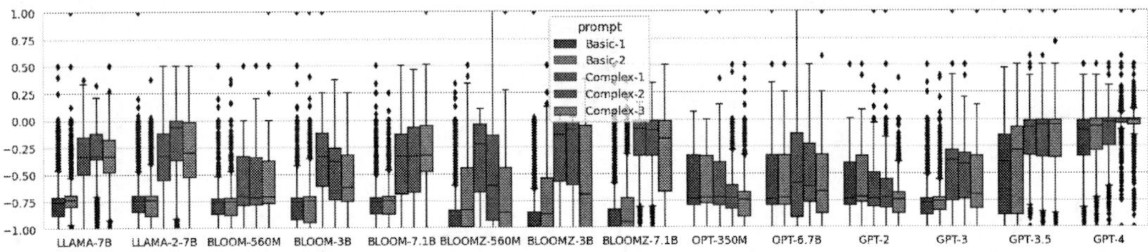

Figure 2: Average of post-correction improvement score across datasets, per model and per prompt, considering post-processed responses to sentence-level text input in the zero-shot setting.

5 Results and Discussion

With eight datasets, three text unit levels, multiple quality bands, fourteen models, five prompts and zero- and few-shot settings, experiments cover many dimensions and yield many results. We first present and discuss metric-based results by iteratively removing dimensions before manually exploring performance factors. Due to to space constraints, some figures are included in the Appendix.

5.1 Metric-based Evaluation

Overall, the performance of LLM-based post-correction is very poor, with a considerable degradation in the quality of original transcriptions across all models, prompts and datasets. Even when considering the most effective setup (sentence level and `Complex-2`), Figure 1 shows that LLMs mostly degrade the input text, occasionally leave it unchanged, and rarely improve it. It is therefore a matter of understanding which setup is the least worst.

Impact of post-processing and text unit level The basic conditions of our experiments include the use or not of response post-processing and the choice of text unit level. Regarding the former, experiments showed that post-processing benefits all models and text units (see Appendix B.2), with GPT-3.5 and 4 requiring the least post-processing and `Complex-2` often being difficult to open models, i.e. requiring most post-processing. Regarding the latter, sentence-level input text yields better results (see Appendix D). Subsequent analyses are therefore based on results from post-processed responses to sentence-level text input.

Impact of prompt template and setup From weak to strong guidance, which prompt template is the best (or causes the least degradation)? Figure 2 provides insights that lead to two observations. First, it is beneficial to provide specific information about the input text, as can be seen with the `Basic-1/2` prompts which systematically produce the strongest degradation. Second, none of the 'best' `Complex` prompts is a clear winner across models and datasets, producing more or less the same magnitude of degradation. Also, changing the execution setup from zero- to few-shot does not bring any improvement. Figure 3 shows that adding three demonstration examples almost systematically further degrades the results for all models except for GPT-3.5 and 4. This is in line with Zhao et al. (2021) who shows the high volatility of results depending on examples and their order.

Impact of models and document type Having eliminated the worst setups, and focusing on zero-shot responses to sentence-level input with the `Complex-2` prompt, which models perform

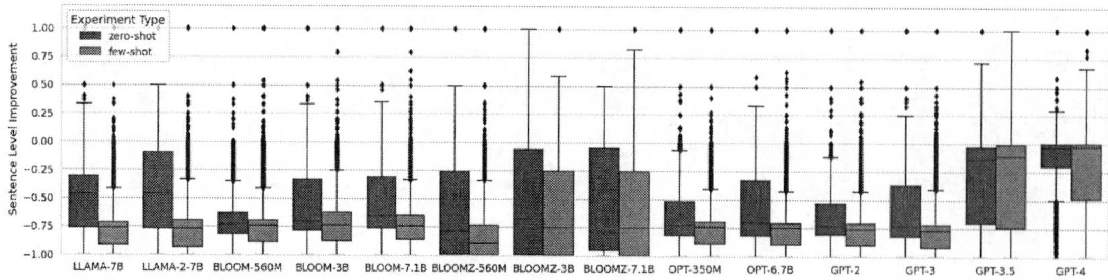

Figure 3: Average of the post-correction improvement score across datasets, per model and in ZS and FS settings, considering post-processed answers to sentence-level text inputs with prompt `Complex-2`.

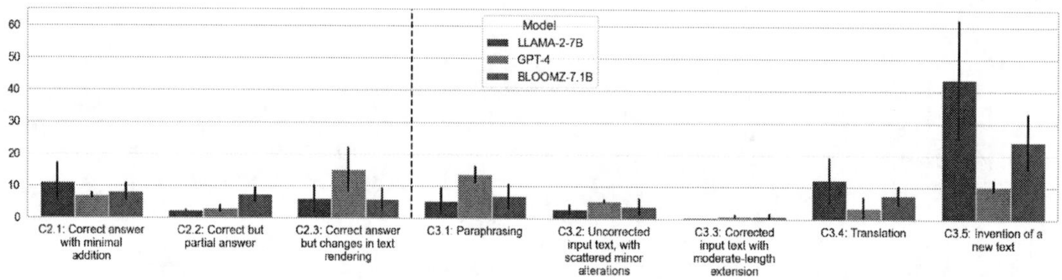

Figure 4: Error category distribution in manually annotated samples across three models, for groups C2 (slight deviation from GT, on the left) and C3 (strong deviation from GT, on the right).

best for which dataset? Regardless of the model, LLM-based post-correction of atypical text material and languages such as in `ajmc` and `htrec` lead to the most severe degradation (Figure 1). For `ajmc-mixed`, the largest multilingual BLOOM and LLaMA models offer some hope, while for `htrec` only GPT-4 seems to be able to save the results from degradation. The situation is less dramatic for `icdar`, `impresso-nzz`, `overproof` and `ina`, with documents closer in language, topics and nature to the training data of the models. As for LLMs, they generally show stability across the datasets, with a few exceptions. Not surprisingly, GPT-3.5 and 4 show the best results. With the exception of `ajmc-mixed`, the cross-lingual multitask fine-tuned BLOOMZ models perform better than their BLOOM counterparts, with no clear difference between model sizes. The smallest models, whether from the LLaMA, BLOOM or OPT series, generally perform on par with GPT-2 and GPT-3.

Impact of OCR quality Finally, the performance distribution among the original transcription quality bands shows that, overall, the noisiest input texts are those that show the least degradation, and sometimes even improvement. This underlines the ability of LLMs to make corrections where necessary, but not to leave almost error-free texts intact (more details in Appendix F).

5.2 Manual Analysis

In addition to improvement scores, we aim to understand the factors influencing transcription quality by manually inspecting around 2,500 LLM-corrected / ground truth transcription pairs, sampled across all datasets and a selection of models, prompts and languages (see Appendix C).

Following initial inspection, we established a tentative taxonomy of LLM errors or behaviours, comprising ten categories organised into four groups:

- C1: unanswered prompts;
- C2: responses with corrected input text but with slight deviations from the GT, thus invalid in terms of PCIS but potentially acceptable within an information retrieval context;
- C3: responses that deviate significantly from the GT, or hallucinations; and
- C4: instances where the GT itself is incorrect.

The error taxonomy, detailed in Appendix C.3, represents cases of instruction inconsistencies, where the model does not do what it is asked to do, and context inconsistencies, where its answer is incorrect (Huang et al., 2023). Figure 4 shows the distribution of errors for three models between C2 and C3, which represent two thirds of the sample. We note that most cases correspond to strong deviations from the GT (C3), with a majority of pure hallucination (C3.5, especially LLaMA-2-7B and BLOOMZ-7.1B), as well as a slight tendency of GPT to propose paraphrases rather than just correct the text. Models also produce smaller deviations (C2), with LLaMA-2-7B marginally continuing the text, BLOOMZ-7.1B giving partial answers, and GPT-4 embellishing the text as it sees fit.

6 Conclusions and Future Work

This exploratory study shows that LLMs are not good at correcting transcriptions of historical documents of any kind, at least in the applied experimental setting. Not only do they not improve the original transcriptions, they usually degrade them, making LLM-based post-correction of historical transcripts a rather distant prospect. Nevertheless, we have found that instructing models about the nature of the input and guiding their output format leads to better results, and that large open-access and multilingual models from the BLOOM(Z) and LLaMA series can compete with commercial GPT models.

On the basis of these findings, future work should investigate in more detail some of the elements that could not be studied due to the scale of the experiments presented here. These include, among others: testing prompts that are even more tailored to the specifics of each document type, distinguishing between error detection and correction prompts (in a chain-of-thought fashion), searching for the temperature hyperparameter, attempting model fine-tuning and model self-evaluation, and consolidating the error taxonomy and error analysis on a few datasets.

Limitations

- Due to time, budget, and computational resource constraints, results are based on single-pass generation.
- Due to the complexity of the materials, text units may be incorrectly segmented and aligned with the GT. Also, the GT may not be 100% correct. This may affect the results.
- Demonstration examples in the few-shot scenario were randomly selected; a manual curation of these could lead to better results in this setting.
- The numerous experiments produced many results that could be further explored and analysed at a finer level for each setting. Nevertheless, we believe that the aggregated results remain informative, further complemented by manual inspection.

Author Contributions

EB and ME formulated the research concept, objectives and methodology, with the contributions of MR and FK. EB was responsible for the code implementation and result visualisation. EB, ME and SNM contributed to data curation and EB and MR worked on data annotation. EB, ME and MR worked on investigation and formal analysis, with the contribution of SNM. EB wrote sections of the original draft, ME wrote the manuscript, and all authors contributed to manuscript revision, read, and approved the submitted version. ME and FK contributed to supervision.

Code and Data Availability

The code used in this work and some datasets are available at `https://github.com/impresso/llm-transcript-postcorrection`.

Acknowledgements

Authors warmly thank the Research and Innovation Department of the French National Audiovisual Institute (INA) for having shared a few radio broadcast transcriptions. Authors also gratefully acknowledge the financial support of the Swiss National Science Foundation (SNSF) for the research projects '*Impresso* - Media Monitoring of the Past II. Beyond Borders: Connecting Newspaper and Radio' under the Sinergia grant CRSII5_213585 and 'Ajax Multi-Commentary' under the Ambizione grant PZ00P1_18603.

References

Chantal Amrhein and Simon Clematide. 2018. Supervised OCR Error Detection and Correction Using Statistical and Neural Machine Translation Methods. *Journal for Language Technology and Computational Linguistics (JLCL)*, 33(1):49–76.

Yejin Bang, Samuel Cahyawijaya, Nayeon Lee, Wenliang Dai, Dan Su, Bryan Wilie, Holy Lovenia, Ziwei Ji, Tiezheng Yu, Willy Chung, Quyet V. Do, Yan Xu, and Pascale Fung. 2023. A Multitask, Multilingual, Multimodal Evaluation of ChatGPT on Reasoning, Hallucination, and Interactivity.

Rishi Bommasani, Drew A. Hudson, Ehsan Adeli, Russ Altman, Simran Arora, Sydney von Arx, Michael S. Bernstein, Jeannette Bohg, Antoine Bosselut, Emma Brunskill, Erik Brynjolfsson, Shyamal Buch, Dallas Card, Rodrigo Castellon, Niladri Chatterji, Annie Chen, Kathleen Creel, Jared Quincy Davis, Dora Demszky, Chris Donahue, Moussa Doumbouya, Esin Durmus, Stefano Ermon, John Etchemendy, Kawin Ethayarajh, Li Fei-Fei, Chelsea Finn, Trevor Gale, Lauren Gillespie, Karan Goel, Noah Goodman, Shelby Grossman, Neel Guha, Tatsunori Hashimoto, Peter Henderson, John Hewitt, Daniel E. Ho, Jenny Hong, Kyle Hsu, Jing Huang, Thomas Icard, Saahil Jain, Dan Jurafsky, Pratyusha Kalluri, Siddharth Karamcheti, Geoff Keeling, Fereshte Khani, Omar Khattab, Pang Wei Koh, Mark Krass, Ranjay Krishna, Rohith Kuditipudi, Ananya Kumar, Faisal Ladhak, Mina Lee, Tony Lee, Jure Leskovec, Isabelle Levent, Xiang Lisa Li, Xuechen Li, Tengyu Ma, Ali Malik, Christopher D. Manning, Suvir Mirchandani, Eric Mitchell, Zanele Munyikwa, Suraj Nair, Avanika Narayan, Deepak Narayanan, Ben Newman, Allen Nie, Juan Carlos Niebles, Hamed Nilforoshan, Julian Nyarko, Giray Ogut, Laurel Orr, Isabel Papadimitriou, Joon Sung Park, Chris Piech, Eva Portelance, Christopher Potts, Aditi Raghunathan, Rob Reich, Hongyu Ren, Frieda Rong, Yusuf Roohani, Camilo Ruiz, Jack Ryan, Christopher Ré, Dorsa Sadigh, Shiori Sagawa, Keshav Santhanam, Andy Shih, Krishnan Srinivasan, Alex Tamkin, Rohan Taori, Armin W. Thomas, Florian Tramèr, Rose E. Wang, William Wang, Bohan Wu, Jiajun Wu, Yuhuai Wu, Sang Michael Xie, Michihiro Yasunaga, Jiaxuan You, Matei Zaharia, Michael Zhang, Tianyi Zhang, Xikun Zhang, Yuhui Zhang, Lucia Zheng, Kaitlyn Zhou, and Percy Liang. 2022. On the Opportunities and Risks of Foundation Models.

Tom Brown, Benjamin Mann, Nick Ryder, Melanie Subbiah, Jared D Kaplan, Prafulla Dhariwal, Arvind Neelakantan, Pranav Shyam, Girish Sastry, Amanda Askell, Sandhini Agarwal, Ariel Herbert-Voss, Gretchen Krueger, Tom Henighan, Rewon Child, Aditya Ramesh, Daniel Ziegler, Jeffrey Wu, Clemens Winter, Chris Hesse, Mark Chen, Eric Sigler, Mateusz Litwin, Scott Gray, Benjamin Chess, Jack Clark, Christopher Berner, Sam McCandlish, Alec Radford, Ilya Sutskever, and Dario Amodei. 2020. Language Models are Few-Shot Learners. In *Advances in Neural Information Processing Systems*, volume 33, pages 1877–1901. Curran Associates, Inc.

Estelle Bunout, Maud Ehrmann, and Frédéric Clavert, editors. 2022. *Digitised Newspapers – A New Eldorado for Historians?: Reflections on Tools, Methods and Epistemology*. Studies in Digital History and Hermeneutics. De Gruyter Oldenbourg.

Guillaume Chiron, Antoine Doucet, Mickaël Coustaty, and Jean-Philippe Moreux. 2017a. ICDAR2017 Competition on Post-OCR Text Correction. In *2017 14th IAPR International Conference on Document Analysis and Recognition (ICDAR)*, volume 01, pages 1423–1428.

Guillaume Chiron, Antoine Doucet, Mickaël Coustaty, Muriel Visani, and Jean-Philippe Moreux. 2017b. Impact of OCR errors on the use of digital libraries: Towards a better access to information. In *Proceedings of the 17th ACM/IEEE Joint Conference on Digital Libraries*, pages 249–252, Toronto, ON, Canada. IEEE, IEEE Press.

Aakanksha Chowdhery, Sharan Narang, Jacob Devlin, Maarten Bosma, Gaurav Mishra, Adam Roberts, Paul Barham, Hyung Won Chung, Charles Sutton, Sebastian Gehrmann, Parker Schuh, Kensen Shi, Sasha Tsvyashchenko, Joshua Maynez, Abhishek Rao, Parker Barnes, Yi Tay, Noam Shazeer, Vinodkumar Prabhakaran, Emily Reif, Nan Du, Ben Hutchinson, Reiner Pope, James Bradbury, Jacob Austin, Michael Isard, Guy Gur-Ari, Pengcheng Yin, Toju Duke, Anselm Levskaya, Sanjay Ghemawat, Sunipa Dev, Henryk Michalewski, Xavier Garcia, Vedant Misra, Kevin Robinson, Liam Fedus, Denny Zhou, Daphne Ippolito, David Luan, Hyeontaek Lim, Barret Zoph, Alexander Spiridonov, Ryan Sepassi, David Dohan, Shivani Agrawal, Mark Omernick, Andrew M. Dai, Thanumalayan Sankaranarayana Pillai, Marie Pellat, Aitor Lewkowycz, Erica Moreira, Rewon Child, Oleksandr Polozov, Katherine Lee, Zongwei Zhou, Xuezhi Wang, Brennan Saeta, Mark Diaz, Orhan Firat, Michele Catasta, Jason Wei, Kathy Meier-Hellstern, Douglas Eck, Jeff Dean, Slav Petrov, and Noah Fiedel. 2022. PaLM: Scaling Language Modeling with Pathways.

Christian Clausner, Apostolos Antonacopoulos, and Stefan Pletschacher. 2019. ICDAR2019 Competition on Recognition of Documents with Complex Layouts - RDCL2019. In *2019 International Conference on Document Analysis and Recognition (ICDAR)*, pages 1521–1526.

Steven Coyne, Keisuke Sakaguchi, Diana Galvan-Sosa, Michael Zock, and Kentaro Inui. 2023. Analyzing the Performance of GPT-3.5 and GPT-4 in Grammatical Error Correction.

Qingxiu Dong, Lei Li, Damai Dai, Ce Zheng, Zhiyong Wu, Baobao Chang, Xu Sun, Jingjing Xu, Lei Li, and Zhifang Sui. 2023. A Survey on In-context Learning.

Maud Ehrmann, Matteo Romanello, Simon Clematide, Phillip Benjamin Ströbel, and Raphaël Barman. 2020. Language Resources for Historical Newspapers: The Impresso Collection. In *Proceedings of the Twelfth Language Resources and Evaluation Conference*, pages 958–968, Marseille, France. European Language Resources Association.

Maud Ehrmann, Matteo Romanello, Sven Najem-Meyer, Antoine Doucet, and Simon Clematide. 2022. Extended Overview of HIPE-2022: Named Entity Recognition and Linking in Multilingual Historical Documents. *CEUR Workshop Proceedings*, (3180):1038–1063.

Elisabeth Engl. 2020. Volltexte für die Frühe Neuzeit. *Zeitschrift für Historische Forschung*, 47(2):223–250.

John Evershed and Kent Fitch. 2014. Correcting noisy OCR: Context beats confusion. In *Proceedings of the First International Conference on Digital Access to Textual Cultural Heritage*, DATeCH '14, pages 45–51, New York, NY, USA. Association for Computing Machinery.

Tao Fang, Shu Yang, Kaixin Lan, Derek F. Wong, Jinpeng Hu, Lidia S. Chao, and Yue Zhang. 2023. Is ChatGPT a Highly Fluent Grammatical Error Correction System? A Comprehensive Evaluation.

Mingqi Gao, Jie Ruan, Renliang Sun, Xunjian Yin, Shiping Yang, and Xiaojun Wan. 2023. Human-like Summarization Evaluation with ChatGPT.

Harsh Gupta, Luciano Del Corro, Samuel Broscheit, Johannes Hoffart, and Eliot Brenner. 2021. Unsupervised Multi-View Post-OCR Error Correction With Language Models. In *Proceedings of the 2021 Conference on Empirical Methods in Natural Language Processing*, pages 8647–8652, Online and Punta Cana, Dominican Republic. Association for Computational Linguistics.

Ahmed Hamdi, Axel Jean-Caurant, Nicolas Sidère, Mickaël Coustaty, and Antoine Doucet. 2020. Assessing and Minimizing the Impact of OCR Quality on Named Entity Recognition. In *Digital Libraries for Open Knowledge*, Lecture Notes in Computer Science, pages 87–101, Cham. Springer International Publishing.

Lei Huang, Weijiang Yu, Weitao Ma, Weihong Zhong, Zhangyin Feng, Haotian Wang, Qianglong Chen, Weihua Peng, Xiaocheng Feng, Bing Qin, and Ting Liu. 2023. A Survey on Hallucination in Large Language Models: Principles, Taxonomy, Challenges, and Open Questions.

Wenxiang Jiao, Wenxuan Wang, Jen-tse Huang, Xing Wang, and Zhaopeng Tu. 2023. Is ChatGPT A Good Translator? Yes With GPT-4 As The Engine.

Philip Kahle, Sebastian Colutto, Günter Hackl, and Günter Mühlberger. 2017. Transkribus - A Service Platform for Transcription, Recognition and Retrieval of Historical Documents. In *2017 14th IAPR International Conference on Document Analysis and Recognition (ICDAR)*, volume 04, pages 19–24.

Md Tahmid Rahman Laskar, M. Saiful Bari, Mizanur Rahman, Md Amran Hossen Bhuiyan, Shafiq Joty, and Jimmy Xiangji Huang. 2023. A Systematic Study and Comprehensive Evaluation of ChatGPT on Benchmark Datasets.

Vladimir I. Levenshtein. 1966. Binary codes capable of correcting deletions, insertions, and reversals. *Soviet Physics Doklady*, (10):707.

Elvys Linhares Pontes, Ahmed Hamdi, Nicolas Sidere, and Antoine Doucet. 2019. Impact of OCR Quality on Named Entity Linking. In *Digital Libraries at the Crossroads of Digital Information for the Future*, Lecture Notes in Computer Science, pages 102–115, Cham. Springer International Publishing.

Pengfei Liu, Weizhe Yuan, Jinlan Fu, Zhengbao Jiang, Hiroaki Hayashi, and Graham Neubig. 2023. Pre-train, Prompt, and Predict: A Systematic Survey of Prompting Methods in Natural Language Processing. *ACM Computing Surveys*, 55(9):195:1–195:35.

Mengsay Loem, Masahiro Kaneko, Sho Takase, and Naoaki Okazaki. 2023. Exploring Effectiveness of GPT-3 in Grammatical Error Correction: A Study on Performance and Controllability in Prompt-Based Methods.

Barbara McGillivray, Beatrice Alex, Sarah Ames, Guyda Armstrong, David Beavan, Arianna Ciula, Giovanni Colavizza, James Cummings, David De Roure, Adam Farquhar, Simon Hengchen, Anouk Lang, James Loxley, Eirini Goudarouli, Federico Nanni, Andrea Nini, Julianne Nyhan, Nicola Osborne, Thierry Poibeau, Mia Ridge, Sonia Ranade, James Smithies, Melissa Terras, Andreas Vlachidis, and Pip Willcox. 2020. The challenges and prospects of the intersection of humanities and data science: A White Paper from The Alan Turing Institute. Technical report, Alan Turing Institute.

Niklas Muennighoff, Thomas Wang, Lintang Sutawika, Adam Roberts, Stella Biderman, Teven Le Scao, M. Saiful Bari, Sheng Shen, Zheng-Xin Yong, Hailey Schoelkopf, Xiangru Tang, Dragomir Radev, Alham Fikri Aji, Khalid Almubarak, Samuel Albanie, Zaid Alyafeai, Albert Webson, Edward Raff, and Colin Raffel. 2023. Crosslingual Generalization through Multitask Finetuning.

Clemens Neudecker and Apostolos Antonacopoulos. 2016. Making Europe's Historical Newspapers Searchable. In *2016 12th IAPR Workshop on Document Analysis Systems (DAS)*, pages 405–410, Santorini, Greece. IEEE.

Thi Tuyet Hai Nguyen, Adam Jatowt, Nhu-Van Nguyen, Mickael Coustaty, and Antoine Doucet. 2020. Neural Machine Translation with BERT for Post-OCR Error Detection and Correction. In *Proceedings of the ACM/IEEE Joint Conference on Digital Libraries in 2020*, JCDL '20, pages 333–336, New York, NY, USA. Association for Computing Machinery.

OpenAI. 2023. GPT-4 Technical Report.

Robert Ostling and Murathan Kurfalı. 2022. Really good grammatical error correction, and how to evaluate it. In *The Ninth Swedish Language Technology Conference (SLTC2022)*.

Long Ouyang, Jeffrey Wu, Xu Jiang, Diogo Almeida, Carroll Wainwright, Pamela Mishkin, Chong Zhang, Sandhini Agarwal, Katarina Slama, Alex Ray, John

Schulman, Jacob Hilton, Fraser Kelton, Luke Miller, Maddie Simens, Amanda Askell, Peter Welinder, Paul F Christiano, Jan Leike, and Ryan Lowe. 2022. Training language models to follow instructions with human feedback. In *Advances in Neural Information Processing Systems*, volume 35, pages 27730–27744. Curran Associates, Inc.

Thomas Padilla. 2019. Responsible Operations: Data Science, Machine Learning, and AI in Libraries. OCLC Research Position Paper. Technical report, ERIC.

Christos Papadopoulos, Stefan Pletschacher, Christian Clausner, and Apostolos Antonacopoulos. 2013. The IMPACT dataset of historical document images. In *Proceedings of the 2nd International Workshop on Historical Document Imaging and Processing*, HIP '13, pages 123–130, New York, NY, USA. Association for Computing Machinery.

John Pavlopoulos, Vasiliki Kougia, Paraskevi Platanou, Stepan Shabalin, Konstantina Liagkou, Emmanouil Papadatos, Holger Essler, Jean-Baptiste Camps, and Franz Fischer. 2023. Error Correcting HTR'ed Byzantine Text.

Paraskevi Platanou, John Pavlopoulos, and Georgios Papaioannou. 2022. Handwritten Paleographic Greek Text Recognition: A Century-Based Approach. In *Proceedings of the Thirteenth Language Resources and Evaluation Conference*, pages 6585–6589, Marseille, France. European Language Resources Association.

Alec Radford, Jeff Wu, Rewon Child, D. Luan, Dario Amodei, and Ilya Sutskever. 2019. Language Models are Unsupervised Multitask Learners.

Jeff Rasley, Samyam Rajbhandari, Olatunji Ruwase, and Yuxiong He. 2020. DeepSpeed: System Optimizations Enable Training Deep Learning Models with Over 100 Billion Parameters. In *Proceedings of the 26th ACM SIGKDD International Conference on Knowledge Discovery & Data Mining*, KDD '20, pages 3505–3506, New York, NY, USA. Association for Computing Machinery.

Christian Reul, Dennis Christ, Alexander Hartelt, Nico Balbach, Maximilian Wehner, Uwe Springmann, Christoph Wick, Christine Grundig, Andreas Büttner, and Frank Puppe. 2019. OCR4all—An Open-Source Tool Providing a (Semi-)Automatic OCR Workflow for Historical Printings. *Applied Sciences*, 9(22):4853.

Christophe Rigaud, Antoine Doucet, Mickaël Coustaty, and Jean-Philippe Moreux. 2019. ICDAR 2019 competition on post-OCR text correction. In *2019 International Conference on Document Analysis and Recognition (ICDAR)*, pages 1588–1593. IEEE.

Matteo Romanello, Sven Najem-Meyer, and Bruce Robertson. 2021. Optical character recognition of 19th century classical commentaries: The current state of affairs. In *The 6th International Workshop on Historical Document Imaging and Processing*, HIP '21, pages 1–6, New York, NY, USA. Association for Computing Machinery.

Nipun Sadvilkar and Mark Neumann. 2020. PySBD: Pragmatic Sentence Boundary Disambiguation. In *Proceedings of Second Workshop for NLP Open Source Software (NLP-OSS)*, pages 110–114, Online. Association for Computational Linguistics.

Teven Le Scao, Angela Fan, Christopher Akiki, Ellie Pavlick, Suzana Ilić, Daniel Hesslow, Roman Castagné, Alexandra Sasha Luccioni, François Yvon, Matthias Gallé, et al. 2022. Bloom: A 176b-parameter open-access multilingual language model.

Robin Schaefer and Clemens Neudecker. 2020. A Two-Step Approach for Automatic OCR Post-Correction. In *Proceedings of the The 4th Joint SIGHUM Workshop on Computational Linguistics for Cultural Heritage, Social Sciences, Humanities and Literature*, pages 52–57, Online. International Committee on Computational Linguistics.

Pit Schneider and Yves Maurer. 2022. Rerunning OCR: A Machine Learning Approach to Quality Assessment and Enhancement Prediction. *Journal of Data Mining & Digital Humanities*, 2022(Digital humanities in...):8561.

Mohammad Shoeybi, Mostofa Patwary, Raul Puri, Patrick LeGresley, Jared Casper, and Bryan Catanzaro. 2020. Megatron-LM: Training Multi-Billion Parameter Language Models Using Model Parallelism.

Elizabeth Soper, Stanley Fujimoto, and Yen-Yun Yu. 2021. BART for Post-Correction of OCR Newspaper Text. In *Proceedings of the Seventh Workshop on Noisy User-generated Text (W-NUT 2021)*, pages 284–290, Online. Association for Computational Linguistics.

Phillip Ströbel and Simon Clematide. 2019. Improving OCR of black letter in historical newspapers: The unreasonable effectiveness of HTR models on low-resolution images. In *Proceedings of the Digital Humanities 2019, (DH2019)*.

Phillip Benjamin Ströbel, Simon Clematide, and Martin Volk. 2020. How Much Data Do You Need? About the Creation of a Ground Truth for Black Letter and the Effectiveness of Neural OCR. In *Proceedings of the Twelfth Language Resources and Evaluation Conference*, pages 3551–3559, Marseille, France. European Language Resources Association.

Melissa M. Terras. 2011. The Rise of Digitization. In Ruth Rikowski, editor, *Digitisation Perspectives*, Educational Futures Rethinking Theory and Practice, pages 3–20. SensePublishers, Rotterdam.

Konstantin Todorov and Giovanni Colavizza. 2020. Transfer Learning for Historical Corpora: An Assessment on Post-OCR Correction and Named Entity

Recognition. In *Proceedings of the Workshop on Computational Humanities Research (CHR 2020)*, pages 310–325.

Konstantin Todorov and Giovanni Colavizza. 2022. An Assessment of the Impact of OCR Noise on Language Models.

Hugo Touvron, Thibaut Lavril, Gautier Izacard, Xavier Martinet, Marie-Anne Lachaux, Timothée Lacroix, Baptiste Rozière, Naman Goyal, Eric Hambro, Faisal Azhar, Aurelien Rodriguez, Armand Joulin, Edouard Grave, and Guillaume Lample. 2023a. LLaMA: Open and Efficient Foundation Language Models.

Hugo Touvron, Louis Martin, Kevin Stone, Peter Albert, Amjad Almahairi, Yasmine Babaei, Nikolay Bashlykov, Soumya Batra, Prajjwal Bhargava, Shruti Bhosale, Dan Bikel, Lukas Blecher, Cristian Canton Ferrer, Moya Chen, Guillem Cucurull, David Esiobu, Jude Fernandes, Jeremy Fu, Wenyin Fu, Brian Fuller, Cynthia Gao, Vedanuj Goswami, Naman Goyal, Anthony Hartshorn, Saghar Hosseini, Rui Hou, Hakan Inan, Marcin Kardas, Viktor Kerkez, Madian Khabsa, Isabel Kloumann, Artem Korenev, Punit Singh Koura, Marie-Anne Lachaux, Thibaut Lavril, Jenya Lee, Diana Liskovich, Yinghai Lu, Yuning Mao, Xavier Martinet, Todor Mihaylov, Pushkar Mishra, Igor Molybog, Yixin Nie, Andrew Poulton, Jeremy Reizenstein, Rashi Rungta, Kalyan Saladi, Alan Schelten, Ruan Silva, Eric Michael Smith, Ranjan Subramanian, Xiaoqing Ellen Tan, Binh Tang, Ross Taylor, Adina Williams, Jian Xiang Kuan, Puxin Xu, Zheng Yan, Iliyan Zarov, Yuchen Zhang, Angela Fan, Melanie Kambadur, Sharan Narang, Aurelien Rodriguez, Robert Stojnic, Sergey Edunov, and Thomas Scialom. 2023b. Llama 2: Open Foundation and Fine-Tuned Chat Models.

Daniel van Strien, Kaspar Beelen, Mariona Ardanuy, Kasra Hosseini, Barbara McGillivray, and Giovanni Colavizza. 2020. Assessing the Impact of OCR Quality on Downstream NLP Tasks:. In *Proceedings of the 12th International Conference on Agents and Artificial Intelligence*, pages 484–496, Valletta, Malta. SCITEPRESS - Science and Technology Publications.

Ashish Vaswani, Noam Shazeer, Niki Parmar, Jakob Uszkoreit, Llion Jones, Aidan N Gomez, Łukasz Kaiser, and Illia Polosukhin. 2017. Attention is all you need. In *Advances in Neural Information Processing Systems*, volume 30, pages 5998–6008, Long Beach, California, US. Curran Associates, Inc.

Haoran Wu, Wenxuan Wang, Yuxuan Wan, Wenxiang Jiao, and Michael Lyu. 2023. ChatGPT or Grammarly? Evaluating ChatGPT on Grammatical Error Correction Benchmark.

Ismet Zeki Yalniz and R. Manmatha. 2011. A Fast Alignment Scheme for Automatic OCR Evaluation of Books. In *2011 International Conference on Document Analysis and Recognition*, pages 754–758.

Bowen Zhang, Daijun Ding, and Liwen Jing. 2023. How would Stance Detection Techniques Evolve after the Launch of ChatGPT?

Susan Zhang, Stephen Roller, Naman Goyal, Mikel Artetxe, Moya Chen, Shuohui Chen, Christopher Dewan, Mona Diab, Xian Li, Xi Victoria Lin, Todor Mihaylov, Myle Ott, Sam Shleifer, Kurt Shuster, Daniel Simig, Punit Singh Koura, Anjali Sridhar, Tianlu Wang, and Luke Zettlemoyer. 2022. OPT: Open Pretrained Transformer Language Models.

Wayne Xin Zhao, Kun Zhou, Junyi Li, Tianyi Tang, Xiaolei Wang, Yupeng Hou, Yingqian Min, Beichen Zhang, Junjie Zhang, Zican Dong, Yifan Du, Chen Yang, Yushuo Chen, Zhipeng Chen, Jinhao Jiang, Ruiyang Ren, Yifan Li, Xinyu Tang, Zikang Liu, Peiyu Liu, Jian-Yun Nie, and Ji-Rong Wen. 2023. A Survey of Large Language Models (v11).

Zihao Zhao, Eric Wallace, Shi Feng, Dan Klein, and Sameer Singh. 2021. Calibrate Before Use: Improving Few-shot Performance of Language Models. In *Proceedings of the 38th International Conference on Machine Learning*, pages 12697–12706. PMLR.

A LLMs hyperparameters

Experiments with OpenAI API were conducted using `gpt2`, `davinci`, `gpt-3.5-turbo` and `gpt-4` models with the default temperature of 0.7. Experiments with the open-source models were conducted using a default temperature of 1.0.

B Post-processing

B.1 Post-processing heuristics

Post-processing of LLMs answers involves the following heuristics:

- Removal of leading and trailing white spaces and double quotes from the response.
- Removal of (parts of) prompts from the response.
- Trimming of the predicted text so that it does not exceed 1.5 times the length of the input text. This constraint ensures that the prediction does not deviate excessively in length from the original digitised text.
- Removal of specific phrases such as "There is no text provided to correct" or "No correction needed" from the response.

B.2 Impact of post-processing on post-correction improvement score

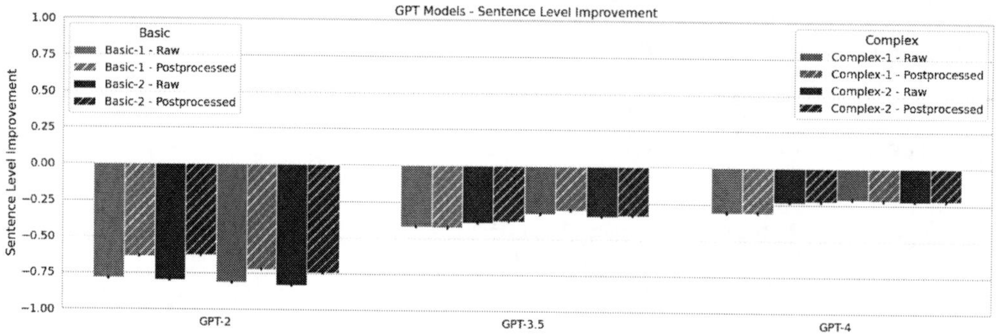

Figure 5: Post-correction improvement scores across datasets for GPT-2, GPT-3.5 and GPT-4 per prompt to sentence level input with (post-processed) and without (raw) post-processing.

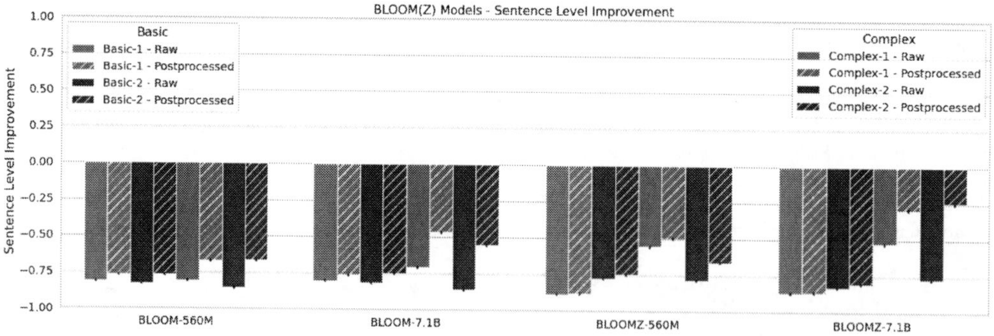

Figure 6: Post-correction improvement scores across datasets for BLOOM-560M, BLOOM-7.1B, BLOOMZ-560M and BLOOMZ-7.1B per prompt to sentence level input with (post-processed) and without (raw) post-processing.

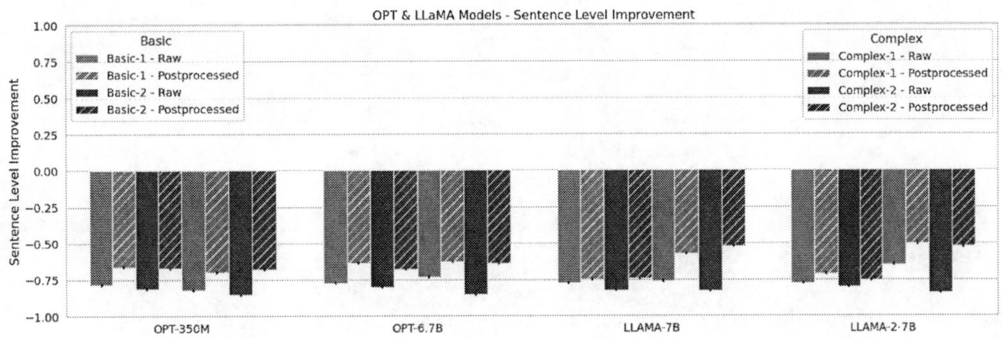

Figure 7: Post-correction improvement scores across datasets for OPT-350M, OPT-6.7B, LLaMA-7B and LLaMA-2-7B per prompt to sentence level input with (post-processed) and without (raw) post-processing.

C Manual Analysis

C.1 Sampling

To manually inspect pairs of LLM-corrected vs. ground truth transcriptions, we sampled a total of 2,459 post-correction items at sentence level. One item was sampled from each dataset (from different quality bands), considering three models (GPT-4, LLaMA-2, BLOOMZ), two prompts (`Basic-2` and `Complex-2`), and four languages (en, de, fr, grc). Table 4 shows the number of items selected per datasets.

Dataset	# items	Percentage
`ajmc-mixed`	41	10%
`ajmc-primary`	14	51%
`htrec`	8	100%
`icdar-2017`	85	18%
`icdar-2019`	61	15%
`impresso-nzz`	45	7%
`ina`	44	15%
`overproof`	36	9%

Table 4: Number and percentage of sampled items per dataset.

C.2 Error category distribution

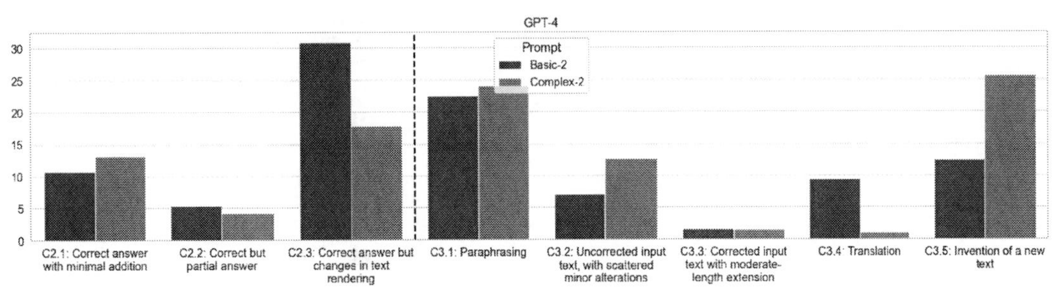

Figure 8: Error category distribution in manually annotated samples per prompt across datasets for GPT-4.

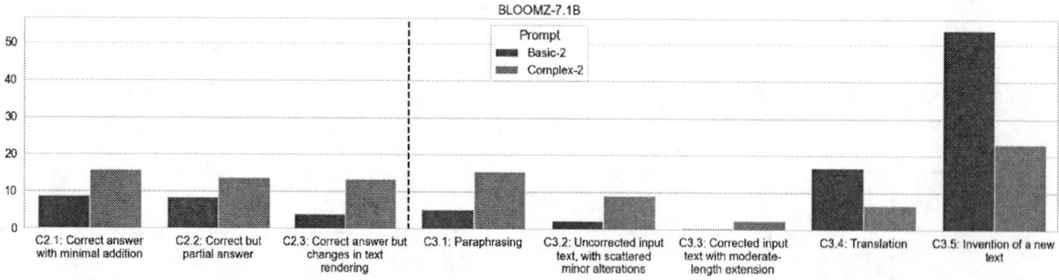

Figure 9: Error category distribution in manually annotated samples per prompt across datasets for BLOOMZ-7.1B.

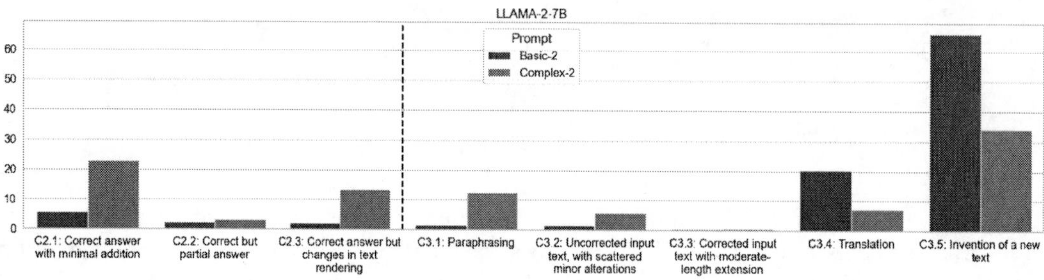

Figure 10: Error category distribution in manually annotated samples per prompt across datasets for LLAMA-2-7B.

C.3 Taxonomy of errors

	CATEGORY	DESCRIPTION	EXAMPLE
		Post-correction task not completed	
C1	**Empty answer** (*instruction inconsistency*)	Unanswered prompt. This includes: empty answers, answers containing some introductory text, and repetitions of (part of) the prompt.	**GT:** - καί gehört zu θανών. **Input:** — zei: gehört zu θανών. **Output:** **Dataset:** `ajmc-mixed` **Model:** BLOOMZ-7.1B **Prompt:** `Basic-2`
		Post-correction task partially completed	
C2.1	**Correct answer with minimal addition** (*context inconsistency*)	The input text is corrected, but extra characters or words (up to a small sentence) are added without changing the meaning.	**GT:** The occupation of the Trobriands and the Woodlark area was successfully accomplished without opposition, and apparently unbeknown to the enemy. **Input:** The occupation of the Trobriands and the Woodlark area was success- fully accomplished without opposition, and apparently unbeknown to the enemy. **Output:** "The occupation of the Trobriands and the Woodlark area was successfully accomplished without opposition, and apparently unknowingly to the enemy. Thank you for your assistance</s>" **Dataset:** `overproof` **Model:** BLOOMZ-7.1B **Prompt:** `Complex-2`
C2.2	**Correct but partial answer** (*context inconsistency*)	The input text is corrected but incomplete (the model did half of the work).	**GT:** Les deux hommes ont été arrêtés, ils se réclament de l'Armée de Libération palestinienne, on ignore leur motif. **Input:** les deux hommes ont été arrêtés il se réclame de l' armée de libération palestinienne en irlande u **Output:** les deux hommes ont été arrêtés **Dataset:** `ina` **Model:** LLAMA-2-7B **Prompt:** `Basic-2`

C2.3	**Correct answer but changes in text rendering** (*instruction inconsistency*)	The input text is corrected, but the model makes changes that improve the formatting and/or readability of the text (carriage returns, case adjustment, de-hyphenation, diacritic correction, spelling normalisation).	**GT:** Fryer Bacon wondered at this man's resolution then asked hee of him, who set him on worke to bee a murderer ? **Input:** Fryer Bacon wondered at this man's resolution then asked hee of him, who set him on worke to bee a murderer ? **Output:** Friar Bacon wondered at this man's resolution, then asked him, "Who set you to work to be a murderer? **Dataset:** `icdar-2017` **Model:** GPT-4 **Prompt:** `Basic-2`
		Post-correction task not completed, with various types of hallucination	
C3.1	**Paraphrasing**	The produced text is close to the input text, but it is a rephrased version of it.	**GT:** Il gémissait des paroles que l'histoire a fidèlement gardées. **Input:** il paie des paroles que l'histoire fidèlement garder **Output:** Il peint des paroles que l'histoire fidèlement garde **Dataset:** `ina` **Model:** GPT-4 **Prompt:** `Complex-2`
C3.2	**Uncorrected input text, with scattered minor alterations** (*instruction inconsistency*)	The original text has not been corrected. Small changes have been made throughout.	**GT:** So little is, in this Cafe, the Do ctrine of Nature beholding to the Philosophy of Des-Cartes. **Input:** So little is, in this Case, the Do- ctrine of Nature beholding to the Philosophy of Des-Cartes. **Output:** It is so little the doctrine of nature that it looks upon the philosophy of Descartes.</s> **Dataset:** `icdar-2019` **Model:** BLOOMZ-7.1B **Prompt:** `Complex-2`
C3.3	**Corrected input text with moderate-length extension** (*instruction inconsistency*)	Some elements of the input text are retained in the answer, which is also continued over several sentences that still relate to the input text.	**GT:** Diesbach hatte nach Wurstisen für die päbstliche Anerkennung seiner vom Bischof und Domkapitel getroffenen Wahl zum Coadjutor zu entrichten: **Input:** Diesbach hatte nach Wurstisen für die päbstliche Anerkennung seiner vom Bischof und Domkapitel getroffenen Wahl zum Coadjutor ru cntrtdbten: **Output:** Dießbach hatte nach Wurstisen für die päbstliche Anerkennung seiner vom Bischof und Domkapitel getroffenen Wahl zum Coadjutor für den tts-oder die nach Wurstisen für die</s> **Dataset:** `impresso-nzz` **Model:** BLOOMZ-7.1B **Prompt:** `Complex-2`
C3.4	**Translation** (*instruction inconsistency*)	The model translates the input text or generates another text in another language.	**GT:** Menelaos, früherer Dienste vergessend, redet, als hätte Aias eben erst Gelegenheit gege- ben, ihn zu erproben. **Input:** Menelaos, früherer Dienste vergessend, redet, als hätte Aias eben erst Gelegenheit gege- ben, ihn zu erproben. **Output:** "Menelaos, forgetting the previous services, speaks as if Aias had recently provided him an opportunity to be tested." **Dataset:** `ajmc-mixed` **Model:** LLAMA-2-7B **Prompt:** `Complex-2`
C3.5	**Invention of a new text** (*context inconsistency*)	The input text disappears and the model hallucinates by inventing a completely different story, usually in the same style as the input text.	**GT:** Nostro in aliis et alieno in omnibus jure salvo. **Input:** Nostro in aliis et alieno in omnibus jure salvo. **Output:** Eodem tempore ut etiam ab aliis ad aliendos personam ad omnes juris iuri **Dataset:** `icdar-2019` **Model:** LLAMA-2-7B **Prompt:** `Complex-2`

D Detailed overviews of results with different text unit levels

D.1 Line level

D.1.1 `overproof` and `impresso-nzz`

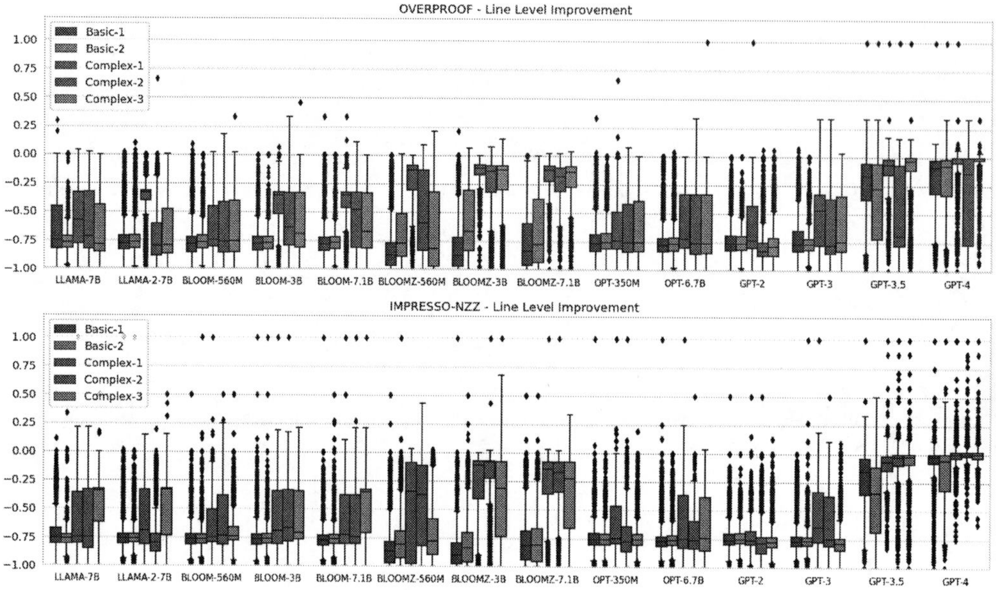

Figure 11: Post-correction improvement score for **`overproof`** and **`impresso-nzz`** datasets, considering all models and prompts based on post-processed responses to **line-level input** in the zero-shot setting.

D.1.2 ajmc, htrec and ina

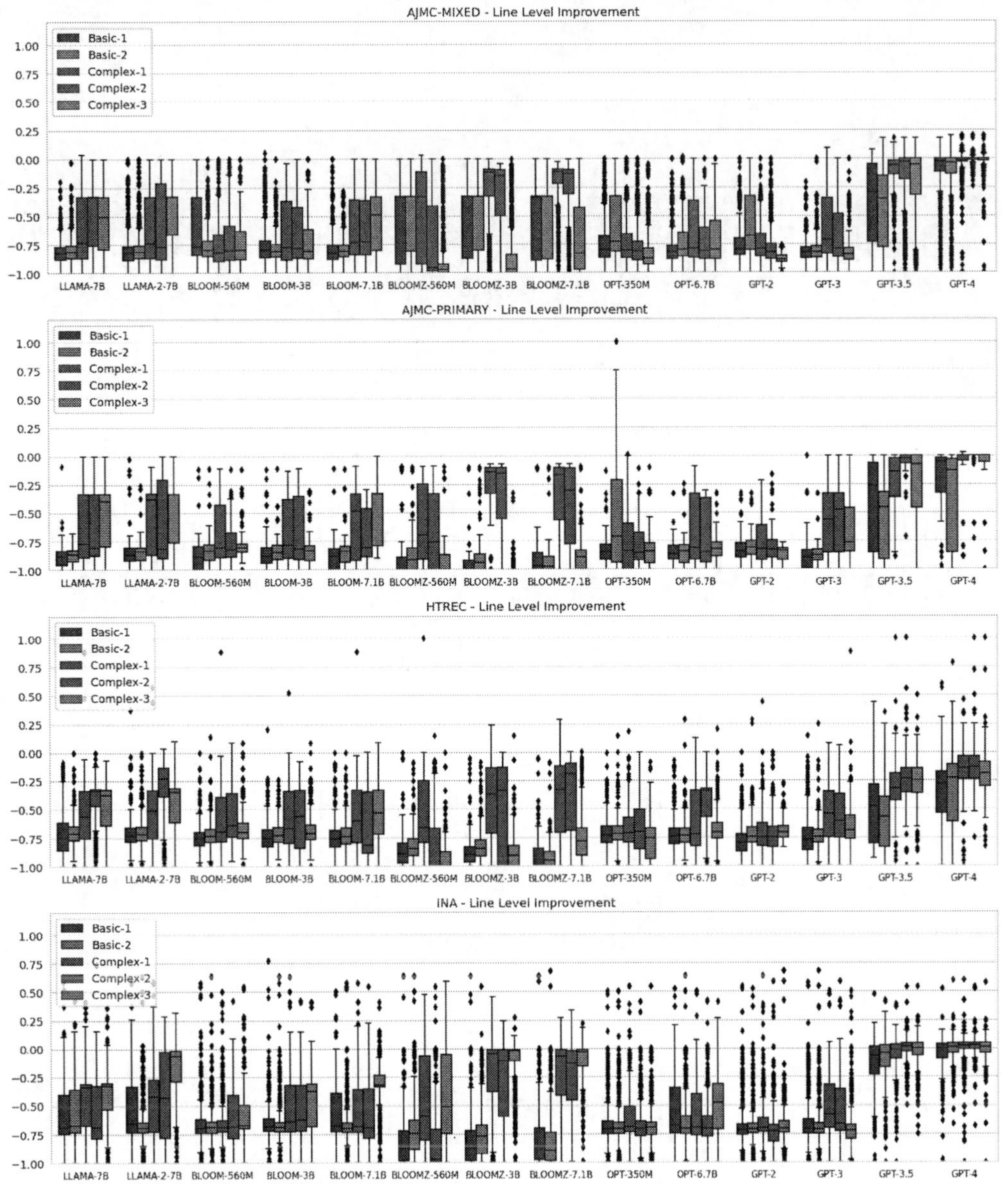

Figure 12: Post-correction improvement score for **ajmc**, **htrec** and **ina** datasets, considering all models and prompts based on post-processed responses to **line-level inputs** in the zero-shot setting.

D.2 Sentence level

D.2.1 `icdar`, `overproof` and `impresso-nzz`

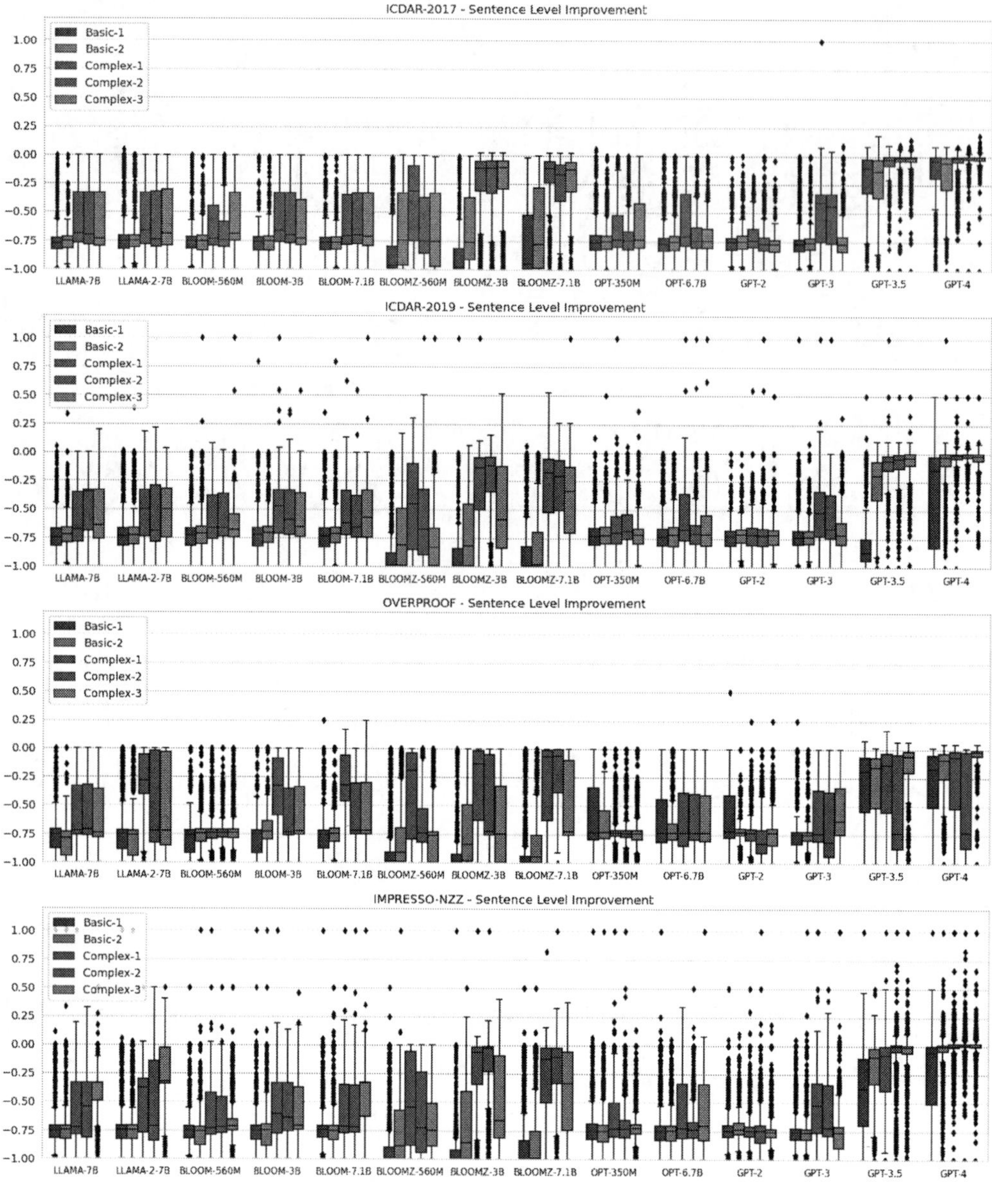

Figure 13: Post-correction improvement score for **`icdar`**, **`overproof`** and **`impresso-nzz`** datasets, considering all models and prompts based on post-processed responses to **sentence-level input** in the zero-shot setting.

D.2.2 `ajmc`, `htrec` and `ina`

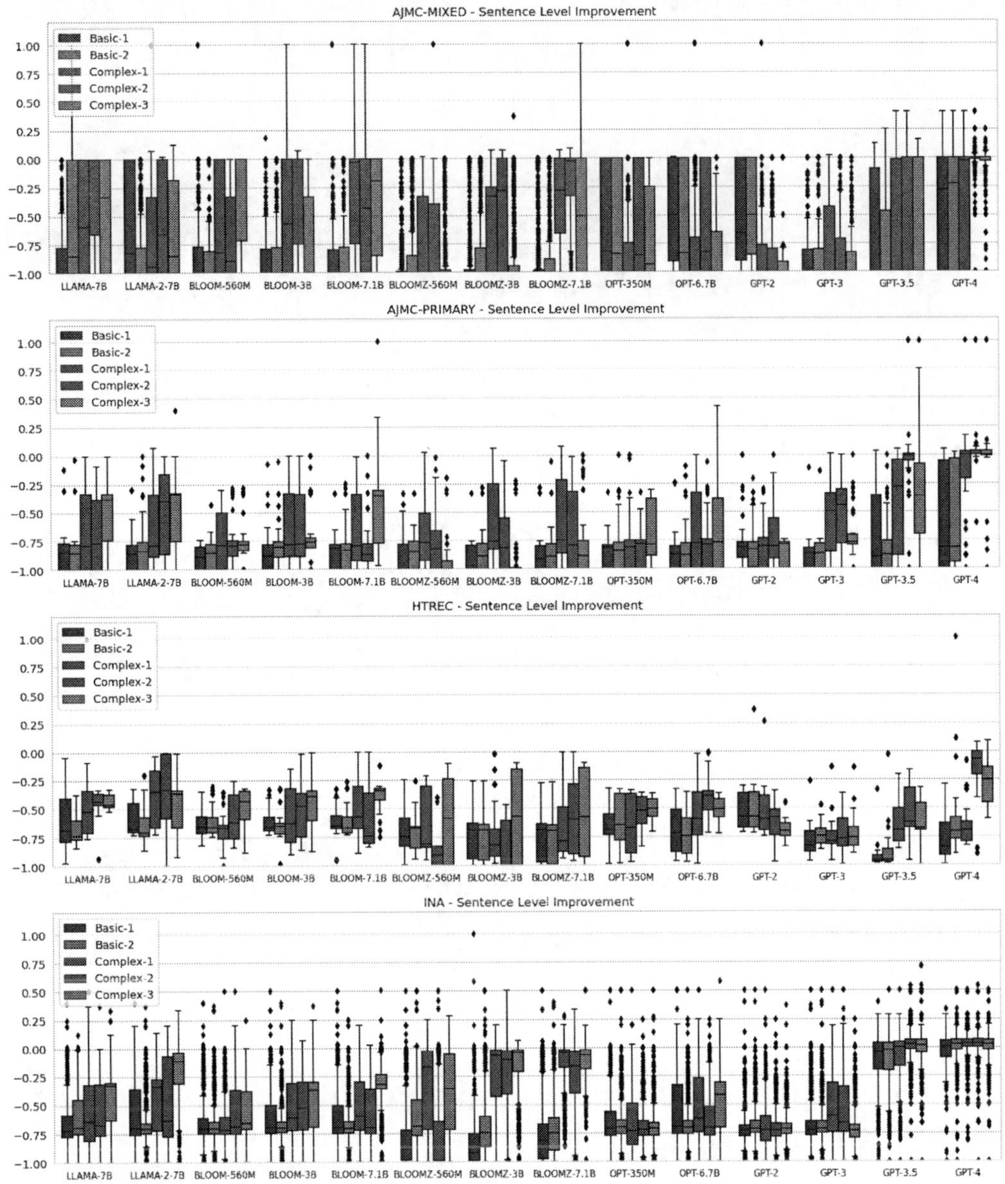

Figure 14: Post-correction improvement score for **`ajmc`**, **`htrec`** and **`ina`** datasets, considering all models and prompts based on post-processed responses to **sentence-level inputs** in the zero-shot setting.

D.3 Region level

D.3.1 icdar, overproof and impresso-nzz

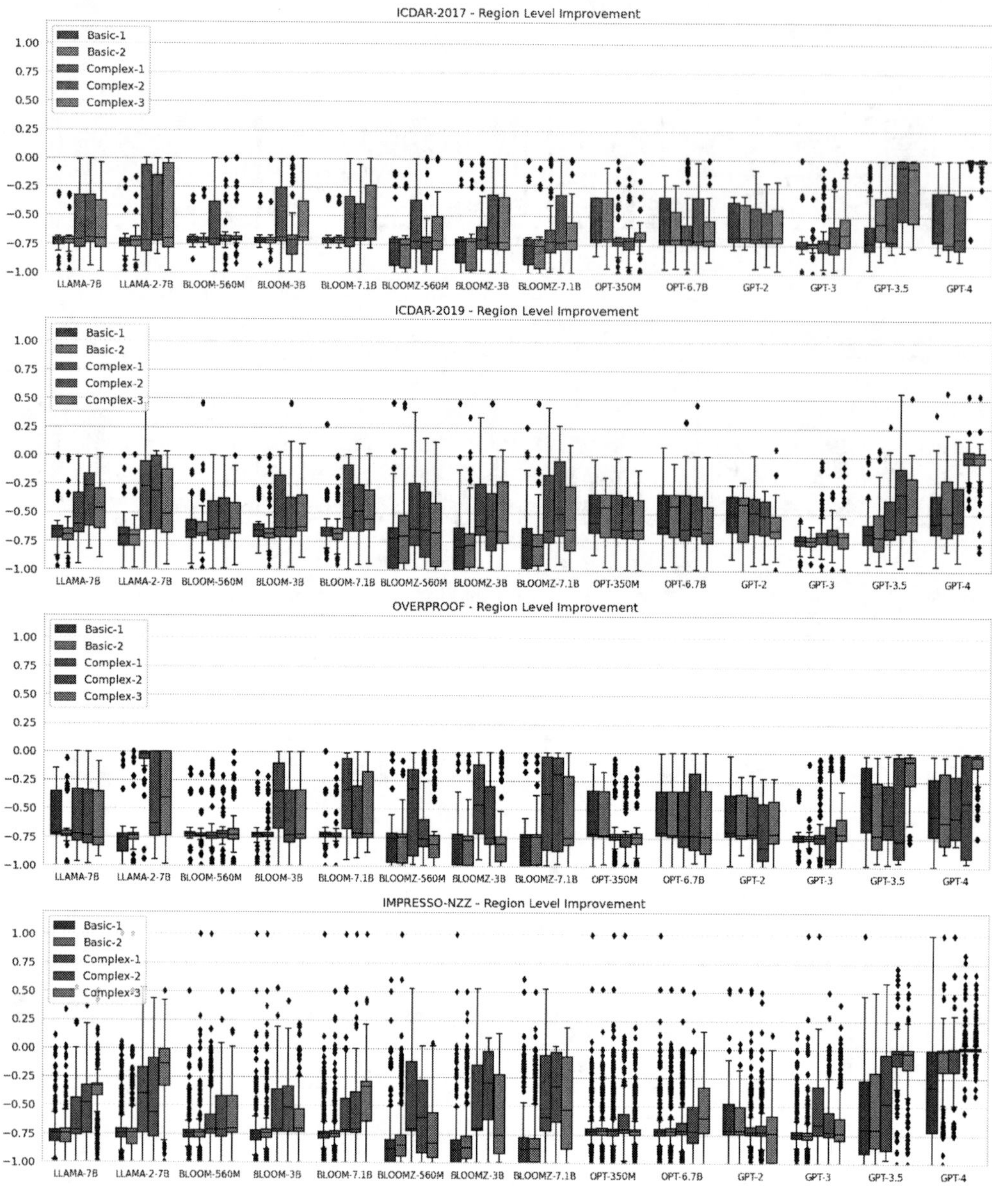

Figure 15: Post-correction improvement score for **icdar**, **overproof** and **impresso-nzz** datasets, considering all models and prompts based on post-processed responses to **region-level input** in the zero-shot setting.

D.3.2 ajmc, htrec and ina

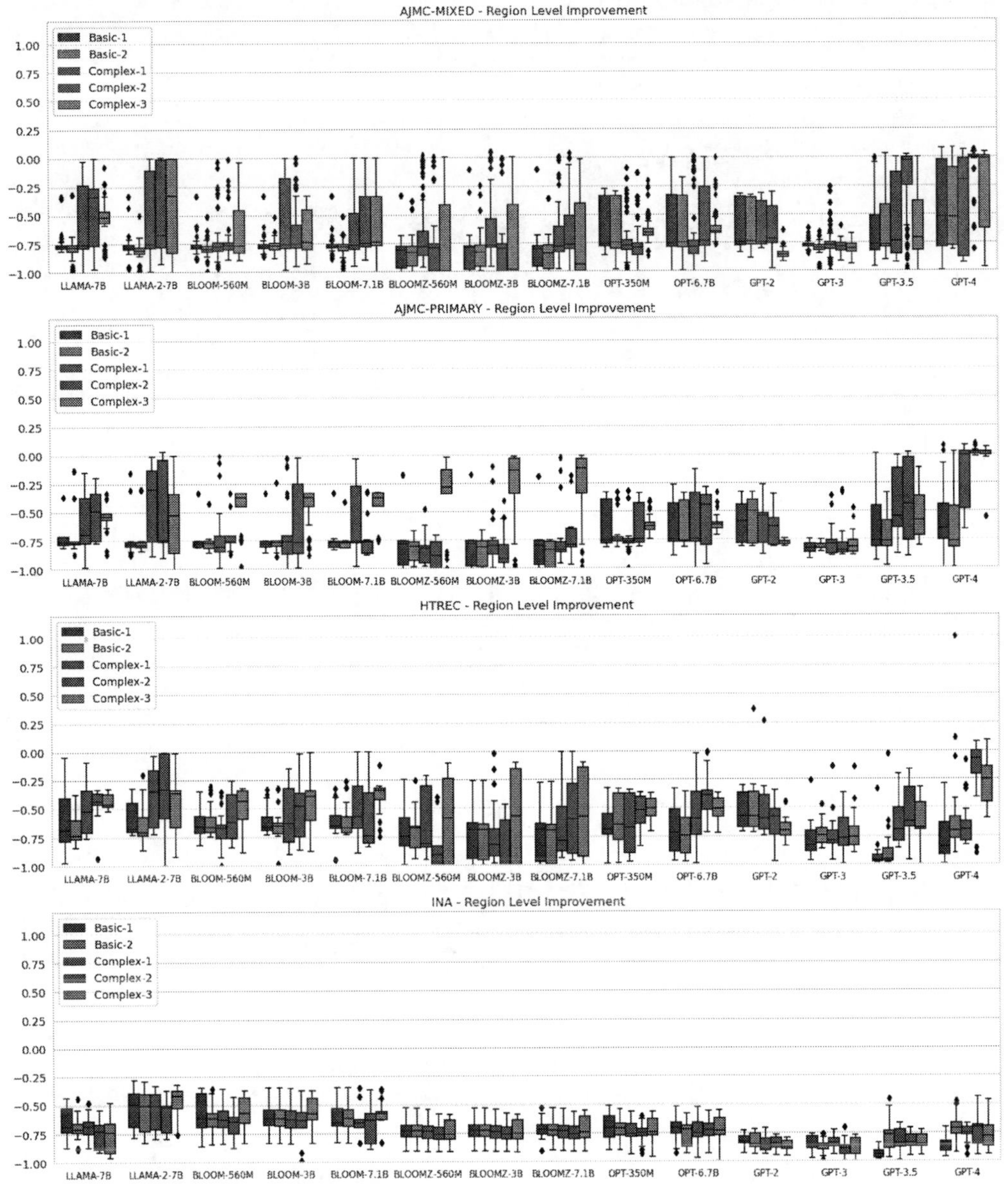

Figure 16: Post-correction improvement score for `ajmc`, `htrec` and `ina` datasets, considering all models and prompts based on post-processed responses to **region-level inputs** in the zero-shot setting.

E Detailed overviews of results in the zero- and few-shot scenarios

E.1 `icdar`, `overproof` and `impresso-nzz`

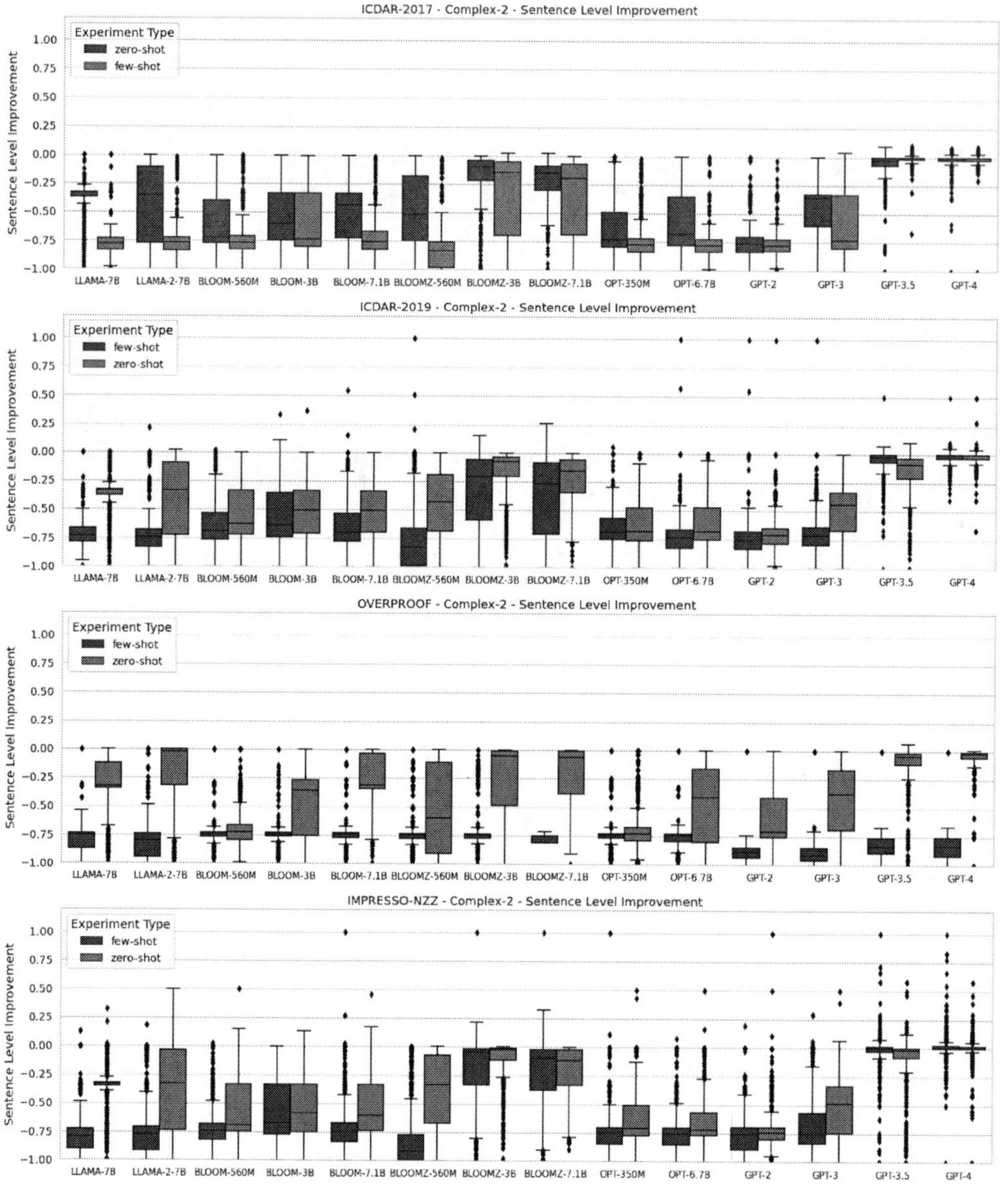

Figure 17: Post-correction improvement scores per model for **`icdar`**, **`overproof`** and **`impresso-nzz`** datasets, considering post-processed responses to **sentence-level input** with `Complex-2` prompt in the zero and few-shot settings.

E.2 ajmc, htrec and ina

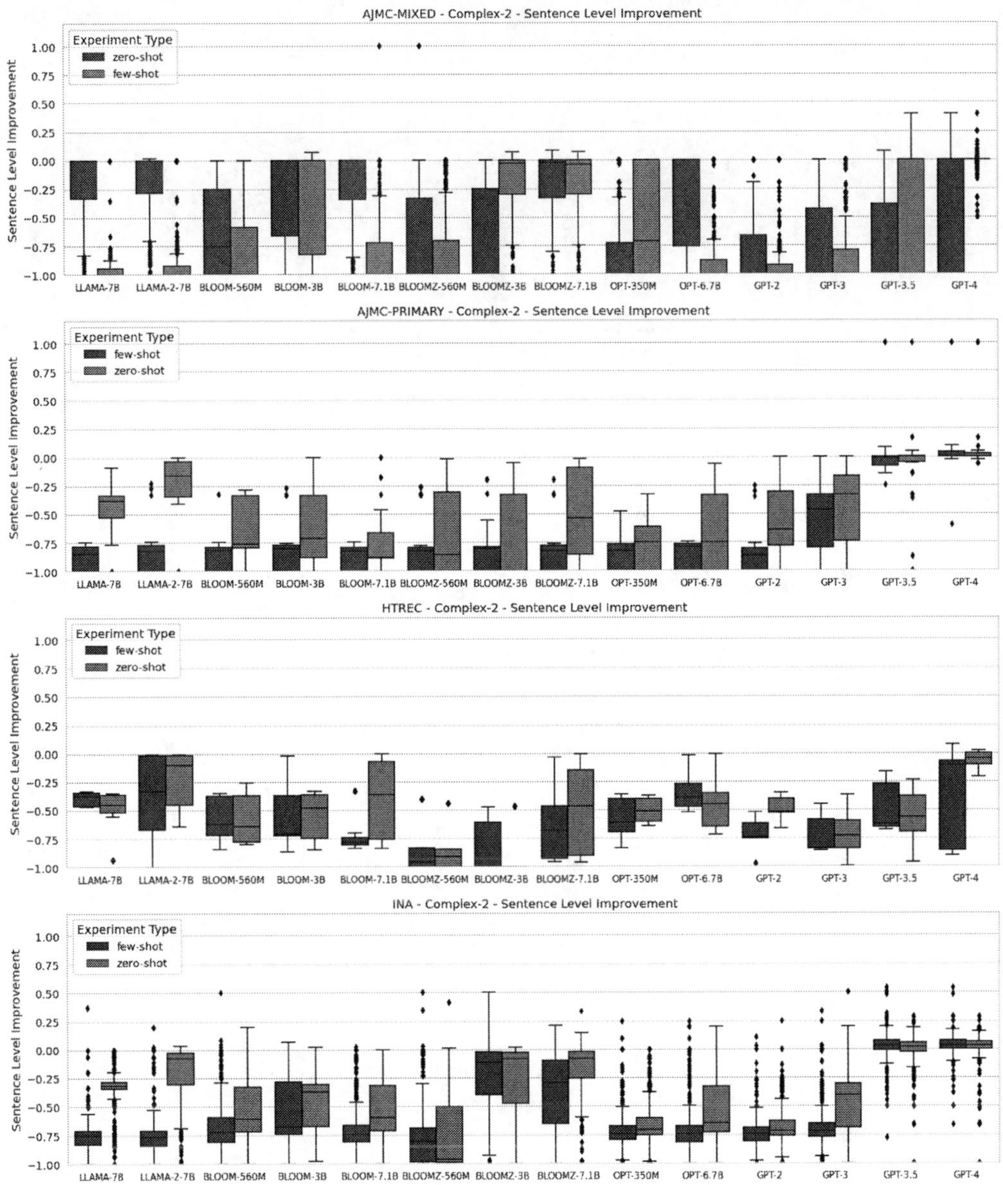

Figure 18: Post-correction improvement scores per model for **ajmc**, **htrec** and **ina** datasets, considering post-processed responses to **sentence-level input** with Complex-2 prompt in the zero and few-shot settings.

F Detailed overviews of results with different quality bands

F.1 `icdar`, `overproof` and `impresso-nzz`

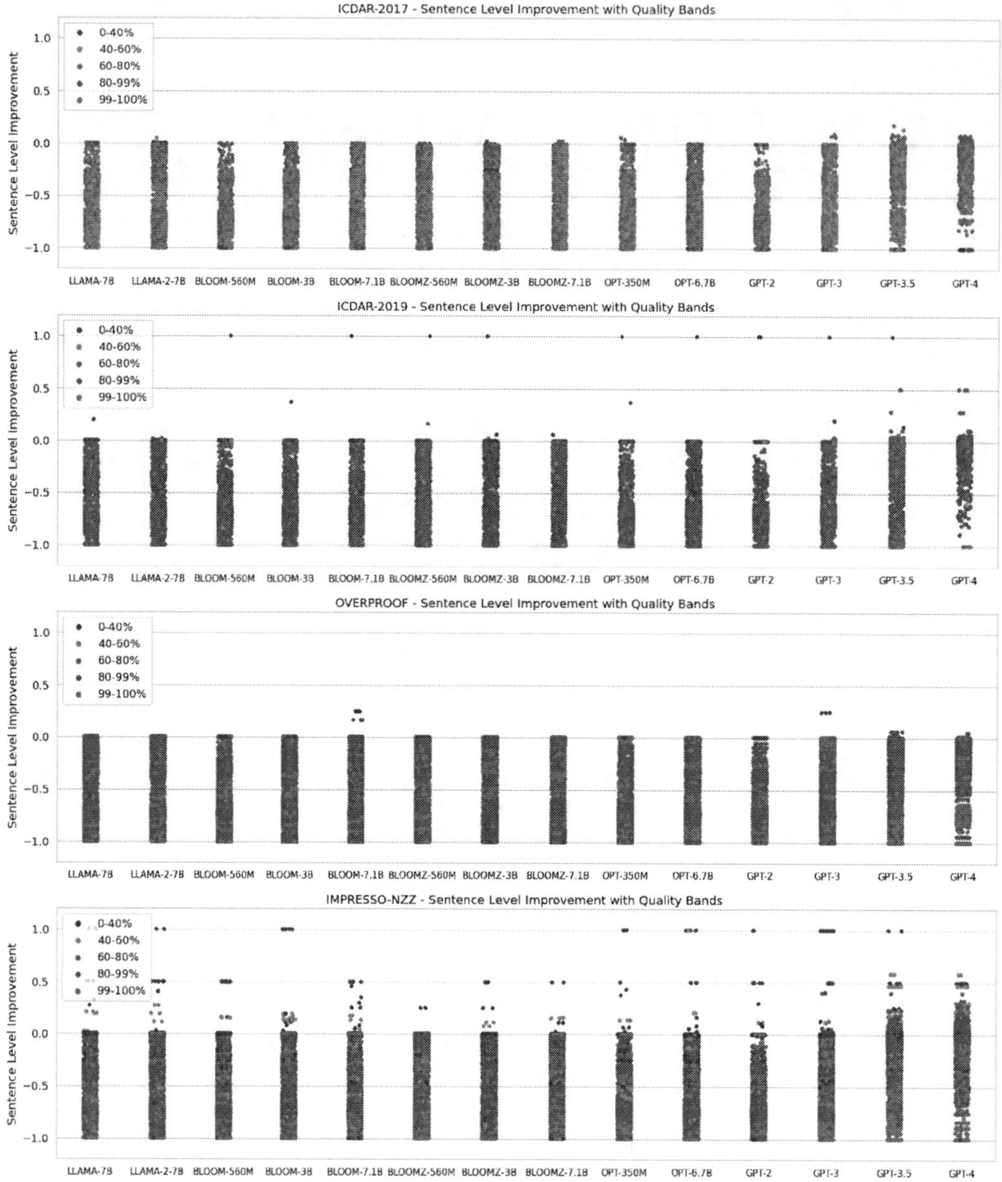

Figure 19: Post-correction improvement scores per quality band and model for **`icdar`**, **`overproof`** and **`impresso-nzz`** datasets, considering post-processed responses to **sentence-level input** in the zero-shot setting.

F.2 ajmc, htrec and ina

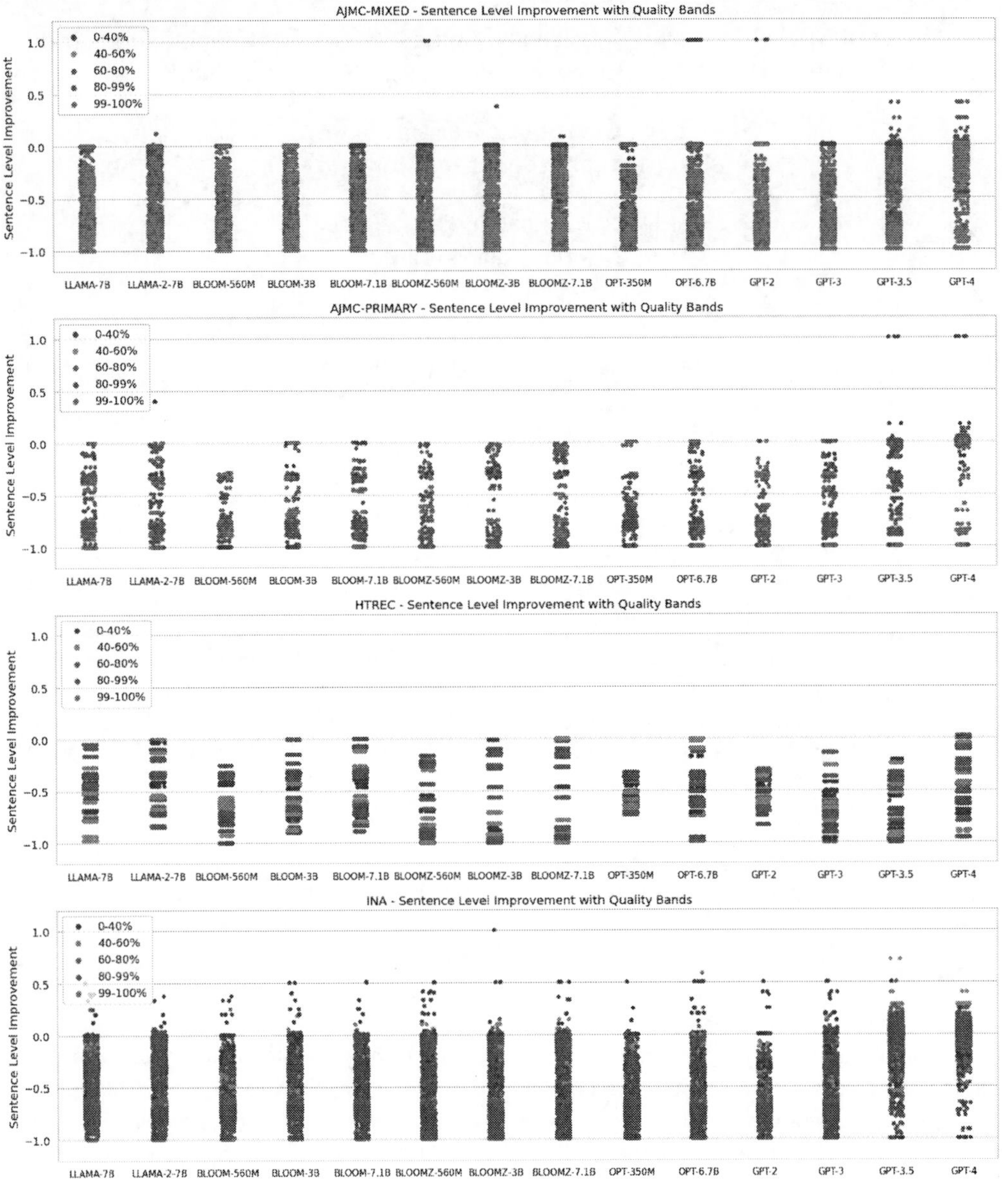

Figure 20: Post-correction improvement scores per quality band and model for `ajmc`, `htrec` and `ina` datasets, considering post-processed responses to **sentence-level input** in the zero-shot setting.

Distinguishing Fictional Voices: a Study of Authorship Verification Models for Quotation Attribution

Gaspard Michel[†*]
gmichel@deezer.com

Elena V. Epure[†]
eepure@deezer.com

Romain Hennequin[†]
rhennequin@deezer.com

Christophe Cerisara[*]
christophe.cerisara@loria.fr

[†] Deezer Research, Paris, France
[*] Loria, Nancy, France

Abstract

Recent approaches to automatically detect the speaker of an utterance of direct speech often disregard general information about characters in favor of local information found in the context, such as surrounding mentions of entities. In this work, we explore stylistic representations of characters built by encoding their quotes with off-the-shelf pretrained Authorship Verification models in a large corpus of English novels (the Project Dialogism Novel Corpus). Results suggest that the combination of stylistic and topical information captured in some of these models accurately distinguish characters among each other, but does not necessarily improve over semantic-only models when attributing quotes. However, these results vary across novels and more investigation of stylometric models particularly tailored for literary texts and the study of characters should be conducted.

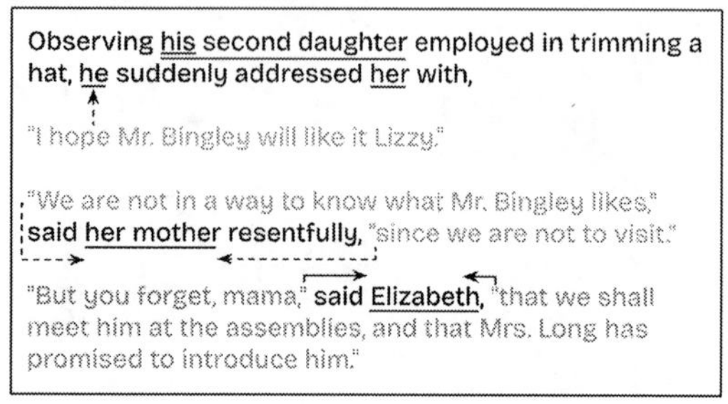

Figure 1: Example of quotation attribution on an excerpt of *Pride and Prejudice* by Jane Austen (1813). Underlined text are identified mentions, and arrows link quotes to their relevant entity mention (solid arrows are explicit references and dashed arrows are anaphoric references). In a separate step, coreference resolution is used to link entity mentions to their canonical character.

1 Introduction

In prose fiction, entire universes come to life. Different techniques are employed by authors to create engaging narratives and use a combination of narrator and character words to build the atmosphere and unveil the story. Characters in the fictional world reveal aspects of their personalities through dialogues. In Bakhtin's idea of *polyphony* (Bakhtin, 1984), characters participate in dialogues in their own voice, according to their own ideas about themselves and the fictional world. Automatically identifying parts of dialogues and attributing them to the character that utters them is central to many studies of large literary corpora (Elson et al., 2010; Muzny et al., 2017a; Sims and Bamman, 2020)

The detection of direct-speech has been widely performed for English literature, and simple regular expression systems achieve almost perfect performances on well-formatted texts. Attributing characters to quotes is more challenging and often requires solving multiple tasks: quotation identification, character identification and speaker attribution (Muzny et al., 2017b; Vishnubhotla et al., 2023). A speaker is attributed to a quote by training a separate model to find the nearest relevant *entity mention*, which is then linked to a *canonical character* with coreference resolution models. Figure 1 summarizes this process. Although many approaches have been explored in this direction, there is still room for improvement

Using a recently proposed corpora of English novels annotated with speakers, our current work first investigates to which extent *voices* of characters in novels are distinguishable using authorship verification approaches applied to character utterances. Then, we analyze quotes of characters in this large corpus and evaluate to which extent character-related features encoded by pretrained authorship verification models contain a predictive signal for *quotation attribution*. Our intuition is that character-level information (such as style, preferences in topic, persona) might be used in addition to contextual information to improve quotation at-

Proceedings of LaTeCH-CLfL 2024, pages 160–171
March 22, 2024 ©2024 Association for Computational Linguistics

tribution models. Prior stylometric studies have shown that canonical drama authors are able to create memorable characters with distinguishable voices (Vishnubhotla et al., 2019; Šeļa et al., 2023). Nonetheless, the stylometric analysis of characters in novels remains scarce, mainly due to the lack of available corpora annotated with speakers. To the best of our knowledge, exploring this type of character representations for quotation attribution has not been done before.

Consequently, with this work, we make the following contributions:

1. We investigate recent neural authorship verification models for the study of characters in novels and benchmark them on their ability to attribute authorship for distinguishing character voices in a large corpus.

2. Framing quote attribution as an authorship verification task, we are the first work to evaluate the usefulness of stylometric character representations encoded by off-the-shelf authorship verification models to attribute quotes to characters.

Results suggest that most characters in the PDNC corpus own distinct voices, and that they are best distinguished by models that encode both semantic and stylistic information. Semantic-only models, however, seem to be better at attributing quotes than models that encode style. Besides, representing characters with the quotes they uttered in a single chapter appear to contain a predictive signal for attributing quotes in other chapters, but this varies per novel. Finally, our results suggest that there are semantic variations between *explicit* quotes (i.e. quotes where the relevant gold mention is a named mention of the speaker) and other type of quotes (*anaphoric* and *implicit* quotes, introduced in Section 3), and that including stylistic information alleviates the impact of these semantic shifts when distinguishing characters voices based on *explicit* quotes only.

2 Related Work

2.1 Quotation Attribution

Quotation attribution models in novels often assume given utterances of direct speech. Elson and McKeown (2010) introduce the CQSC corpus and attribute automatically extracted quotes to named entities ("Elizabeth") and nominals ("her daughter") with a mention ranking model. Instead, He et al. (2013) attribute quotes directly to *speakers* with a supervised ranking system using features such as speaker alternation patterns and character-level features (He et al., 2010). The deterministic sieve-based model of Muzny et al. (2017b) regards quotation attribution as a two-step process: quote-*mention* linking and mention-*speaker* linking.

The NLP pipeline dedicated to books, BookNLP[1], went a step further by replacing the deterministic sieves with fine-tuned language models. Vishnubhotla et al. (2022) introduce the largest-to-date corpus of quotation attribution, PDNC, and show a similar accuracy score of around 63% for both BookNLP and the sieve-based model. However, better results were obtained later by fine-tuning BookNLP on PDNC (Vishnubhotla et al., 2023). Although these works are considered state-of-the-art in quotation attribution, they inherently lack character-level information in the mention-speaker linking step.

2.2 Character Representations

Most works focus on creating distributed *embeddings* that encode the persona of characters (i.e. characters with similar properties such as gender, job, relationships should have similar persona-based representations). Bamman et al. (2014) propose a Bayesian model that infers latent character personas as a distribution over various dependency relations. Brahman et al. (2021) introduce LiSCU, a dataset containing literary texts along with their summaries and descriptions of characters participating in the narrative. They train a language model to generate accurate descriptions of characters, showing that the model has a complex understanding of personas. Inoue et al. (2022) propose to represent characters in novels using a graph-based character network and positional embeddings. The character network contains book-level and authorial information, and captures the attributes of characters, while positional embeddings encode the dynamics of character activity throughout the narrative.

In this work, we rather focus on *what characters say* and *how they say it*, building stylometric representations of characters with off-the-shelf pretrained authorship verification models.

2.3 Authorship Verification

Authorship verification aims to predict whether two texts have been written by the same author. Re-

[1] https://github.com/booknlp/booknlp

cently, these models have employed a contrastive learning framework to build a representation space where works written by the same author are close together while being distant to texts written by other authors. Evaluation is made by building disjoint sets of *queries* and *targets*. Queries are pieces of text written by an author, and targets are other texts written by the same author and other authors. Based on a similarity measure such as cosine similarity, a ranking distribution is created by scoring a query against all targets. Area Under the Receiver Operating Characteristic Curve (AUC) is often used to evaluate if this distribution gives a high rank to the correct target.

Recent advances exploit language models to distinguish hundred of thousands of authors. Rivera-Soto et al. (2021) fine-tune SentenceBERT (Reimers and Gurevych, 2019) using thousands of Reddit users, Amazon reviews and Fanfiction stories. Their model, LUAR, uses both stylistic and content information (such as topical preferences) to distinguish between authors. Similarly, Wegmann et al. (2022) fine-tune RoBERTa (Liu et al., 2019) on posts of thousands of Reddit users. By controlling for content in the creation of their training data, they ensure that their model, STEL, mostly encodes stylistic information.

Although both models perform well on their respective authorship verification tasks, they are blackbox models that do not offer an interpretation of aspects of style captured in their representations. Wegmann et al. (2022) present a clustering analysis of learned representations of Reddit posts and showed that STEL mostly captures variations of punctuation, casing and contraction spelling. These stylistic variations do not apply to quotes in novel, we thus expect STEL to struggle to transfer from Reddit to our domain. Rivera-Soto et al. (2021) do not study aspects of style captured in LUAR's representations, but offer an interpretation of the model's performance based on the domain it was trained on. Particularly, they show that LUAR is prone to overfit to the training domain style features. While training on Reddit data, they conclude that the model rely less on topical diversity to distinguish among authors, which can be favorable to distinguish novel characters that usually speak in a wide range of topics.

2.4 Stylometric Analysis of Characters

Stylometric analysis of literary characters has been mostly focused on drama characters because of existing large annotated corpus. Most works focus on the style of character, aiming at capturing syntactic, lexical and phonological variations that can occur when they are quoted. Vishnubhotla et al. (2019) propose to study the distinctiveness of character stylistic and topical patterns with text classification. Šeļa et al. (2023) propose a measure of distinctiveness based on character 3-grams, which they apply to a large number of drama characters. They show that it is able to capture interesting aspects of stylistics such as phonological differences, accents and dialects, as well as topical and lexical differences. To the best of our knowledge, Dinu and Uban (2017) is the only work that focuses on novel characters. Their supervised bag-of-word classification model was able to accurately classify some characters, but fell short on the main character of the epistolary novel "Liaisons Dangereuse".

Other related works leverage dialogues in movie scripts to build character representations. Azab et al. (2019) train a Word2Vec model where the context window consists of the surrounding speaker identities as well as the current speaker utterance. Similarly, Li et al. (2023) encode all utterances of a script with a pre-trained language model, and extract representations by pooling all encoded quotes of a character together. A contrastive learning objective is used to create a fine-grained representation space where characters are well separated. Although the methods presented above are quite similar to the way we build character representations, authors did not release the code publicly at the time of writing, precluding comparison in our experiments.

In this work, we analyze novel characters at a larger scale using the PDNC corpus containing 28 English novels. Instead of employing classification accuracy as a measure of character distinctiveness, we frame the task as an authorship verification problem to evaluate to what extent characters voice can be distinguished. We are also the first to evaluate if these character-level features contain a predictive signal to attribute unseen quotes to the right speaker.

3 Experimental Setup

Our goal in this work is to investigate if fictional voices of literary characters in novels are distinguishable from a stylistic point-of-view. We also want to know if a partial signal of a character's voice derived from its *explicit* quotes (i.e. the gold *mention* linked to the quote is any named mention such as "Elizabeth") is a good proxy for its overall voice. Explicit quotes are straightforward to attribute to characters since they are linked to a named mention, which can then be linked to canonical characters (*e.g.* with coreference resolution or name clustering) more easily than when dealing with pronominal mentions (Muzny et al., 2017b). We hypothesize that if we can construct representative character embeddings based on explicit quotes only, then these representations can in turn enhance quotation attribution solutions to detect the speaker of other type of quotes. Other types of quotes include *anaphoric* quotes (i.e the gold *mention* is a pronoun or noun phrase) and *implicit* quotes (often happens during a conversation, when no *mention* is linked to the quote but the speaker can be inferred from the context). Finally, using the same set of character representations, we want to evaluate to which extent they contain information to attribute quotes that were not used to build the representations.

To evaluate these representations, we formulate the task as the authorship verification task: given a corpus of quotes from character A (the *query*), a corpus of other quotes from character A and similar corpora for other characters in a given novel (the *targets*) and a similarity measure, we evaluate the ability of pretrained models to predict if the targets have been written by character A or not. AUC is used to assess models' performances, as it accounts for how well models can rank predictions, without concerns of threshold values (Tyo et al., 2022). We chose to frame the task as an authorship verification problem rather than closed-set authorship attribution because the number of targets (*i.e.* number of candidate speakers) vary for each query, which is further described in Section 3.4

We first present how character representations are derived from pretrained models, and then describe how we evaluate the capacity of these representations to answer the above questions. We publicly release our code for further research[2].

3.1 Building Character Representations

Transformer-based models are widely used to encode textual information. To build character representations, we leverage various publicly available pretrained models (PM) trained on different tasks as quote encoders. For each novel, we assume that we have access to all utterances of direct speech $Q = \{q_1, \ldots, q_n\}$ as well as each character in the novel $C = \{c_1, \ldots, c_m\}$. Let $g : Q \mapsto C$ be a function that assigns a quote q_i to its speaker c such that $g(q_i) = c$ implies that character c is the speaker of the quote q_i. To build the representation of a character c in a given subset of quotes $\tilde{Q} \subset Q$, we first extract all quotes of character c in the subset: $\tilde{Q}_c = \{q_i : q_i \in \tilde{Q}, g(q_i) = c\}$. A quote representation is obtained by encoding each quote with a pretrained model, denoted as PM_θ:

$$\mathbf{h}_{q_i} = \text{PM}_\theta(q_i)$$

We then derive an embedding of character c in the subset $\tilde{Q}$ by pooling all embeddings of quotes spoken by c in $\tilde{Q}$:

$$\mathbf{H}_{\tilde{Q}_c} = \text{POOL}(\{\mathbf{h}_{q_i} : q_i \in \tilde{Q}_c\})$$

In our experiments, the POOL function is the average of all quote representations, except for the LUAR model that uses an attention-based POOL function with attention weights trained to focus on the relevant texts of an author. By pooling over the subset of quotes of a character, we expect the resulting representation to contain general information of *what a character say* and/or *how he says it*, depending on the PM used. Compared to some of the previous approaches to character representations presented in section 2.2, we do not use any contextual information (surrounding passages of narrative text, sequence of speaker turn, or surrounding quotes) so that that the representations focus mainly on stylistic and/or content information. We conduct different experiments by varying the construction of the subset $\tilde{Q}$.

Chapterwise: we extract all quotes of a character in a given chapter T to build its query representation. The targets are created by using quotes contained in the held-out chapters.

Explicit: we only extract *explicit* quotes of a character in a given chapter T with similar targets as in the chapterwise experiment. We thus build representations for a character with quotes that are linked to a named mention of the character. This experiment is designed such that we can quantify the amount of information lost compared to the chapterwise experiment that uses all types of quotes. It

[2]https://github.com/deezer/quote_AV

might happen that some characters are not explicitly quoted in chapter T. In this case, we do not build representations for these characters.

Reading Order: we use the first n quotes of a character in the first half of novels (segmented by chapter) as a basis of its query representation. Targets are built using quotes in the remaining half. With this experiment, we want to see the impact of increasing the amount of available character information on the capacity of models to distinguish their voices.

3.2 Data

We use the PDNC dataset[3] (Vishnubhotla et al., 2022), containing annotations of speakers at the quote level for 28 English novels written by 21 authors and published between the 19th and early 20th century. This dataset consists of mostly literary novels, and a few children, crime and science-fiction novels. Characters in each novel are labelled with *minor*, *intermediate* and *major* roles, depending on the total number of quotes they uttered. We only focus on *intermediate* and *major* characters that uttered at least 10 and 100 quotes respectively, and discarded *minor* characters that participate less in the narrative. Quotes are often subject to *incises*, where a narrative segment giving indication on who and how the quotes is being said is inserted within the quote (*e.g.* "said her mother resentfully", third paragraph in Figure 1). In this case, we use the full text of the quote, discarding the incise, as a single character's utterance.

We build character embeddings using the methodology explained in Section 3.1 that we further use to derive sets of queries and targets. For a character c and its quote subset $\tilde{Q}_c$, the associated query is the character representation built from the subset, $\mathbf{H}_{\tilde{Q}_c}$. Using the held-out subset, O, the associated set of targets are embeddings of every character that utters quotes in O: $\{\mathbf{H}_{O_{c'}}\colon\ c' \in C\}$. We only construct queries for characters that utter at least 5 quotes in $\tilde{Q}_c$ to mitigate the amount of uninformative queries. We chose to use 5 quotes based on preliminary results showing that some queries would have only 1 quote and that the resulting character representations were not really informative. Results of the reading order experiment presented in Section 4.3 further support this observation.

[3] https://github.com/Priya22/project-dialogism-novel-corpus

	Chapterwise	Explicit
Total queries	1606	562
# Speakers	11.1 (4.6)	11.1 (4.6)
Activity (%)	93 (10)	53 (28)
Queries	57.4 (29.3)	21.6 (17.9)
Query length	21.4 (11.5)	10.5 (3.5)
Targets/query		
Character	11.0 (4.6)	11.2 (4.7)
Quote	1142 (600)	1176 (597)

Table 1: Summary statistics of our set of queries and targets on the PDNC corpus. Bottom part is averaged over novels with (standard deviation).

Table 1 summarizes the main statistics of the resulting data. For the chapterwise experiment, we derived 1606 queries on the entire corpus, but only 562 for the explicit experiment. Indeed, explicit quotes represent around 31% of the total number of quotes in the corpus, with large discrepancy across novels (the minimum is 10% and the maximum is 81%), thus leading to many characters that do not utter at least 5 explicit quotes in $\tilde{Q}_c$. As a result, the percentage of active characters (i.e characters that have at least one query) drops from 93% to 53% and, out of the 28 novels, we could not create queries for two novels because they did not contain enough explicit quotes to build representations (*The Gambler* by Fyodor Dostoevsky, 1887, and *The Sport of the Gods* by Paul Laurence Dunbar, 1902). Queries in the Chapterwise experiment also contain twice as many quotes on average than in the Explicit one. Nonetheless, the number of character targets and the number of quotes in target is roughly the same between the two experiments. We thus expect the task of distinguishing voices and attributing unseen quotes based on representation of explicit quotes only to be generally harder.

3.3 Models

We build representations with two pretrained authorship verification models: STEL and LUAR and introduce two baseline models: SentenceBERT (SBERT)[4] (Reimers and Gurevych, 2019) and a RoBERTa-based multi-label emotion classification model[5].

[4] We use all-mpnet-base-v2

[5] https://huggingface.co/SamLowe/roberta-base-go_emotions

3.3.1 Baselines

The SBERT and Emotion models are referred to as baselines because their purpose is not to encode stylistic information of characters. SBERT is trained to recognize semantically similar sentences, hence encoding rich semantic textual information. We expect this semantic-only model to distinguish characters voices based on the content of their corpus of quotes, such as topical preferences. The Emotion model is a RoBERTa model fined-tuned to classify emotions in a multi-label setup (28 emotions), allowing predictions of multiple emotions conveyed at once in the same sentence. We use this model as a benchmark based on prior analysis we made, showing that some characters were conveying certain emotions more than others. Thus, our intuition was that it could be used as a discriminative feature of a character's voice. We use representations contained in the last RoBERTa transformer layer before the classification head when encoding quotes.

3.3.2 Authorship Verification Models

Authorship verification models are trained to predict if two texts (or corpus of texts) have been written by the same author, enabling them to capture authorial style to some extent. STEL is a RoBERTa model fine-tuned on the Contrastive Authorship Verification (CAV) task with millions of Reddit users. In the CAV task, a model is asked to distinguish which from three pieces of texts (triplets) have been written by the same author. Using triplets that have similar topic, STEL is trained to distinguish between authors using stylistic information only. Although its base model, RoBERTa, encodes semantic to some extent, restraining training triplets to texts that essentially cover similar topic forces the model to focus on stylistic cues.

LUAR fine-tunes SentenceBERT to encode corpora of utterances. Unlike STEL, they do not force training examples to have similar topic, leading to a model that encodes both content and stylistic information in author representations. For the same author, different representations are built using distinct collections of documents written by the author. LUAR encodes stylistic information by being trained on the authorship verification task. Compared to STEL, we expect LUAR to build more robust character representations since it uses an attention mechanism that allows focus on texts with strong authorial signal.

For all models, we use a maximum sequence length of 64, truncating longer quotes (only 14% of the total number of quotes are longer than 64 tokens). We use publicly available versions of LUAR[6] and STEL[7].

3.4 Evaluation

3.4.1 Character-Character

Given a query character representation built from a subset of quotes $\mathbf{H}_{\tilde{Q}_c}$, a similarity function ϕ, and the held-out subset O, we evaluate the similarity of the query with the targets built from O. In this work, we use cosine similarity for the ϕ function. Ideally, we want a high similarity between a character query and the target linked to the same character, $\mathbf{H}_{O_c}$, and low similarity between the character query and other characters target $\mathbf{H}_{O_{c'}}$:

$$\phi(\mathbf{H}_{\tilde{Q}_c}, \mathbf{H}_{O_c}) > \phi(\mathbf{H}_{\tilde{Q}_c}, \mathbf{H}_{O_{c'}}),\ \forall\, c' \neq c \quad (1)$$

In practice, we evaluate the capacity of pretrained models to give a high rank to corresponding character target $\mathbf{H}_{O_c}$ using AUC. In this context, the AUC measures the probability that Equation 1 holds when randomly selecting a character c' different than c. We chose AUC over standard authorship attribution metrics (such as macro-averaged accuracy) because of its ability to evaluate the output ranking distribution, $\{\phi(\mathbf{H}_{\tilde{Q}_c}, \mathbf{H}_{O'_c}), c' \in C\}$. Besides, unlike accuracy, AUC does not require a threshold value for predicting the speaker of a quote, which can be tricky when using cosine similarities. We refer to this evaluation as Character-Character (CC) as it measures how unique are characters voices.

3.4.2 Character-Quotes

We now introduce how we evaluate the performances of such character representations at attributing quotes from the held-out subset. Similar query representations are used, but targets are replaced by quote representations (encoded by the same PM) rather than character representations. Let $q_i \in O_c$ be a target quote from character c in the held-out subset O and $q_j \in \bar{O}_c = \bigcup_{c' \neq c} O_{c'}$ be any quote spoken by a different character in O, we evaluate the following hypothesis:

$$\phi(\mathbf{H}_{\tilde{Q}_c}, \mathbf{h}_{q_i}) > \phi(\mathbf{H}_{\tilde{Q}_c}, \mathbf{h}_{q_j}),\ \forall\, q_i \in O_c,\ q_j \in \bar{O}_c \quad (2)$$

[6]https://huggingface.co/rrivera1849/LUAR-MUD

[7]https://huggingface.co/AnnaWegmann/Style-Embedding

	CC	CQ
Semantics	67.3 (11.6)	**55.1** (2.5)
STEL	58.1 (8.3)	52.8 (1.9)
Emotions	56.0 (8.0)	51.7 (1.5)
LUAR	**81.6** (6.2)	53.6 (2.4)

Table 2: AUC results of the **chapterwise** experiment. Results are averaged over novels (standard deviation). Best results are highlighted in **bold**.

	CC	CQ
Semantics	63.9 (15.8)	54.4 (4.6)
STEL	56.2 (15.6)	52.7 (3.6)
Emotions	53.4 (14.4)	51.4 (3.1)
LUAR	**80.1** (10.0)	53.5 (4.4)

Table 3: AUC results of the **explicit** experiment. Results are averaged over novels (standard deviation). Best results are highlighted in **bold**. Results for the CQ evaluation are not highlighted because the large standard deviations prevent to chose a best model.

We also use AUC in this Character-Quote evaluation setup (CQ) to assess how well the target quotes spoken by character c are ranked compared to quotes of other characters. Here, the AUC measures the probability that Equation 2 holds when randomly selecting a quote $q_i \in O_c$ and a quote $q_j \in \bar{O}_c$. Intuitively, a high AUC indicates that character representations are more similar to quote representations of the same character, thus showing that they contain useful information to attribute the right speaker to quotes.

4 Results

4.1 Chapterwise

Results for the chapterwise experiment are displayed in Table 2. In the CC evaluation setup, semantic-only representations built from the SBERT model appear to be quite good at distinguishing the voices of characters. We believe that SBERT particularly captures topical preferences, which appear as a useful discriminative feature of voices. Nonetheless, purely stylistic information seems to be worse at distinguishing voices than semantic-only embeddings, as suggested by STEL results. LUAR's high performance suggests that a combination of both content and stylistic information is desirable to achieve better and more stable discrimination among characters. Overall, the Emotions model seems quite misleading, as the AUC is the closest to random attribution (a random attribution would lead to an AUC of 50%).

When evaluating the capacity of these representations to attribute quotes, we see a drastically different picture. The performance of all models is just slightly higher than random attribution, indicating that the task is generally harder. This is not surprising, deciding which among thousands of quotes have been spoken by character c given a corpus of around 10 quotes spoken by c without access to contextual information is a challenging task, probably even for humans. Interestingly, the semantic-only baseline achieve the best results here. We hypothesise that the drop of performance of LUAR is mostly due to how it encodes quotes: it was trained to produce fine-grained author representations based on a corpus of multiple texts rather than to build rich text representations. In contrast, SBERT directly produces meaningful quote embeddings, leading to better performance for quotation attribution even if resulting character representations are less informative than LUAR's.

The high standard deviation in these results also suggests that distinguishing voices of characters is easier in some novels than in others. We analyze to which extent the semantic model and LUAR complement each other by looking at performance per novel in Appendix A and per character role in Appendix B.

4.2 Explicit

We present the results of the explicit experiment in Table 3. As expected, the performance of all models is worse than in the chapterwise experiment. Indeed, character representations built from explicit quotes have access to fewer quotes, reducing the amount of available information for each character. In the CC evaluation setup, LUAR still performs best at distinguishing voices of characters, followed by the SBERT model. Interestingly, even though queries are built with twice as few quotes on average than in the chapterwise experiment, we observe only a slight performance drop for LUAR and STEL. This observation suggests that explicit quotes constitute a strong signal of characters voice. However, we observe a larger drop for the SBERT model, indicating that there might be semantic variations between explicit quotes and other types of quotes. We hypothesize that such variations should occur less in stylistic cues of quotes, which is fur-

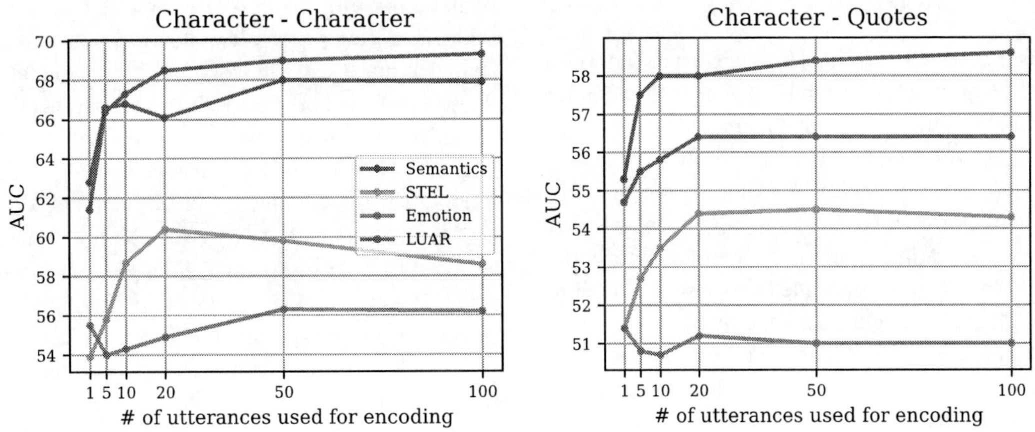

Figure 2: Results of the reading order experiment for the CC (left) and the CQ (right) evaluations. We look at AUC performance when varying the number of utterances used to create character representations.

ther supported by the lower AUC drop of STEL and LUAR.

Evaluating with the CQ setup, we can draw similar conclusions. Performances are worse than in the chapterwise experiment, and we see a larger AUC drop for the SBERT model than for models that encode style. However, the semantic model seems to remain the best at attributing unseen quotes on average, but it's not true for all novels.

Compared to the chapterwise experiment, we see very large standard deviations across novels. This is not surprising, some novels contain only a very small number of explicit quotes, leading to a smaller amount of queries as explained in Section 3.2. Although aggregated results suggest that the semantic model and the LUAR model still contain information for attributing quotes, when looking at results per novel, we observe that they can sometimes provide misleading attributions with AUC worse than 50%, but also provide a good ranking of quotes in other novels (the highest AUC is of 68% for *The Age Of Innocence* by Edit Wharton). Interestingly, we also observe a larger performance gap between the two models on some novels, indicating that they are more complementary when using explicit quotes only.

4.3 Reading Order

Results for the reading order experiment are displayed in Figure 2. Looking at the CC evaluation, we see that all models except Emotions have better performances when increasing the number of available utterances from 1 to 20. Increasing the number of quotes always improves the LUAR model, which successfully creates more fine-grained representations when accessing additional quotes. However, the STEL model peaks at 20 utterances, indicating that it can't really capture the style of characters with more quotes. Interestingly, the semantic model performance only varies slightly when using 5, 10 or 20 utterances, suggesting we can build meaningful semantic representations with a small number of quotes. This result further supports our hypothesis that the drop of performance between the Chapterwise and Explicit experiments is closely linked to semantic variations between explicit quotes and other types of quotes rather than simply due to lower query sizes. Overall, LUAR and Semantics build more informative representations using an increasing number of quotes from, 20 to 50 quotes of a character.

Results for the CQ evaluation show a similar trend, where the AUC of all models plateaus starting from 10 or 20 utterances, except for the Semantics that have increased performance with more data starting from 10 quotes. We hypothesize that stylistic information and topical preferences of characters can thus be captured by these models with a fairly low amount of quotes. A more complex understanding of characters does not always help to attribute quotes when using quote embeddings built with the same models, highlighting the need for additional contextual information.

5 Discussion

We conducted experiments to understand how character representations built from explicit quotes could help to improve quotation attribution. These quotes are particularly easy to attribute to characters and can thus be detected automatically to build *informative* character representations that can serve as additional inputs to quotation attribution systems. Results presented above suggest that explicit quotes might be a good proxy for the voice of fictional characters and that semantic and stylistic information of quotes can help attribute quotes. Nonetheless, we think that there might be semantic variations between explicit and other types of quotes and that adding stylistic information in representations of characters alleviates this shift.

Experiments conducted in this work are focused on *intermediate* and *major* characters, i.e. characters that participate more and shape the narrative. Although they represent a large number of different characters, *minor* characters often have less impact on the story and do not contribute significantly to the overall number of quotes that we want to attribute. However, even with characters that are more quoted, we observed discrepancies in authorial patterns of explicit quoting. While some authors quote all their characters explicitly at least 5 times in a chapter, some do not. As a result, we could build queries for only 53% of *intermediate* and *major* characters in the PDNC corpus. When looking at whole novels rather than at chapters, only 11% are explicitly quoted less than 5 times, among which 17% are major characters. Therefore, we can still build representations for a majority of characters, which motivated our work.

We studied stylistic information encoded in two off-the-shelf pretrained authorship verification models, LUAR and STEL. These models have been trained to distinguish thousands of authors of Reddit posts, and have been shown to transfer poorly to other domains (Rivera-Soto et al., 2021). Most novels do not contain stylistic traits captured by STEL, which probably explains why it is performing badly. We were aware of this limitation at first, but decided to test the model as an off-the-shelf solution to obtain stylometric representations. In the future, we plan to re-train a STEL-like model on literary texts such as drama. LUAR encodes both semantic and stylistic information, it is thus hard to infer the dimensions of content and style it captures as well as their respective contribution to the task. Its good performance on the Character-Character evaluation setup suggests that it gets dimensions of style that make sense in literature. More generally, interpretable authorship verification models (Patel et al., 2023) are an interesting direction as they combine the performance of neural approaches with the interpretability of frequency-based methods.

The high standard deviations across novels indicate that the task of distinguishing voices of characters is easier in some novels than in others. In the Chapterwise experiment (CC evaluation), the AUC of LUAR goes as low as 68% and as high as 91%. Ideally, we would like to understand the reasons behind these variations: Are some authors better at creating memorable voices? Is it easier in a particular genre? Interpretability and literary knowledge are key to answer these questions, that we leave for future work.

6 Conclusion

We presented a study of recent neural approaches to authorship verification applied to literary characters. We designed three experiments to assess if such models can be used to create meaningful character representations and to assess if explicit quotes were a good proxy of a character's voice. Our first evaluation focuses on the ability of these representations to distinguish characters, while our second quantifies the amount of information they contain to attribute unseen quotes. Results at the character level suggest that their voices are better distinguished when using a combination of stylistic and semantic information. Using style also helps to reduce the impact of the semantic shift observed between explicit quotes and other types of quotes. When attributing quotes, our results suggest that adding stylistic information does not necessarily improve over semantic-only models. We believe that the main cause is a poor domain transfer from Reddit to English novels. In the future, we plan to further analyze representations built from models trained on movie scripts (Azab et al., 2019; Li et al., 2023), which we argue should contain stylistic patterns more similar to the ones found in literary works. We also want to investigate how such representations can be incorporated into quotation attribution systems. Finally, we believe our approach could be used at a larger scale to investigate which authors/genre are better at constructing unique voices for their characters.

References

Mahmoud Azab, Noriyuki Kojima, Jia Deng, and Rada Mihalcea. 2019. Representing movie characters in dialogues. In *Proceedings of the 23rd Conference on Computational Natural Language Learning (CoNLL)*, pages 99–109, Hong Kong, China. Association for Computational Linguistics.

Mikhail Bakhtin. 1984. *Problems of Dostoevsky's Poetics*. University of Minnesota Press.

David Bamman, Ted Underwood, and Noah A. Smith. 2014. A Bayesian mixed effects model of literary character. In *Proceedings of the 52nd Annual Meeting of the Association for Computational Linguistics (Volume 1: Long Papers)*, pages 370–379, Baltimore, Maryland. Association for Computational Linguistics.

Faeze Brahman, Meng Huang, Oyvind Tafjord, Chao Zhao, Mrinmaya Sachan, and Snigdha Chaturvedi. 2021. "let your characters tell their story": A dataset for character-centric narrative understanding. In *Findings of the Association for Computational Linguistics: EMNLP 2021*, pages 1734–1752, Punta Cana, Dominican Republic. Association for Computational Linguistics.

Liviu P. Dinu and Ana Sabina Uban. 2017. Finding a character's voice: Stylome classification on literary characters. In *Proceedings of the Joint SIGHUM Workshop on Computational Linguistics for Cultural Heritage, Social Sciences, Humanities and Literature*, pages 78–82, Vancouver, Canada. Association for Computational Linguistics.

David Elson, Nicholas Dames, and Kathleen McKeown. 2010. Extracting social networks from literary fiction. In *Proceedings of the 48th Annual Meeting of the Association for Computational Linguistics*, pages 138–147, Uppsala, Sweden. Association for Computational Linguistics.

David Elson and Kathleen McKeown. 2010. Automatic attribution of quoted speech in literary narrative. *Proceedings of the AAAI Conference on Artificial Intelligence*, 24(1):1013–1019.

Hua He, Denilson Barbosa, and Grzegorz Kondrak. 2013. Identification of speakers in novels. In *Proceedings of the 51st Annual Meeting of the Association for Computational Linguistics (Volume 1: Long Papers)*, pages 1312–1320, Sofia, Bulgaria. Association for Computational Linguistics.

Hua He, Greg Kondrak, and Denilson Barbosa. 2010. The actor-topic model for extracting social networks in literary narrative.

Naoya Inoue, Charuta Pethe, Allen Kim, and Steven Skiena. 2022. Learning and evaluating character representations in novels. In *Findings of the Association for Computational Linguistics: ACL 2022*, pages 1008–1019, Dublin, Ireland. Association for Computational Linguistics.

Dawei Li, Hengyuan Zhang, Yanran Li, and Shiping Yang. 2023. Multi-level contrastive learning for script-based character understanding.

Yinhan Liu, Myle Ott, Naman Goyal, Jingfei Du, Mandar Joshi, Danqi Chen, Omer Levy, Mike Lewis, Luke Zettlemoyer, and Veselin Stoyanov. 2019. Roberta: A robustly optimized BERT pretraining approach. *CoRR*, abs/1907.11692.

Grace Muzny, Mark Algee-Hewitt, and Dan Jurafsky. 2017a. Dialogism in the novel: A computational model of the dialogic nature of narration and quotations. *Digital Scholarship in the Humanities*, 32:ii31–ii52.

Grace Muzny, Michael Fang, Angel Chang, and Dan Jurafsky. 2017b. A two-stage sieve approach for quote attribution. In *Proceedings of the 15th Conference of the European Chapter of the Association for Computational Linguistics: Volume 1, Long Papers*, pages 460–470, Valencia, Spain. Association for Computational Linguistics.

Ajay Patel, Delip Rao, and Chris Callison-Burch. 2023. Learning interpretable style embeddings via prompting llms.

Nils Reimers and Iryna Gurevych. 2019. Sentence-BERT: Sentence embeddings using Siamese BERT-networks. In *Proceedings of the 2019 Conference on Empirical Methods in Natural Language Processing and the 9th International Joint Conference on Natural Language Processing (EMNLP-IJCNLP)*, pages 3982–3992, Hong Kong, China. Association for Computational Linguistics.

Rafael A. Rivera-Soto, Olivia Elizabeth Miano, Juanita Ordonez, Barry Y. Chen, Aleem Khan, Marcus Bishop, and Nicholas Andrews. 2021. Learning universal authorship representations. In *Proceedings of the 2021 Conference on Empirical Methods in Natural Language Processing*, pages 913–919, Online and Punta Cana, Dominican Republic. Association for Computational Linguistics.

Matthew Sims and David Bamman. 2020. Measuring information propagation in literary social networks. In *Proceedings of the 2020 Conference on Empirical Methods in Natural Language Processing (EMNLP)*, pages 642–652, Online. Association for Computational Linguistics.

Jacob Tyo, Bhuwan Dhingra, and Zachary C. Lipton. 2022. On the state of the art in authorship attribution and authorship verification.

Krishnapriya Vishnubhotla, Adam Hammond, and Graeme Hirst. 2019. Are fictional voices distinguishable? classifying character voices in modern drama. In *Proceedings of the 3rd Joint SIGHUM Workshop on Computational Linguistics for Cultural Heritage, Social Sciences, Humanities and Literature*, pages 29–34, Minneapolis, USA. Association for Computational Linguistics.

Krishnapriya Vishnubhotla, Adam Hammond, and Graeme Hirst. 2022. The project dialogism novel corpus: A dataset for quotation attribution in literary texts. In *Proceedings of the Thirteenth Language Resources and Evaluation Conference*, pages 5838–5848, Marseille, France. European Language Resources Association.

Krishnapriya Vishnubhotla, Frank Rudzicz, Graeme Hirst, and Adam Hammond. 2023. Improving automatic quotation attribution in literary novels. In *Proceedings of the 61st Annual Meeting of the Association for Computational Linguistics (Volume 2: Short Papers)*, pages 737–746, Toronto, Canada. Association for Computational Linguistics.

Anna Wegmann, Marijn Schraagen, and Dong Nguyen. 2022. Same author or just same topic? towards content-independent style representations. In *Proceedings of the 7th Workshop on Representation Learning for NLP*, pages 249–268, Dublin, Ireland. Association for Computational Linguistics.

Artjoms Šeļa, Ben Nagy, Joanna Byszuk, Laura Hernández-Lorenzo, Botond Szemes, and Maciej Eder. 2023. From stage to page: language independent bootstrap measures of distinctiveness in fictional speech.

A Performance per Novel

We display the performance by novel for the Chapterwise experiment in Figure 3 and for the Explicit experiment in Figure 4. Note that for the Explicit experiment, novels 18 and 24 (*The Gambler* by Fyodor Dostoevsky (1887) and *The Sport of the Gods* by Paul Laurence Dunbar (1902) respectively) were not considered because we could not build queries due to the lack of explicit quotes. For the chapterwise experiment in the CQ evaluation setup, we see that LUAR's performances is higher than SBERT in 4 novels, indicating complementarity between these models. The picture is even more evident in the explicit experiment (CQ setup), where LUAR's outperformns SBERT in 8 novels. Overall, some novels exhibit characters voices where style information have more impact than on other novels.

B Performance per Character Role

Table 4 displays results of the Chapterwise and Explicit experiments by character role. For the CC evaluation setup, LUAR performs very well on major characters, but struggles with intermediate characters. On the other hand, the semantic-only model performs better on intermediate characters. These results suggest complementarity between the two models, and that major characters exhibit more stylistic variations among them than intermediate characters. The latter result can be linked to the authorial process of creating memorable major characters, with more unique voices than intermediate characters.

For the CQ evaluation setup, it seems that all models are better at attributing quotes of intermediate characters, and we see a quite large gap between the two roles.

C Computing information

We encode quotes with models on a 32-core Intel Xeon Gold 6244 CPU @ 3.60GHz CPU with 128GB RAM equipped with 3 RTX A5000 GPUs with 24GB RAM each. For each model tested, one GPU was enough to encode all quotes in the 28 novels. In total, running the full experiments took around 5 minutes for the Semantics and STEL models, 10 minutes for the Emotions model, and 1 hour for LUAR.

	Chapterwise				Explicit			
	CC (M)	CC (I)	CQ (M)	CQ (I)	CC (M)	CC (I)	CQ (M)	CQ (I)
Semantics	62.9 (15.6)	**75.6** (12.8)	**53.1** (3.6)	**59.6** (5.0)	58.0 (18.3)	**79.1** (16.9)	51.8 (3.8)	**61.2** (7.3)
STEL	55.4 (14.6)	62.2 (11.1)	52.2 (3.1)	53.6 (3.3)	52.5 (18.9)	64.5 (23.7)	51.5 (3.7)	55.0 (10.5)
Emotions	53.1 (15.1)	59.5 (10.0)	50.2 (3.2)	53.6 (7.6)	49.9 (18.2)	59.6 (23.9)	50.2 (3.2)	53.6 (7.6)
LUAR	**91.2** (4.3)	63.0 (12.7)	52.1 (3.9)	56.6 (4.9)	**87.6** (9.0)	57.6 (25.1)	51.6 (4.5)	58.5 (7.3)

Table 4: AUC results by character role for the Chapterwise and Explicit experiments. (M) means major and (I) intermediate.

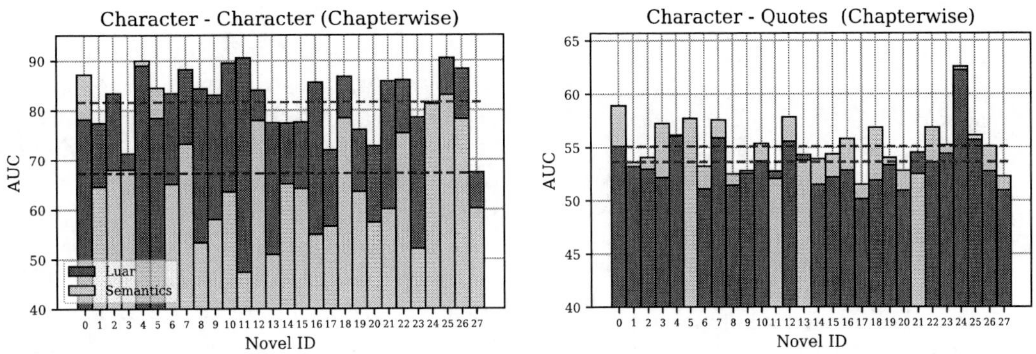

Figure 3: AUC per novel for the *Chapterwise* experiment.

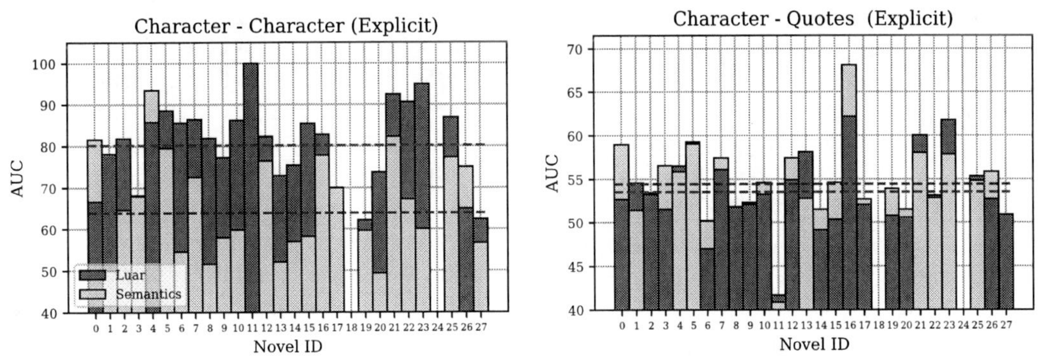

Figure 4: AUC per novel for the *Explicit* experiment.

Perplexing Canon: A study on GPT-based perplexity for canonical and non-canonical literary works

Yaru Wu
Uppsala University
yaru.wu.6038@student.uu.se

Pascale Feldkamp Moreira
Center for Humanities Computing
Aarhus University
pascale.moreira@cc.au.dk

Kristoffer L. Nielbo
Center for Humanities Computing
Aarhus University
kln@cas.au.dk

Yuri Bizzoni
Center for Humanities Computing
Aarhus University
yuri.bizzoni@cc.au.dk

Abstract

This study extends previous research on literary quality by using information theory-based methods to assess the level of perplexity recorded by three large language models when processing 20th-century English works deemed to have high literary quality, recognized by experts as canonical, compared to a broader control group. We find that canonical texts appear to elicit a higher perplexity in the models and we explore which textual features might concur to create such effect. We find that the usage of a more heavily nominal style, together with a more diverse vocabulary, is one leading cause for the difference between the two groups. These traits could reflect "strategies" to achieve a more informationally dense literary style in the canonical groups.

1 Introduction

The question of what "literary quality" is has been at the center of a millennia-long debate in aesthetics and literary studies.While literary judgment is almost by definition subjective, reflecting individual reader preferences, quantitative studies have shown that such preferences tend to converge at the large scale, and that both textual features, like coherence and style (Bizzoni et al., 2023c,a; Koolen et al., 2020; van Cranenburgh and Bod, 2017; Archer and Jockers, 2017), and text-extrinsic features, such as reader or critic demographics (Lassen et al., 2022; Koolen, 2018; Wang et al., 2019), significantly influence appreciation or perceived quality. Most schools of thought in literary research tend to see literary quality as either a perceived quality – an effect of reception and cultural dynamics (Bourdieu, 1993; Casanova, 2007; Guillory, 1995) – or as the effect of certain textual features, such as, among others, authorial strategies of defamiliarization and foregrounding (Shklovsky, 1917; Mukařovský, 1964; Peer, 2008; Attridge, 2004). While consensus on a single gold standard of quality is hard to achieve (Bizzoni et al., 2022), reader preferences and expert valuations can offer a range of measurable levels of appreciation. An often discussed dimension of literary quality is that of the so-called "literary canon", a complex concept generally representing a set of works that have survived or/and (by the same token) remain distinguished in the memory of a literary culture (Bloom, 1995). A community, usually over large periods of time, defines as outstanding and worthy of attention; yet this process is not devolved to any individual authority, which makes the very definition of what is within the canon complex. As such, the canon is often scrutinized in cultural approaches to literary quality. Some schools of thought have seen it as representing nothing but entrenched interests (von Hallberg, 1983) and thus as the cultural capital of ruling classes (Guillory, 1995), while others have considered "canonic" works to excel in terms of intrinsic features (Bloom, 1995), whether stylistic (Brottrager et al., 2022; Barré et al., 2023; Algee-Hewitt et al., 2016) or narrative (Bizzoni et al., 2023d). In his work on the dynamics in the literary field, Bourdieu (1993) placed "popular success" and "consecration" at opposed positions.[1] Recent quantitative studies of the literary field often follow a similar distinction between popularity and prestige (Porter, 2018; Manshel et al., 2019), where more prestigious books and genres are what we could call the more "literary" ones (Porter, 2018;

[1] "There are few fields in which the antagonism between the occupants of the polar positions is more total [than in the literary]" (Bourdieu, 1993, p. 46).

Proceedings of LaTeCH-CLfL 2024, pages 172–184
March 22, 2024

Lassen et al., 2023). Supporting the idea that such literariness may be distinguished by certain text-intrinsic features, Koolen et al. (2020) have shown that readers agree more on the "literariness" of books, and that it is easier to model literariness ratings from textual features than overall enjoyment ratings.

In this work, we approximate what can be considered canonical in a large corpus of around 9,000 novels. Based on this corpus, we ask two main questions: (1) Are canonical novels more "perplexing", as measured through different Large Language Models, than a non-canonical control group? (2) If they are, which linguistic and stylistic features might contribute to the difference?

Our reason for using perplexity (see Chapter 4 for the formal definition of perplexity) is at least two-fold. On one hand, canonical works of fiction are often examples of either "virtuous" (Bloom, 1995) or defamiliarizing usage of language (Mukařovský, 1964; Peer, 2008), thus an uncommon usage of language. Such characteristics may make canonical works of fiction more surprising with respect to non-canonical. Even when perplexity is operationalized as a measure of information theory, these works might elicit a higher perplexity on average. On the other hand, perplexity is a central measure of informativity in information theory (Shannon, 1949). Since perplexity is a function of surprisal, more perplexing texts tend to be more informationally dense. A highly specialized scientific paper – like a highly complex and articulate page of James Joyce – is unusually informative in the sense that it constantly relays novel information (highly specialized or new words – neologisms – or words in a new order) to the reader. In theory, a communicative system that manages to be as dense as possible without breaking down or being "too dense" for its own readers indicates elements of a heightened communicative efficiency – a feature that communities might tend to optimize over time (Rubino et al., 2016; Biber and Gray, 2011).

2 Related works

Studies seeking to predict literary success or perceived literary quality have often followed the intuitive idea that readers perceive a difference between more difficult and easier texts, and approximate some form of stylistic complexity. Such studies use features related to the readability indices developed in linguistics research, such as sentence length, vocabulary richness, or redundancy (Brottrager et al., 2022; van Cranenburgh and Bod, 2017; Crosbie et al., 2013; Koolen et al., 2020; Maharjan et al., 2017; Algee-Hewitt et al., 2016). Additionally, readability formulas find integration in editing tools such as the Hemingway or Marlowe applications,[2] which prioritize more "readable" texts. Yet the relation between stylistic aspects of text complexity and reader appreciation appears complex: while it is suggested that readers prefer more stylistically complex or informationally dense texts (Algee-Hewitt et al., 2016), it is a widespread conception that bestsellers are easier to read (Martin, 1996). In literary studies, reading ease has also been proposed as a marker of "better" style as far back as 1893 (Sherman, 1893). While Martin (1996) and Maharjan et al. (2017) found that readability formulas were weak for predicting reader appreciation, more recent work has shown that preference for the type of text difficulty measured by readability formulas may vary across different audiences: novels with higher readability are preferred by raters on large online platforms, while award-winning novels tend to have lower scores (Bizzoni et al., 2023a). Measures that are more explicitly related to information density or entropy, such as word and bigram entropy (Algee-Hewitt et al., 2016), surprisal (McGrath et al., 2018), and text compressibility (Ehret and Szmrecsanyi, 2016) have also been used to assess the complexity of literary texts.[3] Liddle (2019), for example, shows a diachronic evolution of literary texts towards a greater density of information. Surprisal has been shown to correlate with the cognitive effort of processing words (Hale, 2001; Levy, 2008; Balling and Baayen, 2012) and is as such a measure of the information density of text. The connection of information density or surprisal with a text's relative "quality" (in this case intended as communicative effectiveness) has been linked more explicitly in studies about non-literary domains. For example, Degaetano-Ortlieb and Teich (2022) found that scientific prose has gradually developed informationally denser prose, optimized for expert-to-expert communication.

[2] See https://hemingwayapp.com/help.html, https://authors.ai/marlowe/

[3] In the latter case, the aim is to approximate Kolmogorov complexity, i.e., the complexity of e.g. a string is defined as the length of the shortest possible description of it, as in Ehret and Szmrecsanyi (2016) and Liddle (2019).

Perplexity, as a closely related measure of the probability of words in context, may be applied as another measure of difficulty or as a measure of the *information density* of a text (Rubino et al., 2016). While perplexity is primarily used as an internal evaluation metric for the performance of language models, it has also been used variously as a descriptive and predictive metric to distinguish between the domain and style of texts, for example between formal and colloquial tweets (Gonzalez) or between speech production by people with dementia and without (Fritsch et al., 2019).

Like surprisal, LLMs' perplexity also shows a relationship to human word processing or perception of text difficulty, for example with gaze duration in reading (Goodkind and Bicknell, 2018), though the similarity of model perplexity to, for example, human reading time may change with larger model size (Oh and Schuler, 2021). Still, the relation between the "difficulty" level of a text and perplexity is not clear-cut, and perplexity seems to capture something different than what can be estimated with traditional readability formulas from linguistics research. Miaschi et al. (2020) show no relation between model perplexity and one readability measure, while Martinc et al. (2021) suggest that models might actually attribute less perplexity to texts aimed at adults compared to texts aimed at younger audiences. Similarly, there seems to be no clear connection of perplexity to stylistic features of texts connected to readability, suggesting that different textual features affect readability and model perplexity (Miaschi et al., 2020).[4] Some work has been done to estimate surprise or narrative coherence in fiction (McGrath et al., 2018; Underwood, 2020; Wu, 2023), still the question of quality or reader appreciation of more or less "surprising" texts remains underexplored. In this context, perplexity may constitute an additional measure easily related to different types of reader appreciation. Notably, in text generation, model perplexity is explored to retrieve more or less diverse output, given that a higher likelihood text (with less perplexity) does not necessarily mean that it is of better quality for human raters (Zhang et al., 2020).

[4]Perplexity appears to be estimated consistently across different (and also smaller) models (Goodkind and Bicknell, 2018)

3 Data

3.1 Corpus

We use a corpus spanning 9,089 novels published in the US between 1880 and 2000 (see Table 1 and Figure 1). It is a unique resource both in terms of size [5] and diversity, as it contains relatively recent novels from various genres. It was compiled based on the number of libraries holding each novel with a preference for higher holding numbers, i.e., for more circulated works. As library holdings reflect a diverse demand, the corpus is not homogeneous in terms of genre and features both prestigious and popular works ranging from Mystery to Science Fiction (Long and Roland, 2016).[6]

Table 1: Number of titles, authors, and average titles per author in the dataset.

Titles	Authors	Titles per author
9089	3166	2.88

For example, the corpus contains several National Book Award winners (including Don DeLillo, Joyce Carol Oates, and Philip Roth), as well as important works of genre-fiction (i.e., Tolkien or Philip K. Dick), influential authors of mainstream fiction (such as Agatha Christie and Stephen King), and highly canonical names (such as James Joyce and Ernst Hemingway). Books in the corpus vary in length, from 341 words (Beatrix Potter's *The Story of Miss Moppet*) to 714,744 words (Ben A. Williams' *House Divided*), though only 255 books – 2.9% of the corpus – are shorter than 35,000 words – roughly the average length of a novella like Orwell's *Animal Farm*. The total word count of the corpus is 1,060,549,793 words.

3.2 Canonical novels

The definition of "canonical works" used here adheres to a comprehensive principle, relying on the amalgamation of different expert perspectives on canonicity. We considered four main sources (see Fig. 8 for the number of works gathered from each source and the overlap between sources):

[5]Studies on literary quality often rely on corpora of $<$ 1,000 books (Ashok et al., 2013; Koolen et al., 2020).

[6]While the corpus has no reference publication, several other works have used the same dataset (Underwood et al., 2018; Cheng, 2020). See `https://textual-optics-lab.uchicago.edu/us_novel_corpus` for an overview of the corpus.

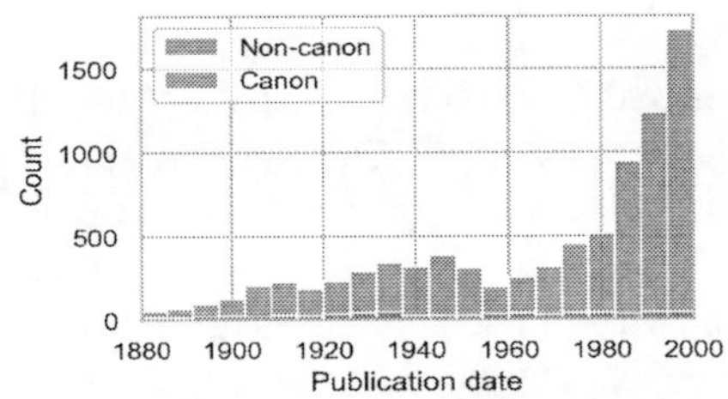

Figure 1: Distribution of canonic titles in the Chicago Corpus over time.

(i) **The Norton Anthology**: This is a leading anthology dedicated to authors considered canonical (Pope, 2019; Ragen, 1992). We consulted both the English and the American Norton Anthology

(ii) **College Syllabi**: The frequency with which college syllabi include an author's work can measure their level of canonization (Barré et al., 2023). We used OpenSyllabus, a database that has compiled 18.7 million college syllabi[7]. Using this data, we tallied all works in our collection from the top 1000 most frequent authors in *English Literature* syllabi.

(iii) **Classics Series**: Numerous major publishers, such as Vintage and Penguin[8], feature a series dedicated to "classic" (e.g. canonic) literature. Given Penguin's status as a leading publisher of English-language literature (Alter et al., 2022), we marked all works in our corpus that featured in this series.

(iv) **Prizes**: We collected long-listed titles (winners and finalists) for prestigious literary awards: The Nobel Prize in Literature, the Pulitzer Prize, the National Book Award. Manshel et al. (2019) have shown that winning an award contributes to the long-term prestige – but also popularity – of titles in academia and on GoodReads. The choices of award-committees seem to be in touch with the general public, but prize-winning books also seem to be connected to disagreement between readers at the large scale (Kovács and Sharkey, 2014).

These sources divide our dataset in two groups: 745 canonical and 8344 non-canonical works. Naturally, we consider this division artificial, as a necessary rule of thumb to make the study possible. In fact, canonicity is not a defined and boolean variable (Barré et al., 2023), but would be best represented as a continuum on several dimensions. To contrast against these proxies, we also collected books in our corpus that are in Publisher's Weekly American 20th century bestseller list.[9]

[7] https://www.opensyllabus.org

[8] https://www.penguin.com/penguin-classics-overview/

4 Perplexity

Perplexity is an information-theoretic measurement of how well a probability model predicts a sample (Goldberg, 2022). The perplexity of a well-trained language model on a test text can be interpreted as the exponential of its average level of surprisal (Hao et al., 2020), namely

$$e^{-\frac{1}{N}\sum_{i=1}^{N} ln(P(token_i|tokens_{j<i}))} \qquad (1)$$

where N is the number of tokens of the text and $P(token_i|tokens_{j<i})$ is the probability assigned to the ith token after the model has processed the first $i-1$ tokens. Thus, lower perplexities indicate that the model is less uncertain about its predictions. In information theory and linguistics, this measure

[9] Extracted from the database collected by John Unsworth at the University of Illinois: https://web.archive.org/web/20111014055658/http://www3.isrl.illinois.edu/~unsworth/courses/bestsellers/picked.books.cgi. Publishers Weekly is a trade news magazine which is published once a week (from 1872) and targeted at agents in the field: publishers, literary agents, booksellers, and librarians. Although based on sales numbers, the full set of selection criteria for the list are unknown.

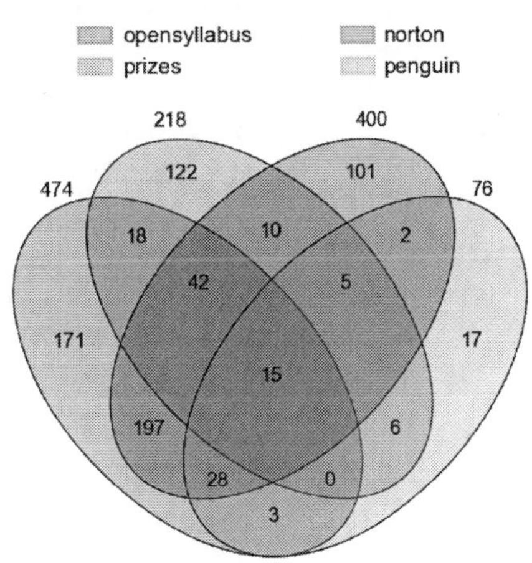

Figure 2: Number and overlap of the canonicity sources used in this study. Note that the largest overlap appears to be between the Norton Anthology and Opensyllabus, indicating the near relation between the two proxies, possibly due to the institutional affiliation of the Norton Anthology.

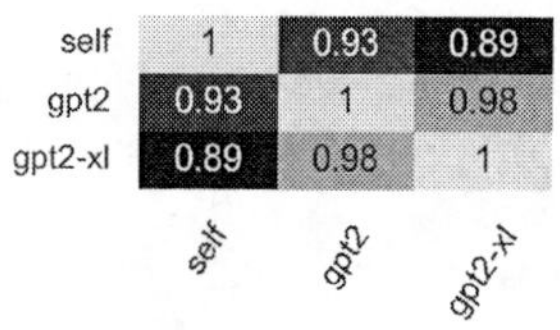

Figure 3: Spearman's correlation between the three GPT-2 based models' mean perplexity scores on each novel of our corpus

is often used to approximate how surprising or complex a text can be for humans as well. As language models are trained on word sequences, perplexity has the benefit of encapsulating lexical, grammatical and syntactic phenomena alike. Strictly in this sense, perplexity-based approaches are able to model a text more holistically than approaches that focus only on one linguistic dimension.

In this study, we calculate the perplexity of three language model on the same corpus. We based all perplexity calculations on the byte pair encoding tokenization (Sennrich et al., 2016) used in the series of gpt2 models. Due to constraints imposed by the maximum input length, we employed a stride-based methodology to gauge perplexity at the text level. This method incorporates a strided sliding window, wherein the context is shifted by fixed-length strides, affording the model an expansive context for making predictions at each iteration. In this specific framework, the window's size is 1024 tokens long, with a stride length of 512 tokens. By doing so, the second half of the previous context window served as the first half of a new context window to calculate perplexity estimates for the remaining 512 tokens (Oh and Schuler, 2023). Therefore, the surprisal for each book is comprised of perplexity values for the initial 1024 tokens, intermediate segments of 512 tokens, and the residual tokens of varying lengths. The aggregate-mean value is designated as the textual perplexity within the confines of this study.

5 Models

We use three alternative, large language models to assess the average perplexity of the novels (see Table 2 for details). For each novel, we thus have three perplexity measures.

The two standard versions of GPT2 models (Radford et al., 2019), namely the gpt2 and the gpt2-xl, are used in this paper since they are based on neural networks with billions of parameters and trained on terabytes of text, achieving very good results both in generating natural text and in estimating the perplexity of unseen texts. However, there is a substantial risk that some of the books of the corpus may have been included within the dataset that these models were trained on, especially when OpenAI has not yet published its dataset until now. Therefore, the main methodology is to train a model of the same architecture as the series of gpt2 models from scratch using a dataset outside the corpus (hereinafter referred to as the self-trained model).

If the corpus perplexity estimation observed from the self-trained model is in close correlation with results from the series of gpt2 models, then the potential bias risk can be excluded. In this context, a new text generator based on the gpt2 model is trained from the beginning on the "article" content of the CNN Dailymail Dataset[10]. The primary reason for not employing other literary works as the training set is due to the potential bias associated with the selection of these books. Moreover, the CNN Dailymail dataset is chosen for its compilation of approximately one million news stories designed for reading and comprehension tasks (Hermann et al., 2015), offering a narrative consistency more closely aligned with that of novels than other datasets, such as WikiText. Then, we use the Adam optimizer with a learning rate of 5e-5 and a cross-entropy loss criterion to train the model for 10 epochs.

Table 2: Architecture hyperparameters and training set sizes for the three models.

	self_model	**gpt2**	**gpt2-xl**
parameters	117M	117M	1542M
layers	12	12	48
heads	12	12	25
dimensions	768	768	1600
dataset size	535M	40G	40G

The Spearmann Correlation test results presented in Figure 3 show a robust correlation in perplexity values between the self-trained model and the other gpt2 models, indicating that a potential data bias can be excluded at least within this corpus. Therefore, the models forming the final hierarchy can be viewed as a sequential examination on the hypotheses and the consistency of our results across the models of varying sizes, ranging from the smallest version of the self-trained model to the largest version of the gpt2-xl model (see Table 2).

[10]https://huggingface.co/datasets/ccdv/cnn_dailymail

6 Perplexity & the Canon

These three variants of GPT2 models based on the Transformer architecture are employed to calculate perplexity values using the stride-based method across the entirety of the novels in the Chicago Corpus. A first mean of evaluation is to observe whether the mean perplexity changes with the models' size, as we would expect larger models to display lower perplexity. Consistently with our expectations, the mean perplexity values decrease when the model size increases, as delineated in Table 3 [11]. Largest models are likely to be less perplexed by unusual linguistic structures, as they have been trained on much larger datasets and have, in some sense, "seen more". It is also a matter of debate, in this respect, whether larger is always better when it comes to correlations with human intuition. It is possible that very large models are harder to surprise than human readers, and their levels of perplexity may not correspond with human readers' experiences as much as those of smaller models (Oh and Schuler, 2021). In our case, we find that the distinction between canonical and non-canonical works, defined by humans, is most strongly reproduced by the smallest of the three models.

Despite some potential fluctuations, the outcomes exhibit general consistency across the three language models. Notably, the highest and lowest perplexity values are elicited from the same two books, namely *The Graduate* by Charles Richard Webb (the least perplexing novel overall) and *Finnegans Wake* by James Joyce (the most perplexing).

Table 3: An outlook on the perplexity values estimated by the three models.

	self_model	gpt2	gpt2-xl
min	16.307	8.9058	6.5862
max	998.4872	306.1784	229.1857
mean	67.1944	28.8428	18.2334

Then, the Mann-Whitney test is used to examine the perplexity difference between canonical and non-canonical works. As shown in Table 6 , in terms of perplexity the difference between canonical and non-canonical novels is significant over all of the three models, with canonical books being more perplexing than non-canonical in all cases. This can be in turn surprising: canonical works, due to their status, might influence other works and become more typical. Yet it seems that they retain a unique originality, or a specially distinctive usage of language. Moreover, there seems to be an internal variation within the canon.

[11] Also see Figure 7 in Appendix

Table 4: Correlation between perplexity and readability with GoodReads' rating count and number of libraries' holdings for each novel - proxies for the popularity or circulation of the works.

	GR rating count	Libraries
self_model	-.23	-.31
R Dale-Chall	-.22	-.25

When inspecting works of different types of canonicity (contrasting literary prizes with other types of collections) we find that works judged canonical by experts and that are more closely affiliated to institutions (the Norton Anthology, Opensyllabus, and Penguin Classics) have a higher perplexity (Table 7). If we contrast with bestsellers, we also find that these appear to even have a lower perplexity than non-canon works (Table 7).

It is important here to note here once again that perplexity is not an absolute measure, but is the result of a model's training. Models trained on large enough datasets will capture fundamental regularities and find idiosyncratic uses of language more perplexing, but every model will consider elements closer to its training set as more normal. In this paper we assume the large training sets of the models as representative enough of contemporary English.

7 Correlations with textual features

Table 5: Correlation Matrix of Readability Metrics and PPLs (Spearmann correlation)

	self_model	gpt2	gpt2-xl
Flesch Ease	-0.530	-0.483	-0.428
Flesch Grade	0.581	0.530	0.470
Smog	0.532	0.480	0.422
ARI	0.636	0.571	0.506
Dale-Chall	0.608	0.603	0.550

Perplexity is a powerful measure of linguistic predictability, as it results from large-scale modelling of word sequences. It can also be, and usually is, the effect of a composition of several factors, so that it is not always easy to understand what elements are driving its values. The richness of a large corpus of narrative fiction only adds to this difficulty. According to all our models, the most perplexing "novel" in the corpus is James

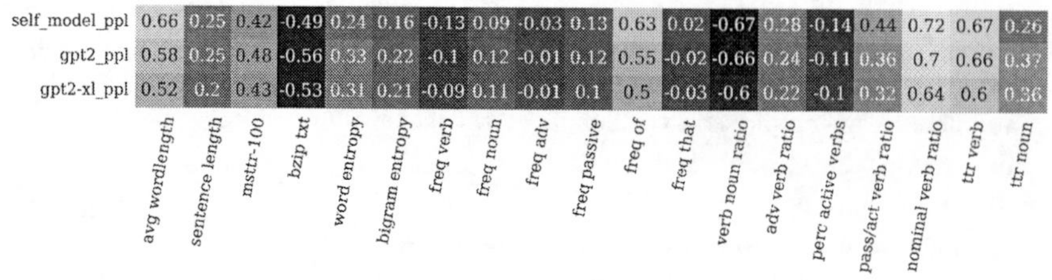

Figure 4: Correlations (Spearman) of perplexity with stylistic and syntactic features.

Joyce's *Finnegans Wake*, while the least perplexing is Webb's *The Graduate*. A look at the first few lines of these books suffices to align our intuition to the models' results.[12] But the reasons for scoring a high perplexity can be different even among those texts that are "clearly" unusual: for example, another high-perplexing novel, Harris' *Nights with Uncle Remus*, often reads as a fairy tale, but is heavily interspersed with heavy use of almost unintelligible eye dialect.[13] While the models' scores clearly pick from the same elements - recording internal Spearman correlations between 0.89 and 0.93 (Fig. 3) - it is not easy to determine which linguistic features have the highest role in determining a given level of perplexity, and, more importantly, in determining which are the perplexing elements in a text that help tell canonical from non-canonical works. In the next sections, we will check the correlation between perplexity and some textual features often considered in the discourse over literary quality and canonicity. We refer to Figure 4 for a summary of the findings.

7.1 Stylometric features

A novel's high perplexity score can be the effect of stylistic complexity. A simple conceptualization of this dimension of style is represented by readability measures, a family of algorithms developed in linguistics that gauge prose difficulty based on simple elements such as sentence and word length, and frequently used in relation to concepts of general literary quality (Bizzoni et al., 2023b; Weigel, 2016; Ashok et al., 2013).[14] The models' perplexity shows robust correlations with all readability measures: books with a higher perplexity are harder to read (Table 5), at least to an extent.

This is not an obvious correlation, as the central elements in readability algorithms, such as sentence length, are not directly factored in the language model's computation of perplexity. Yet, average sentence length alone has >.2 correlations with all our models: texts that are challenging at other levels also tend, to an extent, to feature longer sentences. Other features that affect formulae of readability, such as average word length, also show robust correlations with perplexity.It seems to indicate that canonical works present on average a prose that is more difficult to read than non-canonical works. The inverse relation of readability and perplexity with some proxies of mere popularity, as shown in Table 4, additionally indicates that there is at least one "type" of novel that aggregates different strategies of simplicity - unsurprising usage of language, shorter sentences, shorter words etc. - to achieve a higher level of diffusion. While this, too, can be considered a distinct form of quality, it appears that canonical works tend to the opposite stylistic pole.

Another typical metric often associated with more complex and challenging novels is Type-Token Ratio (Kao and Jurafsky, 2012). As TTR shows a significant relation with our perplexity measures, it is likely that more perplexing novels use a more diverse lexicon or more complex lexical structures rather than simpler and more repetitive alternatives, as also shown by the negative correlation with text compressibility, often a proxy for formulaicity or information density (Fig. 4).[15]

7.2 Syntactic features

We looked into selected syntactic and grammatical features often considered in discussions about

[12] **Finnegans Wake**: "riverrun, past Eve and Adam's, from swerve of shore to bend of bay, brings us by a commodius vicus of recirculation back to Howth Castle and Environs.". **The Graduate**: "Benjamin Braddock graduated from a small eastern college on a day in June. Then he flew home. The following evening a party was given for him by his parents."

[13] "Ez ter dat," responded Uncle Remus, "dey mought stan' on one foot an' drap off ter sleep en fergit deyse'f. Deze yer gooses".

[14] Explicating the formulas is out of the scope of this paper, but can be consulted via the package we used to extract readability scores: `https://pypi.org/project/textstat/`

[15] As it is used in (Ehret and Szmrecsanyi, 2016; Liddle, 2019).

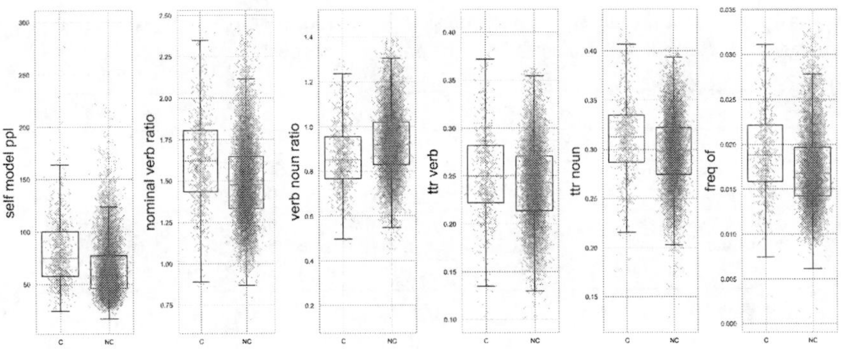

Figure 5: Features distribution for canonical (C) and non-canonical (NC) titles in our corpus. The nominal verb ratio is intended as the ratio of both adjectives and nouns over verbs.

Table 6: Mean and standard deviation for canonical (c) and non-canonical (nc) works regarding features displaying the highest correlations with perplexity. Mann-Whitney's z score and size effect r are reported. * p-value <.005. Numbers in parenthesis report the means, stds, z and r values when running the measures on a corpus where we have randomly selected 1 book per author (thus a smaller corpus of 3153 works of which 200 are canonical).

Measure	Mean_c	Std_c	Mean_nc	Std_nc	z	r
Perplexity (self)	**81.57** (80.17)	53.27 (76.70)	65.01 (64.32)	74.92 (32.26)	3.1* (2.7*) (m)	.33 (.27)
Perplexity (gpt2)	**34.21** (34.33)	15.17 (22.74)	28.00 (28.39)	9.39 (7.91)	3.1* (2.8*) (m)	.38 (.33)
Perplexity (gpt-xl)	**21.81** (22.06)	10.70 (16.97)	17.74 (17.91)	7.03 (4.87)	3.2* (2.8*) (m)	.39 (.35)
Adj+Noun/Verb Ratio	**1.62** (1.60)	0.29 (0.28)	1.50 (1.50)	0.24 (0.25)	3.0* (2.6*) (m)	.27 (.22)
Verb/Noun Ratio	0.874 (0.881)	0.159 (0.153)	**0.929** (0.924)	0.151 (0.15)	1.8* (1.7*) (m)	.23 (.17)
Adverb/Verb Ratio	**0.406** (0.399)	0.069 (0.067)	0.386 (0.378)	0.066 (0.065)	2.7* (2.5*) (m)	.17 (.18)
TTR verbs	**0.253** (0.252)	0.052 (0.053)	0.242 (0.245)	0.042 (0.043)	2.5* (2.3) (m)	.17 (.10)
TTR nouns	**0.312** (0.312)	0.046 (0.053)	0.298 (0.299)	0.037 (0.038)	2.7* (2.4*) (m)	.12 (.15)

the quality of literary (and general) writing: frequency of passive voice and adverbs (Strunk Jr and White, 2007) and relative ratios of Parts-of-Speech, especially looking for traces of so-called "nominal style" (McIntosh, 1975; Bostian, 1983).

The frequency of the passive voice has a faint positive correlation with perplexity, and the active voice a slight negative correlation, suggesting that the passive is slightly more unusual than the active voice. While the percentage of adverbs and verbs plays no role in the perplexity of the novels, the adverbs-to-verb ratio does show a positive correlation.

The verb/noun ratio of each novel displays a very robust correlation with the texts' perplexity. This effect is even more pronounced when we compute the ratio of nouns plus adjectives against verbs. It displays one of the strongest correlations with model perplexity along the three models (see Figures 4 and 6) and delineates a significant difference between the canonical and non-canonical groups (Table 6). We also checked for the relative frequency of the "function words" *of* and *that*: the first is associated with the presence of more nominal phrases, while the latter is typical of more declarative and verb-centered prose. The fact that *of* has a stronger correlation with perplexity than *that*, and is more frequent in the canonical group (Figure 5), is another hint to the larger presence of nominal phrases in more perplexing works. Interestingly, these differences can be extended to subcategories *within* the canonical category: longlisted novels exhibit less perplexity, reading difficulty and traces of nominal style than the rest of the canon group (more "classically" canonical) but more so than the non-canon group, bestsellers included (Table 7).

Nominal style is often considered "heavier" (Huckin, 1993). Several studies on linguistic and information theory also found that non-fiction domains tend to optimize their communication strategies by increasingly relying on nominal phrases – a strategy that works for "expert" audiences (Rubino et al., 2016; Degaetano-Ortlieb et al., 2019; Juzek et al., 2020; Bizzoni et al., 2020). It is possible that the canons' higher perplexity is partly due to including more cognitively demanding, "heavily nominal" texts. One example is Jack Kerouac's

Table 7: Means and standard deviations (in parentheses) for measures across proxies. Note how bestsellers are closer to non-canonical works than canonicals in terms of overall perplexity.

	Non-canon	Bestsellers	Prizes	Canon lists
Perplexity (self model)	67.85 (71.44)	64.1 (24.69)	73.08 (28.82)	**85.17** (54.17)
Nominal/verb ratio	1.51 (0.27)	1.55 (0.25)	1.56 (0.28)	**1.64** (0.29)
Verb/noun ratio	**0.92 (0.15)**	0.91 (0.15)	0.90 (0.15)	0.87 (0.16)
TTR verb	0.24 (0.04)	**0.25** (0.05)	**0.25** (0.05)	**0.25** (0.06)
TTR noun	0.30 (0.04)	0.30 (0.04)	**0.31** (0.05)	**0.31** (0.05)
Dale-Chall readability	5.10 (0.32)	5.01 (0.29)	5.15 (0.35)	**5.29** (0.46)

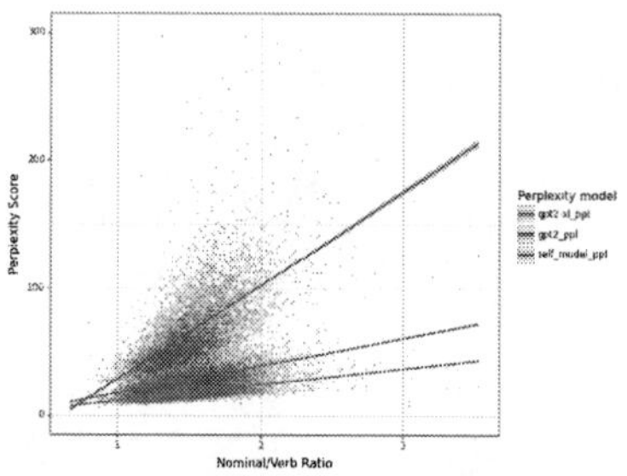

Figure 6: Correlation between perplexity scores and nominal/verb ratio of texts.

Doctor Sax which is one of the top books in our corpus in terms of perplexity and also of nominal/verb ratio. Its prose is rich with adjectives and nouns, sometimes skipping verbs altogether, as in: "not as if idiot but as if sensual or senseless and bitter with venoms of woe". Combined with its frequent neologisms this work offers a good example of text-intrinsic features of perplexity.

8 Conclusions

We have explored some features of canonical vs non-canonical works based on a corpus of 9,000 novels from the late 19^{the} and the 20th century. We first found that canonical novels seem to elicit higher perplexity scores based on three LLMs, with the difference remaining significant across different model sizes. Perplexity seems to reflect a higher complexity in style of canonical novels, compared to that of non-canonical works that enjoy a vast readership.

We have then explored some specific features that might contribute to this effect. Based on our collection, the higher perplexity of the canonical group is linked to different distributions of grammatical constructions: heavier use of nominal phrases, paired with average longer sentences, words, and a higher lexical diversity. Specifically, the presence of a more marked nominal style might be an important cause for the difference in perplexity between the two groups, although it is clear that the overall effect is a result of an ensemble of features at the syntactic, stylistic, and semantic level. The idea that "canonical" novels, on average, are more challenging for readers than non-canonical ones, while the opposite holds for widely spread but non-canonical texts (such as texts rated very often on GoodReads), mirrors existent findings (Bizzoni et al., 2023b).[16] The characteristics of this difference are of particular interest as they seem to be at least partly linked to the communication efficiency observed in expert-domain prose for other fields. A heavily nominal style has been linked with the development of refined and diverse vocabulary, a higher cognitive load for the reader, and more effective communication of information, as nouns can be highly specific and diverse, bringing a higher amount of information at the cost of higher decoding effort. It is a hypothesis worth considering that canonical works might achieve a lower communicative *immediacy* in favor of a higher communicative *efficiency*. What this means for a literary work and what it implies for the reader's experience – given the unique communicative functions of literary texts – remains an open question to explore in future studies.

Finally, it is important to consider that in this work we have intentionally ignored the dimension of time: we are interested in which features distinguish canonical, awarded, best-selling texts etc., independently from their distribution within the corpus. This means that we are treating our models as an abstract "contemporary reader" who, in front of the corpus, reacts to the canonical group differently from the bestseller group and so on. In future, we intend to observe how the features we have studied in this work correlate with time.

[16]Naturally, there are important overlaps, as these are intermingling categories. *The Hobbit* features in our list of canonical works, and so does Twain's *The Prince And The Pauper*.

References

Mark Algee-Hewitt, Sarah Allison, Marissa Gemma, Ryan Heuser, Franco Moretti, and Hannah Walser. 2016. *Canon/Archive. Large-scale Dynamics in the Literary Field*. Stanford Literary Lab.

Alexandra Alter, Elizabeth A. Harris, and David McCabe. 2022. Will the Biggest Publisher in the United States Get Even Bigger? *The New York Times*.

Jodie Archer and Matthew Lee Jockers. 2017. *The bestseller code*. Penguin books, London.

Vikas Ganjigunte Ashok, Song Feng, and Yejin Choi. 2013. Success with style: Using writing style to predict the success of novels. In *Proceedings of the 2013 conference on empirical methods in natural language processing*, pages 1753–1764.

Derek Attridge. 2004. *The Singularity of Literature*. Routledge, London; New York.

Laura Winther Balling and R. Harald Baayen. 2012. Probability and surprisal in auditory comprehension of morphologically complex words. *Cognition*, 125(1):80–106.

Jean Barré, Jean-Baptiste Camps, and Thierry Poibeau. 2023. Operationalizing Canonicity: A Quantitative Study of French 19th and 20th Century Literature. *Journal of Cultural Analytics*, 8(3).

Douglas Biber and Bethany Gray. 2011. The historical shift of scientific academic prose in english towards less explicit styles of expression. *Researching specialized languages*, 47(11).

Yuri Bizzoni, Stefania Degaetano-Ortlieb, Peter Fankhauser, and Elke Teich. 2020. Linguistic variation and change in 250 years of english scientific writing: A data-driven approach. *Frontiers in Artificial Intelligence*, 3:73.

Yuri Bizzoni, Ida Marie Lassen, Telma Peura, Mads Rosendahl Thomsen, and Kristoffer Nielbo. 2022. Predicting Literary Quality How Perspectivist Should We Be? In *Proceedings of the 1st Workshop on Perspectivist Approaches to NLP @LREC2022*, pages 20–25, Marseille, France. European Language Resources Association.

Yuri Bizzoni, Pascale Moreira, Nicole Dwenger, Ida Lassen, Mads Thomsen, and Kristoffer Nielbo. 2023a. Good Reads and Easy Novels: Readability and Literary Quality in a Corpus of US-published Fiction. In *Proceedings of the 24th Nordic Conference on Computational Linguistics (NoDaLiDa)*, pages 42–51, Tórshavn, Faroe Islands. University of Tartu Library.

Yuri Bizzoni, Pascale Moreira, Nicole Dwenger, Ida Lassen, Mads Thomsen, and Kristoffer Nielbo. 2023b. Good reads and easy novels: Readability and literary quality in a corpus of us-published fiction. In *Proceedings of the 24th Nordic Conference on Computational Linguistics (NoDaLiDa)*, pages 42–51.

Yuri Bizzoni, Pascale Moreira, Mads Rosendahl Thomsen, and Kristoffer Nielbo. 2023c. Sentimental matters - predicting literary quality by sentiment analysis and stylometric features. In *Proceedings of the 13th Workshop on Computational Approaches to Subjectivity, Sentiment, & Social Media Analysis*, pages 11–18, Toronto, Canada. Association for Computational Linguistics.

Yuri Bizzoni, Pascale Feldkamp Moreira, Mads Rosendahl Thomsen, and Kristoffer L. Nielbo. 2023d. The Fractality of Sentiment Arcs for Literary Quality Assessment: the Case of Nobel Laureates. *Journal of Data Mining & Digital Humanities*, NLP4DH:11406.

Harold Bloom. 1995. *The Western Canon: The Books and School of the Ages*, first riverhead edition edition. Riverhead Books, New York, NY.

Lloyd R. Bostian. 1983. How active, passive and nominal styles affect readability of science writing. *Journalism quarterly*, 60(4):635–670.

Pierre Bourdieu. 1993. *The field of cultural production: essays on art and literature*. Columbia University Press, New York.

Judith Brottrager, Annina Stahl, Arda Arslan, Ulrik Brandes, and Thomas Weitin. 2022. Modeling and predicting literary reception. *Journal of Computational Literary Studies*, 1(1):1–27.

Pascale Casanova. 2007. *The World Republic of Letters*. Convergences: Inventories of the Present. Harvard University Press, Cambridge, MA.

Jonathan Cheng. 2020. Fleshing out models of gender in English-language novels (1850–2000). *Journal of Cultural Analytics*, 5(1):11652.

Tess Crosbie, Tim French, and Marc Conrad. 2013. Towards a model for replicating aesthetic literary appreciation. In *Proceedings of the Fifth Workshop on Semantic Web Information Management*, SWIM '13, pages 1–4, New York, NY, USA. Association for Computing Machinery.

Stefania Degaetano-Ortlieb, Katrin Menzel, and Elke Teich. 2019. Typical linguistic patterns of english history texts from the eighteenth to the nineteenth century. *Writing History in Late Modern English: Explorations of the Coruña Corpus*, pages 58–81.

Stefania Degaetano-Ortlieb and Elke Teich. 2022. Toward an optimal code for communication: The case of scientific english. *Corpus Linguistics and Linguistic Theory*, 18(1):175–207.

Katharina Ehret and Benedikt Szmrecsanyi. 2016. An information-theoretic approach to assess linguistic complexity. In Raffaela Baechler and Guido Seiler, editors, *Complexity, Isolation, and Variation*, pages 71–94. De Gruyter.

Julian Fritsch, Sebastian Wankerl, and Elmar Noth. 2019. Automatic Diagnosis of Alzheimer's Disease Using Neural Network Language Models. In *ICASSP 2019 - 2019 IEEE International Conference on Acoustics, Speech and Signal Processing (ICASSP)*, pages 5841–5845, Brighton, United Kingdom.

Yoav Goldberg. 2022. *Neural network methods for natural language processing*. Springer Nature.

Meritxell Gonzalez. An Analysis of Twitter Corpora and the Differences between Formal and Colloquial Tweets. In *"Proceedings of the Tweet Translation Workshop 2015"*, pages 1–7, Alicante, Spain. CEUR-WS.org.

Adam Goodkind and Klinton Bicknell. 2018. Predictive power of word surprisal for reading times is a linear function of language model quality. In *Proceedings of the 8th Workshop on Cognitive Modeling and Computational Linguistics (CMCL 2018)*, pages 10–18, Salt Lake City, Utah. Association for Computational Linguistics.

John Guillory. 1995. *Cultural Capital: The Problem of Literary Canon Formation*. University of Chicago Press, Chicago, IL.

John Hale. 2001. A Probabilistic Earley Parser as a Psycholinguistic Model. In *Second Meeting of the North American Chapter of the Association for Computational Linguistics*.

Yiding Hao, Simon Mendelsohn, Rachel Sterneck, Randi Martinez, and Robert Frank. 2020. Probabilistic predictions of people perusing: Evaluating metrics of language model performance for psycholinguistic modeling. In *Proceedings of the Workshop on Cognitive Modeling and Computational Linguistics*, pages 75–86, Online. Association for Computational Linguistics.

Karl Moritz Hermann, Tomas Kocisky, Edward Grefenstette, Lasse Espeholt, Will Kay, Mustafa Suleyman, and Phil Blunsom. 2015. Teaching machines to read and comprehend. *Advances in neural information processing systems*, 28.

Thomas N Huckin. 1993. Stylistic prescriptivism vs. expert practice. *Discourse and Writing/Rédactologie*, 11(2):17–Jan.

Tom S Juzek, Marie-Pauline Krielke, and Elke Teich. 2020. Exploring diachronic syntactic shifts with dependency length: the case of scientific english. In *Proceedings of the Fourth Workshop on Universal Dependencies (UDW 2020)*, pages 109–119.

Justine Kao and Dan Jurafsky. 2012. A computational analysis of style, affect, and imagery in contemporary poetry. In *Proceedings of the NAACL-HLT 2012 workshop on computational linguistics for literature*, pages 8–17.

Corina Koolen, Karina van Dalen-Oskam, Andreas van Cranenburgh, and Erica Nagelhout. 2020. Literary quality in the eye of the Dutch reader: The national reader survey. *Poetics*, 79:1–13.

Cornelia Wilhelmina Koolen. 2018. *Reading beyond the female: the relationship between perception of author gender and literary quality*. Number DS-2018-03 in ILLC dissertation series. Institute for Logic, Language and Computation, Universiteit van Amsterdam, Amsterdam.

Balázs Kovács and Amanda J Sharkey. 2014. The paradox of publicity. *Administrative Science Quarterly*, 1:1–33.

Ida Marie S Lassen, Pascale Feldkamp Moreira, Yuri Bizzoni, Mads Rosendahl Thomsen, and Kristoffer L. Nielbo. 2023. Persistence of Gender Asymmetries in Book Reviews Within and Across Genres. In *CEUR Workshop Proceedings*, pages 14–28, Paris, France.

Ida Marie Schytt Lassen, Yuri Bizzoni, Telma Peura, Mads Rosendahl Thomsen, and Kristoffer Laigaard Nielbo. 2022. Reviewer Preferences and Gender Disparities in Aesthetic Judgments. In *CEUR Workshop Proceedings*, pages 280–290, Antwerp, Belgium.

Roger Levy. 2008. Expectation-based syntactic comprehension. *Cognition*, 106(3):1126–1177.

Dallas Liddle. 2019. Could Fiction Have an Information History? Statistical Probability and the Rise of the Novel. *Journal of Cultural Analytics*, page 22.

Hoyt Long and Teddy Roland. 2016. Us novel corpus. Technical report, Textual Optic Labs, University of Chicago.

Suraj Maharjan, John Arevalo, Manuel Montes, Fabio A. González, and Thamar Solorio. 2017. A multi-task approach to predict likability of books. In *Proceedings of the 15th Conference of the European Chapter of the Association for Computational Linguistics: Volume 1, Long Papers*, pages 1217–1227, Valencia, Spain. Association for Computational Linguistics.

Alexander Manshel, Laura B McGrath, and J.D. Porter. 2019. Who Cares about Literary Prizes?

Claude Martin. 1996. Production, content, and uses of bestselling books in quebec. *Canadian Journal of Communication*, 21(4).

Matej Martinc, Senja Pollak, and Marko Robnik-Šikonja. 2021. Supervised and Unsupervised Neural Approaches to Text Readability. *Computational Linguistics*, 47(1):141–179. Place: Cambridge, MA Publisher: MIT Press.

Laura McGrath, Devin Higgins, and Arend Hintze. 2018. Measuring Modernist Novelty. *Journal of Cultural Analytics*, 3(1).

Carey McIntosh. 1975. Quantities of qualities: Nominal style and the novel. *Studies in Eighteenth-Century Culture*, 4(1):139–153.

Alessio Miaschi, Chiara Alzetta, Dominique Brunato, Felice Dell'Orletta, and Giulia Venturi. 2020. Is Neural Language Model Perplexity Related to Readability? In *Proceedings of the Seventh Italian Conference on Computational Linguistics CLiC-it 2020*, pages 303–309. Accademia University Press.

Jan Mukařovský. 1964. Standard language and poetic language. In Paul L. Garvin, editor, *A Prague School Reader on Esthetics Literary Structure, and Style*, pages 17–30. 1932. Georgetown University Press.

Byung-Doh Oh and William Schuler. 2021. Contributions of propositional content and syntactic category information in sentence processing. In *Proceedings of the Workshop on Cognitive Modeling and Computational Linguistics*, pages 241–250, Online. Association for Computational Linguistics.

Byung-Doh Oh and William Schuler. 2023. Why does surprisal from larger transformer-based language models provide a poorer fit to human reading times? *Transactions of the Association for Computational Linguistics*, 11:336–350.

Willie van Peer, editor. 2008. *The quality of literature: linguistic studies in literary evaluation*. Number v. 4 in Linguistic approaches to literature. John Benjamins Publishing.

Colin Pope. 2019. We need to talk bout the canon: Demographics in 'The Norton Anthology'.

J.D. Porter. 2018. Popularity/prestige: A new canon. *Stanford Literary Lab*.

Alec Radford, Jeffrey Wu, Rewon Child, David Luan, Dario Amodei, Ilya Sutskever, et al. 2019. Language models are unsupervised multitask learners. *OpenAI blog*, 1(8):9.

Brian Abel Ragen. 1992. An uncanonical classic: The politics of the "Norton Anthology". *Christianity and Literature*, 41(4):471–479.

Raphael Rubino, Stefania Degaetano-Ortlieb, Elke Teich, and Josef van Genabith. 2016. Modeling diachronic change in scientific writing with information density. In *Proceedings of COLING 2016, the 26th International Conference on Computational Linguistics: Technical Papers*, pages 750–761, Osaka, Japan. The COLING 2016 Organizing Committee.

Rico Sennrich, Barry Haddow, and Alexandra Birch. 2016. Neural machine translation of rare words with subword units. In *Proceedings of the 54th Annual Meeting of the Association for Computational Linguistics (Volume 1: Long Papers)*, pages 1715–1725, Berlin, Germany. Association for Computational Linguistics.

Claude E Shannon. 1949. Communication in the presence of noise. *Proceedings of the IRE*, 37(1):10–21.

Lucius A. Sherman. 1893. *Analytics of Literature: A Manual for the Objective Study of English Prose and Poetry*. Athenaeum Press. Ginn.

Viktor Shklovsky. 1917. Art as technique. In J Rivkin and M Ryan, editors, *Literary Theory: An Anthology*, pages 15–21. Blackwell Publishing Ltd.

William Strunk Jr and Elwyn Brooks White. 2007. *The Elements of Style Illustrated*. Penguin.

Ted Underwood. 2020. How predictable is fiction?

Ted Underwood, David Bamman, and Sabrina Lee. 2018. The transformation of gender in english-language fiction. *Journal of Cultural Analytics*, 3(2):11035.

Andreas van Cranenburgh and Rens Bod. 2017. A data-oriented model of literary language. In *Proceedings of the 15th Conference of the European Chapter of the Association for Computational Linguistics: Volume 1, Long Papers*, pages 1228–1238, Valencia, Spain. Association for Computational Linguistics.

Robert von Hallberg. 1983. Editor's Introduction. *Critical Inquiry*, 10(1):iii–vi. Publisher: The University of Chicago Press.

Xindi Wang, Burcu Yucesoy, Onur Varol, Tina Eliassi-Rad, and Albert-László Barabási. 2019. Success in books: Predicting book sales before publication. *EPJ Data Science*, 8(1):31.

Sigrid Weigel. 2016. Literature, literary criticism and the historical index of the readability of literary texts. *Social Sciences in China*, 37(3):175–185.

Yaru Wu. 2023. Predicting the unpredictable–using language models to assess literary quality. Master's thesis, Uppsala University.

Hugh Zhang, Daniel Duckworth, Daphne Ippolito, and Arvind Neelakantan. 2020. Trading off diversity and quality in natural language generation.

A Appendix

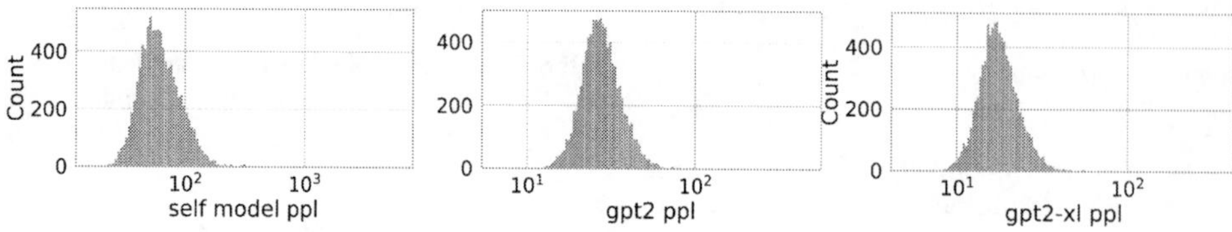

Figure 7: Histogram of the distribution of perplexity per model in our corpus. Note that perplexity has a log normal distribution.

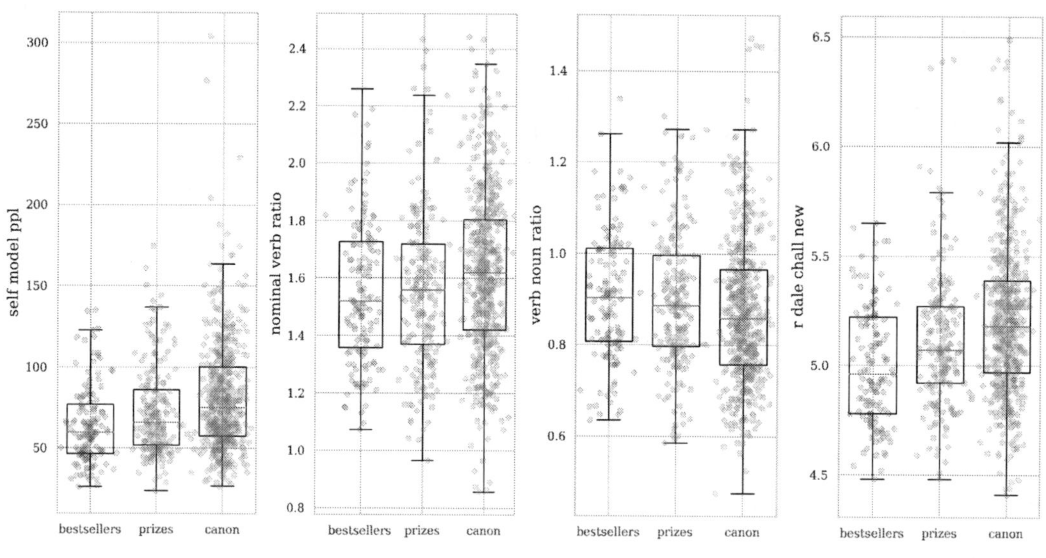

Figure 8: Nominal style features for each canon-type: Bestselling books, Prizewinning books, and books contained in one of the Canon lists. Note that outliers (points beyond the 99.5th percentile of our data) have been removed for this visualization.

People and Places of the Past - Named Entity Recognition in Swedish Labour Movement Documents from Historical Sources

Crina Tudor
Stockholm University, Sweden
first.last@ling.su.se

Eva Pettersson
Uppsala University, Sweden
first.last@lingfil.uu.se

Abstract

Named Entity Recognition (NER) is an important step in many Natural Language Processing tasks. The existing state-of-the-art NER systems are however typically developed based on contemporary data, and not very well suited for analyzing historical text. In this paper, we present a comparative analysis of the performance of several language models when applied to Named Entity Recognition for historical Swedish text. The source texts we work with are documents from Swedish labour unions from the 19th and 20th century. We experiment with three off-the-shelf models for contemporary Swedish text, and one language model built on historical Swedish text that we fine-tune with labelled data for adaptation to the NER task. Lastly, we propose a hybrid approach by combining the results of two models in order to maximize usability. We show that, even though historical Swedish is a low-resource language with data sparsity issues affecting overall performance, historical language models still show very promising results. Further contributions of our paper are the release of our newly trained model for NER of historical Swedish text, along with a manually annotated corpus of over 650 named entities.

1 Introduction

The Swedish labour movement is strong by tradition and has played a crucial role in the development of the Swedish welfare society and in shaping the structure of the labour market. The Swedish trade union federations play an important role internationally, and their archives offer a unique possibility to study the development of the trade unions and their key topics over time, and thereby also the social development nationally and internationally.

In the project *Labour's Memory. Digitization of annual and financial reports of blue-collar worker unions 1880-2020* , we aim to collect and digitize annual and financial reports from local, regional, national and international trade union organisations from 1880 onwards. The collection is to be stored in a database, and will be made searchable for people with an interest in diachronic labour movement documents through a user portal. This is achieved in collaboration between labour history experts, archivists, computational linguists and image analysis specialists.

In this paper, we aim to investigate to which extent current state-of-the-art models for Swedish can be used to extract named entities from historical sources, a key topic for enhanced searchability in the trade union documents. Secondly, we focus on maximizing usability for the intended end product by combining the strengths of different models. Last but not least, we evaluate the performance of these models in terms of accuracy, as well as F1 score. On a more practical level, we also release a new model that is fine-tuned for NER and trained on historical Swedish text, as well as a manually annotated gold-corpus of named entities extracted from Swedish labour union documents dated between 1892 and 1974.

The choices that we made in order to optimize the results and usability of our system were made in consultations with a group of experts from the Labour's Memory project, whose competence overlaps with that of the intended user.

2 Background

Named Entity Recognition (NER) is the process of automatically identifying and classifying name-like entities in text, such as names of persons, organizations and locations (Nadeau and Sekine, 2007). NER is an important subtask in many Natural Language Processing (NLP) applications, e.g., in information extraction/retrieval (see for example Brandsen et al. (2022)) and for anonymisation/pseudonymisation of sensitive personal data in a text (e.g. Bridal (2021) or Papadopoulou et al. (2022)).

For Swedish, researchers have recently worked

Proceedings of LaTeCH-CLfL 2024, pages 185–195
March 22, 2024 ©2024 Association for Computational Linguistics

with developing a gold standard for Swedish named entity recognition (Ahrenberg et al., 2020), trying to merge and accommodate previous NER annotation schemes used for Swedish. There are also initiatives to adapt this standard to the task of annotating named entities in historical Swedish text, where the needs and features to consider differ slightly (Borin et al., 2007).

Outside the topic of NER itself, it is important to acknowledge that Swedish is still a low resource language, which does not have the same large-scale NLP infrastructure as other high-resource languages such as English, Spanish or Chinese. This is evident in terms of data sets, language models and tools, and even more so in the case of historical Swedish text. While there are efforts currently being made to build large language models for Swedish by organizations such as AI Sweden,[1] or historical resources from the side of SWE-CLARIN (e.g. Pettersson and Borin (2022)), it is still a tough undertaking to achieve high benchmark scores for NLP tasks on Swedish.

3 Method

The aim of our work is to perform Named Entity Recognition (NER) for trade union documents from the late 1800s and onwards, with the goal of enhancing searchability in the documents by automatically extracting metadata on persons, locations, organisations, events etc. An important subtask is therefore to adapt our tools to handling historical text, which is further elaborated on in Section 3.1. We move on by describing the different language models we use for the NER task in Section 3.2. In Section 3.3, we introduce the evaluation method that we use, and the gold standard created for this purpose.

3.1 Handling historical text

With the aim of improving the performance of our chosen language models on historical text, we apply several pre-processing steps in order to modernize the original text and bring it closer to the kind of text the readily-available models were originally trained on, as illustrated in Figure 1 and further described below.

The first step in our pipeline concerns abbreviations. The abbreviations used in historical times do not always follow the same standards as present-day abbreviations, meaning that NLP tools trained on contemporary sources may be confused by these. Therefore, we use a dictionary of abbreviations taken from Swedish family history sources[2] to automatically expand as many abbreviations as possible. Since our data contains a large amount of names in the form of *initial* + *surname* (e.g. *F. Linden*), we remove one-letter abbreviations from the list of abbreviations, in order to avoid confusion. For example, the list contains abbreviations for Swedish counties using one upper-case letter, such as 'F' for *Jönköping*, which would coincide with the 'F' in *F. Linden*, so expanding these would be counterproductive.

In the second step, we use the dictionary *Ordbok Öfver Svenska Språket* by Dalin to map historical Swedish spellings to their contemporary counterpart. This dictionary is available in digital format, with over 62,000 entries of words with their historical spelling mapped to its modern version (Borin et al., 2011).

Lastly, we perform spelling normalization of the words not covered by the Dalin dictionary. Spelling normalization is the process of automatically transforming historical spelling to a more modern, standard spelling. This can be done in several ways. In this paper, we choose to use a rule-based approach, with rules based on the Swedish spelling reform in 1906 and previously implemented in Pettersson (2016). The motivation for using this approach, is that since the documents are not several hundreds of years old, the spelling differences are rather modest and assumingly pretty well covered by a rule-based approach. Furthermore, the rules are already defined and described, and thereby easy to include in our pipeline.

Throughout the rest of the paper, when we mention normalization, we refer to the inclusion of all the pre-processing steps described above with the purpose of normalizing the original text.

3.2 NER modelling

After the historical texts have been pre-processed, the actual NER process takes place, through the use of language models. We try three off-the-shelf models for contemporary Swedish, and one model trained on historical Swedish text, as further described below.

As our point of departure, we choose an off-the-shelf model for contemporary Swedish developed

[1] https://www.ai.se/en

[2] https://www.familysearch.org/en/wiki/Sweden_Abbreviations_in_Family_History_Sources

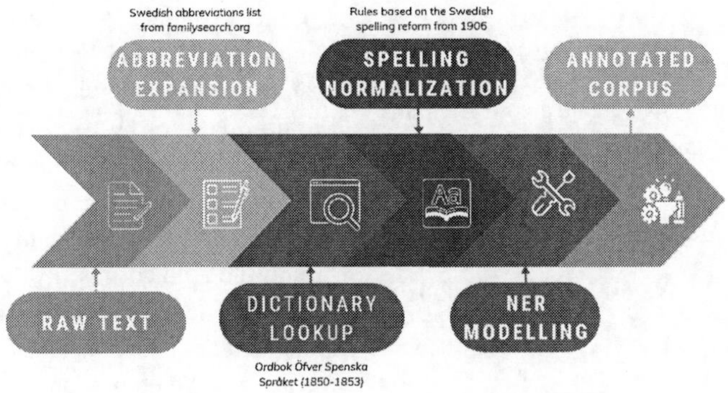

Figure 1: Handling historical texts among the labour movement documents.

by spaCy.[3] SpaCy is an open-source NLP software library which provides language models for over 65 languages, for a wide array of practical applications. In our case, we had three different pipelines to choose between which all can perform NER for Swedish. We ended up going for *sv_core_news_lg*, as that one had slightly better reported F1 score for the task at hand in comparison to the other two. This model is trained on data from news and media sources, as well as the Stockholm-Umeå corpus, v3.0 (SUC3), a balanced corpus of texts from different genres (Språkbanken, 2023).

The second model we try is also built on the spaCy infrastructure, but produced by the Swedish National Library.[4] The training data for this model largely overlaps with that of the previously mentioned model, but the reported F1 score is 4 percentage points higher.

The third model was selected after further investigating the work done by the NLP lab (i.e. KB lab) at the Swedish National Library. It is an updated version of the aforementioned model that makes use of Hugging Face[5] and their transformer architecture. For this model, they are experimenting with Hyper Parameter Optimization (HPO) leading to additional increases in F1 score for NER, reaching up to 91%.

Due to the fact that language models for historical text are in short supply, even more so when it comes to languages such as Swedish, there is no readily available model that can perform NER for historical Swedish text, to the best of our knowledge. In order to overcome this, we try a recently developed BERT model for historical Swedish text and fine-tune it using the same SUCX 3.0 corpus as the model developed by KBLab, so that we can run the same NER experiments and compare accordingly. The original model is released by the National Archives of Sweden and is using data from the 15th up to the 19th century, as well as the Hugging Face ecosystem. Our fine-tuned NER model is freely available to the public on Hugging Face.[6] The self-reported training statistics for our model are available in Appendix A.

For the sake of readability, we will refer to these models by an acronym for the rest of the paper, as follows:

DEF the default spaCy model for Swedish

BIB the spaCy model built by the Swedish National Library (i.e. Kungliga Biblioteket in Swedish)

KB the Hugging Face model developed by the KBLab group at the Swedish National Library

RA the model developed by the Swedish National Archives (i.e. Riksarkivet in Swedish) and fine-tuned for NER by us

We partially summarize the attributes of all the models that we experiment with in Table 1.

Model	Platform	Time	NER corpus
DEF	spaCy	Contemporary	SUC3.0
BIB	spaCy	Contemporary	SUC3.0
KB	Hugging Face	Contemporary	SUCX 3.0
RA	Hugging Face	15th-19th century	SUCX 3.0

Table 1: Summary of the models we use for NER.

[3] https://spacy.io/

[4] https://github.com/Kungbib/swedish-spacy

[5] https://huggingface.co/

[6] https://huggingface.co/crina-t/histbert-finetuned-ner

3.3 Evaluation

To be able to compare the performance of language models on equal grounds, we create a gold standard dataset that is manually labelled by a human annotator, and validated by a second annotator in order to settle eventual uncertainties. For the annotation, we use the same standard as presented by Borin et al. (2007). We use a total of 8 labels, as follows:

PRS "person" names of people
LOC "location" names of locations and other types of geographical entities
TME "time" temporal expressions
EVN "event" well-known events and celebrations
ORG "organisation" names of corporations and other kinds of organisations
WRK "work of art" names of movies, sculptures, periodicals etc.
MSR "measure" numerical expressions, such as monetary expressions or distances
OBJ "artifact" names of food/wine products, vehicles etc.

For the gold corpus, we select a total of 50 pages of sample text. In order to account for the shift in spelling conventions introduced through the 1906 Swedish spelling reform (Jansson, 2023), we select 25 pages which are dated before 1906, and the remaining 25 pages from years dated post-reform. To the best of our ability, we attempt to make sure that these pages are equally spaced out in terms of time elapsed between the dating of each one, as well as that they contain a reasonable body of text (i.e. at least half a page), and not just a few lines.

It can be noted that quite general phrases, not referring to a well-defined point in time, such as *under året* 'during the year' or *de senaste åren* 'in recent years' are labelled as time expressions ('TME') by most models. However, we choose to omit them from our analysis since our group of experts deem them irrelevant. We therefore only keep those that contain numerical expressions and/or names of months or their respective acronyms (e.g. *December* or *dec*). We take a similar approach when it comes to other kinds of named entities as well in the cases where they are too vague and do not point to a specific, individual entity (e.g. *förbund* 'trade union' is too vague, but *Typografförbundet* 'Typographers' Union' would be included in the manual annotation).

Other than the aforementioned 50 pages, we annotate an additional 10 pages from the same time span as the original gold standard (i.e. 1892–1974). We do this in order to be able to evaluate our final hybrid approach on unseen data so that we can more accurately assess its performance, following the same principles for data selection and annotation as the gold corpus.

In total, our gold corpus contains 570 manually annotated entities, plus an additional 85 entities in the test set, which we summarize by label in Table 2. Both of these are freely available to the public on Hugging Face.[7] We mention here that a total of 35 entities representing names of people were replaced with a placeholder in the released version of the corpus at the request of the archive in order to comply with their privacy policy. The documents containing placeholders are clearly pointed out in the description of the dataset.

	Gold set	Test set
EVN	19	6
LOC	86	19
MSR	97	7
ORG	71	13
PRS	162	17
TME	134	22
WRK	1	1

Table 2: Label count for manually annotated entities.

When comparing the gold standard with the automatically extracted entities, we identified some consistent differences between the different kinds of matches we encountered. For this reason, we create 8 distinct categories to differentiate between them in the evaluation phase. While this is a more fine-grained evaluation when compared to what is more widely used in the field (e.g. Chinchor and Sundheim (1993), Tjong Kim Sang and De Meulder (2003) or Segura-Bedmar et al. (2013)), we believe that our evaluation schema can greatly help in easily identifying the source of prediction errors generated by the model. We define and exemplify these categories below:

- **EXM** – exact match
  Both the entity and the label overlap exactly between the model and the annotator.
- **PAM** – partial match

[7] https://huggingface.co/datasets/crina-t/UnioNER

A substring of the gold standard entity is identified by the system, with the same label - e.g. *J.E Blomkvist* (PRS) in the gold standard, while the system outputs *Blomkvist* (PRS).

- **ENM** – entity match
  The exact same string is annotated by both the annotator and the system, with different labels (e.g. manually annotated *Harg* (LOC) is output as *Harg* (PRS) by the system).
- **VAM** – vague match
  The system predicts part of the gold standard entity, but with a different label - e.g. the annotator would label *E Lund* (PRS), while the system outputs *Lund* (LOC).
- **COM** – compound match
  The system merges several entities that the annotator identified as being separate units. E.g. *Hilmer Johansson* (PRS) and *Ernst Hörngren* (PRS) in the gold standard are predicted as *Hilmer Johansson Ernst Hörngren* (PRS).
- **SPM** – split match
  The system splits an entity from the gold standard into separate entities (e.g. gold standard *Uppsala Typografiska Förening* (ORG) vs. the automatically annotated *Uppsala* (LOC) and *Typografiska Förening* (ORG), referring to the Uppsala branch of the Typographers' Union).
- **FP** – false positive
  The system labels a unit that is not in fact a named entity.
- **FN** – false negative
  The system fails to identify an entity that the annotator has identified.

4 Results

In order to identify which approach gives us the best results, we calculate the accuracy of each model, and in doing so we also look at the count for each type of match per individual model. By accuracy we mean the percentage of entities from the gold standard which have a counterpart in the output predicted by the model, regardless of the type of match. The matches we look at are detailed in Section 3.3, and we do not include the counts for FP and FN in calculating accuracy. We also calculate the (accuracy) count for all the different kinds of matches, as well as NER labels, which we present in Figures 2 through 10. We calculate both these metrics first on the original text, then on the normalized version of the text in the gold standard. Our goal is to reach as many exact matches as possible (at best) and to minimize the number of cases where the model returns no match for a given entity in the gold standard (FN).

As a secondary step, we provide calculations for F1 score as applied to our text, since F1 score is a widely used metric for NER, and which also accounts for the FP and FN tags in our case. We present our results for F1 score in Section 4.4

4.1 Baseline

After applying the default spaCy model (DEF) to historical text, we obtain an accuracy of only 57.54%, due to the fact that the number of entities that are left unannotated (i.e. FN) by the DEF model exceeds the number of exact matches. In this case, normalization is detrimental to the model's performance, bringing accuracy down to 51.57%. Given the fact that more than half of our entities are not recognized by the system, we opt out of using this model further.

Moving onto the next spaCy model developed by the Swedish National Library, we immediately notice an improvement in performance. The BIB model predicts significantly more exact and partial matches than its predecessor, while the occurrence of false negatives is also decreased by almost 30% when compared to the DEF model, leading to an overall accuracy of 69.64%.

Normalization does help in this case, but it is barely enough to get the model over the 70% mark. We suspect that this jump in performance between the DEF and the BIB model is due to the fact that the DEF model was trained mainly on news and media text, while the BIB model was trained on a more balanced corpus of text from different sources. While this is clearly an improvement, it is not satisfactory enough to motivate using this model for our purposes.

The Swedish National Library KB model (Kurtz and Öhman, 2022) is an updated version of the previous BIB model. In comparison with its predecessor, the KB model, while not much better at extracting exact matches, does help decrease the number of FNs, as demonstrated in Figure 2. This happens as a result of the increase we see when it comes to partial matches, and at a smaller level in entity matches, vague matches, compound matches and split matches. The overall accuracy for the model lands at 77.34%, with normalization ebbing this number by only 0.29%.

Lastly, we evaluate the performance of our fine-

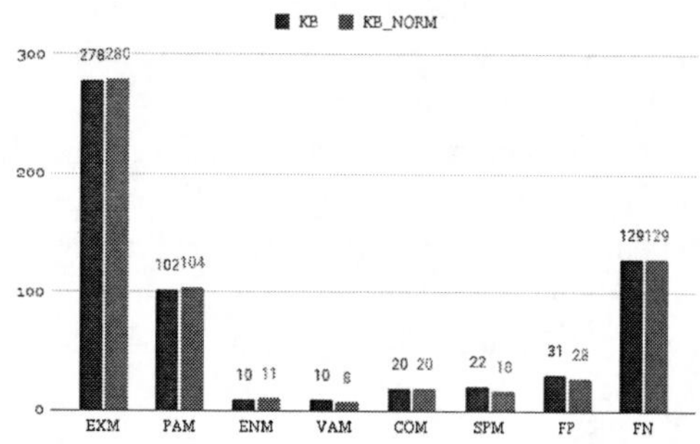

Figure 2: Accuracy count for the Hugging Face model from the Swedish National Library. KB = original text, KB_NORM = normalized text.

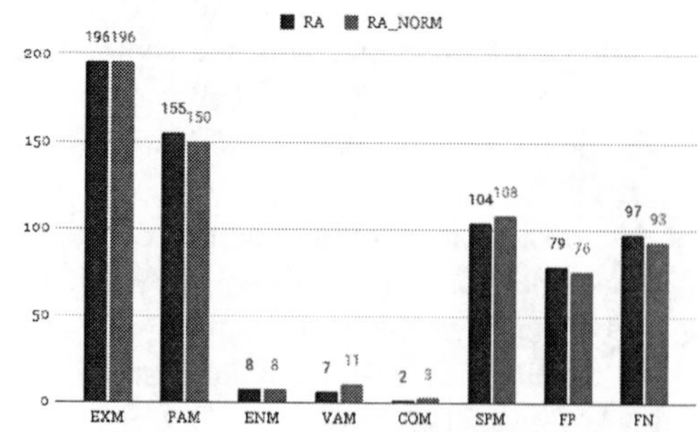

Figure 3: Accuracy count for the model from the Swedish National Archives. RA = original text, RA_NORM = normalized text.

tuned RA model, which is based on a model created by the National Archives of Sweden and trained exclusively on historical data, but fine-tuned for NER on the same SUCX3.0 corpus as the previously evaluated KB model. In this case, we do expect an increase in performance due to the fact that the model is trained on data from the same time period as our gold standard corpus, as opposed to the aforementioned models which are all trained on contemporary text.

When conducting the analysis of this model, we were surprised to see that the number of exact matches dropped significantly. Even more surprising is the fact that despite this, the model shows the least amount of false negatives among all the models we evaluated, which means that it manages to capture (to some extent) about 80% of the entities from the gold corpus. After normalization, the overall accuracy of the model reaches up to 83.41%, which is the highest we were able to reach in our experiments. However, it is worth noting that this high accuracy does not account for the doubled amount of false positives compared to previous models, or the staggering increase in split matches. We investigate this further in Section 4.2.

We summarize the accuracy of each model in Table 3.

Model	Original	Normalized
DEF	57.54%	51.57%
BIB	69.64%	70.35%
KB	77.34%	77.05%
RA	82.60%	83.41%

Table 3: Overall accuracy for each NER model.

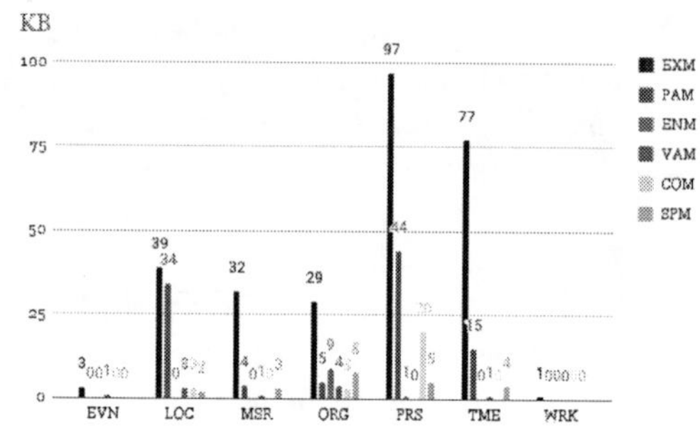

Figure 4: Accuracy count per label for the Hugging Face model from the Swedish National Library, applied to the original text.

4.2 A closer look

After the evaluation described in Section 4.1, it is clear that our two front runners are the KB and the RA models. Were it not for the notable increases in split matches and false positives, the RA model would take precedence, but as it stands, it is worth investigating more in-depth what could be causing these fluctuations. We therefore take a closer look at the way it performs for each individual label, while also extracting the same statistics for the KB model as a point of comparison.

Figure 4 shows how the KB model consistently extracts more exact matches for all different label types, with partial matches being a close second. Same pattern is visible after normalization as well, which can be observed in Figure 5, with slight improvements in exact matches for the person (PRS) and organisation (ORG) labels.

In the case of the RA model, there is a clear decrease in the number of exact matches across labels, and significantly more split matches, as shown in Figure 6. Among all the labels, time expression

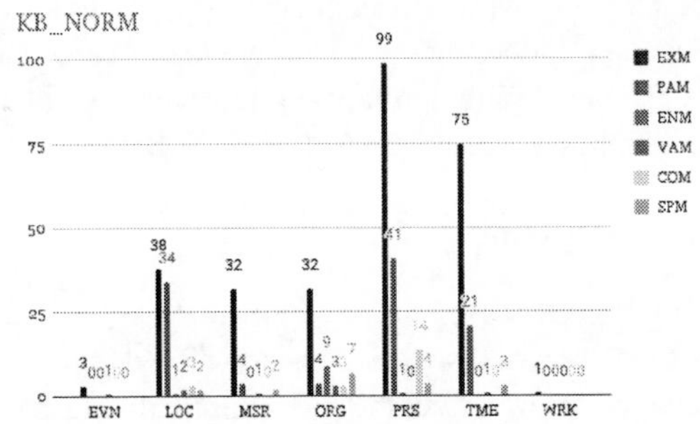

Figure 5: Accuracy count per label for the Hugging Face model from the Swedish National Library, applied to the normalized version of the text.

(TME) is the one that is most affected by the high number of split matches, which we suspect is due to a tokenization issue. There is a high chance that, since the original model is trained on a smaller corpus, there were not enough numerical values for the model to know how to handle years, dates etc. From Figure 7, we can see that the trend remains the same even after normalization, which reinforces the theory that the errors are stemming from the tokenization process.

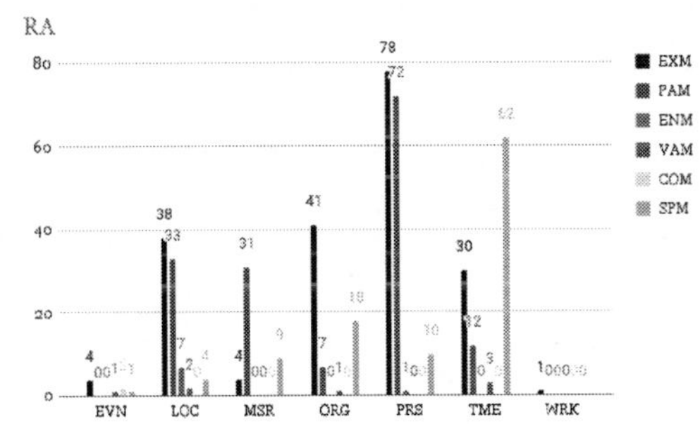

Figure 6: Accuracy per label for the model from the Swedish National Archives, applied to the original text.

4.3 A hybrid approach

After looking in-depth at the strengths and weaknesses of the KB and RA models, we want to investigate to which extent combining their outputs could benefit the end results. More specifically, we aim to avoid overgenerating split matches in the RA model and to try to increase the accuracy of the KB model. For this reason, we prioritize high counts of exact and partial matches, and take specific labels from the RA model (PRS, ORG), merging them with the rest of the labels from the KB model.

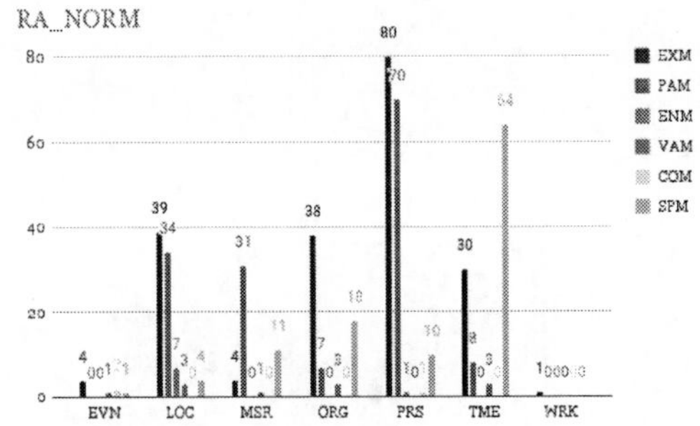

Figure 7: Accuracy count per label for the model from the Swedish National Archives, applied to the normalized version of the text.

By doing this hybrid approach (HYB), we reduce the number of false negatives that were initially present in the KB model, and we also manage to drop the number of split matches that were problematic for the RA model, as shown in Figure 8.

From Figures 9 and 10, we can clearly see that this approach is beneficial in reducing the number of split matches for those categories that are prone to having numerical expressions, such as MSR and TME, and which the RA model could not handle very well.

For accuracy, we obtain an increase from the KB model, reaching 79.82% on the original text, which drops slightly after normalization - to 79.47%.

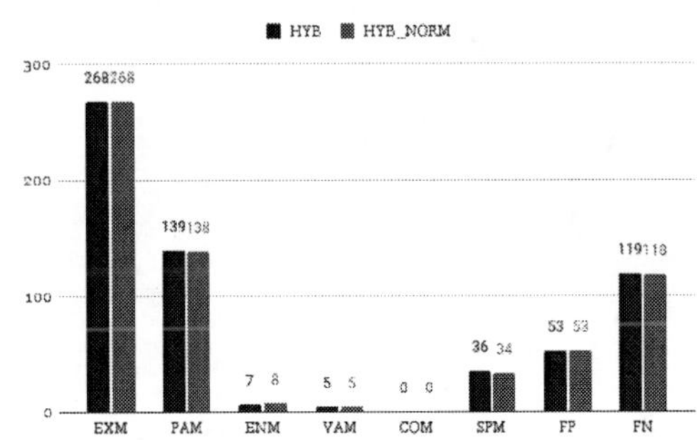

Figure 8: Accuracy count for the hybrid approach. HYB = original text, HYB_NORM = normalized version text.

4.4 F1

As a last evaluation step, we calculate F1 score for the KB, RA and HYB models using seqeval (Nakayama, 2018), which is presented in Table 4. The reason why we do this is two-fold - on the one hand, we want to assess performance on new, unseen data, while on the other hand we want to see

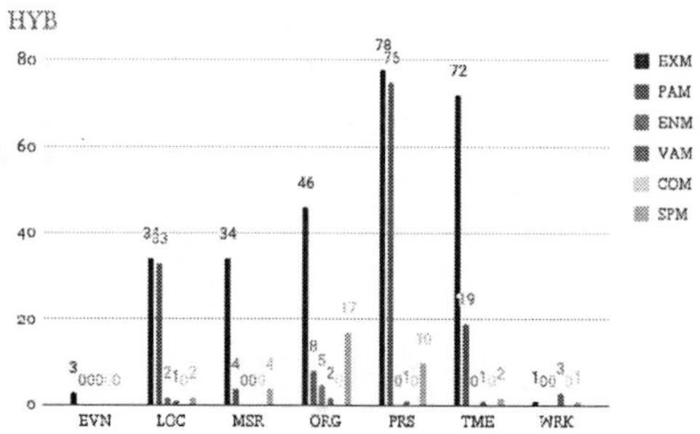

Figure 9: Accuracy count per label for the hybrid approach, applied to the original text.

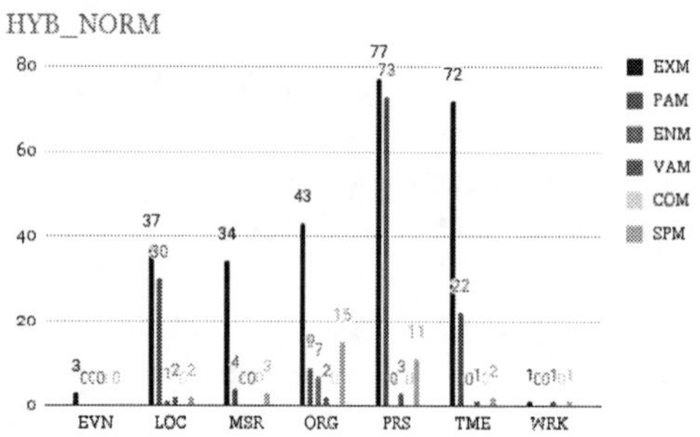

Figure 10: Accuracy count per label for hybrid approach, applied to the normalized version of the text.

how the score is affected by a metric that accounts for false negatives and false positives.

Model	Gold	Test
KB	75.68%	66.23%
KB_NORM	76.79%	71.14%
RA	71.23%	67.36%
RA_NORM	71.68%	66.66%
HYB	76.25%	68.23%
HYB_NORM	76.66%	71.85%

Table 4: F1 score for the KB, RA and HYB models, before and after normalization, from the gold corpus as well as the test set.

Not surprisingly, the RA model performs the worst in this case, due to the high volume of false positives that it predicts. Even though it has a lower false negative count, this is not enough to counterbalance the effect of PAM where the predicted entities did not match the gold standard entirely, or the split entities where the gold entity span was split into several different ones.

It is however interesting to see that the HYB model overtakes the KB model on almost all accounts, and while normalization did not help for accuracy, it does increase F1 score in this case. The HYB model with normalization manages to obtain the highest score on the test set at 71.85%.

5 Discussion

Our study focuses on the application of NER to historical Swedish text, specifically documents sourced from Swedish labor unions dating back to the 19th and 20th centuries. The primary challenge lies in adapting contemporary state-of-the-art NER systems to effectively process and extract entities from historical text, which often differs significantly in linguistic norms, vocabulary, spelling, and syntactic structures from contemporary Swedish.

Our research delves into a comparative analysis of multiple language models applied to NER for historical Swedish text. Three off-the-shelf models designed for contemporary Swedish text were experimented with, alongside a custom-built language model trained on historical Swedish text. This unique approach allowed us to explore the adaptability of existing models and assess the feasibility of fine-tuning historical language models for NER tasks. Through our experiments, we show that current off-the-shelf models have the capability to extract named entities from historical text, but at the same time they can benefit from training on historical data, as shown by the high accuracy of our RA model.

Moreover, we believe that the inconsistent effect of the normalization rules could be partly due to the rather small amount of normalization rules, as well as the nature of a rule-based approach to spelling normalization, where it is hard to write efficient rules without risking overgeneration. Another, more data-driven approach, might have given more consistent results.

It is also important to keep in mind that our evaluation metrics were customized according to the needs of our future users. Since our target groups are looking for as many named entities as possible, we attempt to adapt our approach in order to maximize the usability for the end product - which is the archival database of the Labour's Memory project, while at the same time maintaining a good level of quality for the automatically extracted named entities.

For future work, we would like to investigate the way different data augmentation methods can improve our results, since previous work done on

English text shows promising results when it comes to applications on pretrained transformer models (see, for example, Dai and Adel (2020)), such as the RA model we propose in this paper. Moreover, given the fact that our source material comes from labour union documents, it could also be interesting to look at a more fine-grained analysis of the PRS label in order to be able to identify potential biases in NER systems - similar to the work conducted by Lassen et al. (2023) for Danish text.

6 Conclusion

In this paper, we show that current off-the-shelf models for Swedish can perform NER on historical text, but using a historical language model shows more promising results. However, data from historical sources could also be beneficial for training in order to achieve better F1 score and reduce errors. An alternative path we would like to explore in the future is training on multilingual data from other Scandinavian languages, given that multilingual models show great promise when it comes to cross-lingual transfer learning (see, for exasmple, Chi et al. (2020) or Katsarou (2021)), with the added bonus that Scandinavian languages have similar vocabulary and structure.

A significant contribution of this study lies in the release of the newly trained RA model tailored for NER of historical Swedish text. Additionally, we introduce a manually annotated corpus comprising over 650 named entities, offering a valuable resource for future research endeavors. We also show that combining the strengths of multiple models can be beneficial to our NER task.

In conclusion, while our study provides valuable insights and tools for NER in historical Swedish text, it also underscores the necessity for further advancements and novel methodologies to address the challenges posed by data sparsity in low-resource languages.

Acknowledgements

We would like to extend our heartfelt gratitude to our colleagues in the Labour's Memory project for their invaluable historical expertise and support.

This work has been supported by Riksbankens Jubileumsfond, grant IN20-0040, *Labour's Memory. Digitization of annual and financial reports of blue-collar worker unions 1880-2020.*

References

Lars Ahrenberg, Johan Frid, and Leif-Jöran Olsson. 2020. A new gold standard for Swedish named entity recognition: Version 1 contents. SWE-CLARIN Report Series SCR-01-2020.

Lars Borin, Markus Forsberg, and Christer Ahlberger. 2011. Semantic Search in Literature as an e-Humanities Research Tool: CONPLISIT – Consumption Patterns and Life-Style in 19th Century Swedish Literature. In *NEALT Proceedings Series (NODALIDA 2011 Conference Proceedings)*, volume 11, pages 58–65.

Lars Borin, Dimitrios Kokkinakis, and Leif-Jöran Olsson. 2007. Naming the past: Named entity and Animacy recognition in 19th century Swedish literature. In *Proceedings of the Workshop on Language Technology for Cultural Heritage Data (LaTeCH 2007).*, pages 1–8, Prague, Czech Republic. Association for Computational Linguistics.

Alex Brandsen, Suzan Verberne, Karsten Lambers, and Milco Wansleeben. 2022. Can bert dig it? named entity recognition for information retrieval in the archaeology domain. *J. Comput. Cult. Herit.*, 15(3).

Olle Bridal. 2021. Named-entity recognition with BERT for anonymization of medical records.

Ethan A. Chi, John Hewitt, and Christopher D. Manning. 2020. Finding universal grammatical relations in multilingual BERT. In *Proceedings of the 58th Annual Meeting of the Association for Computational Linguistics*, pages 5564–5577, Online. Association for Computational Linguistics.

Nancy Chinchor and Beth Sundheim. 1993. MUC-5 evaluation metrics. In *Fifth Message Understanding Conference (MUC-5): Proceedings of a Conference Held in Baltimore, Maryland, August 25-27, 1993.*

Xiang Dai and Heike Adel. 2020. An Analysis of Simple Data Augmentation for Named Entity Recognition.

Martin Jansson. 2023. *Samtidens gränser : Om språkreformer och historisk tid runt sekelskiftet 1900.* Ph.D. thesis, Uppsala University, Department of History of Science and Ideas.

Styliani Katsarou. 2021. Improving Multilingual Models for the Swedish Language : Exploring CrossLingual Transferability and Stereotypical Biases. Master's thesis, KTH, School of Electrical Engineering and Computer Science (EECS).

Robin Kurtz and Joey Öhman. 2022. The KBLab Blog: SUCX 3.0 - NER.

Ida Marie S. Lassen, Mina Almasi, Kenneth Enevoldsen, and Ross Deans Kristensen-McLachlan. 2023. Detecting intersectionality in NER models: A data-driven approach. In *Proceedings of the 7th Joint SIGHUM Workshop on Computational Linguistics for Cultural Heritage, Social Sciences, Humanities and Literature*, pages 116–127, Dubrovnik, Croatia. Association for Computational Linguistics.

David Nadeau and Satoshi Sekine. 2007. A Survey of Named Entity Recognition and Classification. *Lingvisticae Investigationes*, 30.

Hiroki Nakayama. 2018. seqeval: A python framework for sequence labeling evaluation. Software available from https://github.com/chakki-works/seqeval.

Anthi Papadopoulou, Yunhao Yu, Pierre Lison, and Lilja Øvrelid. 2022. Neural text sanitization with explicit measures of privacy risk. In *Proceedings of the 2nd Conference of the Asia-Pacific Chapter of the Association for Computational Linguistics and the 12th International Joint Conference on Natural Language Processing (Volume 1: Long Papers)*, pages 217–229, Online only. Association for Computational Linguistics.

Eva Pettersson. 2016. *Spelling Normalisation and Linguistic Analysis of Historical Text for Information Extraction*. Ph.D. thesis, Uppsala University, Department of Linguistics and Philology.

Eva Pettersson and Lars Borin. 2022. *Swedish Diachronic Corpus*, pages 561–586. De Gruyter, Berlin, Boston.

Isabel Segura-Bedmar, Paloma Martínez, and María Herrero-Zazo. 2013. SemEval-2013 Task 9 : Extraction of Drug-Drug Interactions from Biomedical Texts (DDIExtraction 2013). In *Second Joint Conference on Lexical and Computational Semantics (*SEM), Volume 2: Proceedings of the Seventh International Workshop on Semantic Evaluation (SemEval 2013)*, pages 341–350, Atlanta, Georgia, USA. Association for Computational Linguistics.

Språkbanken. 2023. SUCX 3.0 - Stockholm-Umeå corpus 3.0, scrambled.

Erik F. Tjong Kim Sang and Fien De Meulder. 2003. Introduction to the CoNLL-2003 shared task: Language-independent named entity recognition. In *Proceedings of the Seventh Conference on Natural Language Learning at HLT-NAACL 2003*, pages 142–147.

Appendix A. Self-reported raining results for the RA model

Training Loss	Epoch	Step	Validation Loss	Precision	Recall	F1	Accuracy
0.0403	1.0	5391	0.0316	0.8496	0.8866	0.8677	0.9903
0.0199	2.0	10782	0.0308	0.8814	0.9034	0.8923	0.9915
0.0173	3.0	16173	0.0372	0.8698	0.9197	0.8940	0.9913
0.0066	4.0	21564	0.0397	0.8783	0.9239	0.9005	0.9921
0.0029	5.0	26955	0.0454	0.8855	0.9181	0.9015	0.9923
0.0035	6.0	32346	0.0454	0.8834	0.9211	0.9019	0.9922
0.0009	7.0	37737	0.0495	0.8784	0.9261	0.9017	0.9922

Part-of-Speech Tagging of 16th-Century Latin with GPT

Elina Stüssi, Phillip Benjamin Ströbel
Department of Computational Linguistics
University of Zurich
{elina.stuessi,phillip.stroebel}@uzh.ch

Abstract

Part-of-speech tagging is foundational to natural language processing, transcending mere linguistic functions. However, taggers optimized for Classical Latin struggle when faced with diverse linguistic eras shaped by the language's evolution. Exploring 16th-century Latin from the correspondence and assessing five Latin treebanks, we focused on carefully evaluating tagger accuracy and refining Large Language Models for improved performance in this nuanced linguistic context. Our discoveries unveiled the competitive accuracies of different versions of *GPT*, particularly after fine-tuning. Notably, our best fine-tuned model soared to an average accuracy of 88.99% over the treebank data, underscoring the remarkable adaptability and learning capabilities when fine-tuned to the specific intricacies of Latin texts. Next to emphasising GPT's part-of-speech tagging capabilities, our second aim is to strengthen taggers' adaptability across different periods. We establish solid groundwork for using Large Language Models in specific natural language processing tasks where part-of-speech tagging is often employed as a pre-processing step. This work significantly advances the use of modern language models in interpreting historical language, bridging the gap between past linguistic epochs and modern computational linguistics.

1 Introduction

Understanding parts-of-speech (POS) is fundamental in linguistic analysis (Jurafsky and Martin, 2019). Automatic POS tagging offers vital clues for parsing and language analysis. Despite Latin's extensive dataset in the Universal Dependencies treebanks,[1] many historical texts lack syntactic analysis (Nehrdich and Hellwig, 2022).

Latin's enduring relevance in domains like the Catholic Church and classical studies persists despite its decline post-1800 (Leonhardt, 2013). However, this enduring relevance is intertwined with its extensive historical significance, contributing to the language's vast evolutionary timespan.

The evolution of the Latin language spans significant changes over time, notably evident in alterations to case endings and lexical transformations, particularly during the transition from Old Latin to Classical Latin (Allen, 1989). These alterations extend beyond mere word changes, reshaping meanings and structures and resulting in diverse linguistic variations. The historical evolution of the language continued until the Early Modern Latin period of the 16th century, thereby posing challenges for POS tagging systems that have been mostly trained on Classical Latin (Schmid, 2019).

Despite its historical significance, Latin remains classified as a low-resource language due to the scarcity of digitized texts and annotations (Hedderich et al., 2021).[2] The absence of speakers poses difficulties in creating a gold standard,[3] a process notably more labor-intensive and error-prone than that for modern languages. Nonetheless, Latin benefits from a wealth of linguistic expertise derived from its extensive historical legacy, offering substantial aid in overcoming these obstacles (McGillivray, 2013).

The nuances in 16th-century epistolary Latin pose challenges for POS taggers, especially. Tagging a sentence from the correspondence of Swiss reformer Heinrich Bullinger (1504–1575) by various systems[4] highlights discrepancies, as illustrated in Figure 1. *RDRPOSTagger* misclassified punctuation and the name "Erasmus" as verbs. *Lat-*

[1] There are five in total: Latin-ITTB, Latin-Perseus, Latin-PROIEL, Latin-LLCT, Latin-UDante, all of which we introduce in Section 3.1. Also, see https://universaldependencies.org/la.

[2] Although there are large text collections like the *Corpus Corporum*, see https://mlat.uzh.ch.

[3] i. e., a manually compiled and verified annotated version of a text (in our case, the annotation would concern POS tags only).

[4] We will introduce the different taggers in Section 3.2.

Proceedings of LaTeCH-CLfL 2024, pages 196–206
March 22, 2024

	Dominus	Erasmus	plurimam	salutem	tibi	adscribere	iussit	.
GS:	NOUN	PROPN	ADJ	NOUN	PRON	VERB	VERB	PUNCT
LC:	NOUN	PROPN	ADJ	NOUN	PRON	NOUN	VERB	PUNCT
RDR:	NOUN	VERB	ADJ	NOUN	PRON	VERB	VERB	VERB
GPT-4:	NOUN	PROPN	ADJ	NOUN	PRON	VERB	VERB	PUNCT

Figure 1: Demonstration of a sentence tagged with Gold Standard (GS), LatinCy (LC), RDRPOSTagger (RDR), and GPT-4.

inCy tagged "adscribere" as a noun while *RDR-POSTagger* and *GPT-4* identified it correctly as a verb. *GPT-4*'s similarity to the gold standard underscores the potential of Large Language Models (LLMs) to enhance accuracy in language processing tasks.

Our project's core revolves around tagging 16th-century Latin data with multiple taggers, showcasing the disparities and revealing the potential of LLMs to increase accuracy in the POS tagging process. Motivated by the need to enhance linguistic analysis for historians and linguists, our work addresses the challenges in POS tagging within this historical context. Moreover, our efforts in refining POS tagging algorithms preserve cultural heritage and drive advancements in natural language processing (NLP), extending their impact across machine learning and AI beyond linguistic analysis.

Our contributions encompass a detailed investigation into how fine-tuning influences POS tagging accuracy and the customization of models to distinct datasets for improved precision. We underscore the role of fine-tuning and prompting in notably enhancing performance, particularly when tailoring models to domain-specific data. By conducting extensive comparative analyses between fine-tuned and pre-trained models, we reveal each approach's distinct strengths and limitations, emphasizing the nature of domain-specific training for achieving superior accuracy in POS tagging. These evaluations offer insights important for future research, underscoring the need for tailored models and their potential applications in NLP tasks.

2 Recent Work

Exploration of Latin within the field of NLP has remained limited despite the existence of various methodologies designed to enhance its processing efficiency. The inaugural *Workshop on Language Technologies for Historical and Ancient Languages* (LT4HALA) held in 2020 represented a step forward in developing language technologies tailored for historically documented languages, including Latin (Sprungoli and Passarotti, 2020).

As a part of LT4HALA, the *EvaLatin* initiative focused specifically on Latin and investigated lemmatization and POS tagging, scrutinizing their performance across diverse temporal contexts (Sprungoli and Passarotti, 2020). *EvaLatin* encompassed works such as *LSTMVoter* (Stoeckel et al., 2020) and the *UDPipe2*-based system (Straka and Straková, 2020), showcasing advancements in techniques customized for historical Latin texts. Additionally, the *LiLa* project[5] significantly fortified the lexical foundation for Latin, fostering a symbiotic relationship between textual and lexical resources (Passarotti et al., 2023; Pellegrini et al., 2021).

However, despite efforts like Chu[6] highlighting the strengths of GPT models for POS tagging, there remains a conspicuous gap in research specifically exploring LLMs as POS taggers.

3 Data and Methodology

3.1 Datasets

This study focused on leveraging LLMs, particularly different flavours of GPT, for the POS tagging of historical texts from different periods. Utilizing UPOS tags[7] for consistency, our experiments encompassed samples from our own *Bullinger Digital* corpus (Bullinger Digital, 2023) and five treebanks: ITTB (Cecchini et al., 2018; Passarotti and

[5]See https://lila-erc.eu/.
[6]See https://bit.ly/3vUyqNu.
[7]See https://universaldependencies.org/u/pos.

Dataset	time	# of sentences	# of token-tag pairs
Bullinger	c. 16	200	3664
ITTB	c. 13	24,876	420,672
LLCT	c. 8 – c. 10	8,173	218,223
PROIEL	c. 1 BCE – c. 4	11,851	110,774
UDante	c. 13 – c. 14	1,157	38,086
Perseus	c. 1 BCE – c. 4	4,236	68,283
Total		**50,493**	**859,702**

Table 1: Overview of different datasets (c. = century).

Dell'Orletta, 2010), LLCT (Korkiakangas, 2021), UDante (Cecchini et al., 2020), PROIEL (Haug and Jøhndal, 2008), and Perseus (Bamman and Crane, 2006). Table 1 provides an overview of the data used.

The Bullinger corpus, derived from Heinrich Bullinger's 16th-century correspondence, offers insights into early modern societal aspects and the reformation process in Switzerland and Europe. This study uses a sample from a corpus comprising approximately 220k sentences, with the selected subset comprising 200 sentences. The sample intentionally includes only the Latin sections from digitized letters structured into XML format, excluding the Early New High German sentences.

The five treebanks served as training material and fine-tuning data for POS tagging models. The ITTB dataset offers morphosyntactic disambiguation and sentence-level syntactic annotation for Latin. The training and test sets provided in CoNLL-U format include 24,876 tagged sentences, totalling 420,627 token-tag pairs.

Similarly, the Universal Dependencies (UD) version of the Late Latin Charter treebank (LLCT) sheds light on 521 Early Medieval Latin records (charters) from 774 CE to 897 CE. These charters present a non-standard Latin variety, focusing on legal documentary genres, and pose linguistic challenges due to their formulaic nature.[8] The dataset utilized in this work encompasses 8,173 tagged sentences, totalling 218,223 token-tag pairs.

Additionally, UDante, a project annotating Dante Alighieri's Latin works, includes 1,157 tagged sentences amounting to 38,086 token-tag pairs, focusing on 14th-century literary Medieval Latin.[9]

Moreover, the Pragmatic Resources in Old Indo-European Languages (PROIEL) project comprises 11,851 tagged sentences totalling 110,774 token-tag pairs, involving annotated texts such as the New Testament and Latin works like Cicero's "Epistulae ad Atticum" (Eckhoff et al., 2009).

Lastly, the Perseus dataset (version 2.1) features semi-automatically annotated texts like Cicero's "In Catilinam", Ovid's "Metamorphoses," and Augustus' "Res Gestae." Perseus did not originally use UPOS tags, so we mapped the Perseus tags[10] to UPOS tags. Notably, not all UPOS tags had direct equivalents in the Perseus tags. For instance, Perseus employed only "c" to represent conjunctions, lacking the differentiation between subordinating conjunctions (SCONJ) and coordinating conjunctions (CCONJ) as observed in UPOS tags. We omitted the files that included Caesar's "Commentarii de Bello Gallico" and Jerome's "Vulgata," as these texts were already included in the PROIEL dataset. The shortened Perseus dataset utilized in this project comprises 4,236 tagged sentences, totalling 68,283 token-tag pairs.

3.2 POS Tagging Models

We evaluated the performance of various POS tagging models on 16th-century epistolary Latin sourced from the Bullinger letters (i. e., the Bullinger sample mentioned in Section 3.1 and Table 1). The comparative analysis involved *LatinCy*, *CLTK*, *UDPipe*, *RDRPOSTagger*, and *TreeTagger*, alongside the examination of GPT-3.5-Turbo and GPT-4. The taggers compared in this study encompassed a spectrum of approaches, such as Single Classification Ripple-Down Rule (SCRDR) trees, statistical methods, and other distinct methodologies.

LatinCy, a *spaCy*-based Latin NLP toolkit introduced in 2023, employs *spaCy*'s (Montani et al., 2023) POS tagger,[11] backed by statistical models based on neural networks trained on the OntoNotes 5 corpus (Weischedel et al., 2013). With three core models, including "la_core_web_lg" utilizing sub-word vectors (Burns, 2023), *LatinCy* comprehends extensive vocabularies beyond its training data (Ács et al., 2021). Training incorporates diverse sources like Latin Universal Dependencies treebanks (Celano, 2019), Wikipedia or a preprocessed version of the cc100-latin corpus (Ströbel, 2023). Notably, the "la_core_web_lg" model we used for our research achieves an impressive

[8] See https://github.com/UniversalDependencies/UD_Latin-LLCT.

[9] See https://github.com/UniversalDependencies/UD_Latin-UDante.

[10] See https://github.com/PerseusDL/treebank_data/blob/master/v2.1/Latin/TAGSET.txt.

[11] See https://spacy.io/api/tagger.

97.41% accuracy for POS tagging on the respective test data (Burns, 2023).

The *Classical Language Toolkit* (CLTK),[12] established in 2014, caters to ancient languages like Latin and Greek, among others. CLTK's architecture supports various pre-modern languages, providing functionalities for POS tagging, tokenization, and lemmatization (Johnson et al., 2021). Utilizing *Stanza* (Qi et al., 2020) with bidirectional Long Sort-Term Memory networks (Hochreiter and Schmidhuber, 1997), it attains average accuracies of 68% for unigrams and 82% employing a 1, 2, 3-gram back-off tagger on the Perseus test data.[13]

UDPipe2 operates as a multifaceted pipeline, incorporating a neural network with a single joint model for tasks like POS tagging and dependency parsing. It leverages CoNLL-U format data and pre-trained word embeddings, where, e. g., the "Latin-ITTB" model achieved a high accuracy of 98.28% on the ITTB test data (Straka, 2018). Its flexibility spans over 50 languages, including non-Indo-European ones like Arabic and Irish (Wijffels, 2023).

RDRPOSTagger employs SCRDR trees for POS tagging across approximately 80 languages, with three available models showcasing varying accuracies for Latin (Nguyen et al., 2014). For our research, we employed the "UD_Latin-ITTB" model. Its conditional rule structure allows controlled interactions between rules, proving adaptable to languages like Latin. We used the "UD_Latin-ITTB" model that yielded an accuracy of 96.85% on the ITTB test set.

TreeTagger, developed through the University of Stuttgart's textual corpora project, adeptly annotates POS and lemma information in numerous languages like German, English, Chinese, Russian, Greek, and Latin. Its adaptability to new languages hinges on a lexicon and tagged training corpora, underscoring its versatility (Schmid, 1994). There are parameter files for numerous languages available; for Latin, we used the parameter file by Gabriele Brandolini. Functionally resembling traditional *n*-gram taggers, *TreeTagger* estimates transition probabilities using a binary decision tree and achieves accuracies ranging from around 95.8% to 96% on the Penn-Treebank for bigram and trigram versions (Schmid, 1995). However, its output does not directly use UPOS tags, necessitating a post-process tag mapping for compatibility.

Our study assessed two LLMs developed by OpenAI: GPT-3.5-Turbo and GPT-4. GPT-3.5, launched in 2022 and based on GPT-3 (Brown et al., 2020), boasts 175 billion parameters and excels in tasks like translation, text completion, and question-answering (OpenAI, 2023). Its architecture, excluding the encoder attention part, relies on an unmodified transformer decoder (Gupta, 2023). GPT-4, despite improvements, shares limitations like occasional unreliability and context window constraints. While GPT-4 shows superior task performance and visual data processing, only GPT-3.5-Turbo currently supports fine-tuning with custom data.[14]

The various models underwent a thorough assessment, revealing their capabilities and limitations in dealing with historical Latin texts. We applied each model mentioned above to the (test) datasets mentioned in Section 3.1 and compared the obtained accuracies. Incorporating conventional POS taggers and contemporary (fine-tuned) LLMs allowed for a direct comparison between traditional and LLM approaches.

4 Experiments and Results

4.1 Gold Standard

The initial phase involved the curation of a condensed Bullinger corpus comprising 200 sample sentences extracted from the Bullinger letters. Manual verification ensured a representative compilation spanning various editions, authors, and temporal contexts, subsequently stored in text files for further processing.

After the data curation process, the text was tokenized using the *spaCy* tokenizer with the "la_core_web_lg" model. We removed punctuation, including internal parentheses within words.[15] The subsequent application of the UDPipe tagger allowed for assigning reference tags to individual tokens, forming the foundation for creating an accurate gold standard dataset.

Multiple annotators, including a Latin expert, were involved in the verification and correction process of reference UPOS tags assigned by UDPipe. Any discrepancies between the assigned tags and the ideal classifications were addressed through

[12] See http://cltk.org/.

[13] For further details, see http://cltk.org/blog/2015/08/02/updated-accuracies-pos-taggers.html.

[14] As of 07.11.2023, when we conducted our experiments.

[15] E. g., the transcription could contain "vestr[um]" (EN *your*), where the editors added the "um" in parentheses. We removed the parentheses to obtain "vestrum".

manual verification. The collaboration with the Latin expert played a significant role in establishing a strong gold standard, incorporating mutually agreed-upon tagging principles. We employed Cohen's Kappa to assess inter-annotator agreement (IAA) on the corrected tag versions of the Bullinger corpus, yielding a noteworthy IAA of 0.97.

4.2 POS Tagging

Our study employed diverse POS tagging models, as detailed in Section 3.2, each utilizing distinct tagging methods. As test sets, we used the tokenized and manually tagged sample of the Bullinger corpus on the one hand and the tokenized test sets of the treebanks introduced in Section 3.1 on the other hand. We conducted manual post-processing on the taggers' output to ensure consistent token placement, aiming for uniformity in the models' outputs. This manual review became necessary because the taggers occasionally performed additional tokenization on certain words. Specifically, in the case of GPT models, they sometimes added extra text to the response, requiring careful verification to ensure uniform and comparable outputs.

Our experimentation also involved GPT-3.5-Turbo and GPT-4, which required specific prompts for accurate tokenization. We exclusively used system and user prompts, keeping all other parameters (like, e. g., temperature) unaltered. After encountering tokenization issues with the prompts used for the Bullinger test set, we refined the input by incorporating both the original sentence and a tokenized version aligned with our manually created gold standard. Figure 2 displays the used prompt. The variable "tokens" refers to the list of tokens and with the variable "sentence" we entered the sentence that should be tagged. Furthermore, we explored a token-only approach for the Bullinger corpus, submitting only tokens without a reference sentence in the prompt. The utilized prompt for this approach is displayed in Figure 3. Since we had used the already tokenized version of the corpora, we explicitly instructed the models in the user prompt not to perform additional tokenization. In contrast to the sentence-included approach, we focused solely on obtaining tags for individual tokens. Consequently, we requested only the tag for each token inserted into the prompt, replacing the "token" variable.

For the application of GPT models on treebank data lacking sentence boundaries, such as PROIEL, we developed an alternative strategy. Instead of providing complete sentences, we utilized sets of 65 tokens in the prompts, bypassing the requirement for punctuation to delineate sentences. This adaptation enabled the effective use of the GPT models without explicit sentence boundaries. The package size of 65 tokens was selected randomly, aiming to encompass the majority of sentences almost in their entirety. Even when complete inclusion was not possible, the chosen number ensured the presence of contextual information from the sentence, facilitating the disambiguation of words.

4.3 Fine-Tuning of GPT-3.5-Turbo

For the fine-tuning of GPT-3.5-Turbo, we obtained the training and test data from treebanks specified in Section 3.1 in the form of samples with an 80/20 split. When a pre-defined test set was absent, as was the case for PROIEL and Perseus, we randomly selected the test set. To explore how the model performance varies when provided with differently sized training sets, we crafted subsets for fine-tuning in sizes ranging from 50 to 10,000 sentences. We used stratified sampling to obtain the required examples from each training set to represent the different treebank sizes adequately. These subsets used for fine-tuning were formed by concatenating the chosen samples from the training sets from each resource listed in Section 3.1. E. g., "train5000" specifies a model fine-tuned on 5,000 sentences sampled from the different treebanks, taking the size of each treebank into account. We then prepared the data as required by the OpenAI API guidelines.[16]

4.4 POS Tagging Results

The pre-trained models' output required some manual post-processing, albeit not to the same extent as the GPT models' outputs. Significant discrepancies were noted within the GPT-generated content, encompassing repetitions, omissions of passages, instances of unexpected text occurrences (as illustrated in Figure 4), and irregularities such as unspecified tags and incorrect formats. These findings underscore limitations within the model's performance, notably occurring more frequently with models trained using larger datasets, such as train5000 and train10000.[17]

[16]See https://platform.openai.com/docs/guides/fine-tuning.

[17]The best-performing model on the Bullinger sample (train100) can be accessed with the model name `ft:gpt-3.5-turbo-0613:cl-uzh:train-100:8GWMiGKN`,

```
completion = openai.ChatCompletion.create(
    model = model,
    messages=[
        {"role":"system","content": """You are a Latin linguist and part-of-speech tagging expert.
        You are using UPOS (universal part of speech tags). UPOS tags are ADJ,ADP,ADV,AUX,CCONJ,DET,
        INTJ,NOUN,NUM,PART,PRON,PROPN,PUNCT,SCONJ,SYM,VERB and X. X stands for 'other'."""},
        {"role":"user",
        "content":f"""Return the UPOS tag for the tokens of the sentence: {sentence} The sentence should
        be tokenized like that: {tokens}. Return the tags in the format TOKEN \t Tag. Every Token-Tag
        pair should be on a new line in the output file, so add a newline character after the tags.
        Only output the token and the tag (no explanations, no translations, no additional text)."""}
        ]
    )
```

Figure 2: Prompt employed for POS tagging using the GPT API.

```
completion = openai.ChatCompletion.create(
    model = model,
    messages=[
        {"role":"system","content": """You are a Latin linguist and part-of-speech tagging expert.
        You are using UPOS (universal part of speech tags). UPOS tags are ADJ, ADP, ADV, AUX, CCONJ,
        DET, INTJ, NOUN, NUM, PART, PRON, PROPN, PUNCT, SCONJ, SYM, VERB and X. X stands for 'other'."""},
        {"role":"user",
        "content":f"""Do not tokenize the words further, they are already tokenized. Only output the tag
        (no explanations, no translations, no additional text). Return the UPOS tag for the token: {token}."""}
        ]
    )
```

Figure 3: Prompt employed for the token-only POS tagging approach using the GPT API.

```
Vuido PROPN
Nopqrstuvwxyz
gratia NOUN
```

Figure 4: Example of GPT API output displaying unforeseen textual anomalies

After the manual clean-up of the output of all taggers on the Bullinger test set, involving the correction of tokens to adhere to the gold standard tokenization, especially in cases where taggers had further tokenized the input tokens, *LatinCy* demonstrated the highest accuracy (79.8%) among pre-trained models, slightly surpassing CLTK by 2.7%. RDRPOSTagger displayed the lowest accuracy (64.5%), indicating limitations in processing 16th-century data. Table 2 shows an overview of the results.

The token-only approach on the Bullinger corpus yielded the highest accuracy with the fine-tuned model train2000, reaching 78.2%. Remarkably, despite the absence of a reference sentence and the model being provided with only an individual token, the accuracy was nearly as high as for LatinCy. In contrast, the baseline model GPT-3.5-Turbo achieved only 62.2% accuracy in this approach, emphasizing the significant improvement brought about by fine-tuning. The non-fine-tuned GPT-4 achieved an accuracy of 74.3%, showcasing a clear performance difference between GPT-3.5-Turbo and GPT-4. The lowest accuracy, at 58.8%, was observed with the train500 model.

In the sentence-included approach, the best result was obtained using the train100 model, reaching an accuracy of 85.5% on the Bullinger corpus, surpassing the traditional tagging models by a significant margin. In this approach, the differences between the fine-tuned and the baseline models GPT-3.5-Turbo and GPT-4 were less pronounced. GPT-3.5-Turbo achieved an accuracy of 80.2%, and GPT-4 reached an accuracy of 83.5%. The model with the lowest accuracy in this scenario was train500, with an accuracy of 77.2%.

On the test data from the treebanks, *LatinCy* emerged with the highest average accuracy of the pre-trained models (83.22%), indicating effective performance as a POS tagger. The fine-tuned train1000 model exhibited the most effective performance (88.99%), whereas RDRPOSTagger had the lowest (72.36%). Notably, performance across various test sets varied, with ITTB showing the highest accuracy (84.95%) and PROIEL the lowest (74.73%).

the overall best model (train1000) is available under the name `ft:gpt-3.5-turbo-0613:cl-uzh:train-1000:8HUHOHgt`.

Tagger	Bullinger	ITTB	LLCT	UDante	Perseus	PROIEL	Avg TB
LatinCy	**79.8**	87.93	92.01	80.94	72.38	82.84	83.22
CLTK	77.1	88.45	79.32	77.36	72.44	80.63	79.64
UDPipe	72.8	71.59	71.45	70.51	69.2	84.49	73.45
RDRPOSTagger	64.5	82.67	67.41	71.72	64.79	75.22	72.36
TreeTagger	74.3	70.18	70.25	69.86	82.51	89.39	76.44
GPT-3.5-Turbo	62.2/80.2	74.82	78.82	74.33	68.81	79.22	75.2
GPT-4	74.3/83.5	79.73	84.89	77.62	73.9	84.38	80.1
train50	70.3/84.8	89.59	89.2	83.55	73.2	79.37	82.98
train100	69.4/**85.5**	89.73	91.03	85.26	74.19	82.19	84.48
train200	68.2/80.0	91.57	90.93	**85.8**	73.46	83.5	85.05
train500	58.8/77.2	93.2	93.85	82.71	72.09	86.72	85.71
train1000	65.8/82.5	**94.88**	**94.5**	84.94	81.39	89.25	**88.99**
train2000	**78.2**/78.3	87.95	87.43	81.31	**84.31**	87.83	85.77
train5000	71.9/76.6	88.11	84.85	74.62	81.99	**90.0**	83.91
train10000	74.4/76.4	83.84	85.39	75.36	76.34	86.01	81.39

Table 2: Tagger performance across different datasets. Bold numbers indicate the highest accuracy within each test set's column. The taggers starting with "train" are our fine-tuned GPT-3-5-Turbo models. For the GPT models, two numbers for the Bullinger data indicate the token-only and sentence-included approach (see Section 4.2). The average calculated over the test sets of the five treebanks is displayed in column Avg TB.

4.5 Tag Distribution

The taggers exhibit variations in their outputs. Some taggers allocate certain tags more frequently than others, owing to their dissimilar training data and learning algorithms. Moreover, not all taggers have been exposed to datasets encompassing all UPOS tags. In Figure 5, depicting tag distribution across four taggers and the gold standard on the Bullinger corpus data, common POS tags like NOUN and VERB are consistently assigned across all versions. However, notable differences emerge in the frequency of tags such as adverbs (ADV), determiners (DET) and pronouns (PRON). DET, for instance, appears significantly more in the gold standard compared to *LatinCy* or the basic GPT models. Only the fine-tuned model train100, boasting the highest accuracy on the Bullinger corpus, mirrors a similar frequency in assigning this tag. Conversely, *LatinCy* frequently uses ADV but assigns the tag for adpositions (ADP) less frequently than other taggers. The gold standard employs PRON less frequently, while GPT-4 allocates this tag almost twice as often as our gold standard did.

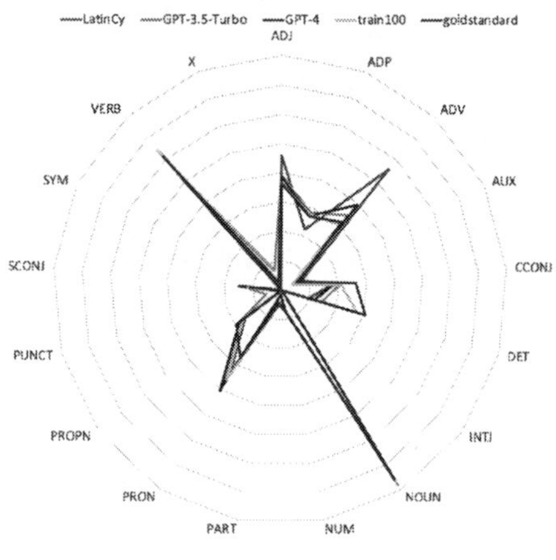

Figure 5: POS tag distribution in the Bullinger corpus.

In analyzing the LLCT treebank data, a distinct disparity emerges in tag distribution when juxtaposed with the Bullinger corpus. Figure 6 illustrates the tag distribution of the LLCT data. Our comparison involves the tagging outputs of *LatinCy*, GPT-3.5-Turbo, GPT-4, the fine-tuned model *train1000*, and the gold standard. Notably, a greater convergence among the models is evident, signifying more consistent tag assignments. Once again, NOUN and VERB exhibit striking similarities across these models, as do auxiliary verbs (AUX). However, a significant deviation surfaces with the other tag (X). *LatinCy* and the gold standard exclude its usage, while GPT-3.5-Turbo predominantly assigns this tag, potentially indicating problems encountered during tagging processes. A comparable pattern emerges when examining the distribution of coordinating conjunctions (CCONJ) and DET across Figures 5 and 6. While CCONJ dis-

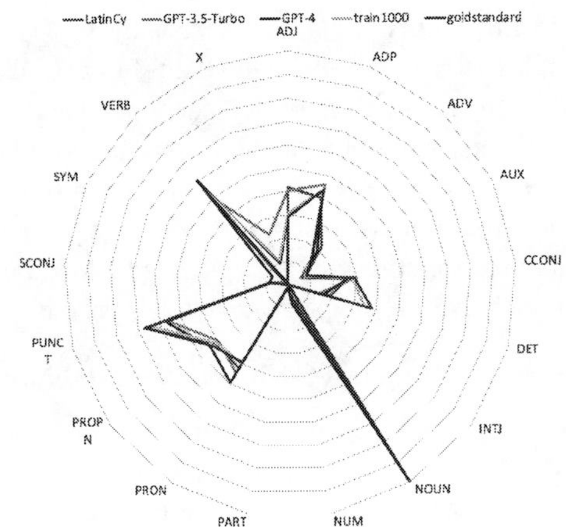

Figure 6: POS tag distribution in the LLCT test set.

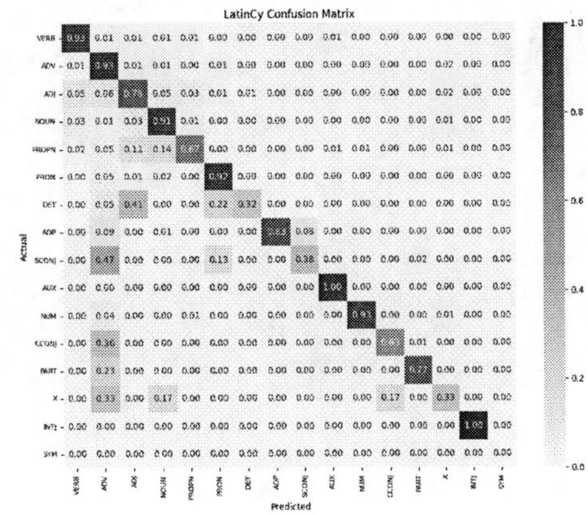

Figure 7: Confusion matrix for LatinCy on the Bullinger sample.

plays similarity across both test sets, the gold standard and fine-tuned models demonstrate a higher frequency in assigning this tag. Similarly, the DET tag exhibits a parallel pattern, with the fine-tuned models and the gold standard assigning this tag noticeably more frequently than the other three models.

5 Discussion

Evaluating part-of-speech tagging models within the context of 16th-century Latin texts provides valuable insights into language processing methodologies, particularly within historical frameworks. This comprehensive assessment reveals several noteworthy observations.

5.1 Fine-Tuning and Model Performance

One key finding is the significant impact of fine-tuning LLMs, such as GPT-3.5-Turbo, on POS tagging accuracy. Despite the superior performance of GPT-4 and GPT-3.5-Turbo, even without fine-tuning, the fine-tuned GPT-3.5-Turbo models outperformed conventional pre-trained taggers, especially on specific test sets. Especially the dominance over LatinCy, the most recent tagger that operates with transformer pipelines, is striking. This underscores the potential for domain-specific fine-tuning to enhance LLM efficacy in linguistically nuanced domains.

The evaluation aimed to assess the performance of various POS taggers on the Bullinger corpus and treebank test corpora. Evaluation of GPT models using token-only versus sentence-included approaches revealed notable differences. The sentence-inclusive method consistently achieved higher accuracy across all models, with a difference of over 11 percentage points compared to the token-only method. The model train500 showed the most significant difference between the two methods with 18.4 percentage points, while train2000 had only a difference of 0.1 percentage points.

The study also emphasizes the importance of prompting strategies when employing LLMs like GPT-4 and GPT-3.5-Turbo for POS tagging. Variations in accuracy between token-only and sentence-included approaches underscore the necessity of prompt engineering to improve contextual comprehension and enhance tagging performance.

5.2 Tag Assignment Challenges and Contextual Cues

Inconsistencies in tag assignments, especially for determiners and coordinating conjunctions, highlight the critical need for standardized definitions and categorizations. The study underscores the role of contextual cues in accurate POS tag assignments, particularly for ambiguous word classes like modal verbs and participles.

Confusion matrices were created to assess differences in tag assignment for the Bullinger sample. Figure 7 illustrates the comparison between the gold standard tags in the Bullinger sample and those assigned by LatinCy, while Figure 8 displays the tags assigned by GPT-4 using the sentence-included approach. These matrices present taggers' predictions along the x-axis and gold standard tags along the y-axis, providing insights into their performance.

LatinCy exhibits a nearly diagonal line, indicating generally accurate predictions. However, it

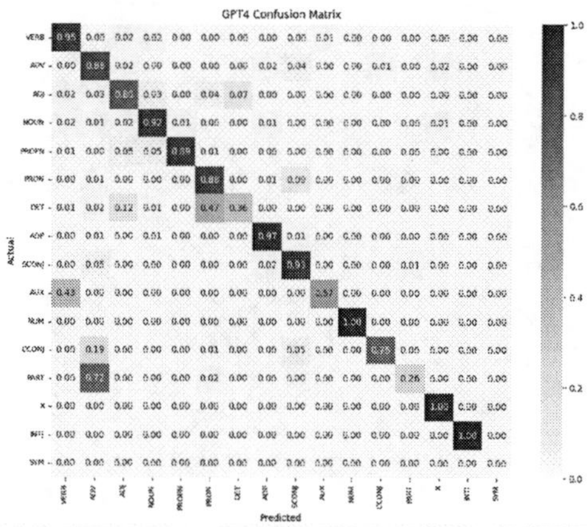

Figure 8: Confusion matrix for GPT-4 on the Bullinger sample.

correctly predicts the SCONJ tag only 38% of the time, incorrectly predicting ADV 47% of the time and PRON 13% of the time. In contrast, GPT-4 displays a more uniform and darker diagonal line, suggesting higher accuracy in tag assignments. GPT-4 demonstrates less dispersion in tag assignments than LatinCy, encountering difficulties in assigning the PART tag, mislabeling it as ADV (26%) and PRON (0.02%).

5.3 Comparative Analyses and Challenges in Applying Taggers

Comparative analyses, akin to prior studies such as Chu (2023), underscore the significance of prompting in part-of-speech tagging, emphasizing both similarities and disparities in the performance among various GPT models. Additionally, this investigation unveils challenges encountered when applying taggers to the Bullinger corpus, revealing notable differences in tagging standards and word usage.

The tagging process was time-consuming, particularly for GPT-4, hence each model was tested only once. While pre-trained models were faster, other GPT models occasionally necessitated several hours, contingent upon the overall global demand for GPT resources. Optimal efficiency was observed during off-peak hours for model testing, contrasting with markedly prolonged processing durations experienced during evening hours (UTC+1), reflecting heightened usage.

5.4 Implications and Future Directions

The study's findings underline the potential and constraints of traditional part-of-speech taggers and LLMs in historical Latin text analysis. The research serves as a pivotal impetus for future studies, prompting advancements in tagging precision and adaptability within historical and resource-limited language contexts. Further exploration of refined contextual models, standardized categorizations, and improved efficiency in deploying LLMs for extensive historical language analyses is encouraged.

5.5 Considerations for Resource Scalability

Despite the competitive performance, especially post-fine-tuning, concerns arise regarding the pragmatic utilization of LLMs in historical text analysis due to resource scalability challenges. The time-intensive nature of tagging procedures, particularly with models like GPT-4, raises considerations for their efficiency and scalability in large-scale historical language studies.

6 Conclusion

In conclusion, these multifaceted findings contribute to our understanding of part-of-speech tagging in historical Latin texts and pave the way for nuanced and targeted advancements in natural language processing within this domain. We could show that fine-tuning Large Language Models like OpenAI's GPT-3.5-Turbo can significantly heighten accuracy in part-of-speech tagging performance. We also provided insights into different prompting techniques for obtaining optimal results. However, the challenges related to stability and resource scalability, especially with time-intensive tagging procedures, raise considerations for the pragmatic utilization of Large Language Models in large-scale historical language studies.

Limitations

The study faced the following limitations: Tests, especially with GPT-4, were time-consuming, limiting the number of test runs due to extended processing times influenced by global demand and usage peaks. Performing only one test run per model with a single-epoch testing approach constrained a more thorough assessment of fine-tuning capabilities. Furthermore, formatting complexities in the output of models posed challenges, impeding the ability to adjust incorrectly formatted passages manually. This limitation hindered a more comprehensive analysis that could have been achieved through re-tagging sections if the process had been less time-intensive. Additionally, it is important to note that our fine-tuning was exclusively conducted on the treebank data due to the absence of large-scaled gold standards for the 16th-century dataset. The 16th-century test set, comprising only 200 sentences, might not have fully represented that era's language complexities. Consequently, this limitation might have introduced an abundance of edge cases, potentially leading to decreased accuracy in the assessment.

References

Judit Ács, Ákos Kádár, and Andras Kornai. 2021. Subword pooling makes a difference. In *Proceedings of the 16th Conference of the European Chapter of the Association for Computational Linguistics: Main Volume*, pages 2284–2295, Online. Association for Computational Linguistics.

William Sidney Allen. 1989. *Vox latina*. Cambridge University Press.

David Bamman and Gregory R. Crane. 2006. The design and use of a latin dependency treebank. In *Proceedings of The Third Workshop on Treebanks and Linguistic Theories*, pages 67–78, Tübingen.

Tom B. Brown, Benjamin Mann, Nick Ryder, Melanie Subbiah, Jared Kaplan, Prafulla Dhariwal, Arvind Neelakantan, Pranav Shyam, Girish Sastry, Amanda Askell, Sandhini Agarwal, Ariel Herbert-Voss, Gretchen Krueger, Tom Henighan, Rewon Child, Aditya Ramesh, Daniel M. Ziegler, Jeffrey Wu, Clemens Winter, Christopher Hesse, Mark Chen, Eric Sigler, Mateusz Litwin, Scott Gray, Benjamin Chess, Jack Clark, Christopher Berner, Sam McCandlish, Alec Radford, Ilya Sutskever, and Dario Amodei. 2020. Language models are few-shot learners. *CoRR*, abs/2005.14165.

Bullinger Digital. 2023. Bullinger Digital.

Patrick J. Burns. 2023. Latincy: Synthetic trained pipelines for latin NLP.

Flavio M. Cecchini, Marco Passarotti, Paola Marongiu, and Daniel Zeman. 2018. Challenges in converting the index Thomisticus treebank into Universal Dependencies. In *Proceedings of the Second Workshop on Universal Dependencies*, pages 27–36, Brussels, Belgium. Association for Computational Linguistics.

Flavio M. Cecchini, Rachele Sprugnoli, Giovanni Moretti, and Marco Passarotti. 2020. UDante: First steps towards the universal dependencies treebank of dante's latin works. In *Proceedings of the Seventh Italian Conference on Computational Linguistics*, pages 99–105, Torino. Accademia University Press.

Giuseppe G.A. Celano. 2019. *The Dependency Treebanks for Ancient Greek and Latin*, pages 279–298. De Gruyter Saur, Berlin, Boston.

Lai-Sik Fan Chu. 2023. GPT-4 is a very good hongkongese POS tagger.

Hanne Eckhoff, Marek Majer, Eirik Welo, and Dag Haug. 2009. Breaking down and putting back together: Analysis and synthesis of new testament greek. *Journal of Greek Linguistics*, 9(1):56–92.

Yashu Gupta. 2023. Chat GPT and GPT 3 detailed architecture study-deep NLP horse.

Dag T. T. Haug and Marius L. Jøhndal. 2008. Creating a parallel treebank of the old indo-european bible translations. In *Proceedings of the Second Workshop on Language Technology for Cultural Heritage Data*, pages 27–34.

Michael A. Hedderich, Lukas Lange, Heike Adel, Jannik Strötgen, and Dietrich Klakow. 2021. A survey on recent approaches for natural language processing in low-resource scenarios. In *Proceedings of the 2021 Conference of the North American Chapter of the Association for Computational Linguistics: Human Language Technologies*, pages 2545–2568, Online. Association for Computational Linguistics.

Sepp Hochreiter and Jürgen Schmidhuber. 1997. Long short-term memory. *Neural computation*, 9(8):1735–1780.

Kyle P. Johnson, Patrick J. Burns, John Stewart, Todd Cook, Clément Besnier, and William J. B. Mattingly. 2021. The Classical Language Toolkit: An NLP framework for pre-modern languages. In *Proceedings of the 59th Annual Meeting of the Association for Computational Linguistics and the 11th International Joint Conference on Natural Language Processing: System Demonstrations*, pages 20–29, Online. Association for Computational Linguistics.

Daniel Jurafsky and James H. Martin. 2019. Part-of-speech tagging. In *Speech and Language Processing*.

Timo Korkiakangas. 2021. Late latin charter treebank: Contents and annotation. *Corpora*, 16:191–203.

Jürgen Leonhardt. 2013. *Latin: Story of a world language*. Harvard University Press, Cambridge, Massachusetts.

Barbara McGillivray. 2013. *Methods in Latin computational linguistics*, volume 1. Brill, Boston.

Ines Montani, Matthew Honnibal, Adriane Boyd, Sofie Van Landeghem, and Henning Peters. 2023. spaCy.

Sebastian Nehrdich and Oliver Hellwig. 2022. Accurate dependency parsing and tagging of Latin. In *Proceedings of the Second Workshop on Language Technologies for Historical and Ancient Languages*, pages 20–25, Marseille, France. European Language Resources Association.

Dat Quoc Nguyen, Dai Quoc Nguyen, Dang Duc Pham, and Son Bao Pham. 2014. RDRPOSTagger: A ripple down rules-based part-of-speech tagger. In *Proceedings of the Demonstrations at the 14th Conference of the European Chapter of the Association for Computational Linguistics*, pages 17–20, Gothenburg, Sweden. Association for Computational Linguistics.

OpenAI. 2023. GPT-4 technical report.

Marco Passarotti and Felice Dell'Orletta. 2010. Improvements in parsing the index thomisticus treebank. revision, combination and a feature model for medieval latin. In *Proceedings of the Seventh International Conference on Language Resources and Evaluation*, pages 1964–1971, Malta.

Marco Passarotti, Eleonora Litta, Flavio Massimiliano Cecchini, Matteo Pellegrini, Giovanni Moretti, Paolo Ruffolo, and Giulia Pedonese. 2023. The LiLa knowledge base of interoperable linguistic resources for latin. architecture and current state.

Matteo Pellegrini, Eleonora Litta, Marco Passarotti, Rachele Sprugnoli, Francesco Mambrini, and Giovanni Moretti. 2021. LiLa linking latin tutorial. In *Proceedings of the Workshops and Tutorials-Language Data and Knowledge*, pages 229–234, Spain.

Peng Qi, Yuhao Zhang, Yuhui Zhang, Jason Bolton, and Christopher D. Manning. 2020. Stanza: A Python natural language processing toolkit for many human languages. In *Proceedings of the 58th Annual Meeting of the Association for Computational Linguistics: System Demonstrations*, pages 101–108.

Helmut Schmid. 1994. Probabilistic part-of-speech tagging using decision trees. In *Proceedings of International Conference on New Methods in Language Processing*, Manchester.

Helmut Schmid. 1995. Improvements in part-of-speech tagging with an application to German. In *Proceedings of the ACL SIGDAT-Workshop*, pages 13–25, Dublin. Springer.

Helmut Schmid. 2019. Deep learning-based morphological taggers and lemmatizers for annotating historical texts. In *Proceedings of the 3rd International Conference on Digital Access to Textual Cultural Heritage*, DATeCH2019, page 133–137, Brussels, Belgium. Association for Computing Machinery.

Rachele Sprungoli and Marco Passarotti. 2020. *1st Workshop on Language Technologies for Historical and Ancient Languages, Proceedings*. European Language Resources Association, Paris, France.

Manuel Stoeckel, Alexander Henlein, Wahed Hemati, and Alexander Mehler. 2020. Voting for POS tagging of Latin texts: Using the flair of FLAIR to better ensemble classifiers by example of Latin. In *1st Workshop on Language Technologies for Historical and Ancient Languages, Proceedings*, pages 130–135, Marseille, France. European Language Resources Association.

Milan Straka. 2018. UDPipe 2.0 prototype at CoNLL 2018 UD shared task. In *Proceedings of the CoNLL 2018 Shared Task: Multilingual Parsing from Raw Text to Universal Dependencies*, pages 197–207, Brussels, Belgium. Association for Computational Linguistics.

Milan Straka and Jana Straková. 2020. UDPipe at evalatin 2020: Contextualized embeddings and treebank embeddings.

Phillip Benjamin Ströbel. 2023. pstroe/cc100-latin · datasets at hugging face.

Ralph Weischedel, Sameer Pradhan, Lance Ramshaw, Martha Palmer, Nianwen Xue, Mitchell Marcus, Ann Taylor, Ann Houston, Eduard Hovy, Robert Belvin, Mohammed El-Bachouti, and Michelle Franchini. 2013. Ontonotes release 5.0.

Jan Wijffels. 2023. udpipe: Tokenization, parts of speech tagging, lemmatization and dependency parsing with the 'UDPipe' 'NLP' toolkit.

Two Approaches to Diachronic Normalization of Polish Texts

Kacper Dudzic, Filip Graliński, Krzysztof Jassem, Marek Kubis, Piotr Wierzchoń
Adam Mickiewicz University, Poznań, Poland
{firstname.lastname}@amu.edu.pl

Abstract

This paper discusses two approaches to the diachronic normalization of Polish texts: a rule-based solution that relies on a set of handcrafted patterns, and a neural normalization model based on the text-to-text transfer transformer architecture. The training and evaluation data prepared for the task are discussed in detail, along with experiments conducted to compare the proposed normalization solutions. A quantitative and qualitative analysis is made. It is shown that at the current stage of inquiry into the problem, the rule-based solution outperforms the neural one on 3 out of 4 variants of the prepared dataset, although in practice both approaches have distinct advantages and disadvantages.

1 Introduction

This paper discusses two solutions to the problem of diachronic normalization, that is, the task of determining contemporary spelling for a given historical text. Diachronic normalization may concern the writing of individual words, punctuation, hyphenation, or separation of tokens. We believe that the methods described in this paper may be useful for linguistic research on historical texts. A practical use case for our work is to facilitate full-text search in historical texts – a query written in contemporary spelling may trigger a search for historical variants through the use of reversed-order diachronic normalization.

Similar experiments, for text normalization in a speech synthesis system from text, were described in (Sproat and Jaitly, 2016). Those authors claim that text normalization remains one of the few tasks in the field of natural language processing where handcrafted rules may yield better results than machine learning. This is due to the following reasons:

- Lack of training data; there is no economic motivation for creating training data for text normalization – unlike machine translation, for example, for which training data are created "naturally";
- Low data density of interesting cases, i.e. words that should be somehow changed – unlike for example, phonemic transcription, where all words are converted to a new representation;
- Standard methods of evaluation which do not reward trivial cases (copying of input words), thus favoring human labor.

In our experiments, we compare the results of a rule-based approach with one based on machine learning. The rule-based approach relies on a set of handcrafted rules to normalize text. In the ML approach, we train a supervised normalization model on the basis of a corpus of Polish books for which both historical and current spellings are available.

2 Related work

The first attempts at rule-based diachronic normalization used for historical text in English were described by Rayson et al. (2007) and Baron et al. (2009). Similar studies were conducted for German (Archer et al., 2006). There, context rules operated at the level of letters instead of words. The normalization rules may be derived from corpora, as Bollmann et al. (2011) showed for German. Diachronic normalization may be also performed using a noisy channel model, as described by Oravecz et al. (2010) using the example of Old Hungarian texts. Research on diachronic normalization has also been conducted for Portugese (Reynaert et al., 2012), Swedish (Pettersson et al., 2012), Slovene (Scherrer and Erjavec, 2013), Spanish (Porta et al., 2013), and Basque (Etxeberria et al., 2016).

Bollmann (2019) surveys historical spelling normalization methods for eight languages. He reports word-level accuracy for the evaluated systems. He claims that using CER is not justified, because it

Proceedings of LaTeCH-CLfL 2024, pages 207–212
March 22, 2024

strongly correlates with WER for systems showing reasonable accuracy. Bollmann and Søgaard (2016) use bi-directional LSTMs and multi-task learning to normalize texts in Early New High German. Their dataset consists of 44 texts from the Aselm corpus. he model presented is evaluated with respect to word-level accuracy. Robertson and Goldwater (2018) discuss the problem of evaluating historical text normalization systems. They emphasize the necessity of reporting accuracy for unobserved tokens and recommend confronting the normalization systems with a simple baseline that memorizes training samples.

Jassem et al. (2017, 2018) present an automatic method for diachronic normalization of Polish texts. The proposed method uses a formal language to model diachronic changes. Graliński and Jassem (2020) introduce a method for finding spelling variants in a diachronic corpus using word2vec.

3 Data

Training and evaluation of a diachronic normalizer requires a corpus of texts that preserve historical spelling along with their contemporized counterparts. As our aim is the normalization of Polish prose, we decided to collect texts for our corpus from two sources. Texts that preserve historical spelling were drawn from the Polish edition of the Wikisource project (Wikimedia Foundation, 2023), which provides proof-read transcriptions of printed books that have fallen into the public domain, encoded in the MediaWiki format. For contemporized texts, we used Wolne Lektury (Modern Poland Foundation, 2023), a digital library that aims to deliver new editions of school readers, free of charge. Although both sources encompass a wide variety of texts, ranging from poems and works of philosophy to dictionaries and historical documents, we narrowed our attention to novels, to facilitate the process of matching the original texts from Wikisource to their contemporized versions in Wolne Lektury with the use of metadata information available for novels in both sources. We initially sourced 308 novels from Wikisource and 279 from Wolne Lektury.

3.1 Preprocessing

All of the texts then underwent preprocessing. First, we split the texts into paragraphs, with the use of markup information preserved in XML files sourced from Wolne Lektury, and MediaWiki content collected from Wikisource. Next, regular expressions were used to remove leftover markup information, such as in-text metadata, formatting, or HTML tags, and to normalize some atypical characters. Accordingly, diacritical marks were removed from letter characters not belonging to the Polish alphabet, and non-ASCII variants of standard letter characters of the Latin alphabet were replaced by their ASCII counterparts. Finally, the same method was used to remove dialogue-specific text formatting and punctuation in paragraphs consisting of dialogue utterances, such as quotation dashes or character cues.

3.2 Alignment

To create aligned paragraph data, we first automatically matched all editions of novels existing across both data sources using fuzzy information similarity for author and title metadata. We then narrowed the matches to those that contained at least one edition in each of the sources.

Next, for each match of all editions of a novel, the oldest edition from Wikisource and the most recent edition from WolneLektury were identified using metadata information. Subsequently, the text paragraphs of both editions were extracted and aligned using the Hunalign tool, version 1.1 (Varga et al., 2005). Specifically, it was used to automatically create paragraph pairs consisting of a given text fragment with historical spelling from the oldest edition of a novel and the same text fragment but with contemporized spelling found in its newer edition, optionally automatically joining or splitting paragraphs where it was applicable. The paragraph alignment quality metric returned by Hunalign was consulted to provide additional filtering. The average alignment quality score across the entire text contents for each edition pair was used to identify and discard very low-scoring edition pairs, which turned out to be Polish translations of foreign novels made by different translators. In turn, per-paragraph alignment quality scores below 1.0 were used as an indicator to discard singular misaligned paragraphs.

3.3 Dataset creation

After completing all of the above steps and performing deduplication at the very end, we obtained a final corpus of 248,645 paragraph pairs originating from 87 eligible pairs of matched novel editions. Four dataset variants were created with this as the basis. All variants involve a training and test split, but they differ in the following two respects:

Pruning was either applied or not. *Pruned* versions of the dataset are reduced in size by removing samples in which the paragraphs of the pair are identical. Applying pruning leads to a 64.83% decrease in the number of samples, a 47.34% decrease in the number of words, and a 47.23% decrease in the number of characters.

Separation of novels prior to the train/test split was either performed or not. In *separated* variants of the dataset, train and test sets are created from separate pools of novels with no overlap, so that all paragraphs from a given novel are contained in only one of the sets. Four novels were sampled from each of the quartiles determined with respect to the number of paragraphs contained in the corpus, to guarantee that each data subset contained a balanced volume of text. In the case of *non-separated* variants, the paragraphs are randomly sampled from the entire set of novels following the standard 80%/20% sampling ratio for train/test splits.

4 Experiments

4.1 Rule-based model

Our first solution to the problem of diachronic normalization relies on a set of deterministic rules. Henceforth, we will refer to this solution as *Transducers*. The rules were handcrafted initially and then adjusted semi-automatically. They were created mostly based on the expert literature describing changes in the Polish spelling system and by looking at a list of similar words having close embeddings. For most of the work on the rules, datasets for supervised learning were not consulted. Originally, the rules were written using the Thrax language (Tai et al., 2011) for defining transducer grammars, but more recently have been rewritten into a Java code base with normalization rules encoded using regular expressions. For instance, the rule:

```
Rule(
    "([cs]|(?:\\A|(?<![cdsr]))z)
     y([aąeęiou])",
    "$1j$2")
```

handles normalization of *y* into *i* in some circumstances (e.g. *decyzya* into *decyzja*). The decision to switch to Java was motivated by the fact that such a module can be easily incorporated, as a plugin, into Java-based open-source search engines (Lucene and Solr). When writing the rules, a conservative approach was taken: a rule was added only when the probability of unwanted changes to texts was very low. Apart from regular expressions, the rule-based solution uses a dictionary of transformations for specific words and dictionaries of exceptions, based on the ideas outlined in (Graliński and Jassem, 2020). The *Transducers* module also handles some OCR errors, but the coverage is rather low (only high-precision rules were applied).

Some further examples of the rules used are included in appendix A.

4.2 Neural normalization models

Diachronic normalization is an example of a language processing task that accepts text at the input and returns text at the output. Therefore, we decided to use the text-to-text transfer transformer architecture (T5, Raffel et al., 2020) as a basis for our supervised normalization models. Initial weights were taken from the pre-trained plT5 model (Chrabrowa et al., 2022), an encoder-decoder model that follows the T5 architecture. The plT5 model was initialized from its multilingual counterpart (mT5, Xue et al., 2021) and further trained on Polish language corpora. It achieves better performance than mT5 on Polish language benchmark tasks with a smaller number of parameters. For our experiments, we used the largest variant of this model available at Hugging Face.[1]

We finetuned four neural diachronic normalization models, with one model for each variant of our dataset. The models were trained for three epochs, using Adam as the optimizer and a learning rate of 5e-05 with a linear scheduler. The batch size was kept at 1 due to the memory limitations of the GPU used for the experiments. Maximum input and output sequence token lengths followed the T5 model family's default of 512. Longer input sequences were split into chunks of maximum length, processed separately, and then joined.

Table 2 reports the results of the evaluation of the neural normalization models, and compares them with the rule-based model. One may observe that the rule-based model is a strong baseline for

[1] `https://huggingface.co/allegro/plt5-large`

Pruning	Separation	Split samples		Characters	Words
		Train	Test		
No	No	198,916	49,729	92,306,901	14,438,223
Yes	No	69,952	17,488	48,710,393	7,603,573
No	Yes	199,004	49,641	92,306,901	14,438,223
Yes	Yes	63,921	23,519	48,710,393	7,603,573

Table 1: Dataset statistics

Method	Pruning	Separation	CER	WER
Transducers	No	No	**0.0164**	**0.0466**
Neural	No	No	0.0488	0.0654
Transducers	Yes	No	**0.0319**	**0.0827**
Neural	Yes	No	0.0728	0.1011
Transducers	No	Yes	**0.0182**	**0.0560**
Neural	No	Yes	0.0632	0.0932
Transducers	Yes	Yes	**0.0281**	0.0844
Neural	Yes	Yes	0.0398	**0.0737**

Table 2: Evaluation results

the task, outperforming the neural models with respect to character error rate (CER) and word error rate (WER). However, the supervised model surpasses the rule-based solution in the case of a test set that consists of a separate set of novels (*Separation=Yes*) and excludes samples that should remain unmodified in the normalization process (*Pruning=Yes*).

5 Discussion

After performing a qualitative analysis of the results obtained using rule-based and neural normalization models, we observed for the neural networks: (1) flexibility in context interpretation, i.e., the ability to adapt to various contexts and understand linguistic nuances; (2) recognition of irregular patterns, i.e., the ability to identify and process non-standard and complex language forms; (3) context-based changes, i.e., considering a broad context, which can lead to changes that go beyond simple spelling rules. On the other hand, for rule-based normalization, it was noted that: (1) relying on specific, defined rules, i.e., focusing on the strict application of established spelling rules, *Transducers* are less flexible in interpretation, meaning that they have limited abilities to cope with irregularities and linguistic nuances; (2) *Transducers* follow a literal interpretation of rules, which may not take into account the full context. The neural approach effectively normalizes examples of former single-word spelling, especially for conjunctions: *przyczem* → *przy czym* (Eng. *at the same time*), *poczem* → *po czym* (Eng. *thereafter*), *napewno* → *na pewno* (Eng. *certainly*), *niema* → *nie ma* (Eng. *there is no*). The rule-based approach, in turn, aptly converts regular orthographic phenomena: *egzystencya* → *egzystencja* (Eng. *existence*), *jenerał* → *generał* (Eng. *general*), *teorya* → *teoria* (Eng. *theory*). It also accurately transforms proper nouns: *Anglja* → *Anglia*, *Marjetka* → *Marietka*. The spelling changes – from *egzystencya* to *egzystencja*, *Anglja* to *Anglia*, etc. – were part of the Polish orthographic reform of 1936. This reform was aimed at simplifying and standardizing the Polish language's spelling. It introduced several changes, including the replacement of the letter 'y' with 'j' or 'i' in certain contexts, and the introduction of the letter 'j' in place of 'i' in some cases to better reflect pronunciation. This reform significantly influenced the modern Polish language, aligning it more closely with its phonetics.

6 Conclusion

This paper has discussed two approaches to the diachronic normalization of Polish texts. We presented *Transducers*, a rule-based solution that relies on a set of deterministic, handcrafted rules, and a family of neural normalization models based on a text-to-text transfer transformer architecture. The experiments that we conducted showed that the rule-based approach is effective in the diachronic normalization task. However, the neural model surpassed the rule-based solution in the case of a test set that consists of a separate set of novels and excludes samples that should remain unchanged in the normalization process.

As the presented research is preliminary in nature, there are several promising directions to explore, which we are committed to doing in the near future. Among other ideas, we want to test the performance of hybrid solutions combining both approaches in distinct ways. We are also considering testing different model architectures and conducting further work on improving the quality of the training data used for the neural approach, as we believe it has the potential to eventually surpass the rule-based solution in most typical scenarios.

Limitations

We restrict our attention to the diachronic normalization of Polish texts. Generalizing the proposed methods to new languages will require, firstly, a new, handcrafted set of normalization rules being developed for the rule-based model presented in section 4.1; and secondly, a parallel corpus of texts that encompass both historical and current spelling, for the neural normalization models discussed in section 4.2.

Acknowledgments

The diachronic normalization methods presented in this work have been developed as part of the „Tools for text normalization and diachronic analysis" module of the Dariah.lab[2] infrastructure hosted at the Faculty of Mathematics and Computer Science of Adam Mickiewicz University in Poznań, Poland. Construction of Dariah.lab was the aim of the project: *Digital Research Infrastructure for the Arts and Humanities DARIAH-PL*, funded by the Intelligent Development Operational Programme, Polish National Centre for Research and Development, ID: POIR.04.02.00-00-D006/20.

[2] `https://lab.dariah.pl/en/project/about-project/`

References

Dawn Archer, Andrea Ernst-Gerlach, Sebastian Kempken, Thomas Pilz, and Paul Rayson. 2006. The identification of spelling variants in English and German historical texts: manual or automatic? In *Digital Humanities 2006. Paris, France: CATI, Université Paris-Sorbonne.*

Alistair Baron, Paul Rayson, and Dawn Archer. 2009. Automatic standardization of spelling for historical text mining. In *Digital Humanities 2009.*

Marcel Bollmann. 2019. A large-scale comparison of historical text normalization systems. In *Proceedings of the 2019 Conference of the North American Chapter of the Association for Computational Linguistics: Human Language Technologies, Volume 1 (Long and Short Papers)*, pages 3885–3898, Minneapolis, Minnesota. Association for Computational Linguistics.

Marcel Bollmann, Florian Petran, and Stephanie Dipper. 2011. Rule-based normalization of historical texts. In *Proceedings of the International Workshop on Language Technologies for Digital Humanities.*

Marcel Bollmann and Anders Søgaard. 2016. Improving historical spelling normalization with bidirectional LSTMs and multi-task learning. In *Proceedings of COLING 2016, the 26th International Conference on Computational Linguistics: Technical Papers*, pages 131–139, Osaka, Japan. The COLING 2016 Organizing Committee.

Aleksandra Chrabrowa, Łukasz Dragan, Karol Grzegorczyk, Dariusz Kajtoch, Mikołaj Koszowski, Robert Mroczkowski, and Piotr Rybak. 2022. Evaluation of transfer learning for Polish with a text-to-text model. In *Proceedings of the Thirteenth Language Resources and Evaluation Conference*, pages 4374–4394, Marseille, France. European Language Resources Association.

Izaskun Etxeberria, Inaki Alegria, Larraitz Uria, and Mans Hulden. 2016. Evaluating the noisy channel model for the normalization of historical texts: Basque, Spanish and Slovene. In *Proceedings of the Tenth International Conference on Language Resources and Evaluation (LREC-2016).*

Filip Graliński and Krzysztof Jassem. 2020. Mining historical texts for diachronic spelling variants:. *Poznan Studies in Contemporary Linguistics*, 56(4):629–650.

Krzysztof Jassem, Filip Graliński, and Tomasz Obrębski. 2017. Pros and Cons of Normalizing Text with Thrax. In *Proceedings of the 8th Language and Technology Conference. Human Language Technologies as a Challenge for Computer Science and Linguistics.*

Krzysztof Jassem, Filip Graliński, Tomasz Obrębski, and Piotr Wierzchoń. 2018. Automatic diachronic normalization of polish texts. *Investigationes Linguisticae*, 37:17–33.

Modern Poland Foundation. 2023. About the Project. https://wolnelektury.pl/info/o-projekcie/. Accessed: 2023-12-16.

Csaba Oravecz, Balint Sass, and Eszter Simon. 2010. Semi-automatic normalization of Old Hungarian codices. In *Proceedings of the ECAI 2010 Workshop on Language Technology for Cultural Heritage, Social Sciences, and Humanities (LaTeCH 2010)*.

Eva Pettersson, Beata Megyesi, and Joakim Nivre. 2012. Rule-based normalisation of historical text – a diachronic study. In *Empirical Methods in Natural Language Processing: Proceedings of the 11th Conference on Natural Language Processing (KONVENS 2012)*.

Jordi Porta, Jose-Luis Sancho, and Javier Gomez. 2013. Edit transducers for spelling variation in Old Spanish. In *Proceedings of the workshop on computational historical linguistics at NODALIDA*.

Colin Raffel, Noam Shazeer, Adam Roberts, Katherine Lee, Sharan Narang, Michael Matena, Yanqi Zhou, Wei Li, and Peter J. Liu. 2020. Exploring the limits of transfer learning with a unified text-to-text transformer. *J. Mach. Learn. Res.*, 21(1).

Paul Rayson, Dawn Archer, Alistair Baron, and Nicholas Smith. 2007. Tagging historical corpora – the problem of spelling variation. In *Dagstuhl Seminar Proceedings. Schloss Dagstuhl-Leibniz-Zentrum fur Informatik*.

Martin Reynaert, Iris Hendrickx, and Rita Marquilhas. 2012. Historical spelling normalization. a comparison of two statistical methods: Ticcl and vard2. In *Proceedings of the Second Workshop on Annotation of Corpora for Research in the Humanities (ACRH-2), Lisbon*, pages 87–98. Edicoes Colibri.

Alexander Robertson and Sharon Goldwater. 2018. Evaluating historical text normalization systems: How well do they generalize? In *Proceedings of the 2018 Conference of the North American Chapter of the Association for Computational Linguistics: Human Language Technologies, Volume 2 (Short Papers)*, pages 720–725, New Orleans, Louisiana. Association for Computational Linguistics.

Yves Scherrer and Tomasz Erjavec. 2013. Modernizing historical Slovene words with character-based SMT. In *BSNLP 2013-4th Biennial Workshop on Balto-Slavic Natural Language Processing*.

Richard Sproat and Navdeep Jaitly. 2016. RNN approaches to text normalization: A challenge. *CoRR*, abs/1611.00068.

Terry Tai, Wojciech Skut, and Richard Sproat. 2011. Thrax: An open source grammar compiler built on OpenFst. In *IEEE Automatic Speech Recognition and Understanding Workshop*.

Dániel Varga, László Németh, Péter Halácsy, András Kornai, Viktor Trón, and Viktor Nagy. 2005. Parallel corpora for medium density languages. In *Proceedings of the RANLP 2005*, pages 590–596.

Wikimedia Foundation. 2023. About Wikisource. https://wikisource.org/wiki/Wikisource:About_Wikisource. Accessed: 2023-12-16.

Linting Xue, Noah Constant, Adam Roberts, Mihir Kale, Rami Al-Rfou, Aditya Siddhant, Aditya Barua, and Colin Raffel. 2021. mT5: A massively multilingual pre-trained text-to-text transformer. In *Proceedings of the 2021 Conference of the North American Chapter of the Association for Computational Linguistics: Human Language Technologies*, pages 483–498, Online. Association for Computational Linguistics.

A Appendix

Here we present further examples of rules used in the rule-based diachronic normalization solution.

```
Rule("izk", "isk")
Rule("yja\\b", "ja")
Rule("(le|ó)dz\\Z", "$1c")
Rule("\\Aanti-?", "anty")
Rule("iemi\\Z", "imi")
Rule("emi\\Z", "ymi")
Rule(
   "(ąc|owan|yjn|owat|jsz|tyczn|logiczn)
   em\\Z",
   "$1ym")
Rule(
   "([dfglmnprt])[jy]([aąeęiou])",
   "$1i$2")
```

Enriching the Metadata of Community-Generated Digital Content through Entity Linking: An Evaluative Comparison of State-of-the-Art Models

Youcef Benkhedda[*,1], **Adrians Skapars**[*,1], **Viktor Schlegel**[1,2],
Goran Nenadic[1] and **Riza Batista-Navarro**[1]
[1]Department of Computer Science, University of Manchester, UK
[2]ASUS Intelligent Cloud Services (AICS), Singapore
youcef.benkhedda@manchester.ac.uk, adrians.skapars@postgrad.manchester.ac.uk,
viktor_schlegel@asus.com, {gnenadic,riza.batista}@manchester.ac.uk

Abstract

Digital archive collections that have been contributed by communities, known as community-generated digital content (CGDC), are important sources of historical and cultural knowledge. However, CGDC items are not easily searchable due to semantic information being obscured within their textual metadata. In this paper, we investigate the extent to which state-of-the-art, general-domain entity linking (EL) models (i.e., BLINK, EPGEL and mGENRE) can map named entities mentioned in CGDC textual metadata, to Wikidata entities. We evaluate and compare their performance on an annotated dataset of CGDC textual metadata and provide some error analysis, in the way of informing future studies aimed at enriching CGDC metadata using entity linking methods.

1 Introduction

Community-generated digital content (CGDC) pertains to digital-born archive collections that have been developed by communities. In the UK, for instance, libraries and museums such as the Morrab Library in Cornwall[1] and the Sherborne Museum in Dorset[2] employ volunteers to catalogue their archive collections, consisting of historic photographs and papers, respectively. Since 1994, the UK National Lottery Heritage Fund has awarded grants to around 5000 community history projects,[3] leading to the proliferation of CGDC.

Encapsulating the collective experiences and narratives of communities over time, such collections serve as indispensable sources of knowledge, offering a window into the past that deepens our understanding of human history and culture (Konstantelos et al., 2019). However, despite their important role in enhancing people's appreciation of their heritage, CGDC items remain hard to find (Hanna et al., 2021). This can be attributed to the fact that semantic information on CGDC items tends to be buried within their textual metadata, e.g., titles and descriptions, making it difficult to search for and link items related to a given query. Such a challenge can be potentially overcome by enriching CGDC metadata using natural language processing (NLP) methods. As a first step, for example, named entity recognition (NER) can be employed to automatically label the names of any entities mentioned within a piece of text (Humbel et al., 2021; Jehangir et al., 2023). This is often followed by entity linking (EL), a task concerned with normalising name variants (e.g., the canonical and vernacular names of a place) to the same real-world entity (Oliveira et al., 2021); typically, this is implemented as a disambiguation task where a unique identifier (denoting an entity) used within a knowledge base, is assigned to a given named entity.

In this paper, we focus on assessing the performance of state-of-the-art EL models on CGDC textual metadata. These models have demonstrated impressive EL performance in the general domain, e.g., on the task of Wikification which involves linking entities within text to Wikipedia (Moro et al., 2014). CGDC metadata, however, are not as well-formed as general-domain texts such as news articles, mainly due to the fact that there are no established standards that require communities to write their textual metadata in a consistent way. For instance, many CGDC descriptions are short, consisting only of phrases rather than full sentences; misspellings and obsolete names are also commonplace. We thus aim to evaluate how well existing state-of-the-art models perform on CGDC textual metadata and analyse cases on which these models tend to fail. This will help researchers working in the areas of digital humanities and cultural analytics in identifying ways on how existing EL approaches can be adapted or optimised for CGDC.

[*]These authors contributed equally to this work.
[1]https://morrablibrary.org.uk/
[2]https://www.sherbornemuseum.com/
[3]https://www.heritagefund.org.uk/our-work/museums-libraries-and-archives

Proceedings of LaTeCH-CLfL 2024, pages 213–220

To the best of our knowledge, ours is the first work to explore EL for CGDC. The handful of efforts that employed EL on archive collections focussed mostly on historical newspapers (Labusch and Neudecker, 2020; Ehrmann et al., 2020; Linhares Pontes et al., 2022; Hamdi et al., 2021), specific centuries (Brando et al., 2015, 2016) or events such as the Second World War (Heino et al., 2017), but not on CGDC.

2 Dataset

To support our evaluation of state-of-the-art entity linking models, we set out to develop our own annotated dataset of CGDC textual metadata.

2.1 Data Collection

We collected textual metadata written in English for items in the following CGDC archives:

Spratton Local History Society Collection (Spratton). Based in the village of Spratton, Northamptonshire in the UK, the Spratton Local History Society[4] have created web pages containing short biographies of Spratton men who served in the First World War.

National Lottery Heritage Fund (NLHF) Archives. Various community projects that were given grants by the UK NLHF have created web pages documenting the lives of people relevant to the history of the communities. These include: Vale People First,[5] The Friends of Hemingfield Colliery,[6] Dorset Ancestors,[7] Farnhill World War I Volunteers[8] and The Haringey First World War Peace Forum.[9]

The Morrab Library Photographic Archive (Morrab). This archive[10] contains over 15,000 digitised photographs capturing Cornish history and culture. Each photograph comes with textual metadata such as title and description.

People's Collection Wales (PCW). PCW[11] is an online platform that allows individuals, community groups and small museums/libraries to contribute items pertaining to Welsh culture and history, including photographs, documents, and audio and video recordings. For each of the more than 150K items in PCW, a title and a description are provided.

We sampled 20 items from the Spratton collection, 25 from the NLHF archives, 50 from the Morrab collection and 50 from PCW. Based on these items, we created the documents that comprise our CGDC dataset. In the case of the Spratton and NLHF subsets, each document contains the title and full text of a web page. Meanwhile, each document in the Morrab and PCW subsets consists of the concatenation of the title and description of the corresponding item.

2.2 Data Annotation

The documents in our collected data were labelled according to the two types of annotations described below, with the help of the brat[12] rapid annotation tool (Stenetorp et al., 2012).

Annotation of Named Entities. The span and semantic type of any named entity that falls under any of the following types were annotated: `Person (Per)`, `Organisation (Org)`, `Location (Loc)`, `Miscellaneous (Misc)` and `Date`.

Annotation of Entity Links. All annotated named entities (except those that were given the `Date` label[13]) were linked to their unique identifiers in Wikidata.[14] If an entity cannot be found in Wikidata, it was linked to the NIL entity.

Guidelines (an overview of which is provided in Appendix A) were prepared, outlining details of the annotation task. Following these guidelines, one annotator labelled all 145 documents in our CGDC dataset. To allow for assessment of reliability of their annotations, a second annotator independently labelled a subset of 20 documents.

Based on the work of the two annotators, we measured inter-annotator agreement (IAA) for each of the two annotation types. When it comes to the annotation of named entities, an IAA of 74.8% in terms of F1-score was obtained. Taking only the named entities whose spans were labelled in the same way by both annotators, we measured IAA with respect to the annotation of entity links. The IAA in terms of Cohen's Kappa (Cohen, 1960) is

[4]http://www.sprattonhistory.org/

[5]https://www.valepeoplefirst.org.uk/dejavu/

[6]https://hemingfieldcolliery.org/people-lives-and-loss/

[7]https://dorset-ancestors.com/

[8]http://www.farnhill.co.uk/volunteers/articles/articles-people/

[9]https://hfwwpf.wordpress.com/

[10]https://photoarchive.morrablibrary.org.uk/

[11]https://www.peoplescollection.wales/

[12]https://brat.nlplab.org/

[13]In our study, temporal expressions are not considered to be real-world entities that need to be linked to Wikidata.

[14]https://www.wikidata.org/wiki/Wikidata:Main_Page

77.79%, which is considered to be substantial (Landis and Koch, 1977). The labels provided by the second author of this paper serve as gold standard annotations.

The 45 annotated documents in the Spratton and NLHF subsets were held out and were used to identify the values of parameters that need to be configured to run the EL models that we selected for comparison (described in the next section). Meanwhile, the annotated documents in the Morrab and PCW subsets (100 overall) were considered as test data, forming the basis of the evaluation of the performance of the chosen EL models.[15] Table 3 in Appendix B summarises the number of named entities per type in the said test data.

3 Problem Formulation and Models

We first provide a formal definition of the EL task: given a target knowledge base containing a set of entities E and a textual document in which a set of named entities N have been identified, an EL model maps each $n \in N$ to the corresponding entity $e \in E$ in the knowledge base. If the entity that n corresponds to does not exist in E, then n is considered to be unlinkable and is thus linked to a NIL entity. In our work, the context in which n appears is also provided as input (together with n itself) and the target knowledge base is Wikidata.

Three state-of-the-art EL models were investigated in this study. For a given named entity (NE), each of the models predicts the best matching entity in the knowledge base that it should be linked to by specifying its identifier (ID) together with a similarity score, if it is linkable; otherwise, it is linked to NIL.

BLINK. This model (Wu et al., 2020) employs BERT-based architectures (Devlin et al., 2019) for two subtasks: retrieving candidate entities by encoding the context containing an NE and the definitions of candidate entities in Wikipedia, and ranking the candidates. Its predicted Wikipedia IDs are mapped to Wikidata IDs.

Entity Profile Generation for Entity Linking (EPGEL). This model (Lai, 2022) makes use of the BART sequence-to-sequence model (Lewis et al., 2020) and a dictionary-based method to generate a "profile", i.e., a title and description, for a given NE based on the context in which it appears. These profiles are then used to retrieve candidate matching entities within Wikidata.

Multilingual Generative Entity Retrieval (mGENRE). Unlike the two models above, mGENRE (De Cao et al., 2022) is capable of linking named entities to a multilingual knowledge base. It employs a pre-trained multilingual BART model that takes an NE and auto-regressively generates its Wikipedia name, which is then mapped to the corresponding Wikidata ID.

In order to identify what configuration of the above models should be used in applying them on our CGDC test data, we utilised our held-out data to determine: (1) how much context should be provided as input to the model together with an NE, and (2) the threshold for the similarity score, whereby an NE is linked to NIL if the similarity score of its top-matching candidate is lower than the threshold. We observed that for all models, providing the sentence immediately preceding and succeeding the sentence containing a given NE, leads to optimal results. Meanwhile, the following values were found to be ideal similarity thresholds: 0.7, 0.8 and 0.4 for BLINK, EPGEL and mGENRE, respectively.

4 Results and Discussion

The models were applied to the gold standard `Person`, `Organisation`, `Location` and `Miscellaneous` NEs in our CGDC test set, i.e., the Morrab and PCW subsets. It is worth noting that we utilised each of the chosen EL models out-of-the-box, i.e., without extending their functionality. All models make use of the text span of a given NE in their analysis, but none of them consider the NE type as a feature, although it is available as part of the input to EL.

A preliminary check was performed to detect `Person` NEs that contain only one token; such NEs were automatically given NIL as their ID, as our preliminary experimentation with the held-out dataset showed that the three EL models are unlikely to be able to correctly disambiguate them.

4.1 Evaluation Metrics

EL performance is typically evaluated in terms of accuracy, i.e., the number of correctly linked NEs over the total number of NEs in the evaluation data. Taking inspiration from the work of Zhu et al.

[15] Our annotations, provided in the standoff format supported by the brat tool, are available for download at https://github.com/OurHeritageOurStories/cgdc_annotations.

NE Type	Model	Non-NAC	NAC	OAC
Per	BLINK	0.412	0.782	0.735
	EPGEL	**0.588**	0.681	0.669
	mGENRE	0.389	**0.925**	**0.855**
Org	BLINK	0.694	0.000	0.426
	EPGEL	**0.895**	0.444	0.720
	mGENRE	0.772	**0.946**	**0.840**
Loc	BLINK	0.808	0.000	0.652
	EPGEL	**0.795**	0.524	**0.743**
	mGENRE	0.708	**0.746**	0.716
Misc	BLINK	**0.750**	0.000	0.488
	EPGEL	0.714	0.357	0.595
	mGENRE	0.607	**1.000**	**0.738**
ALL	BLINK	0.767	0.392	0.621
	EPGEL	**0.795**	0.582	0.712
	mGENRE	0.695	**0.885**	**0.769**

Table 1: EL results on the test data according to named entity (NE) type. Key: Non-NAC = non-NIL accuracy; NAC = NIL accuracy; OAC = overall accuracy.

(2023), we report the performance of the three EL models according to three types of accuracy: (1) non-NIL accuracy (Non-NAC), which considers only NEs that are linked to Wikidata IDs according to the gold standard; (2) NIL accuracy, which considers only unlinkable NEs, i.e., those that are linked to NIL, according to the gold standard; and (3) overall accuracy (OAC), which considers all NEs regardless of whether they are linked to Wikidata IDs according to the gold standard or not.

Table 1 presents the performance of each of the models for each NE type and for the entire CGDC test data (ALL). Overall, EPGEL is best at predicting the IDs of linkable NEs. However, mGENRE is much better at identifying unlinkable (NIL) named entities, which are quite common in CGDC collections as many entities described in such collections are known only to local communities and thus do not have Wikidata entries. This positively impacted overall accuracy, leading to mGENRE obtaining optimal performance on the entire test set. The same trend can be observed for every NE type, except for the Loc type, where EPGEL obtained the best overall performance. A similar observation can be made when considering the performance of the models on each of the CGDC subsets that comprise the test data (see Table 4 in Appendix C).

4.2 Error Analysis

In Table 2, we provide examples of NEs that were wrongly linked by any of the three EL models, highlighting cases within CGDC that led to erroneous predictions. Firstly, lesser-known NEs that coincidentally share names with other entities pose a challenge to all models. For instance, the unlinkable NE *"Constance Amelia Browne"* was linked to *"Q75857857: Constance Browne"*, a member of the British peerage, by EPGEL (Example 1); *"Sir James Jebusa Shannon"* was linked to a painting with a similar name, *"Q28051261: James Jebusa Shannon"*, by BLINK (Example 2). All models wrongly linked *"Morrison Road"* to a road in Australia with the same name (Example 3).

A case that was found difficult by mGENRE in particular is Example 4. It wrongly linked *"Duenna"*, a play, to *"Q1519901: chaperone"*, as *"dueña"* happens to be a synonym for *"chaperone"* in Spanish.

All models seem to struggle to correctly link obsolete names (i.e., names that entities were formerly known as). An example of this is *"County Club hotel"* which is the old name of the entity *"Q1045316: Kings Head Hotel"* (Example 5). Both BLINK and EPGEL linked it to the wrong entity, while mGENRE considered it to be unlinkable and thus linked it to NIL.

4.3 Potential Applications

In this work, we have demonstrated the linking of NEs within CGDC textual metadata to Wikidata, a centralised knowledge base containing structured information on entities and concepts. In this way, our approach has a strong potential to improve the searchability of CGDC items. In the current scenario in which CGDC is made available by communities, a historian might struggle to find CGDC items that are described in their metadata using a vernacular name of a place, for instance. Mapping entities to Wikidata (or any other relevant knowledge base) will enable finding of such items, as all name variants of the same entity will have been assigned the same identifier by an EL model.

Currently, CGDC items collected by different archives or communities are siloed: they are findable only within a community's own catalogue or archive, but not across different archives. Linking CGDC textual metadata to a central knowledge base (Wikidata) via EL will make it possible to create a knowledge graph whereby CGDC items are linked based on the identified entities that they contain. This, in turn, will support seamless searching for CGDC items that pertain to particular entities of interest. Ideally, such a knowledge graph would be editable, allowing for human-in-the-loop data curation whereby human contributors can correct any erroneous identifiers assigned by EL models.

	NE with Context	NE Type	Gold Std.	BLINK	EPGEL	mGENRE
1	**Constance Amelia Browne** was the maternal...	Per	NIL	NIL	Q75857857: Constance Browne	NIL
2	The Bathers/ **Sir James Jebusa Shannon/** 1900-23...	Per	Q731056: James Jebusa Shannon	Q28051261: Sir James Jebusa Shannon	Q731056: James Jebusa Shannon	Q731056: James Jebusa Shannon
3	Sandfields Branch Library, **Morrison Road**,...	Loc	NIL	Q6914046: Morrison Road	Q6914046: Morrison Road	Q6914046: Morrison Road
4	...Theatre Playbill, Advertising the play **Duenna**, to be staged at...	Misc	Q7731154: The Duenna	Q7731154: The Duenna	NIL	Q1519901: chaperone
5	...outside the old **County Club hotel** (a hospital), now...	Loc	Q1045316: Kings Head Hotel	Q6772978: London Marriott Hotel County Hall	Q55782270: Club Hotel	NIL

Table 2: Example input named entities (in bold) and context for which any of the three EL models produced erroneous predictions (shown in grey). The full context for each example can be found in Appendix D.

5 Conclusion and Future Work

In this paper, we present the results of evaluating BLINK, EPGEL and mGENRE— three of the state-of-the-art, general-domain entity linking models— on an annotated dataset of CGDC textual metadata. Our evaluation shows that mGENRE obtains superior performance overall and on unlinkable (NIL) named entities more specifically, which tend to be prevalent in CGDC. Our future work will focus on handling cases that make CGDC textual metadata particularly challenging, e.g., lesser-known named entities and obsolete names, and on combining the strengths of EPGEL and mGENRE in predicting IDs for linkable and unlinkable named entities, respectively. Furthermore, we will investigate how the performance of these models can be enhanced by making them leverage the NE type of any given named entity as a semantic feature that can inform the EL process.

Acknowledgement

This work was supported by the Arts and Humanities Research Council [grant number AH/W00321X/1 – Our Heritage, Our Stories: Linking and searching community-generated digital content to develop the people's national collection].

References

Carmen Brando, Francesca Frontini, and Jean-Gabriel Ganascia. 2015. Disambiguation of named entities in cultural heritage texts using linked data sets. In *New Trends in Databases and Information Systems: ADBIS 2015 Short Papers and Workshops, BigDap, DCSA, GID, MEBIS, OAIS, SW4CH, WISARD, Poitiers, France, September 8-11, 2015. Proceedings*, pages 505–514. Springer.

Carmen Brando, Francesca Frontini, and Jean-Gabriel Ganascia. 2016. REDEN: named entity linking in digital literary editions using linked data sets. *Complex Systems Informatics and Modeling Quarterly*, (7):60–80.

Jacob Cohen. 1960. A coefficient of agreement for nominal scales. *Educational and psychological measurement*, 20(1):37–46.

Nicola De Cao, Ledell Wu, Kashyap Popat, Mikel Artetxe, Naman Goyal, Mikhail Plekhanov, Luke Zettlemoyer, Nicola Cancedda, Sebastian Riedel, and Fabio Petroni. 2022. Multilingual autoregressive entity linking. *Transactions of the Association for Computational Linguistics*, 10:274–290.

Jacob Devlin, Ming-Wei Chang, Kenton Lee, and Kristina Toutanova. 2019. BERT: Pre-training of Deep Bidirectional Transformers for Language Understanding. In *Proceedings of the 2019 Conference of the North American Chapter of the Association for Computational Linguistics: Human Language Technologies, Volume 1 (Long and Short Papers)*, pages 4171–4186, Minneapolis, Minnesota. Association for Computational Linguistics.

Maud Ehrmann, Matteo Romanello, Alex Flückiger, and Simon Clematide. 2020. Overview of CLEF HIPE 2020: Named entity recognition and linking on historical newspapers. In *Experimental IR Meets Multilinguality, Multimodality, and Interaction: 11th International Conference of the CLEF Association, CLEF 2020, Thessaloniki, Greece, September 22–25, 2020, Proceedings 11*, pages 288–310. Springer.

Ahmed Hamdi, Elvys Linhares Pontes, Emanuela Boros, Thi Tuyet Hai Nguyen, Günter Hackl, Jose G Moreno, and Antoine Doucet. 2021. A multilingual dataset for named entity recognition, entity linking and stance detection in historical newspapers. In *Proceedings of the 44th International ACM SIGIR Conference on Research and Development in Information Retrieval*, pages 2328–2334.

Emma Hanna, Lorna M. Hughes, Lucy Noakes, Catriona Pennell, and James Wallis. 2021. Reflections on the Centenary of the First World War: Learning and Legacies for the Future. Technical report, Arts and Humanities Research Council (AHRC).

Erkki Heino, Minna Tamper, Eetu Mäkelä, Petri Leskinen, Esko Ikkala, Jouni Tuominen, Mikko Koho, and Eero Hyvönen. 2017. Named entity linking in a complex domain: Case second world war history. In *Language, Data, and Knowledge: First International Conference, LDK 2017, Galway, Ireland, June 19-20, 2017, Proceedings 1*, pages 120–133. Springer.

Marco Humbel, Julianne Nyhan, Andreas Vlachidis, Kim Sloan, and Alexandra Ortolja-Baird. 2021. Named-entity recognition for early modern textual documents: a review of capabilities and challenges with strategies for the future. *Journal of Documentation*, 77(6):1223–1247.

Basra Jehangir, Saravanan Radhakrishnan, and Rahul Agarwal. 2023. A survey on Named Entity Recognition — datasets, tools, and methodologies. *Natural Language Processing Journal*, 3:100017.

Leo Konstantelos, Lorna Hughes, and William Kilbride. 2019. The Bits Liveth Forever? Digital Preservation and the First World War Commemoration. Technical report, IWM War and Conflict Subject Network.

Kai Labusch and Clemens Neudecker. 2020. Named Entity Disambiguation and Linking Historic Newspaper OCR with BERT. In *CLEF (Working Notes)*.

Ngoc Lai. 2022. LMN at SemEval-2022 task 11: A transformer-based system for English named entity recognition. In *Proceedings of the 16th International Workshop on Semantic Evaluation (SemEval-2022)*, pages 1438–1443, Seattle, United States. Association for Computational Linguistics.

J. Richard Landis and Gary G. Koch. 1977. The Measurement of Observer Agreement for Categorical Data. *Biometrics*, 33(1):159–174.

Mike Lewis, Yinhan Liu, Naman Goyal, Marjan Ghazvininejad, Abdelrahman Mohamed, Omer Levy, Veselin Stoyanov, and Luke Zettlemoyer. 2020. BART: Denoising sequence-to-sequence pre-training for natural language generation, translation, and comprehension. In *Proceedings of the 58th Annual Meeting of the Association for Computational Linguistics*, pages 7871–7880, Online. Association for Computational Linguistics.

Elvys Linhares Pontes, Luis Adrián Cabrera-Diego, Jose G Moreno, Emanuela Boros, Ahmed Hamdi, Antoine Doucet, Nicolas Sidere, and Mickaël Coustaty. 2022. MELHISSA: a multilingual entity linking architecture for historical press articles. *International Journal on Digital Libraries*, pages 1–28.

Andrea Moro, Alessandro Raganato, and Roberto Navigli. 2014. Entity linking meets word sense disambiguation: a unified approach. *Transactions of the Association for Computational Linguistics*, 2:231–244.

Italo L Oliveira, Renato Fileto, René Speck, Luís PF Garcia, Diego Moussallem, and Jens Lehmann. 2021. Towards holistic entity linking: Survey and directions. *Information Systems*, 95:101624.

Pontus Stenetorp, Sampo Pyysalo, Goran Topić, Tomoko Ohta, Sophia Ananiadou, and Jun'ichi Tsujii. 2012. BRAT: a web-based tool for NLP-assisted text annotation. In *Proceedings of the Demonstrations at the 13th Conference of the European Chapter of the Association for Computational Linguistics*, pages 102–107.

Ledell Wu, Fabio Petroni, Martin Josifoski, Sebastian Riedel, and Luke Zettlemoyer. 2020. Scalable Zero-shot Entity Linking with Dense Entity Retrieval. In *Proceedings of the 2020 Conference on Empirical Methods in Natural Language Processing (EMNLP)*, pages 6397–6407, Online. Association for Computational Linguistics.

Fangwei Zhu, Jifan Yu, Hailong Jin, Juanzi Li, Lei Hou, and Zhifang Sui. 2023. Learn to Not Link: Exploring NIL Prediction in Entity Linking. In *Findings of the Association for Computational Linguistics (ACL 2023)*, pages 10846–10860, Toronto, Canada. Association for Computational Linguistics.

A Annotation Guidelines

A.1 Annotation of Named Entities

Any named entity that falls under any of the following entity types should be annotated: `Person`, `Organisation`, `Location`, `Miscellaneous` and `Date`.

`Person:` names of people, e.g., *"Mary"*, *"John Smith"*.

`Organisation:` names of companies, authorities, institutions, agencies, groups of people, e.g., *"Navy"*, *"Home Office"*.

`Location:` names of places, cities, towns, streets, e.g., *"Camden"*, *"Abbey Road"*. Notes:

- depending on the context, the name of a place might be used to refer to an organisation or geo-political entity rather than the place itself, e.g., *"Westminster"* in *"Westminster made the announcement."* In such cases, the name should be annotated as an `Organisation` rather than as a `Location`.
- if the text mentions an address, i.e., a street name immediately followed by its city, the street name and city names should be annotated separately, e.g., *"Princess St"* and *"Manchester"* instead of *"Princess St, Manchester"*.

`Date:` temporal expressions, including both specific and ambiguous mentions of time, e.g., *"December 1950"*, *"early 50s"*, *"previous year"*. If the expression pertains to a range, each constituent temporal expression should be annotated separately, e.g., *"1970"* and *"1980"* instead of *"1970-1980"*.

`Miscellaneous:` a catch-all category for named entities that do not fall under any of the above entity types and yet might be of interest to historians/researchers, e.g., names of warships (e.g., *"Aida Lauro"*), infrastructure (e.g., *"HS2"*), demonyms (e.g., *"French"*). Importantly, this category includes named events, e.g., *"World War II"*.

Handling nested entities. Some sentences might contain nested entities, i.e., an entity within another entity, e.g., *"London"* in *"London Bridge"*. In such cases, only the outer entity, e.g., *"London Bridge"*, should be annotated.

Handing discontinuous entities. Some sentences might contain discontinuous entities, i.e., an entity whose tokens do not appear in one contiguous text span, e.g., *Lord Eskrine* in *"Lord and Lady Eskrine"* and *Battle of Gaza* in *"Battle of Rafa, Gaza and Jerusalem"*. In such cases, the text span should be decomposed into its constituent entities, e.g., *"Lord"* and *"Lady Eskrine"* (`Person` entities); and *"Battle of Rafa"*, *"Gaza"* and *"Jerusalem"* (`Miscellaneous` entities). Note how *"Gaza"* and *"Jerusalem"* were labelled as `Miscellaneous` entities; this is because they were interpreted as pertaining to the *Battle of Gaza* and the *Battle of Jerusalem*, rather than just *"Gaza"* and *"Jerusalem"*.

Handling co-referring expressions. Although a co-referring expression (e.g., *"he"*, *"the company"*) might pertain to a named entity mentioned within the text, we are not annotating coreference in this task so such expressions should simply be ignored.

A.2 Annotation of Entity Links

All annotated named entities should be linked to their Wikidata identifier (by specifying the full URL to the identified item in Wikidata), with the exception of entities that were given the `Date` label. In determining the correct identifier, it is acceptable to make use of any information available within Wikidata, e.g., definitions, synonyms or properties of a candidate item. If an entity cannot be found in Wikidata, the entity should linked to the NIL entity, indicating that it is unlinkable.

B Frequency of Annotations in the CGDC Test Data

NE Type	# Non-NIL NEs	# NIL NEs	# Total NEs
Per	17	119	136
Org	62	39	101
Loc	266	64	330
Misc	28	15	43
TOTAL	373	237	610

Table 3: The number of linkable (non-NIL) named entities (NEs) and unlinkable (NIL) NEs in our CGDC test set, broken down by named entity type.

C Performance of EL Models on CGDC Test Subsets

Test set	Model	Non-NAC	NAC	OAC
Morrab	BLINK	0.720	0.326	0.558
	EPGEL	**0.746**	0.615	0.692
	mGENRE	0.631	**0.912**	**0.747**
PCW	BLINK	0.793	0.432	0.656
	EPGEL	**0.817**	0.569	0.725
	mGENRE	0.726	**0.868**	**0.779**

Table 4: EL results on the CGDC test data, broken down by subset. Key: Non-NAC = non-NIL accuracy; NAC = NIL accuracy; OAC = overall accuracy.

D Further Information on Examples with Wrong EL Predictions

	NE with Full Context	URL of Source Item
1	Constance Browne. **Constance Amelia Browne** was the maternal Aunt of Caldwell. She was born on 10th March 1833 at Market Rasen, Lincolnshire, the eldest daughter of Henry Albert...	`https://photoarchive.morrablibrary.org.uk/items/show/17268`
2	The Bathers/ **Sir James Jebusa Shannon** / 1900-23. Oil painting in the collections of Newport Museum and Art Gallery.	`https://www.peoplescollection.wales/items/28049`
3	Library. Programme for the Official Opening of Sandfields Branch Library, **Morrison Road**, Sandfields in 1961.	`https://www.peoplescollection.wales/items/517688`
4	Penzance Theatre Playbill. Advertising the play **Duenna**, to be staged at the New Theatre, Penzance. Location possibly Chapel Street area.	`https://photoarchive.morrablibrary.org.uk/items/show/15667`
5	VADs, doctors and patients (including many Belgian refugees and Belgian soldiers), outside the old **County Club hotel** (a hospital), now the county library, Beaufort Road, Llandrindod, circa 1915.	`https://www.peoplescollection.wales/items/28537`

Table 5: Full context for each of the examples shown in Table 2 and the URL of the corresponding CGDC item.

Recognising Occupational Titles in German Parliamentary Debates

Johanna Binnewitt
German Federal Institute for Vocational Education and Training, Bonn
johanna.binnewitt@bibb.de

Abstract

The application of text mining methods is becoming more and more popular, not only in Digital Humanities (DH) and Computational Social Sciences (CSS) in general, but also in vocational education and training (VET) research. Employing algorithms offers the possibility to explore corpora that are simply too large for manual methods. However, challenges arise when dealing with abstract concepts like occupations or skills, which are crucial subjects of VET research. Since algorithms require concrete instructions, either in the form of rules or annotated examples, these abstract concepts must be broken down as part of the operationalisation process.

In our paper, we tackle the task of identifying occupational titles in the plenary protocols of the German Bundestag. The primary focus lies in the comparative analysis of two distinct approaches: a dictionary-based method and a BERT fine-tuning approach. Both approaches are compared in a quantitative evaluation and applied to a larger corpus sample. Results indicate comparable precision for both approaches (0.93), but the BERT-based models outperform the dictionary-based approach in terms of recall (0.86 vs. 0.77). Errors in the dictionary-based method primarily stem from the ambiguity of occupational titles (e.g., *baker* as both a surname and a profession) and missing terms in the dictionary. In contrast, the BERT model faces challenges in distinguishing occupational titles from other personal names, such as *mother* or *Christians*.

1 Text Mining in VET research

Thanks to the spread of the internet in general and social media in particular, more and more communication is now taking place in written form. And communication that takes place outside the internet also finds its way into web archives and repositories, for example in the form of minutes or transcripts. Text documents can therefore be a valuable source for (Social Science) research, from which conclusions about social processes and contexts can be derived. The challenge often lies in building bridges between what is said or written and the extra-textual phenomena, i.e. the actual objects of research (see Krippendorff (2019)). In qualitative content analysis, this is done by including a small number of texts in the manual analysis, in which the theoretical concepts are then related to specific text passages, for example using a hermeneutic approach. However, as soon as larger volumes of text are to be analysed, manual methods reach their limits.

Like other disciplines from the social science or humanities, research on the labour market and vocational training deals with fuzzy concepts, such as occupations, skills or job tasks, which are often characterised by the fact that they are defined in an abstract and complex way (Rodrigues et al., 2021, p. 4f.) (Alexopoulos, 2020). As interdisciplinary research field, VET research connects many disciplines, like Social Sciences, Education Sciences, Economics or Psychology, and deals with research questions on apprenticeships, learning designs or labour market needs. Within the intersection of VET research and text mining, many studies analyse skills, competencies or qualifications based on job advertisements as data source (Buchmann et al., 2022; Stops et al., 2020). Recent studies also include training regulations and curricula in the quantitative text analysis (Fischer et al., 2021). In many cases, skills extraction is operationalised by using dictionary-based approaches. Initial approaches are also testing the use of machine learning to recognise skills in job advertisements (Zhang et al., 2022). Khaouja et al. (2021) provide an extensive overview on methods for skills extraction.

Alongside skills, a central concept in VET research is the one of occupation. At first glance, this concept seems easy to grasp, but it harbours various challenges when it comes to (automated)

Proceedings of LaTeCH-CLfL 2024, pages 221–230
March 22, 2024 ©2024 Association for Computational Linguistics

identification of references to occupations in texts. We will use the example of identifying occupational titles automatically in the plenary protocols of the German Bundestag to demonstrate these challenges. The plenary protocols are well suited to this demonstration as they contain around 900,000 speeches, which would be difficult to process manually. The corpus is briefly described in the following section. Section 3 then introduces the concept of occupational titles. Section 4 is devoted to the concrete implementation by describing two different approaches to operationalisation and comparing their results on a small data basis. Section 5 finally describes the application of both operationalisations on a larger data basis in order to compare the varying results. The code is available on GitHub: https://github.com/johannabi/ProfRec_Bundestag

2 Plenary Debates as research object

Parliamentary debates have been in focus for recent research in multiple disciplines, like Political Sciences, Corpus Linguistics or Computational Linguistics. Research interest ranged from network analysis (Padó et al., 2019) over rhetorical analysis (Rehbein et al., 2021) to argument mining (Eide, 2019) or sentiment analysis (Abercrombie and Batista-Navarro, 2020). To our best knowledge, there has not yet been any research in the context of parliamentary debates that has dealt with the identification of personal nouns, i.e. common nouns referring to (groups of) persons, in general or occupational titles in particular. For VET research, the identification of occupational titles in plenary debates could provide valuable insights into how politicians – as representatives of society – talk about certain professions. For example, it could be analysed to what extent the interests of certain professional groups are addressed and asserted in the speeches. Or, for research into inequality and stereotypes, occupational titles could be analysed to determine the extent to which the mention of certain professions within debates on inequality is characterised by stereotypes.

The presented experiments are based on the *Open Discourse* corpus (Richter et al., 2020), but the experiments could also be adopted to other corpora of German parliamentary debates, such as GermaParl (Blaette and Leonhardt, 2023). The Open Discourse corpus was developed by using the transcriptions of plenary sessions that are published by the German parliament in an XML format. In addition to the German-language speech content, the corpus contains metadata such as the date, the legislative period as well as various information on the speaker such as their name or fraction. Documents are separated by speakers and interjections are stored in a different structure. The *Open Discourse* corpus contains 907,644 different speeches from the period 1949 to 2021. Sections 4 and 5 use samples from the *Open Discourse* corpus to show how occupational titles can be automatically identified in the plenary transcripts and what challenges arise in the process. So, in order to better describe these challenges, the following section will first introduce the concept of occupational title.

3 Occupational Titles as research object

From a linguistic point of view, occupational titles are common nouns that represent a subgroup of personal nouns. These in turn are linguistic expressions that refer to individual persons or groups of persons. In this context, both personal and occupational nouns stand in contrast to proper names. While proper names refer to concrete persons, personal and occupational nouns refer to more abstract concepts. In the case of occupational titles, the terms are characterised by the fact that the person or group of persons performs a profession. While other research have already focused on identifying personal nouns in German texts automatically (Sökefeld et al., 2023), the focus on occupational titles as a separate group was only set for the task of classifying Spanish tweet to whether they contain occupational titles. (Miranda-Escalada et al., 2021). Occupational titles can refer to a specific person or group (examples 1 & 2), they can be more generic (example 4 & 5), or they can be attributes of (specific or generic) individuals (example 3).

(1) Mein *Friseur* hat ein Wunder vollbracht.
My *hairdresser* worked a miracle.

(2) Die *Lehrer* an unserer Schule bereiten das Schulfest vor.
The *teachers* of our school are preparing for the school festival.

(3) Der neue Nachbar ist *Tischler*.
The new neighbour is a *carpenter*.

(4) Als *Krankenschwester* musst du heute sehr belastbar sein.
As a *nurse* today, you have to be very resilient.

(5) Ich spreche hier im Namen aller *Busfahrer*.
I am speaking here on behalf of all *bus drivers*.

Further characteristics of occupational titles, which are mainly related to the German language, concern the formation of compounds and gender forms. Since compounding is very productive in German, occupational titles can either be part of other lexemes that do not refer to occupations (as in *Bauernverband* (farmers' association)) or the occupational title can be a specification of another occupational title (as *Versicherungsmaklerin* (insurance broker) being a specification of *Maklerin* (broker)). Productivity of occupational titles in compounds is a first indicator that dictionary-based approaches might be insufficient to identify all occupational title within a text. With regard to the gender forms of occupational titles, dictionary-based approaches can be adapted to the extent that the word list is enriched with masculine, feminine and neutral forms (see section 4.2). As the use of gendered forms and gender-inclusive language can itself be of research interest (see Carla Sökefeld (2021); Damelang and Rückel (2021); Hodel et al. (2017); Horvath et al. (2015)), the correct extraction of all mentioned categories is crucial to avoid bias in subsequent analysis.

Occupational titles can semantically cover different aspects of the profession. In some cases, the activity is emphasised, as in *Dachdecker/in* (roofer), *Lehrer/in* (teacher) or *Verkäufer/in* (salesperson). Other occupational titles originate from the subject that the person deals with during work (*Stahlarbeiter/in* (steelworker), *Immobilienmakler/in* (real estate agent)) or the place where the profession is usually practised (*Grundschullehrer/in* (primary school teacher), *Bankkaufmann/frau* (bank clerk)) (Stooß and Saterdag, 1979; Schierholz et al., 2018). Like many other expressions, occupational titles can also be affected by ambiguities. On the one hand, many (German) surnames originate from traditional professions, such as *Bäcker* (baker), *Müller* (miller) or *Fischer* (fisherman). In example 6, the two meanings of the lexeme *Müller* can be clearly separated from each other, as it belongs to the group of proper names mentioned above and not to the profession of miller. Another type of ambiguity arises particularly with occupational titles that are derived from the verb that describes the activity, such as *Pfleger/in* (caregiver) or *Verkäufer/in* (salesperson) (see example 7). Here, the resolution of the ambiguity between professional and non-professional activity on the basis of a sentence is not always clear. In example 7, however, the lexeme *Verkäufer* refers to the legal meaning of a seller, so that all persons who sell something are meant here, regardless of whether they do so professionally or non-professionally[1]. Finally, another type of ambiguity has emerged from a rather metonymic use of occupational titles. In example 8, the occupational title is used to refer to the business type rather than the person because *beim Bäcker* could also be replaced by *bei der Bäckerei* without changing the meaning of the sentence.

(6) Frau *Müller* kennt sich damit aus.
Ms. Müller knows all about it.

(7) Damit wird ein Vertrag zwischen Käufer und *Verkäufer* geschlossen.
This concludes a contract between buyer and seller.

(8) Beim *Bäcker* um die Ecke gibt es die besten Brötchen.
The bakery around the corner has the best bread rolls.

In addition to these ambiguities, where the textual context – i.e. the sentence – determines whether a particular lexeme is an occupational title, there are other personal nouns where the decision whether it is an occupational title depends heavily on the definition of occupation. As with many concepts in the humanities and social sciences, this definition varies greatly depending on the discipline and the research question being asked. Sailmann (2018) provides a detailed overview of the conceptual history of the profession. Sombart (1959), for example, divides the term into an objective meaning, which focuses on the social function, and a subjective meaning, which emanates from the individual. He defines the social function of occupations very broadly, so that, for example, husband also becomes a profession. In comparison, two other criteria are decisive for Weber: the gainful character of work and a minimum level of qualification required (Weber and Winckelmann, 1985). According to this definition, voluntary activities, such as working as a lay judge, would be excluded from the definition of an occupation. As Weber's definition often forms the basis for occupational statistics today, the operationalisation here will also be based on it.

[1] see also https://www.dwds.de/wb/Verk%C3%A4ufer

4 Operationalising for automatic language processing

After introducing the concept of occupations, this next section will now compare two ways to identify occupational titles automatically, namely a dictionary-based approach and a machine-learning approach. As we have stated above, occupational titles can be affected by ambiguities and lexical productivity, which might make it difficult to apply a simple keyword search (see Widmann and Wich (2023)). Nevertheless, dictionary-based analysis are often applied in DH and CSS, because they are feasible if a dictionary already exists (see Calanca et al. (2019); Stops et al. (2020); Djumalieva et al. (2018)). So, we aim to evaluate such an approach in order to investigate error sources of word lists in a more detailed way. For both approaches, the identification of occupational titles takes place at token level, i.e. for each word in a sentence, the algorithm decides whether it is an occupational title. It is also possible for an occupational title to be represented by a multiword expression, such as *medical assistant*.

4.1 Data Annotation

Since we aim to evaluate both approaches, we need test data as gold standard. Additionally, for the BERT fine-tuning, we also need training data, so this next section describes the annotation process. Since we assume that most occupational titles can be identified at sentence-level, we apply a sentence tokenizer and build our annotation corpus on sentences rather than on whole debates. Since professions are seldom the main topic of debates in the Bundestag and occupational titles are therefore rather rare, a seed list of keywords [2] was used to search for sentences that could be considered for the gold standard. The keywords were selected to include words that are not an occupational title in every context, such as *Bauer* (differentiation from surname) or *Sportler* (differentiation from non-professional). For each keyword, random sentences were selected from the entire corpus, so that the annotation corpus finally comprises 817 sentences, whereby a sentence can also contain several keywords from the list.

The selected sentences were then annotated using the INCEpTION software (Klie et al., 2018). In order to enhance the annotation process, the keywords found were initially marked as potential occupational titles. These annotations could then be corrected during the annotation process and supplemented with additional occupational titles that were not included in the initial word list. Compounds in which an occupational title is not the root of the compound were not annotated (e.g. *Bauernverband* (farmers' association)). The annotation process was carried out by a single person, so no inter-annotator agreement could be formed. The distribution of tokens in train and test set as well as the share of annotated tokens can be seen in table 1. In addition to the initial list of keywords mentioned above, the training and test sentences also contain less common occupational titles, such as *Textilingenieurin* (textile engineer) (textile engineer) or *Agrarsoziologe* (agricultural sociologist). The test sentences contain 54 occupational titles that do not appear in the train sentences.

	All Tokens	Tokens PROF	Types PROF
Train	20,176	1,094 (5.4%)	201
Test	4,941	269 (5.4%)	91

Table 1: Distribution of Labels in Train and Test

4.2 Dictionary-based approach

The basis for the dictionary-based approach was a search term list from the Federal Employment Agency (BA), which was initially developed for processing search queries on the BA portals, such as BERUFENET[3]. It contains a total of 179,002 different German-language terms, which are grouped into male, female and neutral search terms. Neutral terms include both valid occupational titles, such as *Bürokaufleute* (office clerks), but also expressions such as *Pflanze* (plant), which can support the search for occupational information but are not occupational titles. In the case of neutral occupational titles, these were in some cases also assigned to the male and female group, such as *Archivfachkraft* (archivist).

We used SpaCy's PhraseMatcher module to search for all occupational titles from the list (Honnibal et al., 2020). The module enables the rule-based search of words and multi-word expressions in a text. Since the dictionary is divided into male,

[2]The following keywords were used: Bauer, Bäuerin, Landwirt, Landwirtin, Arzt, Ärztin, Mediziner, Medizinerin, Sportler, Sportlerin, Verkäufer, Verkäuferin, Krankenpfleger, Krankenpflegerin, Krankenschwester, Pfleger, Pflegerin.

[3]see https://download-portal.arbeitsagentur.de/

ID	name	level	groups	#keywords
1	mfn_{lemma}	lemma	male female neutral	179,002
2	mf_{token}	token	male female	107,020
3	mf_{lemma}	lemma	male female	107,020

Table 2: Configuration for rule-based operationalisation

female and neutral search terms, we ran different experiments with different subsets of the keyword list. The different configurations are summarised in table 2. Firstly, the length of the keyword list was varied by excluding the neutral terms from the keyword list in Experiment 2 & 3. In addition, we varied whether the phrase matching was applied on token (experiment 2) or on lemma level (experiment 1 & 3).

4.3 BERT-based approach

For the machine learning approach, we decided to apply a fine-tuning on a pre-trained BERT model (Devlin et al., 2019). To our best knowledge, there does not exist any BERT model that is trained on German parliamentary debates, so we chose bert-base-german-cased [4] as base model. All hyperparameters of the finetuning itself were left on default values (see table 3). But since compounds, such as *Lehrerverband* (teachers' association), might pose a challenge for the identification of occupational titles, particular attention was paid to aggregation strategies within the configuration. Since BERT-based models divide tokens in further subtokens, the labels of subtokens can be aggregated in different ways. We varied these aggregation strategies to evaluate their effect on token classification result (experiment 4 to 7).

4.4 Evaluation

In order to assess the quality of the operationalisations described above, all algorithms are applied to the same 163 sentences from the test data. Table 4 summarises the evaluation results for all seven experiments. The metrics are computed at token-level, i.e. multi-word expressions are split into tokens and then counted separately. All configurations of BERT fine-tuning achieve the best recall of 0.86, showing that the aggregation strategy has no effect on identifying more true positives within the

[4] https://huggingface.co/bert-base-german-cased

ID	name	Aggregation strategy
4	$bert_{simple}$	whole token is annotated as PROF if at least one subtoken is annotated as PROF
5	$bert_{first}$	label of first subtoken is taken as label for the whole token
6	$bert_{average}$	highest mean probability of all labels for whole token
7	$bert_{max}$	highest probability of all labels

Table 3: Configuration for BERT fine-tuning (further hyperparameters: learning rate: 5^{-5}; epochs: 5; optimizer: $adamw_{torch}$)

ID	name	pre	rec	f1
1	mfn_{lemma}	0.261	0.784	0.391
2	mf_{token}	0.925	0.463	0.617
3	mf_{lemma}	0.935	0.769	0.844
4	$bert_{simple}$	0.926	**0.863**	0.893
5	$bert_{first}$	0.932	**0.863**	0.896
6	$bert_{average}$	0.932	**0.863**	0.896
7	$bert_{max}$	**0.936**	**0.863**	**0.898**

Table 4: Evaluation results for all experiments (the best scores are bold)

test set. The fewest occupational titles were found by the PhraseMatcher at the tokenised level. The BERT model also performs best in terms of precision. Here, the aggregation strategy **max** achieved the best results, closely followed by the PhraseMatcher at the lemmatised level with all male and female occupational titles. The difference to all other aggregation strategies is also marginal, at one percentage point. The PhraseMatcher, which also includes neutral terms, achieved the most false positives, leading to a precision of 0.26. This result is not surprising, as the keyword list also contained terms such as *Steuerwesen* (taxation), which describe the topic of a professional activity, but are no occupational titles.

In the qualitative error analysis, the dictionary-based approaches also show that ambiguous occupational titles (sportsperson, salesperson, trader) lead to false positives. This problem also affects surnames, as the context is not taken into account. Two causes can be identified with regard to the low recall of the PhraseMatcher: on the one hand, incorrect lemmatisation sometimes impedes the identification of occupational titles. Initial qualitative analyses indicate that female plural forms, such as *Erzieherinnen* (female educators), are more frequently affected by this problem than other lexemes, but quantitative analyses on this are still pending. This would not fulfil the requirement that the method for identifying occupational titles would not include any systematic bias regarding gendered forms. Secondly, valid occupational titles, such as *Agrarsoziologe* (agricultural sociologist), are not included in the keyword list and therefore cannot be found. This clearly shows that even a comprehensive word list with over 100,000 terms can be inadequate, as language is productive and new occupational titles are constantly being added.

The model-based experiments also reveal various causes for false extractions. False positives are often other personal nouns, such as *Bürgerin* (citizen) in example 9[5], or cases in which the distinction between profession and company is blurred, as in example 10. In addition, the aggregation strategy influences the extractions, especially in the case of compound nouns such as in example 11. False negatives mainly affect expressions such as *Beamte* (civil servants), *Angestellte* (employees) or *Beschäftigte* (staff) (see example 12). In addition, multi-word expressions such as in example 13 are often annotated in abbreviated form. Here, *Verkäufer* was extracted correctly, but without the specialisation. Depending on the subsequent downstream task, a distinction between different specialisations of salespersons would be crucial.

(9) Als Medizinerin, als Politikerin, aber auch als **Bürgerin** sage ich: [...]
As a doctor, as a politician, but also as a **citizen**, I say: [...]

(10) Wenn einer Diplom-Landwirtin [...] dort empfohlen wird, Bäuerinnen in den alten Bundesländern einmal zum **Friseur** oder zum Einkaufen zu fahren, dann muß man zumindest beachten, daß ihr vorgeschlagen wird, Bäuerinnen zu fahren.
If a qualified farmer [...] is recommended there to drive women farmers in the old federal states to the **hairdresser** or to the shops, then one must at least note that she is suggested to drive women farmers.

(11) Wir haben die **Junglandwirteförderung** und in der Familienpolitik das Erziehungsgeld für die Bäuerin durchgesetzt.
We have pushed through **young farmers support** and, in family policy, the child-raising allowance for female farmers.

(12) Es ist mit den staatlichen und den Hoheitsaufgaben des *Beamten* einfach nicht vereinbar, daß er sich nebenbei noch als Verkäufer betätigt.
It is simply not compatible with the state and sovereign tasks of the *civil servant* that he also works as a salesman.

(13) Um die notwendige Aufklärung und Beratung sicherzustellen, sind Regelungen über die fachlichen Kenntnisse der *Verkäufer im Einzelhandel* zu treffen.
In order to ensure that the necessary information and advice is provided, regulations on the specialist knowledge of *sales staff in the retail sector* must be put in place.

5 Application on further parliamentary protocols

As the test corpus is comparatively small at 163 sentences, we applied the best dictionary-based and the best BERT-based model[6] to further 2,000 speeches from 2010 in order to compare the extractions where both models disagree. Since we do not have manually annotated sentences here, we can not report evaluation scores in this section. The most common types that were annotated by each model are reported in figures 1 & 2. In total, the PhraseMatcher identified 3,285 tokens (397 types) and the BERT model 2,509 tokens (866 types) as occupational titles. Of these, both models agree with their decision for 1,185 tokens (272 types). The diverging type-token-ratio indicates that the PhraseMatcher mostly annotated more frequent types, such as *Präsident/Präsidentin* (president), which are usually part of the salutation at the beginning of the speech. Meanwhile, BERT annotates more different types, which indicates that the context is taken into account and the lexical variance of the occupational titles themselves is not an obstacle for the model.

If we look at the cases where only the dictionary-based model has marked an occupational title, it is noticeable – as in the previous section described – that these are often words that are not occupational titles in the respective context, such as surnames, or where an incorrect lemmatisation has led to the

[5]FP are shown in bold, FN are shown in italics.

[6]https://huggingface.co/johannabi/german_tc_professions_debates

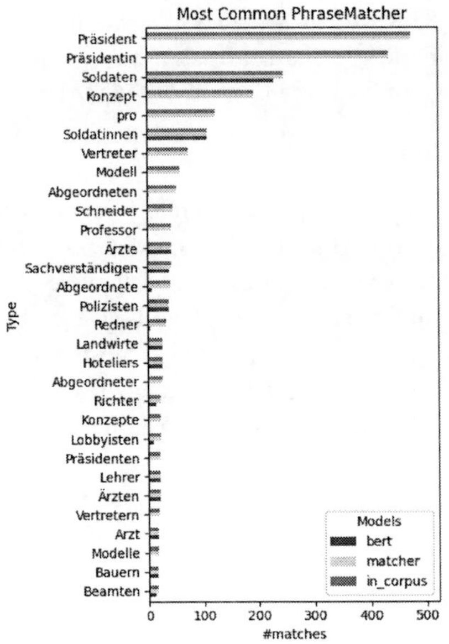

Figure 1: Most Common Types found by best PhraseMatcher in 2000 debates. *in corpus* refers to how often the type appeared.

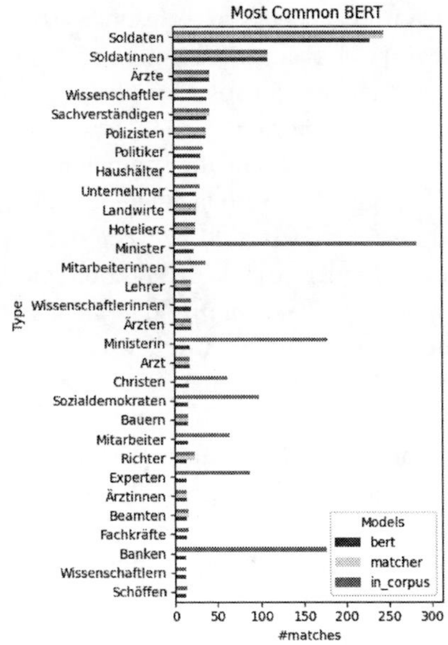

Figure 2: Most Common Types found by best BERT model in 2000 debates. *in corpus* refers to how often the type appeared.

annotation. For example, *Koch* (cook) is marked seven times by the PhraseMatcher, although the occupation is only meant once and the surname in all other cases. In contrast, the BERT model was able to correctly distinguish between the two meanings. There are also some valid occupational titles, such as *Milchbauer* (dairy farmer), *Banker* (banker) or *Pfleger* (carer), that were only found by the BERT model because they were missing from the keyword list.

In contrast, the BERT-based model often annotates other personal nouns that do not refer to professions, such as *Christen* (Christians), *Spekulant* (speculator), *Rentner* (pensioner) or *Schöffen* (lay judge) (see figure 1). In addition, in some cases, company types, such as *Banken* (banks), are annotated as occupations. To prevent these false extractions, the training data for a future model should include more personal nouns or company types as negative examples, so that the distinction between occupational groups and other personal nouns or types of organizations becomes clearer. Finally, the BERT model annotates many generic terms such as *Spezialist* (specialists) or *Akademiker* (academics) as occupational titles. These terms are (for the most part) not included in the keyword list because they do not reflect the specialised nature of an occupation like the dictionary of the Federal Employment Agency does. Nevertheless, these terms could be a starting point for subsequent analysis, since they group together various professions. In this case, the decision whether these terms are occupational terms again depends heavily on the occupational definition and the subsequent content analysis.

6 Conclusion

The evaluation using the test data (section 4.4) as well as the application of the best models on further debates (section 5) have shown that both approaches have various strengths and weaknesses. The weakness of dictionary-based approaches lies in the context-free consideration of keywords and the treatment of unknown occupational titles. With regard to the false negatives, the word list could first be enriched by searching for similar words in a type embedding, such as Word2Vec. Regarding false positives, some errors could be minimised by setting up additional rules. For example, surnames could be excluded by not annotating a potential token if the word *Kollege* (colleague) precedes it. However, it is clear that these rules reach their limits as soon as a distinction has to be made between profession and businesses, like for *Friseur* (hairdresser). The BERT model presented here also has problems with these distinctions, regardless of which aggregation strategy was chosen. In addition, the BERT model still seems to overgeneralise the concept of occupational title, as many of the annotated terms refer to other groups of people. As stated in the previous section, this overgeneralisation could be prevented by adding more examples of personal nouns to the training data in order to improve the distinction between occupational groups and other groups. In addition, the BERT base model could be compared to more specified models, such as jobBERT-de[7], which is domain-adapted on German-language job advertisements from Switzerland (Gnehm et al., 2022). This model may be able to depict occupational concepts more clearly than the BERT base model. Finally, other hyperparameters should be varied in training to determine the best possible configuration for fine-tuning.

One point that usually follows the identification of expressions in texts is the grouping of the expressions on the basis of existing classifications. This is because it is often not the term as such that is to be analysed, but the referenced concept or the terms in relation to the referenced concept. The classification of occupations (KldB) is often used for statistical analyses on occupational activities. However, Schierholz et al. (2018) have already shown that occupational titles are only suitable for coding according to the KldB to a limited extent, because occupational activities, as defined by the KldB, and occupational titles do not fully correspond to each other. For example, when a *Handwerker* (craftsman) is mentioned in the plenary protocols, it is often not recognisable which occupational activity is meant since labour market research often distinguishes between for example carpenters and mechanics. Alternatively, the extracted data could be used for analyses that are based on structuring features other than occupational specialisation. Initial ideas for groupings would be, for example, gender forms (*Lehrer vs. Lehrerin*) or industry affiliation (*employee in the automotive industry*).

Finally, lexical change of occupational titles could be examined at the level of occupational titles, for example by comparing whether a renaming of certain occupations or corresponding apprenticeships also led to a change in language usage or whether a preceding change in language usage has finally led to a change in official training regulations. In addition, occupational titles could be grouped according to profession and gender in order to investigate whether changes in the gender distribution in the profession have also led to a change in language (Oksaar, 1976).

[7]https://huggingface.co/agne/jobBERT-de

Limitations

All experiments presented in the paper were evaluated on a rather small test set (163 sentences). Furthermore, training and test data were annotated by a single person, which might have led to rather subjective annotations. Finally, most assumptions on compounds or gendered occupational titles refer to German-language data. This might not apply to other languages.

References

Gavin Abercrombie and Riza Batista-Navarro. 2020. ParlVote: A corpus for sentiment analysis of political debates. In *Proceedings of the Twelfth Language Resources and Evaluation Conference*, pages 5073–5078, Marseille, France. European Language Resources Association.

Panos Alexopoulos. 2020. *Semantic modeling for data: Avoiding pitfalls and breaking dilemmas*, first edition. O'Reilly, Beijing and Boston and Farnham and Sebastopol and Tokyo.

Andreas Blaette and Christoph Leonhardt. 2023. GermaParl Corpus of Plenary Protocols.

Marlis Buchmann, Helen Buchs, Felix Busch, Simon Clematide, Ann-Sophie Gnehm, and Jan Müller. 2022. Swiss Job Market Monitor: A Rich Source of Demand-Side Micro Data of the Labour Market. *European Sociological Review*.

Federica Calanca, Luiza Sayfullina, Lara Minkus, Claudia Wagner, and Eric Malmi. 2019. Responsible team players wanted: an analysis of soft skill requirements in job advertisements. *EPJ Data Science*, 8(1).

Carla Sökefeld. 2021. Gender(un)gerechte Personenbezeichnungen: derzeitiger Sprachgebrauch, Einflussfaktoren auf die Sprachwahl und diachrone Entwicklung. *Sprachwissenschaft*, 46(1).

Andreas Damelang and Ann-Katrin Rückel. 2021. Was hält Frauen von beruflichen Positionen fern? Ein faktorieller Survey zum Einfluss der Gestaltung einer Stellenausschreibung auf deren Attraktivitätseinschätzung. *KZfSS Kölner Zeitschrift für Soziologie und Sozialpsychologie*, 73(1):109–127.

Jacob Devlin, Ming-Wei Chang, Kenton Lee, and Kristina Toutanova. 2019. BERT: Pre-training of Deep Bidirectional Transformers for Language Understanding. *Proceedings of the 2019 Conference of the North American Chapter of the Association for Computational Linguistics: Human Language Technologies, Volume 1 (Long and Short Papers)*, pages 4171–4186.

Jyldyz Djumalieva, Antonio Lima, and Cath Sleeman. 2018. Classifying Occupations According to Their Skill Requirements in Job Advertisements: Economic Statistics Centre of Excellence (ESCoE) Discussion Papers.

Stian Rødven Eide. 2019. The Swedish PoliGraph: A semantic graph for argument mining of Swedish parliamentary data. In *Proceedings of the 6th Workshop on Argument Mining*, pages 52–57, Florence, Italy. Association for Computational Linguistics.

Andreas Fischer, Patrick Hilse, and Sören Schütt-Sayed. 2021. Curricula, Ausbildungsordnungen und Lehrpläne – Spiegel der Bedeutung nachhaltiger Entwicklung.

Ann-Sophie Gnehm, Eval Bühlmann, and Simon Clematide. 2022. Evaluation of Transfer Learning and Domain Adaptation for Analyzing German-Speaking Job Advertisements. *Proceedings of the Thirteenth Language Resources and Evaluation Conference*, pages 3892–3901.

Lea Hodel, Magdalena Formanowicz, Sabine Sczesny, Jana Valdrová, and Lisa von Stockhausen. 2017. Gender-Fair Language in Job Advertisements. *Journal of Cross-Cultural Psychology*, 48(3):384–401.

Matthew Honnibal, Ines Montani, Sofie van Landeghem, and Adriane Boyd. 2020. spaCy: Industrial-strength Natural Language Processing in Python.

Lisa K. Horvath, Elisa F. Merkel, Anne Maass, and Sabine Sczesny. 2015. Does Gender-Fair Language Pay Off? The Social Perception of Professions from a Cross-Linguistic Perspective. *Frontiers in Psychology*, 6:1–12.

Imane Khaouja, Ismail Kassou, and Mounir Ghogho. 2021. A Survey on Skill Identification From Online Job Ads. *IEEE Access*, 9:118134–118153.

Jan-Christoph Klie, Michael Bugert, Beto Boullosa, Richard Eckart de Castilho, and Iryna Gurevych. 2018. The INCEpTION Platform: Machine-Assisted and Knowledge-Oriented Interactive Annotation. In *Proceedings of the 27th International Conference on Computational Linguistics: System Demonstrations*, pages 5–9. Association for Computational Linguistics.

Klaus Krippendorff. 2019. *Content analysis: An introduction to its methodology*, fourth edition. SAGE, Los Angeles and London and New Delhi and Singapore and Washington DC and Melbourne.

Antonio Miranda-Escalada, Eulàlia Farré-Maduell, Salvador Lima-López, Luis Gascó, Vicent Briva-Iglesias, Marvin Agüero-Torales, and Martin Krallinger. 2021. The ProfNER shared task on automatic recognition of occupation mentions in social media: systems, evaluation, guidelines, embeddings and corpora. In *Proceedings of the Sixth Social Media Mining for Health (#SMM4H) Workshop and Shared Task*, pages 13–20, Stroudsburg, PA, USA. Association for Computational Linguistics.

Els Oksaar. 1976. *Berufsbezeichnungen im heutigen Deutsch: Soziosemantische Untersuchungen Mit deutschen und schwedischen experimentellen Kontrastierungen*, 1 edition. Schwann, Düsseldorf.

Sebastian Padó, Andre Blessing, Nico Blokker, Erenay Dayanik, Sebastian Haunss, and Jonas Kuhn. 2019. Who Sides with Whom? Towards Computational Construction of Discourse Networks for Political Debates. In *Proceedings of the 57th Annual Meeting of the Association for Computational Linguistics*, pages 2841–2847, Florence, Italy. Association for Computational Linguistics.

Ines Rehbein, Josef Ruppenhofer, and Julian Bernauer. 2021. Who is we? Disambiguating the referents of first person plural pronouns in parliamentary debates. In *Proceedings of KONVENS 2021*, pages 147–158.

Florian Richter, Philipp Koch, Oliver Franke, Jakob Kraus, Fabrizio Kuruc, Anja Thiem, Judith Högerl, Stella Heine, and Konstantin Schöps. 2020. Open Discourse.

Margarida Rodrigues, Enrique Fernández-Macías, and Matteo Sostero. 2021. A unified conceptual framework of tasks, skills and competences.

Gerald Sailmann. 2018. *Der Beruf: Eine Begriffsgeschichte*, volume 147 of *Histoire*. transcript Verlag, Bielefeld.

Malte Schierholz, Miriam Gensicke, Nikolai Tschersich, and Frauke Kreuter. 2018. Occupation Coding During the Interview. *Journal of the Royal Statistical Society Series A: Statistics in Society*, 181(2):379–407.

Carla Sökefeld, Melanie Andresen, Johanna Binnewitt, and Heike Zinsmeister. 2023. Personal noun detection for german. In *Proceedings of the 19th Joint ACL - ISO Workshop on Interoperable Semantic Annotation (ISA-19)*, pages 33–39.

Werner Sombart. 1959. Beruf. In Alfred Vierkandt, editor, *Handwörterbuch der Soziologie*, pages 25–31. Ferdinand Enke Verlag, Stuttgart.

Fridemann Stooß and Hermann Saterdag. 1979. Systematik der Berufe und der beruflichen Tätigkeiten. In Franz Urban Pappi, editor, *Sozialstrukturanalysen mit Umfragedaten*, Monographien sozialwissenschaftliche Methoden, pages 41–57. Athenäum-Verl., Königstein/Ts.

Michael Stops, Ann-Christin Bächmann, Ralf Glassner, Markus Janser, Britta Matthes, Lina-Jeanette Metzger, Christoph Müller, and Joachim Seitz. 2020. Machbarkeitsstudie Kompetenz-Kompass: Teilprojekt 2: Beobachtungen von Kompetenzanforderungen in Stellenangeboten.

Max Weber and Johannes Winckelmann. 1985. *Wirtschaft und Gesellschaft: Grundriss der verstehenden Soziologie*, 5. rev. aufl. edition. Mohr, Tübingen.

Tobias Widmann and Maximilian Wich. 2023. Creating and Comparing Dictionary, Word Embedding, and Transformer-Based Models to Measure Discrete Emotions in German Political Text. *Political Analysis*, 31(4):626–641.

Mike Zhang, Kristian Nørgaard Jensen, Sif Dam Sonniks, and Barbara Plank. 2022. SkillSpan: Hard and Soft Skill Extraction from English Job Postings.

Dynamic embedded topic models and change-point detection for exploring literary-historical hypotheses

Hale Sirin
Center for Digital Humanities
Johns Hopkins University
hsirin1@jhu.edu

Tom Lippincott
Center for Digital Humanities
Johns Hopkins University
tom.lippincott@jhu.edu

Abstract

We present a novel combination of dynamic embedded topic models and change-point detection to explore diachronic change of lexical semantic modality in classical and early Christian Latin. We demonstrate several methods for finding and characterizing patterns in the output, and relating them to traditional scholarship in Comparative Literature and Classics. This simple approach to unsupervised models of semantic change can be applied to any suitable corpus, and we conclude with future directions and refinements aiming to allow noisier, less-curated materials to meet that threshold.

1 Introduction

Characterizing and interpreting linguistic novelty has a long tradition in both humanistic scholarship. A foundational study in comparative literature (Auerbach, 1959) hinges empirically on shifts in the meanings of particular words, most notably *figura*. He claims that *figura* went from particularly abstract (as a translation of Plato's *schema*), to concrete (due in part to several particularly novel authors), and finally was usable in both senses in the writing of early Church fathers. We refer to this type of semantic shift as *bimodality*, the degree to which a word makes a sharp transition between having one or two senses.[1] In our attempts to reproduce and extend this humanistic hypothesis, we make the following contributions:

- Propose a novel combination of unsupervised machine learning methods for surfacing relevant phenomena
- Demonstrate viewpoints on model output that move readily between general trends and specific observations
- Derive legible humanistic insights and lines of inquiry regarding shifts in Latin through the Classical and early Christian periods

2 Background

Our goals and methods in this paper have connections to research tracking semantics across time in embedding spaces (Hamilton et al., 2016), which we differ from in our focus on modality rather than the geometric position. Also related is the long-standing task of word sense disambiguation (WSD) (Ide and Véronis, 1998), which we differ from by not operating with a gold standard sense inventory to target, or other supervised task.

The dynamic embedded topic model (DETM) (Dieng et al., 2019) extends topic models (Blei et al., 2003) to operate over word embeddings, and capture topic evolution over time. Change-point detection (Killick et al., 2012) considers the problem of determining if and where the distribution generating a sequence of observations changes, typically w.r.t. time. The simplest approach, employed here, uses dynamic programming to find the optimal piecewise-linear fit to the observations. The Jensen-Shannon divergence (JSD) (Lin, 1991) is a symmetric distance measure based on the Kullback-Leibler divergence.

The Perseus project (Crane, 2023) is a long-standing database and interface to a curated corpus of primary sources from the Classical and early Medieval world.

3 Materials and methods[2]

We derive our corpus from the Perseus project by extracting all XML documents from the underlying repositories, and extract all text marked as *Latin* along with the name of the purported author. We then manually assign years to the set of unique authors based on rough scholarly consensus, and keep

[1] For simplicity we limit this study to *bi*modality, and leave higher complexity to future work.

[2] Code from the study is available at https://github.com/comp-int-hum/diachronic-latin

Proceedings of LaTeCH-CLfL 2024, pages 231–236
March 22, 2024

materials that fall between 250 BCE and 500 CE. This leads to a corpus of 574 documents from 101 authors. We use the Classical Language Toolkit (Johnson et al., 2014–2021) to lemmatize each token and filter non-Latin vocabulary. We group documents into 75-year windows, and split documents into sub-documents of at most 500 tokens.

Word	Neighbors		
bellum	proelium:0.53	optatus:0.49	bello:0.46
hasta	clipeus:0.46	sarisa:0.46	tragula:0.44
terra	caelum:0.52	introgredior:0.50	inhabitabilis:0.50
ignis	flamma:0.55	exuro:0.52	ardeo:0.51
debeo	cumulatus:0.57	oppignero:0.56	faeneratio:0.54

Table 1: Nearest neighbors of several words in the initial word2vec embedding space.

We initialize a 50-topic DETM with skip-gram embeddings (Mikolov et al., 2013) trained on the corpus. Table 1 shows the nearest neighbors for several words, to demonstrate the intuitiveness of the initial embedding space. We fit the DETM using the hyper-parameters listed in Appendix A, monitoring perplexity on the dev set for learning rate adjustment and early termination.

3.1 Measuring static and diachronic semantics

We define a word's *bimodality*, within a particular window, as the degree to which its probability mass is evenly and exhaustively between two topics. At each time window and for each word, we use the two highest values from the word's empirical distribution over topics, $first$ and *second*, to compute a score:

$$evenly\_distr = 1.0 - (first - second)$$

$$exhaustive = first + second$$

$$bimodality = \frac{evenly\_distr + exhaustive}{2}$$

This *bimodality* takes its maximal value of 1.0 when the word is evenly split between two topics. Using the word's sequence of bimodality scores, we apply change-point detection with an L2 cost to find the window constituting the most-prominent shift in modality, which we refer to as the word's *change-point*. Finally, we compute the absolute value of the difference between the means on each side of the change-point, which we refer to as the word's *delta*.

We define the *novelty* of an author as the degree to which their topic distribution diverges from that of the time window immediately preceding their own. For this we calculate the Jensen-Shannon divergence. Note that, while deltas and novelties are derived from the same model output and aren't independent, they can provide different useful perspectives on change, as our results show.

4 Results and analysis

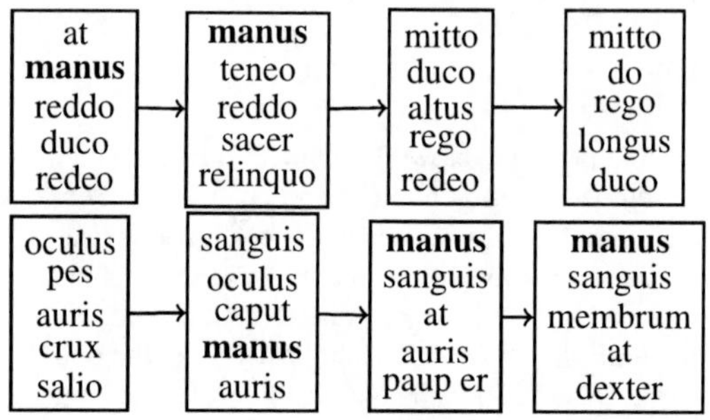

Figure 1: Top words of two topics, at four windows evenly spread across our temporal range, illustrating the semantic shift of *manus* (*hand*).

To exemplify the phenomenon of interest, and as an initial qualitative example, Figure 1 places snapshots of two topics side-by-side. The first topic focuses on actions (commanding, holding, sending, ruling), the second on body parts (eye, head, limb, ear). The word *manus* (*hand*) moves from the former to the latter, which we interpret as a shift from a figurative to corporeal sense. The overlap in the second window corresponds to bimodality. Emergent examples like this lend credibility to our approach as we aggregate and look for broader patterns.

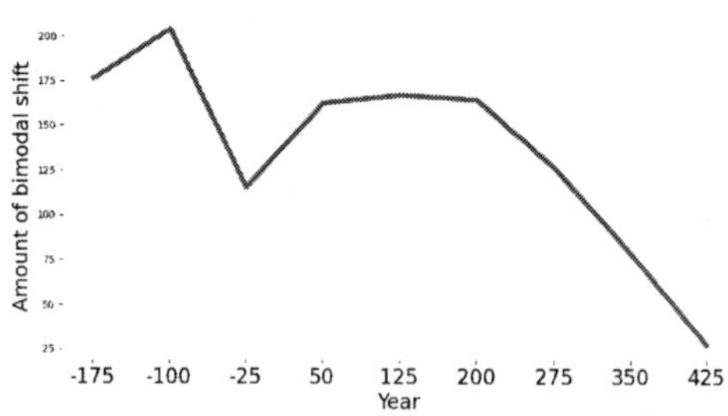

Figure 2: Sum of deltas (bimodal shift) for words with their change-point in the given window.

Our highest-level view is from summing, in each window, the deltas from all change-points identified therein. Figure 2 plots these sums across time: the overarching trend is a substantial decrease in modality shift starting around 200CE with the early Christian era.

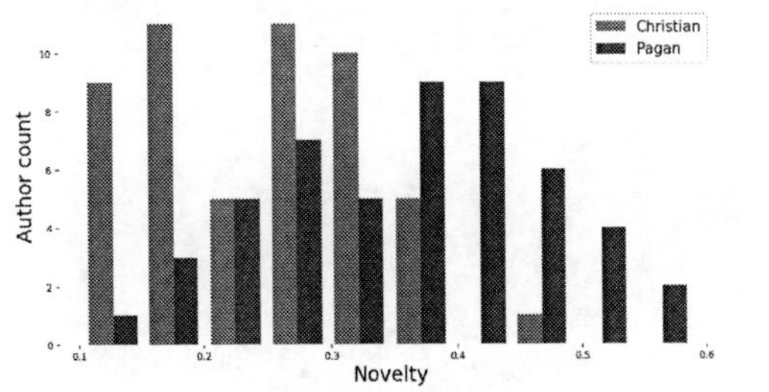

Figure 3: Counts of Christian and pagan authors binned into 10 ranges according to their novelty.

Figure 3 demonstrates that this is not merely a broader linguistic trend projected onto the increasing dominance of Christian writers. The lowest-novelty non-Christian (leftmost blue) is Terentius Afer, one of the earliest writers in the data, while the most-novel Christian (rightmost red) is Saint Hilary, who falls in the middle of the Christian range. This is the opposite of the expected outcome if Latin had simply undergone a general reduction in novelty over time. It supports the view that the Christian writers were, intentionally or naturally, standardizing their language along with their religion.

Author	Window	JSD
Apicius	425	0.589
Vitruvius	-100	0.553
Vergil	-100	0.526
Julius Caesar	-100	0.507
Musonius Rufus	50	0.506
...		
Terence	-175	0.126
Rufinus of Aquileia	350	0.124
Hegemonius	350	0.122
Augustine	350	0.106
Saint Jerome	350	0.103

Table 2: The most and least novel authors in the corpus and their temporal window, according to JSD between their topic distributions and the topic distribution of the preceding temporal window. Early Christian writers are italicized.

The five most and least-novel authors are shown in Table 2. The most striking pattern is the dominance of early Christian authors as the least-novel: this supports the trend seen in Figure 2. The one non-Christian author in the bottom five, Terence, is an interesting case: as a former slave from North Africa one might expect his writing to be rather novel, but his position in our results might align with the common view that his Latin is particularly clear and standard, or be affected by data sparsity in the preceding time period (the earliest in our corpus).

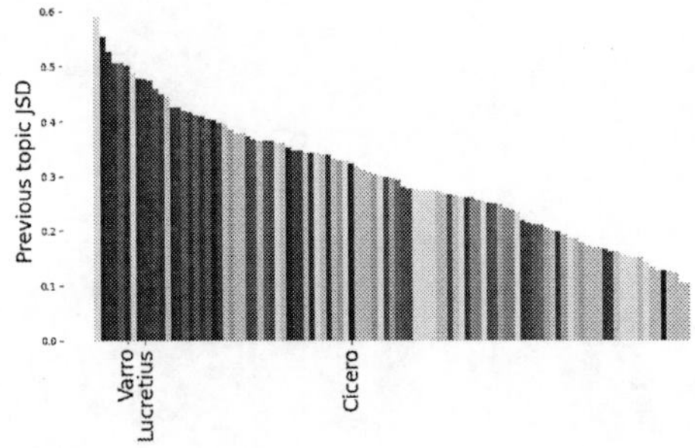

Figure 4: All author novelties in descending order, indicating the position of several authors singled out by Auerbach. Darker colors correspond to earlier windows.

The most-novel authors often focus on a unique domain: Apicius is the (likely composite, Vehling (1936)) author of a recipe collection, while Vitruvius produced the first technical treatise on architecture. It's unsurprising that specialized domains lead to outliers, while Vergil and Caesar may be unsurprising for narrative and stylistic properties. To our knowledge Rufus (a philosopher of the early empire) has not before been highlighted as particularly distinctive, and so might be a compelling target for closer analysis.

Earlier authors have higher novelty, as shown by the darker lefthand columns in Figure 4, and aligning with the trend in word deltas. Of authors Auerbach considered novel w.r.t. *figura*, Lucretius and Varro indeed fall in the top range of novelty, while Cicero is only slightly above the median (in fact, he falls lower than his less-famous brother).

Word	Year	Delta
cathedra (*chair*)	-175	0.947
cicatrix (*scar*)	425	0.944
conlatio (*bring together*)	350	0.939
auster (*south wind*)	350	0.927
recte (*upright*)	350	0.915
...		
probo (*make good*)	350	0.004
obsidio (*siege*)	-25	0.004
sollicitudo (*anxiety*)	350	0.003
declaro (*disclose*)	350	0.002
corpus (*body*)	125	0.001

Table 3: Words whose primary change-point divides their modality with the greatest and least deltas. The year is the start of the change-point's window, with negative numbers corresponding to BCE.

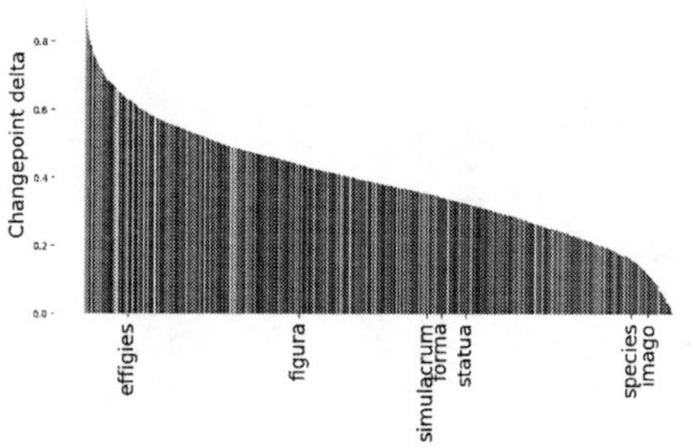

Figure 5: Words sorted by degree of bimodal shift (their change-point delta).

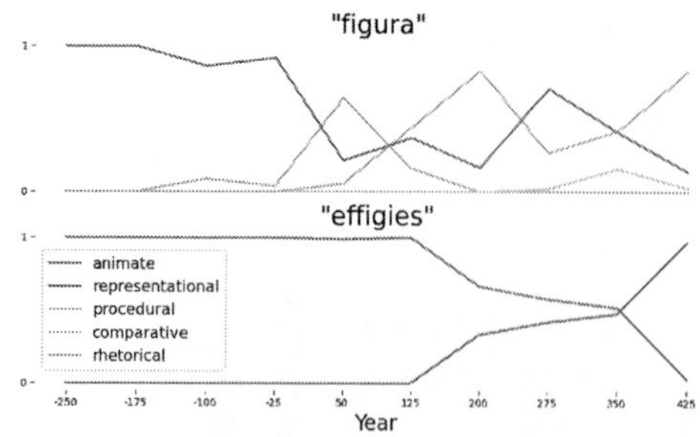

Figure 6: The temporal evolution of topics responsible for the words *figura* (*form, shape*) and *effigies* (*copy, imitation*), with provisional characterizations of meaning. Both words are initially dominated by the *tangible* topic.

The five words with the highest and lowest deltas, shown in Table 3, contrasts with the pattern of decreasing change in summed deltas and author novelty. Most of the top words are excellent examples of the early Christian church's adaptation of Classical vocabulary. *Cicatrix* (*scar*), for instance, takes on figurative meaning when speaking of Christ's wounds as a portal to salvation. *Auster* (*south wind*) may have taken a similar turn: Cicero makes the poetic, but grounded, statement that his ship was carried back to Rome by the south wind, while Augustine compares the Holy Spirit's wrath against wrongdoers to the south wind scattering dust. *Conlatio* (alternate form of *collatio*, *bring together, unify*), and *recte* (*upright, vertical, well-guided*) seem intuitive shifts for the early Christian era. *Cathedra* (*chair, office*), whose 175BCE change-point comes before it is well-attested, may be an artifact of high variance: an important future goal is to leverage data sparsity information within the modeling process, ideally to produce a measure of robustness for change-points.

When the vocabulary is arranged by decreasing delta, we can inspect the positions of several words from Auerbach's study of *figura*. Interestingly, *figura* is the second-highest of the terms, a considerable distance below the high-delta *effigies*.

Inspecting the two words more closely, Figure 6 shows their empirical topic distributions over time. Both words are initially unimodal, generated from the same topic that focuses on animate nouns, particularly the human body, but they evolve quite differently:

effigies is the simpler case: it remains unimodal in the animate topic until about 125CE, at which point it begins shifting to a topic focused on representing, referring, imitating, and equating. After 300 years, *effigies* is again unimodal, but with respect to this *representational* topic.

figura is more complex: rather than directly swapping the animacy topic for another monotonically, it fluctuates between three other topics that themselves are somewhat dynamic. The *rhetorical* spike involves vocabulary related to argumentation and speaking.[3] The later *comparative* spike has vocabulary used to establish (particularly, temporal and spatial) relationships. The largest shift, however, is to the *procedural* topic, which ends our time-frame as the dominant sense. It is also the most difficult to interpret: the gloss was chosen because of the unusual strength of verbs denoting a change of state or coming-to-be (proceed from, generate, come forth, burst, grow), and related "source" nouns (seed, fountain, sea, earth). This final sense may come to dominate due to the expanding use of Christian idioms ("brought forth on the earth", etc), but is well-attested throughout the Classical era.

Taken together, these different viewpoints may begin to disentangle two distributional shifts: one an acute, limited adaptation in a small number of lexical items in the early Christian era, the other a longer, more diffuse process that appears to be slowing down over the same time period.

Unfortunately, the vast majority of scholarship regarding liturgical language is born in, and concerned with, theology. Exceptions, e.g. Liddicoat (1993), do highlight the critical early need to *define orthodoxy* and then *create stability*. These two concerns map to the two distributional shifts highlighted above: focused modification of specialized vocabulary, and broader linguistic consistency to

[3]An interesting topic in its own right, it seems to temporally proceed from a focus on learning and understanding, to a focus on the tension between groups and individuals.

consolidate the early Church.

5 Future Work

Deeper scrutiny of model output, involving scholars from Classics, would benefit from *in situ* examples drawn automatically from the underlying sources. Having established its ability to surface historically distinctive authors and vocabulary, we are augmenting the pipeline in this direction, in anticipation of implementing a frontend for humanists to apply and explore their own diachronic corpora.

A critical facet of Auerbach's arguments is the permeability and comingling of the languages, and a suitable Greek lexicon and lemmatizer would make it a straightforward to include prior and contemporary Greek writing.

The greatest barrier to extending our methodology to arbitrary languages and time periods is imperfect and low-coverage data. In parallel with this research we have applied the same method to a noisy Latin corpus derived from the HathiTrust (HathiTrust Foundation, 2023), which offers considerably higher coverage of sources. Unfortunately the level of noise (from OCR, commentary, etc) and redundancy renders it challenging to use credibly without extensive post-processing. We plan to use this research as a case study for developing a core set of methods for gathering, deduplicating, and rectifying an arbitrary HTC-based corpus such that it approaches the fidelity of a manually-curated resource like Perseus.

References

Erich Auerbach. 1959. *Scenes from the Drama of European Literature: six essays*. Meridian Books.

David M. Blei, Andrew Y. Ng, and Michael I. Jordan. 2003. Latent Dirichlet Allocation. *J. Mach. Learn. Res.*, 3(null):993–1022.

Gregory R. Crane. 2023. Perseus Digital Library.

Adji B. Dieng, Francisco J. R. Ruiz, and David M. Blei. 2019. The Dynamic Embedded Topic Model.

William L. Hamilton, Jure Leskovec, and Dan Jurafsky. 2016. Diachronic Word Embeddings Reveal Statistical Laws of Semantic Change. *CoRR*, abs/1605.09096.

HathiTrust Foundation, 2023. 2023. HathiTrust Digital Library.

Nancy Ide and Jean Véronis. 1998. Introduction to the special issue on word sense disambiguation: the state of the art. *Computational linguistics*, 24(1):1–40.

Kyle P. Johnson, Patrick Burns, John Stewart, and Todd Cook. 2014–2021. CLTK: The Classical Language Toolkit.

R. Killick, P. Fearnhead, and I. A. Eckley. 2012. Optimal Detection of Changepoints With a Linear Computational Cost. *Journal of the American Statistical Association*, 107(500):1590–1598.

Anthony J. Liddicoat. 1993. Choosing a liturgical language: Language policy and the catholic mass. *Australian Review of Applied Linguistics*, 16(2):123–141.

J. Lin. 1991. Divergence measures based on the Shannon entropy. *IEEE Transactions on Information Theory*, 37(1):145–151.

Tomas Mikolov, Kai Chen, Greg Corrado, and Jeffrey Dean. 2013. Efficient Estimation of Word Representations in Vector Space.

Joseph Dommers Vehling. 1936. *Cooking and Dining in Imperial Rome*. Walter M. Hill.

A Hyper-parameters

word2vec

Name	Value
Method	skip-gram
Window size	5
Embedding size	300
Epochs	10

Dynamic embedded topic model	
Name	Value
Topics	50
Epochs	1000
Batch size	2000
Learning rate	0.016

B Caveats

We note that our aim in *Results and analysis* is to illustrate productive exploratory methods and seed discussion with Classicists and literary theorists regarding if and how the patterns relate to traditional scholarship such as Auerbach's. Observations, and certainly interpretations, are provisional. Document dates were assigned as precisely as possible after a light survey, but most often are approximated as the midpoint of the author's life, or of the century they are believed to have flourished (the assignments are included in the experimental repository, for scrutiny and revision). Where English is used to characterize a topic, it is a provisional gloss of a complex, dynamic concept; where used to translate a Latin word, it is derived from the Lewis dictionary.

Post-OCR Correction of Digitized Swedish Newspapers with ByT5

Viktoria Löfgren
Department of Computer Science and Engineering
Chalmers University of Technology
viktoria.lofgren@live.se

Dana Dannélls
Språkbanken Text
University of Gothenburg
dana.dannells@svenska.gu.se

Abstract

Many collections of digitized newspapers suffer from poor OCR quality, which impacts readability, information retrieval, and analysis of the material. Errors in OCR output can be reduced by applying machine translation models to 'translate' it into a corrected version. Although transformer models show promising results in post-OCR correction and related tasks in other languages, they have not yet been explored for correcting OCR errors in Swedish texts. This paper presents a post-OCR correction model for Swedish 19th and 20th century newspapers based on the pre-trained transformer model ByT5. Three versions of the model were trained on different mixes of training data. The best model, which achieved a 36% reduction in CER, is made freely available and will be integrated into the automatic processing pipeline of Språkbanken Text, a Swedish language technology infrastructure containing modern and historical written data.

1 Introduction

The OCR (Optical Character Recognition) quality of printed documents in general and historical documents in particular is often low. Historical documents often suffer from stains, faded print, and ink bleed-through from other pages, which leads to poor OCR accuracy. This, in turn, causes a range of challenges for Natural Language Processing (NLP) systems such as information retrieval and analysis. One way to achieve higher accuracy is to apply a post-OCR correction method to the OCR output. In this context, post-OCR can be compared to machine translation where the input is a set of character strings in one form that should be mapped onto the corrected form (Nguyen et al., 2021).

Since the transformer architecture was introduced in 2017 (Vaswani et al., 2017), it has pushed the state-of-the-art in many NLP tasks, including machine translation. It has also led to the emergence of large pre-trained models. One of

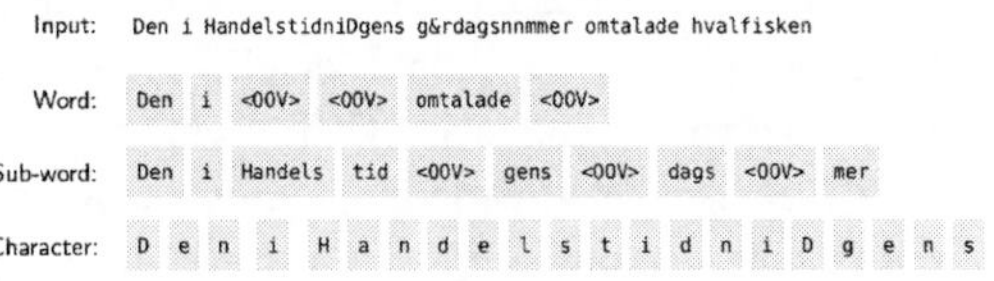

Figure 1: Word, sub-word and character-level tokenization of the sequence. *Den i HandelstidniDgens g&rdagsnnmmer omtalade hvalfisken*.

these is ByT5, which is pre-trained on the large web-scraped multilingual dataset mC4 (Xue et al., 2021b).

ByT5 operates on the character level, as illustrated in Figure 1. This approach preserves words that are not covered by the model's vocabulary due to, for example, OCR errors (*HandelstidniDgens*) or age (*hvalfisken*), at the cost of increased sequence length. Since the sizes of language models' vocabularies are fixed, a word-level model would map all out-of-vocabulary words (e.g., misspelled or obsolete words) to the same out-of-vocabulary token <OOV>, losing all information about these words. This character-level approach has reached state-of-the-art results in transliteration and grapheme-to-phoneme tasks (Xue et al., 2021a), diacritics restoration in 13 languages (Stankevičius et al., 2022), and post-OCR correction in Sanskrit (Maheshwari et al., 2022). However, it has not yet been explored for Swedish post-OCR correction.

The main contributions of this work are: (i) We demonstrate how effective a fine-tuned ByT5 is in the task of correcting OCR errors in 19th and 20th century Swedish newspapers. (ii) We show what effect does further training on data from books and other domains have on the model's performance on newspapers. (iii) We release a freely available post-OCR correction model with state-of-the-art performance on historical Swedish text, and a demo for testing the model. The model is available at `https://huggingface.`

Proceedings of LaTeCH-CLfL 2024, pages 237–242
March 22, 2024 ©2024 Association for Computational Linguistics

co/viklofg/swedish-ocr-correction, with a demo at https://huggingface.co/spaces/viklofg/swedish-ocr-correction-demo.

2 Related Work

Previous work in post-OCR correction of Swedish historical text have explored both statistical and neural network based approaches. Persson (2019) used an SVM classifier in combination with a word list to detect and correct OCR errors in 17th to 19th century texts. Dannélls et al. (2021) proposed a method for increasing OCR accuracy of the Swedish newspapers by merging outputs from two OCR engines. Lundberg and Torstensson (2021) explored using the reference material prepared by Dannélls et al. to train an LSTM-based model from scratch, but found that it was not large enough to yield satisfactory results.

Another successful method for correcting OCR errors in Swedish historical text involves deep CNN–LSTM hybrid models (Drobac and Lindén, 2020; Brandt Skelbye and Dannélls, 2021). Drobac and Lindén (2020) utilized deep CNN–LSTM hybrid networks for the post-OCR task. They employed both Finnish and Swedish historical newspapers from 17th to 18th century, and reached state-of-the-art results for both. Brandt Skelbye and Dannélls (2021) experimented with mixed deep CNN–LSTM hybrid models directly on the character model within the OCR engine. While they have achieved state-of-the-art results for Swedish OCR, their method is not directly comparable to ours as it was not applied as a post-processing step.

In many other languages, post-OCR correction approaches based on neural machine translation have shown promising performance. Examples include the winner of the 2019 ICDAR competition (Rigaud et al., 2019), which was trained on ten European languages (but not Swedish). More recent examples include models for Finnish (Duong et al., 2021), Icelandic (Jasonarson et al., 2023), and English (Nguyen et al., 2020; Soper et al., 2021). Nguyen et al. (2021) note that while these models tend to outperform other techniques, they need a lot of training data to be successful. Nevertheless, the emergence of pre-trained transformer models, which require less training data and perform better than traditional methods such as LSTM networks, gives us hope that these models will overcome some of the previously reported limitations for Swedish OCR.

Dataset	Partition	Time period	Chars (k)	CER
Newspapers	Tesseract	1818–2018	6,957	4.86
	Abbyy Finereader		6,928	3.85
Literature		1836–2001	7,267	1.63
Blackletter	Swedish fraktur	1626–1816	282	17.61
	Then swänska Argus	1732–1734	259	19.06

Table 1: An overview of the datasets

3 Data

This project's main source of data is a manually transcribed subset of the National Library of Sweden's digitized newspapers.[1] In addition to this dataset, three other datasets are used: one dataset containing OCRed literature and two datasets containing OCRed blackletter texts.

All datasets come with a ground truth. An overview of all datasets is given in Table 1.[2]

Newspapers The newspaper dataset was prepared by Dannélls et al. (2021) and comprises almost 44,000 text segments identified by layout analysis of 400 Swedish newspaper pages printed between 1818 and 2018. The dataset includes two versions of each segment, one processed with Abbyy Finereader and one with Tesseract. Spanning two hundred years, the dataset is diverse in both typography and orthography. A majority of the 19th century pages are printed in blackletter typefaces, which often results in worse OCR accuracy and other kinds of errors compared to modern typefaces. The contemporary Swedish spelling was largely settled with the 1889 and 1906 spelling reforms (Pettersson, 2005), which means that the dataset contains both modern and historical spelling, for example *vad* and *hvad* ('what'), and *kvarn* and *qvarn* ('mill').

Literature The literature dataset consists of 79 titles of Swedish literature provided by the Swedish Literature Bank.[3] In total these texts amount to about 7.3M characters, making it slightly larger than the newspapers. It is contemporary with the newspaper dataset, but the OCR quality is generally much higher, likely because of higher print quality and simpler page layout.

Blackletter The blackletter dataset is a combination of two datasets prepared by Borin et al. (2016):

[1] https://tidningar.kb.se/

[2] A quantitative description of the size of the diachronical component of the dataset can be found in Brandt Skelbye and Dannélls (2021).

[3] https://litteraturbanken.se/

Swedish fraktur and *Then swänska Argus*. Both contain OCRed texts printed in blackletter typefaces along with the ground truth. *Swedish fraktur* contains texts from 199 pages from the collections of Gothenburg University Library. *Then swänska Argus* is a dataset consisting of 25 issues of the periodical of the same name by Olof von Dalin.

4 Methodology

4.1 Preparing the data

The main pre-processing step was to split the datasets into short samples. Careful consideration was taken to keep the OCR output and its ground truth aligned, since misaligned training samples may encourage the model to delete or insert text. Each pair of OCR output and ground truth was aligned line-by-line using a modified version of Myers' difference algorithm (Myers, 1986). In our version, we consider two lines 'equal' if their CER is low enough (the threshold was adjusted manually to suit each dataset), which compares the two texts and returns the lines that are present in both texts.

The aligned texts were split on line breaks into samples of typically 1-2 lines. These samples were filtered based on the following conditions: (a) both the OCR output and ground truth should be at least four characters long, (b) the CER should be below 50%, and (c) the ground truth may not contain @, which is used to indicate illegible text.

The newspaper samples were randomly assigned to three splits: train (70%), test (15%), and evaluation (15%). The two versions of each newspaper sample (one processed by Tesseract, one by Abbyy Finereader) were put in the same split to ensure that there was no contamination between the sets. The literature and blackletter samples were randomly assigned to two splits each: train (85%) and test (15%). These datasets were not used in evaluation, since the model's target domain is newspapers.

Dataset	Train	Test	Eval.
Newspapers	125,637	26,456	26,960
Literature	63,867	11,271	0
Blackletter	4,881	861	0

Table 2: Sizes of the three datasets (number of samples)

4.2 Fine-tuning setup

We fine-tuned three models using the following setup. The base model, `byt5-small`, was accessed through Huggingface's Transformers library (Wolf et al., 2020). The maximum input and output lengths were set to 128 UTF-8 bytes, which corresponds to slightly less than 128 characters of Swedish text.[4] The models were fine-tuned for three epochs using the Trainer API provided by Huggingface. Adafactor (Shazeer and Stern, 2018) was used as optimizer with a constant learning rate of 0.001, mimicking the setup used by Xue et al. (2021a) and Raffel et al. (2019) in fine-tuning ByT5 and T5, respectively. The batch size was set to 32, giving a total batch size of $128 \cdot 32 = 2^{12}$ tokens (bytes) per batch.

4.3 Models

Three models were fine-tuned: Model 1, Model 2 and Model 3. The only difference between them is what mix of the datasets, described in Section 3, they were fine-tuned on. The first model, Model 1, was trained on the newspaper dataset only, consisting of 126,000 training samples. Model 2 was fine-tuned on the newspaper and literature datasets, giving a total of 190,000 training samples. Since the literature dataset is contemporary with the newspapers, our ambition with this mix was to provide more examples of 19th and early 20th century Swedish. Model 3 was fine-tuned on the newspaper and blackletter datasets, giving a total of 131,000 training samples. Our ambition with this training mix was to provide more examples of typical errors in OCR of blackletter text, and in turn improve Model 1's performance on older newspapers.

4.4 Evaluation

Each fine-tuned model was evaluated on the 15% subset of the newspaper data. This evaluation set was aligned and filtered in the same way as the training data. The predicted corrections were computed using greedy decoding, i.e., at each decoding step, the highest-probability token was selected. The CER and WER were computed using the Python library `jiwer`.[5]

5 Results and Discussion

Table 3 shows the error rates of the evaluation set before and after processing with each model. All three models successfully reduced the error rates at

[4] ByT5 uses UTF-8 encoding, in which most characters occupy one byte, but non-ASCII characters such as *å*, *ä*, and *ö* occupy at least two bytes.

[5] Version 3.0.3., available at `https://pypi.org/project/jiwer/`, accessed November 6, 2023.

Period	CER (%)				WER (%)			
	BL	M1	M2	M3	BL	M1	M2	M3
1818–1859	8.39	4.39	4.63	**4.30**	32.46	**15.34**	15.80	15.54
1860–1899	4.04	**2.29**	2.61	2.38	16.51	**8.06**	8.63	8.22
1900–1939	2.60	2.01	1.97	**1.92**	11.24	7.03	7.08	**6.99**
1940–1979	1.46	1.39	1.49	**1.29**	6.45	4.43	4.54	**4.39**
1980–2018	0.83	**0.67**	0.75	0.73	3.74	**2.67**	**2.67**	**2.67**
1818–2018	3.20	2.06	2.20	**2.04**	13.21	**7.17**	7.42	7.23

Table 3: CER and WER of Model 1 (M1), Model 2 (M2) and Model 3 (M3) compared to baseline (BL).

both character and word level. This improvement can be seen in both modern and historical texts. Even though it can be assumed that ByT5 has not seen much historical Swedish in its pre-training data, the models did not seem to struggle disproportionately with correcting OCRed historical texts. It is possible that the error patterns are more predictable in the older material than the newer material, and thus easier to find and correct.

Over the entire set, the results in Table 3 show that Model 3 achieved the lowest CER of 2.04%, which corresponds to a 36% reduction from the baseline 3.20%. At the same time, Model 1 achieved the lowest WER, corresponding to a reduction of 46% (from 13.21% to 7.17%). These results are comparable to previously reported results in post-OCR correction of historical Icelandic texts using the larger `byt5-base` (Jasonarson et al., 2023), indicating that `byt5-small` may be sufficiently large for the task.

Although the differences between the three models' error rates listed in Table 3 are small, Model 1 and Model 3 tended to perform slightly better than Model 2. A possible explanation of this tendency is Model 2's relatively large portion of non-newspaper testing data. However, when inspecting the corrections produced by the models, we could not find any evident differences in quality. As an example, consider the evaluation sample shown in Figure 2. The three models agreed that *ko»unqen«* was incorrect, but only Model 3 managed to correct it to *Konungen* ('the king'). At the same time, Model 3 was unable to correct *alk* to *att* ('to').

The example in Figure 2 also displays the models' unwanted tendency to occasionally introduce new errors, for example *sä* $\rightarrow$ *få* ('get') instead of *sä* $\rightarrow$ *så* ('so'). In fact, the best model in terms of CER, Model 3, increased the CER in 7.7% of the evaluation samples. It is possible that the corrections could benefit from using another decoding strategy than greedy decoding.

OCR output (Model input)
— tz. M. ko»unqen« tillfrifFnanbe kor lock,
ligtwis nu sä fortgått alk H. M. den >6 för för,

Expected output
— H. M. konungens tillfrisknande har lyck-
ligtwis nu så fortgått att H. M. den 16 för för-

Model 1 output
— H. M. kommißens tillfrisknande kor lock,
ligtwis nu få fortgått att H. M. den 16 för för-

Model 2 output
— H. M. kommens tillfrisknande för lock-
ligtwis nu så fortgått att H. M. den 16 för för-

Model 3 output
— H. M. Konungens tillfrisknande kor lock-
ligtwis nu så fortgått all H. M. den 16 för för-

Figure 2: A sample from the evaluation set with corrections suggested by the three models. Errors and corrections are highlighted in bold.

6 Conclusion

In this paper, we present state-of-the-art results in post-OCR correction of Swedish 19th to 21th century newspapers. We fine-tuned three models from `byt5-small`, the smallest available version of Google's pre-trained character-level transformer model ByT5, using mixes of training data from different domains. The most successful model in terms of CER was fine-tuned on a mix of Swedish newspapers and blackletter texts. It achieved a 36% reduction in CER over the entire evaluation set, but despite this, it was found to increase the CER in 7.7% of the evaluation samples. We made this model freely available and will integrate it into the automatic processing pipeline of Språkbanken Text,[6] a Swedish language technology infrastructure containing modern and historical written data. Further work aims to minimize the amount of introduced errors taking context information into account. We also intend to conduct several evaluations to learn more about the type of errors the model makes, in particular, on new digitized resources.

Limitations

The proposed model operates directly on text output from OCR engines. This makes it engine-agnostic and not reliant on any specific OCR output format, but may also limit its performance since it is unable to consider metadata such as character confidence scores. Without this knowledge, the model is equally prone to change a (possibly correctly recognized) character regardless of how confident the OCR software is.

Acknowledgements

This research was funded jointly by Nationella språkbanken and HUMINFRA, both received financial support by the Swedish Research Council (grant no. 2017-00626; and 2021-00176).

The authors would like to thank the Swedish Literature Bank for providing us with the literature dataset and its transcription. We would also like to thank the reviewers for their valuable comments on an earlier version of this paper.

References

Lars Borin, Gerlof Bouma, and Dana Dannélls. 2016. A free cloud service for OCR / En fri molntjänst för OCR. Technical report, University of Gothenburg, Gothenburg.

Molly Brandt Skelbye and Dana Dannélls. 2021. OCR processing of Swedish historical newspapers using deep hybrid CNN–LSTM networks. In *Proceedings of the International Conference on Recent Advances in Natural Language Processing (RANLP 2021)*, Held Online. INCOMA Ltd.

Dana Dannélls, Lars Björk, Ove Dirdal, and Torsten Johansson. 2021. A two-OCR engine method for digitized Swedish newspapers. In *CLARIN Annual Conference*. Linköping Electronic Conference Proceedings.

Senka Drobac and Krister Lindén. 2020. Optical character recognition with neural networks and post-correction with finite state methods. *International Journal on Document Analysis and Recognition (IJDAR)*, pages 1–17.

Quan Duong, Mika Hämäläinen, and Simon Hengchen. 2021. An unsupervised method for OCR post-correction and spelling normalisation for Finnish. In *Proceedings of the 23rd Nordic Conference on Computational Linguistics (NoDaLiDa)*, pages 240–248, Reykjavik, Iceland (Online). Linköping University Electronic Press, Sweden.

Atli Jasonarson, Steinþór Steingrímsson, Einar Freyr Sigurðsson, Árni Davíð Magnússon, and Finnur Ágúst Ingimundarson. 2023. Generating errors: OCR post-processing for Icelandic. In *The 24rd Nordic Conference on Computational Linguistics*, pages 286–291, Tórshavn, Faroe Islands. University of Tartu Library.

Arvid Lundberg and Mattias Torstensson. 2021. *Deep learning for post-OCR error correction on Swedish texts*. Master's thesis, Chalmers University of Technology, Gothenburg.

Ayush Maheshwari, Nikhil Singh, Amrith Krishna, and Ganesh Ramakrishnan. 2022. A benchmark and dataset for post-OCR text correction in Sanskrit. In *Findings of the Association for Computational Linguistics: EMNLP 2022*, pages 6258–6265, Abu Dhabi, United Arab Emirates. Association for Computational Linguistics.

Eugene W. Myers. 1986. An O(ND) difference algorithm and its variations. *Algorithmica*, 1:251–266.

Thi Nguyen, Adam Jatowt, Mickaël Coustaty, and Antoine Doucet. 2021. Survey of post-OCR processing approaches. *ACM Computing Surveys*, 54:1–37.

Thi Tuyet Hai Nguyen, Adam Jatowt, Nhu-Van Nguyen, Mickael Coustaty, and Antoine Doucet. 2020. Neural machine translation with BERT for post-OCR error detection and correction. In *Proceedings of the ACM/IEEE Joint Conference on Digital Libraries in 2020*, JCDL '20, page 333–336, New York, NY, USA. Association for Computing Machinery.

Simon Persson. 2019. *OCR post-processing of historical Swedish text using machine learning techniques*. Master's thesis, Chalmers University of Technology, Gothenburg.

Gertrud Pettersson. 2005. *Svenska språket under sjuhundra år*. Studentlitteratur.

Colin Raffel, Noam Shazeer, Adam Roberts, Katherine Lee, Sharan Narang, Michael Matena, Yanqi Zhou, Wei Li, and Peter J. Liu. 2019. Exploring the limits of transfer learning with a unified text-to-text transformer. *arXiv e-prints*.

[6]https://spraakbanken.gu.se/en

Christophe Rigaud, Antoine Doucet, Mickaël Coustaty, and Jean-Philippe Moreux. 2019. ICDAR 2019 competition on post-OCR text correction. In *International Conference on Document Analysis and Recognition (ICDAR)*, pages 1588–1593. IEEE Xplore.

Noam Shazeer and Mitchell Stern. 2018. Adafactor: Adaptive learning rates with sublinear memory cost. *arXiv e-prints*.

Elizabeth Soper, Stanley Fujimoto, and Yen-Yun Yu. 2021. BART for post-correction of OCR newspaper text. In *Proceedings of the Seventh Workshop on Noisy User-generated Text (W-NUT 2021)*, pages 284–290, Online. Association for Computational Linguistics.

Lukas Stankevičius, Mantas Lukoševičius, Jurgita Kapočiūtė-Dzikienė, Monika Briedienė, and Tomas Krilavičius. 2022. Correcting diacritics and typos with a ByT5 transformer model. *Applied Sciences*, 12(5).

Ashish Vaswani, Noam Shazeer, Niki Parmar, Jakob Uszkoreit, Llion Jones, Aidan N. Gomez, Lukasz Kaiser, and Illia Polosukhin. 2017. Attention is all you need. Red Hook, NY, USA. Curran Associates Inc.

Thomas Wolf, Lysandre Debut, Victor Sanh, Julien Chaumond, Clement Delangue, Anthony Moi, Pierric Cistac, Tim Rault, Rémi Louf, Morgan Funtowicz, Joe Davison, Sam Shleifer, Patrick von Platen, Clara Ma, Yacine Jernite, Julien Plu, Canwen Xu, Teven Le Scao, Sylvain Gugger, Mariama Drame, Quentin Lhoest, and Alexander M. Rush. 2020. Transformers: State-of-the-art natural language processing. In *Proceedings of the 2020 Conference on Empirical Methods in Natural Language Processing: System Demonstrations*, pages 38–45, Online. Association for Computational Linguistics.

Linting Xue, Aditya Barua, Noah Constant, Rami Al-Rfou, Sharan Narang, Mihir Kale, Adam Roberts, and Colin Raffel. 2021a. ByT5: Towards a token-free future with pre-trained byte-to-byte models. *arXiv e-prints*.

Linting Xue, Noah Constant, Adam Roberts, Mihir Kale, Rami Al-Rfou, Aditya Siddhant, Aditya Barua, and Colin Raffel. 2021b. mT5: A massively multilingual pre-trained text-to-text transformer. In *Proceedings of the 2021 Conference of the North American Chapter of the Association for Computational Linguistics: Human Language Technologies*, pages 483–498, Online. Association for Computational Linguistics.

The Kronieken Corpus: an Annotated Collection of Dutch/Flemish Chronicles from 1500–1850

Theo Dekker[1], **Erika Kuijpers**[2], **Alie Lassche**[1], **Carolina Lenarduzzi**[1], **Roser Morante**[2] **and Judith Pollmann**[1]
[1]Faculty of History, Leiden University
[2]Faculty of Humanities, VU Amsterdam
{t.m.a.m.dekker,a.w.lassche,j.pollmann}@hum.leidenuniv.nl
{erika.kuijpers,r.morantevallejo}@vu.nl

Abstract

In this paper we present the Kronieken Corpus, a new digital collection of 204 local chronicles, containing almost 24 million words, written in Dutch/Flemish between 1500 and 1850. About half of these texts had not been published before. The manuscripts were photographed in 39 archives and libraries in The Netherlands and Belgium and subsequently transcribed and manually annotated by volunteers. The annotations include named entities and dates, as well as source mentions and attributions. The result is a unique, enriched historical corpus of original hand-written, non-canonical and non-fictional text by lay people from the early modern period.

1 Introduction

We present a newly transcribed and annotated dataset of local chronicles in Dutch from the period 1500-1850. The corpus has been compiled with the goal of developing a method to track and analyse the circulation, reception, evaluation and acceptance of old and new knowledge over time and across geographical locations by a lay public of mainly middle class authors. This work is part of the project *Chronicling novelty. New knowledge in the Netherlands, 1500-1850*[1] and the corpus is available for public use.[2] The historic period of 1500-1850 was chosen because it covers a number of societal changes that impacted knowledge production and circulation, such as the rise of the printing press, church reformations and the scientific revolution. This period also covered the so-called eighteenth century enlightenment and revolutionary era, as well as the political 'restoration' period of the early nineteenth century.

Local chronicles are chronologically organized accounts of events in the author's community. Following Pollmann (2016), who argued that historians of early modern Europe should more actively exploit the potential of the thousands of local chronicles that Europeans wrote between 1500-1850, we approached chronicles as collections of useful knowledge created by authors for future reference. Chroniclers collected information on a range of topics including local politics and history, crime, prices, public space and natural or cultural events that they deemed remarkable. Most of these texts were not written with a view to publication in print, but as manuscripts circulated among the literate middle classes of early modern towns and villages. Chronicles are one of the very few genres of narrative European texts that remained both ubiquitous and relatively stable throughout the early modern period. Therefore they can be used for comparative studies across both time and space about a wealth of topics. In the context of the research project Chronicling Novelty, we analysed what sources of information people considered reliable and how new information changed the way people reasoned over time (Dekker, 2022; Lassche and Morante, 2021; Lassche et al., 2022; Kuijpers, 2022). We believe that this dataset will be of unique value for research in history, digital humanities and historical linguistics, as well as for students of e.g. local politics, state formation, religious history, social conflict, and history of emotions.

After the discussion of some related work in Section 2, we describe the composition of the corpus in Section 3, the transcription process in Section 4, the annotations in Section 5 and the usage, distribution and maintenance in Section 6. Finally, we present a discussion in Section 7 and put forward some conclusions in Section 8.

2 Related Work

Digital historical texts in Dutch are made available by different institutions, and in different ways. Ex-

[1]https://www.nwo.nl/en/projects/vcgw17073.
[2]https://kronieken.transkribus.eu/.

Proceedings of LaTeCH-CLfL 2024, pages 243–252
March 22, 2024

amples can be found at the website of CLARIN,[3] the Huygens Institute[4] and the Institute for Dutch Lexicology.[5] Many texts can be searched and accessed via the Nederlab portal especially catering for historical linguists,[6] such as the Gysseling corpus, the Corpus Middelnederlands and the Corpus Oudnederlands. Most of these corpora consist of documents produced by institutions, such as the currently being digitized proceedings of the States General of the Dutch Republic (1576-1796).[7] Other resources contain Newspapers,[8] or the writings of important political or literary figures and scientists.[9]

In comparison to these existing corpora, this corpus is unique in several ways. It brings together a large set of **non-institutional** writings by a broad range of lay - often unknown - authors that are not archived in one place but scattered all over the Netherlands and Belgium. Similar to the collection of private letters confiscated from Dutch ships during the Anglo-Dutch Wars in the seventeenth and eighteenth century,[10] this collection represents the voices of individuals that belong to various social strata of society, who write on their own initiative and on topics that matter to them. Other than the seized correspondences, however, the chronicles are written in a larger geographical area comprising also current day Belgium and the Eastern and Southern inland provinces of the Netherlands (Rutten and Wal, 2011, 2014). We are not aware of a similar dataset in other languages.

3 Composition of the Corpus

When searching for chronicles that suited our goals we used the following selection criteria: First, we excluded family chronicles and regional chronicles – family chronicles lack the focus on public affairs, while regional chronicles were more often written for publication and by semi-professional historians. In order for our corpus to be searchable, we also decided we could only include texts that were (mainly) written in Dutch, even though French was also an important language in the Southern Low Countries, and there were also chronicles in Yiddish and Latin. Finally, we decided to focus on texts that were not only retrospective, but that also covered events in the (adult) lifetime of the authors, and were written contemporaneously.

The selection of the chronicles that would make up the corpus was carried out by the project leaders, both senior researchers in history, with the help and advice of student assistants, historians and archivists. The list of Chronicles that were selected can be found in our GitHub repository.[11] The collection process lasted from 2016 till 2018. After that time some more chronicles were identified and added.

98 local chronicles consisting of 131 volumes had been edited and published or transcribed for local archives or historical associations before. The DBNL,[12] an online database for literary texts in Dutch hosted by the Royal Library of the Netherlands, had already digitized some of these titles. The chronicles that were not already in the online database of DBNL, were newly digitized and added to it. The rest of the chronicles were manuscripts located in libraries and archives across Belgium and the Netherlands, or owned by private persons.

To find manuscripts we searched the digital inventories of the provincial archives in the Netherlands and Belgium for (variants of) words such as chronicle, annals, journal, history and diary. We did the same for local archives and a number of important libraries of which we knew or suspected that they could host chronicles. In this way we were able to add 106 unpublished chronicles (177 volumes) to our collection, that were sourced from 39 different archives and libraries and a few private collections. These archives and libraries had to be visited one by one, and every page of a chronicle manuscript had to be scanned. Some archives took on the task of scanning the chronicles themselves, but in most cases the ScanTent was used by the project team.[13] In combination with the DocScan app, the ScanTent enables the user to hold a document with both hands and scan it with their smartphone without pressing any button. DocScan

[3] https://www.clarin.eu/resource-families.

[4] https://www.huygens.knaw.nl/en/resources/.

[5] https://ivdnt.org/corpora-lexica/.

[6] https://www.nederlab.nl/onderzoeksportaal/?action=verkennen.

[7] https://republic.huygens.knaw.nl/.

[8] https://www.delpher.nl/nl/kranten.

[9] https://ckcc.huygens.knaw.nl/epistolarium/.

[10] https://brievenalsbuit.ivdnt.org/corpus-frontend/BaB/search/, https://prizepapers.huygens.knaw.nl/.

[11] https://github.com/chroniclingnovelty/chronicles-datasets.

[12] https://www.dbnl.org/.

[13] The ScanTent was developed as part of the READ project by members of the Computer Vision Lab of the Technical University Vienna and the Digitisation Preservation group of the University of Innsbruck. See https://readcoop.eu/scantent/.

automatically takes a picture once a page is turned.

The texts are all in Dutch/Flemish with sometimes quotations in other languages (mainly French or Latin). Spelling is very heterogeneous. Some texts, especially some sixteenth-century chronicles from the North-Eastern Netherlands have elements of the local dialect. Figure 1 shows a map of the Low Countries with the distribution of manuscripts over time and space.

Figure 1: Map with number of chronicles per period and geographical points.

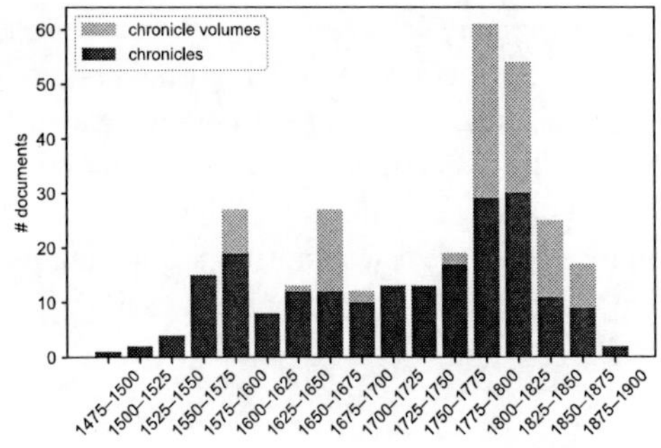

Figure 2: Distribution of chronicles in the Kronieken Corpus, visualized in bars of 25 years.

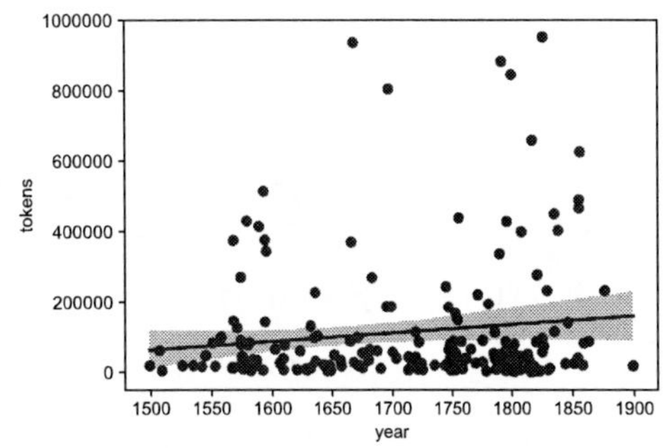

Figure 3: Number of tokens per chronicle in the Kronieken Corpus. For reasons of readability, one chronicle with 2.2 million tokens (written during many years until 1807) was excluded from this plot.

3.1 Units and size of corpus

Statistics about the full corpus can be found in Table 1. The total number of transcribed tokens is 23,871,380, belonging to 204 chronicles.

unit	amount
chronicles	204
chronicle volumes	308
tokens	23,871,380

Table 1: Size of the Kronieken Corpus.

In Figure 2, the distribution of the chronicles per time period is visualized in bars per 25 years. 1750 to 1800 is the period with more chronicles, whereas there are fewer for the first decades until 1525.

The scatter plot in Figure 3 shows the length of each chronicle in number of tokens. As can be observed, most chronicles contain less than 200,000 tokens, which applies to all time periods. The longest chronicles were written after 1650.

3.2 Data bias

Like any historical corpus there is both an institutional and a social bias in this corpus. Some categories of chronicles have had a better survival rate than others because of their content. Chronicles written in periods that were deemed important by later generations, such as the Dutch Revolt, or the Age of Revolutions have stood the test of time better than others. The fate of chronicles was also determined by the institutional context in which they were created. Thus, chronicles written by Catholic parish priests, who had no heirs, often remained in the parish. The same goes for chronicles written in convents. Town secretaries often passed on manuscripts to their successors, and in the course of our period some cities began to collect chronicles themselves. While most towns in the Low Countries had arrangements to keep their records safe, manuscripts that were written in villages may have been more vulnerable. Generally we may assume that many chronicles written by private individuals may still remain in private collections while the majority got lost over time. Figure 4 shows the number of tokens dedicated to every year in the period 1500-1850, reflecting a bias in periods of war and upheaval. This graph is based on the 196 volumes that have date annotations allowing us to count the number of words on each year.

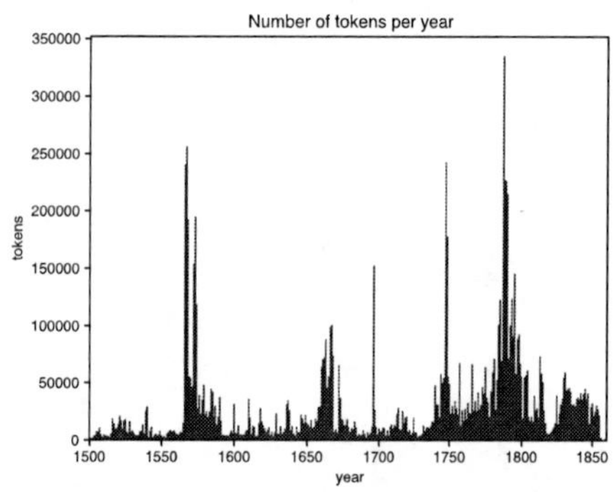

Figure 4: Number of tokens written per year based on the 139 annotated chronicles (196 volumes).

Based on the information that we collected about the authors[14] we could reconstruct the following social profile of the authors: Around 20% of the authors was anonymous, so all our knowledge about them comes from their texts. While the majority of the authors were men, we also identified 14 chronicles written by 16 female authors. 11 of them were nuns who wrote chronicles, probably in service of their convent. Although we had decided not to include convent chronicles, we made an exception for women's convents provided the chronicle focused on local rather than institutional events and resembled other local chronicles in style and content. Our assumption that chronicling was a typically urban activity seems to be correct. 79% of the chronicles in our corpus is written by urban dwellers, 21% in rural areas. For about 70% of the chroniclers we could establish their profession. 21% of all chroniclers were town secretaries, notaries, councillors, tax collectors or otherwise working in public administration. Another important group were clergymen, monastics, ministers and schoolmasters. All in all about half of the authors must therefore have had some form of (higher) education. However, over a quarter of the chroniclers earned their living in urban crafts and trades and almost 7% were farmers or farm hands. Both the real upper classes and nobility as well as unskilled labourers and the poor are underrepresented in this corpus (Kuijpers et al., 2024).

4 Transcription

Once the 106 unpublished chronicles (177 volumes) were photographed or scanned, they had to be transcribed. The scans of the chronicles were uploaded to a collection in Transkribus, a tool for handwritten text recognition (HTR) of historical documents by READ-COOP (Kahle et al., 2017). After uploading the scans, text regions and baselines were automatically detected. It turned out that in manuscripts with irregular hands or staining, text lines were missing or disrupted. In some cases the reading order of the lines was incorrect. Therefore, line segmentation had to be corrected manually by the team members and student assistants, which proved very time-consuming. After this, the scans were ready to be transcribed. This was done with the help of volunteers on the platform *VeleHanden* (ManyHands) which is being run by Picturae, a firm that specializes in the digitization of historical archives.[15] Picturae integrated the Transkribus web tool in the user interface of *VeleHanden*, allowing the volunteers to manually enter transcriptions that could later be used for training HTR models.

Every scan would be transcribed by one volunteer, and checked by another volunteer. On *VeleHanden*, these two roles were respectively the *invoerder* (transcriber) and *controleur* (controller). Every volunteer that was interested in the project could register as *invoerder*. The project team assigned specific volunteers (those who performed above average) the role of controller. Around 15,000 words of manually transcribed text were needed to train a HTR model that could be used to generate a transcription of the rest of the text. For the genre of a chronicle, this meant that about 40 pages of every handwriting needed to be transcribed by the volunteers. After training a model, its quality was evaluated using a test set. A model was considered good enough when the character error rate on the test set was below 4%. The automatically transcribed pages became visible for volunteers on *VeleHanden* to check. The *invoerder* now checked the transcription of the computer, and the controller performed a double check (Dekker et al., 2023).

To guide the volunteers in their work, transcrip-

[14] https://chroniclingnovelty.github.io/corpus-documentation/chronicles/.

[15] http://www.velehanden.nl.

tion guidelines were provided by the project team. These guidelines were based on the guidelines used by another *VeleHanden* project by the Amsterdam City Archive for the transcription of notarial deeds.[16] They contained transcription rules (about for example the use of capitals, punctuation marks, and illegible text), examples of often-used abbreviations in early modern written text, and lists of commonly used symbols and their meaning.[17]

The digitized texts of the other set of chronicles, those 98 chronicles that had been edited and published in the past, had to be uploaded to the same Transkribus collection as the manuscripts, to enable annotation. The digitized versions of these published chronicles contained all sorts of paratext, including introductions, footnotes, margin texts, and page numbers of the publication. All text that was not part of the original manuscript was removed. The varied manner in which the editorial additions to the chronicle were structured meant that most of this curation had to be done manually. Afterwards, the cleaned publications were converted to page XMLs, and uploaded to the Transkribus collection. Because the original page numbering was missing in these chronicles, we defined a page as a collection of 50 lines. However, since many of the chronicles lacked punctuation, some of these lines could turn out to be extremely long, while others were relatively short.

As a small team, with only five years' funding, we were unable to check and correct the transcriptions by the crowd by ourselves. Much of the proofreading was done by volunteers we selected and invited for that task. Even though the average quality of the transcriptions is good, the corpus is not consistent in the use of capitals, punctuation, and quite a few transcription mistakes remain. Most manuscripts until ca. 1710 were written in Gothic script, which would only be readable for a small group of experienced volunteers. Some handwritings are more difficult to read than others and also the condition of the volume, paper and ink could cause problems for even proficient transcribers. Missing or unreadable characters would be indicated by the transcribers with # or @ respectively.

The transcription work started in July 2019, while the *Vele Handen* project closed by the end of 2022. Up until now a small group of volunteers is still transcribing directly in the Transkribus webtool. All but 5 volumes of the scanned manuscripts have been transcribed by December 2023.

5 Annotations

Because of the complexity of the task, annotation projects of historical corpora still make use of manual work by experts or volunteers although tools for automatic annotation are currently being developed (Tonelli and Menini, 2021; Arnoult et al., 2021; Sluijter et al.; Koolen et al., 2020; Koolen and Hoekstra, 2020). We performed the annotations with the Transkribus tool.

Once the chronicles had been transcribed we performed three annotation tasks. (i) We labeled named entities, dates, and page numbers. These labels should improve the searchability of the corpus for future users as well as enable our own analysis. Due to limited time, we were not able to annotate the full corpus. Instead, a subset of 139 chronicles (196 volumes) was annotated. (ii) In a smaller subset of 66 chronicles (85 volumes) the referencing to sources of information by the authors was annotated. (iii) In a third annotation project, attribution relations were tagged in another subset of the corpus (17 chronicles, 22 chronicle volumes). In the first task, we chose to annotate the corpus manually because our goal was to create the largest possible gold standard annotated data set. This differed from the annotation tasks 2 and 3, where the goal was to explore whether a limited set of manually annotated data would be sufficient to train computer models that would be able to automatically label source mentions and attribution relations. In the subsections below, the three annotation tasks are discussed in more detail.

units	amount
chronicles	139
chronicle volumes	196
tokens	12,709,875
`date`	172,974
`location`	292,726
`person name`	189,356

Table 2: Size of the subcorpus annotated with dates and named entities and number of annotations.

[16] `https://www.amsterdam.nl/stadsarchief/alleamsterdamseakten/`. The project was named 'Crowd leert de computer lezen'.

[17] `https://github.com/chroniclingnovelty/chronicles-datasets/tree/main/handleidingen/Invoerinstructie_Transkribus_Lite.pdf`.

5.1 Annotation of dates, named entities, and layout features

Chronicles that were completely transcribed and controlled in the transcription project on *VeleHanden*, were made available in a second project on *VeleHanden*, in which volunteers annotated the chronicles. Guidelines were drawn up in which nine different labels were introduced and explained, accompanied by examples of text fragments in which the label had or did not have to be applied. Three content tags and six layout tags were determined: `date`, `location`, and `person name` were the content tags, and `pagenumber`, `margin text`, `lists and tables`, `copied text`, `image`, and `printed text` were the layout tags. The annotation guidelines are publicly available.[18] In Table 2, statistics can be found on the size of the subset, as well as the number of annotations of the three content labels (`date`, `location`, and `person name`).

The `date` tag contained an attribute, which meant that volunteers added the normalized date in an input field in the ISO 8601 format `yyyy-mm-dd`. This normalization step was essential since the chronicles showed a wide variety of ways in which dates were written. If volunteers were unsure about the normalized date (for example when a chronicler refered to 'St. Elizabeth's Eve'), they still tagged the text as `date`, but entered `xxxx-xx-xx` in the input field. They also used the `xx` if they were not sure about the exact day or month.

A mention of a land, region, place, street, water, or other known location or building, was tagged as `location`. If a location was conjugated to an adjective (for example 'a corps of Brandenburg troops'), the adjective was also tagged as `location`. The same was true for references to population groups, such as 'the Turcks' or 'the Venetians': they were also tagged as a `location`. The label `person name` was applied to mentions of a person's name. Titles of persons were tagged as well, and the same was true for professions, as long as they were accompanied by a person's name, such as 'Heer en Raed en advocaat Fiscaal Boreel' and 'Jan Stampijoen lantmeter'. The mention of a title or a profession only were not tagged.

The remaining six tags considered the layout features of the manuscript, rather than the content. If the author had used pagenumbers, this was annotated with the tag `pagenumber`. A reference to a folio number was also annotated, but when the page number or folio number was part of a reference '(see page X)', the label was not applied. The tag `margin text` was used when text was added in the margin or as a footnote. If a chronicler had noted information in a list or a table, for example the number of deaths per month, or price fluctuations, this was labeled as `lists and tables`. Text that was copied from another source and was recognized as such, was tagged as `copied text`. These fragments were in some chronicles indicated with quotation marks and/or a colon, in other chronicles words such as 'copy', 'extract' or 'resolution' were indications for a copied piece of text. Printed text, for example a pasted newspaper clipping, was tagged as `printed text`. Finally, if a scan contained an image, the label `image` was used.

Since the chance of errors was considered smaller in the annotation project than in the transcription project, the annotations were not double checked.

5.2 Annotation of sources

In order to get more insight into the reception of news and information by chroniclers, an annotation task was set up to label source mentions in chronicles (Lassche and Morante, 2021). A group of four volunteers, all having an above-average knowledge of the early modern Dutch language and culture, performed the task. They were provided with extensive guidelines in which source mentions were explained.[19] To extract source-related information, three labels were distinguished: `receiver`, the person receiving information; `source`, the instance bringing information to the receiver; and `perception`, how the source is bringing information to the receiver.

The label `perception` had four possible attributes: `oral/heard`, `written/read`, `seen`, or `else`. See the following examples, taken from the chronicles:

1. Deze morgen kwam `<source>` burgemeester Vorsterman `</source>` `<receiver>` ons `</receiver>` `<perception: oral/heard>` aanzeggen, dat wegens de ziekte, niemand in de kerk `</perception>`begraven mocht worden.

   This morning `<source>` mayor Vorsterman `</source>` came `<perception: oral/heard>`

[18] https://github.com/chroniclingnovelty/chronicles-datasets/tree/main/handleidingen/Annotatie_instructie_Vele_Handen.pdf.

[19] https://github.com/chroniclingnovelty/chronicles-datasets/tree/main/handleidingen/Annotatie_instructie_bronnen_Vele_Handen.pdf.

telling </perception> <receiver> us </receiver> that because of the disease, no one was allowed to be buried in the church.

2. 18 Februarij hebben <receiver> Wij </receiver> het Eerste in deze Stad in de <source> Amsterdammer Courant </source> van dien dag <perception: written/read> gezien </perception> dat Mevrouw Haere Koninglijke Hoogheijd Gemalin van de Heere Prince Erfstadhouder in 's Hage op den 16 dezer des Avonds te 11 Uuren Voorspoedig en Gelukkig was Verlost van een Gezonde en Welgeschapen Prins!

   On 18 February <receiver> we </receiver> have <perception: written/read> seen </perception> in the <source> Amsterdammer Courant </source> of that day that Her Royal Highness had given birth to a healthy and shapely Prince on the 16th at 11 in the evening in The Hague!

3. <receiver> Men </receiver> <perception: oral/heard> hoorde </perception> hoedat eenen boer sig zeer ongeluckiglijck verhangen hadt.

   <receiver> They </receiver> <perception: oral/heard> heard </perception> how a farmer had very miserably hanged himself.

Inter-annotator agreement (IAA) was calculated at two moments during the process of improving the guidelines, using the balanced F-measure (Hripcsak, 2005) (see Table 3). After the first calculation of the IAA, the F-scores were analysed. They showed that the guidelines caused the most confusion among the annotators regarding the label source. Annotators found it hard to distinguish between the description of an event ('Our Aldermen Court was heard') and the mention of a source ('We heard a strange rumour'). Guidelines were also not clear about self-references of a chronicler ('as I wrote on p. 23'). Some annotators interpreted this wrongly as a source mention.

	F-score 1		**F-score 2**	
	A1–A2	*A2–A1*	*A1–A2*	*A2–A1*
all	0.589	0.589	0.755	0.729
source	0.208	0.208	0.768	0.760
receiver	0.777	0.777	0.667	0.571
perception	0.707	0.707	0.754	0.699

Table 3: Inter-Annotator Agreement for the source annotation task in the first and second calculations.

The F-scores obtained in the second calculation of inter annotator agreement after improvement of the guidelines made it clear that much of the confusion was cleared up: especially the F-score of the label source was much higher than before, as shown in Table 3. Statistics on the size of the subset that was annotated, and the number of annotations that were made are in Table 4. An average of 93 sources were annotated per chronicle, compared to an average of 24 for receivers. The annotated data was used to train a classifier for automatic source annotation, but the low F-scores (below 0.4) of these models indicated a lack of success in this regard (Lassche and Morante, 2021; Lassche, 2024).

	amount
chronicles	66
chronicle volumes	85
source	6167
receiver	1597
perception	3391

Table 4: Size of the subcorpus annotated with sources and number of annotations.

5.3 Annotation of attribution

The extraction of attribution relations from text plays a relevant role in different NLP tasks such as the extraction of quotations and perspectives (Chen et al., 2019). An attribution relation (AR) is 'a relation ascribing the ownership of an attitude towards some linguistic material, i.e. the text itself, a portion of it or its semantic content, to an entity' (Pareti, 2012). An AR is typically expressed by three components: a *source*, a *cue*, and a *content*. A *source* is the entity that is the owner of the attributed abstract object, and can be a named entity, a noun or a pronoun. A *cue* is a lexical item which explicitly signals the ownership relationship between a source and a content. It is often a verb, but it can also be a noun, prepositional phrase, adjective or adverb. A *content* is a text portion which is perceived as meant to be attributed to the source. The following are examples of ARs:

1. <source> D'eene </source> <cue> gelooft </cue>, <content> dat ons Cristus suyvert van alle sonden </content>, d'ander heeft daertoe een vagevier gevonden.

   <source> Some </source> <cue> believe </cue> <content> that Christ purifies us from all sins </content>, others have found purgatory for this purpose.

2. <source>Een Heer, die destijds in Gecommitteerde Raden zat,</source> <cue> verhaalde </cue> mij eens, <content> dat hij driemaal bij den Hertog om audientie had laten vragen, zonder die te kunnen verkrijgen.</content>

   <source>A man, who was on the Committed Council at the time,</source> once <cue> told </cue> me, <content> that he had asked for an audience with the Duke three times, without getting it. </content>

One annotator who followed a training process labeled all the attribution relations in the chronicles under supervision of a senior researcher. Because the only existing guidelines for labeling attribution apply to contemporary English, guidelines that explained attribution relations in early modern Dutch texts had to be made. In Table 5, statistics can be found on the size of the subset that was annotated, and the number of annotations that were made.

	amount
chronicles	17
chronicle volumes	22
`source`	2880
`cue`	3546
`content`	3646

Table 5: Size of the subcorpus annotated with attribution and number of annotations.

During the process of improving the guidelines IAA was calculated for a sample of documents at two moments using the balanced F-measure[20] as shown in Table 6. Currently, experiments are run in which the manually annotated data is used to train a token classifier using BERT, as well as to let a generative model annotate more data.

	F-score 1		**F-score 2**	
	A1–A2	*A2–A1*	*A1–A2*	*A2–A1*
all	0.590	0.578	0.721	0.721
`source`	0.670	0.667	0.757	0.771
`cue`	0.624	0.601	0.812	0.801
`content`	0.503	0.497	0.570	0.574

Table 6: Inter-Annotator Agreement in the attribution annotation task.

6 Usage, Distribution and Maintenance

The corpus, including the transcriptions, meta-data, manual and automatic annotations and documentation has been made publicly available for future use under the creative commons license CC 4.0. All data is stored in a GitHub repository.[21] The digitized versions of published material are published on the DBNL website. The scans of the manuscripts that were uploaded in the Transkribus tool are accessible side by side with their transcriptions and annotations on the read and search website by READ-COOP.[22] Transcripts, annotations and images can be downloaded from this website by any user. Moreover at the 'back side' of this published collection it is still possible to correct transcripts if misreadings are found, and to add new scans of chronicles or missing transcriptions.

The options for future usage of the corpus are diverse. Chronicles belong to the type of material that are underrepresented in the digital resources for the humanities: original hand-written, non-canonical and non-fiction pre-modern material. However, they are considered of prime importance to historical linguists, and literary scholars as well as historians. Historical linguists are interested in chronicles because they give access to a historical linguistic variety that was 'filtered out' by professional printers, proofreaders and editors. For literary scholars, they offer vital access to reading and writing practices beyond the canonical authors. While medieval chronicles have been very well studied as a genre, and for the Netherlands have been digitally available for many years now, [23] early modern chronicles have only recently been rediscovered as an important resource. They provide a very valuable insight in the everyday experiences of life in historical urban and village communities.

The corpus of chronicles is also of great value for the digital humanities and computational linguistics communities. To begin with, corpora of this size and diversity of historic variants are very scarce, especially for Dutch. Such a corpus will allow us to make progress in processing historic variants of Dutch not only because it can be used to improve linguistic normalization tools, but also because it will allow users to train new tools. The additional layers of semantic annotation that will be provided with the corpus will allow the computational linguistics community to train new tools for the semantic processing of historical variants of Dutch. The corpus can be used for research purposes, as well as for teaching purposes. Students can be taught how to process this type of corpora with hands-on assignments. Finally, the corpus can be used to organize international shared tasks on processing historic variants of languages.

Finally, users should take into account that although we believe that chronicles are a genre of texts that have much in common, the diversity in size, topics, writing styles, motives and the pro-

[20] IAA was calculated between the annotator and one other expert.

[21] `https://github.com/chroniclingnovelty/chronicles-datasets`.

[22] `https://kronieken.transkribus.eu/`.

[23] `http://www.narrative-sources.be/colofon_nl.php`

ficiency of the authors make for a very heterogeneous corpus that sometimes hinders comparisons over time and across space.

7 Discussion

Our initial plan was not only to annotate a part of the corpus, but also to use the annotations to train machine learning systems to complete the annotations, for example to annotate source mentions and attribution relationships. However, this has proven to be more challenging than anticipated. Our exploratory experiments on automatically labeling source mentions demonstrated that the mentioning of sources showed so much variation and complexity that the training set was still too small, and the model used (CRF) was not the most powerful (Lassche and Morante, 2021; Lassche, 2024). In ongoing experiments aiming to annotate attribution relationships automatically, similar challenges are arising. Because the ways to automatically annotate data are rapidly expanding due to the swift developments in the field new avenues are opening for experimentation. We plan to train BERT classifiers (Devlin et al., 2019) and to annotate more data using generative models and appropriate prompting.

The corpus has several limitations. First, due to limited budget, time and staff, it was not possible to annotate the full corpus. We manage to annotate 197 out of 308 volumes, which amounts to 63% of the corpus. For the same reason, only 179 volumes have normalised date labels.[24] Second, some errors and misreadings remain. The transcription and annotation tasks were carried out by volunteers with varying proficiency in paleography and comprehension of historical language. The team of experts could not correct all transcriptions themselves but was assisted in this task by a selected group of volunteers. Third, apart from the earlier mentioned bias due to selection procedures by the team as well as the ravages of time, the following types of chronicles may be underrepresented in the corpus: chronicles written by women, chronicles written in rural areas, and chronicles written by lower class authors. Moreover, chronicles that are part of private collections, smaller archives, smaller towns and especially in archives that have not yet digitized their catalogues or inventories had a much smaller chance to be located by us.

[24] An overview with all chronicles and their annotation status can be found on https://github.com/chroniclingnovelty/chronicles-datasets/blob/main/handleidingen/Overview_Chronicles.xlsx.

8 Conclusions

We presented a corpus of 204 Dutch language chronicles from the period 1500-1850 counting almost 24 million words. The corpus has been transcribed manually by volunteers combined with automatic Hand Written Text Recognition as offered in the Transkribus Tool. The transcriptions have also been annotated by volunteers in three annotation tasks: A first general annotation of named entities, mentions of dates as well as elements in the lay out of the pages such as images, printed matter, tables and copied text. A second task focused on the annotation of sources of information mentioned by the author as well as the receiver of this information and the medium of communication, and a third task focused on attribution relations.

The result will be of value to both historians, students of historical literature as well as historical linguists. The additional layers of semantic annotation that are provided with the corpus will allow the computational linguistics community to train new tools for the semantic processing of historical variants of Dutch. Although a big effort was made to provide a quality resource, it was not possible to surmount some limitations posed by the magnitude of the project and the nature of textual data. In future work we will explore ways to surmount these limitations.

Acknowledgements

Research for this paper was funded through the NWO VC project 'Chronicling Novelty. New knowledge in the Netherlands, 1500-1850' directed by Judith Pollmann (Leiden University and Erika Kuijpers (VU Amsteram) and by the Network Institute of the VU Amsterdam, via the project "The Cycle of News in Chronicles from Eighteenth Century Holland: A Stylometric Approach".

References

Sophie I. Arnoult, Lodewijk Petram, and Piek Vossen. 2021. Batavia asked for advice. pretrained language models for named entity recognition in historical texts. In *Proceedings of the 5th Joint SIGHUM Workshop on Computational Linguistics for Cultural Heritage, Social Sciences, Humanities and Literature*, pages 21–30, Punta Cana, Dominican Republic (online). Association for Computational Linguistics.

Sihao Chen, Daniel Khashabi, Chris Callison-Burch, and Dan Roth. 2019. PerspectroScope: A window to the world of diverse perspectives. In *Proceedings of the 57th Annual Meeting of the Association for Computational Linguistics: System Demonstrations*, pages 129–134, Florence, Italy. Association for Computational Linguistics.

Theo Dekker. 2022. God's Invisible Particles as an Explanation for the Rinderpest Outbreak (1713-1714): The Reception of Medical Knowledge in the Dutch Republic. *European journal for the history of medicine and health*, 79(1):152–168.

Theo Dekker, Erika Kuijpers, and Carolina Lenarduzzi. 2023. Van crowdsourcing naar echte burgerwetenschap. Investeer in de kwaliteit van samenwerking. *Stadsgeschiedenis*, 18(2):105–117.

Jacob Devlin, Ming-Wei Chang, Kenton Lee, and Kristina Toutanova. 2019. BERT: Pre-training of deep bidirectional transformers for language understanding. In *Proceedings of the 2019 Conference of the North American Chapter of the Association for Computational Linguistics: Human Language Technologies, Volume 1 (Long and Short Papers)*, pages 4171–4186, Minneapolis, Minnesota. Association for Computational Linguistics.

G. Hripcsak. 2005. Agreement, the F-Measure, and Reliability in Information Retrieval. *Journal of the American Medical Informatics Association*, 12(3):296–298.

P. Kahle, S. Colutto, H. Hackl, and H. Mühlberger. 2017. Transkribus - A Service Platform for Transcription, Recognition and Retrieval of Historical Documents. In *2017 14th IAPR International Conference on Document Analysis and Recognition (ICDAR)*, volume 04, pages 19–24.

Marijn Koolen and F.G. Hoekstra. 2020. The semantics of structure in large historical corpora. Digital Humanities 2020 : intersections, DH2020 ; Conference date: 20-07-2020 Through 25-07-2020.

Marijn Koolen, F.G. Hoekstra, I.J.A. Nijenhuis, R.G.H. Sluijter, Rutger Koert, van, Esther van Gelder, Gijsjan Brouwer, and H. Brugman. 2020. Modelling Resolutions of the Dutch States General for Digital Historical Research. Collect Connect: Archives and Collections in a Digital Age ; Conference date: 23-11-2020 Through 24-11-2020.

Erika Kuijpers. 2022. De informatiebronnen van Albert Louwen (1722-1798), kroniekschrijver te Purmerend. In Erika Kuijpers and Gerrit Verhoeven, editors, *Makelaars in kennis: Informatie verzamelen, verwerken en verspreiden in de vroegmoderne Nederlanden*, pages 131–158. Universitaire Pers Leuven.

Erika Kuijpers, Carolina Lenarduzzi, and Judith Pollmann. 2024. Profiling local chroniclers in the early modern Low Countries.

Alie Lassche. 2024. Information Dynamics in Low Countries' Chronicles (1500-1860). A Computational Approach.

Alie Lassche, Jan Kostkan, and Kristoffer Nielbo. 2022. Chronicling Crises: Event Detection in Early Modern Chronicles from the Low Countries. In *Proceedings of the Computational Humanities Research Conference 2022*, volume 3290 of *CEUR Workshop Proceedings*, pages 215–230. CEUR.

Alie Lassche and Roser Morante. 2021. The early Modern Dutch mediascape. detecting media mentions in chronicles using word embeddings and CRF. In *Proceedings of the 5th Joint SIGHUM Workshop on Computational Linguistics for Cultural Heritage, Social Sciences, Humanities and Literature*, pages 1–10, Punta Cana, Dominican Republic (online). Association for Computational Linguistics.

Silvia Pareti. 2012. A database of attribution relations. In *Proceedings of the Eighth Conference on International Language Resources and Evaluation (LREC'12)*, pages 3213–3217. ELRA.

Judith Pollmann. 2016. Archiving the Present and Chronicling for the Future in Early Modern Europe. *Past & Present*, 230(suppl 11):231–252.

Gijsbert Rutten and Marijke J. van der Wal. 2011. Local dialects, supralocal writing systems. The degree of orality of Dutch private letters from the seventeenth century. 14(2):251–274.

Gijsbert Rutten and Marijke J. van der Wal. 2014. *Letters as Loot: A sociolinguistic approach to seventeenth- and eighteenth-century Dutch*. John Benjamins.

Ronald Sluijter, Joris Oddens, Rik Hoekstra, Marijn Koolen, Rutger van Koert, Menzo Windhouwer, Hennie Brugman, and Femke Gordijn. Opening the Gates to the Dutch Republic: A Comparison between Analogue and Digital Editions of the Resolutions of the States General. In *Proceedings of the Digital Parliamentary Data in Action (DiPaDA 2022) Workshop*, volume 3133 of *CEUR Workshop Proceedings*, pages 158–166. CEUR. ISSN: 1613-0073.

Sara Tonelli and Stefano Menini. 2021. FrameNet-like Annotation of Olfactory Information in Texts. *Proceedings of the 5th Joint SIGHUM Workshop on Computational Linguistics for Cultural Heritage, Social Sciences, Humanities and Literature*.

Direct Speech Identification in Swedish Literature – an Exploration of Training Data Type, Typographical Markers, and Evaluation Granularity

Sara Stymne
Department of Linguistics and Philology
Uppsala University
sara.stymne@lingfil.uu.se

Abstract

Identifying direct speech in literary fiction is challenging for cases that do not mark speech segments with quotation marks. Such efforts have previously been based either on smaller manually annotated gold data or larger automatically annotated silver data, extracted from works with quotation marks. However, no direct comparison has so far been made between the performance of these two types of training data. In this work, we address this gap. We further explore the effect of different types of typographical speech marking and of using evaluation metrics of different granularity. We perform experiments on Swedish literary texts and find that using gold and silver data has different strengths, with gold data having stronger results on token-level metrics, whereas silver data overall has stronger results on span-level metrics. If the training data contains some data that matches the typographical speech marking of the target, that is generally sufficient for achieving good results, but it does not seem to hurt if the training data also contains other types of marking.

1 Introduction

The main narrative of literary works is typically interspersed with dialogues representing direct speech utterances by the characters in the work. Distinguishing narrative and direct speech is important for work on digital literature studies, for tasks including identifying the social networks of novels (Elson et al., 2010) and analyzing the sentiment of characters towards each other (Nalisnick and Baird, 2013). In addition to speech segments, we are also interested in speech tags, or reporting clauses, Speech tags can have different lengths and positions with respect to the speech, exemplified in (1–3).[1] Speech tags are also relevant for work in literary studies, such as Allison (2018) who study them as a means of analyzing Dickens' narrative perspective.

(1) – Står morsan och drömmer? sade hon skarpt. Raska på.
'– Are you dreaming, mum? she said sharply. Hurry up.'
(M. Sandel, *Hexdansen*, p. 46)

(2) Han sa:
Varför står du här och skräpar?
'He said:
Why are you idling here?'
(H. Bergman, *Chefen fru Ingeborg*, p. 15)

(3) – Min chef, sade jag till domaren med en röst som jag förgäves sökte göra stadig, får jag ge honom en spruta till?
'– My boss, I said to the judge with a voice that I tried to keep stable to no avail, may I give him another shot '
(K. Boye, *Kallocain*, p. 264)

Speech segments are often marked typographically to distinguish them from the narrative. In English, the standard is to mark them with quotation marks, which makes both the start and end of such segments easily identifiable. However, in other languages, there is a variety of ways to mark speech, such as using a dash at the start, but not at the end of speech segments or at the restart after speech tags, as in Example 1. In some works, speech is not marked at all, as in Example 2. In these cases, it is much more challenging to identify speech segments, since the typography is not enough, and there is a need to use textual cues, such as reporting verbs and tense shifts. In this work, we focus on Swedish literary works from 1809–1940, containing a mix of speech marking styles.

Most previous work on direct speech identification for literature is based on different types of machine learning. Such systems have been trained

[1] All translations into English from the original Swedish are our own. In examples, we mark direct speech in blue and speech tags in purple.

Proceedings of LaTeCH-CLfL 2024, pages 253–263
March 22, 2024 ©2024 Association for Computational Linguistics

on two types of data: gold or silver. Gold data consists of humanly annotated data. Such data is typically of high quality and may contain a variety of typographical markings. However, it is typically relatively limited in size. By silver data, we mean data that has been automatically extracted from literary texts, normally by identifying works that use quotation marks, and assuming that text within quotation marks constitutes a speech segment. The advantage of such data is that it is easy to collect large annotated corpora. However, the quality is typically lower than for gold data since quotation marks can also be used for other purposes, such as marking quotations, irony, and unusual usage of words or terms. To the best of our knowledge, all previous work on direct speech identification for a single target language has either used gold or silver data, which means that a direct comparison between the usefulness of the two types of data is lacking. The only exception is Kurfalı and Wirén (2020) who worked on zero-shot cross-lingual classification, and compared English silver data to an in-language gold baseline. In this work, we fill that gap, by contrasting the use of a large silver dataset with a smaller manually annotated gold dataset, taken from the SLäNDa corpus (Stymne and Östman, 2022), for the same language, Swedish. As far as we are aware, this is also the first effort to use silver data for the identification of speech tags. While extraction of speech is straightforward in texts using quotation marks, automatically extracting speech tags requires additional heuristics.

There is also little previous investigation of the impact of the use of different typographical markers in the training and test data of classifiers. Stymne and Östman (2022) provided separate test sets for different types of marking but performed only a small pilot experiment. In this work, we extend their study and explore the issue in more detail. The task setup as well as the metrics used in previous works have also varied between studies. In this work, we model the task of identifying direct speech and speech tags as a token-classification problem. Unlike previous studies, we evaluate it on two levels of granularity, both at the token level and at the span level, which requires the exact matching of a full span. This allows us to investigate the effect of metric choice on the results.

To sum up, we investigate the following research questions, in the context of identification of direct speech segments and speech tags in literary works:

RQ1 Is it preferable to use smaller gold data or larger automatically annotated silver data for direct speech identification?

RQ2 Can heuristically constructed silver data be useful for speech tag identification?

RQ3 Is it possible to improve speech and speech tag identification by mixing gold and silver data?

RQ4 What is the effect of different typographical marking of speech in training and test data?

RQ5 What is the effect of using span-level versus token-level evaluation metrics for direct speech identification?

In addition, we provide a detailed overview of related work for the task of direct speech identification.

2 Related Work

In this section, we focus on reviewing related work on the identification of direct speech in literary works for cases where quotation marks are not predominant. This excludes some distantly related work, e.g. targeting other genres such as news texts (e.g. Pouliquen et al., 2007; Quintão, 2014), and work on languages that predominantly use quotation marks, such as English (e.g. Elson et al., 2010; Muzny et al., 2017). Table 1 gives an overview of a selection of relevant work, and summarizes the main setup of each study. In the following, we will go through and discuss each category of Table 1.

Language Most work focuses on one language, in most cases either German or Swedish, with one study on French. Two works explore multiple languages, including a cross-lingual setup (Kurfalı and Wirén, 2020) and multilingual training (Byszuk et al., 2020). The latter found that for many languages, including English, a rule-based system based on punctuation marks gave near-perfect accuracy. However, for other languages, especially Norwegian, which is closely related to Swedish, the rule-based system performed poorly, due to mixed graphical speech marking.

Training data All papers but one use either existing gold data or collect silver data for their experiments. Only one paper, Kurfalı and Wirén (2020) use both variants. However, their main point of investigation is to explore the feasibility of cross-lingual zero-shot training for direct speech identification, so they compare using English silver data,

Work	Language	Training data	Modelling/Eval.	Method	Marks	Miscellaneous
Brunner (2013)	German	Gold	Sentence, work	Rule, Random forest	Mixed, incl. QM	STWR
Schöch et al. (2016)	French	Gold	Sentence	SVM, MaxEnt, ...	Dash/Mix(?)	Applied
Jannidis et al. (2018)	German	Silver	Sentence, token	Log. regr., LSTM, ...	Mixed	Applied
Ek and Wirén (2019)	Swedish	Gold	Token	Log. regr., rule	Stripped speech lines	
Tu et al. (2019)	German	–	Sentence, token	Rule	No-QM	
Brunner et al. (2020b)	German	Gold	Token	BiLSTM-CRF+BERT/FLAIR	Mixed (often QM)	STWR
Byszuk et al. (2020)	9 languages	Gold	Token	BERT-ft, rule	Mixed	
Kurfalı and Wirén (2020)	4 languages	Silver (En)	Token	mBERT-ft	Stripped	Cross-lingual
Dahllöf (2022)	Swedish	Silver	Segment	Multi-layer perceptron	Stripped dash lines	Applied
Stymne and Östman (2022)	Swedish	Gold	Token/Span	BERT-ft	Mixed	Speech tags

Table 1: Summary of work on direct speech identification of literary works. Data type distinguishes training on human annotated gold data, and automatically extracted silver data. Method refers to the main method used in the paper (ft: fine-tuning, rule: rule-based modeling). For modeling and evaluation, it is stated if it is performed on the token level, span level (i.e. for each speech sequence), segment level (i.e. segment between punctuation marks), sentence level (i.e. does a specific sentence contain speech), or on the work level (i.e. based on the percentage of speech predicted for a full work). We also make a best effort to categorize the type of typographical marking used in each study, which is challenging since it is not always directly stated; here QM stands for quotation mark. STWR stands for speech, thought, and writing representation, works marked as such are not restricted to only identifying direct speech. Works marked with Applied, apply the classifiers to a large set of literary works, for further analysis.

to using in-language gold data for German (Brunner et al., 2020a), Portuguese (Quintão, 2014) and Swedish (Stymne and Östman, 2022), which does not constitute a fair comparison with respect to only data type. They do also use English gold data (Papay and Padó, 2020), for which they found that the performance is better with the gold data, with a token-level F1-score of 0.89 compared to 0.85 with the silver data. The silver data contained English books from Project Gutenberg, where speech was extracted based on quotation marks.

Modelling and Evaluation The direct speech identification task has been set up in different ways, the two most common options being either to identify lines containing speech or a token-level classification of tokens as being part of a speech segment or not. For token-level classification, some works feed only speech lines to the classifiers, while some feed the full text, also including non-speech lines. The modeling of slightly different tasks also affects the evaluation choice. The metrics presented for each granularity are accuracy or precision, recall, and/or F1-score. Normally the evaluation granularity follows the modeling, with the exception of (Stymne and Östman, 2022) where token-level classification was evaluated on the span-level. None of the surveyed studies evaluated on more than one level of granularity for a single task formulation. The variety of task formulations, metrics, languages, and datasets used, makes direct comparisons between different papers difficult.

Method The methods used mainly follow the evolution of the computational linguistics field, with some older work using rule-based methods, followed by classical machine learning approaches like logistic regression and SVM, while the majority of newer studies use neural methods, mainly fine-tuning of transformer models. Relatively few works directly compare different types of approaches. Ek and Wirén (2019) found that an SVM-based method worked considerably better than a rule-based baseline, and Brunner (2013) found that a random forest approach was better than a rule-based approach at identifying direct speech, especially for unmarked cases, and noted that the rule-based method suffered in the absence of quotation marks. Brunner et al. (2020b) found that FLAIR character embeddings performed better (for direct speech, but not for other types) than BERT-embeddings as input to a BiLSTM-CRF. Two works also compared different classical machine learning approaches (Schöch et al., 2016; Jannidis et al., 2018).

Typographical marks In Table 1 we attempt to describe the typographical markers of speech in each article. However, it is typically not clearly stated what the mix is, more than at a very high level, as indicated in the table summary. In a few studies, typographical markers are stripped from the data to investigate how well the task can be done in their absence. However, in most other studies, there seems to be a mixture of typographical markers in both training and test data. The exception is our previous work (Stymne and Östman, 2022) where we used a mixed training dataset, but with separate test sets for works with quotation marks, dashes, and no consistent marking. In addition, we explored stripped versions of these datasets. Our overall finding was that it was preferable for both speech and speech tag identification to use training data that matched the graphical speech marking of the intended target data. However, the experiments were limited, and only strict span-level metrics were used. In several other works, the analysis of the results reveals insights relating to typographical markers. Brunner et al. (2020b) noted that a main source of misclassification is the absence of quotation marks and Byszuk et al. (2020) noted that mixing data using quotation marks and dashes may have introduced noise, affecting the performance negatively.

Miscellaneous Several papers classify not only direct speech, but also indirect, free, and free indirect speech, thought, and writing, marked with STWR in Table 1. These papers use the German corpus REDEWIEDERGABE (Brunner et al., 2020a) for training, which contains all these levels, based on principles for English (Leech and Short, 1981). None of the corpora used for training of the other languages contain STWR annotations.

The only study that attempted to identify speech tags in addition to speech segments is Stymne and Östman (2022). In the training data of most other papers, speech tags are not annotated, and can thus not be extracted. The German REDEWIEDERGABE corpus do include annotations of speech tags. However, we are not aware of any work that has used this corpus for speech tag identification.

In Table 1, we also marked works that apply the direct speech identification to analyze a high number of additional literary works. Schöch et al. (2016) investigated the proportion of direct speech in different genres and over time in French novels and Jannidis et al. (2018) investigated the proportion of direct speech over time in German low- versus high-brow novels. Dahllöf (2022) performed a stylometric exploration of differences between the narrative and direct speech in modern Swedish novels.

3 Data

In this section, we give an overview of the SLäNDa corpus that we used for evaluation and gold training data. We then go on to describe the extraction of a new large silver training dataset, based on literary works with quotation marks.

	Tokens	Speech	Tags
Gold train	110K	1881	863
Gold dev	17K	201	90
Gold test:dash	38K	883	325
Gold test:none	25K	577	336
Silver training	6290K	88097	34114

Table 2: Size of data in total number of tokens (for stripped versions), number of speech (segments) and number of (speech) tags.

3.1 Gold Dataset: SLäNDa

Our gold training data comes from the SläNDa corpus version 2.0 (Stymne and Östman, 2022), a collection of excerpts from 19 novels from 1809–1940, manually annotated for speech and other features not forming part of the main narrative, such as thoughts, quotes, and letters. Since all classes except speech and speech tags are rare, they grouped all non-speech classes into an *other* class for their experiments. We use the suggested training and development splits[2] and further adapt it by not considering the *other* class, and only distinguishing between speech segments, speech tags, and narrative (including the *other* class). The training data of SLäNDa contains a mix of typographical markings and is available in two versions, the original version, which contains a mix of quotation marks, dashes, and no marking, which we will call *Gold-mix*, and a stripped version, with quotation marks and dashes removed, which we call *Gold-strip*. We also experimented with a concatenated version containing both variants: *Gold-combo*.

We use the recommended test sets in SläNDa v2.0, which contains two main sets: data from works with dash marking, and from works with with no consistent marking, mainly with no marking at all. We refer to these datasets as *Dash* and *None* respectively, and further also use the provided stripped version of the dash test set: *Dash-strip*. Table 2 summarizes the size of these sets in the number of tokens (for stripped versions), number of speech segments, and number of speech tags.

3.2 Silver Dataset

We collect a new silver dataset by gathering novels and collections of short stories from the same period as the SLäNDa data from Litteraturbanken, a publicly available collection of Swedish literature

[2]Available at `https://lindat.cz/repository/xmlui/handle/11372/LRT-4739`

Grefvinnan	log	och	betraktade	henne	innerligt	.	Var	icke	rädd	för	mig	,
The countess	smiled	and	watched	her	dearly	.	Be	not	scared	for	me	,
O	O	O	O	O	O	O	B-SPE	I-SPE	I-SPE	I-SPE	I-SPE	I-SPE

mitt	barn	–	kom	närmare	!	sade	hon	.
my	child	–	come	closer	!	said	she	.
I-SPE	I-SPE	I-SPE	I-SPE	I-SPE	I-SPE	B-TAG	I-TAG	I-TAG

Figure 1: IOB2 scheme for a sample paragraph, with English glosses for clarity ('The countess smiled and watched her dearly. Don't be afraid of me, my child – come closer! she said.' C. J. L. Almqvist, *Syster och bror*. p. 27).

works.[3] From Litteraturbanken, we selected works of high-quality proofread OCR, which we filtered to only keep those that use quotation marks for speech marking and do not have dashes at the start of lines (dashes can be used for other purposes, but typically sentence-internally). This filtering resulted in 141 works from 1821–1931.

From this data, we extracted speech segments by selecting all sequences surrounded by quotation marks. Speech tags are identified using two heuristics, in relationship to the first speech segment in a paragraph. (1) If the first speech segment is preceded by a colon (either within the paragraph, or in the previous paragraph), we search for the preceding punctuation mark or the start of a line, and mark the tokens in this stretch as a speech tag. (2) If the first speech segment of a line is not followed by a period, we mark any tokens up until a sentence-final punctuation mark or another quotation mark as a speech tag. These two heuristics would cover instances similar to examples (1–3). To further improve the quality, and have data that is not overly imbalanced, we applied two filtering strategies, based on the extracted entities. We only kept works where speech tokens constituted at least 20% of the total number of tokens and where there was at least a ratio of 20% speech tags, compared to speech segments. After this filtering, we were left with 88 works. The proposed heuristics are not perfect and the silver data still contains some noise. However, it is considerably larger than the gold data, as shown in Table 2.

We prepare three versions of the silver data: *Silver-quote*: with original quotation marks kept (not matching the SLäNDa test data), *Silver-dash* with quotation marks replaced by an initial dash, and *Silver-strip*, with all quotation marks removed. The data was prepared in the same format as SLäNDa. The silver data is publicly available under the CC BY-NC-SA license.[4]

[3] https://litteraturbanken.se/

[4] https://github.com/UppsalaNLP/LitDialogSilver/

4 Experimental Setup

In this section, we describe how we model the task, the system we use, and the evaluation metrics used.

4.1 Modelling

We model the task of identifying direct speech segments and speech tags as a token classification task. We follow Stymne and Östman (2022) and use the IOB2-scheme for representing the data, with tags for speech segments, *SPE* and speech tags *TAG*, and all other tokens marked with an *other* tag, *O*.

Figure 1 exemplifies the IOB2-scheme used, from a novel without speech marking. In case there would have been a dash or quotation marks indicating speech, they would have been included in the speech segment annotation. Also, note that dashes can be used for other purposes than speech marking; here one is used within a speech segment.

4.2 System

Based on previous work, summarized in Table 1, we choose to fine-tune a BERT model for token classification based on the IOB2-schema of our data, which has been used in the majority of the most recent works. We use the Machamp toolkit (van der Goot et al., 2021), a toolkit for various NLP tasks, based on fine-tuning an LLM, with support for using multiple datasets. Machamp has given competitive results on several tasks and has features that suit our experimental design. We use their *seq_bio* encoder, which is a CRF model enforcing consistency with IOB-schemes. As the base LLM, we use the Swedish BERT-model KBBert (Malmsten et al., 2020).

For experiments where we train on both gold and silver training data, with very different sizes, we take advantage of the dataset smoothing feature of Machamp, used to control how to sample instances from different datasets. The sampling is based on a multinomial distribution, controlled by the variable α, where $\alpha = 1.0$ means that the original

	Span-level						Token-level macro					
Test data→	Dash		Dash-strip		None		Dash		Dash-strip		None	
Training data↓	**P**	**R**	**P**	**R**	**P**	**R**	**P**	**R**	**P**	**R**	**P**	**R**
Gold-mix	**82.52**	**87.73**	74.12	74.35	**76.66**	**81.05**	92.41	**93.01**	92.47	**92.57**	94.14	**92.12**
Gold-strip	46.48	50.39	**75.70**	**80.06**	74.09	79.45	**93.32**	91.54	**93.41**	92.02	**94.18**	91.51
Gold-combo	79.49	84.36	74.56	78.46	73.49	78.28	92.41	**93.01**	92.47	**92.57**	94.14	**92.12**
Silver-quote	**67.55**	6.00	15.98	3.00	14.17	5.33	78.29	41.68	28.97	2.04	32.03	5.53
Silver-strip	59.93	35.24	**92.15**	**87.68**	**85.88**	**79.60**	91.72	51.95	94.04	**86.74**	87.58	**76.63**
Silver-dash	52.79	**50.02**	44.66	29.78	49.90	33.39	**95.57**	**65.52**	**95.11**	54.99	**95.31**	52.58

Table 3: Macro-average results with different variants of gold or silver training data.

data sizes are used, and $\alpha = 0.0$ means that an equal amount of data from each dataset is used. We experiment with different values of α for mixing gold and silver data. We use the default Machamp settings for *seq_bio* for all other hyper-parameters. With gold data we run for 20 epochs, and when using the much larger silver data, for 10 epochs. In all our experiments, we use the development set from SLäNDa to select the best model across all epochs, to be used for testing.

4.3 Evaluation

For evaluation, we use both span-level and token-level metrics. For span-level evaluation, which is a strict metric requiring the exact matching of a span, including any graphical marker of speech, we use the conlleval script, originally used to evaluate chunking in CoNLL 2020 (Tjong Kim Sang and Buchholz, 2000).[5] For the token-level evaluation, we ignore punctuation and the distinction between *B*- and *I*-tags. The reason for ignoring punctuation in token-level evaluation is to ensure a fair comparison between the original and stripped data versions, which differ in the punctuation marks used for speech marking. We use our own implementation of token-level evaluation. For both granularities, we report precision, recall, and F1-score for speech segments and speech tags separately, as well as macro-averaged scores over the two classes. We repeat all experiments three times with different random seeds and report average results

5 Results

In this section, we present and discuss the results, followed by a summary of our main findings.

6 High-Level Results

In our first experiment, we compare macro-average precision and recall for all variants of gold and silver training data. For F1-scores, we refer to the detailed results in Tables 4–7. Results are shown in Table 3.

Gold Versus Silver Data

For the *Dash* test set, which contains dashes for speech marking, the performance is overall higher with gold data than with silver data, except for token-level precision, which is slightly higher, but with a considerably lower recall.

For the two test sets with no (consistent) marking, *Dash-strip* and *None*, there is a precision/recall tradeoff on the token-level metrics, with considerably higher recall when trained on gold data, and higher precision with silver data. On the span-level evaluation, results are overall better with silver data.

Token- Versus Span-Level Evaluation

For the two test sets without marking, we see a clear difference between the two metrics. On span-level evaluation, matching silver data performs better than gold data, whereas the recall is considerably higher for gold data than for silver data when evaluated on the token level, however, with slightly lower precision. On the *Dash* test set, all gold training data sets perform well on token-level evaluation, whereas there is a large difference between the span-level results, which is due to dashes not being identified as speech markers, which means that the whole span is not matched.

A preliminary investigation into the difference between the two metrics, especially on the two unmarked test sets, showed that the gold SLäNDa data has some inconsistencies in the annotation of punctuation marks between speech segments and speech tags, as well as at the end of speech segments and tags. The silver data, on the other hand, is consistent in this respect, since it was annotated by rule-based heuristics. This seems to be one reason why it is harder to match full segments with gold training data since just missing a punctuation

[5] Retrieved from `https://www.cnts.ua.ac.be/conll2000/chunking/conlleval.txt`.

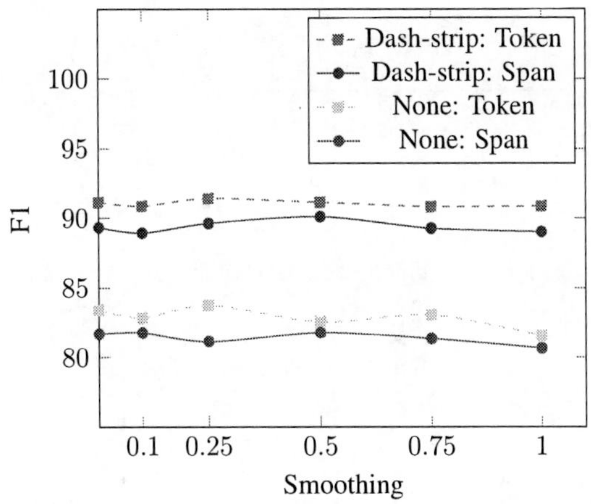

Figure 2: F1-scores at the span and token level (macro), for models trained on both gold and silver data, with different smoothing values.

	Speech			Tags		
	P	R	F	P	R	F
Gold-mix	93.57	**95.82**	**94.68**	93.78	**87.52**	**90.54**
Silver-dash	93.52	77.37	84.68	**97.63**	53.67	69.25
Mixed .25	93.72	91.62	92.65	89.47	77.08	82.81
Mixed .50	**94.51**	88.36	91.33	92.57	76.38	83.68

Table 4: Token-level results for speech (segments) and (speech) tags for the best models on the *Dash* test set.

	Speech			Tags		
	P	R	F	P	R	F
Gold-mix	85.03	**91.47**	88.13	80.01	**84.00**	81.95
Silver-dash	67.78	69.27	68.50	37.80	30.77	33.89
Mixed .25	87.24	86.11	86.66	88.38	81.13	84.59
Mixed .50	**91.20**	88.49	**89.82**	**90.74**	81.44	**85.83**

Table 5: Span-level results for speech (segments) and (speech) tags for the best models on the *Dash* test set.

mark will mean missing a full segment, whereas such an error will not be included in the token-level metrics, which ignores punctuation.

Impact of Typographical Marking

For the *Dash* test set, it is overall best to use training data containing dashes, i.e. *Gold-mix* and *Silver-dash*, with a few exceptions with higher precision at a cost of a lower recall. For the two test sets without marking, the difference between the three types of gold training data is generally very small for both types of evaluation. With silver data, the clearly best option is to use matching training data in the form of *Silver-strip*. It is interesting to see that when training on the silver training data, the recall is much better for *Dash-strip* than for *Dash*, without hurting precision. When training on gold data, these two data sets have similar results on token-level metrics, but *Dash* performs better on the span-level metrics.

We note that the very low recall with *Silver-quote* training is due to the mismatch of punctuation marks between the training and test data, leading to the system rarely predicting speech without punctuation marks. When training with *Silver-strip*, the performance is higher when testing with dashes, on the *Dash-strip* test set than without marking, on the *None* test set, indicating that literary works with some kind of graphical marks may share some similarities compared to original unmarked speech.

6.1 Mixing Gold and Silver Data

To further explore the usefulness of gold versus silver data, we perform an experiment where we combine *Gold-combo* and *Silver-strip* training data. We choose these variants based on initial results, with the main focus on the two test sets without marking, but with the goal of also achieving reasonable performance on the test data with dashes.

Figure 2 shows the macro-average F1-scores for the two test sets without dashes with different values for α, which controls the smoothing of dataset sizes. Overall the differences are quite small, with slightly worse results with original sizes ($\alpha = 1.0$). For both test sets, $\alpha = 0.25$ gives the best token-level scores and $\alpha = 0.5$ gives the best span-level scores. We thus chose those two values for further analysis.

6.2 Detailed Results

We now show detailed results for speech segments and speech tags separately, for the best training data for each type of test set. Tables 4–7 show these results. Note that we use different gold and silver training data for the test sets with and without dashes, to present the best option for each type of test data.

Again, we see a clear difference in results between the token-level and span-level metrics. With token-level evaluation, we always have the highest recall for a system trained on gold data, and while the precision can sometimes be slightly better with silver or mixed training, the difference in precision is quite small, whereas the difference in recall often is large, especially for speech tag identification.

	Dash-strip						None					
	Speech			Tags			Speech			Tags		
	P	R	F	P	R	F	P	R	F	P	R	F
Gold-strip	92.01	96.40	94.15	94.81	87.63	91.06	93.01	94.14	93.56	**95.36**	88.87	92.00
Gold-combo	89.53	**96.96**	93.08	**95.42**	**88.18**	**91.59**	93.47	**94.39**	**93.92**	94.81	**89.86**	**92.27**
Silver-strip	**94.91**	94.34	94.60	93.16	79.15	85.26	**96.12**	90.66	93.30	79.04	62.60	69.76
Mixed .25	93.88	95.37	**94.61**	90.36	80.52	85.16	96.09	89.92	92.87	72.62	65.01	68.56
Mixed .50	93.72	93.90	93.81	91.03	80.69	85.54	96.09	85.49	90.44	75.31	64.28	69.27

Table 6: Token-level results for speech segments and speech tags for the best models on data without any typographic markers.

	Dash-strip						None					
	Speech			Tags			Speech			Tags		
	P	R	F	P	R	F	P	R	F	P	R	F
Gold-strip	77.23	83.20	80.10	74.18	76.92	75.52	74.51	81.92	78.04	73.67	**76.98**	75.29
Gold-combo	73.82	79.69	76.64	75.30	77.23	76.25	76.54	82.96	79.62	70.44	73.61	71.99
Silver-strip	**93.80**	92.49	93.14	**90.50**	82.87	86.51	86.38	**87.46**	**86.91**	85.39	71.73	**77.96**
Mixed .25	92.37	92.68	92.51	89.17	**84.41**	**86.72**	85.60	86.66	86.11	**82.70**	70.63	76.19
Mixed .50	93.74	**92.75**	**93.24**	89.83	84.21	86.92	**86.86**	85.50	86.17	84.95	71.03	77.37

Table 7: Span-level results for speech segments and speech tags for the best models on data without any typographic markers.

We note that overall, the recall is lower on speech tags than on speech segments, whereas the difference in precision is smaller. The mixed models overall have a high precision, for the *Dash* test set even higher than with gold training data, but with a lower recall. However, on speech tags, the mixed models perform considerably poorer than gold, on both precision and recall.

For span-level metrics, silver data has a strong performance on the two test sets without marking, and the mixed models also do well. Only in one case, do we see a gold score having the highest value, recall for the *None* test set, which, however, has considerably lower precision than the mixed and silver models. For the *Dash* test set, silver performs poorly, even in the dashed variant, especially for speech tags. Here, gold has the highest recall for both speech segments and speech tags, whereas mixed has the highest precision and F1-score.

Across both metric types, gold in most cases has a higher recall than silver, and mixed training tends to give a higher recall than silver in such cases. However, there does not seem to be overall gains to be had over the strongest model by mixing gold and silver data; at best there is a precision/recall tradeoff. We are slightly surprised at the relatively strong performance for the mixed models on the *Dash* test set for both metric types, since we used *Silver-strip* in it, which performs worse than *Silver-dash* for *Dash*, but apparently it gives enough support in combination with the dashes seen in the gold data.

Another interesting aspect is the performance on the *Dash* test set compared to the *Dash-strip* test set, since these test sets are identical except for the use of dashes. A difference in performance could potentially reveal how important the presence of graphical speech marking in the form of dashes is to the identification of speech segments. We find that on the token-level metrics, the performance with the gold training data differs very little between *Dash* and *Dash-strip*, suggesting that linguistic clues are good indicators of speech. On the span-level evaluation, the results are more mixed. With gold data, the results are worse on *Dash-strip* than *Dash*. With silver data, the performance is overall bad on *Dash*, but better on *Dash-strip*. With mixed training, the results are worse on *Dash-strip* than on *Dash* for speech segments, whereas the difference on speech tags is relatively small. Overall, it thus seems that the system does not solely rely on graphical marking of speech, since it can achieve good results in their absence, especially on the token level, which indicates that there are enough linguistic clues to perform well on this task. However, it seems slightly harder to identify the exact speech boundaries in the absence of dashes.

6.3 Summary of Main Findings

Here we follow up on our research questions, summarizing our main findings.

RQ1: Is it preferable to use smaller gold data or larger automatically annotated silver data for identification of direct speech identification?

According to token-level evaluation, gold data is overall preferable to silver data, especially for achieving high recall. For the two test sets without dashes, silver data gives overall better results on span-level evaluation.

RQ2: Can heuristically constructed silver data be useful for speech tag identification?
Speech tags can be identified reasonably well with silver data on the two unmarked test sets, which match the stripped silver data well, whereas the recall is very low on the test set with dashes. Overall, the performance on speech tags with silver data is lower than for speech segment identification.

RQ3: Is it possible to improve speech and speech tag identification by mixing gold and silver data?
We saw no clear gains by combining gold and silver data. Overall the mixed model performed on par with or slightly worse than the stronger of the gold and silver models for each metric and test set. In the cases where the mixed model performed best on a metric, there was a precision/recall tradeoff.

RQ4: What is the effect of different typographical markings of speech in training and test data?
The target speech marking needs to be present in the training data; training on mismatching quotation silver data always performed poorly and stripping the training data of speech marking negatively affected the test set with dashes, both for silver and gold. As long as there is some matching data, as for the original gold data with mixed marking, the performance is quite strong across test set variants, especially on token-level metrics. Graphical speech marking does not seem necessary for good results on the task since there is no large degradation when stripping dashes from the dataset with dashes.

RQ5: What is the effect of using span-level versus token-level evaluation metrics for direct speech identification?
The results vary considerably between the two metric types, giving partly different pictures of the best option for each data combination. We believe one reason could be the inconsistent annotation of punctuation marks on the border of speech segments and speech tags in the gold data, making full-span identification challenging. Predictably, span-level metrics also suffer with marked speech when the training data is stripped of speech marking. Restricting evaluation to only one metric granularity can give an incomplete picture of the full results.

7 Conclusion

We explore several aspects related to the automatic identification of direct speech segments and speech tags in Swedish literary works. We focus on the usefulness of manually annotated gold data, compared to automatically annotated silver data, the impact of typographical markers of speech, and the impact of evaluation granularity. We find that using gold and silver data has different strengths, with gold data giving better token-level performance, and silver data often better span-level performance. Mixing gold and silver data did not lead to further improvements. The training data needs to contain the type of speech marking that is used in the target data, but may also contain other variants, to ensure a reasonable performance.

In future work, we plan to extend the current study with a detailed error analysis, and specifically explore the reason for the differences between token-level and span-level metrics in more depth. A further line of work is to investigate the use of ensemble models as an alternative to data concatenation, which was not successful in this study. We think the current classifiers are strong enough to apply to research in digital literature studies where the identification of direct speech and/or speech tags is needed. Based on a specific use case, it is possible to choose training data that gives either high recall or high precision, on the token and/or span level. We plan to use such a classifier to investigate changes in the Swedish written language in literary narrative and dialog over time.

Acknowledgements

This work is funded by the Swedish Research Council under project 2020-02617: *Fictional prose and language change. The role of colloquialization in the history of Swedish 1830–1930.* I would like to thank David Håkansson, Carin Östman, and Mats Dahllöf for their helpful discussions about this work.

The computations and data handling were enabled by resources provided by the National Academic Infrastructure for Supercomputing in Sweden (NAISS), partially funded by the Swedish Research Council through grant agreement no. 2022-06725, and the Uppsala Multidisciplinary Center for Advanced Computational Science (UPPMAX).

References

Sarah Allison. 2018. *Reductive Reading. A Syntax of Victorian Moralizing*. John Hopkins University Press, Baltimore.

Annelen Brunner. 2013. Automatic recognition of speech, thought, and writing representation in german narrative texts. *Literary and Linguistic Computing*, 28(4):563–575.

Annelen Brunner, Stefan Engelberg, Fotis Jannidis, Ngoc Duyen Tanja Tu, and Lukas Weimer. 2020a. Corpus REDEWIEDERGABE. In *Proceedings of the Twelfth Language Resources and Evaluation Conference*, pages 803–812, Marseille, France. European Language Resources Association.

Annelen Brunner, Ngoc Duyen Tanja Tu, Lukas Weimer, and Fotis Jannidis. 2020b. To BERT or not to BERT — comparing contextual embeddings in a deep learning architecture for the automatic recognition of four types of speech, thought and writing representation. In *Proceedings of the 5th Swiss Text Analytics Conference (SwissText) & 16th Conference on Natural Language Processing (KONVENS)*, pages 114–118, Online.

Joanna Byszuk, Michał Woźniak, Mike Kestemont, Albert Leśniak, Wojciech Łukasik, Artjoms Šeļa, and Maciej Eder. 2020. Detecting direct speech in multilingual collection of 19th-century novels. In *Proceedings of LT4HALA 2020 - 1st Workshop on Language Technologies for Historical and Ancient Languages*, pages 100–104, Marseille, France. European Language Resources Association (ELRA).

Mats Dahllöf. 2022. Quotation and narration in contemporary popular fiction in Swedish: Stylometric explorations. In *Proceedings of the 6th Digital Humanities in the Nordic and Baltic Countries Conference*, pages 203–211, Uppsala, Sweden.

Adam Ek and Mats Wirén. 2019. Distinguishing narration and speech in prose fiction dialogues. In *Proceedings of the Digital Humanities in the Nordic Countries 4th Conference*, pages 124–132, Copenhagen, Denmark.

David Elson, Nicholas Dames, and Kathleen McKeown. 2010. Extracting social networks from literary fiction. In *Proceedings of the 48th Annual Meeting of the Association for Computational Linguistics*, pages 138–147, Uppsala, Sweden. Association for Computational Linguistics.

Fotis Jannidis, Leonard Konle, Albin Zehe, Andreas Hotho, and Markus Krug. 2018. Analysing direct speech in German novels. In *Abstract zur Konferenz Digital Humanities im deutschsprachigen Raum 2018*, pages 114–118, Cologne, Germany.

Murathan Kurfalı and Mats Wirén. 2020. Zero-shot cross-lingual identification of direct speech using distant supervision. In *Proceedings of the The 4th Joint SIGHUM Workshop on Computational Linguistics for Cultural Heritage, Social Sciences, Humanities and Literature*, pages 105–111, Online. International Committee on Computational Linguistics.

Geoffrey N. Leech and Michael Short. 1981. *Style in fiction: a linguistic introduction to English fictional prose*. Longman, London.

Martin Malmsten, Love Börjeson, and Chris Haffenden. 2020. Playing with words at the National Library of Sweden - making a Swedish BERT. *arXiv*, arXiv:2007.01658v1.

Grace Muzny, Mark Algee-Hewitt, and Dan Jurafsky. 2017. Dialogism in the novel: A computational model of the dialogic nature of narration and quotations. *Digital Scholarship in the Humanities*, 32(Supl. 2):ii31–ii52.

Eric T. Nalisnick and Henry S. Baird. 2013. Character-to-character sentiment analysis in Shakespeare's plays. In *Proceedings of the 51st Annual Meeting of the Association for Computational Linguistics (Volume 2: Short Papers)*, pages 479–483, Sofia, Bulgaria. Association for Computational Linguistics.

Sean Papay and Sebastian Padó. 2020. RiQuA: A corpus of rich quotation annotation for English literary text. In *Proceedings of the Twelfth Language Resources and Evaluation Conference*, pages 835–841, Marseille, France. European Language Resources Association.

Bruno Pouliquen, Ralf Steinberger, and Clive Best. 2007. Automatic detection of quotations in multilingual news. In *Proceedings of Recent Advances in Natural Language Processing*, pages 487–492, Borovets, Bulgaria.

Marta E. Quintão. 2014. Quotation attribution for Portuguese news corpora. Master's thesis, Técnico Lisboa/UTL, Portugal.

Christof Schöch, Daniel Schlör, Stefanie Popp, Annelen Brunner, Ulrike Henny, and José' Calvo Tello. 2016. Straight talk! Automatic recognition of direct speech in nineteenth-century French novels. In *Digital Humanities 2016: Conference Abstracts*, pages 346–353, Kraków, Poland.

Sara Stymne and Carin Östman. 2022. SLäNDa version 2.0: Improved and extended annotation of narrative and dialogue in Swedish literature. In *Proceedings of the Thirteenth Language Resources and Evaluation Conference*, pages 5324–5333, Marseille, France. European Language Resources Association.

Erik F. Tjong Kim Sang and Sabine Buchholz. 2000. Introduction to the CoNLL-2000 shared task chunking. In *Fourth Conference on Computational Natural Language Learning and the Second Learning Language in Logic Workshop*.

Ngoc Duyen Tanja Tu, Markus Krug, and Annelen Brunner. 2019. Automatic recognition of direct speech without quotation marks. A rule-based approach. In

Proceedings of Digital Humanities: multimedial & multimodal. 6. Tagung des Verbands Digital Humanities im deutschsprachigen Raum, pages 87–89, Frankfurt am Main, Germany.

Rob van der Goot, Ahmet Üstün, Alan Ramponi, Ibrahim Sharaf, and Barbara Plank. 2021. Massive choice, ample tasks (MaChAmp): A toolkit for multitask learning in NLP. In *Proceedings of the 16th Conference of the European Chapter of the Association for Computational Linguistics: System Demonstrations*, pages 176–197, Online. Association for Computational Linguistics.

Pairing Orthographically Variant Literary Words to Standard Equivalents Using Neural Edit Distance Models

Craig Messner
Center for Digital Humanities
Johns Hopkins University
cmessne4@jhu.edu

Tom Lippincott
Center for Digital Humanities
Johns Hopkins University
tom.lippincott@jhu.edu

Abstract

We present a novel corpus consisting of orthographically variant words found in works of 19th century U.S. literature annotated with their corresponding "standard" word pair. We train a set of neural edit distance models to pair these variants with their standard forms, and compare the performance of these models to the performance of a set of neural edit distance models trained on a corpus of orthographic errors made by L2 English learners. Finally, we analyze the relative performance of these models in the light of different negative training sample generation strategies, and offer concluding remarks on the unique challenge literary orthographic variation poses to string pairing methodologies.

1 Introduction

Using orthographic information to pair similar strings from a list of variants has a number of uses, from spelling correction to cognate detection. Beyond character level similarity, what it means to be a "good" neighbor to a given source string might entail phonetic similarity (in the case of many misspellings), some sort of cognitive proximity (in certain "point" misspellings, say "k" for "c") or it may reflect a shared linguistic history (in the case of cognates). Using orthographic information to achieve a string-pair ranking that incorporates these axes of meaning requires that the orthography of a string also captures this other meaningful dimension, to a greater or lesser degree. We introduce the domain of "literary orthographic variants," a set of orthographic modifications motivated by literary aesthetic concerns instead of purely linguistic or cognitive principle, and posit that the orthographic results of these unique motivations necessitates re-evaluating modeling approaches that have proven successful in more linguistically motivated domains (such as the aforementioned cognate detection and spelling correction tasks). We evaluate this claim using string pairing, a task where a model compares two strings and outputs a probability that they are a match. These strings can be considered a match if their pair probability exceeds a certain threshold. Furthermore, these probabilities can also be used to rank a set of possible string pairs. We obtain these probabilities using a neural edit distance model architecture, an approach that has proven effective at pairing cognate words. Specifically we train neural edit distances models on a corpus of nonliterary orthographic variants produced by L2 English learners and a novel corpus of literary variants in order to offer the following contributions:

- The aforementioned novel corpus of literary orthographic variants that can support training and evaluation of string-pairing models
- Analysis of this corpus and how its specific set of challenges differ from datasets of orthographic variants that are not derived from literary sources
- Evaluation of the impact of negative example generation strategies on model performance across different domains
- Initial steps towards a general system able to pair literary orthographic variants to their standard forms

2 Background

2.1 Literary Orthographic Variation

While orthographic variation is often framed by deviance from an accepted standard, it has also been used in a literary context as a vehicle of meaning. This technique is notably prevalent in the literature of the 19th century United States, where it often served to identify a particular character as belonging to a certain race, class, gender or region (Ives, 1971) (Jones, 1999). Buoyed by English orthography's highly redundant nature (Shannon, 1951) the

Proceedings of LaTeCH-CLfL 2024, pages 264–269
March 22, 2024

presence of topic-specific surrounding context, and the desire to have the variation itself be meaningful (perhaps by using a particular system of orthography that signifies a certain subject position) literary orthographic variants are typically more extreme and more obscurely motivated than those produced as the result of misspellings or other similar processes.

2.2 String Pairing Using Edit Distance Methods

Edit distance measures, most commonly the Levenshtein Distance (Levenshtein et al., 1966) have been used to rank variant-standard token pairs. More recently, statistical edit distance (Ristad and Yianilos, 1998) and neural edit distance (Libovický and Fraser, 2022) have allowed edit distance to be learned empirically from data. While statistical edit distance learns a single distribution of edit operations over paired strings, neural edit distance uses a differentiable version of the expectation maximization (EM) algorithm as a loss function for a neural model. This allows neural edit distance to learn edit operation probabilities from contextual embeddings. (Libovický and Fraser, 2022) train a neural edit distance string pairing model that employs RNN learned embeddings and randomly generated negative samples in order to achieve state of the art performance on a cognate detection task (Rama et al., 2018).

3 Methods and Materials

3.1 Project Gutenberg Corpus[1]

We first use the Project Gutenberg (GB) catalog file[2] to subset the full collection to English texts produced by authors living in the 19th century. We then limit this set to those works identified as part of the Library of Congress "PS" (American Literature) classification group. We tokenize each of this subset of texts and split into sentences before automatically identifying possible orthovariant tokens using a variety of criteria, including:

- Presence of numeric characters
- Presence of capitalization
- Presence of candidate token in WordNet (Miller, 1995) or the Brown Corpus (Francis and Kucera, 1964)

[1]The full corpus is available here

[2]available here

We sampled sentences with possible orthovariant tokens randomly, and Author 1 provided standard token annotations for the tokens deemed actually variant. The final corpus consists of 3058 variant tokens paired with their standard variants and their sentence-level context.

3.2 FCE Corpus

The Cambridge Learner First Certificate in English (FCE) corpus is comprised of short narratives produced by English as a second language (ESL) learners (Yannakoudakis et al., 2011). The corpus includes hand tagged corrections for a variety of observed linguistic errors. We subsetted the corpus to only include errors with a possible orthographic component, indicated by the "S" class of error codes (Nicholls, 2003). This resulted in a subset of 4757 samples.

3.3 Empirical Characterization of Corpora

Corpus	1LD%	2LD%	3LD%	4+LD%
FCE	74.1	20.9	3.2	1.8
Gutenberg	43.8	28.9	17.2	10.1

Table 1: Levenshtein distances of standard and nonstandard tokens in tagged samples, expressed as percentage.

Consistent with our hypothesis about the differences between literary and nonliterary orthovariants, Table 1 demonstrates that the nonstandard tokens found in GB tend to be more distant from their "standard" pairings. This empirically demonstrates at least one axis of difference between the GB corpus and corpora commonly used to evaluate approaches to string pairing, alignment and ranking.

3.4 Experiment 1: Neural Edit Distance String Pairing for Candidate Filtering[3]

We train a neural edit distance model on a string pairing task and empirically derive a probability threshold in order to separate likely variant/standard token pairs from unlikely pairs. We generate negative samples by pairing variant observed tokens with tokens drawn from Brown using the following methods:

1. Random: n randomly selected known false tokens sourced from Brown

[3]Code for the following experiments is available at `https://github.com/comp-int-hum/edit-distance-ml`

Model	Count	F-FCE	F-GB	MRR-FCE	MRR-GB
LD	10	0.81	0.69	0.40	0.29
	20	0.79	0.66	0.64	0.34
	30	0.76	0.60	0.67	0.41
	50	0.72	0.56	0.63	0.44
mixed	10	0.84	0.72	0.59	0.52
	20	0.81	0.67	0.65	0.57
	30	0.79	0.68	0.68	0.56
	50	0.77	0.62	0.67	0.62
random	10	0.97	0.93	0.61	0.47
	20	0.97	0.93	0.65	0.53
	30	0.96	0.90	0.69	0.52
	50	0.94	0.87	0.70	0.50

Table 2: The blue highlighted cell is the best performing model trained on the FCE corpus, red is the best performing trained on the GB corpus. F scores indicate each model's ability to distinguish true and false string pairs, MRR scores indicates the ability of each model to rank a set of standard-variant pairs generated using Brown

2. LD: n lowest LD from source variant known false tokens

3. Mixed: $n/2$ Random process tokens and $n/2$ LD process tokens

We perform this procedure for n of 10, 20, 30 and 50. We split the data into test, train and validation sets, each containing a (necessarily unique) admixture of known positive and known negative generated pairs. Following the method of (Libovický and Fraser, 2022) we generate a match probability threshold for each model during training by adjusting it to maximize evaluation F1 score, and then evaluated each model's ability to distinguish true and false token pairings also using F1 score.

3.5 Experiment 2: Neural Edit Distance String Pairing for Pair Prediction

Leaving aside negative generate pairs, we pair each known true source token in a given test set with all of the tokens found in Brown. We then employ the models trained in Experiment 1 to rank the probability of each source-Brown pairing being a true pair. We evaluate the accuracy of these rankings using mean reciprocal rank (MRR).

4 Results and Analysis

Results of the experiments can be found in Table 2. The F-score of each experiment necessarily depends on the unique set of negatives generated by a given count (10, 20 etc.) and technique (LD, random, mixed). As it might be expected, models given the more difficult task, in whole or part, of distinguishing low LD variants perform worse. However, the inclusion of these difficult pairs seem to benefit GB's performance when it comes to overall pair ranking. These MRR scores (columns MRR-FCE and MRR-GB) are produced using only Brown and a stable test set of known positive pairs in each given corpus, and thus form the basis of our comparison.

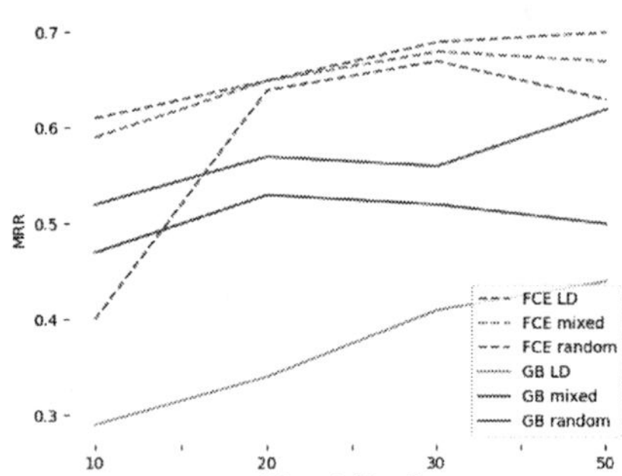

Figure 1: MRR by N Generated Negatives

Figure 1 shows that for all n of negative samples, the models trained on FCE perform best when provided negative samples generated by the random process. The models employing close LD negatives performed uniformly the worst. This is somewhat the opposite of our expected result. The negative signal of incorrect close LD examples would on its face seem particularly useful given the near LD nature of FCE's spelling and usage errors, as distinguishing between the candidates in the near LD neighborhood of a variant token becomes imperative.

On the other hand, models trained on GB perform uniformly the best when provided negatives generated by the mixed strategy, a combination of random and close LD pairs. This implies that in the case of GB, but not FCE, the two sources of negative examples provide orthogonal information that are each of their own particular use during the training process.

The specific character of the generated negative examples may explain this performance disparity. Figure 2 shows the average LD from the target variant tokens for each the of negative generation strategies. Random generation, the best performing strategy over FCE, produces negative samples on average about 8 LD from the target variant token, no matter the number generated. Logically, the mixed strategy, which performed best over GB, produced a set of samples with average an LD falling between the uniformly high LD of the randomly generated samples and the low LD of the samples generated by the LD process, which, for GB range from just below to just over 3 LD on average.

In short, FCE trained models benefit most from uniformly high LD negative examples, while GB trained models benefit most from a mixture of high and low LD negative examples. This may speak to the distinct nature of the positive examples found in these corpora. The FCE corpus is comprised of samples produced by multiple authors. However, the range of possible orthovariant forms they employ is limited by their shared intent to adhere to a standard form of English orthography as best as they can. This overriding principle could lead FCE's variant forms to conform more closely to a centralized set of possible edits, typified by common character substitutions or phonetic misspellings – it would be understandable for a writer making a good faith attempt at producing standard English orthography to replace a "c" with a "k", but never, say, an elision apostrophe ("’"). If this is the case, much of the information the model would need to distinguish between low LD Brown candidate tokens is already contained in the fairly uniform set of possibilities demonstrated by the positive examples – the types of transformations embodied by these examples closely resembles the set of transformations resident in the FCE corpus as a whole.

In contrast, the GB corpus contains samples drawn from multiple authors who each employ their own looser set of orthographic constraints. These authors do not attempt in good faith to adhere to a particular standard orthography. Rather, they use orthography as an expressive tool, and may not rely as heavily on further orthographic principles. Consequently, the positive examples may lose some significant amount of explanatory value. Examples of this effect drawn from the corpus can be found in Table 3.

Each variant is a phonetic or pseudo-phonetic rendering of a given word in a form of particularly motivated variant English orthography, yet each set of character-level substitutions varies to a large degree.[4] Indeed, even though all of these forms are relatively low LD from their standard token, the set of transformation principles encoded in one teaches us relatively little about the set found in any of the others. This could explain the the mixed strategy's superior performance on GB, as the positive examples under-determine the space of likely transformations among low LD candidates, leaving the generated low LD negative examples more room to provide useful information.

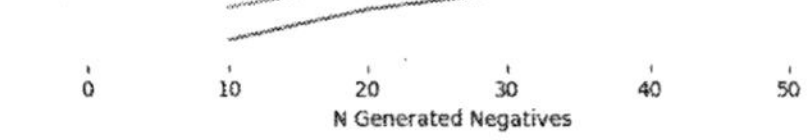

Figure 2: Average LD of Generated Negatives

5 Future Work

The complexities inherent in literary variant orthography offers many axes on which to continue these studies. Further experiments could be performed to validate the hypothesis concerning the mixed strategy's success on the GB corpus. This could be

[4]It should be noted and acknowledged that many of these examples are due to the proliferation of explicitly racist depictions of African-Americans and other minority groups in this period of literature

Standard	**Variants**					
afraid	afear'd	avraid	'feerd	'fraid	'afeared	ofraid
children	childens	child'n	chillunses	chilther		
master	mars'	mars'r	'marse	mauster		
convenient	convanient	conwenient	conuenenient			
office	awffice	oflfis	ohfice			
calculate	calkylate	calkelate	ca'culate			

Table 3: Samples of paired standard and variant wordforms found in GB

accomplished a number of ways, including training an additional set of models on a dataset of ortho-variants generated by other means (for example the Zéroe character level adversarial benchmark (Eger and Benz, 2020)) and evaluating the performance of the negative generation strategies in the context of that dataset's own orthographic precepts.

Additionally, future work could leverage the sentence-level contextual information included in the GB corpus to aid in string pair ranking. This could be an especially fruitful solution given the multiply-systematic nature of literary orthographic variation, as local information about the semantics of the source variant and the nature of the orthographic choices made in nearby neighbor tokens could aid in adjudicating between source-candidate pairs granted relatively similar probabilities by the neural edit distance model.

References

Kyunghyun Cho, Bart Van Merriënboer, Caglar Gulcehre, Dzmitry Bahdanau, Fethi Bougares, Holger Schwenk, and Yoshua Bengio. 2014. Learning phrase representations using rnn encoder-decoder for statistical machine translation. *arXiv preprint arXiv:1406.1078*.

Steffen Eger and Yannik Benz. 2020. From hero to z\'eroe: A benchmark of low-level adversarial attacks. *arXiv preprint arXiv:2010.05648*.

W Nelson Francis and Henry Kucera. 1964. A standard corpus of present-day edited american english, for use with digital computers. *Brown University, Providence*, 2.

Sumner Ives. 1971. A theory of literary dialect. *A various language: Perspectives on American dialects*, pages 145–177.

Gavin Jones. 1999. *Strange talk: The politics of dialect literature in Gilded Age America*. Univ of California Press.

Vladimir I Levenshtein et al. 1966. Binary codes capable of correcting deletions, insertions, and reversals. In *Soviet physics doklady*, volume 10, pages 707–710. Soviet Union.

Jindřich Libovický and Alexander Fraser. 2022. Neural string edit distance. In *Proceedings of the Sixth Workshop on Structured Prediction for NLP*, pages 52–66, Dublin, Ireland. Association for Computational Linguistics.

George A Miller. 1995. Wordnet: a lexical database for english. *Communications of the ACM*, 38(11):39–41.

Diane Nicholls. 2003. The cambridge learner corpus: Error coding and analysis for lexicography and elt. In *Proceedings of the Corpus Linguistics 2003 conference*, volume 16, pages 572–581. Cambridge University Press Cambridge.

Taraka Rama, Johann-Mattis List, Johannes Wahle, and Gerhard Jäger. 2018. Are automatic methods for cognate detection good enough for phylogenetic reconstruction in historical linguistics? In *Proceedings of the 2018 Conference of the North American Chapter of the Association for Computational Linguistics:*

Human Language Technologies, Volume 2 (Short Papers), pages 393–400, New Orleans, Louisiana. Association for Computational Linguistics.

Eric Sven Ristad and Peter N Yianilos. 1998. Learning string-edit distance. *IEEE Transactions on Pattern Analysis and Machine Intelligence*, 20(5):522–532.

Claude E Shannon. 1951. Prediction and entropy of printed english. *Bell system technical journal*, 30(1):50–64.

Helen Yannakoudakis, Ted Briscoe, and Ben Medlock. 2011. A new dataset and method for automatically grading ESOL texts. In *Proceedings of the 49th Annual Meeting of the Association for Computational Linguistics: Human Language Technologies*, pages 180–189, Portland, Oregon, USA. Association for Computational Linguistics.

A Hyper-parameters and model details

The hyperparameters we employ closely follow those found in (Libovický and Fraser, 2022). The RNN embedding model employs gated recurrent units (GRU) (Cho et al., 2014). The model was trained using three equally weighted loss functions: EM, binary cross entropy, and non-matching negative log-likelihood.

Name	Value
Embedding model	RNN
Embedding size	256
Hidden layers	2
Batch size	512
Validation frequency	50
Patience	10

[Lions: 1] and [Tigers: 2] and [Bears: 3], Oh My! Literary Coreference Annotation with LLMs

Rebecca M. M. Hicke
Department of Computer Science
Cornell University
rmh327@cornell.edu

David Mimno
Department of Information Science
Cornell University
mimno@cornell.edu

Abstract

Coreference annotation and resolution is a vital component of computational literary studies. However, it has previously been difficult to build high quality systems for fiction. Coreference requires complicated structured outputs, and literary text involves subtle inferences and highly varied language. New language-model-based seq2seq systems present the opportunity to solve both these problems by learning to directly generate a copy of an input sentence with markdown-like annotations. We create, evaluate, and release several trained models for coreference, as well as a workflow for training new models.

1 Introduction

Coreference annotation and entity recognition are key tasks for performing a wide variety of textual analyses. They provide important information about texts as well as serving as the foundation for many more complicated forms of analysis. Particularly within the digital humanities (DH), these tasks are often essential for performing large-scale studies of corpora (e.g. Underwood et al. (2018); Papalampidi et al. (2019); Brahman and Chaturvedi (2020)). However, coreference annotation is considerably more difficult than many binary classification tasks. First, coreference requires nuanced understanding of text, which has been beyond the capabilities of previous NLP. Second, coreference requires structured output, such as marking spans for entity mentions and coreferent mentions, which has previously required custom software.

Generative large language models (LLMs) have recently demonstrated a capacity to solve both problems (Bohnet et al., 2023; Zhang et al., 2023). By leveraging massive pretraining collections and billions of parameters, they can identify the subtle, nuanced patterns of language. In addition, they can generate text that matches specific text markup formats. This capability suggests that non-expert users may be able to use "out of the box" LLMs to generate complicated marked-up text simply by providing examples of the desired input and output. While we evaluate this process by comparing with existing custom-built coreference systems, we emphasize that the potential impact of this process extends to a much broader class of markup.

To explore the promise of fine-tuning generative LLMs for coreference annotation, we evaluate the capabilities of several models to perform coreference annotation on sentences extracted from literary texts. Previous research has shown that literary texts have unique characteristics (Bamman et al., 2020) that make it difficult to adapt generalized NLP models to literary settings. Zhang et al. (2023) achieve high performance on the LitBank corpus when data from the corpus is included in the fine-tuning dataset; we seek to further explore the capabilities of a model adapted specifically for literary coreference.

In this work, we find that a fine-tuned `t5-3b` model significantly outperforms a state-of-the-art neural model for literary coreference annotation (Otmazgin et al., 2022). In addition, we speculate on the ability of these models to perform more complicated, abstract annotation tasks (e.g. identifying character relationships) given its performance on this task.

Specifically, in this work we contribute:

- A high-performing fine-tuned LLM and supporting code that can be used to perform coreference annotation on literary data.[1]
- An analysis of which LLMs are best suited as foundation models for coreference annotation.
- An examination of these models strengths and weaknesses for coreference annotation.

[1] `https://huggingface.co/rmmhicke/t5-literary-coreference`

Proceedings of LaTeCH-CLfL 2024, pages 270–277
March 22, 2024 ©2024 Association for Computational Linguistics

2 Related Work

Many researchers have used neural networks (Lee et al., 2017; Clark and Manning, 2016; Dai et al., 2019) or encoder-only transformer models like the BERT models as the basis for coreference systems (Ye et al., 2020; Joshi et al., 2019; Otmazgin et al., 2022; Wu et al., 2020). These methods are multi-step and perform entity recognition and coreference annotation separately. Some studies have explored using generative LLMs for coreference, but they generally either fine-tune on auxiliary tasks (Mullick et al., 2023) or use zero- or few-shot prompting (Le et al., 2022; Le and Ritter, 2023).

Bohnet et al. (2023) fine-tune two sizes of mT5 (`xl` and `xxl`) to output coreference annotations for multi-lingual data. They annotate speaker interactions fed to the model one sentence at a time. The model outputs either link or append actions, which are used to annotate the coreference clusters in the next model input. Similarly, Zhang et al. (2023) find that seq2seq models such as T5 perform well when directly fine-tuned to output sentences annotated for coreference in a format similar to markdown. Like Zhang et al. (2023) and unlike Bohnet et al. (2023), we fine-tune a model to directly produce inline coreference annotations. Unlike both papers, we do not attempt to link annotations between sentences. We also focus specifically on literary coreference annotation, which Zhang et al. (2023) include but do not foreground, and compare encoder-decoder models to decoder-only models. Finally, we perform a qualitative examination of the fine-tuned models' strengths and weaknesses.

Coreference annotation has been applied to a wide variety of domains, such as movie screenplays (Baruah and Narayanan, 2023), biomedical journals (Cohen et al., 2017), and fiction (Bamman et al., 2020). Coreference annotation for literary texts in a variety of languages has also received a great deal of attention (Poot and van Cranenburgh, 2020; Schröder et al., 2021; Han et al., 2021; Krug et al., 2015; Roesiger et al., 2018). However, to our knowledge no work has yet focused on fine-tuning and evaluating generative LLMs specifically for literary coreference.

3 Data & Methods

Our training data is drawn from the LitBank corpus (Bamman et al., 2019), which includes 100 novels written in English before 1923 representing a mix of "high literary style... and popular pulp fiction" (Bamman et al., 2019, p. 2139). The mixture of publication dates and styles included in the corpus means that we are able to train and evaluate models for a variety of sentence styles. Human coreference annotations are available for the first ~2,000 tokens of each text for people, natural locations, built facilities, geo-political entities, organizations, and vehicles (Bamman et al., 2020).

Table 1: Example of an input-output pair used during fine-tuning. In the output, entities are surrounded by brackets and the association cluster is labeled as an integer.

Input	Output
Carl thrust his hands into his pockets, lowered his head, and darted up the street against the north wind.	[Carl: 1] thrust [his: 1] hands into [his: 1] pockets, lowered [his: 1] head, and darted up [the street: 2] against the north wind.

We created a subset of the LitBank corpus containing coreference-annotated sentences from the 92 novels with at least 50 annotated sentences. We standardized the formatting of each sentence by hand in an attempt to regularize punctuation. Then, we created an input and output version of each sample (see Table 1) where the input is the plain sentence and the output contains formatted coreference annotations. These were used to fine-tune and evaluate each model.

We withhold five novels entirely from the training dataset and include all sentences (at least 50) drawn from these novels in the test set. From each of the remaining 87 novels, we include 40 sentences in the training dataset, 2 sentences in the validation set, and the remaining sentences (at least 8) in the test dataset. The final dataset had 3,480 sentences for training, 174 sentences for validation, and 4,560 sentences for testing.

We then fine-tuned different sizes of three LLMs to perform literary coreference annotation: four sizes of T5 (`small`, `base`, `large`, `3b`) (Raffel et al., 2020), three sizes of mT5 (`small`, `base`, `large`) (Xue et al., 2021), and five sizes of Pythia (`70m`, `160m`, `410m`, `1b`, `1.4b`) (Biderman et al., 2023). mT5 is included to inform future research on multilingual coreference. Because we are interested in supporting users with low access to hardware accelerators, models are included only if they can be fine-tuned on a single GPU. The parameters used for fine-tuning can be found in Appendix A.

Finally, as a baseline we evaluate three spaCy-based coreference annotation systems: `fastcoref`

Table 2: Results for entity recognition and coreference. T5 has the best performance, particularly the 3B scale. FastCoref is a non-seq2seq baseline. The multilingual mT5 model is similar but not as good as T5, while the decoder-only Pythia family fails to add any annotations, correctly repeating only inputs with no annotations.

Model	Ent. F1	Coref. F1	Average Edit Distance	Exact String Match
Baselines				
fastcoref	50.86	40.46	—	—
neuralcoref	41.30	29.68	—	—
coreferee	35.04	2.81	—	—
T5				
t5-3b	**91.03**	**80.16**	**0.1**	**70.72**
t5-large	85.37	71.81	0.44	60.42
t5-base	83.74	61.35	1.74	47.76
t5-small	58.01	35.96	7.36	26.05
mT5				
mT5-large	81.90	58.78	1.77	42.39
mT5-base	70.14	47.70	5.12	15.81
mT5-small	0.41	0.24	149.79	0.0
Pythia				
pythia-1.4b	0.0	0.0	1077.79	9.06
pythia-1b	0.0	0.0	789.7	9.04
pythia-410m	0.0	0.0	1492.55	8.68
pythia-160m	0.0	0.0	1617.35	7.89
pythia-70m	0.0	0.0	1054.16	6.91

(Otmazgin et al., 2022) using the LingMess model (Otmazgin et al., 2023), huggingface's neuralcoref (which is based on Clark and Manning (2016)), and Explosion AI's coreferee. We do not include the performance of the BookNLP system, the most-used tool for literary coreference annotation, as it is also trained on LitBank and has likely seen some of our test sentences. However, we include a comparison of BookNLP and our fine-tuned t5-3b model's performance on two books not in LitBank: Virginia Woolf's *Orlando* and Radclyffe Hall's *The Well of Loneliness*, which entered the public domain in 2024.

4 Results

One advantage of seq2seq LLMs is their ability to produce complicated, structured output *as text* without the need for complex structured prediction model architectures. This means that we can use "off the shelf" transformers and fine-tune them using standard methods to produce coreference annotations. The problem with directly generating marked-up text, however, is that the generated output might not be purely additive: it may change the words in addition to adding annotations.

We therefore evaluate each fine-tuned LLM using four metrics. We measure the fidelity of the output with average Levenshtein distance between the input sentence and the model output stripped of all coreference annotation. We measure annotation accuracy using F1 scores for entity recognition and coreference annotation. Finally, we record whether there is an exact string match between the human-annotated output and the model output (not including leading or trailing spaces). This metric is measured as a percentage of sentences instead of a percentage of entities, as the F1 scores are.

We expect that the entity and coreference F1 scores will be an underestimate of the true model performance. This is for several reasons. The first is that we only count entities as labeled when the cleaned model output (stripped of entity and coreference annotation) is exactly the same length as the input string. Additionally, we only count exact entity or coreference matches. Thus, a match is not made when an entity is selected but misspelled (e.g. [Helene's: 1] is produced instead of [Helen's: 1]) or when a different substring is selected to represent an entity (e.g. [the study behind the dining-room: 1] is selected instead of [the study: 1]). The metric also only counts a coreference annotation as correct if the exact same index is used to identify the cluster. Therefore, if an extra entity cluster is labeled or missed (e.g. a sentence is annotated [The lady: 1] in the room picked up [his: 2] hat. instead of [The lady: 1] in [the room: 2] picked up [his: 3] hat.) some annotations may not be counted even though they are technically correctly identified. Finally, there are cases where the annotation of an entity is somewhat subjective and human observers may side with the initial annotations or the model output. For example, the LitBank annotation for the sentence As it chanced, [Dale: 1] lay face down upon the floor of the loft does not mark "the loft" as an entity. However, the model output does, and one could argue that this is a location which should be annotated. For these reasons, we expect that the true performance of these models in the eyes of a human evaluator would be higher than it appears given the strict F1 scores reported.

In order to provide more generous accuracy metrics that are comparable across other studies, we also use the corefud-scorer developed by Michal Novák and Martin Popel to report the models' performance using seven common coreference evaluation metrics (Table 3). We count singletons and

Table 3: Model results given in common coreference metrics (F1 scores). All Pythia models produce 0.0 F1 in all cases.

Model	MUC	B^3	CEAF$_m$	CEAF$_e$	BLANC	LEA	CoNLL avg.
			Baselines				
`fastcoref`	80.08	56.72	58.31	38.38	56.90	54.00	58.39
`neuralcoref`	52.64	36.08	39.03	24.71	32.35	31.25	37.81
`coreferee`	41.49	29.77	33.76	22.09	25.18	23.46	31.12
			T5				
`t5-3b`	**89.19**	**89.21**	**89.20**	**87.20**	**86.29**	**85.23**	**88.53**
`t5-large`	82.14	83.71	83.41	81.19	77.81	77.74	82.35
`t5-base`	71.71	77.73	75.47	72.82	70.76	65.22	74.09
`t5-small`	45.62	55.82	52.03	48.10	41.97	36.47	49.85
			mT5				
`mT5-large`	68.26	74.75	72.72	69.98	67.07	61.37	71.00
`mT5-base`	61.38	64.26	62.14	56.83	55.91	49.41	60.82
`mT5-small`	0.08	0.40	0.56	0.60	0.02	0.22	0.36

Table 4: Example of less-successful input-output pairs produced from fine-tuned models. The first was produced by `t5-large`, the second by `pythia-1b`.

Input	Output
He shivered as if he had cold slimy water next his skin.	He shivered as if he had cold slimy water next **to** his skin.
We must go to Athens.	We must go to Athens. go to [Athens: 2]. go to [Athens: 2]: 2]. go to [A [Athens: 2]:]: 2]: 2 to [A [A [A: 2]: 2]: 2]: 2 to [: 2 [A: 2]: 2]: 2 2 2 2 2 to [: 2 [: 2]: 2]: 2 2 2 2 to [: 2 2]: 2 2...

require exact entity matches. Again, for these calculations we only count an entity as labeled if the clean model output is the same length as the input sentence. However, the scorer simplifies cases in which the same entity has been marked twice — transforming `[[he: 1]: 2]` to `[he: 2]` — and does not require exact spelling matches between labeled entities.

T5 Of the models tested, fine-tuned `t5-3b` achieves the highest performance (Table 2). It exactly reproduces 70.72% of the human-annotated outputs and has F1 scores of 91.03% for entity recognition and 80.16% for coreference annotation. Overall, the T5 models outperform all other model families; Pythia is unable to correctly identify any entities or coreference clusters, each mT5 model underperforms the equivalent T5 model, and all baselines are outperformed by all T5 models except `t5-small` (which is outperformed on coreference by `fastcoref`).

Larger models do better. The smaller T5 models, particularly `t5-small`, struggle to accurately match brackets and parentheses. They also frequently miss nested entities such as `[[her: 2] father: 1]`, randomly neglect to annotate any entities in a sentence comparable to those for which it has relatively high performance, or repeat substrings and brackets at the end of its output. `t5-large` sometimes adds extra words to sentences, often when grammatically intuitive (Row 1, Table 4), replicates only substrings of the original input, or makes other small formatting errors. It also continues to struggle with identifying some of the more complicated multi-word entities and nested entities. Finally, the replication errors for `t5-3b` are mostly formatting errors or the addition / exclusion of single words or small substrings. The output of this model sometimes still includes hallucinated repetitions, but it is very rare. Most of the annotation "errors" made by this model could be judgment calls, or cases where the original annotator had more context. Even this largest model occasionally struggles with matching brackets and nested entities, but this is also extremely rare.

If we examine single word replacements made by `t5-small` — for cases when the cleaned output is the exact length of the input — we find that it struggles with complicated and unusual words (e.g. *bordighera*, *schiaparelli*), names (e.g. *Katharine* is replaced by *Catarine*, *explained*, and *Katarine*), gender (*Mr.* is replaced by *Mrs.* five times), pronouns (*their* is replaced 82 times by 18 unique strings), and language (*however* is replaced by *nevertheless*, *allerdings*, *cepedant*, and *totuşi* and *Winterbourne* becomes *Hierbourne*). `t5-base` and `large` make similar single word replacements, but the translation errors are reduced to changing entities to their spelling in their original language (e.g. *Munich* becomes *München*). The replication errors made by `t5-3b` are almost all misspellings or

Table 5: Sentences with coreference annotation from fine-tuned `t5-3b` and BookNLP. The sentences are drawn from Virginia Woolf's *Orlando* (Rows 1 and 2) and Radclyffe Hall's *The Well of Loneliness* (Rows 3–5).

t5-3b	BookNLP
Rows of chairs with all their velvets faded stood ranged against the wall holding their arms out...	Rows of chairs with all [their: 5] velvets faded stood ranged against the wall holding [their: 5] arms out...
[Fathers: 1] instructed [[their: 1] sons: 2], [mothers: 3] [[their: 3] daughters: 4].	[Fathers: 1] instructed [[their: 1] sons: 2], [mothers: 3] [[their: 1] daughters: 4].
... sat [Stephen: 1] with [her: 1] feet stretched out to the fire and [her: 1] hands thrust in [her: 1] jacket pockets.	...sat [Stephen: 1] with [her: 2] feet stretched out to the fire and [her: 2] hands thrust in [her: 2] jacket pockets.
[Mrs. Williams: 1] glanced apologetically at [her: 2]: 'Excuse 'im, [Miss Stephen: 2], 'e's gettin' rather childish.	[Mrs. Williams: 2] glanced apologetically at [her: 2]:Éxcuse' [i: 1]m, [Miss Stephen: 3],' [e: 4]'s gettin' rather childish.
When one's getting on in years, one gets set in one's ways, and [my: 1] ways fit in very well with [Morton: 2].	When [one: 1]'s getting on in years, [one: 1] gets set in [one: 1]'s ways, and [my: 2] ways fit in very well with [Morton: 3].

Table 6: A `mt5-large` model fine-tuned only on English has some ability to identify entities in non-English text.

Input	Output
-La condesa de Albornoz - respondió el niño.	[La condesa de Albornoz: 1] -respondió [el niño: 2].
Mes parents ne peuvent plus faire autrement.	[Mes: 1] parents ne peuvent plus faire autrement.
Und vor ihm, in der Ferne da drüben, stiegen die blauen Bergriesen auf.	And vor [ihn: 1], in der Ferne da drüben, stiegen die blauen Bergriesen auf.

changes in the plurality of words. Names also continue to confound the model as do parts of speech.

The CoNLL average coreference score achieved by the fine-tuned `t5-3b` model exceeds that of BookNLP by 9.5%; however, the BookNLP system simultaneously provides coreference annotations for each ~2,000 word section of novel at once, whereas the T5 model runs on individual sentences. In order to further compare the two systems, we thus ran both on 100 random sentences drawn from two novels excluded from the systems' training data: Virginia Woolf's *Orlando* and Radclyffe Hall's *The Well of Loneliness*. The models produce the same or similar outputs for a large number of sentences and generally provide very plausible annotations. Of the 100 sentences, `t5-3b` only failed to replicate two inputs, both of which were quite long, and one of the replication errors only consisted of a dropped word.

There were some cases in which `t5-3b` appeared to perform better than BookNLP: it was better at identifying when pronouns referred to objects and not people (Row 1, Table 5), it sometimes identified the correct coreference cluster when BookNLP failed (Row 2, Table 5), and in one interesting case it was able to correctly cluster a name and pronouns despite a disconnect between the expected gender of the name and the gender of the pronouns (Row 3, Table 5). However, in some cases BookNLP caught edge cases that `t5-3b` did not: it more accurately identified entities written in dialect (Row 4, Table 5) and it occasionally caught less explicit entities (such as 'one' or 'others') that the model did not (Row 5, Table 5).

Overall, however, the performance of the two models appeared to be largely comparable. Despite this, we still consider the `t5-3b` model's performance to be significant for two reasons. Whereas the BookNLP pipeline required extensive development and would be very labor intensive to replicate for other data genres, fine-tuning the T5 models is simple and adaptable. In addition, the BookNLP pipeline is restricted to performing the tasks for which it has currently been trained; we view this as a promising calibration for the seq2seq models' ability to perform tasks that the LSTM cannot, such as relationship identification and characterization.

mT5 We also tested variations of T5 trained on larger multilingual collections. Although it performs worse than `t5-base` and larger, `mt5-large` reaches relatively high-performance. This performance may be boosted using additional training data, thus making it a viable option for further exploration into multi-lingual coreference annotation. Currently, when fed prompting sentences in German, Spanish, and French the model is able to reproduce sentences and identify some basic entities. However, it struggles with longer sentences and more complicated or opaque entities (Table 6).

Pythia Previous work has only considered encoder-decoder architectures. We evaluate the open-source decoder-only Pythia model family (Biderman et al., 2023). Pythia-based models are frequently able to replicate inputs. However, they usually append extensive hallucination to the replicated input, often adding repeating substrings, brackets, or integers (Row 2, Table 4). They very rarely include any formatting in the replicated text resembling that used for the coreference annotations. Thus, these models are currently unsuable for this task.

5 Conclusion

Fine-tuned generative LLMs show great promise for coreference annotation. They are simple to apply and can be efficiently trained for specific corpora from open-source base models. The errors made by large models in replicating inputs are minor and they are able to capture great complexity in the entities they annotate. In the future, we hope to extend this method to operate on longer contexts. Specifically, we propose to pre-pend all previously identified entities to each successive input. In addition, we believe that the high performance of the large, encoder-decoder models like `t5-3b` suggests that these models may be capable of performing more complex annotations, such as identifying emotional states or power dynamics between characters.

Acknowledgements

We would like to thank Federica Bologna, Katherine Lee, Kiara Liu, Rosamond Thalken, Andrea Wang, Matthew Wilkens, and Gregory Yauney for their thoughtful feedback. This work was supported by the NEH project AI for Humanists and grew out of Mimno's experience as a Visiting Researcher with Michael Collins' group at Google Research.

References

David Bamman, Olivia Lewke, and Anya Mansoor. 2020. An annotated dataset of coreference in English literature. In *Proceedings of the 12th Language Resources and Evaluation Conference*, pages 44–54, Marseille, France. European Language Resources Association.

David Bamman, Sejal Popat, and Sheng Shen. 2019. An annotated dataset of literary entities. In *Proceedings of the 2019 Conference of the North American Chapter of the Association for Computational Linguistics: Human Language Technologies, Volume 1 (Long and Short Papers)*, pages 2138–2144, Minneapolis, Minnesota. Association for Computational Linguistics.

Sabyasachee Baruah and Shrikanth Narayanan. 2023. Character coreference resolution in movie screenplays. In *Findings of the Association for Computational Linguistics: ACL 2023*, pages 10300–10313, Toronto, Canada.

Stella Biderman, Hailey Schoelkopf, Quentin Gregory Anthony, Herbie Bradley, Kyle O'Brien, Eric Hallahan, Mohammad Aflah Khan, Shivanshu Purohit, USVSN Sai Prashanth, Edward Raff, et al. 2023. Pythia: A suite for analyzing large language models across training and scaling. In *Proceedings of the 40th International Conference on Machine Learning*, pages 2397–2430, Honolulu, Hawaii, USA.

Bernd Bohnet, Chris Alberti, and Michael Collins. 2023. Coreference resolution through a seq2seq transition-based system. *Transactions of the Association for Computational Linguistics*, 11:212–226.

Faeze Brahman and Snigdha Chaturvedi. 2020. Modeling protagonist emotions for emotion-aware storytelling. In *Proceedings of the 2020 Conference on Empirical Methods in Natural Language Processing (EMNLP)*, pages 5277–5294, Online. Association for Computational Linguistics.

Kevin Clark and Christopher D. Manning. 2016. Deep reinforcement learning for mention-ranking coreference models. In *Proceedings of the 2016 Conference on Empirical Methods in Natural Language Processing*, pages 2256–2262, Austin, Texas. Association for Computational Linguistics.

K Bretonnel Cohen, Arrick Lanfranchi, Miji Joo-young Choi, Michael Bada, William A Baumgartner, Natalya Panteleyeva, Karin Verspoor, Martha Palmer, and Lawrence E Hunter. 2017. Coreference annotation and resolution in the colorado richly annotated full text (craft) corpus of biomedical journal articles. *BMC Bioinformatics*, 18(1):1–14.

Zeyu Dai, Hongliang Fei, and Ping Li. 2019. Coreference aware representation learning for neural named entity recognition. In *Proceedings of the Twenty-Eighth International Joint Conference on Artificial Intelligence, IJCAI-19*, pages 4946–4953.

Sooyoun Han, Sumin Seo, Minji Kang, Jongin Kim, Nayoung Choi, Min Song, and Jinho D. Choi. 2021. FantasyCoref: Coreference resolution on fantasy literature through omniscient writer's point of view. In *Proceedings of the Fourth Workshop on Computational Models of Reference, Anaphora and Coreference*, pages 24–35, Punta Cana, Dominican Republic. Association for Computational Linguistics.

Mandar Joshi, Omer Levy, Luke Zettlemoyer, and Daniel Weld. 2019. BERT for coreference resolution: Baselines and analysis. In *Proceedings of the 2019 Conference on Empirical Methods in Natural Language Processing and the 9th International Joint Conference on Natural Language Processing (EMNLP-IJCNLP)*, pages 5803–5808, Hong Kong, China. Association for Computational Linguistics.

Markus Krug, Frank Puppe, Fotis Jannidis, Luisa Macharowsky, Isabella Reger, and Lukas Weimar. 2015. Rule-based coreference resolution in German historic novels. In *Proceedings of the Fourth Workshop on Computational Linguistics for Literature*, pages 98–104, Denver, Colorado, USA. Association for Computational Linguistics.

Nghia T. Le, Fan Bai, and Alan Ritter. 2022. Few-shot anaphora resolution in scientific protocols via mixtures of in-context experts. In *Findings of the Association for Computational Linguistics: EMNLP 2022*, pages 2693–2706, Abu Dhabi, United Arab Emirates.

Nghia T. Le and Alan Ritter. 2023. Are large language models robust coreference resolvers?

Kenton Lee, Luheng He, Mike Lewis, and Luke Zettlemoyer. 2017. End-to-end neural coreference resolution. In *Proceedings of the 2017 Conference on Empirical Methods in Natural Language Processing*, pages 188–197, Copenhagen, Denmark. Association for Computational Linguistics.

Dhruv Mullick, Bilal Ghanem, and Alona Fyshe. 2023. Better handling coreference resolution in aspect level sentiment classification by fine-tuning language models. In *Proceedings of The Sixth Workshop on Computational Models of Reference, Anaphora and Coreference (CRAC 2023)*, pages 39–47, Singapore.

Shon Otmazgin, Arie Cattan, and Yoav Goldberg. 2022. F-coref: Fast, accurate and easy to use coreference resolution. In *Proceedings of the 2nd Conference of the Asia-Pacific Chapter of the Association for Computational Linguistics and the 12th International Joint Conference on Natural Language Processing: System Demonstrations*, pages 48–56, Taipei, Taiwan.

Shon Otmazgin, Arie Cattan, and Yoav Goldberg. 2023. LingMess: Linguistically informed multi expert scorers for coreference resolution. In *Proceedings of the 17th Conference of the European Chapter of the Association for Computational Linguistics*, pages 2752–2760, Dubrovnik, Croatia. Association for Computational Linguistics.

Pinelopi Papalampidi, Frank Keller, and Mirella Lapata. 2019. Movie plot analysis via turning point identification. In *Proceedings of the 2019 Conference on Empirical Methods in Natural Language Processing and the 9th International Joint Conference on Natural Language Processing (EMNLP-IJCNLP)*, pages 1707–1717, Hong Kong, China. Association for Computational Linguistics.

Corbèn Poot and Andreas van Cranenburgh. 2020. A benchmark of rule-based and neural coreference resolution in Dutch novels and news. In *Proceedings of the Third Workshop on Computational Models of Reference, Anaphora and Coreference*, pages 79–90, Barcelona, Spain (online). Association for Computational Linguistics.

Colin Raffel, Noam Shazeer, Adam Roberts, Katherine Lee, Sharan Narang, Michael Matena, Yanqi Zhou, Wei Li, and Peter J. Liu. 2020. Exploring the Limits of Transfer Learning with a Unified Text-to-Text Transformer. *Journal of Machine Learning*, 21(1):5485–5551.

Ina Roesiger, Sarah Schulz, and Nils Reiter. 2018. Towards coreference for literary text: Analyzing domain-specific phenomena. In *Proceedings of the Second Joint SIGHUM Workshop on Computational Linguistics for Cultural Heritage, Social Sciences, Humanities and Literature*, pages 129–138, Santa Fe, New Mexico. Association for Computational Linguistics.

Fynn Schröder, Hans Ole Hatzel, and Chris Biemann. 2021. Neural end-to-end coreference resolution for German in different domains. In *Proceedings of the 17th Conference on Natural Language Processing (KONVENS 2021)*, pages 170–181, Düsseldorf, Germany. KONVENS 2021 Organizers.

Ted Underwood, David Bamman, and Sabrina Lee. 2018. The transformation of gender in english-language fiction. *Journal of Cultural Analytics*, pages 1–25.

Wei Wu, Fei Wang, Arianna Yuan, Fei Wu, and Jiwei Li. 2020. CorefQA: Coreference resolution as query-based span prediction. In *Proceedings of the 58th Annual Meeting of the Association for Computational Linguistics*, pages 6953–6963, Online. Association for Computational Linguistics.

Linting Xue, Noah Constant, Adam Roberts, Mihir Kale, Rami Al-Rfou, Aditya Siddhant, Aditya Barua, and Colin Raffel. 2021. mT5: A massively multilingual pre-trained text-to-text transformer. In *Proceedings of the 2021 Conference of the North American Chapter of the Association for Computational Linguistics: Human Language Technologies*, pages 483–498, Online. Association for Computational Linguistics.

Deming Ye, Yankai Lin, Jiaju Du, Zhenghao Liu, Peng Li, Maosong Sun, and Zhiyuan Liu. 2020. Coreferential Reasoning Learning for Language Representation. In *Proceedings of the 2020 Conference on Empirical Methods in Natural Language Processing (EMNLP)*, pages 7170–7186, Online. Association for Computational Linguistics.

Wenzheng Zhang, Sam Wiseman, and Karl Stratos. 2023. Seq2seq is all you need for coreference resolution. In *Proceedings of the 2023 Conference on Empirical Methods in Natural Language Processing*, pages 11493–11504, Singapore.

A Fine-tuning Parameters

The fine-tuning parameters for each model can be found below. The batch size varied based on model.

Parameter	Value
evaluation_strategy	epoch
learning_rate	2e-5
weight_decay	0.01
save_total_limit	3
num_train_epochs	10
gradient_checkpointing	True

Stage Direction Classification in French Theater: Transfer Learning Experiments

Alexia Schneider and **Pablo Ruiz Fabo**
Université de Strasbourg, LiLPa UR 1339
67000 Strasbourg, France
alexia.schneider4@etu.unistra.fr, ruizfabo@unistra.fr

Abstract

The automatic classification of stage directions is a little explored topic in computational drama analysis (CDA), in spite of their relevance for plays' structural and stylistic analysis. We developed a 13-class stage direction typology, based on annotations in the FreDraCor corpus (French-language plays), but abstracting away from their huge variability while still providing classes useful for literary research. We fine-tuned transformers-based models to classify against the typology, gradually decreasing training-corpus size to compare model efficiency with reduced training data. A result comparison speaks in favour of distilled monolingual models for this task, and, unlike earlier research on German, shows no negative effects of model case-sensitivity. The results have practical relevance for computational literary studies, as comparing classification results with complementary stage direction typologies, limiting the amount of manual annotation needed to apply them, would be helpful towards a systematic study of this important textual element.

1 Introduction

Machine learning methods have brought important contributions to Computational Literary Studies (CLS). To name just one monograph-length work, Underwood (2019) used such methods to provide insights on complex issues like the long-term evolution of genres and of literary prestige criteria, focusing mainly on fiction and poetry. Drama has also benefited from such approaches. The recent *Computational Drama Analysis* workshop[1] featured work on the automatic classification of dramatic situations, character types, and emotions in drama. In this paper, we approach a little explored dramatic analysis topic: the automatic classification of stage directions, using a French theater corpus. Stage directions introduce indications about performance, decoration or other information to complement character speech, but can sometimes be largely independent from it (Pfister, 1988, 15). Several typologies have been proposed for them in literary studies (see 3.1). However, their automatic classification has scarcely been studied and poses challenges, given types hard to distinguish from each other. Stage directions on characters' entrance and exit indicate changes to character co-presence on stage and are thus tied to play structure and dramatic technique. The frequency and length of stage directions and their types can be stylistic parameters related to author groups or subgenres. Automatically classifying stage directions facilitates large-scale quantitative analyses of this element's structural and stylistic role.

For French theater, the FreDraCor corpus (Milling et al., 2021), based on Fièvre (2007) and covering mostly the 16th to 20th centuries, offers over 38,000 annotated stage directions. Given the large number of categories (over 5,000), exploiting these annotations for supervised learning is a challenge, that we address in the paper.

Pre-trained language models were a game changer in NLP, allowing for transfer learning (e.g. Devlin et al. 2019) that yields viable classifiers even with a reduced number of examples, or, in the case of larger language models (Brown et al., 2020), in-context learning from (almost) zero examples. In our study, we work with specialized categories for which we could develop annotations, and we opted for transfer learning. We examine the extent to which we can reduce manually annotated training data for the supervised classification of stage directions, in French. As producing manual annotations can be costly, and exploring literary questions may require comparing the results of classifying against several, complementary typologies, the question addressed has practical relevance for CLS. The paper's contributions are:

- A new stage direction typology (3.1) based on the related literary theory and on the FreDra-

[1] https://page.hn/anuvah

Proceedings of LaTeCH-CLfL 2024, pages 278–286
March 22, 2024

Cor types, but abstracting away from some of their large variability to obtain a category set amenable to supervised learning and still useful for addressing literary questions.

- Experiments to clarify which language models (LMs) learn most efficiently on such data, focusing on model characteristics that may generalize beyond our corpus language (French).

An overall goal is to start a reflection on good practices to develop methods to classify this textual element, across languages.

The paper is structured as follows: Section 2 reviews related work. Section 3 describes our typology and classification workflow. Section 4 presents results, and section 5 outlines future perspectives.

2 Related Work

Heterogeneous criteria have been used to design stage direction typologies (Dahms, 1978; Gallèpe, 1997; Issacharoff, 1981; Martinez Thomas, 2007; Pfister, 1988). Among other aspects, taxonomies pay attention to whether stage directions refer to verbal/speech-related or visual information, to characters or setting, whether they describe movements (including entrance and exit) or character interactions. Another feature used is their narrative vs. descriptive nature, their relatedness with or independence from spoken text, or their impact on the play's plot. The Text Encoding Initiative (TEI) guidelines (TEI Consortium, 2023) reflect this heterogeneity in their description of possible `@type` attribute values for the TEI `<stage>` element, used for stage directions. Galleron (2021) attempts to reconcile inconsistencies in earlier typologies, systematizing types via a set of values for the `@ana` attribute of `<stage>`.

Automatic stage direction classification was performed in German by Dennerlein (2016), with four classes (*exit*, *entrance*, *dead* and *aside*); per-class results ranged between 0.75 and 0.88 F1 using random forests. The typology is less complex than our 13-class typology and the classes are more distinct. Maximova and Fischer (2019), working with Russian, developed a model to classify against the TEI guidelines' 9 categories, trained on 6,569 manually annotated examples and reaching ca. 0.75 F1.

Pagel et al. (2021) performed a related but not equivalent task. In their study on predicting German plays' structural elements in TEI, one of the five classes was stage directions, besides act and scene divisions, speaker names and speeches. They thus classified stage directions vs. other structural elements, reporting that a binary classification between stage directions and character speech was not trivial (0.81 F1). Stage directions were also the worst performing class in the 5-way classification (0.84 F1, while other classes were above 0.9). To assess the role for language-specific knowledge, they fine-tuned both English and German BERT cased and uncased models, with best results for the German uncased model. Their experimental setup informed our own (3.2).

3 Methods

3.1 Stage Direction Typology

We wanted to start assessing to what extent it is possible to automatically classify stage directions against different typologies useful for literary analysis. We do not intend the typology here to be the only choice, but in a way a testbed for fine-tuning and a means to assess the potential of the models to classify this type of material, using these classes or similar ones according to researchers' needs.

To develop the typology (table 1),[2] we started off from FreDraCor, which has 38,306 `<stage>` elements with 5,109 unique types.

We grouped semantically the 87 most frequent values, covering 25,823 stage directions, into our 13-class typology, creating a mapping between FreDraCor original labels and our own (Appendix B). E.g. FreDraCor labels *location*, *decor* and *décor* yield class *Setting* in our typology, and *kill*, *fight*, *hit*, *suicide*, *threat* yield *Aggression* in our typology. We only considered single-type FreDraCor labels, for simplicity; the 87 categories selected correspond to classes with at least 50 examples.

The typology contains classes that can be very ambiguous, the vocabulary of which is likely to represent different semantic fields, like *Action* or *Narration*, which are intended to be difficult for classifiers. Other classes can often be detected with surface lexical cues, like the presence of certain prepositions in *Toward*. Our choice of classes is meant to reflect different interests that a scholar studying stage directions may have. E.g. *Aggression* stage directions may be more present in a serious subgenre like the tragedy, *Music* stage directions in the *vaudeville*, or long *Narration* types in plays from the 19th century onwards or experimental work. Thus, the detection of such types is

[2]See corpus examples and English glosses in appendix A.

Class	Scope
Action	General character action category
Aggression	Violent action
Aparté	Aside (character addresses audience or is alone)
Delivery	Delivery manner (e.g. *laughs*, *sobs*)
Entrance	Character enters stage
Exit	Character exits
Interaction	Non-verbal character interaction
Movement	Character movement (but not exit/entrance)
Music	Tune names (in plays with songs)
Narration	Long, "narrative quality", for readers
Object	Describes object or interaction with it
Setting	E.g. *the stage represents a bar*
Toward	Indicates the addressee of a speech

Table 1: Stage direction typology

relevant for subgenre characterization. Some types are relevant for dramatic structure, e.g. *Exit* and *Entrance*, which give information about configuration (character co-presence on stage). *Aparte* is related to knowledge distribution in the play, an active CDA research area (Andresen et al., 2024).

After removing duplicates, we obtained a set of 14,613 examples and used it, gradually decreasing training set size, for our fine-tuning experiments (3.2). Label distribution is imbalanced (table 2).

Class	N. examples	Class	N. examples
Music	2863	Delivery	962
Action	2467	Entrance	646
Toward	2144	Movement	583
Exit	1295	Interaction	565
Object	1130	Narration	554
Setting	982	Aggression	350
		Aparté	72

Table 2: Number of examples per class (training corpus)

3.2 Classification Workflow

We first implemented classical machine learning (ML) models, with version 1.0.2 of `scikit-learn` (Pedregosa et al., 2011): Logistic Regression, Ridge Classifier, Random Forest and SGD. For the last two, results reported (macro-F1) are averaged over 5 runs. The implementation used for the first two is deterministic. Hyperparameters were default. The features were character length and the number of sentences, tf-idf-weighted token unigrams, bigrams, and part-of-speech unigrams (obtained with the `fr_core_news_md` module of spaCy by Honnibal et al. 2020) and 2- to 4-character ngrams, with 1% minimum document frequency.

Models for fine tuning were **(1)** **`camembert-base`** (Martin et al., 2020), a French monolingual model trained on the OSCAR corpus (Ortiz Suárez et al., 2019); **(2)** **`distilcamembert-base`** (Delestre and Amar, 2022), a version of (1) that is distilled, i.e. that attempts to preserve result quality while reducing model complexity (thus size and fine-tuning time); **(3)** **`bert-base-multilingual-cased`** and **(4)** **`bert-base-multilingual-uncased`**, case-insensitive version of (3), both by Devlin et al. (2019), which include French among the 102 languages covered. Model **(5)** was **`distilbert-base-multilingual-cased`** (Sanh et al., 2019), a distilled cased version of (3). The final model **(6)** was based on the **SetFit** architecture (Tunstall et al., 2022). This first fine-tunes a Sentence Transformer (S-BERT) model (Reimers and Gurevych, 2019) using contrastive training on positive and negative training pairs, which helps it learn effectively based on a small number of examples. Then, based on the fine-tuned S-BERT model (`distiluse-base-multilingual-cased-v1` in our case), it trains a classifier for the task, with logistic regression in our setup. Fine-tuning was carried out with version 4.34.1 of the `transformers` library (Wolf et al., 2020) on a V100 GPU. Learning rate was 2e-5 and batch size was 16. The trainer was configured with a maximum of 40 epochs, with early stopping monitoring validation loss and a patience of 3, but only `camembert-base` went over 10 epochs on average. For SetFit, as its API has no early stopping callbacks, we chose 6 epochs with 20 contrastive learning iterations each. We report macro-F1 (mean over 5 runs) in table 4.

Our model choices are justified thus: CamemBERT **(1)** is a leading monolingual LM for French. A distilled version **(2)** was also tested because, given that distilled models are smaller and faster, should there be no important difference in result quality, the distilled model is to be preferred. The multilingual BERT models, cased **(3)** and uncased **(4)** were chosen to compare with the monolingual ones, to get an indication of the extent to which language-specific knowledge helps classification, especially as training data is reduced. We chose the distilled version **(5)** for the same reason as (2). Finally, we tested SetFit **(6)** because its contrastive learning approach allows it to learn from limited data, which fits our study's goal. For our experiments, the annotated corpus was increasingly reduced (table 3), and split into training and validation sets. The test-set was always the same (2,923 examples). This was meant to help assess the extent to which models generalize to the test set, even when fine-tuned on a training set smaller than it.

	100%	**50%**	**25%**	**10%**	**5%**
train	9352	4676	2337	935	467
validation	2338	1169	585	234	117
test			2923		

Table 3: Number of examples at each corpus size

4 Results and Discussion

As table 4 and figure 1 show, LMs performed better than classical ML; improvement increases as training set size decreases. With the full corpus, several LMs reach 0.81 F1, and at 50% (5,845 manually annotated examples), macro-F1 ranges between 0.73 and 0.79. Monolingual LMs show an advantage over multilingual ones from 50% on, more so at 25% (2,922 training examples), 10% (1,169 examples) and 5%. Distilled models performed very closely to full ones, either in mono- or multilingual cases. As their fine tuning was taking between 40% and 75% of the time needed by the full model, they are a better choice. SetFit is the only case where a multilingual and distilled model was competitive with monolingual models at 10% (only 0.01 points below distilled CamemBERT), which suggests the effectiveness of its contrastive learning approach. However, fine-tuning time with our setup was much higher than with all other models.

We see no consistent difference between cased vs. uncased models, contrary to Pagel et al. (2021), who observed that a cased model may generalize less well on their German data. The relevance of language-specific knowledge seen in their study is also seen in ours with the higher performance of French language-specific models. The 10% results are interesting, as they were obtained with less than 1,200 manual annotations. The monolingual models provide ca. 0.7 F1 (vs. approx. 0.8 F1 with ca. 6,000 examples). A 0.7 F1 may not be

Model	**100%**	**50%**	**25%**	**10%**	**5%**
Classical ML					
LogisticReg	0.70	0.64	0.57	0.51	0.41
RidgeClassif	**0.73**	**0.71**	**0.62**	**0.55**	**0.49**
RandomForest	0.65	0.61	0.57	0.49	0.45
SGD	**0.73**	0.69	**0.62**	0.54	**0.49**
Transfer learning					
(1) cam-base	0.77	0.77	**0.75**	**0.71**	**0.68**
(2) d-cam-base	**0.81**	**0.79**	0.74	0.7	0.67
(3) mbert-cas	**0.81**	0.74	0.69	0.61	0.51
(4) mbert-unc	**0.81**	0.74	0.7	0.61	0.57
(5) d-mbert-cas	0.8	0.73	0.67	0.61	0.53
(6) setfit-dmc	0.78	0.74	0.69	0.69	0.62

Table 4: Macro-F1 with different training-set sizes, testing on the 2,923 example test-set

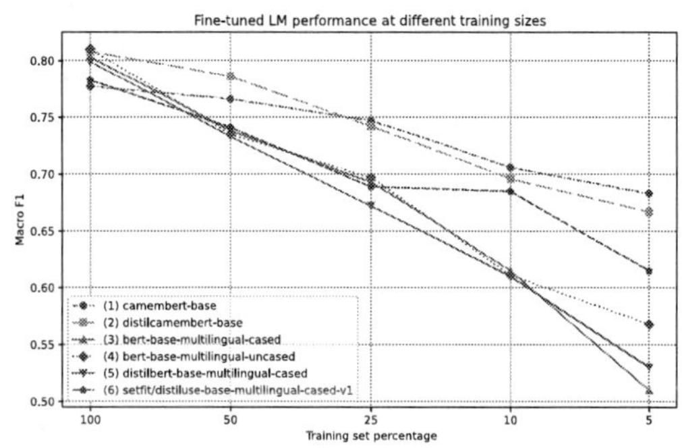

Figure 1: LM performance as training set is reduced

enough for a number of literary studies questions. However, an iterative workflow may be attempted with manual correction of the model outputs and fine-tuning of a better model while keeping the number of manual annotations low. Manual corrections could focus on the worst performing categories. A possible use of the best models would be to automatically annotate FreDraCor stage directions beyond the most frequent 87 single-type labels, which we did not handle here (section 3.1) and account for ca. 30% of the corpus, to assess whether the model's predictions could be a viable way to simplify the corpus' wide variety of labels. The same could be done to corpus examples that bear mixed-type labels.

Confusion matrices for distilled CamemBERT fine-tuned on 100% and 10% of the data are in figure 2,[3] and per-category results in table 5. Cate-

[3]Best F1 of 5 runs; Std Dev 0.012 at 100%, 0.009 at 10%.

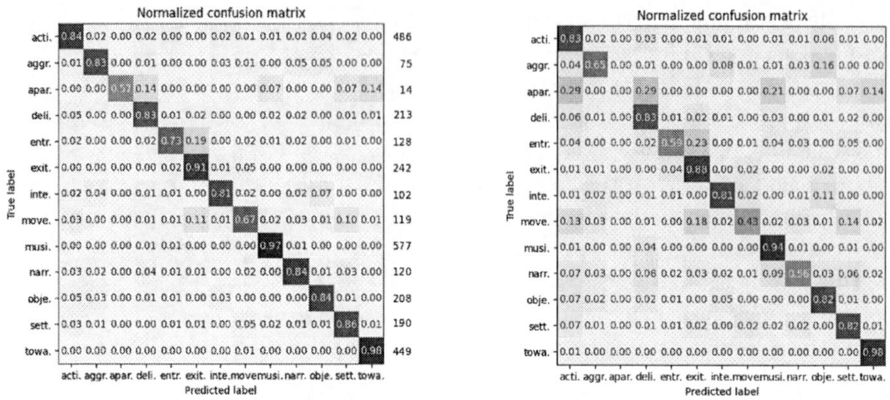

(a) `distilcamembert-base`, 100% of data

(b) `distilcamembert-base`, 10% of data

Figure 2: Confusion matrices for distilled CamemBERT. Values are normalized. The right column shows number of examples per class

	FT on 100% of data			FT on 10% of data				
Class	**P**	**R**	**F1**	**P**	**R**	**F1**	**N**	**Diff**
Action	0.907	0.844	0.874	0.821	0.829	0.825	486	-0.049
Aggression	0.713	0.827	0.765	0.662	0.653	0.658	75	-0.107
Aparte	1	0.571	0.727	0.000	0.000	0.000	14	-0.727
Delivery	0.859	0.831	0.845	0.724	0.826	0.772	213	-0.073
Entrance	0.809	0.727	0.765	0.807	0.586	0.679	128	-0.086
Exit	0.833	0.909	0.87	0.762	0.884	0.818	242	-0.052
Interaction	0.791	0.814	0.802	0.741	0.814	0.776	102	-0.026
Movement	0.702	0.672	0.687	0.761	0.429	0.548	119	-0.139
Music	0.969	0.971	0.97	0.931	0.938	0.934	577	-0.036
Narration	0.765	0.842	0.802	0.744	0.558	0.638	120	-0.164
Object	0.826	0.841	0.833	0.725	0.822	0.770	208	-0.063
Setting	0.823	0.858	0.84	0.757	0.821	0.788	190	-0.052
Toward	0.978	0.984	0.981	0.978	0.978	0.978	449	-0.003

Table 5: Per-category precision, recall, macro-F1 with `distilcamembert-base`, fine-tuned on 100% and 10% of the data. Column *N* is the number of test items per class, and *Diff* is the 10% macro-F1 minus the 100% one.

gories *Movement* and *Entrance* are regularly misclassified as *Exit*; a challenge here is that French verb *rentrer* is a contronym, meaning both to go onstage or offstage. The models have trouble to tease apart *Interaction*, *Aggression*, *Object* and *Movement* from each other; *Agression* and *Movement* are among those most affected by reduced fine-tuning data. Misclassification of various categories towards *Action* also happens, more so as data for fine-tuning decreases or with classical ML.

5 Conclusion and Outlook

The results are encouraging towards automatic large-scale stage-direction classification: 0.7 F1 with a 13-class typology using less than 1,200 manually annotated examples; a more costly set of ca. 5,900 annotations allowed for 0.81 F1. A distilled monolingual model was the best choice, offering satisfactory results and faster fine-tuning than the full model. Besides comparing with large language models and in-context learning, a relevant future task is the detection and classification of *internal* stage directions, implicit from character speech (Galleron, 2018). Reliable multilingual stage direction classification would open the door to large-scale quantitative comparative and diachronic work on an important element of dramatic texts.

Ethics Statement

The study involved the use of GPUs. Given potential carbon footprint, we assessed the necessity of their use. We consider their use justified given that we observed substantially better results at the task with transfer learning than with classical machine learning models. We compared distilled and full models, ascertaining that the distilled ones perform largely equivalently at the task. We thus propose the use of distilled models for the task described, which will mean less data transfer and GPU usage time in fine-tuning.

The study involves a large corpus of theater in French. A bias in this corpus is the underrepresentation of women authors. Relevant future work to counter this bias would be to encode in TEI and publicly release plays by women authors. Resources such as the database by Bourdic (2022) will facilitate the related bibliographic research.

Data and Code Availability

The dataframe derived from the FreDraCor TEI documents is at `https://doi.org/10.34847/nkl.fde37ug3`). Code to run the experiments is at `https://doi.org/10.5281/zenodo.10594104`, both under open licenses.

Acknowledgements

We thank the anonymous reviewers for their insightful comments, which helped improve the paper.

This work was supported by IdEx University of Strasbourg, call Attractivité 2020 (MeThAL project) and Maison Interuniversitaire des Sciences de l'Homme Alsace (MISHA) 2023-24 program (Thealtres project).

References

Melanie Andresen, Benjamin Krautter, Janis Pagel, and Nils Reiter. 2024. Knowledge Distribution in German Drama. *Journal of Open Humanities Data*, 10(1).

Maïwenn Bourdic. 2022. Pièces de théâtre écrites par des femmes, et représentées à Paris entre 1809 et 1906.

Tom Brown, Benjamin Mann, Nick Ryder, Melanie Subbiah, Jared D Kaplan, Prafulla Dhariwal, Arvind Neelakantan, Pranav Shyam, Girish Sastry, Amanda Askell, Sandhini Agarwal, Ariel Herbert-Voss, Gretchen Krueger, Tom Henighan, Rewon Child, Aditya Ramesh, Daniel Ziegler, Jeffrey Wu, Clemens Winter, Chris Hesse, Mark Chen, Eric Sigler, Mateusz Litwin, Scott Gray, Benjamin Chess, Jack Clark, Christopher Berner, Sam McCandlish, Alec Radford, Ilya Sutskever, and Dario Amodei. 2020. Language Models are Few-Shot Learners. In *Advances in Neural Information Processing Systems*, volume 33, pages 1877–1901. Curran Associates, Inc.

Gisela Dahms. 1978. *Funktionen der Ascriptionen zum Sprechtext im russischen Drama von 1747 bis 1903. Eine Typologie*. Ph.D. thesis, Rheinische Friedrich-Wilhelms-Universität Bonn.

Cyrile Delestre and Abibatou Amar. 2022. DistilCamemBERT : une distillation du modèle français CamemBERT. In *CAp (Conférence sur l'Apprentissage automatique)*, Vannes, France.

Katrin Dennerlein. 2016. Automatic recognition of configurations in plays – training a machine learning algorithm.

Jacob Devlin, Ming-Wei Chang, Kenton Lee, and Kristina Toutanova. 2019. BERT: Pre-training of Deep Bidirectional Transformers for Language Understanding. In *Proceedings of the 2019 Conference of the North American Chapter of the Association for Computational Linguistics: Human Language Technologies, Volume 1 (Long and Short Papers)*, pages 4171–4186, Minneapolis, Minnesota. Association for Computational Linguistics.

Paul Fièvre. 2007. Théâtre classique.

Ioana Galleron. 2018. Quel encodage pour les didascalies internes? In *NACLA2 Corpus et textes de la représentation / Corpora and performance texts*, Avignon, France.

Ioana Galleron. 2021. Pour un balisage sémantique des textes de théâtre : le cas des didascalies. *Sens public*. Publisher: Département des littératures de langue française.

Thierry Gallèpe. 1997. *Didascalies : les mots de la mise en scène*.

Matthew Honnibal, Ines Montani, Sofie Van Landeghem, and Adriane Boyd. 2020. spaCy: Industrial-strength Natural Language Processing in Python.

Michael Issacharoff. 1981. Texte théâtral et didascalecture. *MLN*, 96(4):809–823. Publisher: Johns Hopkins University Press.

Louis Martin, Benjamin Muller, Pedro Javier Ortiz Suárez, Yoann Dupont, Laurent Romary, Éric de la Clergerie, Djamé Seddah, and Benoît Sagot. 2020. CamemBERT: a tasty French language model. In *Proceedings of the 58th Annual Meeting of the Association for Computational Linguistics*, pages 7203–7219, Online. Association for Computational Linguistics.

Monique Martinez Thomas. 2007. Typologie fonctionnelle du didascale. In Florence Fix et Frédérique Toudoire-Surlapierre, editor, *La didascale au dans le théâtre du XXème siècle : Regarder l'impossible*, Ecritures, pages 35–46. EUD.

Daria Maximova and Frank Fischer. 2019. Using Machine Learning for the Automated Classification of Stage Directions in TEI-Encoded Drama Corpora. In *TEI Conference*, page 123, University of Graz, Austria.

Carsten Milling, Frank Fischer, and Mathias Göbel. 2021. French Drama Corpus (FreDraCor): A TEI P5 Version of Paul Fièvre's "Théâtre Classique" Corpus.

Pedro Javier Ortiz Suárez, Benoit Sagot, and Laurent Romary. 2019. Asynchronous pipelines for processing huge corpora on medium to low resource infrastructures. Proceedings of the Workshop on Challenges in the Management of Large Corpora (CMLC-7) 2019. Cardiff, 22nd July 2019, pages 9 – 16, Mannheim. Leibniz-Institut f"ur Deutsche Sprache.

Janis Pagel, Nidhi Sihag, and Nils Reiter. 2021. Predicting Structural Elements in German Drama. In *Proceedings of the Second Conference on Computational Humanities Research (CHR2021)*, online.

F. Pedregosa, G. Varoquaux, A. Gramfort, V. Michel, B. Thirion, O. Grisel, M. Blondel, P. Prettenhofer, R. Weiss, V. Dubourg, J. Vanderplas, A. Passos, D. Cournapeau, M. Brucher, M. Perrot, and E. Duchesnay. 2011. Scikit-learn: Machine learning in Python. *Journal of Machine Learning Research*, 12:2825–2830.

Manfred Pfister. 1988. *The theory and analysis of drama*. European studies in English literature. Cambridge University Press, Cambridge [Cambridgeshire] ; New York.

Nils Reimers and Iryna Gurevych. 2019. Sentence-bert: Sentence embeddings using siamese bert-networks.

Victor Sanh, Lysandre Debut, Julien Chaumond, and Thomas Wolf. 2019. Distilbert, a distilled version of bert: smaller, faster, cheaper and lighter. *ArXiv*, abs/1910.01108.

TEI Consortium. 2023. TEI P5: Guidelines for Electronic Text Encoding and Interchange. Version 4.6.0.

Lewis Tunstall, Nils Reimers, Unso Eun Seo Jo, Luke Bates, Daniel Korat, Moshe Wasserblat, and Oren Pereg. 2022. Efficient Few-Shot Learning Without Prompts. In *Efficient Natural Language and Speech Processing Workshop at NeurIPS*.

Ted Underwood. 2019. *Distant Horizons: Digital Evidence and Literary Change*. University of Chicago Press.

Thomas Wolf, Lysandre Debut, Victor Sanh, Julien Chaumond, Clement Delangue, Anthony Moi, Pierric Cistac, Tim Rault, Remi Louf, Morgan Funtowicz, Joe Davison, Sam Shleifer, Patrick von Platen, Clara Ma, Yacine Jernite, Julien Plu, Canwen Xu, Teven Le Scao, Sylvain Gugger, Mariama Drame, Quentin Lhoest, and Alexander Rush. 2020. Transformers: State-of-the-art natural language processing. In *Proceedings of the 2020 Conference on Empirical Methods in Natural Language Processing: System Demonstrations*, pages 38–45, Online. Association for Computational Linguistics.

A Stage direction examples and glosses

For each class, we provide examples from FreDraCor (separated with pipes), followed by their respective English glosses.

Class	Scope	FreDracor examples and English glosses
Action	General character action category	Il désigne le garçon de café I Il lit I Elle s'assied He points to the waiter I He reads I She sits down
Aggression	Violent action	Il tire son épée I Il se donne un coup He draws his sword I He strikes himself
Delivery	Delivery manner, e.g. regarding voice or vocal expression of emotion	En riant I À demi-voix Laughing I In a low voice
Entrance	Character enters stage	Ils entrent en scène I Il rentre chez lui They enter the stage I He enters his home
Exit	Character exits	Il sort I Il rentre She exits I He re-enters
Interaction	Non-verbal character interaction	Elle va aussi pour l'embrasser She moves to kiss him I He takes her hand
Movement	Character movement (but not exit/entrance)	Il continue sa marche I Il recule d'un autre côté I Il veut sortir He continues his walk I He retreats to the other side I He wants to exit
Music	Tune names (plays with songs); music description	Air en duo I Musique céleste Duet melody I Celestial music
Narration	Long, "narrative quality", for readers	Cependant VENDE, qui avait été mandée, survient après les acclamations du peuple, elle commande à son Chancelier de déclarer ses intentions à l'Assemblée However, VENDE, who had been summoned, appears after the cheers of the people; she commands her Chancellor to declare her intentions to the Assembly
Object	Describes object or interaction with it	Il lui donne un écu I Elle froisse la lettre He gives her a coin I She crumples the letter
Setting	Stage description or play location	Le théâtre représente un salon I À Sicilie The theater represents a living room I In Sicily
Toward	Indicates the addressee of a speech	À Julie I Au commandeur et au comte Toward Julie I To the commander and the count

B Mapping between FreDraCor classes and our typology

We list the FreDraCor types that we assigned to each class in our typology. We only worked with single-type labels in FreDraCor, leaving aside stage directions annotated with more than one type (see section 3.1).

For the small number of cases where there was an obvious typo in a FreDraCor label (e.g. *title* spelled as *ttitle*, or *decor* also spelled as *décor*), we accepted both as variants of the same label.

Our types	Corresponding FreDraCor types
Entrance	entrance, entrée
Exit	exit, escape
Setting	location, decor, décor [sic]
Narration	narration, meteo, noise
Toward	toward
Aparte	aparte, alone
Delivery	together, call, interrupt, loud, low, laugh, silence, quiet, cry, shout, nervous, ironic, anger, serious, happy, hesitate, enthousiasm, emotion, emphasis, friendly, grimace, feeling, furious, continue, sing, repeat
Interaction	kiss, touch, help, pull, push
Aggression	kill, fight, hit, suicide, threat
Action	action, watch, show, paint, pray, jump, read, kneel, fall, knock, write, drink, search, open, eat, sleep, stand, sit, move, listen, ring
Movement	closer, away, walk, follow, back
Object	costume, throw, tear, get, give, dress, drop, close
Music	music, title, ttitle [sic], bis

Author Index

Association for Computational Linguistics
209 N. Eighth Street
Stroudsburg, Pennsylvania 18360

ISBN 978-1-7138-9441-4

CURRAN ASSOCIATES INC.
proceedings
.com